Mastering
Modern United States History

Macmillan Master Series

Accounting
Accounting Skills
Advanced English Language
Advanced Pure Mathematics
Arabic
Basic Management
Biology
British Politics
Business Communication
Business Environment
C Programming
C++ Programming
Chemistry
COBOL Programming
Communication
Computing
Counselling Skills
Counselling Theory
Customer Relations
Database Design
Delphi Programming
Desktop Publishing
e-Business
Economic and Social History
Economics
Electrical Engineering
Electronics
Employee Development
English Grammar
English Language
English Literature
Fashion Buying and
    Merchandising Management
Fashion Marketing
Fashion Styling
Financial Management
Geography
Global Information Systems
Human Resource Management

International Trade
Internet
Java
Language of Literature
Management Skills
Marketing Management
Mathematics
Microsoft Office
Microsoft Windows, Novell
    NetWare and UNIX
Modern British History
Modern European History
Modern German History
Modern United States History
Modern World History
The Novels of Jane Austen
Organisational Behaviour
Pascal and Delphi
    Programming
Personal Finance
Philosophy
Physics
Poetry
Practical Criticism
Practical Grammar
Psychology
Public Relations
Shakespeare
Social Welfare
Sociology
Statistics
Strategic Management
Systems Analysis and Design
Team Leadership
Theology
Twentieth-Century Russian
    History
Visual Basic
World Religions

https://www.macmillanihe.com/series/Palgrave-Master-Series-Languages/14073/

Mastering

Modern United States History

2nd edition

John Traynor

First edition 2001
This edition first published 2019 by
RED GLOBE PRESS

Red Globe Press in the UK is an imprint of Springer Nature Limited, registered in England, company number 785998, of 4 Crinan Street, London, N1 9XW.

Red Globe Press® is a registered trademark in the United States, the United Kingdom, Europe and other countries.

ISBN 978–0–230–37224–5 paperback

This book is printed on paper suitable for recycling and made from fully managed and sustained forest sources. Logging, pulping and manufacturing processes are expected to conform to the environmental regulations of the country of origin.

A catalogue record for this book is available from the British Library.

A catalog record for this book is available from the Library of Congress.

Dedication
To Harrison, Evie, Madison, Stanley and Amelie

Contents

List of Tables

List of Presidential Profiles

List of Great American Lives

Acknowledgements

It has taken a long time for me to complete the second edition of this book and as the time taken has grown, so too has the number of people I need to thank. This is a work of synthesis in which I have tried to reflect the debates and interpretations raised by new research into the United States in the twentieth century. I would like to acknowledge the historians whose work is reflected in these pages. Dr Louisa Hotson of Oxford University read my manuscript in its entirety and I am very grateful to her for the valuable suggestions and constructive advice she provided at that time. My friend Martin Griggs, also an historian, read several of the early chapters and again provided excellent advice. At Palgrave, I need to say a big thank you to Suzannah Burywood – a long-time supporter of my work – and Helen Caunce who has been a great source of encouragement and advice.

I would also like to thank Heather Duggan, Head Teacher at Archbishop Blanch School in Liverpool, for giving me the opportunity to teach some of the fantastic students at her school. My GCSE and A Level groups were full of outstanding young people and it was a joy to teach them as well as to take a group of them on a history trip to Berlin and Poland where their interest and enthusiasm was great to see. The History Department at ABS, ably led by Rob Clarke, supported by Paul Wainwright, Daniel Pearson and John Butcher was a really brilliant place of work.

Away from directly writing the book I need to thank some other people who have helped me so much in important ways. Firstly, Dr Aparna Rao, Dr Peter Finigan and Melanie Taylor whose care and professionalism have been first class. Secondly, Anne Coles, David Jacobs and Simon Milton provided tremendous advice and expertise. Mike, Kevin and Sue also offered amazing support.

I would like to thank 'The Lakes Boys' – Robert Furlong, Lee Hopkins, Jon Howarth, Graham Ivory, David Kereszteny-Lewis, Adrian Moulding and Andrew Sharples – for their fantastic friendship. I also need to thank Graham Clark, Jamie Goodfellow and Eric Wilmot – still friends from our days together at Sheffield University.

While I have been working on this project my daughter Hannah got married and so I would like to say to Hannah and Matty Hughes and my son Patrick how proud I am of you and your achievements. Most of all, I would like to thank my wife Linda for all of her love and patience and the practical support, typing and organisation she has brought to this project.

Extracts from *Dear America: Letters Home From Vietnam* have been reproduced with kind permission of The New York Vietnam Veterans Memorial Commission.

JOHN TRAYNOR,
April 2018

◼ М ❚ The beginning of the American twentieth century: 1900–20

1.1 Introduction – A simpler age

Mark Twain (Samuel L. Clemens) was a man of letters, a humourist without parallel, regarded by many as the finest American writer of the nineteenth century. *The Adventures of Tom Sawyer*, published in 1876, evoked magical memories of Clemens' own childhood. *Adventures of Huckleberry Finn* (1884) was his masterpiece, 'the great American novel'. He began the first draft of his autobiography in 1877. In so doing, Mark Twain evoked a picture of an age that now seems long gone.

I was born the 30th of November, 1835, in the almost invisible village of Florida, Monroe County, Missouri. I suppose Florida had less than three hundred inhabitants. It had two streets, each a couple of hundred yards long; the rest of the avenues were mere lanes, with rail fences and corn fields on either side. Both the streets and the lanes were paved with the same material – tough black mud, in wet times, deep dust in dry.

Most of the houses were logs – all of them, indeed except three or four; these latter were frame ones. There were none of brick, and none of stone. There was a log church ... Week days, the church was a schoolhouse ...

There were two stores in the village. My uncle ... was proprietor of a very small establishment, with ... a few barrels of salt mackerel, coffee and New Orleans sugar behind the counter, stacks of brooms, shovels, axes, hoes, rakes and such things...and at the other end of the room was another counter with bags of shot on it, a cheese or two, and a keg of powder; in front of it a row of nail kegs and a few pigs of lead; and behind it a barrel or two of New Orleans molasses and native corn whisky on tap.

Source: Mark Twain, *Autobiography of Mark Twain: Volume 1* (University of California Press 2010)

A long life included work as an apprentice typesetter at the age of 12, a formative period as a steamboat pilot on the Mississippi River and a less fruitful spell as a mining prospector. In February 1863 he signed himself Mark Twain for the first time, not long before he moved to San Francisco to avoid prosecution for duelling. As his literary reputation grew he travelled the world giving lectures, writing a prodigious number of letters and newspaper articles and compiling a body of work so impressive that the writer William Faulkner called him 'the father of American literature'. He died at the family home in Redding, Connecticut on 21 April 1910.

The small-town world Mark Twain so vividly described was one in which he recalled:

[a] great prairie which was covered with wild strawberry plants, vividly starred with prairie pinks, and walled in on all sides by forests. The strawberries were fragrant and fine, and in the season we were generally there in the crisp freshness of the early morning, while the dew-beads still sparkled upon the grass and the woods were ringing with the first songs of the birds ... Doctors were not called, in cases of ordinary illness; the family's grandmother attended to those. Every old woman was a doctor, and gathered her own medicines in the woods, and knew how to compound doses that would stir the vitals of a cast-iron dog. (Twain, 2010, pp. 214–15)

The small-town, agrarian world he left behind with its artisan craftsmen, handmade goods and simple way of life was already embarking on a spectacular and transformative journey. Massive trends of urbanisation, immigration and industrialisation would effectively change the identity of the American nation itself. At the centre of that story was an unprecedented rise in population.

1.2 Population

In 1900, the United States covered a total area of more than 3 million square miles. In that space lived a population of 76,212,168 people. More than 66 million of that total were white (87 per cent), with 8.8 million black people (11.9 per cent). The average male life expectancy was 46.3 years and the average female life expectancy 48.3 years. Each of the closing decades of the nineteenth century had witnessed a rapid increase in population. Between 1880 and 1890 the decennial increase was 25.5 per cent; in the last decade of the nineteenth century it was 20.7 per cent.

Population comparison between 1900 and 2000

Just a century later, in 2000 the US population was calculated to be 281,421,906. The most rapidly growing regions are now in the South and the West, with the single most notable growth hotspot around Austin, Texas, making it the nation's capital for population growth. In terms of numeric growth, 13 of the 15 cities that added the most people at the end of the twentieth century were in the South or West. The exception to this general trend was New York City, which ranked first in numeric population growth. New York maintained its position as the nation's most populous city by some margin, with just over 8 million residents in 2000, followed by Los Angeles and Chicago.

1.3 Women in America at the turn of the twentieth century

The rapid rise of American society at the turn of the twentieth century was based, not least, on the foundation stone of female fertility. With the American economy ready to become the most powerful in the world, a rapidly growing, youthful population was instrumental in what was to come. The average family size through-out the nineteenth century was five and as late as 1910 it stood at 4.5. This cultural drive to raise a family was the single most important factor behind the nation's rapid population growth.

But raising children could represent an almighty struggle. Infant mortality in 1870 was 176 per 1,000. Poor sanitation, contaminated milk and the fact that most American births still took place at home placed a huge burden on mothers. The dangers posed by outbreaks of illnesses such as typhus, scarlet fever, measles and whooping cough lay in wait for young children.

While it is obvious that women played the central role in bringing babies into the world and then taking the prime responsibility for their well-being and upbringing, the rewards for females in American society were more difficult to discern. In almost every sense, women were regarded and treated as second-class citizens even though the society they were building was remarkable for its modernity.

From the outset, young girls were raised in the expectation that they would play second fiddle to their male siblings. The importance of being feminine, learning how to perform domestic chores, assuming a passive role in education, and then, when the time came, finding an appropriate partner and husband were all given paramount importance. Qualities of piety, virtue, domesticity and submissiveness were key ingredients in raising a God-fearing young woman. As Linda Simon puts it: 'The prospect of motherhood shaped every facet of their identity.' (Simon, 2017, p. 37)

Changing perceptions of the role of women

Young women who enthusiastically displayed their housekeeping and maternal skills were more likely to be seen as suitably deferential and spiritually devout. The impor-tant legacy of the Puritan outlook meant that religious and domestic duties were put before any potentially suspect intellectual activity. Prestigious companies, schools and universities were largely dominated by men and by male thinking.

Yet remarkably, while women were treated less favourably than their male counter-parts it is now clear that many people at the time believed the role of women in society was quickly changing and to some (chiefly male) observers, this was the cause of great concern. For example, in 1901, Edward Alsworth Ross, an academic from the Univer-sity of Nebraska, gave a series of lectures in which he

> blamed women for turning away from motherhood – partly because of the phys-ical toll it took on their bodies and the risk of death in childbirth; partly because, availing themselves of higher education, they felt restive. 'Society has put mater-nity out of fashion,' wrote Eliza Lynn Linton, 'and the nursery is nine times out of ten a place of punishment, not of pleasure, to the modern mother.' (In Simon, 2017, p. 39)

As we will see, rapid changes in dress, social interaction and the behaviour of women divided American society between those who were appalled by and those who applauded the changing role of the 'new woman.'

Women and suffrage

The impact of modernity was not necessarily universally reflected in attitudes towards women in general and towards the issue of female suffrage in particular. Two organisations led the way in demanding the vote for women. In 1869 Elizabeth Stanton and Susan Anthony established the National Woman Suffrage Association. The American Woman Suffrage Association led by Julia Ward Howe and Lucy Stone immediately followed. In 1890, the two groups acknowledged the value of joining forces and created the National American Woman Suffrage Association (NAWSA). Despite their efforts, by the turn of the century only four states (Idaho, Colorado, Utah and Wyoming) had given women the same voting rights as men. Those who opposed female suffrage claimed that women lacked the intellect to understand complex political issues and did not need the vote as they were effectively represented by their menfolk. Others claimed that the moral standing of women in general would be degraded by their involvement in the sordid world of politics. Finally, a widely held view was that it was the place of women to devote their time and energy to raising a family, leaving no time for the distractions of politics.

1.4 The Hispanic population

Why did people flock to the United States in such numbers at the start of the twentieth century? It may be that a look at the experience of people from Mexico can reveal some of the characteristics that applied to other immigrant groups as well. Firstly, in common with other sources of migration, the population of Mexico was rapidly increasing, from about 7 million people at the time of the Mexican War with the United States in 1846 to more than 14 million people by 1915. This rapid population growth was not accompanied by a corresponding rise in living standards or employment opportunities.

Across the border in the United States, the picture looked very different. A burgeoning economy, a hunger for cheap labour, employment 'opportunities' in mining, agriculture, fruit harvesting and industry all acted as a magnet to the Mexican people in the same way that this brought in millions of people from Eastern Europe. Sadly, the reality of the reception given to many Mexican migrants was rather different to the one they may have hoped for. Many of the new arrivals from Latin America were Catholic and so prejudice against Hispanic people and their religion was combined by those who saw Protestantism as fundamental to the character of the United States. From the hostility of the American Protective Association in the 1890s at a time of American imperialism, to the Ku Klux Klan in the 1920s during the Red Scare, anti-Catholic sentiment was seldom far from the surface.

Mexicans who entered the United States hoping for a new start were often the victims of 'frontier justice' at a time when Social Darwinism and naked racism went hand in hand. From the 1890s discrimination was applied to Mexican schoolchildren in states such as Texas and California and in courts and policing in Texas, Arizona and Colorado. An example of this thinking was displayed by Senator Albert Beveridge of Indiana when he told Congress in 1900: 'God ... has made us the master organizers of the world ... that we may administer government among savage and senile peoples.' (In Fernandez-Armesto, 2015, p. 629)

Historian Felipe Fernandez-Armesto offers this analysis:

> Discrimination kept Hispanics mired in poverty and excluded from the social and economic opportunities of the 'American Dream' ... More significant for the long-term history of the United States than all the migrants' suffering and all the peculiarities of border life was the diffusion of Hispanics, especially of Mexicans, in the wider territory of the United States ... Migrants penetrated every state of the union and every significant city in the first four decades of the twentieth century. (Fernandez-Armesto, 2015, p. 638)

The Hispanic population of the United States in 2000

The United States Census Bureau defines 'Hispanic' or 'Latino' origin as referring to 'a person of Cuban, Mexican, Puerto Rican, South or Central American, or Spanish culture or origin, regardless of race' (US Census, online). According to the 2000 Census, 282.2 million people resided in the United States on 1 April 2000, of which 35.3 million (or 12.5 per cent) were of Hispanic or Latino origin. Hispanics or Latinos are those people who classified themselves in one of the specific Spanish, Hispanic or Latino categories listed on the Census 2000 questionnaire as 'Mexican', 'Puerto Rican' or 'Cuban' as well as those who indicate that they belong to 'another' Hispanic, Latino or Spanish origin. This may include those whose origins are from Spain, the Spanish-speaking countries of Central or South America, or the Dominican Republic.

1.5 Native Americans and Alaska Natives

Christopher Columbus' legendary arrival in America in 1492 was predated by some ten thousand years or more by migrants from Siberia who travelled across the Bering Strait to settle among the naturally abundant resources of North America. It is estimated that by 1500 up to 7 million people had settled across America, building complex and distinctive cultures. A blissful period without serious interference came to a shocking conclusion in the nineteenth century. The pattern of westward expansion by white men was under way by 1850 and rapidly developed after 1865, so that by 1890 the Census Bureau reported that this process was complete.

Thirty years of constant westward expansion had accelerated after the Civil War as generations of Americans moved into the Trans-Mississippi West and settled on the vast treeless expanses of the Great Plains, the valleys of the Rockies and the drier regions of the south west. In a single generation the west had been wrested from the Native Americans. The bison they had lived on and whose every sinew had been used ingeniously in sustaining their way of life was hunted to the brink of extinction. The massacre of the Sioux tribe at Wounded Knee, South Dakota, in 1890 marked a particularly poignant end to the story of the subjugation of Native American culture.

In place of the Native Americans and the buffalo came white farmers and cattle and eventually barbed wire and fences. In 1862, Congress had created a Department of Agriculture and passed the Homestead Act which gave individual settlers free title grants to 160 acres in return for five years' residency. The consequences for the Native

American tribes were catastrophic. In 1850 there were approximately a quarter of a million Native Americans farming and hunting in the western United States. By 1890, a combination of wars, treaties and the destruction of the buffalo meant that they had been deprived of all but a tiny section of their former lands.

Between 1850 and 1900 the population living in the west expanded from 179,000 to 4.3 million; by 1900 there were 1.5 million people living in California. The state of Colorado saw an increase from just 34,000 in 1860 to around 500,000 by 1900. In the north west the years 1889 and 1890 saw the admission of North Dakota, South Dakota, Montana and Washington (1889) and Idaho and Wyoming (1890).

During this period even those considering themselves to be enlightened wanted to assimilate 'wild', 'savage', 'uncivilised' Native Americans so that the ancient tribal culture was subsumed into the white way of life. The first off-reservation boarding school for Indian children was established in Pennsylvania in 1879 and imposed a strictly white culture upon its students. By 1899, 25 similar boarding schools had been established, placing the last vestiges of the tribal culture under duress. While the Navajo tribe were 'fortunate' in being allocated sizeable lands considered arid and inhospitable in New Mexico and Arizona, the words of a despairing Crow warrior summed up the brutal subjugation of the Native Americans as they were moved onto grim reservations: 'We just lived. There were no more war parties, no capturing of horses ... no buffalo to hunt. There is nothing more to tell.' (Page, 2003, p. 321) Problems of low esteem, poverty, depression, alcoholism, disease and physical punishment of children in schools became a scourge that would plague Native Americans throughout the twentieth century.

Jake Page presents a telling summary of the damage done:

The extent of the catastrophe can barely be imagined. Sheer numbers only give the grossest idea. In 1887, Indian lands totalled 154 million acres, a combined area of a quarter of a million square miles, approximately the equivalent of the state of Texas. A half century later, less than a third of that land remained in Indian hands ... the loss of land, the crowding in of white settlers, railroads, miners, ranchers, the breakdown of tribal authority and independence, the failure of the federal government to provide satisfactorily for the needs of the Indians as promised ... and the mismanagement of most of the reservation resources – all brought about a sense of unease ranging from discouragement to despair among the reservation Indians. No one knows how many simply left for towns and cities, where they hoped to find some kind of employment, and essentially vanished from history. (Page, 2003, p. 331)

American Indians in 2000

The US Census now defines American Indians and Alaska Natives as people having origins in any of the original peoples of North and South America (including Central America) and who maintain tribal affiliation or community attachment. This category includes people who indicate their race as 'American Indian' or 'Alaska Native' or report entries such as Navajo, Blackfeet, Inupiat, Yupik or Central American Indian groups or South American Indian groups. In 2000, 1.9 million people identified themselves primarily as American Indians or Inuit. There are currently more than 550 separate tribes or clans. Approximately a quarter of these people live in lands set aside exclusively for their tribe across more than 50 million acres of reservation land.

1.6 The American economy in 1900

Rapid population growth helped to stimulate economic and social change on an unprecedented scale.

In 1900, the last ever horse-car to be used in the United States made its final run in Washington DC, the nation's capital. In the same year, Bloomingdale's department store in New York City proudly opened its first elevator. In the same city, Buffalo Bill's Wild West Show opened at Madison Square Garden. Also in 1900 the famous railroad engineer, Casey Jones, was killed as he bravely attempted to jam the brakes on a train moments before it crashed. Boston opened its new Symphony Hall and the first advertisement for an automobile appeared in the *Saturday Evening Post*. Meanwhile, in baseball, the American League was formed as a rival to the mighty National League. Eastman Kodak introduced the Brownie Box camera at a cost of just one dollar and the writer L. Frank Baum published his book *The Wonderful Wizard of Oz*. It must have been, in so many senses, an exhilarating time to be in the United States.

Evaluation of the impact of economic growth on American power

A nation that in the nineteenth century had been predominantly rural in character was by the turn of the century hurtling at an intoxicating pace to its destiny as the industrial and financial powerhouse of the capitalist world. Although agricultural output was plentiful, the percentage of the labour force employed in agriculture had sharply declined from 53 per cent in 1870 to 37.5 per cent in 1900. Cities such as New York, Boston and Chicago became the equal of their great European counterparts. This was accompanied by an influx of millions of immigrants, and the rapid rise of major industries. The World's Fair, which opened in Chicago in 1893, was a celebration of American technological progress. One English visitor in 1900 marvelled that 'Life in the States is one perpetual whirl of telephones, telegrams, phonographs, electric bells, motors, lifts and automatic instruments.' (In Whiteclay Chambers II, 1992, p. 2) Although there had been a serious depression in 1893 in which 15,000 businesses went to the wall and 500 banks failed, by 1900 virtually every aspect of the American economy was booming. America was now a modern, urban, industrial society, with immense national wealth and enormous industrial production.

One Harvard historian commented that 'the new American – the child of incalculable coal power, chemical power, electrical power, and radiating energy – must be a sort of God compared with any former creature of nature' (Henry Adams quoted in Whiteclay Chambers II, 1992, p. 2).

By 1900, the American president was at the helm of one of the greatest nations on earth. The once small and vulnerable nation had reached the status of a world power. As Jefferson had once predicted, the republic had moved on to 'destinies beyond the reach of mortal eye'. America's economic performance at the turn of the century was, by any reckoning, outstanding. The natural advantages enjoyed by the nation were considerable. Vast areas of fertile agricultural land enabled American farmers to increase wheat output by 256 per cent and corn by 222 per cent between 1865 and 1898. The sheer expanse of agricultural land combined with up-to-date farming techniques and efficient transport systems made food supplies plentiful and cheap. Industrial development was equally impressive. Coal production increased by 800 per cent between the end of the Civil War and 1898.

The importance of the railway to the American economy

In the same period, new railway track increased by 567 per cent. In 1869 construction workers on the Union Pacific railroad and the Central Pacific came together at Promontory, Utah, to mark the completion of the first transcontinental railroad. By 1893, four railroads joined the West Coast to the East, reducing the journey time to a matter of a few days; in 1883, the Northern Pacific became the first railroad to reach the Pacific Northwest. Between 1880 and 1890, growth in railway mileage increased by an average of 7,000 miles per year. By 1914, America had 250,000 miles of railway, compared to Russia's 46,000 miles over an area twice as large.

The rise of new industries

Performance in the newer industries reflected the general dynamism of the American economy. In 1865, the production of crude petroleum stood at around 3 million barrels; by 1898 this had reached 55 million barrels. Production of steel ingots and castings, which was at a very low level in 1865, had reached almost 9 million long tonnes by 1898. The cumulative effect of all of this was to place America's national income and per capita income way above those of her competitors. In 1914 America's national income stood at $37 billion compared to Britain's $11 billion and Russia's $7 billion. Per capita income in the United States was $377 compared to Britain's $244 and Russia's $41.

1.7 Robber barons or captains of industry?

Why did America change so quickly? The sheer pace and audacity of American economic and technological development should be credited to a great extent to the ordinary men and women (and in some cases, even children) who were employed in the emerging industries of the late nineteenth century. The insular, small-town, artisan and agricultural economy that still existed at the end of the Civil War in 1865 was in some senses swept aside by the bare hands and energy of humble labourers, factory hands, coal and mineral miners and railway navvies. A cheap source of labour was fundamental to profit and to rapid growth.

But at the same time America was fortunate to have at the other end of the business spectrum some outstanding individuals whose leadership, dynamism, risk taking and investment helped to create what writer Charles Morris has called the 'American super-economy'. In *The Tycoons*, Morris states that by 1895:

America was not only the most populous of industrial countries but the richest by any standard – per capita income, natural resource endowment, industrial production, the value of its farmlands and factories. It dominated world markets – not just in steel and oil but in wheat and cotton ... Its people were the most mobile, the most productive, the most inventive, and, on average, the best educated. It did not have much to say for itself in literature and the arts, but that time would come. (Morris, 2005, preface)

These advantages created endless opportunities for those who had the vision, energy, management skills and leadership qualities needed to seize the moment. Morris compares the lives of Andrew Carnegie, a pugnacious talent of Scottish lineage, John D. Rockefeller, diligent and sober from farming stock, Jay Gould, physically unimpressive but filled with ambition, and J.P. Morgan, refined, well-connected and with a powerful intellect. Carnegie with steel, Rockefeller with oil, Gould with railroads and the telegraph and Morgan with banking would become the tycoons who transformed the American economic landscape. Railways, business schools, grain exchanges, cattle markets, meat packing, transatlantic cables, barbed wire for cattle ranching, modern corporate management techniques, and investment capital all came along in the same few decades of bewildering advance.

In this climate, ethics could be marginalised, profits soared and mergers and trusts were the order of the day. To some observers the business tycoons were more like 'robber barons', becoming grotesquely rich at the expense of an exploited proletariat. To their admirers, they had almost single-handedly created an America that we would almost recognise today. Morris cites the 'Model Home' displayed at the 1893 Columbia Exposition's Electricity Building with its 'electric lighting, electric stove, hot plate, electric washing machine, electric carpet sweeper, electric doorbells and fire alarms. In short it looks like us. Ordinary people were reaping the benefits of the vast constructions of the Gilded Age titans' (Morris, 2005, p. 182).

In their slipstream other entrepreneurs also thrived. In the 1880s, Isaac Singer's sewing machine became widely available and the enthusiasm of a merchant from Boston named Albert A. Pope led to the cycling craze of the 1880s and 1890s. In the words of the *Washington Evening Star*, 'On this day of our Lord, January 1, 1907, we are the richest people in the world' (in Morris, 2005, p. xiv). The cumulative effect of all of this was stark. When the immense British Empire went to war with Germany in 1914 it would need to borrow American money.

1.8 Regional contrasts

The American people were spread across an area rich in its physical diversity, from arctic tundra, sub-tropical rain forest and arid deserts to fertile prairies and natural harbours. With three immense continental mountain ranges, vast networks of lakes and rivers, active volcanoes and geysers and ancient swamplands, this unspoiled land offered innumerable opportunities for habitation, exploration and settlement. In *The*

American Century, Harold Evans presents this summary of the regional variations which were so significant in 1900:

> There were still huge regional differences, physical, political and psychological. The eastern seaboard, which had the money, and the Middle West, which had the muscle, contained nearly half the population on a sixth of the land space and most of the imaginative enterprise. Chicago, 'hog butcher for the world,' was shouldering its way out of its boundaries, the paradigm of the new industrial metropolis. It had by 1889 come to surpass Philadelphia as America's second most populous city ... Only the eastern seaboard had the appearance of a settled civilization in city and countryside. Twenty-four years after the Civil War, the melancholy beauty of the South was in weedy ruins. The West had more animals than people and no political clout: the territories of Oklahoma, Arizona and New Mexico had no senators or congressmen in Washington. (Evans, 1998, p. xviii)

1.9 The transition from an agrarian to an industrial economy

Prior to the Civil War, the Southern economy was predominantly rural. It was dominated by the cotton industry and by the institution of slavery. After the Civil War the southern economy began to diversify. For example, in Birmingham, Alabama, there was a rapid rise in the iron and steel industry, and by 1900 the state was enjoying the benefits of its steel, textile and timber output. Birmingham's population grew from 3,000 in 1880 to over 130,000 in 1910. Similarly, in Memphis, the population grew from 23,000 before the end of the Civil War to around 100,000 at the end of the century. The 'New South' was a region of cities, factories, steel mills and blast furnaces. The society engulfed by a bloody Civil War in 1861 was still predominantly rural. The Census of 1860 listed five out of every six Americans as being 'rural dwellers'. Within 40 years this characteristic had been completely reversed and the country had become predominantly urban and industrial. As Ellis W. Hawley explains:

> By 1917 ... the American nation had already passed through a remarkable period of economic change, an era that had witnessed the rapid transformation of a land of farmers, villages, and small enterprises into one of factory production, burgeoning cities, and new and powerful masters of industry and finance ... the rural population had grown, but that of the nation as a whole had expanded much more rapidly. Swelled both by natural increases and by a massive influx of immigrants it had reached a total of 103,000,000, approximately half of whom were now living in urban places ... On the eve of their participation in the Great War that had begun in 1914, Americans had become a predominantly industrial and urban people. (Hawley, 1979, p. 3)

In 1900, 90 per cent of the population of Rhode Island were town dwellers. A section of New York City's Eleventh Ward had a population of 986 per acre, making it possibly the most densely populated area on earth. Between 1860 and 1900 the population of St Louis grew from 161,000 to 575,000. In the same period, the population of Boston increased from 178,000 to 561,000. The same transformation was taking place on the West Coast. The population of San Francisco was a mere 56,000 in 1860 but by 1900 it had reached 342,000. By 1910, 50 American cities had at least 100,000 inhabitants or more. In 1900 the three largest cities in terms of population were New York City (3.4 million), Chicago (1.7 million) and Philadelphia (1.2 million).

At the start of the new century, New York had become a spectacular example of modernity. As Mike Wallace describes in *Greater Gotham*:

> New York had morphed into a City Gigantic. Everywhere one looked, some component part had bulked up to extraordinary size. In these years the city accumulated a sheaf of world records. It had the planet's *tallest* skyscraper, its *biggest* office building, and its *largest* department store ... It boasted the USA's largest corporation, museum, theatre, racetrack, baseball stadium, sugar refinery, building contractor, railroad bridge, Catholic orphanage, high school, university, restaurant, subway system, police force, prison population, system of charities, public workforce, and municipal debt. (Wallace, 2017, pp. 42–43. Emphasis in the original)

As the cities grew in size they became more diverse in their ethnic character. Their neighbourhoods reflected a wide variety of backgrounds, with differences of language, race and religion. Particular ethnic groups became associated with certain cities and trades. Italians formed the major immigrant group in the construction industry of Philadelphia, Pittsburgh and Buffalo. In Chicago, Polish women were predominant in the catering industry. In Pennsylvania, the majority of coal miners were Slovaks.

Great American Lives: The Wright Brothers

The brothers Orville and Wilbur Wright were always close. Born in modest circumstances in Dayton, Ohio, they spent much of their childhood and early adult years tinkering with machinery, fascinated by mechanics and, in all things, applying striking determination to everything they did. Supported by a doting, encouraging father (a bishop) and their sister, Katharine, Orville started his own print shop when he was at school. Wilbur suffered a brutal, unprovoked attack at the age of 18, which damaged his self-confidence and made him reclusive for a time.

In the spring of 1893 the boys opened their own bicycle business, known as the Wright Cycle Exchange. Six years later, Wilbur wrote to the Smithsonian Institute in Washington DC requesting papers and book lists on aviation. In particular, this drew the Wright brothers' attention to developments in France, a centre for those interested in flying machines. They now plunged into a world of physics, the study of birds in flight, aerodynamics and – as they were to discover, as important as anything else to flight – the great variable, the wind. This learning curve took them to the Outer Banks, a remote series of sandbars and islands in North Carolina, close to a tiny settlement named Kitty Hawk.

Thousands of hours were devoted to building their prototype flying machine. The complexity of the scientific adjustments they had to make each step of the way was daunting. When they finally left the ground, with flights of 300–400 feet

Continued

in length, they touched the ground at almost 30 miles per hour. It was now that their bravery and courage came to the fore. Undeterred by some frightening accidents, nosedives and injuries and, at times, a remarkable lack of interest, even scorn, from the media, they refused to give in. At times, their flying machines shattered upon impact and they had to start all over again.

Then, on a winter's day in 1903, they made the first heavier-than-air, powered flight, with a pilot on board. They had paved the way for a century of aviation and exploration. They had changed the world. Two archetypal Americans, boys next door, who had taken to the air.

Further reading: David McCullough, *The Wright Brothers: The Dramatic Story behind the Legend* (London: Simon & Schuster 2015)

1.10 Women at work

The new century saw a gradual increase in the rise of working women. In 1900, the number of working women stood at 5,319,000, or 18.3 per cent of the total working population. By 1930, this had increased to 10,752,000, or 22 per cent of the total working population. Although there was an increase in the number of jobs carried out by women there was little improvement in terms of the quality of their employment opportunities or in their pay. For many families in the 1920s, women played a role as supplementary wage earners similar to that played by children in earlier generations. Households which relied on the woman's wage without an adult male breadwinner, of which there were 3.8 million, endured permanent poverty. Most women remained in poorly paid, low-status, menial occupations. With the exception of teaching and nursing, women were still largely absent from the professions. On a more positive note, the increasing availability of electrical household appliances relieved some of the physical burden of maintaining a home and the wider availability of birth control meant that the birth rate fell from 27.7 per cent in 1920 to 21.3 per cent in 1930.

1.11 The development of the American city

Much of the distinctive appearance and character of America's cities was shaped in the late nineteenth century. Central business districts, ethnic restaurants, theatres, baseball fields and saloons were almost universal features. The use of steel frameworks and the invention of elevators enabled architects to build increasingly ambitious skyscrapers. This initiative stemmed largely from the vision of the Chicago architect Louis H. Sullivan who, with his partner Dankmar Adler, was responsible for the Wainwright Building in St Louis (1891) and the Guaranty Building in Buffalo (1895). However, it was in New York City that 'skyscrapers' really earned the name with the 47-storey Singer Building (1908) and the 60-storey Woolworth Building (1913).

Traffic congestion became steadily worse and led to solutions such as the Brooklyn Bridge (1883) and the Williamsburg Bridge (1903) in New York City. San Francisco's cable car was introduced in 1873, and by the 1890s commuters in more than 50 cities were travelling to work by electric streetcar. Other developments included department stores like Macy's in New York, Wanamaker's in Philadelphia and Marshall Field's in Chicago, and 'five and ten cent' stores such as F.W. Woolworth (1879). Large-scale amusement parks with penny arcades and mechanical rides were opened such as those at Coney Island in Brooklyn and Venice Beach in Los Angeles.

These cultural developments were accompanied by rapid improvements in food supply. During the Civil War of 1861–65 troops from the North were provided with canned meat. Towards the end of the nineteenth century brands of processed foods including Kellogg's cornflakes and Borden's condensed milk became widely used and in 1916 Clarence Birdseye invented a technique for freezing food. Improvements in food processing and refrigerated shipping meant that by the turn of the century city dwellers were being provided with a much improved variety of fruit and vegetables, including the 'iceberg' lettuce, developed in 1903, that was successfully shipped across the country. By 1900 brands such as Quaker Oats, Libby's canned meats and Campbell's soups were all well established.

The problems of urban congestion

The rapidity of economic growth and urban development brought with it brutal working conditions, squalid housing, violent crime and an environment scarred by the consequences of rapid industrialisation. As early as 1793 the authorities in Philadelphia responded to a yellow fever epidemic with an attempt to improve sanitation and water provision. Permanent Health Boards were created in New York City in 1866 and Massachusetts in 1869. The American Public Health Association was created in 1872. Distinguished universities such as Johns Hopkins and Harvard opened medical departments in 1907.

Encouraging developments in medicine were not enough to deal with the problems caused by rapid urban development. Unparalleled growth led to the existence of large-scale slums, which inevitably gave rise to serious health problems, social deprivation, vice and crime. In response, many city authorities began to build upwards. High-rise buildings were first constructed in Chicago in the rebuilding process which followed the great fire of 1871. This solution was then adopted in cities such as New York in the 1880s. This was not a panacea. Poor water supply, impure milk, insanitary accommodation and inadequate garbage disposal led to high rates of infectious diseases.

In New York City, high rents caused poor workers to crowd together in the filth and squalor of the city's notorious Lower East Side. The depravity of one section of New York's West Side led to it becoming known as Hell's Kitchen, a place where in the words of one social reformer 'one could hear human virtue cracking all around'. One account of slum areas in the New York tenements described 'vile privies, dirt-filled sinks, slop oozing down stairwells; children urinating on the walls, dangerously dilapidated stairs; plumbing pipes pockmarked with holes that emitted sewer gases so virulent they were flammable' (in Gordon, 2016, p. 103). In the working-class districts of Pittsburgh as late as 1910 the majority of people were still obtaining their water from outside spigots or sharing communal taps.

Poor living conditions were reflected in alarmingly high rates of infectious diseases. Statistics from the National Center for Health between 1900 and 1904 show a high incidence of typhoid fever and diphtheria, although these diseases were less common than tuberculosis. These problems were so intense that the average life expectancy at birth for Americans born in 1900 was only 47.3; the death rate per 1,000 of the population in 1900 was 17.2.

1.12 Immigration

The rapid population growth created economic opportunities that acted as a magnet to many people from overseas who came to see the United States as a beguiling prospect for a new life. Consequently large numbers of people from Europe and beyond arrived to further boost the American economy.

It has been calculated that between 1820 and 1930, 37,762,012 immigrants entered the United States. Of this total, 32,121,210 came from Europe. A further 4,241,429 entered from the Americas, while 1,058,331 came from Asia. The original American settlers were predominantly Protestant, and largely of English, Scottish, Welsh or Irish descent. The first immigration commenced around 1820 and lasted into the 1880s; this wave of immigrants came chiefly from Germany, Italy, Ireland and Scandinavia. The largest single group came from Germany (5,908,000), followed by 4,651,000 from Italy and 4,579,000 from Ireland. This was then superseded by a fresh wave largely from eastern and southern Europe. Between 1881 and 1920 more than 20 million immigrants entered the United States and in the busiest year (1907) 1.2 million immigrants arrived. After 1890, the majority of immigrants came from Russia, Italy and Austria–Hungary.

The vast majority of these newcomers headed straight for the largest cities. At the turn of the century outbreaks of persecution in Eastern Europe drove a large proportion of Poles and Jews to flee their homeland in the hope that the United States would provide them with a safer haven. As they sailed into New York they passed the Statue of Liberty with its inspiring inscription:

> Give me your tired, your poor,
> Your huddled masses yearning to breathe free,
> The wretched refuge of your teeming shore.
> Send these, the homeless, the tempest-tossed to me.
> I lift my lamp beside the golden door.

However, the massive volume of immigrants began to make some Americans question the tradition of unconditional asylum. Anti-immigrant sentiment had several different strands. One recurring feature was the hostility of the American workforce against what they saw as cheap foreign labour. This sentiment was initially directed most strongly against immigrants from China; many immigrants from Asia tended to settle in California and it was there that the California Workingmen's Party, led by Denis Kearney, began to agitate against Chinese immigrants. The first specific piece of anti-immigrant legislation came in 1882 with the passing of the Chinese Exclusion Act, which placed a ten-year embargo on the admission of immigrants from China. Further pressure from American workers led to the exclusion in 1885 of 'pauper labour' – that is, immigrants who were being brought in as workers under contract.

Restrictions to immigration

In 1900, the government responded to a new wave of immigration by taking steps to restrict entry from Japan. Meanwhile the American Protective Association was agitating for controls against the entry of Catholics. In 1902 the Chinese Exclusion Act became permanent and six years later Japanese immigrants faced further restrictions. The rise of the theory of Social Darwinism led many scientists to contend that the purity and well-being of the American race was being increasingly undermined by the wholesale admission of the flotsam and jetsam of European society. Racialist theories were put forward in influential books such as Madison Grant's *Passing of the Great Race* (1915).

To many observers, the development of the seething cities, with their immigrant make-up and varying culture, seemed to constitute a direct threat to the Anglo-Saxon Protestant culture. In the words of one outspoken nativist, 'the city is the nerve center of our civilisation. It is also the storm center ... the city has become a serious menace to our civilization' (in Whiteclay Chambers II, 1992, p. 3). As wave after wave of immigrants entered the country many Americans contended that their own culture was being swamped. Until 1892, immigrants were cleared for entry at Castle Garden at the Battery in New York City, but such was the sheer volume of immigrants that a larger and more isolated processing station had to be found. From 1892, the immigrants' first port of call before they even set foot on American soil was switched to Ellis Island in New York.

1.13 The presidency: From Progressivism to the New Freedom

Having considered the country's economic, social and demographic background, we will now examine the way in which it was governed. For the nation as a whole, the political and sectional turmoil of the Civil War, marked by the deaths of more than 600,000 people, had been left behind, as had the institution of slavery. The political system was intact and democracy was well established. Two political parties, the Democratic Party, dating back to the presidency of Andrew Jackson (1829–37), and the Republican Party, which was established in 1854, dominated the political scene. In the election of 1900, for example, the Republican and Democratic candidates accumulated more than 13 million votes (Table 1.1), while in third place a Prohibition candidate received a mere 208,914 votes.

Table 1.1   The result of the 1900 presidential election

Candidate	Party	Electoral College votes	Popular votes
William McKinley (Ohio)	Republican	292	7,207,923
William J. Bryan (Nebraska)	Democrat	155	6,368,133

Theodore Roosevelt and the origins of the Progressive Movement

Roosevelt was born to a wealthy family in New York City on 27 October 1858. His father was a merchant and glass importer. Roosevelt served in the New York State Assembly between 1882 and 1884. He worked as Assistant Secretary of the Navy between 1897 and 1898 but resigned that post in order to organise the first regiment of the US volunteer cavalry – Roosevelt's 'Rough Riders' – in the Spanish–American War. He was elected Governor of New York in 1898 and while he established a reputation as an active opponent of corruption and certainly as someone who ruffled the feathers of the Republican Party establishment, his long period in New York politics taught him important lessons. Roosevelt's energy and drive were rewarded when he was nominated as vice presidential candidate on the Republican ticket at the Philadelphia Convention of June 1900. The McKinley–Roosevelt ticket secured 7,207,923 votes compared to the Democrats' 6,368,133 for Bryan and Stevenson.

The broad spectrum of the Progressive Movement makes it difficult to generalise as to who the progressives were. Indeed, some historians prefer to depict Progressivism as a series of quite distinct areas and initiatives, which cannot be easily bundled together as a movement at all. Nevertheless certain common areas exist. The progressives were predominantly middle class. They were moralists, often deeply committed to the old traditional values of rural America. Fundamentally, they believed in the power of energetic and creative government to promote the public good.

On 6 September 1901, President William McKinley visited the Pan-American Exposition at Buffalo in New York. As he stood in line meeting the public, a Polish anarchist named Leon Czolgosz stepped forward and shot him twice at point-blank range. McKinley clung to life for a week but died on 14 September. Roosevelt's biographer, Edmund Morris beautifully evokes the moments of transition:

> Theodore Roosevelt became President of the United States without knowing it, at 2:15 in the morning of 14th September 1901. He was bouncing in a buckboard down the rain-swept slopes of Mount Marcy in the Adirondacks. Constitutionally, not so much as a heartbeat impeded the flow of power from his assassinated predecessor to himself. Practically, more than four hundred miles of mud and rails still separated him from William McKinley's death chamber in Buffalo, where preparations for an emergency inauguration were already under way.
>
> For all Roosevelt knew, he was still Vice President, yet he had already realized that he would soon assume supreme responsibility. Yesterday's telegrams, relayed up the mountain by telephone operators, riders, and runners, had documented the spread of gangrene through his bullet-ridden Chief. (Morris, 2001, Prologue)

With the president's administration brutally curtailed, it fell to his successor, Theodore Roosevelt, to provide the energy and charisma needed to galvanise the Progressive Movement. The assassination meant that Theodore Roosevelt, not yet 43, became the youngest president in the nation's history. Morris describes the sheer wealth of the nation visible to Roosevelt from the procession of McKinley's funeral train that took the new president on a journey marked by sadness and yet illuminating the opportunities that lay ahead for the United States:

> Prosperity was everywhere for Roosevelt to see – if not through drawn blinds at the moment, then memorably on his recent trip to Minnesota. The weather stained barns of poorer days, the drab farmhouses and blistered grain elevators, were pristine with new paint. He had seen corrugated dirt giving way to asphalt, rotten boardwalks smoothing to stone, shards of shacks pushed aside by new redbrick houses. Not so long ago, Midwestern towns had glowed dully at night if they glowed at all. Now they were constellations of electricity, bright enough to wake the sleeping traveller. Equally bright, by day were silver threads of irrigation in the green fields, and new, steel-roofed sheds and schoolhouses. (Morris, 2001, prologue)

It is interesting to note that Roosevelt's stricken predecessor had enjoyed exactly the same financial riches and wealth of opportunities but the power of the presidency as exercised by the two men bears no comparison. It was only when the energy, vision and ambition of the new president was brought to bear that the picture of a modern presidency recognisable to us today began to come into focus. Three years later the Republican Party nominated Roosevelt to run for the presidency in his own right. Roosevelt's popularity was reflected in his majority of 2.5 million over the Democratic candidate and the securing of 336 votes in the Electoral College (Table 1.2).

Few presidents have displayed a more colourful profile than the 26th President. In the words of one authority:

> Energetic, brilliantly intelligent and young (at forty-three the youngest man ever to assume the Presidency) ... He was the ablest man to sit in the White House since Lincoln ... vigorous ... bookish ... All his life he eagerly followed whatever pursuit seemed likely to prove his manliness. He boxed, he wrestled, he swam, he carried a revolver with him wherever he went ... at various times he was a rancher, a big-game hunter in Africa, an explorer in South America, a soldier in the Spanish–American War ... The bitterest disappointment of his life was that he was not allowed to fight in the First World War: he never forgave President Wilson for stopping him ... At all moments between McKinley's death and his own, eighteen years later, he was probably the best-loved man in America. (Brogan, 1990, p. 462)

In a similar vein, Harold Evans presents this picture of Roosevelt's uniquely energetic approach to the presidency:

> He kept up a drumbeat of fire against the 'wealthy criminal class,' the 'malefactors of great wealth,' the 'infernal thieving trusts,' the 'conscienceless less swindlers' ...

Table 1.2 The result of the 1904 presidential election

Candidate	Party	Electoral College votes	Popular votes
Theodore Roosevelt (New York)	Republican	336	7,623,486
Alton B. Parker (New York)	Democrat	140	5,077,911
Eugene V. Debs (Indiana)	Socialist	–	402,283

Theodore Roosevelt

26th President of the United States (1901–09)
Born: 27 October 1858
Birthplace: New York
Died: 6 January 1919, aged 60; buried at Oyster Bay, New York
Education: Harvard College
Political party: Republican
State: New York
Occupations before presidency: Writer and historian; military service
Previous government service: Assistant Secretary of the Navy; Governor of
    New York
Age at inauguration: 42
Dates of office: 14 September 1901–3 March 1909 (Roosevelt was McKinley's
    vice president and therefore succeeded to the presidency on his death)
Election: November 1904, elected in his own right
Vice president: Charles Warren Fairbanks
Length of term: 7 years, 171 days

He sought to regulate big business, not to cripple it, still less destroy it. Above all, he sought to assert the rights of the people against special interests. He used the theatrical powers of the Presidency as no one before him to focus popular discontents in the cause of creative reform, and to fight his battles with reactionary Republican majorities in the House and Senate. The spirit of his administration is symbolic of the Progressive Era, in which aggregates of local and national individuals and groups independently sought gradual reforms in social justice, city government, business, and politics. (Evans, 1998, p. 71)

1.14 President Theodore Roosevelt and the origins of Progressivism

When President Roosevelt delivered his inaugural address at a lavish ceremony on Saturday 4 March 1905, he presented an exposition of the philosophy of Progressivism:

Our relations with the other powers of the world are important; but still more important are our relations among ourselves. Such growth in wealth, in population, and in power as this nation has seen during the century and a quarter of its national life is inevitably accompanied by a like growth in the problems which are ever before every nation that rises to greatness. Power invariably means both responsibility and danger ... Modern life is both complex and intense, and the tremendous changes wrought by the extraordinary industrial development of the last half-century are felt in every fiber of our social and political being. Never before have men tried so vast and formidable an experiment as that of administering the affairs of a continent under the forms of a Democratic Republic. The conditions which have told for our marvelous material well-being, which have developed to a very high degree our energy, self-reliance, and individual initiative, have also brought the care and anxiety inseparable from the accumulation of great wealth in industrial centers. Upon the success of our experiment much depends, not only as regards our own welfare, but as regards the welfare of mankind. If we fail, the cause of free self-government throughout the world will rock to its foundations, and therefore our responsibility is heavy, to ourselves, to the world as it is today and to the generations yet unborn.

Roosevelt and female suffrage

These sentiments did not mean that much was forthcoming from the White House in the way of women's emancipation. In March 1905, President Roosevelt told the National Congress of Mothers:

> The Nation is in a bad way, if the woman has lost her sense of duty, if she is sunk in vapid self-indulgence or has let her nature be twisted so that she prefers a sterile pseudo-intellectuality to that great and beautiful development of character which comes only to those whose lives know the fullness of duty done, or effort made, and self-sacrifice undergone. (Simon, 2017, p. 49)

These arguments faced a growing counter-movement boosted by the rise of the Progressive Movement and the overlap between some of their ideals and the beliefs of the campaigners for women's suffrage. It was claimed that the progressives' campaign against political corruption would be boosted by the purifying impact of giving suffrage to women. Furthermore, the enfranchisement of women would advance the cause of Prohibition. Finally, women would use their vote to support progressive causes such as protection of children in the workplace and improvements in public health and housing. The leaders of the women's suffrage movement presided over a massive increase in their membership (NAWSA had just 17,000 members in 1905 and 2 million by 1917) and a growing acceptance of the validity of their cause. Without ever adopting the militant tactics of their English counterparts the movement led to seven further states introducing woman suffrage between 1910 and 1914.

The rise of Progressivism

The sentiment that sweeping improvements and reforms were needed across a broad range of American society expressed itself in what became known as the 'Progressive Movement', which was influential across the nation between 1900 and 1919. Historian Gary Gerstle has spoken of the 'high-profile reform movements that sought to turn the federal government into a highly centralized, administratively capacious, and redistributionist instrument of reform ... widening its area of authority and stoking its policymaking power' (Gerstle, 2015, p. 5).

Building on prosperity

When President Roosevelt and other influential figures in American society examined their country at the turn of the twentieth century, they saw immense wealth and considerable economic advantages. They had witnessed the rapid construction of great cities, and their country had undoubtedly entered the new century amid a feeling of general prosperity. Indeed, it was the feeling of confidence in the economy fuelled by an upturn after the recession of 1893 and 1894 which led many Americans to decide that the time was ripe for further improvements.

Social concerns

Those who embraced the Progressive Movement were keenly aware of society's ills. Squalid living conditions, exploitation of labour, political corruption, denial of the suffrage to women, poor public health, widespread poverty, crime, vice and alcohol abuse all gave cause for concern. Many Americans came to accept the simple notion that further progress was now necessary.

Fear of social upheaval

Most progressives belonged to the middle class. They perceived disturbing signs that not everyone affected by poor conditions both in the workplace and at home was content to go on merely accepting their lot. President Roosevelt referred in his inaugural address to the dire consequences that could afflict American society if root and branch reform was not implemented. For example, many progressives were alarmed by what they saw as the rapid rise of the radical left, exemplified by the foundation of the Socialist Party of America in 1901. Further cause for concern came in the presidential elections of 1904 and 1912, when the Socialist candidate Eugene V. Debs polled 402,000 and 897,000 votes respectively. In 1910, Victor Berger, representing Milwaukee, became the first Socialist congressman, and by 1912 more than 50 cities had returned Socialist mayors. Fear of the left, then, can be said to be a major factor in the origins of Progressivism.

Influential writers

Certain influential texts played a role in stimulating progressive ideals, for example the publication of *Progress and Poverty* by Henry George (1879). George's powerful demands for social justice and his articulation of the need to reconstruct society made a deep impact on many Americans. Upton Sinclair's *The Jungle* (1906) exposed horrifying conditions in meat-packing factories.

Political corruption

Articles such as Lincoln Steffen's *The Shame of the Cities*, serialised in the popular magazine *McClure's* in 1902, exposed widespread political graft and corruption and led Roosevelt to label the investigative journalists who published such work as 'muckrakers'. The exposure of corruption prompted many progressives to search for improvement.

1.15 The Roosevelt Administration

When Roosevelt entered the Oval Office in 1901 he presided over a country of great extremes of wealth and poverty. As a New York politician he had roamed the slums at night, armed with a pistol and eager to witness for himself the deprivation and poverty which so many Americans endured. Yet at the same time the country for which he now had responsibility had given rise to almost 4,000 millionaires. Constituting a tiny fraction of the nation's population, they owned almost a quarter of its wealth. The richest of the rich, self-made men like Andrew Carnegie, had amassed their fortunes in business. In part, their success had developed through the steady acquisition of smaller businesses by the larger ones. For example, Carnegie had become the richest man in the world through the gradual acquisition of smaller steel companies, culminating in 1901 with the sale to J.P. Morgan of his own massive company which then became US Steel. The company created by this deal comprised 800 separate steel plants brought together to form a billion-dollar corporation.

Roosevelt's belief was that the creation of these gigantic conglomerates, or trusts, was not necessarily in the public interest – for example, a large railroad trust might result in price fixing. Other huge corporations could exploit their workforce or perpetuate unacceptable working practices. Essentially Roosevelt did not object to trusts so much as wish to defend the public interest. Whereas many of his less energetic predecessors in the White House had been content to let big business have its way, Roosevelt came to the highest office with the energy and drive needed to redress the balance. Table 1.3 highlights some of the key areas which Roosevelt now addressed.

Table 1.3	Theodore Roosevelt and domestic issues, 1901–1908
1901 **14 September**	At the age of 42 Roosevelt became the youngest-ever president upon the death of McKinley. As vice president he automatically succeeded to the presidency and became the 26th President of the United States.
1902 **10 March**	Roosevelt began the first of his trust-busting campaigns, in this instance directed against J.P. Morgan's Northern Securities Company, an enormous rail-holding company under the control of J.P. Morgan and associates.
May	The anthracite coal strike of 1902 was based on a demand for higher wages and a shorter working day. When the mine owners refused to make concessions, Roosevelt organised a conference at the White House to resolve matters. This was the first time a president had intervened so directly in a dispute between employers and labour. When this failed, the president compelled the owners to come to terms. The miners went back to work in the spring of 1903, having received a wage rise and a reduction in hours from the Anthracite Coal Commission. Roosevelt stated that he was not taking sides but simply working for a 'fair deal'.
17 June	The Newlands Reclamation Act to promote an irrigation programme for desert lands in the West. Roosevelt's willingness to embrace these issues showed the breadth of his vision of presidential action. As a young boy he had become fascinated by nature; as president, he was happy to embrace conservation issues.
1903 **14 February**	Creation of the Department of Commerce and Labor, including a Bureau of Corporations to investigate trusts.

Continued

19 February	Re-enforcement of Antitrust laws.
1904 14 March	The Supreme Court ordered the dissolution of the Northern Securities Company. This represented Roosevelt's breakthrough in his campaign to regulate big business.
8 November	Roosevelt elected as president in his own right.
1906 June	The Senate passed the Pure Food and Drug Act, following a public outcry over reports of widespread adulteration in food processing. Writer Upton Sinclair's book *The Jungle* exposed in graphic detail horrendous practices in the Chicago meat-packing industry. Roosevelt dispatched US Labor Commissioner Charles Neill and New York reformer James Reynolds to carry out an impartial investigation of the damaging claims. They discovered that some workers were involved in food production while suffering from tuberculosis, and that rancid meat was processed in the production of food for human consumption. Although Roosevelt hesitated to publish the report in the face of business opposition, its details became public and the administration felt compelled to act. A bill was passed through Congress and became law when Roosevelt signed it on 30 June 1906. The problem of enforcement remained. The second dimension of this legislation concerned abuses in the area of patent medicines. Typically these contained ingredients which were either of dubious value or were downright harmful and which could not possibly fulfil the outrageous claims made by those who sold them. The administration's attack on this practice was spearheaded by Harvey W. Wiley, Chief of the Department of Agriculture's Bureau of Chemistry. The crucial test case called into question the value of 'Cuforhedake Brane-Fude', a bestselling headache remedy. When it was established that the qualities of the medicine could not be proven its maker was fined and in future there was a greater degree of regulation in this area. The Hepburn Act (1906) enforced stricter regulation on the railroads, allowing the Interstate Commerce Commission (ICC) to regulate maximum rates. This marked the beginning of effective railroad controls and the initial outcome was generally lower fares in response to passenger complaints to the ICC.
1907 13 March	A major financial crisis led a large number of banks and businesses to collapse. Economic turmoil followed the collapse of the Knickerbocker Trust Company. Roosevelt now sought the co-operation of the Wall Street financiers whom he had earlier confronted. Massive sums of government money were pumped into banks in New York City to keep them afloat. Given the prevailing financial anxiety, Roosevelt was persuaded by business interests to allow the United States Steel Corporation to take over the Tennessee Coal and Iron Company.
1908	Between 1907 and 1908 Roosevelt advocated the introduction of death duties and an income tax, federal supervision of the stock market and the wider implementation of the eight-hour working day. Such progressive measures appealed to the small radical element within his own party but at the same time tended to alienate the substantial bloc which revolved around the interests of big business.
30 March	National Monetary Commission set up under the terms of the Aldrich–Vreeland Act.
3 November	Roosevelt created the National Conservation Commission. William Howard Taft (Republican) elected 27th President.

Roosevelt channelled his boundless energy through his abiding principle that the president was the steward of the people. His political apprenticeship in New York City had left him with an acute sense of unfinished business. He knew that many Americans had fulfilled the American dream and accumulated boundless wealth, yet he was also fully aware of society's ills. In his first message to Congress he drew attention to the 'real and grave evils' of the new giant industrial combinations. Roosevelt was aware of opposition to his ideas within Congress and on Wall Street, but he had correctly judged the public mood. In his outstanding three-volume biography of Roosevelt, Edmund Morris looked back from the perspective of January 1907 at the president's legislative achievements:

> Politically, too, it has been a year of superlatives, many of them supplied, with characteristic immodesty, by the President himself. 'No Congress in our time has done more good work,' he fondly told the fifty-ninth, having battered it into submission with the sheer volume of his social legislation. He calls its first session 'the most substantial' in his experience of public affairs. Joseph G. Cannon, the Speaker of the House agrees, with one reservation about the President's methods. 'Roosevelt's all right,' says Cannon, 'but he's got no more use for the Constitution than a tomcat for a marriage license...'
>
> The editor of the *St. Louis Censor,* who has never forgiven Roosevelt for inviting a black man to dine in the White House, warns that he is now trying to end segregation of Orientals in San Francisco schools. 'Almost every week his Administration has been characterized by some outrageous act of usurpation ... he is the most dangerous foe to human liberty that has ever set foot on American soil.' Another Southerner, by the name of Woodrow Wilson, is tempted to agree: 'He is the most dangerous man of the age.' Mark Twain believes that the President is 'clearly insane ... and insanest upon war and its supreme glories.' (Morris, 1979, p. xiv)

By the time he left office in 1909, Roosevelt's administration had issued suits under the previously inert Sherman Antitrust Act against over 40 corporations, including the Standard Oil Company, the American Tobacco Company and the meat-packers. The consequences of Roosevelt's actions for the American people were clear. His work against the trusts produced more competitive prices and better standards in public transport. His legislation in the food industry addressed serious problems of hygiene and public safety. His work in conservation produced more forest land, irrigation schemes, reclamation programmes, dam building, a National Conservation Commission and an Inland Waterways Commission.

1.16 The Taft Administration

Roosevelt's charismatic style and personal popularity meant that he could have stood for election again in 1908. However, his respect for the long-standing and widely accepted two-term tradition led Roosevelt to promise during the 1904 campaign that that would be his last campaign. Nevertheless, he was instrumental in securing the nomination of his close friend and political ally William Howard Taft as the next

Republican nominee. In the Republican Party Convention of June 1908 Taft was nominated on the first ballot with the distinctively named Philander Chase Knox a distant
second. Taft was uncomfortable with the hurly-burly of the election campaign and was
elected largely because of his close ties to Roosevelt (Table 1.4).

Ironically, given the fact that he was Roosevelt's personal favourite to succeed him,
Taft singularly lacked his predecessor's drive and energy. His expertise lay in the legal
system and he was less well suited to the political complexities of Washington. Taft
retained the key figures from the Roosevelt Cabinet in his administration but he was
unable to build on Roosevelt's achievements or to develop a popular distinctive style
of his own.

In the words of John Whiteclay Chambers II:

Inheriting a difficult situation, Roosevelt's handpicked successor, William Howard
Taft, made the worst of it ... The tide of reform overwhelmed him ... He failed to
mobilize the people or keep his party intact. In the end the electorate repudiated

Table 1.4   The result of the 1908 presidential election

Candidate	Party	Electoral College votes	Popular votes
William H. Taft (Ohio)	Republican	321	7,678,908
William J. Bryan (Nebraska)	Democrat	162	6,409,104
Eugene V. Debs (Indiana)	Socialist	–	420,793

PRESIDENTIAL PROFILE

William Howard Taft

27th President of the United States (1909–13)
Born: 15 September 1857
Birthplace: Cincinnati, Ohio
Died: 8 March 1930, aged 72; buried at Arlington National Cemetery, Virginia
Education: Woodward Hill School, Cincinnati; Yale University
Political party: Republican
State: Ohio
Occupations before presidency: Lawyer; judge
Previous government service: 1901–04: Governor of the Philippines in the
    Roosevelt Administration; 1904–08: Secretary of War (a close friend and
    political ally of Theodore Roosevelt, who saw Taft as his protégé and
    successor)
Age at inauguration: 51
Dates of office: March 1909–March 1913
Election: November 1908
Vice president: James S. Sherman
Length of term: 4 years

him. Taft was not the man for the Presidency. He lacked the imagination and ability to manage contending political forces. He preferred the calm of the courtroom ... Despite his admiration for Roosevelt, Taft was too strict a constitutionalist to emulate TR's bold political ventures and too conservative to go along with continued sweeping reform. (Whiteclay Chambers II, 1992, pp. 184–85)

Within four years Taft had presided over a serious split within the GOP (Grand Old Party, a colloquial term for the Republican Party). Roosevelt had become increasingly dissatisfied with Taft's stance on environment issues, the tariff question, trusts and his ability to lead the Republican Party. Taft's presidency became increasingly factious (Table 1.5). In the early months of 1912 Roosevelt secured victory in a number of state primaries. Although Taft was reselected by the Republican Party for the presidential election in 1912 he trailed in a humiliating third behind Wilson and Roosevelt.

Table 1.5 Timeline: The Taft Administration and domestic issues, 1909–11

1909 **4 March**	Taft delivered his inaugural address inside, in the Senate Chamber. A severe blizzard in Washington disrupted the arrangements and led to most of the inaugural parade being abandoned.
	The Ballinger–Pinchot controversy cast a cloud over the Taft Administration for over a year. It began when Gifford Pinchot, the Chief Forester, publicly accused Richard Ballinger, the Secretary of the Interior, of responding to the pressures of corporate interests ahead of the needs of conservation. In particular, Ballinger was accused of helping a private syndicate mining government-owned coal reserves in Alaska. After examining the case, Taft's response was to dismiss Pinchot, who was fired in January 1910. It soon became clear that Taft had seriously misjudged the political climate on this issue. The majority of Americans favoured Pinchot's position but Taft refused to shift his stance out of a sense of loyalty to a man he was convinced was innocent.
April	The Payne–Aldrich Tariff passes through Congress. A high-tariff act, it had little impact on the prevailing economic climate. Taft supported the Bill, which he declared was the best tariff law ever passed by Congress.
May	Taft allowed the opening to settlers of more than 500,000 acres of land in Idaho, Washington and Montana.
July	Congress put forward the Sixteenth Amendment authorising a federal income tax for the first time, ratified by the states in 1913.
1910 **March**	Turmoil in Congress following protest by progressives against 'Cannonism', the allegedly dictatorial rule of the Speaker of the House of Representatives, 'Uncle Joe' Cannon. Cannon's control of the Rules Committee which organised the order of business in the House gave him immense power. An attempt to dislodge him in 1909 was followed by a move by a bloc of Progressive Republicans in the House to say that members of the Rules Committee should in future be elected by members of the House rather than appointed by the Speaker. Although this motion was passed in 1910 after it was supported by the Democrats the episode damaged Taft's standing because he had given the progressives – or 'Insurgents', as they became known – the impression that he would support them. His change of heart, based on the desire to appease influential conservatives in the Republican Party, was one of several occasions when Taft's judgement proved insecure.

Continued

18 June	Mann–Elkins Act reforms railroad regulation.
August	Rift between Taft and Roosevelt over Antitrust suits.
8 November	Midterm Congressional elections saw a swing to the Democrats, who took control of the House of Representatives for the first time since 1895. Congress now had a reform-minded complexion which Taft found difficult to work with.
1911 15 May	Standard Oil Company dissolved by the Supreme Court in an Antitrust decision.

1.17 Woodrow Wilson and the New Freedom

Wilson's background

We will now consider in some detail the early life, political development and presidency of Woodrow Wilson, who was first elected to the White House in 1912. It is fascinating to observe in Wilson's early life some of the traits which would become deeply significant when he came to occupy the Oval Office.

There were spells in his young life when Thomas Woodrow Wilson was a combination of fragile health and academic excellence. Born in 1856, he had to leave Davidson College in North Carolina in 1874 on health grounds. He graduated from the College of New Jersey (later Princeton) in 1879 and then from the University of Virginia Law School in 1882 but this was disrupted because of illness. In 1886 he received a PhD degree in political science from Johns Hopkins University. Between 1890 and 1902 he was Professor of Jurisprudence and Political Economy at Princeton University and in 1902 he was elected to the prestigious post of President of Princeton University, a position which he retained until 1910. By now the characteristics which were so marked in the later president could be identified: a brilliant mind, a reputation as a gifted speaker, intolerance of those who could not see the point he was making and, above all, granite-like determination. These were the qualities, and faults, which Wilson brought to elected office for the first time in 1910. Just over two years later he would be president. He would be the first president to deliver an address by radio, the first to hold formal press conferences, the only president with a PhD and one of the last to personally craft his own speeches.

From gubernatorial campaign, New Jersey, 1910 to presidential candidate

On 15 July 1910 Wilson formally accepted the New Jersey gubernatorial nomination after Democratic Party State bosses approached him. Two months later, after a meeting at Trenton, New Jersey, the Democratic State Convention nominated Woodrow Wilson for the governorship. Wilson campaigned energetically. Between September and November he made 27 speeches, the contents of which reflected his gradual move towards the left. On 20 October he resigned as president of Princeton and on 8 November he was elected with a margin of almost 50,000 votes over the next candidate. On 17 January 1911 he was inaugurated as the 43rd Governor of New Jersey, his inaugural address emphasising his desire for economic and social reform.

Confirmation that Wilson was already being seen as an outstanding personality with presidential prospects came in March 1911, when he delivered his first major speech outside New Jersey, in Atlanta, Georgia. A setback in the New Jersey State elections of November 1911 was not enough to deflect Wilson. In the Democratic Party primaries held between January and June 1912 he delivered a series of rousing speeches embracing a range of progressive causes which set him apart from the party's southern candidate, Oscar Underwood (Alabama). A more serious rival for the nomination was 'Champ' Clark, who had held senior positions within the Democratic Party leadership in Congress. When the Democratic Party Convention was held in Baltimore in June and July, Clark emerged as the early leader and it was not until the 46th ballot that Wilson obtained the necessary two-thirds majority. On the first ballot Wilson had obtained only 324 votes; on the final ballot this had increased to 990.

The presidential campaign of 1912

Wilson was an able campaigner and placed emphasis on a programme which he labelled the *New Freedom*. He called for the return of free competition in the marketplace, more support for small businesses, tariff reduction and reform of the Antitrust laws and the banking system.

Meanwhile, Roosevelt, who had already served as Republican president from 1901 – upon the death of President McKinley – and was elected in his own right in November 1904 to serve until 1909, had left the Republican Party. Stressing to journalists that he felt as strong as a 'Bull Moose' he became the candidate of the Progressive Party which had developed around a group of insurgents, including the notable progressive Robert La Follette. Roosevelt called his programme, which was a wide-ranging package of economic and social reform including an eight-hour working day and an income tax, 'New Nationalism'. Taft, who had been a relatively lacklustre president since 1909, was somewhat overshadowed by his formidable predecessor and went into the campaign expecting to lose but gaining some comfort from his conviction that the defeat would serve as a lesson to the insurgents. Wilson and Roosevelt dominated the campaign. The most dramatic moment came in October 1912 when Roosevelt was shot by and wounded by a deranged saloonkeeper at a campaign event in Milwaukee. Despite having a bullet lodged in his chest, he insisted on giving his speech to a large crowd before going to hospital. Roosevelt gradually recovered but effectively the attempt on his life meant that his campaign came to an end.

Wilson displayed his astute political instincts by gracefully suspending his own campaign while Roosevelt was ill. It was the final gesture on the way to a decisive victory. On 5 November Wilson cast his own vote at the fire station in Princeton. When the nation's votes were counted it became clear that he had won the popular vote by an emphatic margin: 6,294,327 to Roosevelt's 4,120,207, with Taft in third place at 3,486,343. His Electoral College victory looked even more impressive, with 40 states across all regions of the country and a total of 435 electoral votes. Roosevelt carried 6 states, which were California, Michigan, Minnesota, Pennsylvania, South Dakota and Washington, with a total of 88. Taft won just the states of Utah and Vermont, with a total of 8 electoral votes (Table 1.6).

Table 1.6 The result of the 1912 presidential election

Candidate	Party	Electoral College votes	Popular votes
Thomas Woodrow Wilson (New Jersey)	Democratic	435	6,294,327
Theodore Roosevelt (New York)	Progressive	88	4,120,207
William H. Taft (Ohio)	Republican	8	3,486,343
Eugene V. Debs (Indiana)	Socialist	–	901,873
Eugene W. Chafin (Arizona)	Prohibition	–	206,275

Note: These voting figures mean that Wilson received only a minority of the popular vote (41.8 per cent)

The Democrats also won control of the House of Representatives and the Senate. Although Democrats controlled Congress, southern conservatives within the party dominated the important Congressional committees. This election became known as the 'Big Three' election because Wilson was a Princeton graduate, Taft had attended Yale and Roosevelt had studied at Harvard. Wilson had defeated two candidates who had held the highest office even though his political career was in its infancy. Wilson's vice president was Thomas Riley Marshall.

PRESIDENTIAL PROFILE

Thomas Woodrow Wilson

28th President of the United States (1913–21)
Born: 28 December 1856
Birthplace: Staunton, Virginia
Died: 3 February 1924, aged 67; buried at the National Cathedral, Washington, DC
Education: Davidson College, North Carolina; graduated from the College of New Jersey (later Princeton University) (1879) and from the University of Virginia Law School (1882)
Political party: Democratic
State: New Jersey
Occupations before presidency: Professor of Jurisprudence and Political Economy, Princeton University (1890–1902); President of Princeton University (1902–10)
Previous government service: Governor of New Jersey (1911)
Age at inauguration: 56
Dates of office: 4 March 1913–4 March 1921
Election: November 1912 and 1916
Vice president: Thomas R. Marshall
Length of term: 8 years

Wilson's first term

In February 1913 Wilson stood down from his post as Governor of New Jersey. He was inaugurated as president a month later. In the same month, he became the first president to hold an open news conference, as opposed to an audience with selected journalists. Despite this innovation, Wilson's relationship with the press became troubled and the press conferences were withdrawn in 1915. A further break with tradition came when Wilson addressed the full Congress in person in a speech recommending tariff reduction. These initiatives were characteristic of a dynamic period in American history. Wilson embarked upon an energetic first term, comparable in terms of legislation passed with the great programmes of F.D. Roosevelt and L.B. Johnson.

Tariff reduction

During the presidential campaign Wilson had committed himself to a promise of reducing tariffs. His ability to secure congressional support was reflected in the fact that the House of Representatives quickly pushed through a bill which abolished duties on more than 100 articles and reduced them on almost 1,000 others. Given that the obvious consequence of this was to reduce government revenue, the Sixteenth Amendment was introduced to levy an income tax.

Banking reform

David Reynolds describes Wilson's creation of the Federal Reserve Act, 'to make the rickety American banking system more stable', as 'perhaps the biggest reform of the progressive era' (Reynolds, 2009, p. 281). It could be argued that the American banking system had not kept pace with the burgeoning economy. Even as late as the business panic of 1907, all banks operated independently, making some of the smaller banks less than robust and the system itself somewhat complex. In addition, there was no established framework of support for banks when they encountered financial turbulence. Finally, national banks were only allowed to issue notes in proportion to their holdings of government bonds.

The Federal Reserve Act which was passed in 1913 addressed these weaknesses but attracted fierce opposition from the right-wing press and powerful banking interests who advocated a completely de-centralized, privately controlled reserve system. The new Federal Reserve would be a government agency whose chairman and governors would be appointed by the president while at the same time considerable power was also placed in regional banks with the creation of 12 financial districts across the whole country. While this legislation was of great importance economically it also demonstrates Wilson's political authority, skill and legislative leadership.

Major tariff and banking reform was only the start of Wilson's hectic first term.

Table 1.7 summarises Wilson's domestic preoccupations up to the declaration of war in April 1917.

Table 1.7   Woodrow Wilson and the New Freedom, 1913–17

1913 **4 March**	Wilson inaugurated. Congress divided the Commerce and Labor Department into two distinct but Cabinet-level departments.
12 March	Wilson called Congress into special session for 7 April.
15 March	Wilson delivered his first presidential press conference.
8 April	Wilson became the first chief executive for more than a century to appear before a Joint Session of Congress.
11 April	Wilson gave approval to racial segregation within the American civil service following a Cabinet proposal by the postmaster general (Southern influence in Wilson's support for racial legislation).
22 April	In Congress the Underwood Bill advocated a reduction in the tariffs contained in the Payne–Aldrich tariff. The Bill received Congressional support and in the face of anti-bill lobbyists Wilson publicly condemned those wanting to amend it. The Bill was passed by the Senate in September and signed by the president in October.
31 May	Ratification of the Sixteenth and Seventeenth Amendments to the Constitution, leading to a federal income tax and a change in the way the Senate was elected, replacing a system in which senators were selected by state legislatures by one with direct election of senators.
26 June	A bill was introduced in both Houses of Congress to create a Federal Reserve to act as the country's central bank. Intense debate surrounded the Bill, which was passed through the Senate in December. A Federal Reserve Board, which was based in Washington, directed the bank. This move reflected official disquiet with Wall Street in New York and with the events surrounding the serious financial panic of 1907. The Board was empowered to act independently of the president and given the opportunity to exercise national control over the banking and currency of the United States. A system of 12 regional Federal Reserve banks were created.
1914 **20 January**	Wilson told a joint session of Congress that he would follow a policy of 'quiet moderation' in regard to big business.
4 February	The House passed an Immigration Restriction Bill (the Burnett Bill).
15 February	The House passed a bill calling for a minimum age for child labour, but Wilson refused to support it, and it was also rejected by the Senate.
14 April	The Clayton Bill, introduced by Henry Clayton, an influential member of the House, detailed illegal practices in restraint of free trade. The Bill became law in October but reduced in scope.
12 June	The Stevens Bill sought to bolster the powers of the Federal Trade Commission (FTC) to regulate fair trade practices.
July	Towards the end of the month share prices plummeted as war loomed in Europe.
September	The Federal Trade Commission Act passed, to oversee the activities of corporations and to prevent unfair business practices.
3 November	In the midterm Congressional elections, the Democrats retained control of the House but with a much-reduced majority, losing 61 seats. The Democrats gained five seats in the Senate, for a 56–40 majority.
12 November	Wilson spoke of 'benefits' to African Americans of the segregation system.

Continued

1915 **2 January**	Only seven senators voted against the Burnett Immigration Restriction Bill with its literacy clauses. Wilson used his veto against the Bill at the end of the month. The year marked the sinking of a number of ships in the Atlantic by German submarines, leading to an emphasis on the need for military preparedness.
4 March	The Seaman's Act improved conditions and safety for merchant sailors.
18 December	Wilson married Edith Galt (his first wife died in August 1914).
1916 **January**	With an eye on the presidential election in November, Wilson tried to attract progressives to support him by announcing a new batch of progressive measures. In the same month, Wilson embarked upon a speaking tour in the west of the country to bolster support for military preparedness. Meanwhile, he made one of the most significant appointments of his entire presidency when he placed the Jewish liberal Louis D. Brandeis on the Supreme Court; Brandeis went on to serve with great distinction until 1939. In the House, a new Shipping Bill was introduced, allowing for the creation of a US Shipping Board to operate shipping lanes.
2 February	The Keating–Owen Child Labor Bill passed through the House. It passed the Senate in September but was declared unconstitutional by the Supreme Court in 1918.
4 May	The Hollis–Bulkley Rural Credit Bill passed the Senate.
11 July	The Federal Highway Act approved government aid to states for road building.
17 July	Wilson supported the Farm Loan Act to provide credit through 12 regional Farm Loan banks.
11 August	The Warehouse Act created a national framework for inspection of farm warehouses; farmers could deposit their commodities at licensed warehouses.
19 August	The Kern–McGillicuddy Bill – The Federal Employees' Compensation Act – offered compensation to half a million federal employees.
3 September	Wilson signed the Adamson Act which created an eight-hour day for railroad workers.
8 September	The Emergency Revenue Act doubled the income tax and introduced an inheritance tax.
7 November	Wilson re-elected president.
1917 **5 February**	Congress overrode Wilson's veto to introduce a literacy test for immigrants.
22 February	The Smith–Hughes Act provided funding for agricultural and vocational education.
8 March	Senate voted to amend the cloture rule: if two-thirds of the senators present voted to invoke cloture, each senator was limited to just one hour of debate.
2 April	Jeannette Rankin became the first woman in the House of Representatives. Wilson asked Congress to support a declaration of war against Germany.
4 April	The Senate voted 82–6 in favour of a declaration of war.
6 April	The House voted 373–50 to declare war.

Further reading

Berg A.S., *Wilson* (London: Simon & Schuster UK 2013).

Brogan H., *The Penguin History of the United States of America* (London: Penguin 1990).

Clements K.A., *Woodrow Wilson: World Statesman* (Chicago: Ivan R. Dee 1987).

Cobbs E., *The Hello Girls: America's First Women Soldiers* (Cambridge, Mass.: Harvard University Press 2017).

Cooper J.M., *Woodrow Wilson, A Biography* (New York: Vintage Books 2011).

Evans H., *The American Century: People, Power and Politics: An Illustrated History* (London: Jonathan Cape 1998).

Fernandez-Armesto F., *Our America: A Hispanic History of the United States* (New York: W. W. Norton 2015).

Gerstle G., *Liberty and Coercion: The Paradox of American Government from the Founding to the Present* (New Jersey: Princeton University Press 2015).

Gordon R.J., *The Rise and Fall of American Growth* (New Jersey: Princeton University Press 2016).

Hawley E.W., *The Great War and the Search for a Modern Order: A History of the American People and Their Institutions, 1917–1933* (New York: St Martin's Press 1979).

Jones M.A., *The Limits of Liberty: American History 1607–1992* (New York: Oxford University Press 1995).

Kinzer S., *The True Flag: Theodore Roosevelt, Mark Twain, and the Birth of American Empire* (New York: Henry Holt and Company 2017).

Morris C.R., *The Tycoons* (New York: Holt 2005).

Morris E., *The Rise of Theodore Roosevelt* (New York: Random House 1979).

Morris E., *Theodore Rex* (New York: Random House 2001).

Page J., *In the Hands of the Great Spirit* (New York: Free Press 2003).

Simon L., *Lost Girls: The Invention of the Flapper* (London: Reaktion Books Ltd 2017).

Temperley H. & Bigsby C. (eds.), *A New Introduction to American Studies* (London: Pearson 2006).

Twain M., *Autobiography of Mark Twain: Volume 1* (Berkeley: University of California Press 2010).

Wallace M., *Greater Gotham: A History of New York City from 1898 to 1919* (New York: Oxford University Press 2017).

Whiteclay Chambers J. II, *The Tyranny of Change: America in the Progressive Era 1890–1920* (New York: St Martin's Press 1992).

2 Foreign policy 1900–20

2.1 Theodore Roosevelt and foreign policy

The concept of isolationism

The new industrial powerhouse had, until 1898, reserved its energy for the rigours of industrial development. It had not been put to the test in war since the conflict with Mexico that began in 1846. As one analyst has put it, for the majority of the nineteenth century the United States enjoyed 'an era of free security' (Whiteclay Chambers II, 1992, p. 201). America's geographical position, the huge defensive barrier formed by the Pacific and Atlantic Oceans and the stability generated by the European balance of power, made the task of guiding American foreign policy straightforward.

With modern communication systems still in their infancy the average American citizen's awareness of world affairs was limited. The isolationist ideas of Americans such as George Washington, who cautioned against 'the insidious wiles of foreign influence', and Thomas Jefferson, who advised against 'entangling alliances', remained influential. In the words of John Whiteclay Chambers II:

> Like a young giant flexing newfound muscles, the United States swaggered onto the center of the world stage in the early years of the twentieth century. The rapidly industrializing nation expanded its economic interests and began a policy of diplomatic and military intervention abroad. This new international activism moved beyond America's traditional foreign policy of reacting to events. Policymakers ... began to use American power to shape the international environment, protect American interests, and encourage progress in international relations. (Whiteclay Chambers II, 1992, p. 201)

A hallowed tradition of isolationism had been passed from one president to the next. The received wisdom passed down from Jefferson onwards was that the United States should avoid foreign entanglements. Sheer physical distance from Europe was a major factor in sustaining this outlook. As Hugh Brogan puts it: 'The world was so large, the oceans so wide and their own continent so vast and empty it was impossible for the Americans to be much concerned with foreign affairs.' (Brogan, 1990, p. 448) In addition, the shocking losses of the American Civil War meant that an appetite for bloodshed was conspicuous by its absence. Yet, ironically, as the Progressive Era dawned and as the new century beckoned, the United States found itself at war. An increasingly vocal body of opinion began to express the belief that the United States now needed to adopt a new approach in international affairs, believing that the country could no longer afford to sit back and watch while other nations developed into major powers. The dynamic growth of Germany and Japan, for example, made many Americans wary that the United States would fall behind its rivals.

When the war with Spain broke out in 1898, one vocal senator exclaimed: 'There is no such thing as isolation in the world today.' (Whiteclay Chambers II, 1992, p. 202) In part, the senator was right. The Industrial Revolution had created new weapons and new warships which enabled the European powers and Japan to assert themselves more forcefully than ever before. As these world powers greedily pursued their imperialist aims in Asia and Africa it seemed increasingly unrealistic to expect the United States to remain completely aloof from these developments. A nation in which isolationist feeling ran deep ended the nineteenth century with a victorious war over Spain, the acquisition of territories in Hawaii, Samoa, Guam, the Philippines and Puerto Rico and, as the new century began, the creation of American protectorates in Haiti, Panama, Nicaragua and the Dominican Republic.

Roosevelt's 'big stick' diplomacy

The three presidents who led the United States in the period 1901–17 each had a distinctive approach towards foreign affairs. Theodore Roosevelt, when asked about his foreign policy, liked to quote the African saying: 'Speak softly and carry a big stick.' Roosevelt replaced the broadly reactive nature of American foreign policy with a proactive style based on racial, geographic, strategic and commercial considerations. He aimed to protect America's interests where he felt they were threatened and to develop American control where he felt it was desirable. Under the influence of expansionists such as Admiral Mahan, and the military governor of Cuba, General Wood, Roosevelt was prepared to commit the United States to a policy of realpolitik. America would now actively seek to use diplomacy, economic strength and ultimately naval and military power to further its aims. Roosevelt's more ambitious agenda can be detected in the rapid growth of the navy which he instigated. Between 1901 and 1909 the American Navy virtually doubled in size. Annual naval expenditure at the start of the century amounted to $56 million; five years later this figure had been increased to $118 million.

The Spanish–American War, 1898

The war between Spain and the United States flared up over Cuba. Cuba was the only colony that Spain had retained in the Americas; when Spanish rule came under threat with a series of uprisings in the 1890s, most notably in 1895, many Americans sympathised with the Cuban rebels. The physical proximity of Cuba – just 90 miles off the Florida coast – was a factor, but equally important was the sense of supporting the demand for independence against the colonial power. Some Americans maintained that the United States should go to the aid of the Cuban people in the face of the repressive Spanish regime. Some historians have estimated that thousands of Cuban civilians died in concentration camps on the island; contemporary accounts of Spanish execution squads callously shooting the rebels added to the desire to help Cuba. Religion also played its part, because of the clash between Catholic Spain and Protestant America.

In the presidential election campaign of 1896, the Republicans made a commitment to supporting Cuban independence. The situation was made more volatile by the fact that Spain was absolutely determined to hang on to the last vestiges of its New World empire and by 1898 had deployed almost 200,000 soldiers in a bid to retain it. A pivotal moment came when the American battleship *Maine* was dispatched to Havana. On 15 February 1898, the ship was blown up by a mine in Havana harbour with the loss of 260 crew. While doubt remains as to exactly who planted the mine, newspapers controlled by jingoistic press barons like William Randolph Hearst and Joseph Pulitzer seized upon this 'outrage' and placed the blame firmly on the Spanish. The battle cry, 'Remember the *Maine*!' was taken up across the country. Amid inflamed public opinion Congress voted unanimously to approve $50 million for national defence. With midterm elections looming, and taunted by Roosevelt that he was displaying less backbone than 'a chocolate éclair', President McKinley felt compelled to act. On 11 April 1898 the president urged Congress to seek 'forceful intervention' in Cuba to bring peace to the island. In the face of American action, Spain declared war on the United States on 24 April.

The conflict was fought largely at sea. This was fortunate for the United States, whose army numbered less than 30,000 but which in the previous decade had transformed its navy from a limited and dated affair to a new and powerful fleet. Heavy Congressional spending in 1883 saw the construction of four steel cruisers; by the time the war with Spain came along the United States had 17 battleships and six armoured cruisers. This gave it a huge advantage over a rather weak Spanish fleet. In the key exchanges, the Americans defeated the Spanish Pacific squadron at the Battle of Manila Bay on 1 May and inflicted massive damage on the Spanish fleet off Santiago, Cuba, on 3 July. In addition, an expeditionary force landed in Cuba and inflicted some damage on the Spanish at the Battle of San Juan Hill (1 July 1898).

The battle was reported with great enthusiasm in America and elevated Lieutenant-Colonel Theodore Roosevelt, who was serving as second-in-command of the self-styled 'Rough Riders' (a volunteer cavalry unit), to the status of a hero. Less acclaimed were the valiant efforts of the black troops who fought at San Juan in the 9th and 10th Cavalry. However, the reality was that the American forces were ill-equipped, poorly trained and, given the sub-tropical Cuban heat, ludicrously overdressed in their heavy woollen uniforms. Consequently the land forces became mired in a stalemate and with the American soldiers falling victim to malarial illness and yellow fever it was a relief that the Spanish government decided to seek terms in the face of her heavy naval losses. An armistice was signed on 12 August 1898.

The war had lasted for just over two months. Less than 400 American soldiers had died, although 5,000 American soldiers fell victim to disease. Not least in importance was the fact that the War Department had been galvanised by McKinley from an inept organisation into something more suited to the needs of a major power. The Treaty of Paris that brought an end to the Spanish–American War was signed on 10 December 1898. In addition to recognising Cuban indepdendence, Spain ceded Guam and Puerto Rico to the United States. In exchange for a payment to Spain of $20 million the United States also obtained the Philippines. The treaty was ratified through the Senate, but by a small majority. In the face of criticism of American imperialism, McKinley placed the conflict with Spain in a Christian context, presenting America's influence as civilising and evangelical. In February 1901 Cuba adopted a Constitution based on the American model, but it was not until January 1909 that American troops were withdrawn from Cuba.

The Philippines

Paul Johnson observes: 'At a stroke, the United States emerged as a great power, and a global one, with all kinds of new responsibilities, including administration of the 7100 islands which constitute the Philippines.' (Johnson, 1997, p. 510) Numerically, this added a further 7 million subjects. While some Americans questioned the validity of this colonial acquisition, others believed that the spiritual benefits which Anglo-Saxon civilisation would bring to a nation of backward people was, in Rudyard Kipling's words, 'The White Man's burden'. This rested on the notion that America was acting on the basis of a moral duty rather than for motives of greed or expansionism. This overlooked the fact that the inhabitants of the Philippines had their own religion (Catholicism) and wanted independence rather than American rule. America now blundered into an ill-conceived and protracted struggle, in the wrong place, at the wrong time, with no moral justification and with little to gain. For three years the United States attempted to quell a rebellion of its own making. In the face of a determined and effective insurrection led by Emilio Aguinaldo, American forces began to resort to the type of brutality that had been used by the Spanish in their struggle with the Cuban rebels.

Ultimately, 70,000 American troops were deployed at a cost of almost $200 million. More than 4,000 American soldiers died in a struggle that resembled in terms of guerrilla warfare some of the traumatic moments that would unfold in Vietnam more than 60 years later. In July 1902, the Philippine Government Act was passed, providing for rule by a US Presidential Commission.

Imperialism

The war with Spain had its important short-term causes, but it also signified important psychological and economic changes which combined to give the United States an outlook on foreign affairs which was very different to the mindset of only a few decades earlier. Put simply, it could be argued that while isolationism was still widely accepted the attractions of imperialism had become increasingly important. Several elements can be identified in leading towards this process.

Economic factors

First, there is no doubt that economic pressures were of key importance. The need for fresh markets to buy American products was important, especially when business understood that a fall in domestic demand could cause a recession. Companies such as General Electric, Standard Oil and Singer were set to become increasingly important on the world stage. In addition, the rapidly increasing need for cheap and plentiful raw materials to sustain the new industrial processes was very pronounced. Often such resources existed only outside the United States.

The completion of westward expansion

The drive west, wars with the Native Americans and the process of domesticating the wildernesses had occupied the young nation's energy in a frenetic period between 1840 and 1890. By 1890, the process was complete. Such was the dynamism and restless drive of the country that it seemed natural to look elsewhere to sustain the process of expansion and growth.

Imperial expansion

Towards the end of the nineteenth century many of the powerful European nations were eagerly expanding their empires, particularly in Africa. Those who believed in this trend argued that imperial expansion brought massive economic, spiritual and psychological rewards. Imperialists argued that nations which developed in this way remained strong and vital; those who accepted their lot became weak and withered away. There was also a profound sense of missionary zeal – that the Christian nations would civilise the savages. This sentiment was powerfully expressed by senators such as Albert Beveridge from Indiana, who told the Senate that God had decreed that Americans were 'the master organizers of the world' to rule over those who were 'savage and senile' (in Fernandez-Armesto, 2015, p. 629). Darwin's important ideas on natural selection and the survival of the fittest ('Social Darwinism') were spread in the United States by John Fiske, who believed that the Anglo-Saxon influence would inevitably spread to 'every land on the earth's surface' (Jones, 1995, p. 397).

Strategic considerations

The spectacle of other nations busily using their navies to consolidate their empires and build new bases, for example in the Pacific, made an impression on many Americans in government and in the armed forces. A school of thought believed that if the United States did not move to join in this process, it would be at a significant disadvantage later. Therefore America's future status and security was at stake. The work of Captain Alfred T. Mahan, whose major work, *The Influence of Sea Power Upon History*, was published in 1890, was of great importance in convincing decision makers that the worldwide commercial struggle could not be kept separate from the need for a powerful navy and a sizeable merchant fleet.

The Panama Canal

The Caribbean was of central importance to Roosevelt's foreign policy. He set about the progressive extension of American power and influence in the region and was prepared to pay scant regard to morality or to constitutional limits in the process. An important by-product of the Spanish–American War was that it highlighted to American naval strategists how valuable it would be to connect the Atlantic and Pacific Oceans by building an isthmian canal to be controlled by the United States. In 1901 the United States signed a treaty with Great Britain which would allow America to construct and control a canal, with the proviso that all other nations would have equal access at all times. The option of building it in Nicaragua, where the route was longer but fairly straightforward, was rejected by Congress in 1902 in favour of a shorter but more awkward route in Panama, which at that point in time was a province of Colombia. A year later the United States and Colombia concluded the Hay–Herrán Treaty, which gave the United States a six-mile-wide canal zone with a 99-year lease in return for an annual payment of $0.25 million dollars to begin nine years after the ratification of the treaty. In addition, the United States would make a one-off payment of $10 million. However, this development was stopped abruptly when the Colombian Senate, concerned with the issue of sovereignty, refused to ratify the treaty.

The Colombian rejection caused uproar in Panama, where there was already widespread dissatisfaction with Colombian rule; in November 1903, Panama declared its independence. President Roosevelt was outraged by the Colombians' actions and promptly sent three American ships, most notably the cruiser Nashville, to support Panama. This action prevented Colombian forces from crushing the Panamanian uprising. Roosevelt then received the Panamanian financier, Philippe Bunau-Varilla, in Washington; within days of the meeting, on 18 November 1903, the two men agreed to the terms which Colombia had previously rejected.

In 1906, Roosevelt became the first president to leave the country while in office when he visited the Canal Zone to witness developments in person. Full construction by American engineers began a year later and in 1914 the first ocean steamer passed through the canal. While the canal was a remarkable feat of engineering and brought even more popularity to Roosevelt, in the long term America's actions caused at best disquiet and at worst hostility in Latin America.

The Far East and the 'Open Door' policy

A succession of American presidents regarded the Far East as of prime importance in economic, political and strategic terms. The rapid development of the American economy meant that America's burgeoning manufacturing industries needed to go beyond the domestic market to maintain demand.

In the first instance, many American businessmen and industrialists looked to China. They recognised that its combination of a huge and rapidly growing population and its considerable untapped mineral resources made it of potentially enormous value as a market for American goods. A book by Brooks Adams entitled *America's Economic Supremacy*, published in 1900, stated that 'China is the prize for which all energetic nations are grasping.' It is important to recognise that there was also a desire to have a missionary impact on China. In short, the Americans who looked to China wanted to trade, teach and preach.

The United States sought stability in China and also wanted other countries to keep their distance. Therefore America viewed the conflict between China and Japan of 1895 with great concern, and was also worried by the acquisition of a number of Chinese ports by the European powers. Equally alarming was the Boxer Uprising of 1900, in which foreign diplomats and legations had come under attack by militant Chinese secret societies.

With trade at the centre of their considerations, American politicians devised a policy which they termed the 'Open Door'. This committed the United States to ensuring that the 'door' to China was not 'blocked' by any other nation. President McKinley's Secretary of State, John Hay, circulated a note to the major powers to inform them that 'it was American policy to preserve Chinese territorial integrity and to ensure equality of commercial opportunity, not merely in the foreign spheres of interest, but in the whole of the Chinese Empire' (in Jones, 1995, p. 405). Trade with China would be on an equal footing for all nations. The fact was that no other nation was in a strong enough position to challenge America's stance over China, but that situation would not last.

The Western hemisphere

Roosevelt's foreign policy in the Caribbean was forged during a period when he was becoming increasingly concerned about growing European influence in the region. With one eye on the growing 'threat' from Germany with its rapidly developing navy, the United States annexed Puerto Rico in 1898. Meanwhile, Cuba was effectively controlled by the terms of the Platt Amendment, which gave America a legal entitlement to take military action on the island when necessary. Roosevelt remained particularly concerned about the vulnerability of debt-ridden Latin American countries to European exploitation. In the case of both Venezuela and the Dominican Republic, European warships were sent to the Caribbean to collect outstanding debts for creditors. In 1904, Roosevelt responded with a pronouncement which became known as the Roosevelt Corollary to the Monroe Doctrine. The president stated that in addition to the Monroe Doctrine which prohibited European colonisation in the Western hemisphere, the United States could also take pre-emptive action to defend its interests. Roosevelt's open-ended statement that the United States could respond to 'Chronic wrongdoing or incompetence' in the Western hemisphere by the use of 'force ... however reluctantly' as 'an international police power' (Jones, 1995, pp. 408–09) gave America a wide-ranging brief. In concrete terms, this meant, for example, that in the Dominican Republic the nation's debts were moved from European to American creditors.

2.2 Taft's 'dollar diplomacy'

Although Roosevelt assumed that his protégé, William Howard Taft, would maintain his approach in foreign policy, in fact the new president had his own, distinctive ideas. Whereas Roosevelt was fond of outspoken rhetoric, aggressive posturing and, where necessary, the use of force, Taft came to the presidency in 1909 with different tactics in mind. Taft wanted to adopt a more subtle approach, though his goals remained broadly similar, and he was more inclined to observe constitutional limits in the application of executive power. In dealing with foreign powers he hoped to create an order based on co-operation rather than force. His desire to use America's economic strength in order to influence foreign policy led to the phrase 'dollar diplomacy'; whereas Roosevelt might think first of sending in the navy, Taft believed that the sheer weight of American economic influence would be enough to promote and maintain American interests.

In particular, Taft looked to the Caribbean and China where he wanted to 'substitute dollars for bullets' (Whiteclay Chambers II, 1992, p. 211). However, it should also be noted that when economic influence was not enough, Taft was prepared to use force. Five years later, in Nicaragua, Taft showed that 'dollar diplomacy' was now central to American foreign policy. In 1909, the State Department encouraged American financiers effectively to take over the running of Nicaragua's financial system. With an increasingly unpopular, pro-American, minority government in power America's high-handed actions became extremely resented, and growing unrest culminated in a revolutionary situation. Taft responded by sending in the marines to quell the revolution; they remained there for more than a decade. Despite the change of administration and political party in 1913, elements of Republican foreign policy remained. Wilson's public pledge to steer the direction of American foreign policy away from armed intervention was exposed when increasing unrest and violence in Haiti (1915) and the Dominican Republic (1916) prompted him to become the third president in succession to dispatch the marines to defend American business interests.

2.3 Woodrow Wilson's foreign policy

Wilson's idealism

When Woodrow Wilson became president in 1913 he emphatically rejected both Roosevelt's 'big stick' and Taft's 'dollar diplomacy'. The new Democratic regime placed an emphasis on idealism, as reflected in Wilson's pledge of October 1913 that the United States would 'never again seek an additional foot of territory by conquest'. Taft's economic hold over Latin America was disavowed with a promise that in future dealings would be based 'upon terms of equality and honor' (Jones, 1995, p. 409). Again, in practice, Wilson was unable to maintain his principles to the extent he had desired. For example, when conflict flared in Haiti in 1915, Wilson responded by sending in the marines to restore stability to the country but also to counter the revolution which he felt threatened American interests there.

Wilson ran into potentially more serious difficulty when he involved the United States in the troubled affairs of Mexico as it emerged from the revolution of 1911. In February 1913, General Victoriano Huerta seized control of Mexico by force. With his reactionary policies, he was not an unattractive proposition to American business interests who advocated that the United States should recognise his regime. However, Wilson wanted to see a constitutional ruler and so lent his support to the more liberal figure of Venustiano Carranza. In 1914, Wilson used a dispute over the brief arrest of some American sailors in a Mexican port to increase the pressure on Huerta. With reports that a German consignment of arms for Huerta was on its way, Wilson decided to use military force without waiting for Congress to give its blessing. The US Navy attacked the port of Veracruz before the German consignment arrived. In a heavy bombardment, more than 100 Mexicans were killed: Wilson had not only disregarded his principles, he had also managed to alienate Carranza, the very person he had been trying to support.

The situation became more complex when Carranza ousted Huerta but faced immediate opposition from his former supporter, Pancho Villa. Wilson chose Villa rather than Carranza, in the belief that he would bring genuine reform to Mexico. When Villa was defeated in October, Wilson gave rather lukewarm support to Carranza. Villa responded with a series of outrages calculated to elicit an American military response in Mexico. More than 30 American citizens in Mexico and New Mexico were attacked and killed in two incidents at the start of 1914. Eventually, in the spring of 1916, Wilson felt he had no choice other than to order Brigadier-General Pershing and 6,000 cavalry to track Villa down. During a fruitless and increasingly frustrating search clashes between the American troops and Carranza's forces became increasingly worrying. Wilson recognised the dangers ahead and decided to agree to Carranza's offer of negotiation. With the problems posed by Germany in the Atlantic dominating Wilson's attention he had no desire to become involved in a protracted struggle in Mexico.

2.4 A 'distant conflict': The outbreak of war in Europe

When war broke out in Europe in August 1914 it seemed clear that the position of the United States would rest on the traditional policies handed down by presidents such as Jefferson, based on the principles of avoiding intervention in European diplomacy or politics, avoiding commitments to entangling alliances and thereby sustaining the policy of 'traditional isolation'. For many Americans, the war confirmed their worst feelings about Europe and seemed to emphasise the superiority of the American way: many writers contrasted the militarism, secret alliances and the autocracy of the European powers with the democracy and idealism of the United States.

Several factors seemed likely to keep the United States out of the war. Europe's sheer geographical distance, the fact that the war did not appear to directly threaten any American interest, the widely shared belief that the conflict would soon be over and the fact that most Americans felt that the European powers had themselves to blame for resorting to force rather than arbitration meant that the public mood was firmly against American involvement. In addition, at the outset of war, it seemed clear that the President of the United States had a deep personal commitment to the maintenance of American neutrality.

Woodrow Wilson was 57 when the war broke out. Born in the southern state of Virginia in 1856, he had vivid childhood memories of the American Civil War, and retained an aversion to war throughout his political career. Privately, however, Wilson shared the pro-Allied sentiment of many of his countrymen. The president was an admitted Anglophile, and respected the British parliamentary and education systems. He had enjoyed cycling holidays in the English countryside and, like many men of a similar background, admired the traditional way of life of the English aristocracy. In contrast, in June 1914, two months before war broke out, his friend and confidant Edward House told the president that the German system represented 'militarism run stark mad' (Neiberg, 2016, p. 13).

However, as the president charged with shaping United States policy Wilson felt duty bound to put these personal views to one side. Therefore on 8 August 1914 he solemnly affirmed America's neutrality with an appeal to the American people to remain 'impartial in thought as well as in deed'. Wilson stated that the war in Europe was one 'with which we have nothing to do, whose causes cannot touch us' (in Jones, 1995, p. 412). For those who did not need to be so careful in their public utterances the matter was more clear-cut. As German troops marched through neutral Belgium a well-known judge in Tennessee staged a mock trial which concluded that the invasion was the 'crime of the century' (in Neiberg, 2016, p. 14). An academic at the University of Chicago stressed the planning that must have been needed and said: 'We saw that the whole thing was premeditated; we realized that methods of mobilization, not to speak of strategic railroads, are not mapped out in a moment.' (In Neiberg, 2016, p. 20) In the press the African American Philadelphia *Tribune* looked back at Germany's recent past and said: 'Germany has been the aggressor on nearly every occasion since 1870.' (In Neiberg, 2016, p. 21) Public collections and donations were generously made, but almost entirely destined for Belgium and France.

But Wilson had charted a path of neutrality and as he put it in August 1914, 'When all this half of the world [Europe] will suffer the unspeakable brutalization of war, we shall preserve our moral strength, our political power and our ideals.' (In Neiberg, 2016, p. 25) In the same month he told Congress that 'we must be impartial in thought, as well as in action, must put a curb upon our sentiments, as well as upon every transaction that might be construed as a preference of one party to the struggle before another' (in Neiberg, 2016, p. 37).

It is interesting at this point to consider whether neutrality was ever more than an ideal rather than a practical, sustainable position. Was the United States already too dependent on an Allied victory for it to remain on the sidelines, especially when the final outcome was in doubt? Could the United States ever, truly be neutral, given its trading interests and its views on German militarism? As Michael S. Neiberg states in *The Path to War* (2016):

> Without British shipping, American firms ... simply could not fill the millions of dollars of orders coming in to their firms every month. Economic interest, political preference, and cultural affinity thus coincided nicely. Such circumstances, however, put the United States in an awkward international position given how manifestly they ran counter to Wilson's desire to put a strictly impartial face on American thought and behaviour. (Neiberg, 2016, p. 50)

Beyond this, the prevailing public mood appears to have been that the United States would be highly likely to remain outside the war. Above all, perhaps, it seemed a matter of geographical separation. As the ambassador, Walter Hines Page, said by letter to President Wilson, upon the outbreak of war: 'Again and ever, I thank heaven for the Atlantic Ocean.' (In Neiberg, 2016, p. 39) In addition, in 1914 and even to an extent in 1915 it was widely believed that in any case the war would all be over in relatively short order.

While Wilson steadfastly maintained his public position, most historians agree that he did manage to put his personal preference for the Allies (Great Britain, France and Russia) on one side, at least in public. However, he appreciated that American interests would be damaged by a German victory. As he commented to his private secretary in the autumn of 1914: 'England is fighting our fight.' (In Jones, 1995, p. 414) This policy was more difficult to sustain in practice than he had first imagined. In the first place, powerful cultural ties meant that the majority of Americans supported the Allied cause. Such sentiments were particularly powerful among the East Coast establishment. Harvard historian Samuel Eliot Morison later recalled:

> At the western university where I was teaching when the war broke out in Europe, it seemed to the average student as unreal as the Wars of the Roses; returning to Harvard early in 1915, one was on the outskirts of battle ... Sympathy for the Allied cause was unconcealed; not for a moment was Harvard neutral in thought or deed. (In Traynor, 2001, p. 49)

The impression of Germany as a militaristic, autocratic and aggressive country was also widely held. This view was further sustained when German actions such as the invasion of Belgium in 1914 and the subsequent destruction of Louvain allowed the British to circulate powerful anti-German propaganda to a broadly sympathetic American audience tied by important linguistic and cultural affinities to the British. Despite these factors, the United States attempted to stick to a neutral course when the war began. Just two weeks into the war Secretary of State William Jennings Bryan, the strongest proponent of true neutrality, issued a statement prohibiting loans to belligerents. A French attempt to secure a $100 million loan in the United States was rebuffed because Bryan felt it would violate 'the true spirit of neutrality'. However, by August 1915, American bankers were requesting permission to launch a bond issue of $500 million to Britain and France, on the grounds that failure to do so would lead to a depression in the United States. With Wilson's permission, a loan totalling $2.3 billion and organised by J.P. Morgan was floated. This effectively rendered true neutrality meaningless. John Whiteclay Chambers II points out:

> Even more important than propaganda in influencing the United States was the growth of American economic ties with the Allies. With its control of the sea, Britain drew on American resources – food, arms, and munitions. Total US trade with the Allies more than tripled, from $800 million to $3 billion, between 1914 and 1916. (Whiteclay Chambers II, 1992, p. 218)

By now it was also becoming clear that the war was having a positive impact on the American economy, not least in agriculture. As Neiberg explains:

> Farmers benefited from both increased demand for American crops and meat and the good harvests of 1915 and 1916 ... With the demand for wheat rising sharply in Europe, the American Midwest had already profited handsomely. Of the nation's top 128 urban regions, those that grew fastest in 1914 and 1915 depended on wheat. They included Duluth, Fargo, Lincoln, Minneapolis, Omaha and Wichita. (Neiberg, 2016, p. 120)

Meanwhile, the British blockade of Germany meant that American commerce with the Central Powers virtually collapsed. Nevertheless, Maldwyn Jones states that: 'There is no evidence that bankers or businessmen attempted to persuade Wilson to declare war. They did not believe American intervention was necessary to avert an Allied defeat.' (Jones, 1995, p. 424)

The economic situation prompted German protests, but the United States maintained that it was prepared in principle to sell arms to Germany even though, in practice, British control of the shipping lanes meant that no such trade was possible. Against this background, the German government decided that it had been left with no choice but to act against the British blockade with a campaign of submarine warfare. In February 1915, Germany announced that it would target any enemy merchant shipping within a designated war zone around the British Isles. Above all, it would be the violence and destruction waged by the German submarine fleet in the Atlantic (Table 2.1) that would bring America directly into the conflict. Most of all, the sinking of the *Lusitania* on Friday 7 May 1915 scarred the psyche of the American public in a manner comparable with Pearl Harbor or the terrorist attacks of 11 September 2001. The British passenger liner went down with the deaths of 1,198 people, including 128 American citizens. While Wilson was personally outraged by the attack he was not ready to lead his nation into war and as he told an audience in Philadelphia: 'There is such a thing as a man being too proud to fight.' (In Jones, 1995, p. 416) The fact that this statement caused a degree of public outrage suggests that the mood in the United States was shifting and Wilson's public comments no longer chimed with general attitudes.

Meanwhile, the outbreak of war in Europe forced many Americans to look back at their ancestral roots as immigrants. Many of those with a British background lived on the East Coast, and they expressed articulate support for the Allied cause. Broadly speaking, this was the overriding sentiment of the American people. However, substantial immigrant groups saw the struggle very differently. The largest immigrant group of all was from Germany. Many German–Americans bitterly opposed the pro-Allied view of the war put forward by the middle-class, East Coast establishment. While the Midwest of the country was pro-German, there was also a considerable anti-British sentiment among the Irish–American community and hostility towards Tsarist Russia from the powerful Jewish–American lobby. Indeed, one of Wilson's most pressing concerns as war broke out was its potential for creating racial division and tension at home.

Table 2.1   Submarine warfare, 1915–17

Date	Name of ship	American casualties	Consequences
28 March 1915	*Falaba* (British steamer)	One American seaman drowned when this British ship was sunk without warning	The sinking took place against the background of a peace mission by Colonel Edward House; Wilson was reluctant to undermine House's position and he therefore failed to act.
May 1915	*Gulflight* (American tanker)	Torpedoed but not sunk	Wilson maintained his policy of peace.
7 May 1915	*Lusitania* (British liner owned by Cunard)	Attacked off the Irish Coast en route from New York to Liverpool; 1,198 casualties, 128 of them American	The American press condemned this act of 'mass murder'; Wilson resisted talk of war with the words 'there is such a thing as a man being too proud to fight'. However, Wilson sent a number of messages to the German government warning that further attacks would be regarded as 'deliberately unfriendly'. In the wake of this, Secretary of State Bryan resigned, contending that the administration should ban American citizens from travelling into war zones on ships carrying munitions.
19 August 1915	*Arabic* (British steamer owned by White Star Line)	42 passengers were killed, including two Americans	Public opinion further inflamed, and the White House considered breaking off relations with Germany. The German Ambassador in Washington assured the US Government that passenger ships would not be attacked in future unless they tried to escape or resist. The German Chancellor further pacified the situation by announcing that the submarine commander had exceeded his orders in attacking the *Arabic*. *Continued*

24 March 1916	*Sussex* (Unarmed passenger steamer mistaken for a mine layer and torpedoed)	The ship limped into port with 80 casualties; several Americans were injured	Secretary of State Lansing urged Wilson to break off diplomatic relations. Instead, Wilson sent his most strongly worded message so far. He told Germany that unless it abandoned submarine warfare against passenger- and freight-carrying vessels the United States would be obliged to cut off diplomatic relations. Germany responded with the '*Sussex* pledge', which stated that from now on merchant vessels would be granted traditional rights of stop and search, rather than being attacked without warning. For a short time, the submarine campaign was halted.
26 February 1917	*Laconia* (Cunard liner)	12 people were killed, including two American women	Following a meeting at Pless Castle, the German military leaders and the Kaiser voted to resume unrestricted submarine warfare. Wilson broke off diplomatic relations with Germany but stated that only 'overt acts' would convince him of Germany's course. The sinking of the *Laconia* was such an overt act. Three days later the government published the Zimmermann Telegram.
March 1917	U-boats sank three American merchant ships	More than 20 crew members were killed	This was the final straw for Wilson. This coincided with the abdication of Tsar Nicholas II, which removed the difficulty the United States would have had in supporting an autocratic government in a war.

2.5 The election of 1916 and America's subsequent entry into the First World War

John Milton Cooper Jr's 2011 biography of Wilson provides some helpful insights into the nature of Wilson's 1916 campaign for a second term:

> Wilson's campaign got off to a later start because he had to stay in Washington to attend to public business, yet the delay gave him an advantage. The last measures of the New Freedom helped his re-election prospects much more than any speeches or tours.

At the dedication of the new American Federation of Labor building in July 1916 the incumbent was keen to praise labour. The signing of rural credits and child labour laws were also timely so that Wilson could subsequently claim:

> This record must equally astonish those who feared that the Democratic Party had not opened its heart to comprehend the demands of social justice. We have in four years come very near to carrying out the platform of the Progressive Party as well as our own, for we are also progressives. (Cooper, 2011, p. 348)

Over and above these important domestic considerations, Wilson's campaign for re-election in 1916 was dominated by the matter of war. Initially he intended to rest his platform on the issue of Americanism. However, the election highlighted the extent of anti-war sentiment in the country at large, and as the campaign intensified Wilson decided to play upon the fear that victory for the Republican candidate, Charles Evans Hughes, would certainly lead to direct American intervention in the conflict. Despite Wilson's personal misgivings, the Democrats began to use slogans such as 'He kept us out of the war' and 'War in the East, peace in the West, thank God for Wilson.'

As in 1912, Wilson cast his vote at the Princeton fire station but the nation's verdict appeared, even to his own entourage, to be too close to call. With the *New York Times* initially declaring Hughes the victor it took two days to confirm Wilson as the winner and almost two weeks for Hughes to formally concede defeat.

Wilson had become the first Democrat since Andrew Jackson to win a second consecutive term. Wilson gained 277 Electoral College votes to Hughes's 254. In the popular vote the margin was almost 600,000 votes: 9,129,606 to 8,538,211 (Table 2.2). Compared to 1912, Wilson's popular vote had increased by almost 3 million votes and his share of the total by over 7 per cent. Wilson secured the key state of California by just over 3,000 votes or less than 0.38 per cent of the total.

Table 2.2   The result of the 1916 presidential election

Candidate	Party	Electoral College votes	Popular votes
Thomas Woodrow Wilson (New Jersey)	Democrat	277	9,129,606
Charles E. Hughes (New York)	Republican	254	8,538,221
A.L. Benson (New York)	Socialist	–	585,113

While Wilson's narrow return to office had undoubtedly rested on the conduct of the war issue he was also able to validly present himself as a successful domestic leader with a very significant record of legislative achievement. Hughes had pushed Wilson close, securing traditional Republican support in the North East and Midwest. Wilson was putting in place what would become the foundation for the majority Democratic coalition of the South, farmers and labour. The biggest irony for Wilson was that it would soon become clear that his domestic presidency was at an end and the war he had pledged to stay away from was now looming.

Despite Wilson's election promises, unrestricted submarine warfare had pushed Germany to the edge of war with the United States. In his second inaugural address Wilson made clear the limitations of isolation with the striking phase: 'We are provincials no longer.' Two further events in 1917 made it easier for Wilson to receive the Congressional support he would need for a declaration of war. Firstly, the abdication of Nicholas II, the autocratic ruler of Russia, in the spring of 1917 and his replacement by the liberal-minded Provisional Government removed the moral difficulty many Americans faced in supporting the Allies when Russia was involved. This was an especially pivotal moment for the powerful Jewish–American population who joyously welcomed the Tsar's departure.

Secondly, on 29 February the American Government made public the details of a secret telegram which had been intercepted by British intelligence and handed over to the United States. The telegram had been drawn up by Arthur Zimmermann, the German Foreign Secretary, and was addressed to Count von Bernstorff in Washington, who in turn was to pass on the information to the German Minister for Mexico. The telegram proposed a Mexican–German Alliance in the event of war between the United States and Germany. Mexico was asked to encourage Japan to join this alliance and in return Mexico was offered the prospect of the return of her 'lost territory' in Texas. The contents of the Zimmermann Telegram shocked the American people and brought home to them the extent of German hostility.

Crucially, these events even shifted the position of America's largest immigrant groups, as Italian-Americans, Irish- (Catholic) Americans and Jewish-Americans came to support the Allied position. Even German–Americans, who numbered 8 million and formed approximately 16 per cent of the electorate, were largely at the point where they saw themselves as on the American side. With these seismic changes taking place, only a few weeks elapsed until a further attack by German U-boats pushed Wilson to a position where despite all of his reservations and public commitments, in the face of these further overt acts of German aggression he felt compelled to ask Congress to support a declaration of war. Unrestricted submarine warfare seemed, to the American public and the American media, to be tantamount to a declaration of war. Wilson's room for manoeuvre had disappeared (Table 2.3).

A gentle drizzle fell on 2 April 1917 as President Woodrow Wilson, accompanied by a cavalry troop, made his way to the Capitol for the most sombre occasion of his political career. The splendid buildings were brilliantly lit up and stood out dramatically against the darkening sky. The president was ready to walk into the chamber of the House of Representatives at 8.32 pm. The Speaker of the House called the American Congress to order with the words: 'Gentlemen, the President of the United States.' Wilson strode to the Speaker's platform and commenced his address to the House and Senate, the Cabinet, the Supreme Court and important guests. He was about to deliver what would be acknowledged as the most important speech of his presidency.

Table 2.3 Wilson's search for peace, 1915–17	
Spring 1915	Wilson dispatched his emissary Colonel House to London to explore the prospects for peace. House also visited Paris and Berlin and offered American mediation. However, the Allies informed House that they would prefer America's support, prompting House to issue a sharp reminder of American neutrality.
November 1915	At a meeting with the British Foreign Secretary, Sir Edward Grey, Wilson discussed for the first time the concept of a League of Nations. It was not until November 1916 that Wilson made a public commitment to full American participation in the League.
February 1916	Wilson's continuing search for peace led to a call to France and England to attend a peace conference 'when opportune'. The House/Grey memorandum suggested the possibility that if France and Britain agreed to attend but Germany declined America would, in the words of Wilson, 'probably' enter the war.

Continued

November 1916	The wholesale slaughter on the Somme between July and November 1916 convinced Wilson that both sides were blindly determined to carry on with the fighting to the bitter end. Wilson bitterly criticised both sides for the sheer cost of the war and asked them to state the 'precise objects' for which each side was continuing to fight.
January 1917	At the start of the year Germany accused the allies of prolonging the war merely for territorial gain. In the same month, Wilson addressed the US Senate, criticising the inflexibility of the belligerents and putting forward the concept of 'peace without victory' which under-pinned his concept for the post-war world order.

Wilson's war address

I have called the Congress into extraordinary session because there are serious, very serious, choices of policy to be made, and made immediately, which it was neither right nor constitutionally permissible that I should assume the responsibility of making ... The new policy has swept every restriction aside. Vessels of every kind, whatever their flag, their character, their cargo, their destination ... have been ruth-lessly sent to the bottom without warning and without thought of help or mercy for those on board ... It is a war against all nations. American ships have been sunk, American lives taken, in ways which it has stirred us very deeply to learn of, but the ships and people of other neutral and friendly nations have also been sunk and overwhelmed in the waters in the same way. There has been no discrimination. The challenge is to all mankind. Every nation must decide for itself how it will meet it ... We must put excited feeling away. Our motive will not be revenge ... but only the vindication of right, of human right, of which we are only a single champion ...

With a profound sense of the solemn and even tragical character of the step I am taking and of the grave responsibilities which it involves ... I advise that the Congress declare the recent course of the Imperial German Government to be in fact nothing less than war against the people and government of the United States; that it for-mally accept the status of belligerent which has thus been thrust upon it; and that it take immediate steps not only to put the country in a more thorough state of defense but also to exert all its power and employ all its resources to bring the Government of the German Empire to terms and end the war ... We have no quarrel with the Ger-man people ... the world must be made safe for democracy ...

There are, it may be, many months of fiery trial and sacrifice ahead of us. It is a fearful thing to lead this great peaceful people into war, into the most terrible and disastrous of all wars, civilization itself seeming to be in the balance. But the right is more precious than peace, and we shall fight for the things which we have always carried nearest to our hearts – for democracy ... for a universal dominion of right by such a concert of free peoples as shall bring peace and safety to all nations and make the world itself at last free ... the day has come when America is privileged to spend her blood and her might for the principles that gave her birth and happiness and the peace which she has treasured. God helping her, she can do no other! (Wilson Presidential Library, online)

From the floor of the House and in the galleries there was a wave of applause. The senators waved small, silk flags and cheered the president to the rafters. Wilson took little comfort from the tumultuous reception. He later remarked, 'My message today was a message of death for our young men. How strange it seems to applaud that.' (In Brogan, 1990, p. 491) When he returned to the White House he wept. The House of Representatives approved the war message with a vote of 373 to 50, and the Senate by a vote of 82 to 6. On 6 April the president signed the official declaration. The United States was at war with Germany. Neiberg's analysis is that in the end '[t]he war had finally become impossible to ignore. It would not end soon or on its own, and its effects would eventually engulf America. A German victory would impose a European and global order unacceptable to the American people' (Neiberg, 2016, p. 212).

2.6 America's impact on the First World War

Preparedness

The Americans entered the war in April 1917 at a critical time for the Allies. Great Britain faced huge shipping losses thanks to unrestricted German submarine warfare and her food supplies were sorely limited. In Russia, Tsar Nicholas II had recently abdicated but the Provisional Government was desperately trying to keep the Russian war effort afloat. France was facing a mood of defeatism and mutiny within the ranks. However, America was not militarily prepared to take to the battlefield in 1917. As Neiberg explains:

> Prior to 1915, most Americans, especially those holding the purse strings in Congress, sought to keep spending on the military as low as possible ... Facing few immediate threats, the nation had rarely seen a need for large numbers of soldiers in peacetime. The army, scattered mostly across isolated garrisons in the American West, had fewer than 5,000 officers and 102,000 soldiers ... Numerically, the United States had the seventeenth largest army in the world. Put another way, the French Army had twice as many men killed and wounded in the first twelve days of the war as the entire American army had in its ranks. (Neiberg, 2016, p. 125)

Although the political and military leadership had contemplated large-scale military mobilisation, the prospect of war seemed so unthinkable that serious planning had not been undertaken. Between the autumn of 1915 and May 1916 Wilson had been involved in a prolonged dispute over America's military preparedness. In January 1916 Wilson asked Congress to support a military programme which would provide the country with a Continental Army of 400,000 men and 'a Navy second to none'. Wilson's plans encountered opposition in the Senate and he was forced to compromise by accepting the federalising of the National Guard. Although naval expansions were approved, the Continental Army plan did not come to fruition and despite the National Defense Act of 1916, which doubled the size of the regular army, the army still numbered only 200,000 officers and men at the start of 1917. In *American*

Arsenal, Patrick Coffey makes plain the limitations of American military strength at this time, equipped as it was with 'a twentieth of the German army's strength. It had no gas masks, no airplanes that could match Germany's, and only a few days' inventory of artillery shells, given the rate at which the guns were firing on the Western Front' (Coffey, 2014, p. 46).

Mobilisation for war

Despite these limitations, America responded to the demands of war with energy and enterprise. A national process of economic and social mobilisation was required, and President Wilson brought in high achievers from outside the Cabinet, captains of industry who gave freely of their talent, but it took time for the country to fully mobilise its war effort (Table 2.4). By November 1918, 3.5 million men had been drafted under the terms of the Selective Service Act of May 1917. (The old Civil War practice of hiring a substitute was no longer allowed.) By the time the war came to an end in November 1918, the army had expanded to more than 4 million, of whom 2 million served in the American Expeditionary Forces (AEF). The American Expeditionary Forces were placed under the Command of Major-General John J. Pershing. Robert H. Ferrell believes that they 'were stamped with the personality of their commander, General Pershing, a tough, unrelenting officer. Without him it hardly seems possible that the 2,080,000 American soldiers in France could have been turned into a great fighting army' (Ferrell, 1985, p. 48).

Table 2.4   Economic mobilisation for war

The War Industries Board	Under the leadership of Wall Street financier Bernard M. Baruch, this agency led the drive for greater efficiency in industrial production. The Board was empowered to regulate prices, allocate raw materials and determine industrial priorities. Baruch had immense powers, which he used to control the whole range of American manufacturing.
The Fuel Administration	Led by Harry A. Garfield, this boosted oil and coal production and introduced daylight saving time as an economy measure.
The Railroad Administration	Under the leadership of William G. McAdoo, the railroads were brought under national control; the demands of transporting military items or personnel took precedence over civilian traffic. Federal investment led to the introduction of new equipment and a drive to standardise track gauge.
The Food Administration	Future President Herbert Hoover led this agency, which had control of the production, manufacture and distribution of foodstuffs. Hoover brought about unprecedented increases in American farm production. The Allies, for whom food supplies were critically important, gratefully received exports of food.

Although the economic mobilisation programme was an unqualified success, other aspects of the 'Home Front' were less positive. Although President Wilson had told Congress that the United States was going to war to 'make the world safe for democracy', he was not afraid to take draconian measures to reduce civil liberties at home, for the duration of the war (see Section 2.9 and Table 2.5).

2.7 American casualties

At a meeting in Paris in April 1917, Pershing insisted that American troops be assigned to their own portion of the front line in order to maintain their separate identity, resisting the Allies' desire to slot Americans in as replacements for depleted Allied regiments. In August 1917 the American First Army was formed and took up position in a section of the Western Front near Verdun. Even so, a shortage of troops and shipping meant that by September 1917 the AEF numbered only 61,531. Faced by the major German offensive of March 1918, Pershing agreed that American army and marine units could be deployed under Allied command. In May–June 1918 growing numbers of American troops helped to force the Germans back across the Marne. In September the Americans took part in a massive allied counter-offensive at St Mihiel (12–16 September) and in the campaign launched at Meuse–Argonne (28 September), which involved 1.2 million American troops, took heavy casualties.

By the time the First World War came to an end in November 1918, the United States had committed approximately 4.8 million men to the Allied cause. The final loss of life amounted to 112,000 people. Organisations such as the Bring Home the Soldier Dead League campaigned for the fallen to be returned to the United States. However, the Field of Honor Association argued for the soldiers to be left where they had fallen, and in the words of General Pershing:

> Could these soldiers speak for themselves, they would wish to be left undisturbed, where with their commanders they had fought their last fight. The graves of our soldiers constitute, if they are allowed to remain, a perpetual reminder to our allies of the liberty and ideals upon which the greatness of America rests. (In Meigs, 1997, p. 180)

In September 1919 the War Department decided for the first time in American history to repatriate their dead. Ultimately, at a cost to Congress of $8,451,000, 45,588 fallen Americans were returned to the United States and 764 to their European birthplace. Ten thousand American soldiers were buried without their identity being known. Four such bodies were selected by the Graves Registration Service and in a moving ceremony at Châlons-sur-Marne, a blindfolded sergeant placed a bouquet of white roses on one of the four coffins after circling them three times. This was the coffin of the man who had been selected as the Unknown Soldier. His remains were transported to the United States and laid to rest at the Arlington National Cemetery.

2.8 Peace without victory

On 27 May 1916, President Wilson made an important speech to the League to Enforce Peace. Speaking in Washington, Wilson told the League that he favoured American membership of a post-war collective security association of nations. A positive response to the speech encouraged Wilson to incorporate the theme in his 1916 presidential campaign. On 22 January 1917, almost two years before the war in Europe came to an end, President Woodrow Wilson addressed the Senate with his vision of the peace he would like to see:

> 'It must be a peace without victory ... Victory would mean peace forced upon the loser, a victor's terms imposed upon the vanquished. It would be accepted in humiliation, under duress, as an intolerable sacrifice, and would leave a sting, a resentment, a bitter memory upon which terms of peace would rest, not permanently, but only as upon quicksand. [Such a peace was the] only ... sort of peace that the peoples of America could join in guaranteeing.' While these words were of lasting importance, Wilson's idealistic sentiments were not always reflected in the domestic arena which saw damaging consequences for freedom of speech and the civil liberties which the President so frequently espoused. As the eminent American historian Richard Hofstadter memorably said: 'War has always been the nemesis of the liberal tradition in America.' (From Jill Lepore, *The New Yorker*, September 2015)

2.9 The impact of war on civil liberties: 1917–18

Table 2.5 The impact of war on civil liberties: 1917–18

The Committee on Public Information (April 1917)

Under the leadership of journalist George Creel, the Committee issued over 70 million copies of more than 30 different propaganda pamphlets. It issued 6,000 press releases and organised war exhibitions attended by 10 million people. Through these activities the Committee fuelled the popular anti-German mood and whipped up feelings of '100 per cent Americanism'.

The Espionage Act (15 June 1917)

Made it illegal to 'wilfully and knowingly' obstruct the implementation of the Espionage Act or to encourage disloyalty. Under its terms, punishments of up to 30 years in jail and fines of up to $10,000 faced anyone convicted of obstructing the draft, circulating false rumours, or inciting rebellion among the armed forces. The powers granted under the act were used by the postmaster general to suppress the mailing of a number of radical periodicals, such as *The Masses, American Socialist* and the *Milwaukee Leader*. Under the terms of the Act, a film producer was sentenced to ten years' imprisonment (commuted to three years) for making a film on the American Revolution which portrayed British atrocities.

Trading with the Enemy Act (October 1917)

Granted the president sweeping powers of censorship over all international communications and gave the postmaster general similar authority over all foreign-language publications in the United States.

Continued

The Sedition Act (May 1918)

Free expression was restricted even further by the Sedition Act, which was modelled upon the State of Montana's Criminal Syndicalism Act. The Act made illegal 'any disloyal, profane, scurrilous language' concerning the government, army or navy uniforms. The vague nature of this offence made it possible for the government to use its powers indiscriminately. More than 1,500 people were imprisoned under the Act, most notoriously the Socialist leader, Eugene V. Debs, who received a ten-year sentence for making a speech against the war. Debs would remain in prison until Wilson left office; he eventually received a pardon from President Harding. Beyond the measures contained in this wartime legislation, the prevailing mood became profoundly anti-German and tolerated sweeping revolution in civil rights. In this climate, the Supreme Court upheld both the Espionage Act and the Sedition Act. Of particular significance was the US Supreme Court ruling of *Schenk* vs *United States* (March 1919), which concluded that the Espionage Act did not violate the First Amendment. Other elements of the wartime climate included schools curtailing their teaching of the German language, the removal of German books from libraries, and the banning of German newspapers and the music of Beethoven and other German composers. Individuals with German-sounding names were often coerced into changing them. The movement to prohibit the manufacture, production and consumption of alcohol was boosted by the connection in the public's mind between Germans and the brewing industry.

When Germany took the decision to look for peace terms in October 1918 the Chancellor, Prince Max of Baden, asked that the armistice should be based on Wilson's Fourteen Points. However, it should also be noted that Wilson's attitude towards Germany had stiffened by this time. The United States had suffered heavy casualties in the autumn of 1918; in addition, Wilson was appalled by the German sinking of the Irish ferry the *Leinster* on 12 October, coming as it did one week after the German's original request for an armistice.

2.10 Woodrow Wilson and the quest for peace

Versailles peace settlement

The First World War finally came to an end when the Germans concluded a ceasefire with the Allies on 11 November 1918. All parties were surprised by the sudden collapse of the German war effort and it was agreed that the details of the peace settlement would be determined at a peace conference to be held in the New Year. Germany's hope was that the peace settlement would be based on the principle of 'peace without victory' which President Wilson had set out. However, before Wilson set off on his mission to Paris he suffered a serious setback. The midterm Congressional elections went in favour of the Republican Party, leaving them with a majority over the Democrats of 237 to 190 in the House and 49 to 47 in the Senate. On 18 November Wilson announced that he would personally lead the American delegation at the Paris Peace Conference. Many historians have commented that this was a tactical error, and that Wilson would have been more effective in a detached role. On 4 December the cruiser *George Washington* set sail for the port of Brest in France. J.A. Thompson offers this perspective on the significance of Wilson's mission:

> Woodrow Wilson was the first American President to leave the Western Hemisphere during his period of office, and, as befitted him, the circumstances in which he did so were neither casual nor frivolous. He went to Europe in late 1918 to take part in

the peace conference following a war that the United States had played a crucial part in bringing to a decisive end. His aim was to secure a peace that accorded with the proposals he had set out in his Fourteen Points address of January 1918 and in other speeches – a peace that would be based upon justice and thus secure consent, that would embody liberal principles (the self-determination of peoples as far as practicable, the prohibition of discriminatory trade barriers) and that would be maintained by a new international organisation in which the United States, breaking its tradition of isolation, would take part – a league of nations, that would provide a general guarantee of political independence and territorial integrity to great and small states alike. (Thompson, 1988)

Although Wilson's visit to France was to generate a degree of euphoria, it is important to note that major problems were in store. Wilson's overriding desire for peace meant that he underestimated the damaging psychological impact of the war casualties upon the American public. His ambitions to manage the European peace settlement were out of step with the public mood, which now favoured a return to the isolationist tradition. In addition, Wilson had aroused antagonism when he decided to break with the convention of consultation with the Senate by not including any of its members in the diplomatic team for Paris, which furthermore contained only one member of the Republican Party.

The details of the American delegation were announced on 18 November 1918. Key figures included Secretary of State Robert Lansing – a legal expert, Colonel Edward House, General Tasker H. Bliss and Henry White. Wilson arrived in France on 13 December and was given a rapturous welcome en route to Paris. However, he was also quickly made aware that the French people expected his support in their desire to see Germany punished. In his speech of welcome of 14 December, President Raymond Poincaré told Wilson:

> The French government will furnish you with authentic documents in which the German general staff develops its plan of plunder and industrial annihilation. Should it remain unpunished the most splendid victories would be useless. (In Traynor, 1991, p. 106)

However, Wilson's steadfast belief in the principle of 'peace without victory' placed him on a collision course with those who wanted to see Germany punished to the maximum degree. The peace conference began with preliminary meetings at the French Foreign Ministry in January 1919 and concluded when the terms were presented to the German representatives on 7 May. The talks were dominated by the 'Big Four' – President Wilson of the United States, Prime Minister Lloyd George of Great Britain, Premier Clemenceau of France and Prime Minister Orlando of Italy. Wilson's relationship with Clemenceau steadily deteriorated. The French leader noted: 'God gave us the Ten Commandments and we broke them, Wilson gave us the Fourteen Points. We shall see.' (In Cooper, 2011, p. 491)

When Wilson fell ill in April 1919 it may have been with a severe cold or influenza, but recent biographer A. Scott Berg goes so far as to suggest that Wilson may have already suffered a series of small strokes and was perhaps exhibiting the early signs of dementia. Clemenceau made no attempt to hide his pleasure. These clashes of personality and policies became more damaging when placed against the background of technical difficulties faced by the statesmen. A. Lentin, in his book *Guilt at Versailles*, shows the problems faced by Wilson in trying to implement his ideal of national self-determination:

He was ignorant, when he promised Italy the South Tyrol, that its population was Austrian. When he approved the boundaries of Czechoslovakia, he had no idea that they contained three million Germans. When he assented to the incorporation of Transylvania within Romania, he was unaware of sanctioning an act of annexation. (Lentin, 1985, p. 75)

Lepore notes:

He was especially eagerly received by delegates from stateless and colonized societies: Egyptians, Indians, Chinese, Koreans, Arabs, Jews, Armenians and Kurds. In 'The Wilsonian Moment' (2007), Erez Manela argues that Wilson's rhetoric of self-determination contributed to a wave of popular protests in the Middle East and Asia, including a revolution in Egypt in 1919; made the nation-state the goal of stateless societies; and lies behind the emergence and force of anticolonial nationalism during the past century. (From Jill Lepore, *The New Yorker*, September 2015)

The treaty, with its 440 clauses and more than 200 pages, was finally rushed to a conclusion and presented to the Germans at a strained ceremony held on 7 May 1919. Most historians agree that Wilson succeeded in moderating the extreme demands of the French. Certain clauses such as Article 231, the War Guilt clause, and Article 232, the reparations clause, went beyond what Wilson had hoped for. Nevertheless, Lentin concludes that the treaty

Did not pacify Germany, still less permanently weaken her, appearances notwithstanding, but left her scourged, humiliated and resentful. It was neither a Wilson peace nor a Clemenceau peace, but a witches' brew concocted of the least palatable ingredients of each which, though highly distasteful to Germany, were by no means fatal. (Lentin, 1985, p. 132)

2.11 The Senate and the Versailles Treaty

'He shall have power, by and with the advice and consent of the Senate, to make treaties, provided two-thirds of the Senators present concur.'
Article II, Section 2 of the United States Constitution

Despite the relative success of his mission to restrain French demands for revenge, six months at Versailles had taken a severe toll on Wilson who was exhausted by his illness and by the strain of dealing with Clemenceau. As the *George Washington* headed for home, the president complained to his personal physician of sleeplessness, headaches and indigestion. Although Wilson was given a warm welcome when he reached Union Station in Washington DC, he knew that his reception in the Senate would be less enthusiastic. Wilson now prepared to present the Treaty and the Covenant to the Senate, and it was now that his failure to consult the Senate came back to haunt him. Inside the Senate, a group of around 15 politicians, known as the Irreconcilables, had come together under the leadership of Senator William E. Borah (Idaho) and included James A. Reed (Missouri) and Robert M. La Follette (Wisconsin). These politicians were totally opposed to American membership of the League of Nations, and critically they dominated the Senate Foreign Relations Committee. In addition, a more moderate Republican opposition group, led by Senator Henry Cabot Lodge, insisted that a key clause, Article 10 (Article X) of the Covenant of the League of Nations, be removed before they would support the Treaty. Among the 47-strong Democrat minority in the Senate, supporters of the League and the Covenant numbered around 43.

Wilson formally presented the Treaty to the Senate on 10 July 1919, stating that the United States had 'reached her majority as a world power ... a new role and a new responsibility have come to this great nation.' (In Berg, 2013, p. 606) The Republicans slowed down the Treaty by insisting upon reading the entire document aloud and by packing the foreign relations committee with isolationists. On 6 November 1919, Lodge presented 14 reservations to the committee. The most significant removed all American obligation to defend the territorial integrity of any other country as envisaged in Article X of the Treaty. Faced with this fundamental omission, Wilson instructed his own party to join the Irreconcilables in voting against ratification, which they did in November 1919. Wilson was in no mood for compromise and the final vote came on 15 March 1920. On this occasion, 23 Democrats joined the 12 Irreconcilables in defeating the Treaty by 49 votes to 35.

Against the backdrop of Congressional resistance, Wilson embarked on a gruelling public speaking tour in an attempt to rally public support in place of the political support he had been denied. In less than a month, starting in August 1919, Wilson proposed to deliver almost 40 speeches across 17 states and travel 8,000 miles. At the outset he declared: 'I have come out to fight for a cause. That cause is greater than the Senate. It is greater than the government. It is as great as the cause of mankind.' (Cooper, 2011, p. 523) Physically and mentally, Wilson remained drained from the exertions of the Versailles Conference. By the end of September 1919 it was clear to his aides that he had pushed himself to breaking point. After a speech in Pueblo, Colorado on 25 September Wilson collapsed; he told an adviser, 'I seem to have gone to pieces. The doctor is right. I am not in condition to go on.' (Ferrell, 1985, p. 169)

Wilson was taken back to Washington on the presidential train but by the time he had returned to the White House it was clear that he suffered a catastrophic stroke from which he never really recovered. With almost 18 months of his period of office remaining, the stricken president's iron will was now more implacable than ever. Physically and mentally unable to face the strain of his high office, Wilson now entered a phase of frustration, sadness and even, at times, delusion. As Jill Lepore puts it:

[A]lmost entirely confined to his bed, the state of his health unknown to the public and little known even to his own Cabinet. He could see only out of a tiny corner of his right eye. His thoughts no longer came in trains but in torrents. He could not use his left arm. He could barely walk. By no means could he manage the Capitol steps. He could not possibly attend the Inauguration. 'It cannot be done,' he said quietly. (Jill Lepore, *The New Yorker*, September 2013)

Shielded by his wife and his personal physician but obsessed by his enemies in Congress, his natural obstinacy turned into an outlook that ruled out even the slightest hint of compromise. Even though it was only flexibility that could save his treaty from abject defeat in Congress, the isolated and stricken president refused to compromise with the Republicans. A gradual and limited recovery in his health in February 1920 was only accompanied by an even more destructive attitude towards the notion of compromise. In a statement in March the president proclaimed:

> For myself, I could not look the soldiers of our gallant armies in the face again if I did not do everything in my power to remove every obstacle that lies in the way of this particular Article of the Covenant ... Any reservation which seeks to deprive the League of Nations of the force of Article X strikes at the very heart of the Covenant itself.

Without the cast-iron commitment of Article X the League would merely amount to a 'futile scrap of paper' (in Cooper, 2011, p. 558). Wilson's opponents were delighted because the president appeared so unreasonable and inflexible. When Lodge's amendments were passed, Wilson urged his supporters to vote against the entire document. This placed Wilson on the same side of the vote as Borah and his Irreconcilables. Ironically then, it was Wilson himself, in collaboration, as it were, with his bitterest enemies, who made America take the first steps back down the isolationist path. As a gleeful Senator Brandegee remarked to news reporters, 'The President strangled his own child.' (In Cooper, 2011, p. 558) The final vote came on 19 March based on the Treaty with the Lodge reservations. A two-thirds majority was needed for consent but the vote was 49 in favour and 35 against, seven votes short of the two-thirds of members present. Wilson's fight for the League was at a bitter end. The Treaty would never be ratified, the United States would never join the League and Wilson would never forgive his opponents.

Further reading

Berg A.S., *Wilson* (London: Simon & Schuster 2013).

Brogan H., *Longman History of the United States of America* (London: Longman 1985).

Coffey P., *American Arsenal: A Century of Waging War* (New York: Oxford University Press 2014).

Cooper J.M., *Woodrow Wilson: A Biography* (New York: Vintage Books 2011).

Ferrell R.H., *Woodrow Wilson & World War I 1917–1921* (New York: Harper & Row 1985).

Johnson P., *A History of the American People* (London: Weidenfeld & Nicolson 1997).

Meigs M., *Optimism at Armageddon: Voices of American Participants in the First World War* (London: Macmillan 1997).

Morison S.E., *The Oxford History of the American People* (New York: Oxford University Press 1965).

Neiberg M.S., *The Path to War: How the First World War Created Modern America* (New York: Oxford University Press 2016).

Thompson J.A., *Journal of American Studies* (Cambridge: Cambridge University Press 1988).

Traynor J., *Challenging History: Europe 1890–1990* (London: Macmillan 1991).

Traynor J., *Mastering Modern United States History* (Basingstoke: Palgrave 2001).

Whiteclay Chambers II J., *The Tyranny of Change: America in the Progressive Era 1890–1920* (New York: St Martin's Press 1992).

3 The 1920s

3.1 The transition from war to peace: President Harding and a return to isolationism

When the First World War came to an end after 1,563 days of bloody conflict, the widely held belief in the United States, as well as in Europe, was that this would be 'the war to end all wars'. During the winter of 1918–19 a succession of ships bearing dead and wounded American soldiers sailed into Hoboken Harbor in New Jersey. More than 116,000 American troops had perished. 53,000 American soldiers had been killed in action. 63,000 had died from disease. A further 2,900 were classified as missing in action. The psychological impact of the war on the American public was immense. Many Americans bitterly resented the fact that their country had joined the war at all, and their determination never to repeat that mistake was absolute. The loss of young life left many Americans disillusioned and wary of any future commitment outside the United States.

During the war, the Wilson Administration's Committee on Public Information had whipped up anti-German feeling to a hysterical and damaging extent. The mood of super-patriotism and fervent Americanism which was generated carried with it a hatred of the enemy and a tendency to limit the freedom of speech. The emotions apparent in the 1920s such as hostility towards foreigners, an unhealthy obsession with '100 per cent Americanism' and a fear of radical ideas can all be attributed, in part, to the trauma of the war. This manifested itself in the conduct of American foreign policy with a sharp return to isolationism.

The 1920 presidential election and the shift to isolationism

The Democratic convention of June 1920 was the first by a major party to be held on the West Coast. Even though Wilson was no longer a functional president he remained committed to the League of Nations and entertained a deluded idea that he could somehow secure his party's support for an unprecedented third term and a campaign that would amount to a referendum on his beloved treaty. It was a sign, perhaps, of how detached from reality the president had become that he was so bitterly disappointed when in July 1920, at the party convention in San Francisco, the Democrats chose James Cox of Ohio as its candidate on the 44th ballot.

Even though Wilson's name did not appear on the ballot, from the start of the campaign the Republicans targeted 'Wilson's League' and it quickly became clear that his dogged commitment to American membership of the League of Nations had back-fired. Cox, and his running mate, Franklin D. Roosevelt, tried to keep the League as the main issue, but the electorate was more interested in domestic matters such as rising prices and the wave of industrial action. Maldwyn A. Jones states: 'the presidential election of 1920 showed that the country had wearied of being kept constantly on its toes. Wilsonian moral fervor, and crusading zeal, whether for domestic reform or a new world order, had gone out of fashion.' (Jones, 1995, p. 435) As Robert H. Ferrell puts it, Wilson's obsessive advocacy of the League had made him 'as unpopular as he had once been popular.' In November 1920, when Harding captured more than 16 million votes, with only 9 million for Cox, the Republican victor told a cheering crowd: 'The League ... is now deceased ... We have torn up Wilsonism by the roots.' (Ferrell, 1985, p. 229)

Yet despite Wilson's bitter lament that the country would now embark upon a period of 'sullen and selfish isolation', there remained a degree of interest in international affairs. While the wartime slaughter had truly appalled most Americans, it had also created a desire for future peace and disarmament. So in August 1921, Harding's Secretary of State, Charles Evans Hughes, invited representatives from Britain, China and a number of European countries to attend a disarmament conference to be held in Washington, DC in November. American observers began to attend League of Nations Assembly meetings and delegates were sent to a wide range of international conferences. The United States was maintaining a watching brief in international affairs, and this was reflected in the American initiative which led to the convening of the Washington Conference on disarmament and Pacific Ocean affairs, chaired by Secretary of State Hughes.

3.2 The Washington Naval Conference

American organisation of this important conference indicated that while the United States had rejected membership of the League of Nations it retained interest in international affairs. The conference began in November 1921 and lasted until February 1922; the key issues were naval disarmament and the future of the Pacific and the Far East. America's geographical position meant that it needed a fleet in the Pacific and the Atlantic. The high costs involved in the upkeep of two ocean-going navies prompted America's desire to see agreed limits imposed on the world's largest fleets. In addition, the contribution of the Anglo-German naval race to the war of 1914 had not been forgotten. In February 1922 the major nations signed the Five-Power Treaty (known as the Washington Naval Treaty), which was roughly in line with American requirements. A three-tier tonnage system was agreed: Britain and the United States were limited to 525,000 tonnes, and Japan accepted a ceiling of 300,000 tonnes with 175,000 tonnes for France and Italy.

In terms of affairs in the Far East, America and Canada wanted to see Britain move away from her pre-war alliance with Japan. The Nine-Power Pact signed on the same date as the Five-Power Treaty affirmed the territorial integrity of China and accepted the principle of the 'Open Door' through which each nation could trade with China on an equal footing.

While the United States was satisfied with the Washington Conference, it did not signal the start of a return to the international stage. In addition, the weaknesses of the agreements reached in Washington would be starkly revealed when less amenable forces came to control Japanese policy in the early 1930s.

3.3 Reparations

The issue of war debts soon cast a shadow over relations between the Republican administrations of the 1920s and the financially shattered Allies. During the war, the Allies had borrowed more than $10 billion from the United States. The majority of this money had gone straight back to America, where it had been used to pay for food supplies and munitions. In 1919 Britain took the view that these debts should now be written off, in acknowledgement of the fact that Britain and France had paid a much higher price in human lives than the United States. To Britain's astonishment, the Americans asked for a full repayment of the war loans. As it was clear that both Britain and France were effectively destitute it seemed that the only way to raise the money was to penalise vanquished Germany by imposing harsh economic terms.

The practical problems of inflicting a huge reparation bill on Germany became clear when she failed to keep up with her monthly payments in the bitter winter of 1923. With Germany destabilised, in the grip of runaway inflation and facing occupation in the Ruhr by French and Belgian troops, the United States decided that something needed to be done to resolve the situation. An international commission was established which led to the implementation of the Dawes Plan (April 1924). This created a modified settlement of the reparations issue, with lower-level payments. In addition, American loans to German industry and agriculture helped to restore stability and a degree of prosperity to the shattered German economy. In 1929, a further development came with the Young Plan, in which the reparation payments of the debtor nations were reduced and the repayment period extended. These positive developments were then derailed by the disastrous global impact of the Wall Street Crash and the subsequent worldwide Depression.

3.4 The Kellogg–Briand Pact, 1928

The International Treaty for the Renunciation of War as an Instrument of National Policy (the Kellogg–Briand Pact) was signed at the Quai d'Orsay in Paris on 27 August 1928. Limited to two paragraphs, the Pact declared that the signatories would henceforth try to resolve disputes only by peaceful means. Fifteen nations initially signed, with a final total of more than 60. From an American perspective, the Pact represented national acknowledgement of a vocal domestic peace campaign for the 'outlawing of war'. The sense of optimism created by the peace movement was heightened when the Secretary of State, Frank Kellogg, travelled to Paris to place his signature next to that of his French counterpart, Aristide Briand. In fact, the significance of the Pact was illusory; although the Senate ratified the Pact by 85 votes to 1, this did not signify the return of the United States to an active intervention position in world affairs. In fact, the Senate's ratification of the Pact was swiftly followed by the approval of a $274 million spending programme on 15 heavy cruisers.

3.5 The 'Red Scare'

During the feverish atmosphere of the war many Americans directed their hostility towards the country's substantial German-American population. When the war ended this anti-German sentiment gave way to a mood of xenophobia, heightened by the communist revolution in Russia in October 1917 and directed against anyone with radical or revolutionary ideals. Widespread alarm at the rise of the American communist movement and the American Socialist Party was disproportionate to the size of these organisations and the extent of their activities. An outbreak of industrial unrest, including a five-day general strike in Seattle in February 1919 led to fears of impending social upheaval and even revolution. The mayor of Seattle condemned the strike as 'domestic bolshevism'. Other industries affected by strike action included the railroads, coal and steel with violent clashes between the authorities and the workers.

The Boston police strike

The extent of the fault lines that seemed to be appearing in post-war society are shown by the fact that almost 4 million workers took part in more than 3,000 strikes during the troubled year of 1919. No industrial dispute sparked greater fear of a breakdown in the fabric of American society than the Boston police strike. By the autumn of that year many rank-and-file members of the police force of Boston, Massachusetts, the oldest in the country, felt that they had been pushed to the limit. Some of their station houses were in a state of disrepair, squalid and riddled with vermin. Without a pay rise since 1913 but with inflationary price rises, they made several unsuccessful demands for a cost-of-living increase. In August 1919 the old Boston association, which was known as the Social Club, had formally affiliated with the American Federation of Labor (AFL). This emboldened the police officers to push once again for a pay rise but alarmed those who pointed to the fact that the mere existence of a police union that could strike breached the regulations set out in the Boston Police Department manual.

When the new pay demand was refused, more than two-thirds of a police force of 1,500 men refused to carry out their duties. In the evening of 9 September 1919, carrying their iconic old-style helmets under their arms, more than 1,000 of Boston's finest walked away from their duties. To the general dismay of an alarmed public there was an immediate outbreak of looting and violence as furniture stores, a cigar shop, shoe stores and a jewellers were ransacked. These events seemed to strike at the very heart of the traditional American sense of belief in their system of law and order. With the fabric of Boston apparently unravelling, the national mood was now characterised by paranoia and hysteria.

With perfect timing for his own political fortunes, the Governor of Massachusetts, Calvin Coolidge, called out the entire state guard of Massachusetts. As Bostonians despaired about the future of their beautiful, historic city, Coolidge condemned the actions of the striking police with the words: 'There is no right to strike against the public safety by anybody, anywhere, at any time.' *The New York Sun* praised the decisive action of the 'plain New England gentleman, whose calm determination to uphold the law and maintain order in the situation caused by the Boston police walkout has made him a national figure' (in Shlaes, 2014 p. 174).

With workers seemingly radicalised by the wartime expansion of labour unions and with a mounting sense of bitterness towards what were seen as excessive corporate profits, an unprecedented attack on capitalism seemed possible. However, the wider public mood turned sharply against the police and the dispute quickly came to an end. Meanwhile, following a series of bomb outrages, culminating in an attack in 1920 on the headquarters of J.P. Morgan on Wall Street at the financial heart of New York City in which 39 people were killed, fear of bolshevism swept the country as the fear of German spies had done two years previously.

The Palmer Raids

The prevailing atmosphere was exacerbated by the actions of the Attorney General, A. Mitchell Palmer, himself the victim of an attempted assassination at his Washington home. The nation's most senior lawmaker was possibly motivated by his desire to exploit the national mood as the platform for his personal presidential ambition. A wave of arrests in November 1919, the so-called 'Palmer Raids', targeted anarchists and socialists, many of whom were deported to Russia. Five members were expelled from the New York State Legislature because they were socialists. Palmer also authorised raids on magazines and printing presses and on the offices and private homes of socialists, liberals, feminists, atheists and libertarians, leading to the arrest and detention without trial in often shocking conditions of thousands of radicals. (Brogan, 1985)

Sacco and Vanzetti

It was against the 'Red Scare' background of tension and intolerance that the case of Sacco and Vanzetti unfolded. On Christmas Eve 1919, an armed hold-up in Bridgewater, Massachusetts, was thwarted without bloodshed. Then, in April 1920, a raid in nearby South Braintree, an industrial suburb of Boston, resulted in the murder of a shoe factory paymaster and a factory guard and the theft of $15,000. Within a month, two immigrant Italians, Nicola Sacco, a heel trimmer, and Bartolomeo Vanzetti, a fish peddler, were arrested and charged with armed robbery and murder, although there was little firm evidence against them. The case itself was fairly routine and initially attracted little attention. Yet as the trial progressed it emerged that Sacco and Vanzetti were anarchists and wartime 'draft dodgers' while Webster Thayer, the conservative judge who ran proceedings, made little attempt to conceal his distaste for the accused. The police who had arrested Sacco and Vanzetti testified that they had drawn guns, and this was presented as confirmation of their guilt. The prosecution asked the jury to do its patriotic duty.

While the evidence against Sacco and Vanzetti was far from conclusive, it came as little surprise when they were convicted in July 1921 and sentenced to death. The trial was now receiving widespread attention and divided opinion in America. The judge boasted to his friend of what he had done to 'those anarchist bastards'. On the other hand, many writers and left-wingers alerted world opinion to what they felt was a horrendous miscarriage of justice. In April 1927, The Supreme Court of Massachusetts rejected calls for a new trial on the grounds that there had not been 'a failure of justice'. Sacco and Vanzetti were executed by electrocution on 23 August 1927. This was widely condemned in liberal circles and certainly damaged the reputation of the United States abroad.

Ballistic evidence and the criminal records have been unable to provide a definitive answer to whether they were guilty. In 1977, 50 years after the investigation, the Governor of Massachusetts and future presidential candidate, Michael Dukakis, officially declared on behalf of the state that the trial had been unfair in what was effectively a posthumous pardon. The execution of Sacco and Vanzetti has remained controversial because of the view that they were found guilty primarily because of their radical ideals and their ethnicity rather than any conclusive evidence. Its importance, according to one eminent writer, is that the historian 'could fix upon it as a way of penetrating the deepest conflicts in American life' (Temkin, 2009, p. 7). In fact: 'The Sacco-Vanzetti affair presents us with many eerie and sobering correlations to the present. Global political action, terrorism, justice and injustice, jingoism, xenophobia, radicalism, and the treatment of immigrants and minorities.' (Temkin, 2009, p. 8)

Great American Lives: Emma Goldman, 1869–1946

At the height of the Red Scare, the backlash against those on the left deemed radical or communist was intense and at times brutal. At the same time, women were largely deterred from entering the political arena. Therefore, any female who put forward radical views at this time was certain to come under extreme duress. Emma Goldman's anarchist philosophy placed her at the extreme end of the spectrum of hostility directed against the radical left.

Born in 1869 in the Russian Empire (present-day Lithuania) to a Jewish family, Goldman emigrated to the United States in 1885. Embracing radicalism and giving support to acts of extreme political violence such as the Haymarket Affair (1896), Goldman wrote and lectured on matters such as women's rights, birth control and anarchism.

Goldman was intensely moved by the poverty of many American workers. She believed that America's capitalist government ruthlessly exploited the poor and dispossessed. Goldman claimed: 'The rejection of the ruling classes and absolute freedom from government would best serve ordinary people and foster true equality.' (Reynolds, 2009, p. 324)

When the United States joined the First World War in 1917 she worked alongside fellow anarchist Alexander Berkman in creating the No-Conscription League. This resulted in a two-year prison term from 1917 to 1919. Goldman was released in September 1919 with the Red Scare at its height. But in November, the Attorney General launched the 'Palmer Raids' in which 9,000 suspected radicals, including Goldman, were arrested and held without trial. The young J. Edgar Hoover described Goldman and Berkman as 'beyond doubt, two of the most dangerous anarchists in the country' (Reynolds, 2009, p. 324).

Continued

However, as David Reynolds points out: '... others protested at the ruthless violation of civil liberties. A group of distinguished lawyers, including Felix Frankfurter of Harvard and Ernst Freund of Chicago, condemned "the utterly illegal acts which have been committed by those charged with the highest duty of enforcing the laws – acts which caused widespread suffering and unrest, have struck at the foundation of American free institutions, and have brought the name of our country into disrepute"' (Reynolds, 2009, p. 324).

Academic opinion counted for little in the hysterical climate of the Red Scare and Goldman was deported to Russia. She became disillusioned with the emerging communist dictatorship and spent the rest of her life in England, France and Canada.

Goldman died in Toronto in May 1946. To an extent she continues to divide opinion. Her bravery, principles, feminism and commitment to her ideas led to a revival of interest in her during the 1970s. On the other hand, her support for politically motivated murder and violence means that she is heavily criticised by others.

Further reading: David Reynolds, *America, Empire of Liberty: A New Liberty* (Allen Lane 2009). Coverage of the Red Scare is on pp. 323–327.

3.6 The election of 1920 and the Harding Administration

President Wilson's ill-health

Wilson never recovered from the transient ischaemic attack he suffered in September 1919. This was a precursor to the serious stroke he suffered the following month which, combined with an infection of the prostate gland, constituted a life-threatening illness. He lived out the rest of his administration isolated, in a wheelchair, in the White House. Two recent major biographies of Wilson by A. Scott Berg and John Milton Cooper, Jr cast new light on the extent of his decline. Cooper describes this period as 'the worst crisis of presidential disability in American history' (Cooper, 2011, p. 535). Low mood, physical helplessness, self-delusion and an unbalanced sense of judgement meant that the president was in office but unable to govern. At this time, Wilson's devoted second wife, Edith, protected her husband by acting as a gatekeeper to the president. During what she called 'her stewardship' she decided who could meet with her husband and which official papers could be passed to or withheld from him. Albert Fall, a Republican senator from New Mexico, complained that the United States was now a 'government by petticoat' (Cooper, 2011, p. 537). The seriously ill president was now more stubborn than ever. Any attempt to modify the terms upon which America would join the League of Nations was met with a destructive rage against his enemies. Berg states: 'With another year to his term, Woodrow Wilson became the lamest duck ever to inhabit the White House, residing more than presiding for the rest of his days there.' (Berg, 2013, p. 679)

The political emergence of Herbert Hoover

The death of Theodore Roosevelt in January 1919 and Wilson's poor health removed the two most significant figures of the time from the political landscape. This paved the way, so many insiders thought, for a rising star, the exceptionally driven and industrious Herbert Hoover, to be given the Republican nomination. Born in 1874, the son of Quakers in West Branch, an Iowa village of only 300 people, he had suffered the loss of both of his parents at a young age. Despite this, he attended Stanford University and in adult life became a highly successful and wealthy engineer. In 1914 he was asked to lead an emergency mission to save war-torn Belgium from starvation. Hoover's energetic, purposeful response was to create from scratch the Commission for the Relief in Belgium (CRB). When the United States joined the war in 1917 Hoover became food administrator for the United States but retained control over the Belgian relief programme.

When President Wilson attended the Peace Conference at Versailles in January 1919, Hoover formed part of the US delegation as food adviser. Despite the fact that Hoover had worked so successfully and diligently for the Democratic President Wilson, he frequently let it be known in private that he considered himself a Republican. Above all, Hoover loathed demagogues and 'political mud' and was determined to be his own man. In February 1919, in a speech at Johns Hopkins University in Baltimore, he was prepared to publicly argue that it was in America's self-interest to support the Treaty of Versailles and American membership of the League of Nations with relatively modest amendments. In the prevailing climate, Hoover had placed himself on the wrong side of the political mood. This became crystal clear at the party's convention in Chicago in June where it was apparent that Hoover's pro-League stance and progressive reputation meant that he would not win the nomination.

Warren G. Harding

Out of the wreckage of Hoover's naïve and amateurish campaign a dark horse emerged. Displaying the political skill of a veteran, Warren Harding, a small-time politician and newspaper editor from Marion, Ohio, secured the nomination and at the same time allowed Hoover to believe that he would support the League when he had no intention of doing so. Hoover believed that he had forged an alliance with Harding but the Ohio man left him for dead. Accepting the Republican nomination in July, Harding made it clear that he would be campaigning on an isolationist ticket.

Harding's running mate, Calvin Coolidge, the Governor of Massachusetts, had significantly raised his profile with his timely and high-profile intervention against the Boston police strike. This stance had done a great deal to secure his nomination for the vice presidency and helped Harding to achieve one of the greatest electoral victories in American history. The Republicans ruthlessly placed the stricken incumbent at the centre of their campaign as they denounced 'Wilson's league'. The result was a catastrophic defeat for the Democrats. Harding secured more than 60 per cent of the popular vote, and the gap in the Electoral College was equally dramatic, with 404 to 127. While the Democrats held on in the South, 37 states voted Republican with 11 for the Democrats. The scale of the defeat was made worse by a Congressional victory for the Republicans in both the House and the Senate (Table 3.1).

Table 3.1   The result of the 1920 presidential election

Candidate	Party	Electoral College votes	Popular votes
Warren G. Harding (Ohio)	Republican	404	16,152,200
James M. Cox (Ohio)	Democrat	127	9,147,353
Eugene V. Debs (Indiana)	Socialist	–	919,799

Analysis of Harding

It is not hard to see the election of Harding as evidence of the post-war malaise which had gripped America. The contrast between Wilson's eloquence and idealism and Harding's mind-numbing oratory was there for all to see. His lack of fluency, intellectual limitations, and homespun parochialism contrasted painfully with Wilson's high-minded rhetoric and breadth of vision. An amenable, sociable character, Harding was both unable and unwilling to outgrow his origins. He enjoyed occupying the White House but ultimately found the challenges that lay in wait there for him overwhelming.

PRESIDENTIAL PROFILE

Warren Gamaliel Harding

29th President of the United States (1921–1923)
Born: 2 November 1865
Birthplace: Bloomington Grove, Ohio
Died: 2 August 1923, San Francisco, California, aged 57; buried at the Harding Tomb, Marion, Ohio
Education: Ohio Central College
Political party: Republican
State: Ohio
Occupation before presidency: Newspaper editor
Previous government service: Member of the Ohio Senate; Lieutenant-Governor of Ohio; US Senator
Age at inauguration: 55
Dates of office: 4 March 1921 to 2 August 1923
Election: November 1920
Vice president: Calvin Coolidge
Length of term: 2 years 5 months

Harding's background and achievements

The owner and editor of the *Marion Star* newspaper, Harding became active in local politics and progressed through the state legislature to represent Ohio in the United States Senate. He was regarded as intensely loyal and amenable but rather shallow when it came to the major issues of the day. His knowledge of the world outside Ohio politics was sorely limited. The balance of historical opinion has been heavily against Harding. Brogan's verdict illustrates this point:

> Harding was not intelligent or firm or hard-working enough to be a successful President. His other personal weaknesses hardly mattered. True, he committed adultery in a coat-cupboard at the White House because he was too afraid of his wife to take his mistress to more comfortable quarters ... True he was rather too fond of giving government posts to poker-playing cronies whose honesty turned out to be inadequate. (Brogan, 1985, p. 506)

One authority recently observed that Harding was 'a man with skeletons in his closet more appropriate to Halloween' (Jeansonne, 2012, p. 9).

Analysis: Harding – a case for rehabilitation?

While Harding's standing remains low it is now generally acknowledged that the exclusively critical verdict has probably been unfair, and a slight degree of rehabilitation has taken place. It has been noted that Harding's treatment of the socialist leader Eugene V. Debs, who had been arrested under the terms of President Wilson's Sedition Act, was impressive given the prevailing mood of the country at large. Debs had been sentenced to ten years' imprisonment simply for making a speech against the war. Commendably, Harding commuted the sentence and even invited Debs to a personal meeting at the White House. In a period when industrial relations were difficult, Harding supported demands for an eight-hour working day in the steel industry. Despite pressure from the American Legion, Harding vetoed a soldiers' bonus bill in 1922. Finally, despite the prevailing mood of isolationism in foreign affairs, Harding backed the arms limitation which was at the centre of the Washington Conference of 1921–22. Ellis W. Hawley offers an alternative view of the beleaguered Harding Administration:

> Historians have long looked upon the Presidency of Warren G. Harding as a major debacle. Often missing from their accounts is the fact that the Harding era also came close to combining full employment and rising living standards with stable prices and international peace. For all the scandals the new administration presided over a series of developments that made the American economy the envy of much of the world. (Hawley, 1979, p. 58)

Harding's appointments

Harding was fully, almost painfully, aware of his own limitations and it is to his credit that he sought to compensate for them by appointing a group of men to senior posts who were both able and successful. Andrew Mellon, from Pittsburgh, became the second richest man in America. He made his fortune in the aluminium industry and, subsequently, oil and had built up a huge financial empire. He served with distinction as Harding's Treasury Secretary and remained at the helm in the Treasury until 1932. He believed in high taxation, low tariffs, freedom for business, and opposition to the trade unions. Charles Evan Hughes, the Secretary of State, had previously served as the Governor of New York. Hughes had been the Republican's presidential nominee in 1916 and was probably the country's most eminent lawyer. Harding's Secretary of Agriculture, Henry Wallace, had extensive experience of farming issues and his role as editor of an influential Iowa farm journal had earned him widespread respect. Last but not least, the future president, Herbert Hoover, served with energy and distinction as the Secretary of Commerce. His vision was to use his department to provide a wealth of statistics and information for the nation's economic decision makers. With the appointment of these four gifted, hard-working individuals Harding had some of the most able cabinet-level officers of any administration. However, some of his other appointments were much less impressive.

'The Ohio Gang', the death of Harding and the succession of Coolidge

When he became president, Harding brought with him to Washington a number of his old companions from Marion, Ohio. He enjoyed the company of the 'Ohio Gang' and could be relaxed and informal with them, playing cards and drinking whisky. He rewarded their loyalty with appointments to key posts such as the Director of the Mint and the Superintendent of Federal Prisons. Attorney General Harry M. Daugherty had a long-standing relationship with Harding and had served him as his political manager. It was not long before Daugherty betrayed Harding's trust and damaged the reputation of the Justice Department and its associated law enforcement agencies. In 1923, a group of men including Jesse Smith, a member of the Ohio Gang and a close friend of Daugherty, were accused of using their influence within the Justice Department to sell pardons and immunity from prosecution; as details of the scandal emerged Smith attempted suicide. Daugherty was damaged by the scandal but escaped imprisonment.

The head of the Veterans' Bureau, Charles R. Forbes, abused his position to a massive extent. Between 1921 and 1923 at least $250 million was misappropriated, through fraudulent construction contracts and the selling off of government property at a fraction of its value. Some historians have claimed that when Harding's suspicions were aroused he throttled Forbes into a confession. Forbes left the country and resigned and it was not until after Harding's death that he was finally prosecuted and imprisoned.

The Teapot Dome scandal

The most damaging scandal of all revolved around the activities of Albert Fall, the Secretary of the Interior. A Senate enquiry was set up to scrutinise the leasing to private individuals of government oil areas which had been set aside for naval use. The enquiry discovered that Fall had managed to transfer oil reserves to his own department and then secretly leased those at Elk Hills, California and Teapot Dome, Wyoming to two oil magnates, Edward L. Doheny and Harry F. Sinclair. In return, Fall had received substantial 'loans'. Fall was found guilty of accepting bribes and was fined $100,000 and sentenced to 12 months in prison. Fall had secured the dubious distinction of becoming the first member of the American Cabinet to be convicted on a criminal charge.

For most of his presidency, Harding was largely oblivious to the misdeeds of his friends. However, towards the end of his life it seems likely that he was becoming increasingly worried about their activities. He told a journalist, 'I have no trouble with my enemies but my damn friends, my God-damn friends ... they're the ones that keep me walking the floor nights.' (Hawley, 1979, p. 76) When he set out on a trip to Alaska in July 1923 he had become increasingly preoccupied and profoundly depressed. By the time he reached Seattle on the way home he was on the brink of collapse. He travelled on to San Francisco where, on 2 August, he suffered a coronary thrombosis which proved fatal. The unexpected death of Harding was followed by a flood of allegations and scandals about his private life and public appointments. The damage to the reputation of the Republican Party would have been more severe if it had not been for the patently high moral standards of his successor, Calvin Coolidge.

3.7 Prohibition

The Women's Christian Temperance Union (WCTU)

Long before the federal anti-alcohol laws of 1919–20 the topic of Prohibition was a major issue, causing tension between Americans on both sides of the debate. The WCTU was perhaps the best organised of the groups lobbying for Prohibition. The name of this group reminds us of the fact that pressure for action against alcohol was very much a feminist issue at this time. The consumption of alcohol dated back to the colonial period and had become even more pronounced through the influx of European immigrants in the nineteenth century. The role of alcohol was clear across issues of domestic violence and abuse, the neglect of children, disposal of household income on liquor at the expense of food for the family, absence from work, dismissal from work with ensuing poverty, and the impact of alcohol on personal health and mental well-being.

In a typical example from the late nineteenth century, a female homesteader from Wyoming described how male farmhands would spend their time off indulging in binge drinking that would last for several days. A report from 1899 claimed: 'Ordinary country women in America are for the most part total abstainers ... in the country villages social drinking is not the custom outside the saloon, and drunkenness among women is almost unheard of.' (In Murdock, 1998, p. 65) One detailed regional study of medical admissions from 1884 to 1912 across a range of hospitals and clinics has shown that of those needing care at this time only 15 per cent were women.

An examination of the Annual Report of the Police Commissioner for the City of Boston for the year 1919 (now online) offers some interesting insights into the role alcohol played in crime in the city:

> In arrests for drunkenness the average per day was 97. There were 19,408 fewer persons arrested than in 1918, a decrease of 35.32 per cent; 50.99 per cent of the arrested persons were non-residents and 40.58 per cent were of foreign birth.

Of deaths in which officers were detailed to assist medical examiners, five of 844 deaths were ascribed to alcoholism. In the house of detention for women, located in the court-house, 1,921 of 4,055 women arrested in the city were committed for drunkenness.

It is not surprising then, to see that many women were passionate supporters of Prohibition. Beyond the gender divide the warning issued by the Delaware Moral Society, that the US was becoming a 'nation of drunkards', was a typical clarion call from the sobriety movement. The power of the Protestant work ethic as a cultural counterpoint to indolent drunkenness cannot easily be understated (McGirr, 2016, p. 55).

Catherine Gilbert Murdock observes:

> [A]lcohol abuse in the nineteenth and early twentieth centuries existed on a scale Americans today have trouble conceptualizing. Public drunkards were a pathetic, everyday spectacle in villages and cities throughout America. Drink really did kill men and ruin families, and millions of citizens felt that the best way to meet the crisis would be to eliminate alcoholic beverages. Moreover, the nation's abusive drinking patterns were strictly gendered. At the very most, 20 percent of the alcoholic population was female. Historically, it is not America that had a drinking problem, it is American men. Male drinking gave rise to the American temperance movement, the longest, most popular social cause of the nineteenth century. (Murdock, 1998, pp. 3–4)

With the rise of the saloon, 'consumption of beer increased from 2.3 gallons per capita annually in 1840 to 25.9 gallons in 1910, a rise of over 1,000 per cent.'

The WCTU was formed after a meeting in Cleveland in 1874 which was attended by church representatives from 17 states. They elected Frances E. Willard as their leader. Under her energetic leadership, the WCTU soon had chapters in every state and as early as 1875 the new body was petitioning Congress for a Federal Prohibition Act. Through its 'Department for the Suppression of Social Evil', it set out to demonstrate the links between crime and alcohol consumption. Membership of the WCTU was predominantly middle class; analysis of the membership suggests that typically the women were the wives of doctors, lawyers and landowners. Wearing a white ribbon they campaigned under the slogan of 'home protection' to safeguard families against the excesses of rapid change and industrialisation. Critics of Willard could point to her increasingly strident language such as her claim in 1890: 'Alien illiterates run our cities today; the saloon is their palace.' (In McGirr, 2016, p. 92)

Their ambition was to replace the saloons, which they so despised, with coffee houses. The writer Edward Behr suggests that this tactic shows that the WCTU was basically out of touch with the working classes and with immigrants who sustained so much of the demand for alcohol. Nevertheless, the WCTU undoubtedly gave the Prohibition issue a national profile and, in particular, the lobbying had an impact on thousands of American women who embraced the argument for Prohibition at the same time as they campaigned for the vote.

The Anti-Saloon League

A further cornerstone of the 'dry' movement came with the creation of a pressure group called the Anti-Saloon League (ASL) in 1893. Its leadership, core membership and financial resources came to a considerable extent from the Protestant Church and, in particular, Methodism. Perhaps its most important figure was Ohio-born Wayne Wheeler. He established close contact with powerful political leaders in Congress and even came to exert influence over the White House. Wheeler's influence led to Ohio becoming one of the driest states in the union so that by 1908 85 per cent of its territory was classified as 'dry'. The state came to exemplify Wheeler's vision of America itself, with its emphasis on rural values, hard work and strict observation of the Sabbath. Wheeler persuaded the ASL that the prospect of a national constitutional amendment prohibiting the sale and manufacture of alcohol was achievable. At the 1913 ASL Convention in Columbus, the momentum behind the drive for a constitutional amendment gathered pace. The Anti-Saloon League and its newspaper the *American Issue* were powerful, modern, highly effective elements in the overall drive towards Prohibition. Finally, with the ongoing drive for industrial efficiency it is worth noting that leading industrialists such as John D. Rockefeller were happy to donate millions of dollars to the Prohibition cause.

Opponents of Prohibition

The wave of immigration in the nineteenth century brought to America huge numbers of Germans, Irish and Italians whose culture and customs included the consumption of beer, wine and whisky. This meant that the brewing industry was a highly lucrative business and no group provided more sustained opposition to Prohibition than the United States Brewers' Association. The breweries and distillers whose livelihood depended on the trade in alcohol met formally as the Brewers' Association for the first time in 1862. They launched a series of expensive newspaper campaigns and also lobbied against women's suffrage because they recognised that many of the most active Prohibitionists were women. They saw the WCTU as their mortal enemy.

The impact of the First World War on Prohibition

Approximately half of the 48 states were already 'dry' before America entered the First World War in April 1917. However, the war, the notion of sacrifice, hostility to all things German (the brewing industry) and the overriding need for preparedness changed the national mood and swayed the argument decisively in favour of the Prohibitionists. Pressure for a federal ban on the manufacture and consumption of alcohol assumed new momentum. Proponents of Prohibition put forward practical, moral and religious arguments to support their stand against alcohol. Firstly, they made the practical point that a ban on the production of alcohol would conserve supplies of important grains such as barley. Secondly, it was claimed that the efficiency of both industrial workers and the armed forces would be enhanced by a ban on liquor. Thirdly, they argued that it was wrong for America to continue to enjoy the consumption of alcohol while some of its young men were making the supreme sacrifice on the battlefields of France and Belgium.

Proponents of Prohibition assumed 'the loftiest motives of patriotism' for their cause, casting those who did not want a ban as inherently un-American. New 'scientific' thinking on alcohol as a 'narcotic' was used by the Alabama congressman Richard

P. Hobson to justify his claim that alcohol was a 'poison destructive and degenerating to the human organism ... that lowers to an appalling degree the average standard ... of our citizenship.' (McGirr, 2016, p. 49) The traditional notion of alcohol as a medicinal remedy came under fire from the American Medical Association and the Scientific Temperance Federation, which was founded in Boston in 1906.

The Eighteenth Amendment and the Volstead Act

With concerns about the abuse of alcohol attracting a significant degree of support, 'The noble experiment' of Prohibition was introduced by the Eighteenth Amendment which became effective on 16 January 1920. The new law prohibited 'the manufacture, sale, or transportation of intoxicating liquors within, the importation thereof into, or the exportation thereof from the United States.' John F. Kramer, the first Prohibition Commissioner, proclaimed:

> This law will be obeyed in cities large and small, and in villages, and where it is not obeyed it will be enforced. The law says that liquor to be used as a beverage must not be manufactured. We shall see that it is not manufactured. Nor sold, nor given away, nor hauled in anything on the surface of the earth or under the earth or in the air. (McGirr, 2016, p. 266)

The enforcement of Prohibition and reasons for its failure

From the outset, the water was muddy. Murdock notes:

> The stringency of national prohibition was not at first apparent. The Eighteenth Amendment approved by Congress and forty-six state legislatures (ten more than necessary for ratification) ... did not prohibit purchase of liquor. This loophole, which had been created to obtain purchasers' testimonies against sellers, created an ethical morass ... But the fact remained that drinkers did not get arrested and did not go to jail. In the 1920s a citizen could complain about the failure of government efforts and the breakdown of law and order while tapping comfortably into a new supply of bootleg hooch. (Murdock, 1998, p. 89)

The accompanying Volstead Act, passed by Congress in the autumn of 1919 and named after a member of the House from Minnesota, defined alcohol as any beverage containing more than 0.5 per cent alcohol. However, the act did allow possession and consumption of alcohol within the home, by the house owner, his or her family, and guests. In addition, the production of grain alcohol for medicinal, sacramental and industrial use remained legal.

Nevertheless, President Harding set up a Prohibition Unit under the leadership of Roy Haynes so that during the Prohibition era millions of gallons of wine and spirits were destroyed, and thousands of illegal stills were confiscated. America's prisons filled up with those convicted for contravening the Prohibition laws: in 1932 alone, 44,678 people were given jail sentences for alcohol-related offences. Although these figures show some impact they should not hide the fact that the laws were hugely difficult to enforce and were flouted by many people throughout American society (Table 3.2).

Table 3.2   Reasons for the failure of Prohibition

- Key factors in the failure of Prohibition included the fact that Congress never allocated enough money to make enforcement of Prohibition possible. The ASL contended that Prohibition could be enforced for less than $5 million a year. Congress allocated slightly more than that and provided for around 1,500 Prohibition agents in 1920. By 1930 the figure had increased to 2,836.

- Meanwhile, the sheer size of the United States and the immense boundaries between the United States and Canada in the north and Mexico in the south made the work of this small band of agents almost impossible. The United States had around 29,000 kilometres of coastline to patrol and, in addition, substantial amounts of liquor were smuggled in from the Bahamas and the West Indies.

- The salary received by the agents (on average, $2,000), was low enough to make them prone to bribery and corruption.

- Prohibition never received the full support of the American people. In particular, America's large, predominantly working-class, immigrant community tended to defy the Prohibition laws.

- In addition, the ban was unpopular with the richest element of society, who saw the laws as an infringement of their personal liberty.

Lisa McGirr notes:

[T]he enforcement of Prohibition was notable for its magnitude and its selectivity. Not surprisingly for a movement led at its core by the well-heeled Protestant Anti-Saloon League, enforcement hit working-class, urban immigrant, and poor communities hardest. It was, after all, enacted to discipline their leisure in the first place. (McGirr, 2016, pp. 27–28)

Writing after the Second World War the influential historian Richard Hofstadter described the Eighteenth Amendment as 'a farce' and placed it within the context of the socially restrictive policies that were introduced when the United States went to war, reflecting a 'village' mentality symbolic of 'moral overstrain' with the outlook of 'absolute morality' (in McGirr, 2016, pp. 17–18). In 1973, the commentator Alistair Cooke observed that the noble experiment 'did not noticeably endow Americans with more nobility than they already had. On the contrary, it gave rise to a national underground industry, based in Chicago that turned small-time safecrackers and brothel owners into millionaires' (Cooke, 1973, p. 324). In *The War on Alcohol: Prohibition and the Rise of the American State* (2016) Lisa McGirr states that the Eighteenth Amendment was 'one of the nation's most significant policy debacles: after less than fifteen years it became the first, and it remains the only, constitutional amendment to be rescinded' (McGirr, 2016, p. 12).

Her insights into Prohibition are nuanced and important:

The war on alcohol was a prime example of a recurring theme of United States mass politics. The nation's powerful traditions of evangelical Protestantism and its free-wheeling brand of expansive capitalism emerged in tandem – and in tension with one another. This combination of forces periodically fuelled moral crusades among men and women unsettled by social conflict and change. These reformers turned to the state to stabilize the social order, and secure their place within it, with strong doses of coercive moral absolutes. Their monumental anxieties over industrial capitalism, mass immigration, and the increasingly large and potentially volatile proletarian populations congealed around the campaign against the saloon and the liquor traffic. (McGirr, 2016, pp. 24–25)

Al Capone and organised crime

During the 1920s violent and well-resourced gang leaders, most infamously Al Capone, fought out a brutal battle for territorial control of Chicago with its lucrative speakeasies. Ultimately it was Capone who emerged as the dominant racketeer, to the extent that by 1927 his annual income was estimated to be worth approximately $60 million. Born in 1899, the son of an Italian barber, his early introduction to violent crime took place on the streets of New York City. He moved to Chicago in 1919 and by 1920 his criminal partnerships were generating an income of over $2 million a year. Capone claimed that he was merely a businessman legitimately meeting a public demand for alcohol but between 1927 and 1930 more than 500 gangland murders took place.

In fact, illicit alcohol was only a part of the Capone empire. Deirdre Bair's biography describes a case study by the prestigious Harvard Business School which revealed how Capone's 'Outfit' was run along the lines of a major corporation: 'The HBS study examined the years 1920–33 when Al controlled literally hundreds of "brothels, speakeasies, and roadhouses, which served as venues for gang administered gambling, prostitution, and illegal alcohol sales."' (Bair, 2016, p. 311) Extortion rackets, widespread corruption of politicians and criminal infiltration of the police force added to the scale of the operation. The most notorious of the gangland killings sanctioned by Capone was the 'St Valentine's Day Massacre' of February 1929. Capone's men donned police uniforms and entered a garage where several members of a rival gang were making coffee. While Capone's men slaughtered their rivals, Capone himself was pictured by the press sitting innocently on the beach in Miami, Florida.

The collapse of Capone's criminal career

Later that year Capone was finally arrested by Philadelphia police for carrying a gun, but his operation continued from prison. In 1931, Capone was convicted on the grounds of income tax evasion rather than the murders which he had undoubtedly sanctioned but which remained unpunished. He was sentenced to 11 years in prison but was released in 1939, by which time he was seriously ill with syphilis. He died on his Palm Island estate in Florida in January 1947 at the age of 48.

Capone's career illustrates the indisputable fact that millions of dollars of business was simply transferred from brewers and bar keepers to bootleggers and racketeers, who frequently relied on the support of corrupt officials, judges and senior policemen. Blackmail, extortion and gangland murders became all too common and came to symbolise the Prohibition era. Analysis of cases involving breaches of the Volstead Act shows that the majority of cases failed due to insufficient evidence and the tendency of witnesses to refuse to give evidence or take to the stand in court.

3.8 Religious fundamentalism

For two weeks in the summer of 1925, the attention of the legal world focused on a modest courtroom in the small town of Dayton, Tennessee. In July 1925, *Time* magazine described the scene on the first morning of what it called 'the trial of the decade':

> About 8 o'clock, dusty wagons, gigs, buggies and small automobiles came jogging in along the country roads. In them are gaunt farmers, their wives in gingham and children in overalls, who crowd toward the court house to get seats for the day's proceedings in the trial of teacher John Thomas Scopes, alleged violator of the state's anti-evolution law. (*Time Magazine*, July 1925)

What became known as the 'Monkey Trial' did not concern a murder or sensational crime, and lasted for only a fortnight. However, the issues it raised represented fundamental questions and, in particular, highlighted the tensions which existed between the traditional values of old, rural America and the new, modernist ideas created by advances in science and education. Many American Protestants at this time were religious fundamentalists who staunchly defended what they held to be the literal truths contained in the Bible. Such beliefs were most widely held in the rural areas of the South and the Middle West. For many people in the South, and particularly within what was sometimes referred to as the 'Bible Belt', religious fundamentalism was inextricably linked with a deep-rooted belief in the supremacy of the white race. These fundamentalists took the view that the creation of the world in seven days was something to be taken literally and to be accepted without question.

The movement against modern scientific ideas in the early 1920s was reflected in the prohibition of evolutionary teaching in North Carolina and Texas and a purge of forward-thinking academics at universities in Tennessee. However, rapid progress in education and science had now placed the literal truth of the Bible in question. In American schools and colleges there was an increasing tendency to teach students about the theory of evolution and the ideas of scientists such as Charles Darwin. High-school biology textbooks portrayed the gradual evolution of the human race as a process which had taken millions of years rather than seven days. Many scientists claimed that although their ideas were incompatible with a seven-day creation they by no means ruled out the existence of God.

At the centre of the campaign to defend the fundamentalist view was William Jennings Bryan. At the end of the First World War, Bryan launched an energetic campaign for the passage of laws prohibiting the teaching of evolution. In 1925 the state of Tennessee passed a law which banned the teaching in its public schools of any evolutionary theory which contradicted the view of the creation contained in the Bible's Book of Genesis. Shortly after the bill was passed, John T. Scopes, a young high-school biology teacher in Dayton, was arrested for violating the new law. The American Civil Liberties Union claimed that academic freedom was at stake and offered Scopes the financial support needed to contest the case. The trial which followed highlighted the painful, transitional period between traditional values and the new ideas which America was experiencing at this time.

Bryan took centre stage for the prosecution. Scopes was represented by the country's outstanding defence lawyer, Clarence Darrow, an outspoken agnostic from Chicago. In a key session in the trial, Darrow placed emphasis on several passages in the Bible (such as the story of Jonah and the Whale) which he claimed were not to be taken literally. In a devastating cross-examination Darrow exposed Bryan's ignorance and confusion about many parts of the Bible. However, although Darrow may have won the argument, he was unable to win the case. Scopes was found guilty and fined, although the sentence was later reversed on a technicality. The Tennessee law which had led to the case was upheld and was not repealed until 1967. Nevertheless Bryan's reputation was badly damaged and he died of a stroke on 26 July 1925 within days of the trial's conclusion and before he had left Dayton.

The anti-evolution movement continued after Bryan's death. Organisations which continued the campaign included the Bryan Bible League, the Bible Crusaders and the Supreme Kingdom. Yet despite the efforts of these organisations it would be fair to say that the cause of fundamentalism had probably been done more harm than good by the Monkey Trial. By 1928, the anti-evolution groups had been able to secure the legislation they advocated only in Arkansas and Mississippi. By 1930, it was clear that from a national perspective it was the modernist ideas which were prevailing across the education system.

Great American Lives: Clarence Darrow, April 1857–March 1938

Twentieth-century American legal history is littered with compelling court cases which gripped the public imagination. 'The Monkey Trial', labour leaders accused of anarchism, brutal homicides, the spectre of the electric chair and the eternal themes of law, order, crime and punishment may explain the public fascination with the courtroom.

At the centre of many of the cases was the lawyer Clarence Darrow, defender of the labour movement, outspoken critic of Prohibition and lifelong campaigner against the death penalty. Born in Kinsman, Ohio, to free-thinking parents he attended the University of Michigan Law School, but failed to graduate and so was ultimately self-taught. Initially dealing with the legal issues of small farming communities, he moved to Chicago as his reputation grew. Committed to the Democratic Party he defended Eugene V. Debs, an outspoken socialist and key figure in the American Railway Union Strike of 1894. In doing this, Darrow placed himself outside mainstream public opinion which was ferociously anti-radical at this time.

Although he was ultimately unable to keep Debs from going to prison, Darrow's clarity, eloquence and brilliant legal mind were now recognised. Despite his crumpled appearance he became a 'go-to' lawyer in cases that appeared helpless. This was certainly the case in the notorious trial of two teenage killers, Nathan Leopold and Richard Loeb. Leopold and Loeb came from super-privileged backgrounds and had glittering academic prospects. Bizarrely, they seemed to relish the attention when they were charged with the brutal, depraved murder of a 14-year-old boy. Expressing no remorse Loeb said: 'I did it because I wanted to.' The young men seemed certain to hang but Darrow's highly skilled defence centred on their 'mental condition' led a Chicago newspaper to conclude that he was 'the greatest figure in the greatest moment ... of life and death in the history of American jurisprudence' (p. 347).

The best known of Darrow's cases came when he spectacularly took apart the literal interpretation of the Bible presented by William Jennings Bryan

Continued

in the '7 Days or Forever' 'Monkey Trial.' 'Lost when pinned down in detail,' Bryan's claims that Eve 'was literally, made out of Adam's rib' and that 'a big fish swallowed Jonah' were made to sound outlandish. Within days of the trial, Bryan died in his sleep. He would not be the last man to find a legal encounter with Darrow to be bewildering. Darrow claimed of Bryan's death: 'Busted heart nothing – he died of an overstuffed belly.' (p. 397)

Further reading: John Farrell, *Clarence Darrow: Attorney for the Damned Melbourne* (Scribe 2011).

3.9 Changing attitudes towards immigration

The hostility towards Europe evident in the 'Red Scare' also manifested itself in an increasingly harsh stance against immigrants in general, and particularly those who tried to enter the United States from Asia. This intolerant atmosphere was heightened by the economic impact of the recession of 1920–21. Those who vociferously claimed that American stock was being undermined by the 'flood' of immigrants claimed that the literacy test of 1917 had failed to protect the United States from the influx of immigrants from southern and eastern Europe. The spectre of Lenin's communist regime which had come to power in the Soviet Union in 1917 only added to the clamour for new measures against immigrants. Those who campaigned for a return to 'national purity' argued that new anti-immigrant legislation was urgently needed to protect 'one hundred per cent Americans' against the influx of foreigners. It was not long before Congress gave way to the popular mood and passed the measures outlined in Table 3.3.

Table 3.3   Anti-immigration legislation

The Emergency Quota Act (1921)

Based on the notion of emergency measures against immigrants, the Act set an overall limit of 357,000 per year on immigrants.

The Act established quotas for each national group at 3 per cent of the number of foreign-born residents in the United States in 1910.

By going back to 1910, the Act was clearly designed to engineer a significant reduction in the number of 'new' immigrants.

The National Origins Act (Johnson–Reed Act) (1924)

The Act replaced temporary measures with permanent legislation.

The Act reduced the total number of immigrants allowed per year to 165,000.

The Act reduced the quota for each national group to only 2 per cent, and took the base year back to 1890.

By taking the base date back to 1890, the figure for immigrants from southern and eastern Europe would be much lower.

Most controversially, the Act excluded Asians completely, terminating an agreement of 1907–08 and causing considerable offence in the Far East (particularly Japan).

The Act came into permanent force in 1929, and set an annual quota of 150,000, with each nationality being set a figure based on the existing American population.

In fact, approximately 85 per cent of the quota was allocated to the countries of northern and western Europe.

The case for legislation against 'the foreign-born flood' was most forcibly argued by Senator Albert Fall who claimed in 1924:

> It is no wonder, therefore, that the myth of the melting pot has been discredited. It is no wonder that Americans everywhere are insisting that their land no longer shall offer free and unrestricted asylum to the rest of the world. The United States is our land. We intend to maintain it so. (In Brogan, 1985, p. 512)

3.10 The Coolidge era and the presidential election of 1924

In June 1923 a weary President Harding boarded a train in Washington to take him on a tour to the West Coast and a boat trip off the coast of Alaska. Amid growing rumours of scandal in the nation's capital, it was hoped by his advisers that the president could shake off his tiredness and charm voters ahead of the presidential election due in 1924. However, on both counts the trip failed in its objectives. Those who came to listen to his speeches in cities like San Francisco felt that the president appeared listless and visibly tired. Even the tranquillity of a cruise to South East Alaska seemed to do little to raise Harding's spirits. Meanwhile, in the words of biographer Kendrick A. Clements, 'Reports of unfolding scandals in the Veterans' Bureau and the Justice Department followed the ship like the coastal fog.' (Clements, 2010, p. 266)

By the end of July the president's personal physician and a team of other doctors and consultants were growing increasingly concerned with Harding's ill-health. He deteriorated sharply on the night of 2 August 1923. The public, who generally had a fondness for their leader, were completely shocked when the news of his death was announced. While mystery and rumour surrounded his passing at the time, it is now believed that Harding's death was due to a coronary thrombosis. It is also likely that his increasingly nervous demeanour, caused by the knowledge of his friends' misdeeds, made a significant contribution to his demise.

Calvin Coolidge

President Harding's sudden death brought into the spotlight a politician who was unusually keen to maintain a low profile. John Calvin Coolidge was born on Independence Day 1872, in a tiny hamlet in Vermont. It was a place where the old America was slow to give way to the new:

> A man who remembered Plymouth Notch from Coolidge's time said that the greatest changes have been in everyday sounds; no longer does one hear the axe ring out in the woods, producing the winter's supply of fuel, nor the squeal of the runners of sleighs nor the jingle of bells on horses in winter, nor the bells of cows in the fields, nor the hooting of lovesick bears. Those sounds are gone, replaced by automobile and occasionally airplane sounds. (Ferrell, 1998, p. 1)

The man from New England who succeeded Harding was vividly described by one observer as: 'A small, hatchet-faced, colourless man ... with a tight-shut, thin-lipped mouth, but with a gleam of understanding in his pretty keen eye.' (Ferrell, 1998, p. 1) He had presided over the Senate in a scrupulously impartial manner and enjoyed his 'least busy years' when he occupied the role of vice president. Famously, on the night of Harding's death he was sworn in by the light of a kerosene lamp in his modest New England home.

Harding's death removed Coolidge from the irritations of being a staggeringly inactive vice president. However, his low profile meant that he had some work to do to avoid being more than a temporary stand-in for Harding. Coolidge used the ensuing months to set before Congress a limited programme that suggested a clear sense of continuity with Harding. On virtually all domestic issues he took a conservative stance. As the fallout from Harding's scandals and indiscretions emerged he outmanoeuvred his Republican opponents for the candidacy and let his own honesty, simplicity and integrity stand for him.

The State of the Union Address in December 1923, the most significant statement of his presidency, allowed him to assert: 'We want idealism. We want that vision which lifts men and nations above themselves. These are virtues by reason of their own merit. But they must not be cloistered; they must not be impractical; they must not be ineffective.' (In Ferrell, 1998, p. 61) Above all, Coolidge's emphatically pro-business stance, at a time of general economic well-being, was enough to convince the Republican Party that he could secure a victory in 1924. It was, perhaps, a measure of his growing confidence that he did not even attend in person the Republican Convention held in Cleveland, in June 1924.

In contrast, the Democrats took several weeks in a humid summer convention in New York City to pick the utterly unremarkable John Davis as their candidate. If he was a lacklustre choice, he was, regrettably, an even worse campaigner. Furthermore, the emergence of a third-party Progressive candidate, Robert LaFollette, only added to the miserable prospects of the Democrats. Coolidge made only a small number of speeches, leaving the vice presidential candidate, General Dawes, to hit the campaign trail on his behalf. The result was emphatic. Coolidge secured 15.7 million popular votes, with Davis as far behind, with 8.3 million votes, as a lame horse. Significantly, LaFollette's 4.9 million votes increased the damage visited upon the Democrats who were destined to sit out an entire decade of presidential leadership. The Electoral College vote was equally catastrophic, with 382 for Coolidge, 136 for Davis and 13 for LaFollette (Table 3.4).

Table 3.4 The result of the 1924 presidential election

Candidate	Party	Electoral College votes	Popular votes
Calvin Coolidge (Mass)	Republican	382	15,725,016
John W. Davis (West Virginia)	Democrat	136	8,386,503
Robert M. LaFollette (Wisconsin)	Progressive	13	4,822,856

Calvin Coolidge

30th President of the United States (1923–29)
Born: 4 July 1872
Birthplace: Plymouth Notch, Vermont
Died: 5 January 1933, aged 60; buried at Plymouth Notch Cemetery
Education: Yale University; Harvard Business School
Political party: Republican
State: Vermont
Occupation before presidency: Lawyer
Previous government service: Governor of Massachusetts; vice president
Age at inauguration: 51
Dates of office: 3 August 1923–4 March 1929
Election: November 1924
Vice president: Charles G. Dawes
Length of term: 5 years, 7 months

Historiography and analysis of the Coolidge Administration

Historians have generally been dismissive of the Coolidge presidency. His most well-known statement, made in a speech to the American Society of Newspaper Editors in January 1924, 'the chief business of the American people is business', seemed to many to typify the narrow outlook of the 30th President. His reluctance to talk earned him the nickname 'Silent Cal' and his habit of taking up to a two-hour nap every afternoon seemed to sum up a listless administration, easily caricatured and not worthy of further consideration. However, a new insight was provided in 1998, when American historian Robert H. Ferrell published *The Presidency of Calvin Coolidge*. This presented a new portrait of a president motivated by personal drive and ambition. He sees Coolidge as idealistic and guided by a powerful sense of public service.

In this first full-length account for 30 years, Ferrell demonstrated that the 'odd little man from Vermont' was actually hard-working, sensitive and politically astute. In the speech to the newspaper editors which received so much attention for the statement on business, Coolidge also advocated 'the multiplication of schools, the increase of knowledge, the dissemination of intelligence, the encouragement of science, the broadening of outlook, the expansion of liberties, the widening of culture' (Ferrell, 1998, p. 62). Ferrell points out that Coolidge was the first president to meet regularly with news reporters whom he would laconically greet with the word, 'mawnin.' He frequently invited members of Congress to social breakfasts although the social niceties tended to be provided by his wife Grace.

Coolidge's period in office was marred by the tragic death of his 16-year-old son, Calvin Jr from blood poisoning in July 1924 after playing tennis on the White House court and infecting a blistered toe. Coolidge never recovered from this tragedy and the whole political process lost its allure to him. A biography by Amity Shlaes offers powerful insights into the impact of his loss.

Coolidge knew he had changed since Calvin's death. In darker moments, he told himself that the presidency had caused the event ... Had Coolidge not been president, Calvin would not have played tennis on the court outside. Had Calvin not played tennis, there would have been no blister. Had there been no blister, Calvin would not have died. The process of politics held less interest for him now. But when it came to completing the work that he and Harding had begun, Coolidge found he was more determined than before. Lincoln had not given up when his son had passed away ... Coolidge would not give up until he completed his own campaigns: the campaign to push the government back – back from spiritual life, back from commerce, back from new sectors in the economy – and find prosperity and peace. Protecting the space that faith enjoyed in American culture, the realm of the spiritual, seemed to him especially important. (Shlaes, 2014, p. 302)

Coolidge's less attractive characteristics were perhaps understandably more pronounced after this bereavement and he could frequently be cold, rude and secretive even with those closest to him.

3.11 The economy in the 1920s

In broad terms the 1920s in America was a period of unprecedented prosperity. It was a decade in which big business made enormous profits, investment in new technology and business methods was high, unemployment was low and the general standard of living rose significantly. The stimulation of the First World War and the rapid economic mobilisation which industrial warfare had demanded provided a platform for further growth. Despite these positive factors, the US faced a sharp recession in 1921–22 when approximately 5 million workers became unemployed. As Secretary for Commerce, Hoover urged business leaders and industrialists to maintain wage levels so that consumer spending could be maintained. Hoover actively promoted spending on public works, such as highway construction, and gathered a raft of economic data through the President's Conference on Unemployment to inform effective countermeasures.

From 1923 the peacetime economy took off into a period of rapid expansion. New production methods, the innovation of the assembly line and the adoption of scientific management techniques led to stunning increases in productivity. The 1920s saw a general increase in the per capita output of industrial workers of around 40 per cent. Widespread consumer credit and low levels of taxation combined to create an economy stimulated by new levels of consumerism. These factors coalesced to create the first great economic boom in the history of the United States in the twentieth century. Large-scale consumerism, consistently high demand, rising wages, easy access to credit and a cultural willingness to borrow fuelled what would become popularly known as the 'Roaring Twenties'.

No industry played a greater part in the boom period than the automobile industry. The technological innovation and successful production and marketing techniques of companies such as Ford, Chrysler and General Motors not only enabled many Americans to purchase their first motor car but also led to the rapid development of connected industries such as oil, rubber and glass while also prompting unprecedented levels of road building. The short-term political consequences of the boom were plain to see.

A succession of Republican presidents – Harding, Coolidge and Hoover – were able, at least until the crash of October 1929, to take credit for leading the 'party of prosperity'.

The generally buoyant nature of the economy in the 1920s and the unprecedented availability of consumer goods has tended to create the impression that this was a decade of prosperity for all. However, it is also clear that certain industries, groups and regions did not share in the general economic well-being. Traditional staple industries, such as textiles, entered a period of decline. Groups which tended to remain outside the prosperity included women, African Americans, Native Americans and the elderly. In 1930 around 16 million families, representing 70 million people, were receiving less than $2,000 a year, a figure which was thought to be the minimum to equip a family with the basic necessities. Further examination of life in the 1920s will reveal what a truly diverse country America was, and provide a degree of perspective on this decade of phenomenal economic progress.

3.12 Farmers and agriculture

The period between 1896 and 1915 marked a golden age for American farmers. In that period, they increased their production by 50 per cent but saw a general price increase which maintained their sense of well-being. By 1900 the agricultural workforce numbered 37.5 per cent of the total labour force. However, by the 1920s, when approximately one-third of the American workforce was still employed in the agricultural sector, times had changed. Most American farmers did not share in the general prosperity of the 1920s. Indeed for many farmers the decade was marked by poverty, hardship and an endless struggle against debt; per capita farm income was one-third of the national average. While city dwellers appeared to be enjoying the fruits of prosperity their agrarian counterparts largely endured a decade of economic uncertainty and financial distress.

Overproduction

Overproduction was at the centre of many farmers' difficulties. During the First World War, the federal government had encouraged farmers to produce as much cotton and wheat as possible and to raise the maximum number of livestock. This emphasis on production was maintained even when the war came to an end in November 1918. Better quality seeds, new tractors and generally high levels of borrowing to pay for new machinery meant that the 1920s witnessed a steady increase in farm output. Eventually the farmers were so successful that they created a glut of many of the products they worked so hard to produce. This resulted in farm produce being sold at prices well below the actual cost of production, and formed the context for a continuing drift from the countryside to the towns and cities.

The period 1920–30 saw an overall decline in the agricultural work force. In 1920, 11,390,000, or 27 per cent of the overall labour force, were employed in agriculture. By 1930, this had fallen to 10,321,000, or 21.2 per cent of the total labour force. The total number of farms declined between 1920 and 1930 for the first time in American history, from 6.4 million at the start of the decade to 6.2 million by 1930 (although the average acreage increased in the same period).

The brutal consequence of these trends saw many small American farmers simply give up, leaving 13 million acres of cultivated land abandoned. The economic difficulties faced in agriculture created a mood of rural activism which led many farmers to form a bloc to press their interests at a national level. The leaders of this bloc included conservative Republicans such as Arthur Capper, a member of the House of Representatives, and William S. Kenyon, a senator from Iowa. Their efforts contributed to the passage of a series of favourable farming legislations.

The McNary–Haugen Bill

In addition, in January 1924 two Republicans, Senator Charles L. McNary of Oregon and Congressman Gilbert N. Haugen of Iowa, introduced their Farm Relief Bill, which proposed that the federal government would control farm surpluses and increase prices by purchasing annual surplus stocks at agreed prices and then sell them abroad at world prices. The bill sought to relate farm prices to the period of prosperity between 1910 and 1914 when farm prices had been buoyant. This bill was opposed by Coolidge and defeated in 1924. Although Congress resubmitted versions of the bill in 1927 and 1928 Coolidge again vetoed them on the grounds that the measures were special-interest legislation.

Analysis

It seems unlikely that any amount of favourable legislation could have protected the farming community, or any other group, from the terrible financial storm that began in October 1929. The problem of overproduction was exacerbated by the sudden fall in demand after 1929. Many farmers could not appreciate a connection between their own struggle to make ends meet and the wheeling and dealing of the stock market. At first, it was difficult for many farmers to see the Wall Street Crash as anything other than a remote event. As one farmer said:

> Everybody talks of the Crash of '29. In small towns out West, we didn't know there was a Crash. What did the stock market mean to us? Not a dang thing. If you were in Cut Bank, Montana, who owned stock? The farmer was a ping-pong ball in a very tough game. (In Badger, 1989, p. 14)

However, the urban demand for farm products rested on the ability of the urban workers to purchase food. This was profoundly damaged by the events of October 1929. Although many city dwellers were desperate for food, they could no longer afford to pay good prices. The alternative for American farmers was to sell their goods abroad. However, the worldwide Depression meant that the foreign market had simply disappeared. Therefore conditions in the countryside were made worse as a result of the economic crash. Furthermore, many subsistence farmers in parts of the Appalachians and in the cut-over regions of the Great Lakes lived in remote areas, without modern amenities and with poor soil conditions.

These areas were characterised by disproportionately high population growth. Migrant farm labourers, particularly in California, were often immigrant

Table 3.5 Agricultural legislation, 1921–27

1921	The War Finance Corporation	This was revived to promote the export of farm surpluses.
	The Packers Stockyard Act	This Act empowered the Agriculture Secretary to act against the manipulation of farm prices.
	The Emergency Tariff Act	This Act imposed higher duties on corn, meat, wheat, wool and sugar, initially for six months and then extended.
1922	The Farm Co-operatives Act (Capper-Volstead Act)	Allowed farm produce to be sold through Farmers' Union and other co-operative stores, with stores buying at current prices and stockholders sharing the profits from their own purchases. These co-operatives became major businesses. By the end of the decade the California Fruit Growers' Exchange, for example, controlled almost 90 per cent of citrus fruit trade in that state.
1923	The Agricultural Credit Act	Enabled the US Treasury to provide capital for loans to farmers for between six months and three years.
1927	The McFadden Banking Act	Empowered the Federal Reserve Board to give loans for ten-month periods.

workers enduring squalid living conditions, extremely low pay and having no recourse to justice. More significant numerically were the 8.5 million tenant and sharecropper families living in the South; 3 million of these were African Americans depending on their landlords for housing, supplies, farm equipment and credit. In return, they would provide a year's labour. Each year the landlord would divide the proceeds and the sharecroppers would slip further into debt. The iniquities of the system were plain for all to see and were powerfully summed up in the words of one Alabama tenant farmer who commented: 'Ain't make nothing, don't speck nothing more till I die. Eleven bales of cotton and the man takes all. We just work for de oder man. He git everything.' (In Badger, 1989, p. 28)

3.13 Industry

American industry in the 1920s enjoyed a number of striking advantages. The influence of some outstanding individuals such as Frederick Taylor and Henry Ford was absolutely profound. The Republican Party's attitude towards business tended to encourage investment and stimulated production. Technical innovation, scientific management, consumer confidence and high productivity created a positive economic climate. Although the growth of the automobile industry was crucial in stimulating other industries there were further developments which were also significant in producing such a strong economic performance. The gross national product of the United States stood at $72.4 billion in 1919 and reached $104 billion ten years later. In the same period, annual per capita income grew from $710 to $857.

Whereas the industrial growth of the late nineteenth century had been founded on coal, iron and steel, the economy of the 1920s rested on new industries. These included chemicals, electricity and synthetic textiles. The development of the electrical industry in turn led to the electrification of domestic dwellings, and the equipment of these homes with new appliances such as cookers, refrigerators, toasters and a range of household gadgets. The development of the refrigerator industry reflects the dynamism of the country in general. Whereas only 5,000 a year were in production in 1921, by 1930 this had reached 1 million. The sense of confidence in the economy and the impact of the new technology were reflected in the introduction of the radio (the first broadcasting station, KDKA, began broadcasting in 1920) and the development of the aviation industry. Although the Wright brothers made the first flight in 1903, it was Charles Lindbergh's spectacular flight across the Atlantic in *The Spirit of St. Louis* in 1927 that really captured the public's imagination. Within three years, 50,000 miles of air routes had been established in the United States and almost half a million passengers were being carried per year. In this extract from his biography of Lindbergh, A. Scott Berg evokes the moment when the flight took place:

> A little before ten o'clock, the excited crowd at Le Bourget heard an approaching engine and fell silent. A plane burst through the clouds and landed; but it turned out to be the *London Express*. Minutes later, as a cool wind blew the stars into view, another roar ripped the air, this time a plane from Strasbourg. Red and gold and green rockets flared overhead, while acetylene searchlights scanned the dark sky. The crowd became restless standing in the chill. Then, suddenly unmistakably the sound of an aeroplane ... and then to our left a white flash against the black night ... then nothing. No sound. Suspense. And again a sound, this time somewhere off towards the right ... Then sharp swift in the gold glare of the searchlights a small white hawk of a plane swoops ... down and across the field – C'est lui Lindbergh. LINDBERGH! On May 21, 1927, at 10.24 p.m., *The Spirit of St. Louis* landed – having flown 3614 miles from New York, non-stop, in 33 hours, 30 minutes, and 30 seconds. And in that instant, everything changed – for both the pilot and the planet. (Berg, 1998, p. 5)

Henry Ford and the automobile industry

The publication of the first automobile journal, *Horseless Age*, in 1895, heralded the dawn of a new era in the history of American transport. The late nineteenth century had been dominated by the development of a coast-to-coast railway system. The new century would belong to the car. At the turn of the century the major French and German car manufacturers prided themselves on the sheer quality of the cars they produced. Each car was individually built, but this meant that prices were extremely high. In 1899, 2000 cars were built in the United States.

Nothing contributed more to the economic boom of the 1920s than the automobile industry, and its fortunes are inextricably linked to the remarkable story of a farm boy from Michigan, Henry Ford. Although he was not the first American to produce a motor car, his intuitive grasp of the potential mass market made him unique. His constant drive to improve production techniques had a galvanising effect on his competitors and transformed American industry itself. Although Ford was infinitely more comfortable in the tranquillity of rural America than in the city, he probably did more than any other individual to transform America into a modern, urban society.

Henry Ford was born in Greenfield, Michigan, a country boy of Irish farming stock. He performed modestly at school but qualified as an engineer in 1891 in a Detroit company owned by Thomas Edison. Five years later he produced his first automobile, which had a four-horsepower engine. In 1899, he produced an improved version and in the same year set up the firm that became known in 1903 as the Ford Motor Company. Ford displayed a drive and clarity of purpose that was to make him one of the most influential figures of the century. In 1905 he split from his financial backers at Ford who wanted to specialise in luxury cars. Ford gained absolute control and made the decision to make all of the component parts in his own factory; this would be critical in enabling him to make his cars as cheaply as possible. A year later, the innovation of vanadium steel opened up new possibilities.

The Model T Ford

He set up a small team who worked intensely for a year to produce a new car. The team came up with the Model T that came on the market in the autumn of 1908. Sales of the car were remarkable and in order to meet the demand, and inspired by the popularisation of Frederick Taylor's *Principles of Scientific Management* (1911), Ford perfected his assembly-line techniques. By 1913, a Model T was being produced every 12½ hours; within a year, this had reduced to 96 minutes. Ford was outselling his rivals but employed fewer workers and took less time to make his cars. Then, in 1914, Ford announced that it was doubling its rate of pay to an unprecedented $5 a day. Although the move was denounced as immoral by the *Wall Street Journal*, Ford had calculated that not only had he secured worker loyalty, he had also created a new class of purchasers – his employees. Eventually, Ford's River Rouge plant in Detroit, Michigan became the largest factory complex in the world.

This extract from Studs Terkel's oral history of the Depression, *Hard Times*, shows that working for Ford was not necessarily an easy proposition:

> I sandpapered all the right-hand fenders. I was paid $5 a day. The parts were brought in from the River Rouge plant in Detroit. When I went to work in January, we were turning out 232 cars a day. When I was fired, four months later, we were turning out 535. Without any extra help and no increase in pay. It was the famous Ford speed-up. The gates were locked when you came in at eight o'clock in the morning ... I was aware of men in plain clothes being around the plant, and the constant surveillance ... if you wanted to go to the toilet, you had to have the permission of the foreman. He had to find a substitute for you on the assembly line. (In Terkel, 1986, p. 137)

Other manufacturers such as Chrysler and General Motors produced a more attractive range of cars but Ford had done more than anyone else to ensure that by 1920, 9 million cars had been registered and by 1929, nearly 27 million. The knock-on effect of this was economically and socially profound. As well as employing almost half a million workers the automobile industry also stimulated the growth of plate glass, rubber and nickel, paint, lead, leather and other essential materials. Beyond this, the building of the nation's roads, the movement to the cities, the growth of the suburbs and the development of skyscrapers can all be linked to the fundamental change which Ford had brought to American society.

3.14 Analysis: How widespread was the affluence of the 1920s?

In some respects Harding inherited what appeared to be an unpromising economic situation. The transition from war to peace was accompanied by rising unemployment, business failures and agricultural distress. The wartime boom in orders for armaments, uniforms and food supplies abruptly ended. The economic situation began to deteriorate in May 1920, got worse during 1921 and did not really recover until 1922. During this period up to 5 million people were out of work. Unemployment reached 12 per cent in 1921 and inflation rose by 40 per cent between 1918 and 1920. Deprived of American loans from 1920 onwards, the Allied powers could no longer afford to order American exports. Fortunately for Harding, he had appointed an able man, Andrew Mellon, to the Treasury. By 1922 the country was moving out of recession, partly owing to the measures adopted by the Republican administration.

In broad terms, America's industrial workers performed well in the 1920s. Industrial production almost doubled, and the majority were rewarded for their efforts with a general increase in prosperity. Hours of work declined, real wages increased by 26 per cent and unemployment, which in 1920 had stood at 5.2 per cent, had decreased to a mere 4.2 per cent by 1928. New thinking was sometimes applied to wage policies as well as production. Some enlightened business leaders began to argue that employers should not necessarily pay the lowest wages possible, claiming that higher wages would generate greater productivity. In addition to better pay, many workers saw a gradual improvement in their working conditions, with a new emphasis on safety, recreational facilities and the development of 'company unions' which promoted meetings between workers' representatives and management.

Despite these broad improvements, employers were generally antagonistic towards trade unions. A national drive for an open-shop arrangement was launched under the label the 'American Plan', with the implication that trade unionists were often unpatriotic. The use of strike-breakers, company police and spies was not infrequent. At times this led to serious disorder. In 1922, for example, the Southern Illinois Coal Company brought in strike-breakers to bypass industrial action by its miners. When company guards killed two strikers a full-scale massacre occurred leaving 19 strike-breakers dead. Such incidents served only to heighten public hostility against the unions, which contributed to a general decline in trade union membership from around 5 million in 1920 to 3.5 million in 1929.

The Roaring Twenties

The prodigiously gifted writer F. Scott Fitzgerald helped to create a notion of the 1920s as 'the Jazz Age' or the 'Roaring Twenties', an endless cycle of parties, conspicuous consumption, fabulous houses, flappers and high fashion. This extract from his finest work, *The Great Gatsby*, illustrates the point:

> There was music from my neighbour's house through the summer nights. In his blue gardens men and girls came and went like moths among the whisperings and the champagne and the stars ... I watched his guests ... taking the sun on the hot sand of his beach while his two motor-boats slit the waters of the Sound. On weekends

his Rolls-Royce became an omnibus, bearing parties to and from the city between nine in the morning and long past midnight ... Every Friday five crates of oranges and lemons arrived from a fruiterer in New York ... at least once a fortnight a corps of caterers came down with several hundred feet of canvas and enough coloured lights to make a Christmas tree of Gatsby's enormous garden ...

By seven o'clock the orchestra has arrived ... the cars from New York are parked five deep in the drive, and already the halls and salons and verandas are gaudy with primary colours and hair bobbed in strange new ways ... The party has begun. (F. Scott Fitzgerald, *The Great Gatsby*, 1925/2011, pp. 82–86)

Of course the privileged experience of upper-class Americans in a novel in no sense indicates that the general affluence of the 1920s was evenly distributed. While for better-off Americans the month of October 1929 marked a painful dividing line between prosperity and poverty, for others there was no such distinction. For many people the 1920s as a whole was characterised by poverty, low wages, menial work or irregular employment.

When he came to the White House in 1933 Franklin Delano Roosevelt was acutely aware that many Americans had endured severe economic hardship for generations. In the summer of 1933 the president asked the first lady, Eleanor, to visit the Appalachians to investigate the stories of fearsome poverty which he had heard reported. What she saw shocked her. At Scott's Run, near Morgantown, West Virginia she came across children who did not know what it was like to sit down at a table and eat a proper meal. Later, Eleanor travelled to the Deep South where she found similar conditions. This poverty was in existence long before the Depression of 1929 and reflected a fundamental maldistribution of income in the United States. In 1929, the wealthiest 20 per cent of American families received 54.4 per cent of the total national income. The top 5 per cent received 30 per cent, and the top 1 per cent received 15 per cent. Conversely, the poorest 40 per cent had to make do with just 12.5 per cent of the national income.

The groups which remained outside the general prosperity included working-class women, African Americans, the rural poor and, perhaps the poorest of all, Native Americans. In the case of the Native Americans the later period of the nineteenth century had seen them systematically stripped of their land, their culture and their rights. By 1928 more than 50 per cent of Native Americans had a per capita income of less than $200 a year. Many Native Americans endured truly miserable conditions in squalid reservations, their difficulties reflected in high rates of alcoholism and crime, low life expectancy and high infant mortality. Finally, it should be noted that certain regions, including the textile towns of New England, the rural South and the Appalachian region of West Virginia and Kentucky had very significant issues of poverty.

Great American Lives: F. Scott Fitzgerald, 1896–1940

Along with Ernest Hemingway, Fitzgerald was perhaps the most naturally gifted American writer of his era, and maybe of the twentieth century. Of Irish-Catholic descent, he was born into privileged circumstances in Saint Paul, Minnesota, in 1896. Fitzgerald was largely raised in New York, but returned to his native state to attend a school for the upper middle class, St Paul Academy.

Continued

A spell at an elite Catholic School in New Jersey paved the way for entry to the prestigious university at Princeton, where he enrolled in 1913. Intelligent and artistically talented he nevertheless failed to proceed academically in line with Princeton's expectations. Preoccupied with his own writing and with the highly sought-after membership of the university's eating clubs, he was unable to fulfil the 'college dreams' that meant so much to him.

However, for the aspiring artist and intellectual it is likely that failure helped him to grow more than easy success. Fate meant that in 1917 he left the university for the noble, romantic cause of military service. The war ended before he could reach the battlefields of France but his sense of the sacrifice of the 'lost generation' was profound. Fitzgerald's great writing of the 1920s took on a haunting, wistful feel. His most recent biographer, David S. Brown, contends: 'Fitzgerald's deepest allegiances were to a fading antebellum world he associated with his father's Chesapeake Bay roots. Yet as a Midwesterner, an Irish Catholic, and a perpetually in-debt author he felt like an outsider in the haute bourgeoisie haunts of Lake Forest, Princeton, and Hollywood – places that left an indelible mark on his worldview.' (Brown, Jacket, 2017)

Fitzgerald's undoubted talent was recognised by Scribners and it was this great literary house that published his major works. *This Side of Paradise* (1920) painted a portrait of the privilege and wealth of the Princeton student body. *The Beautiful and Damned* (1922) was strikingly different in tone from Fitzgerald's upbeat first novel and much less successful commercially. Despite the fact that the Jazz Age was at its height, the novel was bleak in its portrayal of wealthy young men whose lives were empty of meaning. The book now considered his master work, *The Great Gatsby*, was published in 1925 but its standing and commercial success were only fully established after his death. *Tender Is the Night* (1934) reflected the personal pain of his troubled marriage to Zelda, her protracted mental illness and their shared problems with alcohol.

The lavish parties, expensive cars and privileged lifestyle depicted in *The Great Gatsby* has meant that Fitzgerald has been simply portrayed as a chronicler of the Jazz Age. Brown contends that 'Fitzgerald was at heart a moralist struck by the nation's shifting mood and manners after World War 1' (Brown, 2017, p. 2). Indeed recent scholarship on Fitzgerald shows his interest not just in the somewhat frivolous indulgences of the Roaring Twenties but in more profound themes of loss, sexual politics and the destiny of America itself as it moved from the Protestant roots of an earlier time.

Despite producing an outstanding body of work, personal peace was illusive for Fitzgerald and Zelda. Poor health, including heart disease and alcoholism, financial difficulties and a mixed critical response to his work troubled Fitzgerald to the end of his life. He was still working on *The Last Tycoon* when he died suddenly in Hollywood, in December 1940.

Further reading: David S. Brown, *Paradise Lost: A Life of F. Scott Fitzgerald* (Belknap Press 2017)

3.15 Republican economic policy

Economic policy between 1921 and 1933 was largely generated by three key departments – the Treasury, Agriculture and Commerce – all staffed by highly competent individuals. Of particular significance in economic terms was Andrew Mellon who presided over the Treasury throughout the 1920s. He favoured high tariffs, low taxation and the support of big business. Mellon was credited with helping to bring about the prosperity of the 1920s but was also partly blamed for causing the Great Depression. The high tariffs introduced in the Fordney–McCumber Tariff and sustained through the 1920s produced a huge budget surplus. Consequently, Mellon was able to reduce taxation levels on a regular basis (Table 3.6). This played a key role in stimulating the buoyant consumer spending patterns of the 1920s. Robert H. Ferrell offers this perspective on the American economy in the 1920s:

> The 1920s saw the triumph of American industry, for its accomplishments stood at every hand. Its organization reached across the continent, its efficiency was known worldwide, its production was nothing short of astonishing. Its relation to American government was so intimate that it could be described as dominating government. And in regard to American labor, its relation to laboring men and women, it was similarly dominant: nominally equal, managing a Hooverian cooperation between its purposes and those of the workforce that achieved them, industry controlled its labour force more closely, tightly, than in any previous era in American history. (Ferrell, 1998, p. 72)

Table 3.6   Key Republican economic legislation, 1921–30

November 1921 **The Federal Aid Highway Act**	Used federal funds to pay for half of the cost of the new trunk roads needed to accommodate the burgeoning automobile industry.
May 1921 **The Emergency Tariff Act**	Faced with deflationary pressures and falling prices for farm goods, Congress pushed through emergency tariffs, placing high duties on wheat, corn and meat – initially for six months but subsequently extended.
March 1922 **The Fordney–McCumber** **Tariff**	Raised tariffs on a range of farm goods to their highest levels ever.
1924–29	Congress created a special Commission to advise on the tariff question.
1928	Herbert Hoover (Republican) stood for the presidency, promising only to raise tariffs needed to help distressed farmers.
1929	In the House, the Chairman of the House Ways and Means Committee, Willis Hawley (Oregon), put forward a Bill which raised most tariffs to new levels. This passed through the House at the end of May.
1930	Further amendments (chiefly sponsored by Reed Smoot of Utah) led to the passage in June of the Smoot–Hawley Tariff, which passed through the Senate by 44 to 42 and was signed by Hoover on 17 June. Tariffs now the highest in American history.

3.16 Coolidge's decision not to seek a second term and the emergence of Hoover

There is little doubt, given the prevailing 'Coolidge Prosperity', that the incumbent would have secured widespread support if he had chosen to stand again. However, Coolidge stunned the political world with a terse statement of August 1927: 'I do not choose to run.' This was revealed to the press while he was on a summer vacation in the Black Hills, Dakota before he had even told his wife. His final political address was delivered at Madison Square Garden in New York City, at a rally for Hoover in 1932. Although 'Silent Cal' had less to say when he was in the White House than any other incumbent, Ferrell shows conclusively that what motivated Coolidge was simply a deep sense of public service. As Coolidge put it, 'I am going to try to do what seems best for the country, and get what satisfaction I can out of that.' (In Ferrell, 1998, p. 24) His decision left the Republican nomination for president open to his energetic and ambitious Commerce Minister, Herbert Hoover.

Hoover's background and personality

Orphaned at an early age and raised as a Quaker in simple circumstances on the frontier by his aunt and uncle, Hoover made his way up the political ladder through drive, intelligence and dedication to public service. He became renowned for his administrative ability, being described by one historian as a 'whirling Dervish' (Jeansonne, 2012, p. 89). Within his first working week as Secretary of Commerce in March 1921 he had set up a system for the distribution of information and statistics to the business community in his drive to make the Commerce Department more accountable to the needs of American business. Hoover rapidly extended the remit of the Bureau of Foreign and Domestic Commerce, and saw the need to present a clear business philosophy which he set out in 1922 with the publication of *American Individualism*, which was reprinted in 1928 to coincide with Hoover's presidential campaign. He worked tirelessly under Harding and then Coolidge to bring efficiency to the business community.

His dedication and drive in bringing relief in Europe and then in the Mississippi River Valley and New England earned him the nickname 'the great humanitarian'. Hoover's reputation was boosted by his response to the Great Mississippi River Flood of spring 1927. When the river overwhelmed its levees in more than 200 places, three-quarters of a million people were left homeless and 25,000 square miles of farms and small communities were devastated. Hoover's decisive leadership of an emergency committee once again illustrated the organisation, drive and skill of the 'Great Engineer'.

Although he was denied the nomination in 1920, the political landscape had shifted sufficiently to allow Hoover an untroubled run in 1928. Boosted by favourable newsreel coverage of his relief effort and with a groundswell of appreciation, not least in the Democratic South, it was clear that Hoover had now become a national figure of great standing. At the Republican Party Convention of June 1928 in Kansas City, Missouri, Herbert Clark Hoover was elected on the first ballot. With 837 votes and his closest rival, Frank Lowden of Illinois, securing only 74 votes, it was an emphatic demonstration of Republican solidarity. Hoover's running mate was Charles Curtis of

Kansas. Hoover's work in the Department of Commerce made him a popular choice in business circles. His campaign rested on continuity with the previous Republican administrations. He advocated further tax cuts and continued tariff protection. Hoover also made it clear that he would maintain the party's stand over Prohibition. In August 1928, at Stanford Stadium, California, a day after his 54th birthday, Herbert Hoover formally accepted the Republican presidential nomination. To an audience of 60,000 people Hoover confidently declared:

> We in America today are nearer to the final triumph over poverty than ever before in the history of any land. The poorhouse is vanishing from among us ... We shall soon with the help of God be in sight of the day when poverty will be banished from the nation. (In Badger, 1989, p. 29)

Hoover was not blessed with the natural communication skills of many other leading politicians. Painfully shy, lacking tact and charm, incredibly sensitive to the criticism of others and a monotonous public speaker, he relied on statistics and factual content rather than easy charm to win people over. Robert Ferrell cites one of Hoover's faults as a tendency to encroach on the authority of other government departments (such as the Department of Labour), behind which was an intense degree of personal ambition which by 1927 had served to alienate and antagonise many colleagues, including Coolidge.

The Democratic candidate 1928 – Al Smith

The Democrats remained divided over issues such as immigration restrictions, the Ku Klux Klan and Prohibition. In 1924, the Catholic governor Alfred Smith of New York had been denied the party nomination because of opposition from Southern, rural, Protestant, 'dry' Democrats. In 1928 the party decided to give Smith his chance. A successful governor of New York, he had established a reputation as a humane progressive. At the Democratic Party Convention held in Houston, Texas, he was nominated on the first ballot. (A sharp contrast with the 1924 convention when he had withdrawn after 103 ballots.) Despite this ostensible show of support, Smith's Catholicism, strongly urban image and his openly expressed hostility to Prohibition made him a candidate with clear limitations. While Smith was an able candidate, there was never any real possibility of him doing well across the country. His Catholic background provoked a fresh wave of support for the Klan in the South, and the campaign itself revealed Smith's ignorance of agricultural issues.

Hoover presented himself as the representative of continuity with the successful business policies of Harding and Coolidge. Sustained reliance on the hard work and business sense of American individualism, a meritocracy with equality of opportunity protected by the state, would bring permanent prosperity. In line with the previous Republican administrations, Hoover advocated tax cuts, a balanced budget, low interest rates and minimal federal interference with the economy. Even though Hoover was naturally shy and sorely limited as a speaker, Republican prosperity, excellent campaign organisation and his personal credibility all ensured that Smith was soundly beaten. Although Hoover had won a resounding victory, Smith had secured 15 million votes compared to Davis' 8 million votes in 1924. In addition, Smith had actually outperformed Hoover in the country's 12 biggest cities. This boded well for the Democrats in terms of their political future (Table 3.7).

Table 3.7 The result of the 1928 presidential election

Candidate	Party	Electoral College votes	Popular votes
Herbert C. Hoover (California)	Republican	444	31,392,190
Alfred E. Smith (New York)	Democratic	87	15,016,443

PRESIDENTIAL PROFILE

Herbert Clark Hoover

31st President of the United States (1929–33)
Born: 10 August 1874
Birthplace: West Branch, Iowa
Died: 20 October 1964, aged 90; buried Herbert Hoover Presidential Library
   and Museum, West Branch, Iowa
Education: Newberg Academy; Stanford University
Political party: Republican
State: Iowa
Occupation before presidency: Engineer
Previous government service: Chairman of Commission for Relief in Belgium;
   US Food Administrator; Secretary of Commerce
Age at inauguration: 54
Dates of office: 4 March 1929–4 March 1933
Election: November 1928
Vice president: Charles Curtis
Length of term: 4 years

3.17 Before the fall – Hoover's domestic agenda

The new president came to the Oval Office with a high reputation for his efficiency, wisdom and sheer capacity for hard work. Once installed in the White House, Hoover's attention to detail seemed all-encompassing. He had the vision to set a much broader agenda than his immediate predecessors. His love of the American wilderness was reflected in pioneering work in the conservation and protection of National Parks and Forests, the development of camping sites, hiking trails, National Monuments, promotion of the scouting movement, preservation of wildlife, prohibition of logging in environmentally fragile areas and preservation of archaeologically precious Indian Nation sites. With an implicit expectation that he would be serving for two terms, Hoover also commissioned an ambitious study of American social problems, named the Committee on Recent Social Trends, to enable his administration to focus on far-reaching economic and social reform based on robust analysis of scientific data and social trends.

In his early months in office the president gave his attention to matters including the health of the nation's children, the education system, national land policy and housing while turning his gaze for the future to railroads, utilities, adult literacy, the banking system and the structure of the federal bureaucracy. In April 1929 the president declared that the most serious problem facing the nation was the matter of law enforcement. Compared to Britain, the US had 20 times more murders and 50 times more robberies, while corruption, forgery, embezzlement and burglary were all endemic. In response, the president personally appointed J. Edgar Hoover as the new Director of the FBI.

To many Republicans the obvious competence and drive of the president suggested that a second term in the White House was a formality. No one was able to foresee the incredible collapse that was just around the corner. In the words of Hoover biographer Glen Jeansonne: 'Hoover before the Depression was Noah before deluge.' (Jeansonne, 2012, p. 112) On 1 January 1929, the *New York Times* wrote in its New Year editorial: 'It has been a twelve months of unprecedented advance, of wonderful prosperity – in this country at least ... If there is any way of judging the future by the past, this new year may well be one of felicitation and hopefulness.' The paper was accurately reflecting the general mood of optimism following several years of sustained economic growth.

In his inaugural address of March 1929, the president stated: 'In no nation are the fruits of accomplishment more secure.' Towards the end of the year the president told Congress: 'The test of the rightfulness of our decisions must be whether we have sustained and advanced prosperity.' But the president was about to endure a test that would have pushed any leader to the limits of their skill and endurance.

3.18 The stock market crash of 1929

In *Lords of Finance*, Liaquat Ahamed leaves us in no doubt as to the scale and importance of the events of 1929:

> The collapse of the world economy from 1929 to 1933 – now justly called the Great Depression – was the seminal economic event of the twentieth century. No country escaped its clutches; for more than ten years the malaise that it brought in its wake hung over the world, poisoning every aspect of social and material life and crippling the future of a whole generation. (Ahamed, 2010, p. 6)

In the autumn of 1929 the very first edition of *BusinessWeek* stated:

> As the fall begins, there is a tenseness in Wall Street ... a general feeling that something is going to happen during the present season ... Stock prices are generally out of line with safe earnings expectations, and the market is now almost wholly psychological. (In Ahamed, 2010, p. 348)

This gloomy tone was by no means shared. Irving Fisher, professor of economics at Yale, declared on 15 October 1929 that: 'Stocks have reached what looks like a permanently high plateau.' At the same time a letter from J.P. Morgan and Co. to the president himself boldly stated that 'the future appears brilliant' (Ahamed, 2010, pp. 353–54).

At precisely the same time as the letter was sent to Hoover, the prices of shares on the Wall Street stock market began to fall steadily. Confident forecasts now began to appear premature as the men at the very top of the Wall Street banking system gathered at the headquarters of J.P. Morgan. While long-term economic trends and global factors were undoubtedly important it may well be that the sheer greed, arrogance and wild judgements of the barons of the US financial system now began to reap the consequences. The first major panic of 24 October was followed by what Ahamed calls 'The "second hurricane of liquidation"' on Black Monday, 28 October. 'It came from every direction: demoralized individual investors, pool operators liquidating, Europeans throwing in the towel, speculators forced to sell by margin calls, banks dumping collateral.' (Ahamed, 2010, p. 356) Almost 10 million shares changed hands that day and $14 billon was wiped off the value of US stocks.

On 25 October, the day after the disastrous events of Black Thursday, Hoover tried to reassure the financial community, stating that the American economy remained sound and prosperous. Those who earned their living judging the mood in the financial district were less convinced. A journalist from the *New York Times* now saw Wall Street as a place of 'vanished hopes, of curiously silent apprehension, and of a paralyzed hypnosis' (in Ahamed, 2010, p. 358).

The sudden and precipitous collapse of the New York Stock Exchange in October 1929 has come to symbolise the start of the Great Depression. Starting in the United States, the developed economy was plunged into a downward spiral from which it would not fully recover until the outbreak of the Second World War. The most catastrophic of all economic avalanches began in the United States, and with increasing speed and ferocity it swept more and more economies into the abyss.

There is a consensus among economic historians that by 1929 stock market speculation had reached unhealthy and unrealistic levels. Successive years of prosperity had been accompanied by a rapid increase in the prices of shares and in the numbers of people willing to buy them. Between 1927 and October 1929 many share prices had soared; by early 1929 at least 1 million people were speculating on the stock market. The boom in share prices could not go on forever, and the bubble burst in October 1929. The classic account of the events of the Wall Street Crash was written by J.K. Galbraith. In this extract he provides a compelling picture of the disastrous events of 24 October 1929:

Thursday, October 24, is the first of the days which history identifies with the panic of 1929. Measured by disorder, fright and confusion, it deserves to be so regarded. That day 12,894,650 shares changed hands, many of them at prices which shattered the dreams and the hopes of those who had owned them ... By eleven o'clock the market had degenerated into a wild, mad scramble to sell. The uncertainty led more and more people to try to sell ... By eleven-thirty the market had surrendered to blind, relentless fear, this indeed, was panic. Outside the Exchange in Broad Street a weird roar could be heard. A crowd gathered. Police Commissioner Grover Whalen became aware that something was happening and dispatched a special police detail to Wall Street to ensure the peace ... A workman appeared atop one of the high buildings to accomplish some repairs, and the multitude assumed he was a would-be suicide and waited impatiently for him to jump ... Rumour after rumour swept Wall Street. Stocks were now selling for nothing.

The Chicago and Buffalo Exchanges had closed. A suicide wave was in progress, eleven well known speculators had already killed themselves ... Tuesday, October 29 was the most devastating day in the history of the markets. It combined all of the bad features of all of the bad days before. Volume was immensely greater than on Black Thursday ... Selling began as soon as the stock market opened and in huge volume. Great blocks of stock were offered for what they would bring; in the first half hour sales were at 33,000,000-a-day rate ... The worst day on Wall Street came eventually to an end. Once again the lights blazed all night. Members of the Exchange and their employees ... by now were reaching breaking point from the strain and the fatigue. In this condition they faced the task of recording and handling the greatest volume of transactions ever. In one house an employee fainted from exhaustion, was revived and put back to work again. (Galbraith, 1955, pp. 95–96, 105–07)

Analysis: Why did the Crash happen when it did?

The financial boom could be sustained only by fresh injections of cash. This could come from two main sources: either new investors attracted by the prospect of quick profits on the stock market, or further investment from existing investors. As the boom had gathered pace no one appeared to have any inkling that it could not carry on indefinitely. The fact that many investors were allowed to buy shares with borrowed money – 'on the margin' – increased the numbers of speculators but did nothing to promote future financial stability. When the level of demand finally began to slow in 1929 there was a sudden appreciation that many investors had purchased stocks and shares at inflated prices. The moment that a general tendency to buy was replaced by a general desire to sell, the market was in serious trouble. It was then that the psychological mood of the stock market became all-important.

Analysis: What were the underlying factors behind the Great Crash?

Significantly, during the 1920s the rapid growth of the American economy had led to New York superseding London as the world's most important financial centre. Most historians would agree that the American economy had long-standing difficulties which went beyond the activities of the stock market. A consensus among economic historians regarding the causes of the Crash remains difficult to find. Four central structural weaknesses in the American economy have been acknowledged, but historians differ in the emphasis placed upon them (Table 3.8).

Charles Rappleye helpfully places the Crash and the Great Depression into context:

As autumn arrived in 1929 the Wall Street Crash was weeks away but the Great Depression – the historic economic disaster that befell Hoover and the nation – was in some manner already under way. The stock market, heaving and squealing like a

Table 3.8 Underlying factors for the Great Crash

1. **The very success of industrial production in the mid-1920s could not be sustained indefinitely.** During the 1920s industrial capacity in many key areas of the economy steadily increased. The decade saw massive increases in industrial output generally, and in particular in the production of consumer goods, the growth of the automobile industry and an expansion in construction. While it was well understood that capitalist economies are cyclical in nature, the captains of industry did not seem to foresee that maximising production would eventually end with a fall-off in demand.

2. **The inherent inequality in wealth and the maldistribution of income meant that there was not enough purchasing power in the economy to sustain this growth into the 1930s.**
The stark facts are that in 1929, one-third of the nation's income was in the hands of only 5 per cent of the population, while at the same time just over 70 per cent of the population received an income below $2,500 a year. Ultimately, there would come a point when too many consumer items, from houses to automobiles to domestic products were being piled up and, at the other end of the process, consumers did not have enough money to simply keep on buying.

3. **It would soon become clear that there were also inherent weaknesses in the banking system.**
At the start of the 1920s there were over 30,000 independent banks in existence in the United States. Far too many of these were small, rural banks with limited capital. A lack of resources, poor or dishonest management and willingness to make purely speculative loans rendered then highly vulnerable to sudden, large-scale withdrawals or 'runs'. The fragility of these banks is indicated by the fact that almost 5,000 of them collapsed between 1923 and 1930. Pressure on the rural banks became even more acute with the onset of the agricultural Depression in 1930. The banking crisis then spread from the rural areas to the metropolitan areas and by autumn 1932 from individual banks to the collapse of banking systems within entire states. By March 1933, 34 states had closed their banks.

4. **There were inherent weaknesses in the international economy and its interconnectedness with the American system.** At the end of the First World War, America was the world's major creditor nation; massive war loans had been paid to the European powers. However, the capacity of the European nations to sell their goods in America and help repay their loans was made difficult by the introduction of prohibitive tariffs, such as the Smoot–Hawley Tariff (1930). Conversely, American investment overseas steadily increased. In particular, major investment in German economic recovery and unsound loans to Latin America were ultimately problematic. In May 1931 the collapse of the Austrian Kreditanstalt bank signalled the general collapse of the European economy. The knock-on effect of this was keenly felt in the United States and underlines the fact that while the depression started in 1929 there were calamitous further collapses such as in 1931.

maxed-out steam engine, peaked in September. Steel production, a more fundamental barometer of industrial activity, began slipping in June; residential construction had been in a slump for several years.

In the popular mind the Depression begins with the crash – the spectacular collapse of stock prices that wiped out billions of dollars in private and corporate wealth and was followed by business failures, an industrial slump, and deep unemployment that lasted ten long years. It's a valid checkpoint; useful for marking the transition from the Roaring Twenties to the Somber Thirties, a reflection and a cause and an emblem of a historic debacle.

But economists will tell you the crash was just one factor in the onset of the Depression, the stock market a victim as much as a catalyst of the general economic breakdown. (One respected analyst goes so far as to assert, 'No causal relationship between the events of late October 1929 and the Great Depression has ever been shown.') Precise reasons remain in dispute. (Rappleye, 2016, p. 99)

3.19 The Great Depression

The Great Depression that began in the autumn of 1929 was without parallel in American history. Its severity blighted an entire decade. The prosperity which preceded it meant that the psychological consequences of more than ten years of misery and mass unemployment were truly profound. Charles R. Morris places the depression in its international context:

> The 'advanced countries' of the world, sixteen countries in Western Europe and North America, taking 1929 as a base of 100, saw their real national output drop by 17 per cent. Prices and trade volumes fell by about a quarter. At the Depression's trough in 1932, nearly a third of all workers were unemployed. (Morris, 2017, p. 306)

The spectre of mass unemployment

By the autumn of 1931 unemployment had reached 8 million and was rising fast. The downward spiral continued and reached its worst point in the winter of 1932–33. By this time, international events such as the failure of the Austrian Kreditanstalt bank in May 1931 and the collapse of the German economy had demonstrated that this was not a short-lived economic downturn, but a major Depression. By 1932 at least 13 million people were unemployed. In addition, between 1 and 2 million other Americans were wandering the country desperately searching for work. By early 1933, approximately one-quarter of the entire work force was unemployed; this accounted for up to 14 million people, and if families are included this means that around 40 million Americans did not have a dependable source of income within the home.

The impact of the Depression upon industry

Between 1929 and 1932 American industrial production was cut by more than half. The average weekly wage in manufacturing dropped from $24.16 in 1929 to $16.65 in 1933. Real earnings dropped by one-third between 1929 and 1933. Between 1929 and 1930 5,000 banks went out of business. Approximately 9 million people lost all their savings. Iron and steel production fell by 59 per cent in the same period. In the summer of 1932 in Gary, Indiana, workers at the United States Steel Corporation were reduced to working one day every fortnight in return for $1.75 a week. By 1933, all of the United States Steel Corporation's workers were employed part time.

The automobile industry which had boomed in the 1920s now experienced its own Depression. At the start of 1929, Henry Ford employed 120,000 workers at his Detroit factory. By August 1931, only 37,000 men were needed. The impact of the failing motor industry on the city of Detroit was immense. One observer noted that Detroit was 'clogged with dead tissue ... and its life is bleeding away' (in Badger, 1989, p. 21). Industries which had flourished because of the boom in the automobile industry now appreciated how much they depended upon it for their own survival. Industries badly hit by the automobile slump included steel, glass, construction and rubber.

Major electrical companies such as Westinghouse and General Electric were sorely damaged. General Electric's net income declined from $60.5 million in 1930 to just $14.7 million by 1932, and Westinghouse reduced its workforce by 54 per cent between 1929 and 1932. Those employed in the building trade were particularly hard hit. Residential construction fell by 82 per cent between 1929 and 1932.

The impact of the Depression on the American people

In November, Hoover met with railroad presidents and urged them not to abandon planned track construction. Two days later he met with business and industrial leaders and asked them to pledge to continue with their investment programmes, production targets and wage levels. At the end of a frantic month the beleaguered president urged mayors and governors across the nation to increase their spending on public works. At all times Hoover was serious, cerebral, analytical and hard-working but reluctant to engage in any sustained attempt to engage with the public. However, as the depression took hold the stark sign 'No men wanted' appeared outside factories and businesses across the country. Given the desperation for work, wages fell to astonishingly low levels. In Connecticut, some sweatshop owners paid women workers a *weekly* rate of between 60 cents to 1 dollar for 55 hours of work. At the other end of the spectrum, Robert S. McElvaine notes that in terms of the stock market crash 'huge losses were taken by certain wealthy investors who saw paper fortunes vanish in the stock-market crash' (McElvaine, 1983, p. 17).

Despite this, McElvaine contends that:

> Most of the rich remained quite comfortable ... Throughout the Depression decade, despite the myths of investors' bodies piling knee-deep after they leaped from Wall Street windows, it was generally not this sort that seriously considered suicide. Rather it was the desperate worker, such as the unemployed Youngstown steel operative who begged for a job in 1932, saying 'If you can't do something for me, I'm going to kill myself.' (McElvaine, 1983, pp. 17–18)

In the autumn of 1930 a despairing mechanic in Houston, Texas sat down and wrote a brief suicide note:

> This depression has got me licked. There is no work to be had. I can't accept charity and I am too proud to appeal to my kin or friends, and I am too honest to steal. So I can see no other course. A land flowing with milk and honey and a first-class mechanic can't make an honest living. I would rather take my chances with a just God than with unjust humanity. (In Badger, 1989, p. 11)

In Chicago, the Roseland garbage dump attracted people who were filled with desperation and despair:

> About twenty-five men and boys and one woman stood in two rows all day, all the way down to the garbage hill waiting for that load to come down. And then, like a flock of chickens, they started to scratch in that smelly pile ... Apples seemed most popular even when half rotted away. Carrots, potatoes, and bread also found their way into the baskets ... Most of them admitted it was for their supper. (In Badger, 1989, p. 13)

In January 1930 the Charity Organization Society of New York reported that it was being 'swamped with appeals for help and in Boston desperate people were offered groceries in return for chopping wood' (Rappleye, 2016, p. 166). Each of the great American cities witnessed scenes of despair. As winter conditions made suffering more intense: 'A Red Cross survey in Lee County, bordering the Mississippi River, found "not only suffering but actual starvation."' (Rappleye, 2016, p. 210) By 1931 the great city of Chicago found itself on the brink of bankruptcy. Industrial towns such as Dayton and Akron now saw unemployment at the barely credible level of 80 per cent. In Tenino, Washington when the last bank closed people resorted to barter.

In December 1932, a university professor noted that 'No one can live and work in New York in this winter without a profound sense of uneasiness. Never in modern times has there been so much widespread unemployment and such moving distress from sheer hunger and cold.' A shopkeeper in Philadelphia was so moved by one family's plight that he allowed them to live on credit rather than see them go hungry: 'Eleven children in that house. They've got no shoes, no pants. In the house, no chairs. My God, you go in there, you cry, that is all.' (In Leuchtenburg, 1963, p. 2)

William Leuchtenburg provides a vivid picture of a nation in Depression:

> By 1932 the unemployed numbered upward of thirteen million. Many lived in the primitive conditions of a ... society stricken by famine. In the coal fields of West Virginia and Kentucky, evicted families shivered in tents in midwinter; children went barefoot. In Los Angeles, people whose gas and electricity had been turned off were reduced to cooking over wood fires in back lots. Visiting nurses in New York found children famished ... On the outskirts of town or in empty lots in the big cities, homeless men threw together makeshift shacks of boxes and scrap metal. St. Louis had the largest 'Hooverville', a settlement of more than a thousand souls, but there was scarcely a city that did not harbour at least one ... 'I come home from the hill every night filled with gloom', one Washington correspondent noted. 'I see on streets filthy, ragged, desperate looking men, such as I have never seen before'. In December 1932, a New York couple moved into a cave in Central Park where they lived for the next year. (Leuchtenburg, 1963, pp. 1, 2, 19)

3.20 Analysis of Hoover's temperament in response to the Crash

Hoover's commitment to a balanced budget and his belief in voluntarism rather than federal control was very powerful; he sincerely believed that private initiatives from business leaders could lead America to recovery. The president was keenly aware of the problems faced by farmers, and as early as April 1929 he was asking Congress to act on their behalf. This led to increased tariff protection and the creation of a Federal Farm Board which could support farm co-operatives, provide loans and purchase surplus crops. Ultimately, these measures, though significant, were unable to address the key problem of overproduction and under-consumption. As the Depression tightened its grip in the winter of 1930, Hoover claimed that the economic trauma was a worldwide rather than an American phenomenon.

However, Hoover's words seemed rather hollow when, just over a week later, the Bank of the United States, a large, private bank with 400,000 depositors and over 50 branches, collapsed. This meant that since October 1929 around 1,300 banks had failed. Having claimed the credit for the boom Hoover now attracted the bitterness of a nation. He was portrayed as cold, callous, unimaginative and hard-hearted. Eventually he became so unpopular that it was unsafe for him to go out onto the streets to campaign. In Detroit, mounted police were called in to disperse an angry mob who had gathered to hear Hoover speak. His friend Henry Ford provided a fleet of limousines and the president was driven through silent streets, while the windows of his car remained tightly closed.

3.21 1931 – Further collapse and Hoover's response

In June 1931 in the wake of the collapse of the Austrian Kreditanstalt bank, the president proposed a one-year moratorium on all intergovernmental debts and reparations. Looking back at this moment Hoover later recalled that: 'Apprehension began to run like mercury through the financial world.' (In Rappleye, 2016, p. 255) The strain on the president was becoming increasingly intense and in private an aide noted: 'The president is dog tired. How he stands up under the pressure is a mystery to me.' (In Rappleye, 2016, p. 266) The moratorium briefly stemmed the tide but within months the downward spiral had resumed its apparently inexorable course. The situation had become so grave that by the end of 1931 Hoover confided to his closest aides that he was now concerned not just with saving Germany or Britain, but with saving the United States itself. This finally compelled Hoover to make his most significant move of the Depression. On 8 December 1931, he asked Congress to set up an Emergency Reconstruction Finance Corporation (RFC) which would authorise massive loans to insurance companies, railroad companies and banks to promote fresh investment in the hope that this would fuel industrial recovery.

The Reconstruction Finance Corporation

The RFC was headed by Charles Dawes and was granted capital of $500 million with the authority to borrow an additional $1.5 billion. The RFC was established on

22 January 1932, and within the first six months of its existence it had provided loans of $1.2 billion. Historian Fiona Venn points out some of the weaknesses of the RFC:

> In this early period, the extension of credit was not particularly significant as individual businesses were too worried by long-term business prospects even to wish to borrow. Moreover, the terms on which the RFC operated were carefully defined. It was given up to two billion dollars to rescue major institutions such as banks, big businesses and mortgage, loan and insurance companies, but many of its resources went to its largest clients. In the first two years of operation, about 7 per cent of its borrowers accounted for over half of the total sum lent. These loans were initially aimed at restoring confidence in the economy as a whole, rather than meeting the needs of the most vulnerable groups within it. (Venn, 1998, p. 18)

3.22 Analysis

Writing in 1983 Robert S. McElvaine observed:

> Hoover was not the heartless ogre that a generation and more of Democrats have depicted. He was, rather, that rarest of politicians, a man of principle ... He believed firmly in individualism, but not the sort connoted by his frequently quoted term 'rugged individualism' ... Hoover not only wanted everyone to have a chance to succeed, but he also opposed heavily concentrated wealth and believed that the unfortunate should be cared for by their own communities. Another term Hoover used, 'progressive individualism', was a more accurate description of his philosophy ... he wanted communities of 'socially responsible individualists' to provide for the unemployed. (McElvaine, 1983, p. 20)

However, even sympathetic accounts point out that Hoover's response of 'voluntary charity, local and state relief' were wholly inadequate in the face of a crisis of unprecedented magnitude. Charles R. Morris notes:

> [T]he market crash occurred in the seventh month of the term of the new president, Herbert Hoover. The subsequent economic collapse overwhelmed him, forever destroying his reputation. That is a pity, because in calmer times, he might have created a positive legacy of progressive policy-making. (Morris, 2017, p. 123)

Swept from office in the most brutal circumstances Hoover carried with him forever the conviction that the first fault lines of the Depression were beyond the influence of the White House. When Hoover sat down to write his memoirs published in 1952, the first sentence read, 'The primary cause of the Great Depression was the war of 1914–1918.' (Hoover, 1952, p. 2)

Further reading

Ahamed L., *Lords of Finance: The Bankers Who Broke the World* (London: Windmill Books 2010).
Badger A.J., *The New Deal: The Depression Years, 1933–1940* (London: Macmillan 1989).

Bair D., *Al Capone: His Life, Legacy and Legend* (New York: Doubleday 2016).

Berg A.S., *Lindbergh* (New York: Macmillan 1998).

Berg A.S., *Wilson* (London: Simon & Schuster UK 2013).

Brogan H., *Longman History of the United States of America* (London: Longman 1985).

Clements K.A., *The Life of Herbert Hoover: Imperfect Visionary 1918–1928* (New York: Palgrave Macmillan 2010).

Cooke A., *Alistair Cooke's America* (London: BBC Books 1973).

Cooper J.M., *Woodrow Wilson: A Biography* (New York: Vintage Books 2011).

Ferrell R.H., *The Presidency of Calvin Coolidge* (Kansas: University Press of Kansas 1998).

Galbraith J.K., *The Great Crash 1929* (London: Hamish Hamilton 1955).

Hawley E.W., *The Great War and the Search for a Modern Order: A History of the American People and their Institutions 1917–1933* (New York: St Martin's Press 1979).

Jeansonne G., *The Life of Herbert Hoover: Fighting Quaker 1928–1933* (New York: Palgrave 2012).

Leuchtenburg W.E., *Franklin D. Roosevelt and the New Deal* (New York: Harper & Row 1963).

McGirr L., *The War on Alcohol: Prohibition and the Rise of the American State* (New York: Norton 2016).

McElvaine R., *Down and Out in the Great Depression: Letters from the Forgotten Man* (North Carolina: Chapel Hill 1983).

Morris C.R., *A Rabble of Dead Money: The Great Crash and the Global Depression: 1929–1939* (New York: PublicAffairs 2017).

Murdock C.G., *Domesticating Drink: Women, Men and Alcohol in America 1870–1940* (Baltimore: Johns Hopkins 1998).

Nash G.H., *The Life of Herbert Hoover: Fighting Quaker, 1928–1933* (New York: Palgrave 2012).

Rappleye C., *Herbert Hoover in the White House: The Ordeal of a Presidency* (New York: Simon & Schuster 2016).

Russell F., *A City in Terror: Calvin Coolidge and 1919 Boston Police Strike* (Boston: Beacon Press 1975).

Shlaes A., *Coolidge* (New York: Harper Collins 2013).

Temkin M., *The Sacco-Vanzetti Affair: America on Trial* (New Haven: Yale University Press 2009).

Terkel S., *Hard Times: An Oral History of the Great Depression* (New York: Pantheon Books 1986).

Venn F., *The New Deal* (Edinburgh: Edinburgh University Press 1998).

■ ⊻ 4 FDR: The Great Depression and the New Deal

4.1 The presidential election of 1932

When the Democratic Party came together at the Chicago Stadium, Illinois, for its Convention of June 1932, party bosses were confident that the candidate they selected as Democratic nominee would go on to win the presidency. As one popular convention button stated, 'Anybody but Hoover'. However, with the White House in plain sight, there would be intense competition for the nomination. Nine candidates went forward, of whom three had substantial backing. Alfred Smith, the Democrats' defeated presidential candidate of 1928, was eager to stand again and commanded considerable support in the urban, industrial states and from within the Democratic Party machine. The speaker of the House of Representatives, John Nance Garner, had the backing of his home state of Texas and the powerful support of the State of California.

Franklin D. Roosevelt

The front runner was Franklin D. Roosevelt. He had been elected Governor of New York in 1928 and had been re-elected by a record margin of 700,000 votes in 1930. This reflected Roosevelt's growing reputation as an energetic, but politically moderate, reformer. To be clear, at this stage he was not regarded as a political heavyweight. Roosevelt was careful not to make strong ideological commitments that would tie him down later.

In January 1932 Roosevelt stepped away from the tradition of reticence when he announced that he hoped to win the Democratic nomination. In a commencement address at Oglethorpe University in May 1932 he told his young audience:

> The country needs and, unless I mistake its temper, the country demands bold, persistent experimentation. It is common sense to take a method and try it: If it fails, admit it frankly and try another. But above all, try something. The millions who are in want will not stand by silently forever while the things to satisfy their needs are within easy reach. (In Morris, 2017, p. 257)

While Roosevelt explicitly advocated a shift away from 'an individualistic society' towards greater 'social planning', these outline ideas were not enough for some observers. The influential *New York Times* bemoaned his capacity for shifting ground and demanding vague action claiming that: 'the man most to be avoided in a time of crisis is the one who goes about wringing his hands and demanding that something be done without explaining or knowing what can or ought to be done.' (In Dallek, 2017, p. 115) Not for the last time, he was being defined as an opportunist, big on personal charm but shallow of intellect.

Conversely, Roosevelt had sustained an interest in issues which served to extend his appeal beyond the urban East. His knowledge of farm issues and enthusiasm for conservation made western Democrats receptive to him. In addition, Roosevelt's long periods of convalescence at Warm Springs, Georgia, enabled him to develop an affinity with the South, which was not shared by his rival, the archetypal New Yorker, Al Smith. Roosevelt now appeared to be a candidate who could appeal to both urban and rural elements within the Democratic Party. The Roosevelt banner attracted blue-collar workers, trade unionists, small farmers and earnest young activists. Despite this broad base of support, Roosevelt's nomination for president in 1932 was no formality. Democratic rules meant that Roosevelt needed a two-thirds majority to secure the party's nomination. Roosevelt was denied a first-ballot victory and appeared vulnerable until Garner dropped out and decisively the State of California gave its backing to him. Roosevelt had come close to losing the nomination, but on the fourth ballot he received 945 votes.

Roosevelt's New Deal campaign pledge

A high-profile but arduous flight in bad weather to the Democratic Convention in Chicago belied concerns about the candidate's physical capacity. When Roosevelt gave his acceptance speech in Chicago Stadium in July 1932 he told the packed convention:

> On the farms, in the large metropolitan areas, in the smaller cities and in the villages, millions of our citizens cherish the hope that their old standards of living and thought have not gone forever. Those millions cannot and shall not hope in vain.

Then came the final rhetorical flourish: 'I pledge you, I pledge myself, to a New Deal for the American People.' (In Dallek, 2017, p. 123) Roosevelt made no attempt to elaborate on the concept of the 'New Deal' and had not anticipated its importance for his future administration. The phrase itself was dreamt up by speechwriter Sam Rosenman, and it remained an ill-defined notion throughout what was generally a flawless campaign. Recent biographer Robert Dallek says: 'The truth is that Roosevelt had no more idea of how he would restore the country's prosperity than Abraham Lincoln had in trying to persuade the rebellious Southern states to remain in the Union.' (Dallek, 2017, p. 2)

Meanwhile, Hoover's shaky prospects looked even slimmer when a veteran's protest march on Washington in July 1932 was met with a violently disproportionate response. The 20,000-strong Bonus Army made camp on Pennsylvania Avenue but its brutal removal by bayonet-wielding cavalry men and, incredibly, six tanks, prompted widespread outrage. Buoyed by Hoover's mounting unpopularity, Roosevelt concentrated on attacking Hoover's record, criticising the incumbent for overspending in what became an increasingly bitter contest. In a speech in Iowa in September 1932, Roosevelt declared: 'I accuse the present Administration of being the greatest spending Administration in peace times in all our history. It is an Administration that has failed to anticipate the dire needs and the reduced earning power of the people.' In Pittsburgh, a month later, Roosevelt returned to the same theme when he stated: 'I regard reduction in Federal spending as one of the most important issues of this campaign.' Finally, in the key cities of Baltimore and Boston, Roosevelt spoke of the 'Four Horsemen of the present Republican leadership – the Horsemen of Destruction, Delay, Deceit, Despair.' (Dallek, 2017, p. 126)

Hoover responded bitterly, seeing his opponent as an inconsistent, incoherent, opportunist:

[T]his campaign is more than a contest between two men ... They are proposing changes and so-called new deals which would destroy the very foundations of our American system. Our system is founded on the conception that only through freedom to the individual, will his initiative and enterprise be summoned to spur the march of progress. (In Dallek, 2017, p. 127)

Despite Hoover's emphasis on ideological differences, voters were also presented with a contrast in style and personality. Jean Edward Smith describes FDR's 'remarkable zest for life – a stark contrast to the starchy, buttoned-up demeanour of Herbert Hoover in the White House' (Smith, 2007, p. 280).

While the clearest difference between the two parties seemed to be that the Democrats were calling for the repeal of Prohibition, what really counted was the state of the economy. The Republicans were universally blamed for the Crash and Hoover had become so unpopular that it became unsafe for him to go out onto the streets to campaign. In the words of William Leuchtenburg:

On the outskirts of town or in empty lots in the big cities, homeless men threw together makeshift shacks of boxes and scrap metal. Meanwhile in the words of Leuchtenburg 'Hooverville', a settlement of more than a thousand souls, but there was scarcely a city that did not harbor at least one. (Leuchtenburg, 1963, p. 2)

The same author describes how the campaign took its toll on the incumbent. 'Toward the end, Hoover was a pathetic figure, a weary, beaten man, often jeered by crowds as a President had never been jeered before.' (Leuchtenburg, 1963, p. 16) The cumulative effect on Hoover was disastrous. This extract from Arthur M. Schlesinger's book, *The Crisis of the Old Order*, shows how the strain of being held responsible for the Depression had finally taken its toll:

The president, white-faced, exhausted, stumbling in speech, repeatedly losing his place in his manuscript, swayed on the platform. Behind him a man gripped an empty chair to be shoved under him in case of collapse. Colonel Starling, chief of the Secret Service broke into a cold sweat. After the speech a prominent Republican took Starling aside and said, 'Why don't they make him quit? He's not doing himself or the party any good. It's turning into a farce. He is tired physically and mentally.' (Schlesinger, cited in Traynor, 1987, p. 11)

The difference in demeanour could not have been clearer. 'If Roosevelt's program lacked substance his blithe spirit –his infectious smile, his warm mellow voice, his obvious ease with crowds – contrasted sharply with Hoover's glumness.' (Dallek, 2017, p. 127)

When Election Day dawned on 8 November 1932 it was clear that the Hoover–Curtis ticket was heading for an emphatic defeat. The Roosevelt–Garner team carried all but six states and 57.4 per cent of the popular vote compared to Hoover's 39.7 per cent. With a turnout of almost 40 million, 4 million more than 1928, Roosevelt gained 22.8 million votes compared to Hoover's 15.8 million. In the Electoral College, FDR took 472 votes to Hoover's 59. The Republicans lost 12 seats and with it their majority in the Senate. In the House, the figures were even more calamitous with a loss of 101 seats (Table 4.1).

Table 4.1   The result of the 1932 presidential election

Candidate	Party	Electoral College votes	Popular votes
Franklin D. Roosevelt (New York)	Democrat	472	22,821,857
Herbert E. Hoover (California)	Republican	59	15,761,841
Norman Thomas (New York)	Socialist	–	881,479

PRESIDENTIAL PROFILE

Franklin Delano Roosevelt

32nd President of the United States (1933–45)
Born: 30 January 1882
Birthplace: Hyde Park, New York
Died: 12 April 1945, aged 63; buried at Hyde Park, New York
Education: Groton, New York; Harvard University; Columbia Law School
Political party: Democratic
State: New York
Occupations before presidency: Lawyer; politician
Previous government service: Assistant Secretary to the Navy in the Wilson
   Administration
Age at inauguration: 51
Dates of office: 4 March 1933–12 April 1945
Election: November 1932, 1936, 1940 and 1944
Vice president: First and second administration: John Garner (Texas); third
   administration: Henry Wallace (Iowa); fourth administration: Harry S.
   Truman (Missouri)
Length of term: 12 years

4.2 FDR's background

Franklin Delano Roosevelt (FDR) was born on 30 January 1882 to a prosperous family of Dutch descent. His father was a wealthy landowner and the family home at Hyde Park, New York State, provided their only child, Franklin, with a sheltered and privileged upbringing. The dominant influence in his early life was his mother who indulged her child in every sense. Roosevelt was educated at Groton, an exclusive preparatory school in upstate New York, followed by Harvard University which he entered in September 1900 and then Columbia Law School. His academic career covering largely classics lacked distinction and Roosevelt placed much more energy into football, billiards, fine dining, drinking and extra-curricular activities than his studies. He did experience success when he was voted managing editor of the student newspaper, *The Crimson*, but was dismayed when he failed to win acceptance to the Porcellian, Harvard's most exclusive campus club. As his Harvard days came to an end, he decided to study law at Columbia University, not because he was fixed on a legal career but more because it would take him back to New York.

Roosevelt seemed destined for a legal career, but displayed little enthusiasm for this. Almost three years after he had entered legal practice he decided in the summer of 1910 to change course and run for political office. He was twice elected to his home county in the New York State Legislature. In 1913, he was appointed Assistant Secretary of the Navy in President Wilson's Administration, for which he served for seven years. Roosevelt showed much more enthusiasm for politics than the law; however, he suffered defeat in his 1914 bid to become a senator for New York. An even heavier reverse came in 1920 with a resounding defeat as the vice presidential candidate on the Democratic national ticket where he was the running mate to James M. Cox. Roosevelt believed this defeat was due to the forces of 'materialism and conservatism' that followed the First World War and claimed that 'people tire quickly of ideals and we are now repeating history' (in Dallek, 2017, p. 73). Not least of the formidable political gifts that were still to emerge from Roosevelt was his ability to find affinity with the public mood. It had not been evident in 1920 but his time was still to come.

The impact of polio on FDR

The ups and downs of political life were placed into sharp perspective in August 1921, while Roosevelt was enjoying a vacation at Campobello, the family's summer home in New Brunswick, Canada. Roosevelt returned home from several days spent sailing, swimming and deep-sea fishing feeling completely exhausted. By morning his temperature was 102 degrees and by the afternoon the paralysis, from which he would never recover, had already set in. At first, a local doctor from Maine believed Roosevelt merely had 'a nasty summer cold.' When his condition worsened an 84-year-old surgeon, Dr William Keen, travelled over 100 miles to see the stricken patient. A detailed study of the treatment he administered, published in 2013, concluded that 'Keen's judgement was wrong in every detail' (Dallek, 2017, p. 77). It eventually became clear that Roosevelt had been struck down by poliomyelitis, although it was hoped that there would be a gradual recovery. Aged 39, he had always enjoyed bracing good health but the disease had disastrous consequences. Roosevelt was permanently crippled and was able to walk only with the aid of leg braces. Nevertheless, he was unstinting in his attempt to restore strength and movement and in October 1924 he travelled to Warm Springs, Georgia, to see if the warming mineral waters could provide a cure. FDR biographer Ted Morgan believes that the experience of a devastating illness subsequently enabled Roosevelt to make a connection with the suffering of the American people in the 1930s:

> His illness made it possible for him to identify with the humiliations and defeat of depression America ... A man who could not walk became president of a country that had lost hope. With a simple set of beliefs ... he transmitted his own confidence to the nation. (Morgan, 1985, p. 771)

After what his wife Eleanor called his 'trial by fire' Roosevelt found new humility, sensitivity and hidden depths. His Labor Secretary, Frances Perkins, felt that 'The man emerged completely warm-hearted, with new humility of spirit and a firmer understanding of profound philosophical concepts.' (Kearns Goodwin, 1994, pp. 16–17)

Political comeback after illness

It took Roosevelt several years before he was fit enough to re-enter political life. He returned to the political arena with a narrow victory over Albert Ottinger, the Republican State Attorney General, in the contest for the governorship of New York in 1928, Roosevelt prevailing by just over 25,000 votes from a total of 4.23 million. To win such a prestigious position, against terrible physical adversity, in a year that had seen the Republican candidate take the presidency in a landslide, made him a genuine contender for the presidential nomination for 1932. Roosevelt's personal triumph was a remarkable one and helped mould the character of the man who was about to face immeasurable pressure and responsibility. Roosevelt used the governorship to demonstrate that he could effectively deal with his disability and at the same time carry out a progressive agenda that would be supported by his constituents. A resounding victory in the governorship election of 1930 cemented Roosevelt's place on the national political stage. In the summer of 1932 he was nominated as the Democratic candidate for the presidency. Four victories in presidential elections then followed (1932, 1936, 1940 and 1944).

In office, Roosevelt faced the most severe Depression in American history and then led the Grand Alliance in the struggle against fascism. The responsibilities he faced could not have been more daunting or unrelenting. Historian Robert Dallek has spoken of 'the success of Franklin Roosevelt, arguably the third of America's greatest presidents, and surely the most important of the twenty-nine since Lincoln' (Dallek, 2017, p. 17). Doris Kearns Goodwin describes how after days filled with tension and decision making Roosevelt would relax in his bed by recalling the blissful childhood memory of sledging in the snow on the Hyde Park estate.

4.3 The Hundred Days and the First New Deal

The inaugural address

A sullen Hoover had 'left office to the sound of crashing banks' and as one writer observed: 'we could smell the Depression in the air, it was like a raw wind.' (Leuchtenburg, 1963, p. 18) Roosevelt was careful to keep a distance from the damaged outgoing president during the long interregnum. Their relationship, never good, had deteriorated even further after the election result and their journey together to Capitol Hill for the formal handover of power was chilly in every sense. The economic situation deteriorated even further between Roosevelt's victory in the November 1932 election and his inauguration in March 1933. Jonathan Alter goes as far as to say: 'It is hard to avoid the conclusion that he intentionally allowed the economy to sink lower so that he could enter the presidency in a more dramatic fashion.' (Alter, 2007, p. 181)

Once he had assumed the presidency, Roosevelt needed to act to combat the popular mood of despair and to address the issue of unemployment, given that a third of the workforce was without a job. Anthony Badger comments that Roosevelt '[u]ndoubtedly lifted the paralysing fear that had settled on the country ... He was the first American President who could carry his message directly to the people' (Badger,

1989, p. 7). This was clearly illustrated on inauguration day, Saturday 4 March 1933, when Roosevelt was sworn in using his family's old Dutch Bible. Exercising an almost visceral leadership, the president told a huge crowd: 'First of all, let me assert my firm belief that the only thing we have to fear is fear itself – nameless, unreasoning, unjustified terror.' Roosevelt used biblical imagery to highlight the nation's plight which he said came 'from no failure of substance. We are stricken by no plague of locusts … plenty is at our doorstep, but a generous use of it languishes in the very sight of the supply'. In terms of blame, FDR placed this at the door of the country's business leaders who had exploited the economy for their own gain and now abdicated responsibility for the ensuing collapse.

The brief inaugural address was remarkably effective in raising the national mood. Meanwhile, Roosevelt was scathing about some of the country's bankers who, having 'failed through their own stubbornness and their own incompetence, have admitted their failure and have abdicated'. The new president concluded that 'our greatest primary task is to put people to work' and promised 'action, and action now' (in Dallek, 2017, p. 5). The response to the speech was overwhelmingly positive. The White House received around 450,000 letters, nearly all of them favourable, in the first week after the speech. Roosevelt had convinced many of the American people that he had the compassion to listen to them directly. Whereas during the Hoover presidency one man had dealt with all of the mail the White House received, under Roosevelt the staff dealing with the mail alone was extended to 50. Roosevelt's instincts for the popular mood were again demonstrated when the Volstead Act was quickly amended so that drinking beer became legal even though the formal undoing of Prohibition would take longer.

But the road to recovery would be immensely challenging and it would need more than fine speeches and warm words, however welcome and well-received they might be. Dallek states:

> Franklin Roosevelt's greatest challenge on assuming office was finding ways to combat the Great Depression with effective federal programs that would not agitate public fears of a swing toward collectivism and away from individualism by a president reaching for too much power. (Dallek, 2017, p. 8)

The collapse of the American banking system

Given the parlous state of the banking system, Roosevelt's capacity to remain calm in the eye of the financial storm was increasingly striking. Even on the very day of inauguration, the banking crisis lurched downward. At 2.30 am on 4 March the banks of New York shut down. The financial system of the entire United States was on the edge of the abyss. Thirty-eight states had now closed their banks. Roosevelt recognised the psychological element of this crisis and declared a nationwide bank holiday which gave some people the opportunity to regain their nerve. Crucially, the administration stopped some way short of a truly radical step such as nationalising the banks but rather confined itself to a series of reforms simply designed to bring stability to the system. The administration now rushed through the Emergency Banking Relief Bill, the first of what would be an avalanche of new legislation. This act, passed by Congress in under eight hours, brought all banks under federal control and allowed those banks considered solvent to reopen under licence. For the time being, it was enough.

The fireside chats

On the evening of 12 March 1933 a CBS newsman made a brief announcement to say: 'The President wants to come into your home and sit at your fireside for a little chat.' For the first of his 'fireside chats' around 60 million Americans gathered round their radio sets and were told in a calm, positive tone that it was now safe for them to return their savings to the banks. 'I can assure you that it is safer to keep your money in a reopened bank than under the mattress.' (Dallek, 2017, pp. 140–141) Roosevelt's ability to communicate with the American people had been amply demonstrated and as William Leuchtenburg comments:

> Roosevelt was the first President to master the technique of reaching people directly over the radio. In his fireside chats, he talked like a father discussing public affairs with his family in the living room. As he spoke, he seemed unconscious of the fact that he was addressing millions. [Roosevelt] undoubtedly lifted the paralyzing fear that had settled on the country … He was … the first American President who could carry his message directly to the people. (Leuchtenburg, 1963, p. 330)

Hugh Brogan sees Roosevelt as:

> The first fully modern President. He used the great crises which swept him into office to accustom the American people to look first to the White House for the solution of their political problems. The torrential activity of his first term greatly assisted this aim … He was always news, always on the front pages of the newspapers … In his 'fireside chats' on the radio he projected himself and his message into millions of homes … He made extensive tours throughout America, so that hundreds of thousands saw for themselves the big smile … At bottom, Franklin Roosevelt was a man of power and vision. He was a master politician, who took command with absolute authority … Franklin Roosevelt … transformed America from a country which had been laid low by troubles which its own incompetence had brought on it, and which it was quite unable to cope with, to a country, as it proved, superbly equipped to meet the worst shocks the modern world could hurl at it. It was enough. (Brogan, 1985, p. 567)

Finally, it is interesting to note that while the fireside chats have become such an important part of the Roosevelt mythology he actually spoke in this way only four times in 1933 and only 27 times in total during a four-term presidency.

Analysis: To what extent was FDR personally responsible for the New Deal?

Jonathan Alter offers this insight:

> When FDR became President, he had no carefully worked out political philosophy or rigorous approach to governing beyond a penchant for action. This sounds like a shortcoming but proved a hidden asset. Had he been an intellectual or ideologue,

he would have lacked the flexibility and spirit of experimentation the times required. (Alter, 2007, p. 32)

Although to the American people the First New Deal and the personality of Roosevelt were inextricably linked, historians now emphasise the collective aspects of the New Deal. Roosevelt was the driving force, the 'remote majesty' in the White House, but he used a myriad of advisers and aides and literally thousands of administrators, supported by loyal battalions of social workers and idealistic college graduates. FDR listened to his Cabinet members but also to unofficial advisers. Most important in terms of advice was 'The Brain Trust', consisting of a small group of university academics and lawyers. Notable members included Professor Felix Frankfurter of the Harvard Law School and Columbia University professors Rexford G. Tugwell and Raymond Moley.

While it has been easy to imagine the New Deal emanating from the White House the reality was that wide-ranging initiatives found energy and leadership across every state. The sheer scope of the New Deal was staggering and transformed the role of the federal government so that the impact of the national government was felt in virtually every household. The power and range of the presidency was also visibly extended but it would be wrong to suggest that every initiative stemmed from the Oval Office. David Kennedy points out that even as the Hundred Days drew to a close:

> The precise battle plan of the New Deal's attack ... remained difficult to define. Little coherent pattern could be detected in the unlikely mixture of policies that had been adopted. They ranged from orthodox budget cutting to expansive spending for relief and public works ... from deliberate crop destruction to thoughtful conservation, from mortgage protection for the middle class to union protection for labor. (Kennedy, 1999, p. 153)

The president's policies were not easy to categorise. Conservatives were dismayed when the administration removed its currency from the gold standard. Democrats found it difficult to accept that their new president could slash government pay-outs to veterans and reduce the salaries of federal workers. Radicals lamented the fact that he had not nationalised the banks. As the eminent historian Richard Hofstadter remarked: 'Only a leader with an experimental temper could have made the New Deal possible.' (In Dallek, 2017, p. 143)

Fiona Venn, in *The New Deal*, states that:

> Recent historical interpretations of the New Deal have tended to emphasize its limitations as a reforming, radical force. Many of its achievements helped to institutionalize and consolidate the existing *status quo* in both economic and political spheres. Certainly, it also reinforced the prevailing gender stereotypes, incorporated organized labor into a regulated contractual relationship with capital and failed to address critical issues such as the racial discrimination endemic in American society. Many of its longest-lasting effects were virtually coincidental, most notably the changes in the role of the federal government, the strengthening of the executive branch and the beginning of an 'imperial presidency'. (Venn, 1998, p. 3)

A further insight comes from Jonathan Alter who quotes FDR's Labor Secretary to illustrate the president's leadership style: '"He put the dynamite under the people who had to do the job and let them fumble for their own methods," as Perkins later put it. This was the presidential leadership that eased the Depression and won World War II.' (Alter, 2007, p. 293)

Charles R. Morris provides some additional, important observations:

> The New Deal programs were a pastiche of income transfers, price and market interventions, and permanent regulatory initiatives ... there is a striking vein of research that suggests that the main factor in the recovery was Roosevelt himself – and it's not nearly as far-fetched as it sounds. It has long been a puzzlement that the economy picked up sharply in the *month* that Roosevelt finally assumed the presidency. (Morris, 2017, p. 262)

A further very important work by Ira Katznelson, *Fear Itself: The New Deal and the Origins of Our Time* is full of insights into the New Deal. Not least is this one about the transformative role played by Congress, not just in the New Deal but in shaping modern America:

> One cannot fully understand the New Deal without appreciating the activist law-making that resulted from many bouts of arguing, bargaining, and voting in the U.S. Senate and House of Representatives. These policy achievements demonstrably challenged the period's common claim that national legislation had become incapable and obsolete.
>
> In the United States, the legislature remained an effective center of political life ... Congress maintained a pride of place in a system of coequal branches. Its constitutional role was not supplanted. The Senate and the House of Representatives continued, when they wished, to say no even to presidents at the peak of their popularity. Working through Congress, the New Deal falsified the idea that legislative policies must ensure democratic failure. To the contrary, Congress crafted policies that changed how capitalism worked, in part by promoting unions that gave the working class a voice both at the work-place and in national politics. (Katznelson, 2013, p. 20)

The scale of the New Deal

The sheer volume of legislation was unprecedented. In the first Hundred Days of his presidency Roosevelt introduced no less than 15 major bills into law. In his biography of FDR, Ted Morgan notes:

> Bills originating in the White House were passed almost daily. This was Presidential power without precedent – FDR could dream up an idea, something that had never been tried, and set the huge machinery of government in motion to implement it. For instance he wanted to take the unemployed out into the woods and give them forestry work. [That became] the Civilian Conservation Corps. (Morgan, 1985, p. 379)

During the first Hundred Days, cornerstone projects such as the Tennessee Valley Authority (TVA) and the Social Security Act came to define the ambition and scope of the New Deal. At this stage it is easy to see the first wave of projects as focusing on emergency measures, relief agencies and urgent personal support. Amid this flurry of activity, at the centre of the storm, was the unruffled figure who was transforming himself from a politician of straightforward dimensions into a giant. It seemed that by merely taking the oath of office a man of great charm but limited depth now seemed capable of single-handedly taking on the Great Depression (Table 4.2).

Table 4.2   The First New Deal

The Federal Emergency Relief Administration (FERA)	For the first time, the federal government accepted that unemployment relief should come from Washington and not just be left to the individual states.
	The Act gave $500 million, to be issued through direct grants to the individual states.
	The scheme was administered by a key Roosevelt aide, Harry Hopkins, who had chaired New York's relief agency
	In his first two hours as boss of the FERA Hopkins allocated $5 million to state relief agencies but in the longer term he came to see these payments as potentially destructive to their recipients and he became a staunch advocate of work relief.
	Hopkins created a range of work-relief schemes such as highway repairs and improvements to public buildings.
	More than 4 million people were occupied in this way by the winter of 1933.
The Civil Works Administration (CWA)	The work-relief principle was at the centre of this initiative which injected $1 billion into the economy during a five-month period from November 1933.
	More than 4 million people were employed in large-scale construction and repair projects around roads, schools, hospitals and airports, while ditches were dug and pipes were laid. Whereas the Civilian Conservation Corps (see below) targeted young people, the CWA was aimed at the middle-aged unemployed.
	This agency was short lived, expensive and heavily criticised for the nature of the mundane tasks it often required.
The Tennessee Valley Authority (TVA)	After a meeting at Muscle Shoals, Alabama, on the banks of the Tennessee River, FDR began to think out loud about 'the widest experiment ever undertaken by a government' (Alter, 2007, p. 287).
	Embracing no less than seven states, this aimed to develop the whole area of the Tennessee River basin.
	Innovations included land reclamation, dam building, hydro-electric power, rehousing and recreation.
	The impact was to boost living standards across the whole region, although lower costs for electricity were not as successful in attracting industry to the area as had been hoped.
	The TVA was criticised by some for its 'socialist' principles but it was ultimately one of the best received and most successful New Deal projects.
The National Recovery Administration (NRA)	This National Recovery Administration (NRA) tried to negotiate agreements with all major industries to create fair prices, wages and working hours. More than 2 million employers displayed a blue-eagle symbol to show that they were taking part in the scheme.
	Section 7a of the Act guaranteed workers the right of collective bargaining.
	Roosevelt gave Hugh Johnson the responsibility for the NRA, but he ran up against insurmountable opposition. On the one hand, employers resisted the support for trade unions. At the same time, big business did not seem to be creating new jobs.

Continued

In 1935 the Supreme Court ruled that the NRA was unconstitutional.

Dallek concludes: 'Although the NRA did add almost two million workers to payrolls, set precedents for minimum wages and maximum hours, and kept the economy on an even keel – or at least from descending into further deflation – it did not come close to ending the Depression.' (Dallek, 2017, p. 157)

The Agricultural Adjustment Administration (AAA)

Farm prices had been damaged by overproduction. The Agricultural Adjustment Administration (AAA) aimed to raise farm prices and income.

Dallek describes Agriculture Secretary Henry A. Wallace as 'a brilliantly effective evangelist for rural America' (Dallek, 2017, p. 145).

The AAA promoted 'organised scarcity in action', sought to reduce production and therefore boost prices.

Farmers who cut down acreage or production would receive compensation.

The AAA was a particularly controversial New Deal agency. More than 5 million pigs were slaughtered at a time when many people were going hungry.

Poorer farmers did not benefit. It was mainly larger landowners who felt the improvement in prices.

Sharecroppers and tenants were actually hard hit by the domestic allotment programme and their poverty worsened.

Alter says 'little or no thought was given to the long-term consequences' (Alter, 2007, p. 280).

Kennedy says 'the New Dealers' faith in agricultural revival as the master key to general prosperity was quaintly anachronistic.' (In Dallek, 2017, p. 145)

The Civilian Conservation Corps (CCC)

The president's personal and long-standing interest in conservation lay at the heart of a plan, breathtaking in its size, ambition and rapidity of execution. This offered short-term work to young men on a variety of conservation projects.

250,000 men (the project excluded women, while black people were mainly in segregated camps) were quickly put to work planting trees, building dams, constructing log cabins in national parks, extinguishing forest fires, restoring historic battlefield sites and reclaiming swampland.

Workers were only paid $1 per day, leading to some criticism, but the scheme was widely popular, attracting almost 3 million men during its nine-year existence.

Three billion trees were planted, a billion fish stocked, 30,000 wildlife shelters built, 20 million acres protected from soil erosion and 800 state parks were created.

The overall impact in limiting the suffering of families in the Depression was limited.

The Public Works Administration (PWA)

Directed by Secretary of the Interior, Harold Ickes, the PWA had a budget of $3.3 billion which was spent building schools, hospitals and other public buildings.

Continued

The Glass–Steagall Banking Act (1933)	Aimed to reform the structure of the banking system separating commercial from investment banking.
	Restricted commercial banks in terms of investment and speculation.
	More reserves were made available to banks.
	Set up the Federal Bank Deposit Insurance Corporation to secure individual deposits under $5,000.
	FDR was a reluctant signatory to legislation described by the economist Milton Friedman as 'the single most important structural change' to the American economy since the Civil War. (Alter, 2007, p. 305)
The Securities and Exchange Act (1934)	Tried to reduce the prospect of a stock market failure such as in 1929.
	The federal government was given power to regulate stock exchanges and purchase of stocks 'on the margin' was prohibited without a deposit of at least 55 per cent of the purchase price.

Noted presidential biographer Jean Edward Smith states:

When the hundred days ended in the early morning hours of June 16, Congress had shattered all precedent for legislative activity. Roosevelt had sent fifteen messages to the Hill, and Congress had responded with fifteen historic pieces of legislation. FDR's mastery of the legislative process was complete. He compromised when compromise was necessary, zigzagged when required, but in the end saw his program through. 'It's more than a New Deal,' said Interior secretary Harold Ickes. 'It's a new world.' (Smith, 2007, p. 332)

Jonathan Alter's excellent study of 'The Hundred Days' looks at what Roosevelt had done to the presidency itself:

The first Hundred days were over, with a new standard in place for all future presidents to measure themselves against. It wasn't just that Roosevelt, with the help of Congress, had pushed though the most legislation in the shortest time in American history. In a flash, he had transformed the presidency and the role of Washington, D.C. Presidents thereafter would have to perform the role of communicator in chief and legislator in chief, or risk irrelevance. Business would have to make room for government in influencing economic life. The American people would come to expect their presidents – from either party – to come to office with ambitious legislative agendas. (Alter, 2007, p. 307)

4.4 Criticism of the New Deal

In the summer of 1934, Roosevelt toured the United States for the first time since his election victory in 1932. He claimed that he now saw hopeful people whereas he had previously seen the look of despair. In the letters that continued to arrive at the White House, Roosevelt continued to receive a considerable degree of adulation. One woman from Wisconsin wrote, 'We all feel if ever there was a saint, he is one.' (McElvaine, 1983, p. 14) After positive results for the Democrats in the 1934 midterm

Congressional elections a journalist for the *New York Times* said, 'the New Deal had won the most overwhelming victory in the history of American politics'. William Allen White proclaimed that FDR had been 'all but crowned by the people'. William Randolph Hearst said simply, 'The forgotten man does not forget.' (Smith, 2007, p. 350)

However, the problem of unemployment stubbornly remained. Despite the huge public spending and hectic legislation of 1933 the fact remained that at the start of 1934 there were still 11.3 million people without work. Although Roosevelt's initial measures enjoyed widespread support, criticism began to emerge by 1934. In a novel published in that year one of the characters bitterly exclaimed:

> What the hell has happened to everything? You read in the paper things have never been so good; there's never been so much prosperity; the God-damned stock market is booming; and then you find out you can't get work; everybody's losing his job, or their wages are being cut. (In Traynor, 1987, p. 32)

In late 1934, a Pennsylvanian observed: 'The forgotten man is still forgotten ... the New Deal and N.R.A. has only helped big business.' (McElvaine, 1983, p. 14) A letter sent to the White House in 1935 exclaimed: 'We're about down and out and the only good thing about it that I see is that there's not much further down we can go.' (McElvaine, 1983, Introduction) A writer from Missouri bitterly claimed that 'Roosevelt's statement some time ago that no one would starve is just another broken promise.' (McElvaine, 1983, p. 13)

Critics of the New Deal

Huey Long

Long was the flamboyant governor of the state of Louisiana. A charismatic and ambitious political operator, he was seen by his opponents as a dangerous demagogue. Known as the 'Kingfish', his dominance of his own state and gradual move from supporter to critic of Roosevelt led him to entertain presidential ambitions. In January 1934 Long launched his 'share our wealth' campaign with the slogan 'Every Man a King', and the promise that, if elected, he would confiscate all personal fortunes over $3 million and distribute it, so that every ordinary citizen would receive between $4,000 and $5,000. The richest members of society, in particular the wealthy bankers and high financiers, would see their wealth capped. While Long's critics maintained that his plans were economically implausible, his energetic delivery and easy promises generated significant support, especially among the poorest farmers in the Southern states. Long delivered substantial social improvement to his home state, with progressive schemes for raising standards of literacy and education, boosting the size and status of Louisiana's State University (LSU), opening state charity hospitals, and constructing roads and bridges. He also quickly came close to bankrupting his state. Long and his entourage were also worryingly ready to indulge in the crude and violent intimidation of his opponents.

Long's burgeoning support, rural progressivism, economic radicalism, evangelical fervour, capacity for self-promotion, ability to come through bruising election campaigns and brash self-assurance was enough to cause deep concern in the White House. Long found Roosevelt's thinking difficult to penetrate and moved away from supporting early elements of the New Deal to criticism of the president. He privately called FDR a 'phony' and told aides, 'I can out promise him and he knows it.' (White,

2006, p. 528) At the age of 42 Long's career was cut brutally short when he was assassi-nated in Baton Rouge, Louisiana in September 1935. Long's biographer, T.H. Williams, describes him as 'a great natural politician who looked, and often seemed to behave, like a caricature of the red-neck Southern politico, and yet who had become at the time of his death a serious rival to Franklin D. Roosevelt for the presidency' (Williams, 1969, Introduction).

Father Charles Coughlin

Coughlin was a Canadian-born Catholic so would never have been eligible to run for the American presidency but nevertheless came to represent a real threat to Roosevelt in terms of his hold on the public imagination. A Catholic priest, he had moved to Royal Oak, Michigan, where from 1926 he attracted increasing attention with his radio sermons on the CBS network, which eventually generated a weekly audience in excess of 30 million people. In 1934 he founded the National Union for Social Justice which lobbied in support of his banking policies but he was also explicitly anti-Semitic. While Long generated support in rural areas, Coughlin developed a significant power base among the urban working classes in the Midwest and the North. Although the radio priest initially expressed support for the president, by 1935 his populist schemes to nationalise the banks, credit and currency and introduce a minimum annual wage made him a further radical and dangerous opponent for Roosevelt to contend with. Ultimately, Coughlin's extremism, radicalism and megalomania meant that his longer-term influence was self-limiting.

Dr Francis Townsend

A doctor from Long Beach, California, Townsend had personally witnessed the impact of the depression on the savings of old people. He devised a plan – the Townsend Old Age Revolving Pension Plan – to boost the American economy, based on the idea of paying a pension of $200 a month to every American over 60. In return, they had to retire at 60 and spend their $200 within the month. Townsend argued that the retirement scheme would create jobs for younger people; the spending plan would increase demand for consumer goods, and in turn create more jobs. For a time, particularly when the honeymoon period of FDR's presidency appeared to be on the wane, speculation that Townsend could help to form an anti-Roosevelt coalition appealing to radicals, labour groups and small farmers was enough to cause some concern in the White House. By January 1934 his following at 'Townsend Clubs' seemed increasingly messianic.

The 'thunder from the left', of men like Long and Townsend, was not the only criti-cism directed at Roosevelt. In the election campaign of 1932, Roosevelt had promised to balance the budget; by 1934 his conservative opponents were criticising him for spending too much money, encouraging the growth of trade unions, increasing tax-ation and regulating working hours and wages. Backed by the wealth of the DuPont family, important businessmen set up the American Liberty League, a group that criticised Roosevelt for betraying his own class. In addition, many ordinary people wrote to Roosevelt to tell him that the New Deal had let them down. Typical was this comment from a man from Los Angeles, California who told Roosevelt: 'You are multi-millionaires, what do you care for the masses of people?' (McElvaine, 1983, p. 177)

4.5 The Second New Deal

It is now widely accepted that the central purpose of the New Deal was to save American capitalism. While some experts have emphasised the continuity of the New Deal across the period 1933–38 others find the concept of a first and second New Deal to be a helpful distinction. The measures which constituted what is sometimes called the Second New Deal have been characterised by historians as a more radical and reformist programme than the first programme, with a less conciliatory attitude towards business. This is contrasted with the First New Deal, with its emphasis on emergency measures of immense scope, a myriad of legislation, a distinctive group of advisers, a sense of firefighting and a spirit of co-operation between government and business.

Several factors combined together in 1934–35 to oblige Roosevelt to give the New Deal a new direction. Firstly, Roosevelt was keenly aware of the forthcoming presidential election in November 1936. Critics such as Long and Townsend had attracted considerable support. Many observers anticipated that Long would run as a presidential candidate in 1936. Secondly, despite the unprecedented legislative activity of 1933–34, at the start of 1935 11 million people were still without work and the economy appeared becalmed. Industrial relations had deteriorated in 1934 and strike action had afflicted the automobile, coal and steel industries.

Some authorities have claimed that the sheer scale and reforming ambition of the fresh batch of legislation instigated in 1935 amounted to a 'Second New Deal'. They contend that the Second New Deal represented a radical programme based on genuine social and economic reform and more concerned with those at the bottom of the economic system. On the other hand, others claim that a clear pattern in the development of the New Deal is more difficult to discern. They claim that FDR had no systematic programme and emphasise that the president was a pragmatist rather than an idealist. Finally, it has been pointed out that some of the measures of the Second New Deal had in fact been in preparation for some time and that some of them were initiated by Congress rather than the president. They see the New Deal change direction and shift its emphasis, but do not accept the notion of two, separate, New Deals.

Key elements of the Second New Deal

The Works Progress Administration (WPA), 1935

The WPA accounted for one-third of the total government money allotted to poor relief. Over eight years the WPA spent around 11 billion dollars and gave work to more than 8.5 million people. Its projects included the construction of schools, hospitals, airport runways and urban renewal. More radically, the WPA encompassed support for writers and artists through agencies such as the Federal Writer's Project and the Federal Arts Project. This was the type of activity that drew the sharpest criticism from opponents of FDR who claimed that the government was completely over-reaching the constitutional limits to its jurisdiction.

The Rural Electrification Administration

This addressed the fact that nine out of ten American farms had no electricity supply. This agency encouraged farmers to join together to borrow money from the government to build power lines. By 1941, four out of ten American farmers had electricity, and by 1951 the figure had reached nine out of ten.

The National Labor Relations Act (Wagner Act)

This Act stemmed from the initiative of Senator Robert Wagner. The Supreme Court had ruled that the National Industrial Recovery Act was unconstitutional and had therefore removed the safeguard to collective bargaining encompassed in its Section 7a. The Wagner Act reaffirmed the government's support for the worker's right to join trade unions. It created a new National Labor Relations Board which campaigned against unfair labour practices, including the use of blacklists for union members.

4.6 The presidential election of 1936 and the 'Roosevelt recession' of 1937

It is tempting to assume that Roosevelt cruised to an untroubled second election victory on a universal wave of gratitude from the thankful American people. In fact, the path to four more years in the White House was much more troubled and complex, even though the outcome was a crushing defeat of the Republican candidate. Firstly, the personal strain of dealing with the economic catastrophe was significant. FDR was finding the responsibility, unrelenting paperwork and massive physical demands of the highest office arduous, leading one observer to describe him, in 1935, as 'on edge' and 'dangerously tired', while an aide noted how 'drawn ... tired ... and nervous' he seemed, compared to how he had been in 1933 (Dallek, 2017, p. 232, 242). On his worst days, the prospect of a further four years made him feel less than enthusiastic. His low-key approach to the second election campaign prompted his 'aghast and angry' (Dallek, 2017, p. 237) wife to write furious memos demanding a more concerted effort from her husband.

Secondly, the initial excitement of the Hundred Days had now given way to the growing realisation that the economic malaise was utterly profound and entrenched, with the limitations of the New Deal increasingly apparent. Thirdly, and of profound importance, was the growing debate about the president's direction of travel. When the Supreme Court ruled in May 1935 that the National Recovery Administration (NRA) had exceeded its constitutional limits, in a test case concerning interstate commerce regarding a poultry corporation, what was at stake were huge questions about the essence of the New Deal and of American government itself. The nine judges in the Supreme Court had taken a 'states-rights decision', what Roosevelt called 'the horse-and-buggy definition of interstate commerce' that placed authority locally (Dallek, 2017, p. 219). The president stood in the opposite corner, advocating in this instance the power of the centralised government. FDR wondered aloud how he could deal with the country's profound economic problems if his authority was being held in check by the judicial branch of the government.

In a cabinet meeting of December 1935 the president anticipated that 'all of the New Deal bills will be declared unconstitutional by the Supreme Court. This will mean that everything that this administration has done of any moment will be nullified.' It is a measure of how much the president divided opinion, that the *Chicago Tribune* hailed the Supreme Court decision as the triumph of 'Constitutionalism' over 'Hitlerism', while one of the judges enthused that 'the New Deal is on the rocks' (Dallek, 2017, p. 244). While some of the wealthiest elements of American society now regarded FDR as a traitor to his class, it was becoming clear that Roosevelt stood not just for economic recovery but what David Kennedy has called 'lasting social reform and durable political realignment' (in Dallek, 2017, p. 248).

These were the background issues, then, that made the 1936 presidential election resemble, to some extent, a referendum on FDR himself and the philosophy of intervention. Many were genuinely grateful to Roosevelt and cheered him when he stated, on the campaign trail in New York in September 1936, that thanks to his policies 'starvation was averted, homes and farms were saved, banks were reopened, crop prices rose, and industry revived' (Dallek, 2017, p. 261). On the other hand, his many opponents found his ideas dangerous and yearned for a return to balanced budgets, reduced national debt and fiscal conservatism.

Despite these tumultuous events, the Democratic Convention of June 1936 acclaimed the achievements of the New Deal and re-nominated Roosevelt as its candidate for the forthcoming presidential election. Roosevelt's opponent was Alfred Landon, the Republican Governor of Kansas. The results showed that despite the difficulties he was facing and the savagery of the criticism he endured, Roosevelt was at the height of his public support and in a landslide victory he secured every state, with the exception of Maine and Vermont. Roosevelt won 60.4 per cent of the popular vote (Table 4.3). In addition the Democrats in Congress gained 76 seats compared to the Republicans' 16 seats; in the House of Representatives they took 331 seats compared to 89 Republican seats. Roosevelt's inaugural speech of January 1937 promised new attention for the 'ill-housed, ill-clad and ill-nourished' and seemed to herald a further radical chapter of reform. In reality, the momentum of the New Deal was ebbing away. The flood of legislation had ended and support for the president's programme within Congress and within his own party was diminished.

The recession of 1937

At the start of 1937 the economic indicators appeared to point towards a continuing improvement in the American economy. During the spring, industrial output finally rose above the levels of 1929. Although the unemployment rate at the start of 1936 was 16.9 per cent of the total workforce, the public work schemes of the second phase of the New Deal had helped to reduce unemployment to 7.7 million. Nevertheless, some of the New Deal agencies attracted criticism on the grounds that the jobs they created

Table 4.3 The result of the 1936 presidential election

Candidate	Party	Electoral College votes	Popular votes
Franklin D. Roosevelt (New York)	Democrat	523	27,751,597
Alfred M. Landon (Kansas)	Republican	8	16,679,583
William Lemke (North Dakota)	Union and Others	–	882,479

were not genuine. For example the Works Progress Administration (WPA) was heavily criticised and the word 'boondoggling' was coined to describe the allegedly trivial nature of the work it offered.

In August 1937 the recovery lost its momentum and the country began to move into recession. Industrial activity suddenly fell away. In just three months steel production declined from 80 per cent of capacity to 19 per cent. On a single day 7 million shares were sold on the stock market, stirring terrible memories of the Crash of October 1929. Roosevelt was stunned by this turn of events and was persuaded to reduce government spending. Thousands of workers employed by the WPA were laid off. The big automobile manufacturers had to restrict production and thousands of unsold cars were stored on huge parking lots.

In his 'fireside chat' of 15 November 1937, Roosevelt announced details of his new programme to combat the recession. This package included new regulation of working hours and wages, new farm legislation, abolition of child labour and new measures against trusts. Despite these measures the recession took a grip and unemployment began to increase, so that by 1938 over 10 million people were once again without work. Some of Roosevelt's critics gloated over the irony of the president presiding over a slump and referred to the 'Roosevelt recession'. The economic reverses of late 1937–38 that saw unemployment levels soar may have led Roosevelt to ease back on his spending programmes.

The serious industrial unrest of 1937 was in sharp contrast to the mood which Roosevelt had been able to exploit in the crisis years of 1933–34. By 1938 the president was increasingly preoccupied with the dark clouds being generated overseas by the rise of dictatorships in Italy and Germany, and concerns about the situation in the Far East. While this partially explains why Roosevelt's second term in office lacked the energy and sense of urgency he had displayed in the first four years, Fiona Venn points out that it would be wrong to conclude that the New Deal came to an end in 1937:

> The WPA and PWA [Public Works Administration] continued with their projects, reaching virtually every corner of the vast United States ... New Dealers, at both local level and in Washington, DC, continued to work enthusiastically for causes in which they believed; but much of what was achieved in the second term amounted to the continuation and consolidation of the achievements of the first term, rather than the recasting of the reform agenda. New initiatives were fewer on the ground, took longer to pass through Congress and were frequently rendered less effective by limited appropriation. (Venn, 1998, pp. 84–85)

Nevertheless, new measures introduced by Roosevelt in 1938 included the second Agricultural Adjustment Act. This allowed the agriculture secretary to fix marketing quotas for export crops and created the Commodity Credit Corporation to store crop surpluses. The Federal Crop Insurance Corporation was introduced to guarantee minimum crop prices for farmers. However, the scale of these measures was limited compared to the great measures of 1933. Some economists contend that Roosevelt simply stopped spending too soon. They argue that he needed to maintain his earlier policy of injecting huge sums of cash into the economy. Once Roosevelt stopped 'priming the pump' the economy was bound to move back into recession. Others would contend that the jobs created by the New Deal did not generate wealth and were essentially artificial.

4.7 A New Deal for women?

In broad terms, women had tended not to enjoy the economic advantages secured by many men during the 1920s. Women were generally employed in menial occupations, paid less than men and subject to the prevailing mentality that their chief responsibility was to raise children and look after the family home. At the same time, the fact that many working-class males needed their partner to supplement their income drove increasingly large numbers of women into the workplace. By 1930 virtually a quarter of the national workforce were women. When the Depression began, many poorly paid women, particularly those working in the textile industry, were quickly laid off. At the same time, middle-class families were quick to shed domestic help when the economic climate deteriorated. Given that domestic service was a major employer of working-class women, this was a crucial factor in increasing female unemployment. The impact on the relatively small number of women employed in the professions was more evident in terms of falling pay rather than outright unemployment. Female teachers, for example, generally retained their jobs, but had to accept sweeping pay cuts. More positively, the fact that many women worked in clerical posts and service industries tended to shelter them from the most damaging forces of the Depression which were felt in the manufacturing industry. Of course, women managing households without an adult male breadwinner were faced with a perpetual struggle against poverty. Many women were placed under immense psychological pressure through the mental suffering of their male partner when they were thrown on the breadline.

The fortunes of women in terms of the New Deal were rather mixed. While the NRA attempted to work with employers to improve working conditions and introduce minimum rates of pay, many women fell outside the remit of its measures. The NRA, for example, did not regulate domestic service. Even when women's jobs did fall within the NRA, the New Deal agency established rates of pay for women which were between 15 to 30 per cent lower than those paid to men. More positively, the jobs provided by WPA helped many women to survive the Depression. Through the Women's and Professional Division of the WPA, women were offered jobs in areas such as librarianship, teaching and nursing. In addition, the work of Eleanor Roosevelt, who led a White House conference on the Emergency Needs of Women, led to women being offered paid work for helping with the distribution of food and clothing to the needy. Anthony Badger (1989) cites the example of 2,600 women in Mississippi who were put to work on sewing projects and produced over 4 million garments. These women were given a sense of purpose and were provided with an amount of money which made a difference between starvation and survival.

4.8 The rural depression

If the banking crisis was seen by most people as the single most pressing issue when FDR came to power, many of those at the very centre of the New Deal believed that the plight of the agricultural economy came in second place. In setting up the Agricultural Adjustment Administration so quickly, Alter notes that 'almost overnight, FDR established the principle that Washington bore responsibility for farm prices and should pay farmers to create scarcity' (Alter, 2007, p. 281). Why was agricultural (perhaps mistakenly?) seen as so central to American recovery? The impact of the Depression was felt across the whole of rural America. Overproduction had dogged American agriculture throughout the 1920s. The events of the Wall Street Crash and the subsequent Depression swept away urban demand for food supplies. Examination of the cotton crop as an example reveals the devastating consequences. A bumper cotton crop in the summer of 1931 – the third largest in history – raised the fearful prospect of a loss of $100 million to the cotton industry in the south. A year later the total yield of the cotton crop was valued at only $465 million. In Mississippi, it was said that times were as 'tough as jail house stew'. In North Carolina, total receipts for the tobacco crop for 1932 were one-third of those in 1929. In 1931 in the Midwestern corn belt, prices for hogs (pigs) went into the sharpest yearly decline ever recorded. Dairy farmers in Vermont were caught between a decline in milk prices and an increase in the cost of feed. Widespread distress led to increasingly bitter scenes. For example in England, Arkansas, in January 1931, 300 desperate farmers announced that if they were not provided with food they would be left with no choice but to loot stores. A judge who attempted to foreclose a number of farms at Le Mars, Iowa, in April 1933 faced a mob of 600 angry farmers.

This song written by Bob Miller in the 1930s sums up the impact of overproduction on American farmers:

> Seven cent cotton and forty cent meat,
> How in the world can a poor man eat?
> Poor getting poorer all around here,
> Kids coming regular every year.
> Fatten our hogs, take 'em to town,
> All we get is six cents a pound.
> Very next day we have to buy it back.
> Forty cents a pound in a paper sack.

(In McElvaine, 1983, p. 67)

The dust bowl

The exceptionally difficult climatic conditions which afflicted many farm states between 1932 and 1936 brought new levels of despair. In this period, virtually no rain fell across the states of Arkansas, Oklahoma, Nebraska, North and South Dakota. Across the whole region, scorched top soil simply turned to dust. A combination of intense heat and strong winds then meant that this dry top soil was blown away. Previously green and fertile land now took on the appearance of a desert. Millions of acres of farmland between the Rockies and the Appalachians were affected. Hurricanes and tornadoes devastated the Midwest; it has been calculated that in April 1933 alone there were 179 dust storms. During a violent dust storm in May 1934 the cities of Boston, New York and Washington were covered with dust blown across from the Southern plains.

Roosevelt sent out observers to the countryside to photograph and document the rural Depression. One of the most famous photographers was Lorena Hickok, who later recalled:

> [T]he children I'd seen running about with bare feet in Bottineau County, North Dakota ... the farmers in South Dakota who were clawing up mildewed Russian thistle out of the stacks they had cut for their cattle and making it into soup ... cattle so weak they could hardly walk. (Lorena Hickok, *One Third of a Nation*, 1981, cited in Traynor, 1987, p. 16)

Perhaps the greatest insight into rural distress came with the publication in 1939 of John Steinbeck's powerful novel *The Grapes of Wrath*. This graphically portrayed the desperate plight of migrant labourers and sharecroppers who had abandoned their homes in Oklahoma and Arkansas and trekked across America to search for a new life in California. Steinbeck described in the most moving terms the plight of farmers who, upon arrival in California, were obliged to take on poorly paid, menial tasks and to live in grim, overcrowded camps.

More recently Timothy Egan's *The Worst Hard Time* looked at some of those who had survived the Great American Dust Bowl. This extract illustrates the plight of those living in Dodge City, Kansas:

> 'My God! Here it comes!'

> Dodge City went black. The front edge of the duster looked two thousand feet high. Winds were clocked at sixty-five miles an hour. A few minutes earlier there had been bright sunshine and a temperature of eighty-one degrees, without a wisp of wind. Drivers turned on their headlights but could not see ahead of them, or even see the person sitting next to them. It was like three midnights in a jug, one old nester said. Cars died, their systems shorted out by the static. People fled to tornado shelters, fire stations, gyms, church basements. There was a whiff of panic, not evident in earlier storms, as a fear took hold that the end was near. A woman in Kansas later said she thought of killing her child to spare the baby the cruelty of Armageddon. (Egan, 2006. p. 204)

The return of rural prosperity

In common with other aspects of the economy it was not so much the New Deal but the stimulus of the wartime economy that eventually restored rural prosperity. Total farm cash income was $9,105 million in 1940 but this had increased to $22,405 million by 1945. By this time, longer-term trends can be observed, such as the demise of the sharecropping system, the decline of tenant farming and a gradual reduction in the number of people employed in the agricultural sector. By 1945, the number of farms in the United States was 5.9 million, compared to 6.4 million in 1920.

New Deal agricultural projects

The Tennessee Valley Authority (TVA)

Created on 18 May 1933, the TVA encompassed projects not just in Tennessee but also in North Carolina, Virginia, Kentucky, Mississippi, Alabama and Georgia. The large-scale projects in these states transformed the whole region and boosted the prosperity of farmers through investment, electrification programmes and the production of nitrate fertilisers.

The Civilian Conservation Corps (CCC)

Set up on 31 March 1933 under the terms of the Unemployment Relief Act, the CCC went into action in April and operated for seven years. At the centre of this agency were projects of reforestation and soil conservation. It offered work in newly created camps for men between the ages of 18 and 25 in return for pay of $30 a month. By the autumn of 1935, over 500,000 young men were working in CCC camps. They constructed more than 30,000 wildlife shelters and restored battlefields from the Civil War and the War of Independence.

The Agricultural Adjustment Administration (AAA)

This was the central farm relief measure of the New Deal. Its basic premise was to pay farmers to reduce crop acreage. Few New Deal agencies aroused as much controversy as the AAA, which was run by George Peek but was under the ultimate authority of Roosevelt's Agriculture Secretary, Henry Wallace. The AAA responded to the problem of low farm prices caused by an abundance of crops and livestock. It was decided to raise prices by destroying surplus crops and livestock. William Leuchtenburg summarises the most notorious incident connected with the policy of 'organised scarcity':

> Wallace reluctantly agreed [on behalf of the AAA] to a proposal by farm leaders to forestall a glut in the hog market by slaughtering over six million little pigs and more than two hundred thousand cows which were due to farrow ... the piglets overran the stockyards and scampered through the streets of Chicago ... the country was horrified. (Leuchtenburg, 1963, p. 73)

Although in 1936 the Supreme Court ruled the AAA unconstitutional, Congress later returned to the policy of subsidising farmers through further legislation.

In addition to the work of the 'alphabetical agencies', a number of bills were passed to further assist farmers.

The Frazier–Lemke Bankruptcy Act (1934)

This attempted to help farmers by delaying the foreclosure of farm mortgages (it was replaced with a modified Act in 1935 after the first Act had been declared unconstitutional).

The Bankhead–Jones Farm Tenancy Act (1937)

This came to the assistance of sharecroppers by creating the Farm Security Administration to lend money to tenants who wanted to buy their own land. The Act also sought to improve the conditions of migratory labour.

Although we live in an age when images of extreme weather events seem increasingly familiar, photographs from the American Dust Bowl in the 1930s still have the capacity to astound. At the start of 1936 some states such as Nebraska, Oklahoma and Arkansas were entering their fourth year of catastrophic weather. Long periods with no rain at all, winds with the power of a tornado and flash flooding reduced once successful farmers to frightened, beleaguered bystanders.

This was the year when the New Deal agency known as the Farm Security Administration began to send out photographers to capture images of a dust bowl that was almost beyond description. No one captured the suffering of the American Dust Bowl more effectively than Dorothea Lange. Born in New Jersey in 1895 to a middle-class family, she contracted polio at the age of 7. This may have given her the strong sense of empathy so evident in her work.

Trained in photography as a young woman by the noted portrait photographer Arnold Genthe, her most important work came in her sensitive, powerful, insightful depiction of the Dust Bowl. Her intimate, iconic portraits with stark captions perfectly captured the suffering of the Depression.

Dorothea Lange's work can been seen at Oakland Museum of California (OMCA Dorothea Lange)

4.9 Industrial relations during the New Deal era

Even at the height of domestic misery in the winter of 1932–33 there was little evidence of genuine militancy among the nation's unemployed, the downtrodden or from those who remained in work. American popular culture in the 1930s continued to extol the virtues of free enterprise and individual pride, and suspicion of radicalism was widespread. Yet a cursory glance at the figures shows the dramatic rise in labour union membership which took place during the New Deal era. The Norris–LaGuardia Act of 1932 outlawed the use of injunctions against striking labour unions. Further support to the growth of the labour unions was provided with the 1933 National Industrial Recovery Act, which guaranteed the right to collective bargaining. Against this background, a split in the American Federation of Labor (AFL) took place at its 1935 Convention. Whereas the majority of the AFL leadership saw their organisation as a craft union of skilled workers, others felt that the union should embrace unskilled workers. The breakaway Committee on Industrial Organizations (CIO) sought to establish itself as a single union for the millions of workers in mass-production industries. In 1937, this evolved into the Congress of Industrial Organizations. Within the year, the CIO and its outspoken leader John L. Lewis were claiming a membership of almost 4 million. Lewis recruited members in key manufacturing areas such as automobiles, steel, glass and rubber.

Alarmed by these developments, many employers turned to the increasing use of 'company spies' – armed bands of private armies and strike-breakers. The test of strength occurred in 1937 and centred on the steel industry. In Massillon, Ohio, two employees of the Republic Steel Company were killed in a violent strike. Even more serious was the Memorial Day Massacre in South Chicago, where police fired upon striking steel workers resulting in four deaths and more than 80 injuries. 'Sit-down' strikes in the automobile industry enabled the CIO to obtain union recognition from every car manufacturer with the exception of Ford. Public concern about the growing power of the unions, Roosevelt's defence of organised labour and an alleged link between the CIO and Democratic campaign funds meant that the industrial unrest of the 1930s served only to undermine Roosevelt's standing with those who were fearful of the risk of labour.

4.10 Assessments of the New Deal

Maldwyn A. Jones pinpoints some of the landmark changes which the New Deal encompassed:

> For all its failures and limitations the New Deal can claim achievements which have stood the test of time and have become part of the national consensus. It laid the foundations of the welfare state and created a new legal framework for industrial relations. It introduced much-needed controls on banks and stock exchanges. It established the principle that government had the primary responsibility for regulating the economy. Roosevelt ... restored national morale. The New Deal permanently enlarged the role of the Federal government. It gave American capitalism a more humane aspect. While it did nothing to redistribute wealth or income, it redistributed power between capital and labor. Finally, Roosevelt raised the presidential office to a new peak of prestige and power. He revitalized and dramatized the Presidency. (Jones, 1995, p. 476)

William Leuchtenburg provides this assessment of the New Deal in which he claims:

> Franklin Roosevelt re-created the modern Presidency. He took an office which had lost much of its prestige and power in the previous twelve years and gave it an importance which went well beyond what even Theodore Roosevelt and Woodrow Wilson had done ... Roosevelt greatly expanded the President's legislative functions ... [However, the New Deal] never demonstrated that it could achieve prosperity in peacetime. As late as 1941, the unemployed still numbered 6 million and not until the war year of 1943 did the army of jobless finally disappear. (Leuchtenburg, 1963, p. 327, pp. 346–47)

In his excellent summary of the New Deal, Anthony Badger states:

> The success of the New Deal's efforts to secure industrial recovery was strictly limited. Between 1933 and 1937 the American economy grew at an annual rate of 10 per cent, but output had fallen so low after 1929 that even this growth left 14 per cent of the work force unemployed. A recession in 1937 quickly shot the unemployment rate back up to 19 per cent. Well into 1941 unemployment remained at over 10 per cent ... It was World War II, not the New Deal, that was to shape the political economy of industrial and financial America ... The deficiencies of the New Deal were glaring. As the 9,000,000 unemployed in 1939 testified, the policies for industrial

recovery did not work … Roosevelt never pretended that his aim was anything other than to save and preserve capitalism. (Badger, 1989, p. 66, 67, 299, 303)

As Badger suggests, historians are now very aware of the relatively conservative parameters of the New Deal in that as a force for radical reform it had clear limitations. It only reinforced the prevailing gender stereotypes and did nothing to address the issues presented by racism. The most significant changes associated with the New Deal were to alter the role of the federal government, enhance the power of the executive branch and to begin the process that would lead to the development of what could be called an 'imperial presidency'.

Julian Zelizer highlights the extent to which Roosevelt was obliged to make concessions to his opponents in order to secure legislative momentum:

During the 1930s … FDR was already forced to compromise his New Deal to appease southern Democrats and Republicans by agreeing to federal legislation that protected the racial order of Dixie and made it difficult for organized labor to gain a foothold in that low-wage non-union region. (Zelizer, 2015, p. 3)

Finally, an outstanding piece of work by Charles R. Morris offers new interpretations and insights:

The very long periods of unemployment that became routine in the 1930s must have inculcated the expectations of failure and attitudes of shiftlessness associated with 'hard core' unemployment. The solution, however, came quickly – fifteen million men were called into service in 1940–1941, military contracts turned on the lights in disused plants, and seven-day, twelve hours a day factory shifts were suddenly routine. (Morris, 2017, p. 297)

More remarkable still is Morris's reference to recent research:

The economist Alexander Field has recently made the striking claim that it 'was not principally the Second World War that laid the foundation for post-war prosperity. It was technological progress across a broad frontier of the American economy during the 1930s' … Field's research casts a new light on the conventional story that World War II 'ended the Depression.' For sure, the flood of war spending was a massive 'demand shock' that quickly mopped up the Depression-era excess workers. But there is little evidence of a wartime 'supply shock' that created the infrastructure to both win the war and power America's post-war success. While the war accelerated some specific technologies – like airframes, antibiotics and munitions – the disruptions caused by rapid-fire national mobilization and demobilization, along with other wartime distortions, probably outweighed the positive developments. (Morris, 2017, pp. 298–300)

4.11 The presidential election of 1940

The Republican Party boasted several strong candidates as it convened for its Convention in Philadelphia in June 1940. Thomas E. Dewey (New York), Arthur Vandenberg, an outspoken isolationist (Michigan) and Robert A. Taft (Ohio) all had strong claims

Table 4.4   The result of the 1940 presidential election

Candidate	Party	Electoral College votes	Popular votes
Franklin D. Roosevelt (New York)	Democrat	449	27,244,160
Wendell L. Willkie (Indiana)	Republican	82	22,305,198

on the candidacy. In the event they cancelled each other out and instead, on the sixth ballot, the convention turned to Wendell Willkie (Indiana), who had received only 105 votes on the first ballot, but 999 on the final one. At the Democratic Party Convention held in July in Chicago, Roosevelt stated that he would not be prepared to break the 'George Washington' precedent and actively seek re-nomination; however, the reality was that the party was ready to support Roosevelt for an unprecedented third term. Roosevelt's campaign staff soon rallied a nomination on the first ballot: FDR polled 946 votes with James Farley a distant second with only 72 votes. The choice of the avowedly liberal Henry A. Wallace as running mate was not universally popular and would be reversed four years later. By October, the campaign revolved chiefly around the issue of the war.

Willkie responded to a disappointing show in the early polls by raising fears that Roosevelt would take the country into the war. In response, a week before polling day, Roosevelt told a large audience in Boston: 'Your boys are not going to be sent to fight in any foreign wars.' (Kennedy, 1999, p. 463) It was enough to secure victory by a comfortable margin but, given the unparalleled experience of his opponent, Willkie did rather well, particularly in the Midwest farm states. FDR gained more than 27 million popular votes with a margin of 5 million over his opponent. In the Electoral College, the gap looked emphatic with 449 to 82 in FDR's favour (Table 4.4). It was a satisfying victory for a groundbreaking third term but new, darker challenges lay ahead for the president.

Further reading

Ahamed L., *Lords of Finance: The Bankers Who Broke the World* (London: Windmill Books 2010).

Alter J., *The Defining Moment: FDR's Hundred Days and the Triumph of Hope* (New York: Simon & Schuster 2007).

Badger A., *The New Deal: The Depression Years, 1933–1940* (London: Macmillan 1989).

Dallek R., *Franklin D. Roosevelt: A Political Life* (London: Allen Lane 2017).

Egan T., *The Worst Hard Time* (Boston: First Mariner Books 2006).

Galbraith J.K., *The Great Crash 1929* (London: Hamish Hamilton 1955).

Jones M.A., *The Limits of Liberty: American History 1607–1992* (New York: Oxford University Press 1995).

Katznelson I., *Fear Itself: The New Deal and the Origins of Our Time* (New York: Liveright Paperbacks 2013).

Kennedy D.M., *Freedom from Fear: The American People in Depression and War 1929–1945* (New York: Oxford University Press 1999).

Leuchtenburg W.E., *Franklin D. Roosevelt and The New Deal* (New York: Harper & Row 1963).

McElvaine R., *Down and Out in the Great Depression: Letters from the Forgotten Man* (Chapel Hill: University of North Carolina 1983).

Morgan T., *FDR: A Biography* (New York: Simon & Schuster 1985).

Morris C.R., *A Rabble of Dead Money: The Great Crash and the Global Depression: 1929–1939* (New York: PublicAffairs 2017).

Rappleye C., *Herbert Hoover in the White House: The Ordeal of the Presidency* (New York: Simon & Schuster 2016).

Smith J.E., *FDR* (New York: Random House 2007).

Terkel S., *Hard Times: An Oral History of the Great Depression* (New York: Pantheon Books 1986).

Traynor J., *Roosevelt's America 1932–1941* (London: Macmillan Education 1987).

Venn F., *The New Deal* (Edinburgh: Edinburgh University Press 1998).

White R.D. Jr, *Kingfish: The Reign of Huey Long* (New York: Random House 2006).

Williams T.H., *Huey Long: A Biography* (New York: Alfred A. Knopf 1969).

Online resource

FDR Library: www.fdrlibrary.org, last accessed in 2018.

■ ⯆ 5 Roosevelt's foreign policy, 1933–45

5.1 Latin America and the 'Good Neighbor policy'

Roosevelt came to the White House with an understandable fixation on the pressing domestic catastrophe so inevitably his initiatives in foreign affairs were modest. While Roosevelt's 1933 inaugural address was largely concerned with the nation's economic crisis, he did make an important reference to foreign affairs: 'In the field of World policy I would dedicate this nation to the policy of the Good Neighbor – who resolutely respects himself and, because he does so, respects the rights of others.' (FDR Library) This principle was not entirely new, and was similar in approach to Republican policy under Hoover. The countries which were uppermost in Roosevelt's mind when he spoke of 'neighbors' were the Latin American countries such as Brazil, Cuba, Chile, Peru and Paraguay. The first significant step in the implementation of the Good Neighbor policy came with the withdrawal in 1934 of American troops from Haiti, where they had been since 1901. In this case, Roosevelt was honouring a promise which had been made by Hoover. In 1935, important trade agreements were reached with Haiti, Honduras, Brazil and Colombia. These positive moves were further enhanced with the staging of important conferences in Montevideo (1933), Buenos Aires (1936) and Lima (1938). In Montevideo, the United States approved a resolution which stated that 'no state has the right to intervene in the internal or external affairs of another'.

The United States renounced the Platt Amendment of 1901, in which the Cuban Constitution conceded to the United States the right to intervene in Cuba, and began to withdraw from its position of unilateral control over the Panama Canal. In 1936 Roosevelt attempted to sum up the purpose behind the Good Neighbor policy: 'Peace, like charity, begins at home; and that's why we have begun at home, here in North and South and Central America ... to banish wars for ever from this vast portion of the earth.' (FDR Library) A sign that Roosevelt intended to stick to the spirit of the Good Neighbor policy came when he resisted calls for American intervention in Mexico, where the government had nationalised its oil industry at the expense of several American companies.

5.2 The road to war: The Far East

Events in the early 1920s implied that there was no need for undue concern. With moderate forces in the government holding sway, Japan seemed prepared to accept the limitations on its empire which the West desired. At the Washington Conference of

1921, Japan, the United States, Great Britain and France agreed to respect each other's interests in the Pacific. Japan signed the treaty, thereby accepting an inferior ratio of battleships to the United States and Britain but with an undertaking that the United States would not construct any naval bases in the Western Pacific. Japan also signed a Nine-Power Pact in 1922 agreeing to respect the sovereignty, the independence and the territorial and administrative integrity of China.

These positive moves were undermined to some extent by deep and abiding Japanese resentment at the Asian exclusion clause in the new American immigration legislation of 1924. Moreover, internal forces in Japan threatened this period of stability. The Japanese economy was rapidly expanding. Population growth, for a relatively small country, moved at a phenomenal rate in the late 1920s with a rise of approximately 900,000 per year. Natural resources such as petroleum, bauxite and rubber were of critical importance to Japanese industry. These were present in surrounding countries such as Burma, Malaya and the Philippines, and the worldwide economic slump of 1929 made access to such resources even more important.

Certain elements within the Japanese government now looked to China as the next stage in its imperial development. The 1920s saw a rapid rise in the number of extreme nationalist associations within Japan; these groups advocated an aggressive foreign policy and placed the onus on Japan's armed forces to make economic expansion possible. While moderate forces wanted to operate within the framework of the treaties with the West, more extreme factions believed that the time was ripe for more radical action. The term 'Greater Asia Co-Prosperity Sphere' was used to describe an economic empire to be dominated by Japan.

Emperor Hirohito

When Emperor Hirohito came to the throne in 1926 important changes began in the conduct of Japan's affairs. Although Hirohito was venerated as a God on earth, his practical influence on daily affairs was fairly limited; temperamentally gentle, he tended to follow others who were more outspoken. In the early 1930s, hard-line generals, aggressive nationalists and militaristic expansionists became increasingly influential. While Roosevelt wanted to concentrate his energy on domestic matters, events in both the Far East and Europe were already moving in a difficult direction before he had even entered the White House. In 1931, Japanese forces in the Kwantung Army, operating outside the control of Tokyo, moved into Manchuria in North-East China. President Hoover was prepared to condemn Japan's actions, but he emphatically rejected proposals for economic sanctions. By the end of 1933, Manchuria was completely under Japanese control.

These developments were the cause of great concern in the Roosevelt White House. In May 1933, Joseph Grew, the American Ambassador in Tokyo, reported on the worrying size and sophistication of the Japanese fighting machine. In August 1933, the president himself remarked in private that the Japanese navy was probably superior to that of the United States. However, it was very clear within the United States that public opinion did not support any significant military action to quell the Japanese forces. The country remained preoccupied with the Depression.

Its armed forces were not sufficiently developed to take on Japan. The limitations of the treaties of the 1920s had been exposed. When the League of Nations criticised Japan, the Japanese simply withdrew its membership of the organisation. Intermittent fighting between Chinese and Japanese troops escalated to all-out war in 1937. On 1 July 1937, an incident near the historic Marco Polo Bridge in Beijing sparked off a war which would last until 1945 (and in the case of the Chinese Civil War, until 1949).

5.3 The road to war: Europe

1933 – Hitler as Chancellor of Germany

Two major political figures came to office in the first months of 1933. In January, Adolf Hitler was appointed Chancellor of Germany. Hitler's opponents believed that they had shackled him by surrounding him with conservative politicians who would limit his room for manoeuvre. They also believed that his inexperience would be ruthlessly exposed when they placed upon his shoulders the burden of leading Germany out of the Great Depression. Yet within days of coming to power Hitler was moving with astonishing speed and skill to dismantle democracy and destroy his opponents. By the time Roosevelt was delivering his inaugural address in March, Hitler was ready to use the Reichstag fire and the elections which followed it to acquire unprecedented emergency powers. Within months, all political parties with the exception of the National Socialists had been prohibited.

Hitler's foreign policy

While these developments alone would have been of concern to the West, Hitler's foreign policy was even more problematic. Hitler had made it clear in his book *Mein Kampf,* and in countless speeches, that he was utterly committed to the reversal of the Versailles Treaty. German rearmament, the reoccupation of the Rhineland, union between Germany and Austria and the return of the Sudetenland from Czechoslovakia and of previously German land from Poland were all on Hitler's agenda. Those who took the time to study Hitler more carefully would also have seen that his territorial ambitions did not rest there. A deep hostility towards France, Poland and the Soviet Union meant that Hitler represented a grave threat to world peace. In Mussolini, the fascist dictator of Italy, Hitler was to find a kindred spirit. And far away in Japan, as the militarists gained control of the complex Japanese decision-making process, Hitler found further support. Germany's withdrawal from the League of Nations in October 1933, and the immediate economic recovery fuelled by a rearmament programme which was initially carried out in secret and became increasingly more blatant demonstrated that Hitler did not intend to bide his time. A more ominous test of the resolve of the West to enforce the Versailles Treaty came in March 1936 when German troops reoccupied the Rhineland. The absence of a firm response from Britain and France made a profound impression upon Hitler, who was now convinced that the West lacked political will and leadership.

America's lack of military readiness

How would Roosevelt react? The country that he now led was by no means geared to war. The National Security State that would become central to the construction of foreign policy was still in the future. In fact, the nation's armed forces had been steadily reduced since the First World War. When Roosevelt came into office the army numbered only 140,000, and in the dire financial climate of 1933 Roosevelt felt that there was scope for even further cuts. It is important to recognise several factors that placed further limits around the president. First, he was well aware of the depth of isolationist feeling which was at its strongest in the Midwest but was present across the whole country at the time. These sentiments were powerfully expressed in 1935, when a Democrat from Pennsylvania declared: 'Let us turn our eyes inward. If the world is to become a wilderness of waste, hatred and bitterness, let us all the more earnestly protect and preserve our own oasis of liberty.' (Kennedy, 1999, p. 386) Comments of this type struck a profound chord with the American people. Secondly, Roosevelt was grappling with the most acute economic crisis in American history. Therefore there was little to suggest that any strong leadership of the kind to discourage the emerging dictatorships would emanate from the White House.

FDR's foreign policy outlook

Nevertheless, Roosevelt's cultivated East Coast background and his political sophistication meant that he had strong Anglophile leanings and an appreciation of the limitations of the blinkered isolationist viewpoint. In a revealing private comment in January 1935 Roosevelt referred to the problem of dealing with 'a large misinformed public opinion' (Dallek, 2017, p. 228). FDR never removed his political vision too far away from the ballot box. He knew only too well that interventionist- or internationalist-type comments would not be appreciated in the American political landscape of the mid-1930s. While Roosevelt genuinely shared Wilson's revulsion of war, this extract from a major election speech in 1936 illustrates his desire to be seen as a leader who would keep well clear of the gathering storm in Europe:

> I have seen blood running from the wounded. I have seen men coughing out their gassed lungs. I have seen the dead in the mud. I have seen cities destroyed. I have seen two hundred limping, exhausted men come out of line – the survivors of a regiment of one thousand that went forward forty-eight hours before. I have seen children starving. I have seen the agony of mothers and wives. I hate war. (In Dallek, 2017, p. 260)

Jean Edward Smith offers a helpful analysis of FDR's leadership in foreign affairs: 'Roosevelt's approach to foreign policy was similar to his conduct of domestic affairs: intuitive, idiosyncratic, and highly personalized.' (Smith, 2007, p. 417)

The Nye Committee, 1936

The sheer strength of the isolationist position was supported by the findings of a Special Senate Committee on Investigation of the Munitions Industry. Under the chairmanship of North Dakota Senator Gerald Nye, the committee spent two years between 1934 and 1936 investigating the role of big business and the armaments industry in the American entry into the First World War. The sensational but unjustifiable conclusion of the Nye Committee, published in 1936, was that Wilson had been led into the First World War by pressure from bankers and industrialists. In the climate of the 1930s the American public were willing to believe that the United States had entered the war because of the greed, powerful lobbying and machinations of the munitions makers and Wall Street financiers. Therefore when Mussolini's Italy blatantly attacked Ethiopia in October 1935 the West, the United States included, responded with fine words but very limited deeds. Even in the wake of well-publicised Italian atrocities, the United States continued to supply Italy with a wide range of important materials. A similar sign that the United States (like the other powers) was not yet prepared to take a stand came when American athletes took part in the heavily stage-managed Olympic Games in Berlin in the summer of 1936. With anti-Semitic excesses toned down for the duration of the Games, the United States had missed an opportunity to make a strong point regarding Hitler's dictatorship.

Chamberlain becomes Prime Minister, 1937

When Neville Chamberlain became Prime Minister of Great Britain in May 1937 he was determined to act in the face of the growing menace from the dictators. However, when he attempted to enlist the support of the Roosevelt White House he quickly reached the conclusion that the United States was not to be trusted. Chamberlain recognised the potential value of the United States as an ally, but knew that FDR was exceptionally mindful of the fervent isolationists; he knew that Roosevelt wanted to avoid another war but confided in his sister that it was best 'to count on nothing from the Americans but words' (Kennedy, 1999, p. 404).

Roosevelt's 'Quarantine Speech', 1937

Despite these misgivings, some indication that the president was beginning to distance himself from the strict isolationists came from a highly publicised speech in Chicago on 5 October 1937. He told his audience:

> The epidemic of world lawlessness is spreading. When an epidemic of physical disease starts to spread, the community approves and joins in a quarantine of the patients in order to protect the health of the community against the spread of the disease ... War is a contagion, whether it be declared or undeclared ... There is no escape through mere isolation or neutrality. There must be positive endeavours to preserve peace. (In Kennedy, 1999, p. 405)

Roosevelt watched the reaction to his 'quarantine' speech with great interest; his conclusion was that the country was by no means ready to follow his lead.

Anschluss and the Sudetenland, 1938

The growing international crisis now began to accelerate. In the spring of 1938, Germany and Austria were reunited when Hitler sent his troops into Vienna, disregarding the fact that *Anschluss* (union) was forbidden under the terms of the Versailles Treaty. At the end of September 1938, at the Munich Conference, the West handed over the Sudetenland area of Czechoslovakia to Hitler in order to avoid war: Hitler's threats had made the West buckle. Meanwhile Roosevelt could do little more than observe these dismal events from a distance. In the words of historian David Kennedy (1999), in 1938 'the American President was ... a weak and resource less leader of an unarmed, economically wounded, and diplomatically isolated country' (Kennedy, 1999, p. 419). Hitler was able to cynically take advantage of the lethal combination of American isolationism and British appeasement.

FDR begins to shift his stance, 1939

Once again, Roosevelt used the State of the Union Address in an attempt to modify public opinion. In January 1939, the president told Congress:

> [S]torms from abroad directly challenge ... There comes a time in the affairs of men when they must prepare to defend not their homes alone but the tenets of faith and humanity on which their churches, their governments and their very civilization are founded.

With the world growing smaller 'and weapons of attack so swift', 'no nation can be safe'. Roosevelt's conclusion was that the United States should look again at the 'many methods short of war' which were open to it. Roosevelt now asked Congress for special funds of $300 million for the building of new aircraft. It was a small start to what would eventually become a monumental enterprise, but at this point in time it did not come close to deterring Hitler. Even so, within days of this address the president was reassuring the press that American 'foreign policy has not changed and it is not going to change' (Kennedy, 1999, pp. 420–21).

Germany invades Czechoslovakia and Poland, 1939

A further sign that Hitler saw little to deter him on the international scene came in March 1939, when he displayed his total contempt for Chamberlain and the Munich Agreement by ruthlessly occupying the rump of Czechoslovakia. The policy of appeasement was now over: Britain finally made it clear to Hitler that it would stand firm if Germany were to invade Poland. In a sneering and sarcastic speech to the Reichstag in April 1939, Hitler also displayed his contempt for Roosevelt and the United States, making a personalised attack on Roosevelt; it became clearer than ever that events had now assumed a dreadful momentum. On 1 September 1939, Roosevelt was woken in the middle of the night to be informed that the invasion of Poland had begun. Roosevelt replied: 'It has come at last. God help us all!' (Kennedy, 1999, p. 425) Even when the 'lightning war' over Poland began, with German fighter planes screaming over

Warsaw and with ominous signs of ill-treatment of the Jews, the United States was not yet ready to step in. In one of his most sombre 'fireside chats', Roosevelt told the American people that the United States 'will remain a neutral nation ... I cannot ask that every American remain neutral in thought ... Even a neutral cannot be asked to close his mind or close his conscience.' Beyond this, Roosevelt repeatedly stressed 'We are not going in.' (Kennedy, 1999, p. 427) His strategy remained the one announced in January 1939 of 'methods short of war'. Meanwhile, the isolationists remained as vocal as ever. Charles Lindbergh, the daring pilot of *The Spirit of St. Louis*, declared:

> The destiny of this country does not call for our involvement in European wars ... One need only glance at a map to see where our true frontiers lie. What more could we ask than the Atlantic Ocean on the east and the Pacific on the west? (In Kennedy, 1999, p. 433)

'The Phoney War', 1940

The isolationists' cause seemed to be borne out when the destruction of Poland was followed by a period of calm dubbed 'the Phoney War'. For a while it seemed as though the drama had come to an end. In fact, it had just begun. In a series of stunning blows in April–June 1940, Hitler seized Denmark, Norway, Holland, Belgium, Luxembourg and then France. Fate now placed the future of Britain in the hands of Winston Churchill. With Chamberlain discredited, bitter and broken, the new prime minister took office on 10 May 1940. As Churchill lamented the fall of France and anticipated the 'Battle of Britain', Roosevelt was also in a grim frame of mind. Speaking in Virginia, he expressed his fear of the United States as a 'lone island in a world dominated by the philosophy of force' (Kennedy, 1999, p. 441). Between that moment and the Japanese attack on Pearl Harbor, Churchill used every ounce of charm, persuasion, blackmail and flattery to persuade Roosevelt to do everything possible to aid the Allied cause. It was this process which culminated in the formulation of what became known as the 'Grand Alliance'.

5.4 The Neutrality Acts, 1935–39

With memories of how the country had been dragged into the European war in 1917 still fresh in the nation's memory, Congress in the early and mid-1930s passed a succession of measures designed to prevent this from happening again. In particular, the Acts sought to avoid two 'mistakes' made under Wilson. First, this time around, America was determined to avoid siding with one belligerent by providing them with economic assistance. Second, Congress was determined to avoid the problems caused by the sinking of belligerent vessels which then turned out to have American citizens on board. With little opposition expressed in Congress, these Acts clearly reflected the public mood which at this point in time was firmly against any intervention (Table 5.1). While Roosevelt had misgivings about the Neutrality Acts, and in particular the fact that they treated aggressive and peaceful states alike, he was acutely aware of the strength of isolationist feeling and for political reasons he was not prepared to go against the tide of opinion at this time.

Table 5.1	The Neutrality Acts, 1935–39
1935 **31 August**	The first Neutrality Act was set against the background of a steadily escalating conflict between Mussolini's Italy and Ethiopia. It stated that if the president proclaimed a state of war existed between foreign states, the United States would prohibit all arms exports to belligerents, and issue warnings to American citizens against travelling on vessels belonging to belligerent nations.
1936 **6 February**	Congress passed a second Neutrality Act which extended for a further year the terms of the first Act and prohibited war loans and credits to belligerents.
1937 **8 January**	Congress extended the terms of the Neutrality Act so that the arms embargo included civil wars, such as the one that had broken out in Spain in the summer of 1936.
1 May	Congress passed an even firmer and 'more permanent' Neutrality Act. It stipulated that whenever the president declared a state of war to exist anywhere in the world, the United States would make no arms sales or loans to belligerents, and forbid US citizens to travel on belligerent vessels.
1939 **4 November**	This Act introduced a 'cash and carry' clause, which allowed the president to make belligerents pay cash for any materials purchased in the United States and take them away in their own ships.

5.5 The Lend-Lease Program

Between May 1940, when he became prime minister, and the end of the year, when he was becoming ever more desperate, Winston Churchill had repeatedly asked Roosevelt to help the Allied cause. In August, the president announced that he would give 50 American destroyers to Britain in exchange for American naval access to British possessions. But with British ships being sunk by German submarines and warships and with money rapidly running out Churchill knew that without further American aid Britain would be in 'mortal danger'. In a letter delivered to the president in December, Churchill presented a stark picture of Britain's dire financial position.

Bolstered by his unprecedented third election victory in November 1940, Roosevelt was placed in a stronger position to speak out against the general tide of isolationism. However, he was aware that under the terms of the Johnson Act of 1934, the United States could not make loans to governments who had defaulted on their debts from the First World War. At his desk, in informal style, on 17 December 1940, FDR used homely language to illustrate the conclusion he had now reached: that it was now in America's best interests to help Britain win the war. Roosevelt told a group of journalists that if a neighbour's house was on fire and he needed your garden hose to put it out, you would not, at that crucial point, argue about the price. Rather you would lend him the fire hose, which he would return when the fire was out. Roosevelt now spoke of lending Britain whatever supplies she needed, rather than lending her money, 'with the understanding that when the show was over, we would get repaid something in kind' (Kennedy, 1999, p. 468).

'The arsenal of democracy'

Roosevelt began his 'fireside chat' of 29 December by underlining the terrible price the United States would pay in the event of a victory for Germany and her allies. He made it clear that he now saw the role of the United States in the war to serve as 'the arsenal of democracy'. Roosevelt wanted the United States to become the major supplier of munitions to the Allies. He pointed out that Britain was not asking the United States to join the war, but was asking 'for the implements of war' (Kennedy, 1999, p. 464). A week later, Roosevelt used his State of the Union Address to personally ask Congress for its support with the Lend-Lease Program. The occasion was also marked by Roosevelt's stirring definition of the 'four essential freedoms' which he believed were central to the Allied cause. These were freedom of speech, freedom of worship, freedom from want and freedom from fear.

Lend Lease, 1941

The isolationists argued that once again the United States was on a slippery slope to outright involvement in the war. Their strength was enough to ensure that when the president signed the Lend-Lease Bill of March 1941 it had been substantially amended from its original form. Despite the amendments, British vessels were soon able to sail away from the United States with supplies of munitions, foodstuffs and other essential materials which would eventually total almost $50 billion in value. The Lend-Lease Program marked a turning point in the war, easing Britain's financial and logistical concerns.

The importance of the Atlantic, 1941

Inadvertently, Roosevelt had also created a situation which would significantly increase the degree of involvement of the United States in what became a virtual undeclared war in the Atlantic. Remaining factors that impeded the immediate impact of the Lend-Lease Program were that the United States was not yet mobi-lised in the way that she would become when she joined the war itself in December 1941. In addition, the isolationists were very wary of sanctioning escorts of precious supplies across the Atlantic. America's concern was that, for the second time, the sinking of ships in the Atlantic by German submarines would drag her into the war. However, the fact that goods were being shipped away from the United States without American convoy meant that Britain faced the prospect of seeing valuable consignments heading for the bottom of the ocean before they had even reached their destination. The shipping lanes of the Atlantic were becoming increasingly dangerous. By spring of 1941 German U-boats were sinking 500,000 tonnes of shipping a month. This devastating level of destruction obliged the president to take a number of measures in response. In April 1941, he extended the zone of neutrality to midway across the Atlantic; United States patrols were now instructed to report the location of German submarines to British warships. In July, American marines were sent to Iceland to deter a German invasion; this allowed the president to sanction the convoying of vessels as far as Iceland.

Roosevelt was now prepared to mislead the American people in order to convince them of the Nazi threat. When in September 1940 the United States destroyer *Greer* instigated an inconclusive skirmish with a German submarine Roosevelt declared, 'I tell you the blunt fact that the German submarine fired first upon this American destroyer without warning ... These Nazi submarines and raiders are the rattlesnakes of the Atlantic.' Raising the stakes still further, Roosevelt warned that Axis vessels 'enter our waters ... at their own peril' (Kennedy, 1999, p. 497). Just over a month later the United States destroyer *Kearny* was attacked off the Icelandic coast, with 11 fatalities. An outraged Roosevelt declared: 'We Americans have cleared our decks and taken our battle stations.' (Kennedy, 1999, p. 499) Yet before the month was over the American destroyer USS *Reuben James* was sunk by a U-boat with the deaths of 115 crew. By narrow majorities Congress now removed the Neutrality restrictions, with the exception of the clauses concerning loans to belligerents and the prohibition for United States citizens of travel on belligerent ships. This period saw a much more pronounced level of hostility between the United States and Germany; however, America's military preparedness was far from complete and so at this stage Roosevelt retained his position of neutrality even though it was now fairly clear that war was imminent.

5.6 The Atlantic Charter

On 3 August 1941, President Roosevelt left Washington, ostensibly for a summer vacation fishing expedition in the waters of Cape Cod. His real destination took him instead to a secret liaison with the heavy cruiser the USS *Augusta*. Amid the closest secrecy, the president was taken through treacherous seas to a meeting with the British Prime Minister, Winston Churchill. The British battleship *Prince of Wales* arrived at Argentina Bay off the Newfoundland coast on Saturday 9 August. Although the United States was not yet directly involved in the Second World War, Roosevelt was ready to strengthen his support for Britain. After three days of talks the United States and Great Britain issued the Atlantic Charter. This was a stirring joint statement of shared principles which would follow 'the final destruction of Nazi tyranny', expressing support for self-determination by the nations of the world and condemning territorial aggression. Churchill left the meeting boosted by the supportive language Roosevelt had used. Richard Crockatt offers this perspective on the significance of the Atlantic Charter:

> From Churchill's point of view, the Charter spelled out a broad agenda in advance of what he took to be an inevitable and much desired event: the entry of the United States into the war. Roosevelt, who had originally proposed the idea of a joint statement, was no less concerned to solidify the relationship with Britain. The United States was already acting as the 'arsenal of democracy', having through lend-lease and other measures committed considerable resources to the British war effort. One further consideration, not mentioned in the Charter but nevertheless of great significance, had a bearing on the Atlantic Conference. Roosevelt and Churchill agreed that both nations should send aid to the Soviet Union, which was reeling in the face of Germany's invasion deep into Soviet territory. In short, the building blocks of the wartime coalition of anti-Axis powers were put in place at the Atlantic Conference. (Crockatt, 1995, p. 41)

5.7 Pearl Harbor and its consequences

Japan's plan to attack Pearl Harbor

The Japanese plan to attack Pearl Harbor was one of the most elaborate and ambitious conceived in modern warfare. Just one element seemed, by itself, to be incredible. It had been decided at the highest level that Japanese naval forces would strike without warning at the very heart of the United States Pacific Fleet. On the morning of Sunday 7 December 1941, Japanese planes, delivered within range by a substantial fleet, would descend upon the huge but largely undefended American base at Pearl Harbor in Hawaii and destroy it. This would deliver such a blow to American forces in the Pacific that the United States would be unable to prevent Japan executing its 'Southern Operation', which would leave Japan dominant over China and the entire Pacific region. The elaborate preparations, masterminded by Admiral Isoroku Yamamoto, Commander-in-Chief of Japan's Combined Fleet, were almost complete. In preparing the air assault the Japanese forces had even gone to the trouble to build a model of the American Pacific base in Saeki Bay. At the same time, Japanese forces were also moving south to take invasion troops to the Philippines, Malaya and – most crucial of all – the Dutch East Indies, with their vast supplies of oil.

7 December 1941

Meanwhile, at Pearl Harbor on the island of Hawaii, most of the American Pacific Fleet was docked on 'Battleship Row', off Ford Island. The American aeroplanes stood on the ground nearby, on the airfields at Wheeler, Bellows and Hickam. With the time approaching 8.00 am most of the men who lived and worked on the base were just beginning their Sunday morning routines. Two hours earlier 183 Japanese planes had taken off from six aircraft carriers and had fallen into their triangular formations for the first strike. As the Americans stirred themselves, the Japanese commander gave the order to begin the attack. Wave after wave of Japanese dive-bombers, torpedo planes and fighters swarmed over the prone base. Within two hours more than 180 American aircraft had been destroyed. The degree to which the Americans had been caught off guard was reflected in the fact that the anti-aircraft guns on the air bases had no ammunition ready when the attack began. Seven battleships and a further ten naval vessels had been sunk or badly damaged. 2,403 men were killed. On the battleship *Arizona* more than 1,000 men were trapped, entombed, as the ship keeled over within moments.

Analysis: Did the United States expect an attack from Japan?

It is sometimes assumed even to this day that the United States had no inkling of this attack. It is now clear that as early as 25 November 1941 the American government was preparing for one. On that day, the American Secretary of State told his

Cabinet colleagues that 'they are poised for attack – they might attack at any time'. On 27 November, an alert was sent out to all American commanders in the Pacific, including Admiral Kimmel and General Short at Pearl Harbor, warning of a likely Japanese attack and urging that 'This dispatch is to be considered a war warning'. However, the same document also suggested that the likely target is expected to be 'The Philippines, Thai Peninsula or Borneo'. The sheer distance of Pearl Harbor from Japan convinced American strategists that the most likely target for a military strike was in the Philippines or South-East Asia; whereas defensive measures were taken at other bases, Pearl Harbor was left completely unprotected (Costello, 1985, pp. 128–29).

In *Pacific War* (1985), military historian John Costello describes how a further warning was almost delivered:

> On Sunday December 7 Japan's Ambassador in Washington phoned the Secretary of State to request an appointment at precisely 1 o'clock, adding 'It is a matter of extreme urgency'.
>
> Alarmed by this, the Army's Chief of Staff, General Marshall drafted a warning to be sent to Panama, the Philippines, San Francisco and Hawaii. 'JUST WHAT SIGNIFICANCE THE HOUR SET MAY HAVE WE DO NOT KNOW BUT BE ON THE ALERT ACCORDINGLY.'
>
> Fatally, General Marshall sent the message by post rather than by radio, and it arrived too late. (p. 140)

Historiography and Pearl Harbor

In the aftermath of the catastrophic disaster of 7 December, conspiracy theorists have been willing to speculate about Pearl Harbor and the possibility of some kind of American deception around these critical events. With the benefit of recent research, however, David Kennedy discounts this possibility:

> Many Americans instinctively believed that an inferior power like Japan could not possibly have inflicted such damage on the United States unless some individual had failed in his duty ... the most extreme accusations have indicted Roosevelt himself for deliberately putting the Pacific Fleet at risk in order to bait Japan to the attack and thus bring the United States into the war – a thesis that simply will not bear close examination in light of the President's unwavering insistence on the priority of the Atlantic and European theaters and the unambiguous conviction of his naval and military advisers that not Japan but Germany was the truly dangerous adversary ... Roosevelt's deepest failure, it might be argued, was his inattentiveness to Asian matters and his unwillingness to be seen as 'appeasing' Japan, when in fact a little appeasement – another name for diplomacy – might have yielded rich rewards ... Despite decades of investigation, no credible evidence has ever been adduced to support the charge that Roosevelt deliberately exposed the fleet at Pearl Harbor to attack in order to precipitate war. (Kennedy, 1999, pp. 524–25)

In *No Ordinary Time: Franklin and Eleanor Roosevelt: The Home Front in World War II* (1994), Doris Kearns Goodwin, firstly, outlines the case made against President Roosevelt by those who believe that the United States could not have been caught so badly off guard without some kind of prior knowledge:

> Historians have focused substantial time and attention trying to determine who knew what and when before the 7th of December – on the theory that Roosevelt was aware of the Japanese plans to attack Pearl Harbor but deliberately concealed his knowledge from the commanders in Hawaii in order to bring the United States into hostilities through the back door. Unable to swing Congress and the public toward a declaration of war against Germany, critics contend, the President provoked Japan into firing the first shot and then watched with delight as the attack created a united America. (Kearns Goodwin, 1994, p. 293)

Kearns Goodwin is a highly respected presidential historian and her considered evaluation of the 'conspiracy theory' against FDR is set out in the extract that follows:

> To be sure, Roosevelt was concerned that, if war came, the Japanese should be the ones to initiate hostilities. Stimson records a conversation on November 25 in which the President raised the possibility that Japan might attack without warning. The question Roosevelt asked 'was how we should manoeuvre them into the position of firing the first shot without allowing too much danger to ourselves?'...
>
> Common sense suggests that, if the President had known beforehand about Pearl Harbor, he would have done everything he could to reposition the fleet and disperse the aeroplanes to ensure minimal damage. For the purposes of mobilizing the American people, one American ship torpedoed by the Japanese at Pearl Harbor would have sufficed. It is inconceivable that Roosevelt, who loved the navy with a passion, would have intentionally sacrificed the heart of its fleet, much less the lives of thirty-five hundred American sailors and soldiers, without lifting a finger to reduce the risk. (Kearns Goodwin, 1994, p. 293)

More recently Craig Nelson offers this final comment:

> The answer to the key and eternal American questions –Why didn't the United States know? Why didn't our intelligence work? Why couldn't our military defend us? – is that in the end, Japanese emotion won out over rational action ... Japan's course to Pearl Harbor was irrational in the extreme. Sense, in the end, did not carry the day. (Nelson, 2016, p. 429)

The consequences of the attack on Pearl Harbor

The strike on Pearl Harbor had clear limitations in terms of Japan's ambition to deliver a terminal blow. First, the carriers of the United States Pacific Fleet were all elsewhere. Even more damaging, in the long run, was Japan's failure to strike at the enormously important fuel-oil store. Had this fuel-oil tank farm been destroyed, American prospects of salvaging the situation in the Pacific would have been even more remote.

The US declares war on Japan, 8 December 1941

On 8 December, in a special address to a packed Congress, a grim-faced President Roosevelt, wearing a black armband of mourning, made an emotional speech:

> Yesterday, December 7, 1941 – a date which will live in infamy – the United States was deliberately attacked by the naval and air forces of the Empire of Japan. [Japan's] unprovoked and dastardly attack [left no doubt] that our people, our territory and our interests are in grave danger. (FDR Library)

The isolationist mood that had constrained Roosevelt for so long vanished amid a wave of anti-Japanese feeling. Only one member of Congress voted against the declaration of war. The country was now firmly united behind the president. On 11 December, Japan's allies, Germany and then Italy, declared war on the United States. Hitler denounced Roosevelt as 'the man who is the main culprit in this war' (Costello, 1985, p. 164). The United States responded by formally declaring war on Germany and Italy. The removal of the question mark as to whether the United States would join in the war was a cause of celebration in China and Great Britain. The British Prime Minister, Winston Churchill, later wrote that 'saturated with emotion I went to bed and slept the sleep of the saved and thankful' (Kennedy, 1999, p. 523). For the second time in the century, the United States had entered a world war.

5.8 America enters the Second World War – the Grand Alliance

The popular mood in December 1941

Unlike the First World War, the United States entered the arena without hysteria, or celebration, and with few illusions about the difficulties in store. In one day, the attack on Pearl Harbor had utterly transformed the popular mood across the entire nation. The sheer sense of outrage over what was seen as a treacherous Japanese attack provided the American people with a powerful unifying emotion. The ambiguity and ambivalence which marked American entry into the First World War was replaced by a deeply felt determination, combined with a basic desire for revenge. The president set the tone with his firm, sober and determined demeanour. Perhaps, too, the American people were more sophisticated than their counterparts of 1917. Newsreel coverage meant that they had a clear idea of the sheer brutality that this war entailed. In Adolf Hitler and in the Japanese the Americans had enemies who were so clearly of malicious intent that the very future of the civilised world seemed to be at stake. The world was a significantly smaller place than it had been in 1917. The Blitzkrieg, the Blitz, anti-Semitism and concentration camps created a darker scenario than the somewhat distant, and to a degree romanticised, trenches of Belgium and France in the First World War.

American mobilisation

No country could match the economic potential of the United States. Its manpower and resources gave it the opportunity to supply the entire war effort. But first of all this potential needed to be realised. The task of organising the country fell to Franklin D. Roosevelt, the man who had done most to alleviate the harshest excesses of the Depression. This process was already in motion before war was declared. The Lend-Lease Program in which America had tried to become the 'arsenal of democracy' had seen considerable increases in production levels. Military preparedness was underway through increased Congressional spending on defence and in addition the Selective Service Act of 1940 had started the process of drafting young men for military service. Roosevelt placed the details of the mobilisation programme in the capable hands of Harry Hopkins.

A series of government agencies was set up to organise the process. The Office of Price Administration (OPA) set prices on literally thousands of products in order to combat inflation. The National War Labor Board (NWLB) set wages, and was empowered to take control of industrial plants if production was disrupted by industrial action. The War Production Board (WPB) was given the immense task of overseeing and co-ordinating war-related industries. The effectiveness of these measures was reflected in some outstanding production figures. A dynamic combination of private enterprise and public control led to the United States reaching unprecedented levels of arms production. Bearing in mind that for so long the country had tried to keep out of the war and to limit spending on armaments, the transformation to a wartime economy was even more remarkable. Within just four years the United States produced almost 300,000 aeroplanes, more than 85,000 warships, 86,000 tanks and almost 50 million tonnes of artillery ammunition. These materials were used not just by American troops, but also by British, Russian and other Allied forces.

5.9 The Home Front

Internment camps

The American people did not in general resort to the mood of xenophobic intolerance which had characterised their society in the early days of the First World War. The exception to this came with the harsh treatment meted out to the substantial Japanese community that had settled on the West Coast. Following recommendations from the military, Roosevelt issued Executive Order 9066, sanctioning the forced removal of an entire racial community along the Pacific Coast where, since Pearl Harbor, public hostility had been pronounced. The process began in the spring of 1942 with the movement of more than 100,000 citizens of Japanese ancestry from the states of California, Oregon and Washington Coast to internment camps across seven states. In 1942 and in 1944, the Supreme Court issued rulings that supported this process.

Domestic sacrifice

In contrast to the treatment of Japanese citizens was American conduct in the war itself when its soldiers and many of its civilians displayed heroism, ingenuity, energy and resolve. The war which the United States had tried so hard to avoid was now upon them; as in 1917, a period of 'fiery sacrifice' was now in store. A measure of the extent that the United States committed itself to the war effort was that from the start of 1942 onwards fashion designers began to produce dresses that could fasten without any need for metal hooks or zips. Household goods traditionally made using metal were replaced by items made from either glass or plastic. DuPont's entire supply of nylon, which was normally used to make women's stockings, was commandeered to make war items such as parachutes and tents.

Rationing

While rationing was not introduced to quite the extent as in Britain, important restrictions were introduced and rigidly enforced. For example, from August 1941 onwards petrol stations across the country were closed every day from 7 pm to 7 am. Within weeks of the Japanese attack on Pearl Harbor, rubber rationing was introduced by the OPA. In 1942, items rationed included sugar, coffee and gasoline (diesel). The sale of new cars and trucks was also prohibited; in the summer, a coupon system of rationing was introduced. Measures of this type remained in place throughout the war. The war had a direct impact upon American society. With the horrors of the battlefield not far away many people married younger and had children sooner. Sexual attitudes became much more relaxed. Leisure time was valued and anything which gave people the chance to escape from the war, such as the cinema, concerts and the reading of books, became more popular than ever before.

5.10 Impact of the war on the American economy

The war transformed the American economy in a way in which the New Deal could never equal. Five years into the Roosevelt presidency, unemployment in 1938 remained obstinately high at 9.5 million (17 per cent of the working population). It was only when the government began huge increases in expenditure on the armed forces during 1940 and 1941 that the long-term scourge of unemployment began to be lifted. In 1944, unemployment fell to just 670,000. Men who had been reduced to selling apples on the street in the 1930s now found work plentiful and 12-hour shifts seven days a week became the norm.

Between 1941 and 1945, America's gross national product (GNP) increased by 35 per cent. The president skilfully shifted his position towards big business as the hostility of the 1930s was replaced by a co-operative drive to increase production rates. FDR told the American people that 'Dr Win-the-war' had replaced 'Dr New

Deal'. The country moved into a period of prosperity not seen since the 1920s. The unemployment rate, which had stood at 14.6 per cent in 1940, fell to just 1.2 per cent four years later. At the same time workers' wages on average doubled. Lucrative overtime was readily available. Prosperity even returned to elements of the agricultural sector (although small farmers continued to struggle) as the stimulation of wartime production breathed new life into virtually every sector of the economy.

Armaments production

Corporate profits soared with the biggest share of military contracts going to huge corporations such as US Steel, Ford and General Electric. Companies which invested in industrial retooling for military production were given substantial tax incentives. The Reconstruction Finance Corporation provided massive government loans so that industrial plant could be expanded.

Doris Kearns Goodwin (1994) describes how the president himself provided the impetus for the sweeping changes that now took place:

> 'We must raise our sights all along the production line,' Roosevelt told the Congress in his State of the Union message on January 6, 1942. 'Let no man say it cannot be done.' He then proceeded to outline a staggering set of production goals for 1942: sixty thousand planes, forty-five thousand tanks, twenty thousand aircraft guns, six million tons of merchant shipping. 'The figures,' *US News* reported, 'reached such astronomical proportions that human minds could not reach around them. Only by symbols could they be understood; a plane every four minutes in 1943; a tank every seven minutes; two seagoing ships a day.' (Kearns Goodwin, 1994, p. 313)

The Liberty Ship

In some cases the emphasis was on quantity rather than quality. This was most evident in the production of the Liberty Ship. David Kennedy states:

> The Liberty Ship was the workhorse of both the British and the American merchant fleets: a 440-foot-long vessel that could steam at a sluggish ten knots and into whose five holds a skilled cargo master could pack 300 freight cars, 2840 jeeps, 440 tanks, 230 million rounds of rifle ammunition ... By 1943 construction crews were splashing Liberty Ships from scratch in forty-one days. In November 1942 workers in Henry Kaiser's mammoth Richmond, California, shipyard put together one ship, the *Robert E. Peary*, complete with life jackets and coat hangers aboard, in exactly four days, fifteen hours, and twenty-six minutes. The *Peary* was a publicity stunt, but it augured a further reduction in average construction time at the extraordinarily productive Richmond yard to just seventeen days. (Kennedy, 1999, pp. 649–50)

Women in the workforce

Further positive developments included the entry of almost 60 per cent of the female population into the labour force. In *The American Century*, Harold Evans describes how:

> Women welded, riveted, cut steel, and assembled bombs and tanks. Half of them were married, and one in five had a husband away in the armed services. Every second worker in ordnance and electrical manufacturing plants and every third worker in aircraft factories was a woman. Women were thought to be better than men for welding in tight corners and fiddling with fuses because of their smaller fingers. They made the fuses for most of their bombs ... Yet on average Rosie earned only 60 per cent of the male wage. Women pilots got 20 per cent less than men of the same grade ...
>
> Nor did the influx of women transform social attitudes. Women were hissed in some workplaces where men feared they would be taking their work ... The working women helped to win the war, but they had no effective champion for their social concerns. The middle-class women's organizations were preoccupied with more general civic issues than Rosie the Riveter's problems in being worker, wife, mother and housekeeper. (Evans, 1998, pp. 348–49)

At the same time the far-reaching Revenue Act of 1942 meant that more Americans paid more income tax than ever before. Taxation levels enabled the United States to cover almost half the total cost of the war, estimated by economic historians as approximately $300 billion.

5.11 The war in Europe

When the United States belatedly entered the war in December 1941 the outcome appeared far from certain. The Japanese attack on Pearl Harbor had delivered a devastating blow to the fleet in the Pacific. The German invasion of the Soviet Union was only six months old and Hitler's forces were yet to suffer the reverses which would prove the turning point in the entire war. In the Atlantic, German submarines were exacting a heavy toll on Allied shipping. The situation in the Middle East and North Africa was equally bleak. It had already been agreed by the military strategists that in the event of the United States entering the war, priority would be given to Anglo-American action against Hitler's forces in Europe. Yet the precarious situation in the Pacific meant that the United States was forced to act there as a matter of urgency.

US bombing raids in Europe

It was not until the summer of 1942 that units of the air force were able to join in the bombing raids over Germany which would eventually prove so decisive in the outcome of the war. Of even greater significance, both strategically and psychologically, were the daylight bombing raids carried out by B-17s in 1943. While the Americans inflicted substantial damage on German cities, it was not yet enough to secure victory; more critical was the reversal in fortune of the German forces in the Soviet Union. From 1943 onwards a combination of Soviet resistance and Russian weather made the task of the German Army in the Soviet Union look increasingly impossible.

Operation Overlord

Meanwhile Churchill and Roosevelt agreed at their meeting in Canada in the summer of 1943 that they would switch the focus of their effort away from the Mediterranean and towards an amphibious invasion of France across the English Channel. The operation, known as Operation Overlord, was put into action on 6 June 1944. In just two weeks, 1 million Allied troops landed in France. By the end of July these forces were able to penetrate German defences and move into France. Paris was liberated at the end of August, followed by Belgium and Luxembourg a month later. By September 1944, Allied forces were in Germany itself. The role of General Eisenhower in masterminding the Allied invasion was of the greatest significance. His efforts were rewarded with the realisation that just as Allied forces were breaking through in the west, the Red Army had forced German forces back into Poland in the east.

Germany's military collapse

Although the Germans launched a desperate counter-offensive at the end of 1944 it was now only a matter of time before the Germans would collapse. Although German resistance had raised doubts in Allied quarters and threatened the solidarity of the Anglo-American leadership, a fresh Soviet assault in January 1945 marked the beginning of the end. As Russian troops moved into Berlin in April, Allied forces moved across the Rhine and eastward with little resistance. The Allied Conference at Yalta of February 1945 took place at a time when the 'Big Three' (the United Kingdom, the United States and the Soviet Union) knew that victory was certain. Roosevelt's death in April 1945 meant that he was unable to see the moment of triumph, but his firm leadership undoubtedly played a major role in the events which culminated in Hitler's suicide and the subsequent German surrender.

5.12 The war in the Mediterranean

The sheer complexity of the Second World War, with its disparate conflicts and the terrible urgency that surrounded every strategic decision, meant that it was unlikely that the newly forged Anglo-American military alliance would always run smoothly. In the early days of the conflict Churchill's views held sway, but as events unfolded the United States military leadership became less willing to fall in line. Churchill was convinced that the Allies could do substantial damage with relatively little cost by launching an attack on the Axis powers in what he termed 'the soft underbelly' of the Mediterranean. General Eisenhower, for the Americans, favoured a more direct approach across the English Channel (this would eventually take shape as Operation Overlord). With the Soviet Union under huge pressure from the German onslaught in the east, FDR had promised the opening up of a 'second front' in Europe before 1942 was over. However, in the first instance Churchill's will prevailed and preparations for an Anglo-American move in French North Africa were approved.

British and American forces under Eisenhower's command landed in November 1942. Within six months, a fierce and costly campaign concluded with the decisive capture of Tunis in May 1943 and the mass surrender of German and Italian troops. It was an important success for the Allies. At the Casablanca Conference of January 1943, it was decided that the next offensive would be to invade Sicily, while the attack on France would be deferred. The Allies now announced that they would accept nothing less than 'unconditional surrender' from the Axis powers. The Sicily invasion of July 1943 quickly achieved its objective and led to the collapse of Mussolini's government in the same month. In September, the new Italian government under Marshal Badoglio changed sides and joined in the war against Germany. Despite this turn of events, the Germans continued to fight stubbornly, moving forces to occupy Rome and to build formidable defences. It was not until June 1944 that the Allies recovered Rome, and fighting continued in Italy until the war came to an end in April–May 1945.

5.13 The war in the Pacific

The Japanese strike on Pearl Harbor gave Japan a massive early advantage from which the United States took months to recover. The Japanese conquest of the Philippines in 1942 underlined the scale of the problem that the United States faced in the Pacific. It was not until the Battle of Midway in June 1942, when American naval and air forces inflicted crippling losses on the Japanese fleet and combined to prevent a Japanese takeover of the strategically important Midway Island, that Japan suffered a serious reversal. To an extent, the United States had regained the initiative in the region. Gradually it gained the upper hand, with major successes at Guadalcanal in February 1943 and with a victory in the First Battle of the Philippine Sea in June 1944. Increasing American control in the Philippines meant that by the spring of 1945 an approach to the Japanese home islands could be made (Table 5.2).

Iwo Jima and Okinawa

The Pacific islands of Iwo Jima and Okinawa assumed massive strategic and symbolic importance in the early months of 1945. These islands could be transformed into air bases for the bombing of Tokyo and other major cities; the advance on the home islands would follow, and the Japanese will to resist would be eroded. The Japanese decided to offer fanatical resistance in order to reduce America's willingness to carry on with an invasion of the Japanese home islands. On Iwo Jima, the Japanese constructed an elaborate network of defensive tunnels, and it took five weeks of bitter fighting, at a cost of more than 24,000 casualties, before the United States took the island. On Okinawa the United States suffered a further 20,195 dead and 55,162 wounded. Japan had now lost the last of its naval force, and a further 691 Japanese aircraft were destroyed. While Japan's forces had suffered irreversible losses, there were those in the Japanese government who remained determined to resist at all costs. The Japanese government was now divided between factions who advocated peace and those who would never surrender. Meanwhile, the capture of the islands of Okinawa and Iwo Jima in the spring of 1945 gave America a base for the bombing of Japan's increasingly vulnerable cities.

The bombing of Japanese cities

America's military leaders now knew that further 'island-hopping' through the Pacific could be achieved only at a terrible cost. In March 1945, in order to try to secure a Japanese surrender, the United States launched a series of massive low-level air raids on key Japanese cities. This intensive bombing campaign was still going on when President Truman entered the White House and was told that the top-secret mission to develop an atomic bomb (the Manhattan Project) was nearing its conclusion. Truman's advisers knew that the annihilation of the Japanese Air Force by the spring of 1945 meant that Japan's densely populated cities were now exposed to the possibility of low-altitude bombing. The Allies had decided that the massive civilian casualties would shatter morale more quickly than a protracted military campaign against determined professional soldiers. The bombing began in March 1945; catastrophic damage was inflicted and huge civilian casualties incurred. However, when Harry S. Truman came to the Oval Office a Japanese surrender remained elusive.

Table 5.2 The war in the Pacific, 1941–45

1941 7 December	Japanese attack on Pearl Harbor and Japanese Air Force attack on United States bases in the Philippines, Wake Island and Guam. British bases at Hong Kong and Singapore under attack. A Japanese invasion force moved in on Malaya and Thailand. Japan declared war on the United States.
8 December	The United States and Great Britain declared war on Japan.
11 December	Germany and Italy declared war on the United States.
13 December	Japanese forces took control of Guam.
23–25 December	The American base at Wake Island fell to Japan.
1942 2 January	Japan took control of Manila.
17 January	Burma invaded by Japan.
15 February	Japan occupied Malaya and Singapore.
4–9 May	Japanese and American navy in exchanges in the Coral Sea.
6 May	American forces surrendered the Philippines to Japan.
4–6 June	Major Japanese defeat in the Battle of Midway.
August	In the Battle of Savo Island, the Japanese Navy sank four Allied cruisers.
7 August	United States troops landed at Guadalcanal, disrupting Japanese construction of an airstrip.
September	Tojo resigned as Japanese Foreign Minister; Japan suffered a significant defeat following their attack on the Guadalcanal airfield.

Continued

October	Japanese aircraft carrier *Yara* sunk in the Battle of Santa Cruz.
November	American Navy achieved a major victory in battle for control of the Solomon Islands.
December	Japan planned to evacuate Guadalcanal.
1943 January	Buna in New Guinea captured from Japan by American forces.
February	Japan withdrew from Guadalcanal.
March	Japan suffered major losses in the battle of the Bismarck Sea.
July	Japan defeated in the sea battle at Kolombangara. United States won the air battle over the Solomon Islands.
November	Allies took Tarawa and Makin Islands from the Japanese. Roosevelt, Churchill and Jiang Jieshi (Chiang Kai-shek) agreed to accept only unconditional Japanese surrender and to seize all Japan's islands in the Pacific.
1944 February	The Allies surrounded the Japanese naval base at Rabaul.
June	The United States launched a sustained air war against Japan, and inflicted heavy losses upon Japan in the first Battle of the Philippine Sea.
July	Moderate elements in the Japanese government began to look for a speedy end to the war.
October	Japanese fleet suffered major losses in the Battle for Leyte Gulf.
1945 February–March	The United States Marine Corps sustained heavy losses in the invasion and capture of Iwo Jima.
March	America began low-level bombing raids of Japanese cities. In a firebombing raid on Tokyo, 185,000 Japanese civilians were killed or wounded.
April	United States marines captured Okinawa in the Ryuku Islands, a major island en route to Japan itself, at a cost of 50,000 casualties. Japan suffered 111,000 dead and lost 4,000 aircraft. Emperor Hirohito appointed Suzuki as prime minister and told him to seek an end to the war.
May	Rangoon fell to British troops, completing the recapture of Burma. Germany surrendered unconditionally on 7 May.
July	US troops liberated the Philippines. In the same month, the Manhattan Project achieved its objective of successfully exploding an atomic bomb.
July–August	At the Potsdam ('Terminal') Conference, Truman told Stalin that the United States had developed a new weapon. The Potsdam Declaration urged Japan to surrender or risk the 'utter devastation of the Japanese homeland'. A split in the government meant that Suzuki was unable to persuade the hard-line military generals to surrender.
6 August	America dropped an atomic bomb on the city of Hiroshima.
8 August	The Soviet Union declared war on Japan.
9 August	America dropped a second atomic device, this time on the port of Nagasaki.
10 August	Japan offered to surrender.

Continued

| 14 August | The Japanese government accepted Allied peace terms which allowed Emperor Hirohito to retain his position; American troops began the occupation of Japan. |
| 2 September | General MacArthur accepted Japan's surrender on board the United States battleship *Missouri* in Tokyo Bay. |

5.14 The election of 1944

Given the nature of the wartime emergency, it was not surprising that the Democratic Party turned once again, and for the last time, to the man who had brought them three successive election victories. At the Democratic Party Convention in Chicago in July 1944 the party nominated Franklin D. Roosevelt by acclamation. On the first ballot Roosevelt received 1,086 votes. Meanwhile in the Republican Convention, also held in Chicago, the GOP turned to Thomas Dewey. Dewey was also nominated on the first ballot, with 1,056 votes. In second place was Douglas MacArthur, who registered just one vote.

During the campaign it did not seem certain that Roosevelt would win. The sacrifices made over the previous three years, including a degree of rationing, shortages of some items and inflationary pressures in the economy did not endear all of the electorate to the incumbent. Roosevelt was obviously weary and unwell, confiding to one distant cousin that he felt 'like a boiled owl'. But 'the old soldier' rallied during the campaign to refute Dewey's claim that FDR's administration had 'grown tired, old and quarrelsome' (Lelyveld, 2016, p. 8).

Vice President Truman

Roosevelt's ticket was bolstered by the arrival on the scene of Senator Harry S. Truman who replaced the incumbent vice president Henry A. Wallace. Truman was from Missouri, and this boosted the party's fortunes in the Midwest and in the South. Dewey was also an energetic campaigner. As Governor of New York, he had established a reputation as a lively and honest man who would appeal to moderate forces within the party. Others claimed he was aloof and formal, with one observer comparing Dewey to the 'bridegroom on the wedding cake'. Dewey accepted large portions of the New Deal, but claimed that the Republicans could manage the war better than the Democrats. The result was the closest of Roosevelt's record four election victories. The Democrats performed particularly well in urban areas and also made significant gains in both elements of Congress (Table 5.3).

Table 5.3 The result of the 1944 presidential election

Candidate	Party	Electoral College votes	Popular votes
Franklin D. Roosevelt (New York)	Democrat	432	25,602,504
Thomas E. Dewey (New York)	Republican	99	22,006,285

5.15 The Manhattan Project

Scientific background

The scientific foundations for America's nuclear weapons programme came with the publication in 1905 of Einstein's *Special Theory of Relativity*, and with the splitting of the atom in 1932. Nevertheless, considerable scientific, technical and financial problems remained. In September 1939, only days after the outbreak of war in Europe, Roosevelt ordered the creation of a government-sponsored Uranium Committee. The pace of scientific development quickened with the creation in June 1941 of the Office of Scientific Research and Development (OSRD), under the leadership of Dr Vannevar Bush. Scientists from universities at Princeton, Chicago, Colombia, California and the Massachusetts Institute of Technology (MIT) were brought into the programme. Nevertheless, concern that Hitler would have scientists working on a similar programme prompted Albert Einstein to write to Roosevelt urging him to accelerate America's research. Sustained work on the uranium chain reaction enabled Dr Bush to report to Roosevelt in the summer of 1942 that the development of an atomic bomb was feasible.

Nuclear test – New Mexico, July 1945

The Manhattan District within the Army Corps of Engineers was set up to co-ordinate developments, and from then on the top-secret development programme became known as the Manhattan Project. The project came under the dynamic leadership of General Leslie R. Groves, who established huge resource plants at Hanford and Tennessee's Oak Ridge. However, early in 1942 the centre of the development plan was moved to Los Alamos, in New Mexico, where it came under the leadership of Dr J. Robert Oppenheimer, the director of Princeton's Institute for Advanced Studies. Three years of scientific endeavour, the efforts of 125,000 people and an expenditure of almost $2 billion culminated in the first-ever test of an atomic device at Alamogordo Air Force Base in the New Mexico desert at 5.29 am on 16 July 1945. Oppenheimer was moved to observe, 'The radiance of a thousand suns ... I am become as death, the destroyer of worlds.' (Bird & Sherwin, 2009, p. 309) The scientists regarded the test as an outstanding success and the news was quickly passed to President Truman who was with Stalin and Churchill at the Potsdam Conference near Berlin.[1]

5.16 The Grand Alliance

Although Churchill had taken some satisfaction from Roosevelt's participation in the Atlantic Charter, what he really wanted was to see the United States enter the war. The moment he had waited so long for then came when the United States joined in the Second World War with the declaration of war on Japan on 8 December 1941 and with Germany's declaration of war on the United States on 11 December. On 1 January 1942, the Allies – numbering 26 nations, principally the United States, Great Britain and the Soviet Union – signed a United Nations declaration affirming the Atlantic Charter and pledging joint military and economic action against the Axis forces. The Grand

Alliance between Britain, the United States and the Soviet Union was now a political and military reality. At the Casablanca Conference of January 1943, British and American military strategists met to share ideas and to declare that they would seek the unconditional surrender of the Axis powers.

Beyond the military commitment and the shared declarations of principles, the Grand Alliance was also a personal alliance. Roosevelt and Churchill quickly established a strong personal relationship, and they were also able to develop a rapport with Stalin. They came together at the Tehran Conference in November 1943 to consider the planned Allied invasion of France and the issue of Soviet entry into the war against Japan. By 1944, Stalin was indicating that he valued his relationship with Roosevelt and that Roosevelt was someone he could communicate with; this relationship was aided by the frequent trips to Moscow made by Roosevelt's personal emissary, Harry Hopkins.

5.17 The Yalta Conference

Despite a rapid deterioration in his health and amid great secrecy, Roosevelt travelled more than 6,000 miles for what would be his last wartime conference with Churchill and Stalin. He arrived in the Crimean resort of Yalta on 3 February 1945 and spent 4–11 February negotiating the whole shape and structure of post-war Europe. On the surface, relations between the Big Three were extremely cordial. The level of compromise reached was so great that one historian has referred to the Yalta Conference as the 'high point of allied unity' (Yergin, 1977, p. 62). An alternative view has presented Roosevelt as a sick and weary president, unable to deal with Stalin's forceful negotiating style and willing to 'give away Eastern Europe' in order to secure agreement on his own, personal priorities such as the establishment of the United Nations.

Much of the goodwill at Yalta stemmed from the fact that the 'Big Three' knew that the military collapse of Germany was imminent. The wartime Grand Alliance had almost achieved its purpose. However, the Soviet military advance which had done so much to secure this victory meant that Stalin was handed a huge territorial advantage. This was of particular importance with regard to the future of Poland, the dominant issue of the Conference. Churchill viewed Poland with great concern. He was wary of Russian ambitions in Eastern Europe and declared that 'Poland should be free and sovereign' (Yergin, 1977, p. 63). Churchill advocated the restoration of the Polish government-in-exile which had been based in London since the Nazi occupation of 1939.

However, Stalin's bargaining position was strengthened by the fact that Russian forces were deep inside Polish territory, and would soon be ready to advance upon Berlin and Prague. The military liberation of Poland was accompanied by the creation of a new government in Poland, based in Lublin and dominated by communists. Stalin claimed:

> [F]or Russia it is not only a question of honour but of security ... Not only because we are on Poland's frontier but also because throughout history Poland has always been a corridor for attack on Russia. [Twice in the last thirty years] our German enemy had passed through this corridor. (In Yergin, 1977, p. 63)

A compromise was reached with acknowledgement of the principle that free elections would be allowed in the states of Eastern Europe. The 'Big Three' agreed that some non-communist members of the London-based government would be allowed to join the Lublin government. In return, Russia was allowed to retain the section of eastern Poland which she had annexed in 1939. However, Roosevelt and Churchill resisted the demand that Poland should receive all German territory east of the rivers Oder and Neisse. Roosevelt left Yalta saying 'we have wound up the conference – successfully I think. I'm a bit exhausted but really all right' (Yergin, 1977, pp. 66–68) (Table 5.4).

Analysis: How did FDR perform at Yalta?

Ultimately the United States would resign itself to Soviet domination of Eastern Europe. In the words of Jacques Rupnik (1989), American policy demonstrated a 'verbal refusal to accept the Sovietisation of Central Europe, without having the means or the determination actually to oppose it' (in Crockatt, 1995, p. 76). The examination of newly released Soviet archive material by Yalta expert S.M. Plokhy offers further insights into Roosevelt's work at his final conference. Plokhy shows that the formidable Soviet intelligence network meant that Stalin knew a great deal about his allies and their intentions. However, he concludes:

> [D]espite his obvious fatigue, the president showed complete command of the major issues under discussion. Throughout the conference FDR demonstrated his trademark ability to make alliances, strike deals, and manoeuvre in order to achieve his main goals. There is no instance at Yalta when he yielded on an important issue spontaneously, in clear violation of his earlier position or without consulting his advisers. And there was a remarkable consistency between Roosevelt's positions at Yalta and in Tehran. He was clearly tired and pressed for the conference's early conclusion, but he did not leave Yalta before his main objectives had been achieved. (Plokhy, 2011, p. 400)

Further insights are provided by Joseph Lelyveld in his recent study of *The Last Months of Franklin Roosevelt*:

> If he failed at Yalta, it wasn't because of his physical or mental capacity. Had he been at a peak of vigor, the results would have been much the same. Like Churchill, who would soon face an election, Roosevelt had his own compelling reasons as the war entered its final phase for putting the best possible face on what had been accomplished. Stalin had committed himself to supporting the United Nations and dispatching mighty armies to the Far East. Seen in that context, it was no time

---

Table 5.4   Main areas of agreement made at Yalta, February 1945

- The Russians agreed to support the creation of the United Nations. It was agreed that each of the Great Powers would be able to exercise a veto within the Security Council.
- It was agreed that Germany would be divided into four military zones (the three powers plus a smaller zone for France). Berlin was also divided into four allied military sectors. Other issues concerning Germany were postponed until a future peace conference. Meanwhile, Austria was similarly divided.
- The issue of compensation to Russia for the war damage was passed on to a separate Reparation Commission.
- Stalin agreed that the Soviet Union would join in the war against Japan. In return, the Soviets would receive Sakhalin Island and some territory in Manchuria.

for a break ... The assessment of the one man who was at Roosevelt's side in every encounter he had with the Soviet dictator still seems trustworthy. Chip Bohlen was no apologist. He didn't find Roosevelt 'a likeable man.' But notwithstanding the president's undeniable decline, his dwindling energy, he remained 'mentally sharp' in the diplomat's view. 'Our leader was ill at Yalta, the most important of the wartime conferences,' Bohlen wrote, 'but he was effective.'

Lelyveld also makes the important point that Roosevelt may have 'considered Yalta part of an ongoing process, not a final testament' (Lelyveld, 2016, pp. 287–90). Roosevelt returned from the Crimea satisfied but exhausted. His message to Congress of 1 March 1945 asking for support for the conclusions reached at Yalta was warmly received.

5.18 The death of Roosevelt and the succession of Truman

Roosevelt had faced the worst Depression in American history and taken on the immense responsibility of leading the alliance of Britain, the United States and the Soviet Union in their titanic struggle against Hitler and his allies. These heavy responsibilities had visibly taken their toll. In April the president was taking a much-needed rest at Warm Springs in Georgia. He had taken the waters there regularly since he had contracted polio in 1921. It had become a spiritual home, and it was perhaps fitting that he was there when he died from a brain haemorrhage on 12 April 1945.

A Harvard history professor, saddened by the president's death, met his class as usual at Harvard Hall and began by quoting the American poet, Walt Whitman: 'Hush'd be the camps today, and soldiers let us drape our war-torn weapons, and each with musing soul retire to celebrate, our dear commander's death' (in Traynor, 1997, p. 61). The professor went on to tell his class that 'Mr Roosevelt was great because he restored men's faith.' Senator Robert A. Taft of Ohio said:

> The President's death removed the greatest figure of our time at the very climax of his career, and shocks the world to which his words and actions were more important than those of any other man. He dies a hero of the war, for he literally worked himself to death in the service of the American people. (In Lelyveld, 2016, p. 327)

Power automatically passed to the vice president, a senator from Missouri named Harry S. Truman. It would soon emerge that Truman had different views on how best to deal with Stalin, and the special relationship between the United States and the Soviet Union which had rested so heavily on the rapport between Roosevelt and Stalin soon became a thing of the past. Finally, while acknowledging Roosevelt's place in the pantheon of great presidents it is worth noting that he appears to have made next to no effort to prepare his successor. As Michael Beschloss states in *The Conquerors:*

> Thus on Friday morning, April 13, 1945, when Harry Truman sat down behind Roosevelt's maple office desk, he was befuddled. He had no idea what Roosevelt, Churchill and Stalin had said or agreed to at Yalta. He had not been allowed to read a single one of the cables that had flowed into Warm Springs. (Beschloss, 2002, p. 217)

It would be a baptism of fire.

Note

1. It would take another decade after the atomic bomb test for the fuller implications of fallout to be more widely understood as this extract from *The New Yorker* magazine of 16 July 1955 by Daniel Lang illustrates:

The explosion of the first atomic bomb, on July 16, 1945, in New Mexico ... among many other things, inflicted burns on a nearby herd of cattle and caused the animals' hair to turn gray. (The cattle were presently sent to Oak Ridge, Tennessee, where they and, more recently, their progeny have been studied ever since by members of the faculty of the University of Tennessee School of Agriculture, who are endeavouring to determine the long-range effects of overexposure to radiation.) Fallout from the first explosion in New Mexico also contaminated cornstalks in Indiana that were later converted into strawboard to make packing cartons; some of these found their way to Rochester, New York, where the Eastman Kodak people innocently used them to ship out a supply of film, which is exceptionally sensitive to radiation. The film was ruinously fogged. (In Lang, 2015, p. 11)

Further reading

Beschloss M., *The Conquerors: Roosevelt, Truman and the Destruction of Hitler's Germany 1941–1945* (New York: Simon & Schuster 2002).

Bird K. & Sherwin M.J., *American Prometheus: The Triumph and Tragedy of J. Robert Oppenheimer* (London: Atlantic Books 2009).

Costello J., *The Pacific War* (London: Pan Books 1985).

Crockatt R., *The Fifty Years War: The United States and the Soviet Union in World Politics, 1941–1991* (London: Routledge 1995).

Dallek R., *Franklin D. Roosevelt: A Political Life* (London: Allen Lane 2017).

Dobbs M., *Six Months in 1945: From World War to Cold War* (London: Arrow Books 2013).

Evans H., *The American Century: People, Power and Politics: An Illustrated History* (London: Jonathan Cape 1998).

Kearns Goodwin D., *No Ordinary Time: Franklin & Eleanor Roosevelt: The Home Front in World War II* (New York: Simon & Schuster 1994).

Kennedy D.M., *Freedom From Fear: The American People in Depression and War 1929–1945* (New York: Oxford University Press 1999).

Lang D., Fallout (On Radioactive Debris) in *The New Yorker Book of the 1950s: Story of a Decade* (London: William Heinemann 2015).

Lelyveld J., *His Final Battle: The Last Months of Franklin Roosevelt* (New York: Alfred A. Knopf 2016).

Morris C.R., *A Rabble of Dead Money: The Great Crash and the Global Depression: 1929–1939* (Philadelphia: PublicAffairs 2017).

Nelson C., *Pearl Harbor: From Infamy to Greatness* (London: Weidenfeld & Nicolson 2016).

Plokhy S.M., *Yalta: The Price of Peace* (New York: Penguin 2011).

Schrijvers P., *The Crash of Ruin: American Combat Soldiers in Europe during World War II* (London: Palgrave 1998).

Smith J.E., *FDR* (New York: Random House 2007).

Traynor J., *USA 1918–1941* (London: Nelson 1997).

Yergin D., *Shattered Peace: The Origins of the Cold War and the National Security State* (Boston: Houghton Mifflin Company 1977).

Online resource

FDR Library: www.fdrlibrary.org, last accessed in 2018.

■ M 6 African Americans 1900–45

6.1 Systemic oppression

In a total population of 75,994,575 the number of African Americans living in the United States in 1900 was 8,833,994. This amounted to approximately 11.6 per cent of the total population. At this time approximately 90 per cent of Black Americans lived in the South. The term 'Deep South' is used to describe a geographic and cultural sub-region in the Southern United States. Most definitions of the Deep South would include the states of Georgia, Alabama, South Carolina, Mississippi, Louisiana, and Texas – as the westernmost extension of the Deep South. Finally, Arkansas is sometimes included to the periphery of the Deep South.

For the vast majority of African Americans in the Deep South, daily life at the turn of the twentieth century was exceptionally difficult. Poverty, disease, racism, illiteracy and the threat of white violence marked the lives of many ordinary people. Black children routinely received an inferior education to their white counterparts. Professional occupations were largely closed to black people, and systems of law, order and justice were heavily slanted against them. In most cases black people worked on plantations and received little or no cash income. Consequently nutritional standards were poor, so that black families faced higher rates of infant mortality and infectious disease and a significantly shorter lifespan than their white neighbours. In this extract from *America's Struggle Against Poverty*, James. Patterson describes some of the difficulties faced by black farmers living in the Deep South:

> Typically, they lived in two to three room unpainted cabins, without screens, doors, plumbing, electricity, running water or sanitary wells. They subsisted on salt pork, flour, cornmeal, molasses, dried peas, and beans. Most tenants had not received any cash income in years ... Disease was rampant – two million cases of malaria alone in 1938. One report in 1938 concluded that the cotton states were a 'belt of sickness, misery, and unnecessary death.' (Patterson, 1994, pp. 38–39)

These pressing issues of poverty and poor living standards would on their own have presented a challenging and difficult way of life. Yet since 1661, when the Virginia Colony began passing America's first black codes, the aggression and hostility of white people towards African Americans made the situation infinitely worse. In the Deep South the long-standing 'Jim Crow' laws of racial segregation further restricted African Americans. These laws, which were deeply rooted in the Southern culture, rigidly segregated facilities in waiting rooms, theatres, schools, restaurants, public parks, transport and other amenities.

Colossal economic growth ensured that the twentieth century would belong to the United States. Even the mighty economies of the British Empire and Germany would be surpassed by America's technology, energy and innovation. But in one, hugely important respect, the US appeared pitiful in its lack of progress. As the twentieth century began, the plight of African Americans was, in so many senses, horrific. An entire system of subjugation had been created to replace the crumbling edifice of slavery. The cruelty, violence and economic exploitation that had allowed slavery to survive for so long were now deployed in a new system of terror: Jim Crow. These two words, an arcane term, stood for a society in which the black minority, particularly in the Deep South, were terrorised and victimised for decade after decade. Indeed, it would not be until the 1960s that the system of segregation between black people and white people finally began to crumble.

Such a system rested on a number of separate but powerful ideas and principles that would prove painfully difficult to overcome. The rise of 'scientific' and 'biological' racism in the late nineteenth century claimed that white people were a superior race. This stemmed to a significant extent from complex, deep-rooted sexual and social fears about the black male. The press sustained these attitudes through its racist coverage of all news relating to black people. The decision of the US Supreme Court in Plessy vs Ferguson meant that the doctrine of 'Separate but Equal' was applied universally across the South. Areas such as health and education for African Americans were significantly underfunded in comparison to the same services for white people.

A complex network of state and local laws and statues ensured that racial segregation pervaded each and every area of life. From railway carriages to steamboats, from schools to theatres, parks, benches and even cemeteries, blacks and whites were rigorously kept apart. Violence against black people could be carried out by individuals, lynch mobs or the Ku Klux Klan. The Jim Crow system demanded black subservience or relative quiescence and this served to undermine basic confidence and self-belief.

Economic resources such as land, money and buildings were largely in the hands of white people. The South's plantation agricultural system based mainly on cotton but also tobacco, rice and sugar formed the platform for the development of the Southern caste system. Black people were largely occupied in the most menial, poorly paid jobs. In terms of the right to vote, disenfranchisement of black voters was based on the Poll Tax, Literacy Tests, Residency and Citizenship Tests. The prevalence of the 'White Primary' meant that black voters were excluded from selecting party nominees even before the general election took place. Meanwhile the Democratic Party had been the party of white supremacy and state rights for most of the nineteenth century. If all of these measures were not enough to prevent black people voting, then violence and intimidation at the ballot box was commonplace. As late as 1938, no more than 4 per cent of African Americans could vote.

6.2 Racial violence and lynching

Historian Amy Wood has a deep understanding of the disturbing topic of lynching. She demonstrates that while lynching was the most terrifying and ghastly example of racial violence it was merely one element among 'myriad forms of terror and intimidation.'

Violent personal assault, rape and murder were in fact all more common than lynching which Wood describes as 'an infrequent and extraordinary occurrence'. However, 'lynching came to stand as the primary representation of racial injustice and oppression as a whole' (Wood, 2009, Introduction, p. 1).

It is difficult to be precise about the exact number of cases but we do know that there was a peak in lynching from the 1890s through to the first decade of the twentieth century. Given the lawlessness inherent in these atrocities it is clear that many of these terrible events simply went unrecorded. It has been estimated that from 1880 to 1940 at least 3,200 men were killed by lynch mobs in the Deep South.

Vigilantism had been widely used to punish alleged crimes and to settle scores as part of an embryonic and erratic system of law and order during the settling of the American West. Towards the end of the nineteenth century in the country at large a transition from public to private executions took place, but in the South public hangings continued, the last recorded one taking place in Kentucky in 1936. Wood makes an important distinction between the lawless, frontier society and those who, for example, carried out a lynching in Arkansas who acted with 'ostentation and self-righteous dignity ... The performance of a lynching created a symbolic representation of white supremacy – a spectacle of demonic and wicked black men against a united and pure white community' (Wood, 2009, pp. 42–44).

Wood explains:

[L]ynching became a predominantly southern, racialized phenomenon, as white southerners sought to restore their dominance in the face of emancipation and the threat of black enfranchisement and social autonomy ... racial violence surged at the turn of the century, however, not because southern communities were cut off from modern institutions and customs but because they were undergoing an uncertain and troubled transformation into modern, urban societies. The devastation and uncertainties of the rural economy after the Civil War pushed increasing numbers of southerners, white and black, off the farm, and as northern investment poured into the South, cities and towns grew in area and population. The most spectacular lynchings took place not in the countryside but in these newly urbanizing places, where mobs hanged their victims from telegraph and telephone poles and where streetcars and railroads brought crowds to witness the violence. (Wood, 2009, pp. 3, 6)

The damage caused by lynching went beyond the trauma suffered by the victim, their friends and family. It is now clear that black communities in the Deep South felt the threat of lynching even when they had not actually seen such an event take place. Lurid, gratuitous, coverage of a lynching in the press and word of mouth from one community to the next were enough to spread terrifying details of what could happen to anyone. The white lynch mobs acted as they did in the knowledge that they operated with complete immunity from the law. Indeed, law enforcement officers were at times willing to play an active part in a lynching as well as turning a blind eye to the actions of others. In a similar way to the Klan, the spectacle, crowd behaviour, ritual and imagery of lynching all served to promote a sense of white supremacy and of black helplessness. As we will see in the section that follows, action from the White House to prevent or punish lynching would be desperately slow to emerge.

6.3 Presidential attitudes from McKinley to Wilson

William McKinley (1897–1901)

The nation's capital is a southern city, and in 1900 racist attitudes in Washington DC were pervasive. The first president of the twentieth century, William McKinley, was born in the state of Ohio in 1843. He became president in 1897 and has the distinction of being the last president to have fought in the Civil War. While he was willing to meet with veterans who had served in both armies in that conflict he showed no visible commitment to the welfare of former slaves. His campaign team cynically used the black vote to garner support at the Republican convention in Philadelphia even though the reality was that few black voters from the South would be able to freely take part in the presidential election. While he made more than 30 presidential appointments of black people this was a largely empty thank-you gesture for those who had helped him to secure the nomination.

In more substantive issues McKinley was lacking. When North Carolina amended its constitution to deny blacks the franchise, in violation of the Fifteenth Amendment, he simply stood by and when the state of Louisiana imposed 'grandfather clauses' in a feigned attempt to meet the Amendment he again chose not to intervene. It should be noted, perhaps, that political leaders at this time had no real incentive to change the very system that had placed them in power. As we will see with McKinley's successor, even the most modest attempts to change the racist system were quick to provoke outrage and condemnation.

Theodore Roosevelt (1901–09)

Altogether more dynamic and impressive than his predecessor, Roosevelt was nevertheless a product of his time in his attitude towards African Americans. Philosophically, Roosevelt was committed to the notion of white supremacy, the need to pick up the 'white man's burden' and the potential for white people to 'civilise' other races. In September 1901 when it emerged that Roosevelt had invited Booker T. Washington, the founder of an educational institute for black people in Alabama, to the White House for dinner, the press (not all of it southern) castigated both men. The political cartoons and racist language used to disparage the meeting were vicious. Hate mail and death threats to both men followed. The southern *Richmond News* declared that: 'at one stroke, and by one act, he has destroyed the kindly, warm regard and personal affection for him which were growing up fast in the South. Hereafter ... it will be impossible to feel ... that he is one of us.' (In Morris, 2001, p. 55) When it came to matters of substance, such as enforcing the Fourteenth and Fifteenth Amendments, or curbing lynching, Roosevelt remained silent in the hope that this would boost support for the Republican Party in the South among the white population.

William Howard Taft (1909–13)

Given that Taft was the only man to serve as President and Chief Justice of the United States it might be reasonable to expect an administration of executive and judicial activism to be forthcoming from the 27th President. This did not materialise. While Roosevelt's actions on race are seen by historians as contradictory, those of his successor were not. He meekly accepted the restrictions southern states had placed on voting and was careful not to name blacks to posts in places where there was even a hint of local white opposition. Neither Taft nor his more dynamic predecessor were able to make inroads into the Democrats' southern stronghold even though they had shown they were prepared to disenfranchise their local black supporters. As the next presidential election came into view, the 'Solid South' took great pride in its own candidate, a southern-born and southern-thinking governor from a northern state.

Woodrow Wilson (1913–21)

Given Wilson's intellect, capacity for moral leadership and outspoken commitment to democracy it might be expected that he would have actively promoted civil rights during his long spell in the White House. Instead his attitude in this area has attracted considerable criticism. Support for two-term Democratic president Woodrow Wilson from the African American electorate was generally limited to between 5 per cent and 7 per cent. When the new Democratic Congress worked on laws barring racial intermarriage in Washington DC, Wilson was happy to go along with this. Public amenities such as public toilets and water fountains displayed segregation signs across the city. Federal agencies including the post office, navy and later the interior, were all headed by southerners. Wilson's 'southern' views on matters of race are apparent in his academic work and public papers. It seems that he would have had no sense of hypocrisy in declaring that the war he entered in April 1917 was 'to make the world safe for democracy' while the nation's black population were ensnared by the system of Jim Crow which he perpetuated.

Wilson's most infamous act in regard to racism was his warm support for the film *Birth of a Nation* which featured the original Ku Klux Klan coming to the rescue of white womanhood. The president presented the film at the White House, the first time a movie had been shown there. Ta-Nehisi Coates describes Wilson in these terms in the context of a speech given by the president at the 50th anniversary commemoration of Gettysburg: 'Wilson, born into the Confederacy and the first postbellum president to hail from the South, was at that very moment purging blacks from federal jobs and remanding them to separate washrooms.' (Coates, 2017, p. 75)

6.4 The role of Black Americans in the First World War

The United States entered the war in April 1917 and deployed almost 400,000 black soldiers to the battlefields of France and Belgium before the conflict came to an end in November 1918. A pamphlet published for black people at the time praised the gallant soldiers:

> [F]ruit and flower of the race who have helped to make the world safe for Freedom and Democracy; many of them have fought, bled, and died that their country's ideals

might triumph ... surely in the hour of victory and prosperity he will not be denied fair treatment and recompense accorded other soldiers because of his valuable services and unswerving patriotism. (In Meigs, 1997, p. 19)

The theme that their service and sacrifice in war might now serve as a turning point was echoed by W.E.B. Du Bois, who wrote in *The Crisis*, the magazine of the National Association for the Advancement of Colored People (NAACP) that: 'This war is an End, and, also, a Beginning. Never again will darker people of the world occupy just the place they have before.' Similarly, an African American teacher speaking to his black audience proclaimed:

When we have proved ourselves men, worthy to work and fight and die for our country, a grateful nation may gladly give us the recognition of real men, and the rights and privileges of true and loyal citizens of these United States. (In Meigs, 1997, p. 19)

Such expectations were quickly dashed. This extract from a pamphlet, 'Record of African Americans and American Indians in the Great War', noted with great disappointment:

In almost every sense, however, African Americans were denied the 'fair treatment and recompense accorded other soldiers'. Of the 400,000 men in uniform ... only two divisions, the Ninety-second and the Ninety-third, or less than 40,000 men, were ever actually designated as combat troops. For the most part, African-American soldiers were used as labor battalions, unloading ships, building roads, digging graves, necessary work but not equal to combat in anyone's mind. And having been denied full participation as combat troops, they found themselves denied the recompense that should have come with that manifestation of their patriotism. (In Meigs, 1997, p. 19)

More than 360,000 African Americans had given military service for the United States in the First World War. For many, the end of the war gave rise to a feeling of optimism that they might now be granted greater equality. They were bitterly disappointed. We have seen that little in the way of support for black people came from the White House. We will now examine some of the key individuals from within the black community who devoted their lives to securing better conditions for their people.

6.5 Black leadership in the period 1900–45

Booker T. Washington, 1856–1915

Booker T. Washington was born into slavery in Virginia in 1856. His mother was an illiterate, enslaved cook while the identity of his white father was unknown. One of his earliest memories was of hearing his uncle being savagely whipped but in his own words, the 'greatest injury' inflicted upon him by slavery was that, 'for 250 years we were taught to depend on someone else for food, clothing, shelter and every move in life' (in Dierenfield & White, 2012, p. 31). In 1872, at the age of 16, he made a gruelling 500-mile journey to enrol at the Hampton Institute in Virginia, where he gained an education and trade skills. Seven years later, after spells spent teaching and studying law, he returned to Hampton as a teacher. Increasingly Washington came to believe that if black people acquired skills and education, and embraced hard work then, eventually, a process of racial uplift would take place, and electoral justice would then follow.

Washington's good character and competence led him to be offered, at the age of 25, the chance to be the first principal of the very modest buildings that formed the embryonic Tuskegee Normal and Industrial Institute of Alabama. This black teacher training college with its strict, spartan regime became increasingly successful under his leadership and eventually attracted very significant funding from charitable donations. Washington's leadership and ability to attract donations meant that much-needed investment was directed towards thousands of other black educational establishments in the South. Dierenfield and White say that Washington was 'the outstanding black educator of his day and Tuskegee was his great monument' (Dierenfield & White, 2012, p. 37).

However, his importance went beyond his achievements in Alabama. He urged his fellow black citizens to accept disenfranchisement and advocated educational and vocational achievement instead. Washington's advocacy of steady economic progress gained some support from the emerging black middle class, but his policies did not find universal favour among his own community. It is possible that his pragmatism, during an upsurge in lynching in the 1890s, may have staved off a further white backlash while promoting educational opportunities. Washington's views were most definitively expressed in his Atlanta Compromise address of 1895:

> No race can prosper till it learns that there is as much dignity in tilling a field as in writing a poem. It is at the bottom of life we must begin and not at the top. Nor should we permit our grievances to overshadow our opportunities ... As we have proved our loyalty to you in the past, in nursing your children, watching by the sick bed of your mothers and fathers, and often following them with tear-dimmed eyes to their graves, so in the future, in our humble way, we shall stand by you with a devotion that no foreigner can approach, ready to lay down our lives, if need be, in defense of yours. (In Dierenfield & White, 2012, p. 38)

The ethos of the Atlanta Address was further addressed in Washington's *Up from Slavery* (1901). In the same year, though, the extent of the racial hostility that he was attempting to overcome was underlined by the hostility that greeted the news that he had dined with President Roosevelt at the White House. Washington nevertheless remained consistent in his outlook but did become a somewhat more emphatic critic of the Jim Crow system in his later life. He died in November 1915 at the age of 59.

William Edward Burghardt Du Bois, 1868–1963

Washington's blend of pragmatism and compromise was fiercely attacked by the most eminent black academic of the time, W.E.B. Du Bois. Du Bois was born to working-class parents in Great Barrington, Massachusetts in 1868. A free black, he attended Fisk University and then became the first African American to gain a PhD from Harvard University. After Harvard he secured a post teaching classics at Wilberforce University in what became a career of outstanding academic achievement and scholarship highlighted by his work at Atlanta University where he taught sociology and history. Du Bois was by no means confined to academia, and his political activism was instrumental in jointly founding the NAACP. Du Bois remained with the NAACP for two decades and through its highly influential and articulate newspaper and persistent challenges to the racist system through the courts, performed outstanding work for the black community.

In his best known work, *The Souls of Black Folk*, published in 1903, he accused Washington, 'The Great Accommodator', of betraying black people. Du Bois argued that black progress rested on active political opposition to the caste system. He believed this leadership would stem from the 'talented tenth' of 'exceptional men' who would provide the African American community with the direction it needed to rise above menial work and circumstances. In 1905 Du Bois and fellow militants founded the Niagara Movement which called for 'every single right that belongs to a freeborn American, political, civil and social' (Jones, 1995, p. 271). Moving in this direction served to alienate Du Bois from Washington, and the Niagara Movement was unable to sustain itself through issues of funding and organisation. Even so, it is seen by many as the forerunner of more organised black protests that would follow in the later twentieth century. While individuals such as Washington and Du Bois are of great significance, the emergence of a highly motivated civil rights organisation in response to the racially charged events of 1908 was of particularly long-lasting importance.

The National Association for the Advancement of Colored People (NAACP)

A horrific lynching which took place in 1908, in Springfield Illinois, attracted national attention, not least because it occurred close to the tomb of the great president Abraham Lincoln. This shocking event prompted a conference a year later which led to the formation of the National Association for the Advancement of Colored People (NAACP). This dynamic organisation would make a long-lasting contribution to the liberation of black people from the evils of segregation. The Association campaigned for the end of segregation and for equal voting rights and educational opportunities for black people. Some of its most effective work came from a protracted series of legal challenges and litigation. Many of those who worked for the NAACP in its early years were white, supported by a number of black activists who were largely middle class. Not least in the organisation was Du Bois who was instrumental in its formation and became the editor of its influential newspaper, *The Crisis*, for the next two decades.

Marcus Garvey, 1887–1940

While the middle-class nature of the NAACP and the National Urban League denied these organisations a significant foothold among the black urban population, this cannot be said of the larger-than-life leadership of Marcus Garvey. Born in Jamaica in 1887 he arrived in the United States in 1916. By this time he had already established the Universal Negro Improvement Association (UNIA). Some basic principles enabled Garvey to attract a substantial following. Firstly, Garvey emphatically argued that equality for blacks was simply not attainable in a society as racially prejudiced as the United States. Secondly, Garvey's charismatic appeal to racial pride and a glorification of the African heritage was extremely attractive. Finally, he urged black people to go 'back to Africa' to embrace their 'Fatherland' and racial heritage.

Garvey became a wildly popular but hugely divisive figure. To his adoring followers in the ghetto the combination of racial pride and beguiling pageantry attracted up to half a million members to the UNIA by 1925. While a mass return to Africa did not take place, membership of Garvey's satellite organisations such as the Universal African Black Cross Nurses and the Black Star steamship line reflected the popularity of his message. However, to the establishment it was easy to see him as a radical and a challenge to the existing order. In 1923 Garvey was found guilty of fraud in relation to the mail and four years later he was deported to Jamaica. He died in London in 1940 at the age of 52. The movement withered without him but the influence of the 'Back to Africa' movement on the Black Power activists of the 1960s is clear to see. Upon laying a wreath to Garvey in 1965, Martin Luther King Jr proclaimed him as 'the first man of color to lead and develop a mass movement. He was the first man on a mass scale and level to give millions of Negroes a sense of dignity and destiny' (in Dierenfield & White, 2012, p. 116).

Great American Lives: Langston Hughes, 1 February 1902–22 May 1967

James Mercer Langston Hughes was born in the small town of Joplin, Missouri but largely raised by his maternal grandmother in Lawrence, Kansas. She imbued Langston with a sense of racial pride and a keen interest in language and black American oral tradition. As a child he immersed himself in reading and developed a love of drama and poetry.

As a young man he travelled widely and worked as a crewman on a ship and then took odd jobs to sustain a living. He subsequently enrolled at Lincoln University, a black college in Chester County, Pennsylvania.

Hughes' poetry first appeared in print for *The Crisis,* the newspaper for the National Association for the Advancement of Colored People (NAACP) in 1921. Five years later, *The Weary Blues* was his first book of poetry. His writing focused on the lives of working-class African Americans but contained humour and joy as well as documenting the struggle and the 'racial mountain' black people faced.

Hughes advocated racial pride and consciousness while his poetry utilised jazz rhythms. His work was widely acclaimed: his first novel *Not Without Laughter* (1930) was awarded the Harmon Gold Medal for literature and in 1935 he was granted a Guggenheim Fellowship.

Hughes' output of poetry and prose was prolific but beyond his individual work he was pivotal in what became known as 'The Harlem Renaissance'. This was a concerted celebration of black culture, dance, poetry, fashion, music and art, which became so powerful in the 1920s as to be considered a re-birth of African American art. Centred in the vibrant Harlem district of New York, the sense of overt racial pride was influential much further afield. Many experts

Continued

have drawn connections between the Harlem Renaissance and the Civil Rights Movement that followed the Second World War.

Hughes also established a theatre troupe in Los Angeles and supported emerging black playwrights in Chicago. His left-wing political views led to accusations of Communism but his later work was perhaps more lyrical than overtly political. He will be remembered, above all, as a great poet.

He passed away in New York City at the age of 65 but his work is still frequently cited during times of racial tension as a source of reconciliation.

6.6 The Great Migration

In 1910 almost 90 per cent of African Americans lived in the South. Within 60 years that figure had fallen to just 53 per cent. The gradual movement over this period of more than 6 million African Americans from the rural South to the urban North has become known as the 'Great Migration'. This movement acquired particular momentum in the period between 1916 and 1920, and can be connected to America's involvement in the First World War. The attraction of higher wages in armaments factories in cities such as Cleveland, Detroit and Philadelphia proved a powerful incentive. In addition, economic hardship and white intimidation, particularly acute for sharecroppers and tenant farmers in areas such as the Mississippi Delta and the Alabama Black Belt, combined to make many families leave the South.

For many, the end of the war gave rise to a feeling of optimism that they might now be granted greater equality. However, the new urban dwellers found that their employment opportunities were largely limited to domestic service and low-paid unskilled work. Living conditions in crowded ghettos added to a feeling of disillusionment and gave rise in some quarters to a new mood of black militancy. As the African American population of the northern cities soared, many black migrants experienced resentment and hostility from northern whites. At the same time the importance of the rapidly increasing black vote was not lost on Democrats in the north of the country. Finally, a notable side effect of the Great Migration was its serious impact in diminishing the source of cheap labour which the South had traditionally exploited. Against this backdrop of raised expectations and dashed hopes took place the most intense period of inter-racial tension in the nation's history. Approximately 25 race riots took place in the last six months of 1919. One of the most serious was started when an African American teenager unintentionally swam in front of a white-only beach on Lake Michigan. The teenager was attacked, stoned and drowned, prompting 13 days of rioting, resulting in the deaths of 23 African Americans and 15 whites and leaving over 1,000 families homeless. Further riots on a significant scale took place in Tulsa, Oklahoma; Elaine, Arkansas; and Knoxville, Tennessee.

6.7 Presidential attitudes from Harding to Hoover

The images of the US in the 1920s that come so readily to mind, of the Jazz Age, the Roaring Twenties, stock market speculation and soaring skyscrapers did not form any part of the experience of the vast majority of black people in this decade. The latest fashions, stocks and shares, ownership of motor cars, and the purchase of domestic appliances were largely white pursuits. In fact, for the majority of African Americans the decade was by no means a period of prosperity. For black people in rural areas the industries of farming and agriculture remained extremely challenging throughout the decade. To what extent did those charged with leading the nation in the 1920s concern themselves with matters of race? It may be the case that the somewhat dismissive attitude of some historians towards both Warren Harding and Calvin Coolidge has led to an assumption that neither post-holder would have any significant contribution to make in this area.

Warren Harding (4 March 1921–2 August 1923)

Perhaps no twentieth-century president has been as lightly dismissed as Warren Harding. The beleaguered gambler and scandal-dodger, the philanderer in a cupboard in the White House, seems almost too frivolous a figure to have engaged in any serious attempt to improve the nature of race relations in the United States. But in a forum held at the President Kennedy Museum in Boston in 1988, historian Alvin S. Felzenberg, author of *Calvin Coolidge and Race: His Record in Dealing with the Racial Tensions of the 1920s* presented important and often overlooked evidence on both Harding and his successor, Calvin Coolidge, on precisely this area. Felzenberg's research showed that:

> both Presidents Harding and Coolidge proposed a commission to bridge the divide between the races. Harding told Congress in 1921 that such a body could formulate 'if not a policy, at least a national attitude' that could bring the races closer together. (Felzenberg, 1988)

Furthermore, in a speech he delivered in the Deep South itself, in Birmingham, Alabama in 1921, Harding boldly – by the standards of that time – condemned lynching and called for greater tolerance in racial matters. Finally, as an interesting counterpoint Linda Gordon states: 'The Klan claimed President Harding as a member.' (Gordon, 2017, p. 165)

Calvin Coolidge (2 August 1923–4 March 1929)

Coolidge in 1923, and again in 1925, echoed some of the themes raised by Harding. He urged the creation of a 'Negro Industrial Commission' to promote a better policy of mutual understanding. Both men were reacting to increased lynching in southern towns and violence against blacks in northern cities. Felzenberg suggests that neither Harding nor Coolidge was able to get Congress to approve a commission:

> The House did pass a bill that would have made lynching a federal crime during Harding's first year. It succumbed to a filibuster in the Senate. Coolidge continued to press for increased toleration and racial reconciliation. His efforts are a much understudied part of his career. (Felzenberg, 1988)

The excellent recent biography of Coolidge by Amity Shlaes makes this observation:

> Black leaders had in the past been disappointed with the cold reception they received in his office, too little aware that this reception was accorded just about

every interest group. Coolidge saw his work as freeing the individual rather than the group. (Shlaes, 2014, pp. 313–14)

And the same author points out a letter written by Coolidge after receiving a letter of complaint about a black man competing for a nomination to Congress. Shlaes cites Coolidge's published reply:

'I was amazed to receive such a letter. During the war 500,000 colored men and boys were called up under the draft not one of whom sought to evade it. A colored man is precisely as much entitled to submit his candidacy' as any other citizen. (Shlaes, 2014, p. 314)

Felzenberg provides further detailed insights into Coolidge's record on racial matters:

Coolidge's party retained only nominal control of the Senate during his presidency, with western Progressives often voting with southern agrarians. Neither group was particularly interested in the welfare of African Americans. Coolidge challenged those who heard him to use lessons learned in the war to establish interracial harmony at home. It was one of the most eloquent speeches he ever gave. I cite a key passage: 'We have come out of the war with a desire and a determination to live at peace with all the world. Out of a common suffering and a common sacrifice there came a new meaning to our common citizenship. Our greatest need is to live in harmony, in friendship, and in good-will, not seeking an advantage over each other, but all trying to serve each other.'

Although sincere in intentions, the Coolidge administration found it hard to eradicate the vestiges of Wilsonian segregation. Political appointees who had come to town with Woodrow Wilson proved apt at burrowing their way into classified positions ... With regard to patronage, Coolidge named blacks to judgeships and other prominent posts. His record here was better than Wilson's and probably better than Taft's. (Felzenberg, 1988)

6.8 The Ku Klux Klan

Beyond the world of presidential politics, the mood of intolerance reflected by the 'Red Scare' and the rejection of Wilsonian idealism can also be seen in the resurgence of the Ku Klux Klan and the introduction of Prohibition. The tension which had contributed to the Chicago race riots of July 1919 had an equally destructive impact in the South. The original Ku Klux Klan had developed in the southern states following the victory of the Northern Union in the American Civil War (1861–65). It was characterised by its violent assertion of white supremacy, elaborate rituals and its white, hooded costume. Although the Klan had declined in the later nineteenth century, the memory of its activities lived on in the folklore of the Deep South.

The revival of the Klan was initiated by William Simmons, a Methodist circuit preacher and travelling salesman from Harpersville, Alabama. As a child, Simmons had been raised on stirring accounts of the first Klansmen and he later dreamed of founding his own secret order based on the original Klan. On the eve of Thanksgiving, in November 1915, he gathered together a small group at Stone Mountain in Georgia where they poured petrol over a pine cross and called for the revival of the 'Invisible Empire'. A week later the film *Birth of a Nation*, directed by D.W. Griffiths, opened in Atlanta, Georgia, an epic work which depicted the Klan in a heroic light. This was the climate in which Simmons published an advertisement in the local press appealing for local men of 'intelligence and character' to join his 'high-class order', which would become the 'World's Greatest Secret, Social, Patriotic, Fraternal, Beneficiary Order' (Chalmers, 1981, p. 30).

By 1919 membership of the Klan had reached several thousand but it was the appointment of two full-time recruitment officers in 1920 that really led to the rapid expansion which Simmons desired. With the business-oriented drive and organisation of Edward Young Clarke and Mrs Elizabeth Tyler, membership grew both in the Deep South and beyond. The wealth and status of many early members made the revived Klan resemble an elite club, although it must be emphasised that 'white supremacy' was at its core.

According to David M. Chalmers, 'in the first fifteen months of the Clarke–Tyler regime, approximately eighty-five thousand members had been added, worth, at ten dollars a head, over three quarters of a million dollars' (Chalmers, 1981, p. 35). Membership of the Klan was confined to 'native born, white American citizens, who believe in the tenets of the Christian religion, and who owe no allegiance ... to any foreign government or institution, religious or political' (Jackson, 1992, p. 23). The Klan's hostility was not confined by any means to black people. Indeed, such was the length of the list that it opposed that well-known historian Robert Ferrell has spoken of a 'merger of bigotry'. The Klan opposed Catholics, Jews and foreigners and condemned alcohol, declining sexual morality, dancing and short skirts.

Linda Gordon, in *The Second Coming of the KKK* (2017), has identified six key ideological components that came together in fuelling the resurgence of the Klan. These were racism, nativism, temperance, fraternalism, Christian evangelicalism and populism (Gordon, 2017, p. 25). Meanwhile, Nancy MacLean in *Behind the Mask of Chivalry: The Making of the Second Ku Klux Klan* demonstrates that the Klan provided credit to the needy, took action against petty criminals, enforced moral standards, and made high-profile donations to charity, while its core purpose, of course, was to instil terror. While the Klan purported to represent the values of Americanism, Christianity and morality it was also a force for militant patriotism, violence and intimidation. Many were also attracted by its spectacular initiation ceremonies and its paraphernalia of oaths, secret grips (handshakes), passwords and absurd titles.

David M. Chalmers (1981) states that:

[The Klan's] greatest selling point was the protection of traditional American values. These were to be found in the bosoms and communities of white, native-born, Anglo-Saxon, Protestants, whether in the small towns or transplanted into a newly minted urban America. The changing world of the 1920s, which saw post war restlessness and new waves of immigration combined with ... the erosion of both the small town and fundamentalist morality, brought the Klan millions of recruits. (Chalmers, 1981, p. 2)

The Klan rapidly extended beyond its southern, rural origins, quickly attracting significant numbers in expanding cities such as Dallas, Memphis, Detroit, Los Angeles, Denver and San Antonio. Typically members were drawn from the lower middle class, such as clerical workers, owners of small businesses and blue-collar workers. The rapid growth in the 1920s meant that at its height the movement could claim (estimates vary) between 2 and 3 million members. The confidence of the organisation was such that the Klan was represented in huge numbers at the Democratic convention of 1924 in Madison Square Garden, New York City.

But the abrupt collapse of the organisation was imminent. Membership reached a peak of 2 million in 1925, after which it went into sharp decline. The Klan was essentially a negative organisation. It relied for its support on the criticism of other groups but lacked positive, constructive ideas of its own and therefore its growth could not be sustained indefinitely. From 1925 onwards criticism of the Klan in the press became more concerted.

In November 1925 David C. Stephenson, the Grand Dragon of the Indiana Klan, was found guilty of the rape and kidnapping of a secretary, Madge Oberholtzer, who died in the aftermath of his horrific attack. The outspoken criticisms of vice and corruption in American society which Stephenson had made at the height of his power now appeared hollow and hypocritical. Faced with a long spell in prison for second-degree murder, Stephenson then revealed details of widespread corruption among other Klan officials. The sickening details of the Stephenson scandal appalled the general public including Klan members. Such was the speed and scale of the Klan's decline that one newspaper, the *Jackson Daily News*, urged its readers not to 'kick the corpse' by supporting unnecessary anti-Klan legislation. (Chalmers, 1981, p. 69)

Gordon believes that the multiple scandals involving Klan leaders were devastating to its membership but she also provides an excellent up-to-date summary of some of the other factors behind the Klan's demise:

In the late 1920s, the Klan waned in influence and membership fell almost as rapidly as it had arisen. By 1927 Klan membership had shrunk from several million to about 350,000. Leaders' profiteering – gouging members through dues and the sale of Klan paraphernalia, not to mention criminal embezzlement – grew harder for members to ignore. Power struggles among leaders produced splits ... Rank-and-file resentment transformed the Klan's already high turnover into mass shrinkage as millions of members either failed to pay dues or formally withdrew. (Gordon, 2017, p. 191)

6.9 Presidential attitudes from Herbert Hoover to Franklin D. Roosevelt

The flood that began in the Mississippi Valley in the winter of 1926 and overwhelmed the region in 1927 was biblical in its scale. Seven states, with a large African American population, including Tennessee, Arkansas, Mississippi and Louisiana noted rainfall significantly above average before Christmas 1926. By Easter 1927 large parts of the Mississippi Delta were beneath water that stretched for 1,000 miles in length and 50 miles wide. More than 200 hundred people were killed, 3 million acres of farmland flooded and dozens of towns and cities were under water by the end of April. No national politician was more eminently qualified to deal with a disaster on this scale than the Republican Secretary of Commerce, Herbert Hoover. The 'great humanitarian' was duly dispatched to Memphis in April 1927 to bring his engineering and organisational gifts to the national disaster that appeared before him.

Despite Hoover's best efforts, reports soon began to circulate that in some of the relief camps set up by the American Red Cross, the ugly face of segregation had become apparent. Hoover was informed that National Guard troops were using their weapons to enforce segregation and that black refugees were receiving significantly inferior treatment. The exact details of what happened conflict and indeed two NAACP members observed that 'never before' had they 'seen the color line obliterated to the same extent' (Clements, 2010, p. 379). However, Kendrick A. Clements offers this definitive assessment:

> The 1927 flood on the lower Mississippi took place in the midst of a society based on absolute white domination in economics, politics, and social relations. With camps patrolled by local National Guard units and relief administered by Red Cross chapters made up of local white citizens, racism pervaded the operation. (Clements, 2010, p. 380)

Hoover performed invaluable work in organising the Mississippi Flood relief but he does not appear to have been willing, on this occasion, to confront the racism that, at times, afflicted this operation. It seems that Hoover was more concerned with the economic implications of the flood than the well-being of African Americans. His own political ambitions were probably uppermost in his mind with the 1928 election looming. There is no doubt that Hoover's role in the flood relief programme enhanced his reputation and was one factor among many that propelled him into the White House. Unfortunately for him, once in office he would face a man-made disaster that would make even the great flood of 1927 look relatively manageable.

President Hoover (1929–33)

It seems fair to say that racial matters were never uppermost in the president's mind once the Great Depression began. From October 1929 the president watched as the American economy crumbled, taking with it a nation's confidence and self-esteem. In the era of mass unemployment, food shortages, worldwide depression and political turmoil the question of race, for the president at least, receded in importance. The Depression exacerbated the plight of many African Americans because a shortage of work made many whites 'resort' to occupations which they had previously regarded as the domain of African Americans. This meant that unemployment rates among their community were extremely high. For example, in 1931 around 33 per cent of African Americans in southern cities were unemployed. Employment opportunities to lift African Americans out of the poverty trap were rare. Hoover's personal industry and resilience were not enough to stem the impact of the Great Depression and there is little in his record to suggest that in his attempts to turn the American economy around any sustained thought was given to the plight of African Americans.

Across the presidents we have considered here, historian Linda Gordon states that: 'neither major political party and none of the presidents in this period – Wilson, Harding, Coolidge, and Hoover – could be persuaded to condemn the Ku Klux Klan.' (Gordon, 2017, p. 165)

Franklin D. Roosevelt, the African American vote and the presidential election of 1932

Hoover's catastrophic defeat in November 1932 brought into office a president who had coped with the terrible adversity of a crippling disease. Many historians believe that in dealing with the consequences of polio, Roosevelt found a sense of empathy with those less fortunate than himself. To what extent did his attempt to save the country from complete ruination provide genuine support for African Americans?

First of all, examination of the presidential election of 1932 shows that intimidation, literacy tests and the imposition of a poll tax combined to dissuade many African Americans from registering their vote. Those who did vote tended to lend their support to the Republican Party, which under Lincoln in the Civil War period had done so much to bring about the end of slavery. In Chicago, for example, Roosevelt won 59 per cent of the white vote but only 23 per cent of the African American vote. In urban areas with a large African American electorate, such as Detroit, Cleveland and Philadelphia, there was also a tendency to remain loyal to Hoover.

6.10 A New Deal for African Americans?

At first it seemed that the character of the New Deal would do little to alter voter behaviour. Indeed some New Deal projects aroused resentment rather than admiration. The TVA constructed a new, showpiece model town called Norris, a 'vision of villages and clean small factories'. However, it emerged that this town was for white people only. Other New Deal agencies seemed equally negative. The Civilian Conservation Corps which carried out projects across the nation's farms, forests and parks generally segregated its camps for workers. In October 1934 in Thornhurst, Pennsylvania, rumours of an all-black camp prompted a petition which stated: 'Many unescorted women of various ages are obliged to travel by the site of these camps at all hours of the day or night ... They should not be exposed to possible, indeed probable, dangers.' In the face of these setbacks, the black newspaper *The Crisis* told its readers in 1935 that they 'ought to realise by now that the powers-that-be in the Roosevelt administration have nothing for them' (Traynor, 1987, p. 30).

In simple terms Roosevelt's New Deal was aiming to save the capitalist system rather than to address in any systematic way the injustices of the South. Recent scholarship leaves no doubt as to the extent that the New Deal was a compromise between Roosevelt's need to secure Congressional support for his policies and his willingness not to challenge pervasive racism. Ira Katznelson has described

the New Deal's intimate partnership with those in the South who preached white supremacy ... No member of Congress at any time during the full New Deal era would have thought that the South did not comprise a discrete and coherent entity. Like that of other Democrats, the patronage, influence, and seniority of southern members depended on these members securing their party's majority status. But as guardians of their region's racial order, they assessed New Deal policies for compatibility with organized white supremacy. (Katznelson, 2013, p. 127)

Consequently, FDR was extremely wary of becoming involved in even the most outrageous injustices. The unjust imprisonment of the Scottsboro Boys in which nine black youths in Alabama were falsely accused of rape in 1931 remained a source of international concern as late as 1938. In that year, the President of the United States wrote a conciliatory letter to the Governor of Alabama suggesting that as an old friend he might commute the sentences of the boys so that they 'could be taken away from Alabama with a guarantee on their part that they would not turn up again' (Traynor, 1987, p. 25). When the request was declined FDR decided to remain silent. The last of the men – they were no longer boys – was not released from jail until 1950, 19 years after he had been arrested.

6.11 Lynching

From 1933 to 1935, lynch mobs murdered 63 African Americans while southern sheriffs made no effort to intervene. In October 1934 a young man named Claude Neil, who was due to face a murder charge in Marianna, Florida was seized by a mob and lynched before a crowd of 4,000 onlookers. In 1937 two African Americans were taken from a jail in Duck Hill, Mississippi, set alight and then hanged. Such incidents prompted civil rights campaigners to press for a federal anti-lynching bill. Although Northern Democrats came out in support of the bill, Roosevelt was acutely aware of the risk of alienating Southern Democrats. In May 1934 he told an African American spokesman:

> I've got to get legislation passed by Congress to save America. The Southerners occupy strategic places on most of the Senate and House Committees. If I come out for the anti-lynching bill now, they will block every bill I ask Congress to pass to keep America from collapsing. (In Traynor, 1987, p. 26)

6.12 1936–40

Despite the clear limitations of the New Deal, analysis of the 1936 elections suggests that there was a clear move by African American voters towards the Democratic Party. In Cleveland, for example, every African American constituency voted Democrat, and Roosevelt's African American vote in Chicago was twice what it had been in 1932. A magazine poll conducted in Chicago in 1938 revealed overwhelming African American support for Roosevelt. It seems that this was largely owing to Roosevelt's decision to pay out relief cheques to individuals; the number of African American receiving relief payments increased from around 18 per cent of the African American population in October 1933 to almost 30 per cent in January 1935.

The 1940 Census shows that only one in 20 black males was employed in a white-collar occupation, compared to one in three white males. Sixty per cent of African American women workers were employed in some type of domestic service. The impact of the Depression meant that some white people now turned to jobs which they hitherto would have regarded as beneath them. This made it even more difficult for African Americans to find employment. In the Deep South employment opportunities were even more restricted. In 1940, for example there was not a single African American policeman in the states of Mississippi, South Carolina, Louisiana, Georgia and Alabama. It seems unpalatable to recognise that the existence of such a powerful racist system was not lost on those trying to design a system of racial oppression of their own – in Nazi Germany – in the same decade as the New Deal. But James Q. Whitman, in *Hitler's American Model: The United States and the Making of Nazi Race Law*, makes the connections plain:

> Nazi lawyers regarded America, not without reason, as the innovative world leader in the creation of racist law; and while they saw much to deplore, they also saw much to emulate. It is even possible, indeed likely, that the Nuremberg laws themselves reflect direct American influence …
>
> In recent years historians have published considerable evidence of Nazi interest in, and even admiration for, a range of American practices, programs, and achievements. Especially in the early years of the regime, the Nazis did not by any means regard the United States as a clear ideological enemy. (Whitman, 2017, p. 5)

6.13 The impact of the Second World War

Roosevelt's four terms in office (1933–45) were not enough to substantially address the manifold problems faced by black people in this period. Roosevelt's focus on passing bills through Congress meant that he was prepared to hand segregationists the local authority to run federal programmes in order to smooth the legislative path. Some of the benefits that should have found their way to black people such as a minimum wage, unemployment insurance and the right to join a union were denied on a local basis. While more assistance came from Roosevelt than from his immediate predecessors, it was black people in the North rather than in the Deep South who received the greater share of material benefits. It has long been maintained that it was the Second World War rather than the New Deal that eventually returned prosperity to the nation as a whole. Sadly, the share of that prosperity for black people would remain sorely limited.

The Second World War had a significant impact upon the status of African Americans. Awareness of racism in America was heightened by the presentation of the Allied war effort as a struggle against Hitler's racist ideology. It seemed ironic to many observers that the United States was fighting against racism in Europe when it prevailed so strongly in American society. Initially, segregation in the American armed forces was retained on the grounds that it would be bad for morale to ask whites to fight alongside African Americans. Young African American men from the North were called up and immediately taken to training camps in the rural South, where they were treated in a shocking way. This tended to heighten African American militancy. Many African

Americans who lived in the northern cities were appalled to see how their southern counterparts were being treated.

African American soldiers were not allowed to serve at all in the United States Army Air Corps or the United States Marine Corps. The best way to combat the prevailing racism was for African American soldiers to demonstrate their capabilities, which they emphatically did. During the winter of 1944–45, as the Battle of the Bulge reached a critical point, African American troops were called up in large numbers to fill the gaps caused by heavy casualties. This process, carried out on the grounds of military contingency, meant that segregation in the armed forces was effectively being broken down. In January 1945 the first formally integrated unit in the history of the Army was introduced. This was followed up in 1948, when President Truman opened up all jobs in the armed services to African Americans. In terms of domestic life, then, the process of desegregation was being led by forces unleashed by the war. In December 1946, President Truman issued Executive Order 9809, creating the President's Committee on Civil Rights, which demanded an end to segregation in all aspects of American life.

Further reading

Coates T., *We Were Eight Years in Power: An American Tragedy* (London: Hamish Hamilton 2017).

Chalmers D.M., *Hooded Americanism: The History of the Ku Klux Klan* (New York: Duke University Press 1981).

Clements K.A., *The Life of Herbert Hoover: Imperfect Visionary 1918–1928* (New York: Palgrave Macmillan 2010).

Dierenfield B.J. & White J.W., *A History of African-American Leadership* (Harlow, UK: Pearson 2012).

Felzenberg A.S., author of 'Calvin Coolidge and Race: His Record in Dealing with the Racial Tensions of the 1920s' (1988), speaking in a forum held at the President Kennedy Museum in Boston, in 1988.

Gordon L., *The Second Coming of the KKK: The Ku Klux Klan of the 1920s and the American Political Tradition* (New York: Liveright Publishing 2017).

Jackson K.T., *The Ku Klux Klan in the City, 1915–1930* (Chicago: Elephant Paperback 1992).

Jones M.A., *The Limits of Liberty: American History 1607–1992* (New York: Oxford University Press 1995).

Katznelson I., *Fear Itself: The New Deal and the Origins of Our Time* (New York: Liveright Paperbacks 2013).

Meigs M., *Optimism at Armageddon: Voices of American Participants in the First World War* (London: Macmillan Press Ltd 1997).

Morris E., *Theodore Rex* (New York: Random House 2001).

Patterson J.T., *America's Struggle Against Poverty 1900–1994* (Cambridge, Mass.: Harvard University Press 1994).

Shlaes A., *Coolidge* (New York: Harper Perennial 2014).

Traynor J., *Roosevelt's America 1932–1941* (London: Macmillan Education 1987).

Whitman J.Q., *Hitler's American Model: The United States and the Making of Nazi Race Law* (Princeton: Princeton University Press 2017).

Wood A.L., *Lynching and Spectacle: Witnessing Racial Violence in America, 1890–1940* (Chapel Hill: University of North Carolina 2009).

■ Ⅴ **7** Post-war America

Harry S. Truman (the S stood for nothing in particular) was born in the small market town of Lamar, Missouri in May 1884. He recalled his childhood on the family farm in idyllic terms: hunting for bird nests, picking strawberries and an abundance of wholesome food. He was born with poor eyesight, as 'blind as a mole', as he put it, and was diagnosed by an optometrist in Kansas City with hyper-metropia, or colloquially, 'flat eyeballs' (McCullough, 1993, p. 41). Equipped with his wire-rimmed spectacles he became a prodigious reader, developed a love of history books and thrived at school in Independence, Missouri.

In 1900 he accompanied his father to the Democratic Convention which was being held in nearby Kansas City. A keen interest in politics was in the family DNA. Then, out of the blue, in 1901, shortly after Harry graduated from high school, financial disaster overwhelmed his father who lost everything in a series of ill-judged investments. The family had to move to a much more modest part of Kansas City. Harry's application to the prestigious West Point military academy was rejected because of his poor eyesight and so, desperate to support the family, he took a job on the Santa Fe railroad. He was regarded by most people who met him as a fine young man and from 1903 to 1905 he worked in banking in Kansas. His military ambitions remained and in 1905 he joined a new National Guard unit. But Harry's own prospects took second place to the family, and in 1906 he was obliged to move with his relatives to a farm in Blue Ridge. This involved prodigious energy and hard work and Harry demonstrated an abundance of both. In 1910 he met the love of his life, Bess Wallace. Harry continued to drive himself, but the death of his father in 1914 and a failed investment in a zinc mine in Oklahoma were painful experiences.

When war came in 1917, Harry helped to organise a new artillery battery in Missouri. He was 33 years old, deeply patriotic and with a bottomless sense of duty to family and country. Posted to France in the spring of 1918 he described the work he undertook in artillery training to be the toughest thing he had ever experienced. As always, he threw himself into this and impressed his superiors to the extent that he was rapidly appointed a captain. He rose to the challenge of moulding the 'wild Irish' Catholics in his command and became known for his strict but fair leadership, commanding widespread respect.

In August 1918 he was plunged into the horrors of war, shelling the enemy with poison gas, seeing young men around him run away in the heat of battle and standing just 15 feet away from a shell burst. He confided in a letter home to Bess that he was simply too frightened to run away but to his commanders he seemed to have remained cool under the most extreme pressure. His regiment, like others, took heavy losses but he had earned immense respect from his men. When Captain Truman was told the war was finally over, he was lying in a dugout eating blueberry pie. Harry and Bess now knew more than ever that they wished to be married and a relieved, excited, battle-hardened man set sail for New York in April 1918. In the blissful period at the end of the war he and Bess were married and at the same time Truman entered into a business partnership to set up a haberdashery store in Kansas City. After a promising start, the business collapsed, with heavy debts, in 1922.

Harry's capacity to bounce back from serious setbacks remained a key characteristic but this time his new avenue was in politics which took him into the orbit of the renowned Democratic 'organisation' of Tom Pendergast. Pendergast was the archetypal machine politician, fixer and insider whose authority within his area was absolute. His network doled out warm clothing or coal in winter, welcomed newcomers to the area all year round and expected their votes in return. With this machine behind him, his impressive war record and his support from the farm base, it was no surprise when Truman was elected as a regional judge in Independence. The rank of judge suited Harry and he fulfilled his duties rigorously and fairly so that from 1927 he was elected to what would become two consecutive terms at the higher level of presiding judge, with a population of almost half a million people. The natural step-up followed with Truman being elected to the US Senate in 1934. Truman's well-known connections with the party machine meant that he was sometimes written off as no more than a party man and his re-election to the Senate in 1940 was relatively close. However, his effective service investigating wartime profiteering and waste for Senate committees significantly enhanced his reputation.

With the presidential election looming in 1944 the question of who would be vice president was unusually important. The visible decline in President Roosevelt's health and the strain of wartime leadership meant that there were real doubts as to whether he would be able to serve the full term. But Henry A. Wallace, the liberal vice president from the 1940 victory, was not universally popular. Truman's reputation as a safe pair of hands and a highly effective domestic politician helped to secure his nomination at the expense of Wallace who was seen as too far to the left. Roosevelt showed relatively little personal interest in this particular issue which, given the extent of his wartime commitments, was perhaps understandable.

In contrast to the tired president, who as 'a good soldier' agreed to run for an unprecedented fourth term, the Republican candidate, Thomas Dewey, who had served as Governor of New York since 1942 was young and dynamic. Truman was not regarded as particularly distinctive but he was effective and reliable. The country recognised that wartime was not the time for a change and for the last time Roosevelt posted a Democratic victory. It was the closest of the four victories with Roosevelt/Truman polling more than 25.6 million popular votes compared to Dewey's 22 million. In the Electoral College the margin was decisive with 432 against 99. In normal times, the office of vice president was often derided, even by the post-holder, but this time things were different. Within months, the domestic politician, the haberdasher from Missouri would be the president, and most importantly of all at that time, the Commander-in-Chief.

7.1 Truman and the post-war economy

American supremacy in 1945

The United States emerged from World War II with unparalleled economic and military supremacy. Protected by its geographical position, it had been neither a battlefield nor the victim of air raids. Its industrial and economic capacity eclipsed all of its rivals and this was used to endow the country with a huge, well-equipped army while its navy and air force were more powerful than those of the rest of the world put together. It was the only country so far to equip itself with the most destructive weapon of all, the atomic bomb. For Harry S. Truman, this presented problems as well as opportunities. The contrast in the economic well-being of the country during the war compared to the pre-war period was quite staggering. The question now was: how would Truman manage the difficult transition from a wartime to a peacetime economy?

The transition to a peacetime economy

Given the fact that it was the Second World War rather than the New Deal which rejuvenated the American economy, many experts believed that the end of the conflict would see the economy move into reverse. In particular, it was felt that as wartime contracts came to an end, a massive increase in unemployment would ensue. Signs of a slowdown were easy to see. From 25 May 1945, military aircraft production was reduced by 30 per cent. During the war the Ford Motor Company had manufactured a total of 8,600 bombers, 278,000 jeeps and 57,000 aircraft engines. However, in June 1945 Ford completed its final wartime project; in August, 100,000 war workers in New York State were laid off.

Despite the fact that government spending was suddenly curtailed after August 1945, the widely predicted return to Depression did not materialise. In fact, an era of prosperity not witnessed since the 1920s now began. Government spending was replaced by unprecedented consumer demand. This consumer spending was sufficient to compensate for government cutbacks and enabled the labour market to employ the services of the millions of ex-service men who had now returned to the workforce. Credit should also be given for the manner in which the Truman Administration managed the transition from war to peace. Taxes were cut and generous loans were provided to businesses.

The issue of price controls

On 15 August, the War Manpower Commission lifted all controls on wages. In the same week, President Truman ordered the full restoration of collective bargaining, civilian consumer production and the complete return of free markets. On 20 August, the War Production Board (WPB) ended consumer production controls on more than 200 products. These constructive measures were supported by a major piece of legislation which had been signed by President Roosevelt in June 1944. The Servicemen's Readjustment Act, popularly known as the 'GI Bill of Rights', gave low-interest loans for housing, and funded education and training for ex-servicemen to pursue business projects.

7.2 Truman's domestic legislation

'The Fair Deal'

On 6 September 1946, President Truman formally announced his economic recovery plan to Congress. In what later became known as the 'Fair Deal', the president presented a vision of full employment, a substantial increase in the minimum wage, national health insurance, considerable federal support for education, government-supported housing for the needy and the extension of social security. Despite the upbeat tone of his Congressional address, Truman was unable to achieve the cohesion he would have liked in post-war American society. While he was able to avoid taking the economy into a post-war recession, the period after 1945 was characterised by inflation and industrial disputes on a large scale. As workers moved from peace to war, their expectations rose. With the period of wartime controls and self-sacrifice coming towards an end many workers demanded, and were encouraged by the president to expect, a large pay rise. The loss of wartime overtime payments also worried many workers and heightened their desire for an increase in the normal hourly rate.

During the war, the government had maintained firm price controls across a wide range of products. When the war came to an end, business leaders and agricultural interests expected to see higher prices for their goods as a reward for their wartime efforts. The Truman Administration, while initially prepared to relax wartime controls, was alarmed by the potential for inflation that this new climate had created. If prices were allowed to increase, wage demands would become even more extravagant. Truman, however, found that Congress, under pressure from business and farm groups, was reluctant to return to price controls. A price control measure that came before Congress in June 1946 was so compromised after intensive debate that Truman vetoed it; this was followed by a steep increase in food prices. Truman belatedly returned to the idea of using the Office of Price Administration (OPA) to curtail prices. However, farmers retaliated by withholding supplies of meat, leading to a serious national shortage: in September, it was being reported that in New York City people were resorting to eating horsemeat. Against this backdrop, Truman was forced to abandon his attempts at price controls.

Industrial unrest

By the end of 1946 the cost of living had reached 30 per cent; higher prices led, in turn, to increased wage demands. Industrial unrest, already present at the start of 1945 became more intense as the year progressed. On 2 March striking workers brought ten Chrysler plants to a standstill. In October a six-hour strike by workers at Bell caused serious disruption to the telephone service. More serious still was a strike in the winter of 1945, led by the United Automobile, Aircraft and Agricultural Implement Workers of America involving 180,000 workers at all General Motors plants.

In the immediate aftermath of the Japanese surrender, President Truman had ordered a complete return to a free market, including an end to wartime price controls, and in what subsequently looked like a serious error he gave the impression that the country could now afford to provide substantial pay increases. On 14 February 1946, the president responded to labour unrest in the steel, automobile and coal industries by easing wage and price controls. Within 24 hours, the steel strike, which had seen 800,000 Pittsburgh steelworkers withdraw their labour since January, was ended with a pay rise of 18.5 cents per hour. In February, the president created the Office of Economic Stabilisation, which was aimed at managing the difficult process of reconversion to a peacetime economy. However, at the same time, major employers were resorting to substantial pay rises in order to bring industrial disputes to an end. A strike at Ford was ended by an 18 cents an hour pay rise. Within a month, a similar deal was reached at General Motors.

The potentially damaging consequences of such actions became clear when on 1 April 1946 more than 400,000 coal miners went on strike to demand a pay rise. The serious unrest in the mining industry was followed by massive upheaval in the railroad system. It was these two industries that caused Truman the greatest difficulty. On 17 May 1946, in order to avert a railroad strike, the federal government seized control of the railroads. Even so, within a week, the railroad workers belonging to the Railroad Trainmen and Locomotive Engineers Brotherhood came out on strike, bringing the nation's railway network to a standstill. Of 24,000 freight trains normally in operation, fewer than 3,000 now ran. *Newsweek* reported poignant scenes: 'The Chicago woman kept from her father's deathbed in Minnesota; the 13-year-old Arizona boy *en route* for an emergency brain operation in California; the woman taking the body of her husband back to Cleveland for burial.' (In McCullough, 1993, p. 498)

Analysis: The limits of presidential authority

Truman was enraged by the action of the striking railway men and appalled by the consequences of their actions. At a Cabinet meeting on 24 May Truman stunned his Cabinet when he told them, with 'gray-blue eyes blazed' and with a mouth that was 'a thin, hard line pulled down at the corners' that he had decided to draft the striking rail workers into the army. Truman reportedly said: 'We'll draft them and think about the law later.' That night, in a national address, a visibly tired president declared:

> I come before the American people at a time of great crisis. The crisis of Pearl Harbor was the result of action by a foreign enemy. The crisis tonight is caused by a group of men within our own country who place their private interests above the welfare of the nation.

In a 'time for plain speaking' he said that it was inconceivable that the labour leaders 'should be placed in a position where they can completely stifle our economy and ultimately destroy our country' (McCullough, 1993, pp. 501–03).

The next day Truman went before Congress to ask for powers to draft the striking railroad strikers into the Army: 'For the past two days the nation has been in the grip of a railroad strike which threatens to paralyze all our industrial, agricultural, commercial and social life ... the disaster will spare no one.' Truman called for 'temporary emergency' legislation to 'authorize the President to draft into the armed forces of the United States all workers who are on strike against their government' (McCullough, 1993, p. 504). Although the strike was brought to a conclusion the next day, the president's controversial 'solution' shocked even his conservative opponents.

7.3 Internal division and the election of 1948

'The Missouri Gang' and the departure of the New Dealers

Between 1945 and 1948, Truman encountered a diverse range of domestic difficulties which collectively seemed to have put paid to his prospects for winning a presidential election in his own right in November 1948. Although he was able to confound his critics and secure an unlikely victory, historians have nevertheless been generally unimpressed with his conduct of domestic affairs. While Truman appeared to be committed to taking the New Deal measures of his predecessor and building a platform for further reform, he was unable to retain the services of several influential members of the Roosevelt Administration. Truman was personally unable to secure the loyalty of certain key figures, and they were further alienated by the influence of the small group surrounding the president from his home state, the so-called 'Missouri Gang'. Unable to work together, Frances Perkins and Henry Morgenthau Jr left the Cabinet in the year of Roosevelt's death. The high-profile dismissal of Henry Wallace, who had publicly criticised Truman's anti-communist stance in foreign policy, damaged Truman's standing among traditionally sympathetic liberals. The resignation of Harold Ickes in the same year created a sense that the administration was in some disarray.

The midterm elections, 1946

The midterm elections of 1946 were fought against a backdrop of seething industrial unrest, rising inflation and political division within the Democratic Party. Such was Truman's standing that he adopted an extraordinarily low profile in the build-up to the elections. Despite this manoeuvre, the Democrats were unable to stave off a significant reverse, which saw them lose control of both the Senate and the House of Representatives for the first time since 1932. Ultimately it was this Republican Congress which set in motion the Twenty-Second Amendment to the Constitution which restricted future presidents after Truman to just two terms in office.

The Taft–Hartley Act

The dominant Republican presence in the 80th Congress, combined with the bloc of conservative Southern Democrats, made it extremely difficult for Truman to pass legislation. Although Congress did not go so far as to unravel the New Deal, it effectively blocked virtually all of his domestic proposals. Despite his use of the presidential veto, Truman was unable to prevent the passage of the controversial national Labor Management Relations (Taft–Hartley) Act. Whereas Roosevelt had tilted the balance of industrial relations towards the workers, the provisions of this Bill comprehensively restored the balance of power to the bosses. Under the new Act, the closed shop and secondary strikes became illegal. Trade unions became directly accountable for any acts of violence committed by their members, and had to accept an 80-day cooling-off period before they could resort to strike action.

Despite the difficulties of his dealings with Congress, Truman announced a new drive for civil rights legislation in 1948. In February, he advised Congress of his desire to make lynching a federal crime and to outlaw segregation in interstate travel. Although no legislation was passed, Truman did secure a landmark in the history of the civil rights campaign when he passed an Executive Order in July 1948 ending the practice of segregation in the armed forces.

7.4 The presidential election of 1948

Given the range of Truman's domestic difficulties, it is hardly surprising that the Republican Party entered the election year in confident mood. The visible signs of division within the ranks of the Democratic Party further boosted their hopes of victory. Truman's commitment to civil rights in 1948 alienated Southern Democrats to such an extent that a faction broke away from the party and set up the States' Rights Democratic Party (the Dixiecrats) with the Governor of South Carolina, Strom Thurmond, as their presidential candidate. At the other end of the spectrum disenchanted liberals rallied around the leadership of Henry Wallace to form the Progressive Party. Following his strong showing in the 1944 election, the Republicans again nominated Thomas E. Dewey for president, with the expectation that he would go on to achieve a Republican victory for the first time since 1928.

Table 7.1 The result of the 1948 presidential election

Candidate	Party	Electoral College votes	Popular votes
Harry S. Truman (Missouri)	Democrat	304	24,105,695
Thomas E. Dewey (New York)	Republican	189	21,969,170
J. Strom Thurmond (South Carolina)	States' Rights Democrat	38	1,169,021
Henry A. Wallace (Iowa)	Progressive	–	1,156,103

Yet, against the odds, Truman seemed to almost release himself from the burdens of office and became increasingly self-confident in his campaign dealings with both the press and the public. At times abandoning prepared speeches, the 'new', more off-the-cuff Truman showed that he remained a highly accomplished politician. During a 9,500-mile whistle-stop excursion which began in June, Truman appeared to be relaxed, witty and pugnacious. On a further epic whistle-stop tour he began in September he appeared young and at ease, in contrast with his rather buttoned-up opponent. As his biographer David McCullough (1992) points out, Truman was a more formidable opponent than the Republicans had bargained for:

> The huge crowds at every whistle stop in the campaign heard Truman, from the back of his railcar, gleefully blaming everything on the 'do nothing' 80th Congress. The cry 'Give 'em hell, Harry!' began to arise, and the delighted President would reply: 'I never give anybody hell. I just tell the truth and they think its hell.' (McCullough, 1993, pp. 671–72)

Despite Truman's resurgence most experts believed that Dewey would defeat him; their predictions were confounded when Truman went on to secure a narrow victory (Table 7.1).

7.5 The rise of McCarthyism

> PARRIS: Thomas, Thomas, I pray you, leap not to witchcraft. I know that you – you least of all, Thomas, would ever wish so disastrous a charge laid upon me. We cannot leap to witchcraft. They will howl me out of Salem for such corruption in my house. (From Arthur Miller, *The Crucible*, 1953)

> Various ground rules had begun to emerge, some of them unprecedented. Witches could be male or female, itinerant beggars of prosperous farmers, young or old, full church members or outsiders ... More and more often, when one of the girls pointed to a spectre someone else saw it too. Vision grew sharper in Salem village. Memories improved. (The Witches: Salem, 1692: A History)

The Wheeling speech, February 1950

The anti-communist movement that became increasingly pronounced in American society during the late 1940s and early 1950s is inextricably linked in the public mind with Joseph McCarthy. A previously little-known senator from Wisconsin, he rejuvenated his jaded political career when he made sensational allegations concerning the degree of communist infiltration of the State Department. More recently, historians have placed McCarthy in perspective, observing that the anti-communist movement was already in full swing when the opportunistic, hard-drinking senator made his infamous speech on 9 February 1950, in Wheeling, West Virginia:

Six years ago there was within the Soviet orbit 180,000,000 people. Today there are 800,000,000 people under the absolute domination of Soviet Russia – an increase of over 400 per cent. As one of our outstanding historical figures once said, 'When a great democracy is destroyed, it will not be because of enemies from without, but rather because of enemies from within'. The truth of this statement is becoming terrifyingly clear as we see this country each day losing on every front.

The reason why we find ourselves in a position of impotency is not because our only powerful potential enemy has sent men to invade our shores, but rather because of the traitorous actions of those who have been treated so well by this Nation. It has not been the less fortunate or members of minority groups who have been selling this Nation out, but rather those who have had all the benefits that the wealthiest nation on earth has had to offer – the finest homes, the finest college education, and the finest jobs in Government we can give.

This is glaringly true in the State Department. There the bright young men who are born with silver spoons in their mouths are the ones who have been worst ... In my opinion the State Department, which is one of the most important government departments, is thoroughly infested with Communists. I have in my hand fifty-seven cases of individuals who would appear to be either card carrying members or certainly loyal to the Communist Party, but who nevertheless are still helping to shape our foreign policy. (In Schreker, 1994, pp. 211–12)

Precursor to McCarthyism

It is important to note that many other politicians in addition to McCarthy played an important part in creating and sustaining the anti-communist mood. For example, as a member of the House Un-American Activities Committee (HUAC), Richard Nixon's energetic pursuit of alleged communists brought him national attention and helped him to rise rapidly through the ranks of the Republican Party. Within the Senate, a key figure in the anti-communist period was Pat McCarran, a Democrat from Nevada. As chair of the influential Senate Judiciary Committee and the main sponsor of the 1950 Internal Security Act, McCarran became extremely powerful. His work with the Senate Internal Security Subcommittee helped to place in the public mind the belief that China had been 'lost' because of the activities of communists who had infiltrated the State Department. The press also played an important part in this period. Sensationalist reporting of communist infiltration, alarmist coverage of the Cold War, unsubstantiated allegations and outspoken support for the robust plain speaking of McCarthy and his supporters helped to sell newspapers and sustain the mood. In the Midwest, for example, where McCarthyism was strongly supported, the *Chicago Tribune* became an outspoken supporter of 'Jolting Joe' as he rocked the East Coast establishment with his allegations of 'red infiltration'.

Historiography and McCarthyism

Historians now stress the importance of other factors in the development of the anti-communist mood which swept America at this time. In particular, fear of the Soviet Union, concern over their development of the atomic bomb and agonising and recrimination over the 'loss' of China to communism played their part. Perhaps even more important was the Korean War that began in 1950 and heightened the conviction that the communists were absolutely relentless in their objectives. Above all, perhaps, McCarthyism reflected the end of certainty. In this period, Americans were no longer convinced that their future safety and security was guaranteed (Table 7.2).

In *The Age of McCarthyism*, Ellen Schrecker offers this analysis of the controversial senator:

McCarthy was a gifted demagogue whose wildly irresponsible charges of communism brought him the publicity he craved. But his antics distracted the attention of contemporaries and historians and caused them to overlook the more profound and enduring aspects of the anti-Communist crusade of the 1940s and 1950s. The word McCarthyism creates problems. Identifying the anti-Communist crusade with Senator McCarthy narrows the focus and slights the more important roles played by people like FBI Director J. Edgar Hoover and President Harry Truman. (Schrecker, 1994, pp. 1–2)

Table 7.2   Timeline: The 'Red Scare', 1938–54

1938	**August**	House Un-American Activities Committee (HUAC) established. Initially intended to protect the United States against the possibility of Nazi espionage, it became the main mechanism for rooting out communists in areas such as government and also in Hollywood.
1940	**June**	Smith Act forbade teaching or advocating the overthrow of the government.
1944	**May**	American Communist Party became the Communist Political Association.
1945	**June**	Six journalists and government employees arrested and charged with leaking classified documents after State Department documents discovered in the offices of the communist magazine, *Amerasia*.
	September	Defection of a Soviet spy revealed existence of communist espionage in Canada.
1946	**November**	In the midterm elections the Republicans took control of Congress. In the same month, Truman set up a Temporary Commission on Employee Loyalty, asked to develop a loyalty–security programme aimed at federal employees.

Continued

1947	March	Under Executive Order 9835, a loyalty–security programme was implemented; this led to the dismissal of hundreds of workers deemed security risks.
	June	Taft–Hartley Act restricted power of trade unions and communist leadership.
	October	In the 'Hollywood Ten' hearings, film directors and screenwriters called before HUAC.
	December	Following a meeting at the famous New York hotel The Waldorf, the major Hollywood film producers issued what became known as the 'Waldorf Statement', in which the studios sacked the 'Hollywood Ten'; this marked the beginning of black lists and effectively terminated the careers of those under suspicion.
1948	July	Twelve communist leaders arrested under the terms of the Smith Act.
	August	The Hiss–Chambers hearings mark the start of HUAC's action against communists in government (Hiss had been a high-level official in the State Department). Richard Nixon came to the fore with the exposure of the 'Pumpkin Papers', revealing microfilms that Whittaker Chambers had hidden in a pumpkin on his farm in Maryland; Nixon enhanced his public reputation and secured the indictment of Hiss for perjury in December.
1949		Beginning of anti-communist measures within the university system; three professors dismissed at the University of Washington and loyalty oaths imposed elsewhere.
	Autumn	Communists take control of China and the Soviet Union explodes an atomic bomb for the first time.
1950	January	Hiss convicted of perjury after a second trial.
	February	Klaus Fuchs charged with passing atomic secrets to the Russians; in the same month Joseph McCarthy delivered the speech which gave new momentum to his previously lacklustre career, alleging that communists had infiltrated the State Department.
	June	Start of Korean War.
	Summer	Tydings Committee investigated McCarthy's charges and concluded they were unfounded and that he was a 'fraud'.
	July	Julius Rosenberg arrested on charges of espionage; his wife Ethel arrested a month later.
	September	McCarran Act (Internal Security Act) introduced sweeping anti-communist measures including the forced registration of all communist organisations and the barring from the United States of anyone who belonged to a totalitarian organisation; Truman's failed attempt to veto the bill on the grounds that it infringed civil liberties only made him look 'soft on communism'.
1951	April	After a trial lasting a month, Julius and Ethel Rosenberg were sentenced to death for their part in the espionage ring revolving around British scientist Klaus Fuchs who passed highly important atomic information to the Soviet Union. Judge Irving Kaufman made these remarks in the sentencing of Julius and Ethel Rosenberg, 5 April 1951: 'I consider your crime worse than murder. Plain deliberate contemplated murder is dwarfed in magnitude by comparison with the crime you have committed ... Only the Lord can find mercy for what you have done. The sentence of the Court upon Julius and Ethel Rosenberg is, for the crime for which you have been convicted, you are hereby sentenced to the punishment of death.' (In Schrecker, 1994, pp. 145–46)
	June	Further wave of arrests under the Smith Act.

Continued

	July	The Senate Internal Security Subcommittee begins enquiry into the 'loss' of China and communist subversion.
1952	November	Eisenhower elected president; privately contemptuous of McCarthy, he was reluctant publicly to confront him.
1953	June	The Rosenbergs were executed.
	December	Robert Oppenheimer, the eminent scientist and director of the Manhattan Project, had his security clearance withdrawn pending investigation.
1954	April–June	In the Army–McCarthy televised hearings, McCarthy made a very poor impression.
	December	The Senate formally censured McCarthy (he died in May 1957).

A list of some of the writers subjected to scrutiny by the Federal Bureau of Investigation (FBI)

W.H. Auden	Truman Capote	John Dos Passos
William Faulkner	Ernest Hemingway	Sinclair Lewis
Robert Lowell	Carl Sandburg	John Steinbeck
Tennessee Williams	Edmund Wilson	Thomas Wolfe

This selective list of authors comes from *The New Yorker*, 5 October 1987. Herbert Mitgang wrote that 'files on these writers contain information compiled by the F.B.I. and, in addition, references and information from the Central Intelligence Agency, the Immigration and Naturalization Service, the State Department, and the intelligence branches of the military services' (Herbert Mitgang in *The New Yorker*, 5 October 1987).

7.6 Truman's foreign policy

Truman's abrasive personal style

As vice president at the time of FDR's death in April 1945, power automatically passed to Harry S. Truman, whose background was chiefly in domestic affairs. He had not been briefed on key elements of foreign policy. Even during the period of his vice presidency, Truman had been kept in ignorance of the Manhattan Project, and initially he found the detail and complexity of foreign affairs difficult. After a succession of high-level briefings, Truman continued to find their intricacies challenging. Nevertheless, within weeks of Roosevelt's death, he made it clear that the direction of American foreign policy towards the Soviet Union was about to change.

On 23 April the Russian foreign secretary, Molotov, had a meeting with President Truman which he would never forget. Truman used 'plain American language' to express his feelings about Soviet conduct in Poland. He told Molotov that in future the Russians should stick by their agreements. Molotov was shocked by Truman's tone and told Truman, 'I have never been talked to like that in my life.' Truman's blunt reply was:

'carry out your agreements and you won't get talked to like that.' (Yergin, 1977, p. 83) Clearly Molotov would have immediately conveyed to Stalin his impression of the new leader in the White House. Even so, there were mixed feelings within the administration about the wisdom of the 'get tough' policy. While some advisers were delighted with the more abrasive style others, including Truman himself, expressed doubts. Truman told his close friend, the former ambassador to the Soviet Union, Joseph Davies, 'I gave it to him straight. I let him have it. It was the straight one-two to the jaw.' Yet he then looked for reassurance asking 'Did I do right?' (Yergin, 1977, p. 101) The chance for Truman to develop his understanding of dealing with the Soviet Union came in July 1945, when it was arranged for him to meet with Stalin and Churchill at Potsdam.

7.7 The Potsdam Conference

This was held between 17 July and 1 August 1945 at Potsdam, near the shattered city of Berlin. Truman adopted a more abrasive style than Roosevelt, but four main points of agreement were reached. Beyond these areas of common ground there was only disagreement and tension. Truman took an independent line from the British. He concluded that the Russians would understand only a forceful approach, and should not be allowed any part in the control of Japan. Joseph Davies was surprised that hostility to Russia was becoming so open and felt that the president was surrounded by advisors hostile to the Russians, even at the expense of Big Three Unity. However, Truman did tell Davies that he was trying his best to save peace and to stick to Roosevelt's plans, but he found the bargaining tactics of the Russians extremely frustrating.

A turning point in the atmosphere of the Conference came on 24 July, when Truman casually informed Stalin that the United States was now equipped with 'a new weapon of special destructive force.' Truman's self-confidence had been boosted by the news that American scientists had successfully carried out a test of an atomic bomb; however, Stalin's low-key response left him wondering whether the Soviet Union had grasped the full importance of what he had been told. In fact, Stalin's intelligence network had already conveyed some inkling of what was behind Truman's words. If Stalin and Roosevelt had departed Yalta with a sense of shared experience and a close working relationship, the atmosphere between the Soviet dictator and Truman could not have been more different.

Outcomes of the Potsdam Conference

Nevertheless, the Potsdam Conference settled some important matters:

- Each Occupying Power was allowed to extract reparations freely from its own zone.
- In addition, the Soviet Union was allowed to take 10 per cent from the western zones, and a further 15 per cent which was to be set against supplies of food and raw materials from the Soviet zone.
- The Soviet Union agreed to hold free elections in Poland.
- The United States accepted the Oder–Neisse Line as Poland's future Western frontier.

7.8 The atomic bomb

During his period as vice president, Truman had not been informed of the Manhattan Project. Now, the responsibility of deciding whether to use the weapon passed into the hands of a man who had only been in office for three months, but he quickly reached the decision that the new weapon should be used against the Japanese. Initially, the United States claimed that the atomic bomb had been dropped to bring the war in the Pacific to a rapid conclusion. The alternative – a long and difficult invasion of the Japanese homeland – was regarded as dangerous and likely to result in massive casualties. It is now also clear that the United States hoped that the use of the bomb would make the Soviet Union more likely to seek agreement than confrontation on territorial and diplomatic issues.

The destruction of Hiroshima

On the morning of 6 August 1945, the American plane *Enola Gay* dropped an atomic device on the crowded Japanese city of Hiroshima. The bomb, named 'Little Boy', used 64 kilograms of rare uranium-235. It is estimated that between 66,000 and 78,000 people were killed while a further 80,000 were injured and 300,000 more were exposed to radiation. A statement from the White House now warned the Japanese people that if they did not surrender they could 'expect a rain of ruin from the air, the like of which has never been seen on this earth' (Costello, 1985, p. 526). On 9 August, a second Japanese city, Nagasaki, was destroyed by a plutonium bomb. On 10 August, the Japanese indicated that they were now prepared to surrender unconditionally. On 14 August the Japanese emperor told his people that 'the enemy has begun to employ a new and most cruel bomb' and 'we have ordered the acceptance of the provisions of the Joint Declaration of the Powers' (Costello, 1985, p. 529). This brought the war in the Pacific to an end. Even with the distance afforded by writing his memoirs, Truman stood by his decision:

> Let there be no mistake about it. I regarded the bomb as a military weapon and never had any doubt that it should be used. The top military advisers to the President recommended its use, and when I talked to Churchill he unhesitatingly told me that he favoured the use of the atomic bomb if it might aid to end the war. (In McCullough, 1993, p. 442)

Historiography – Did Truman have to use the atomic bomb?

Despite Truman's personal conviction, it seems fair to suggest that there is a broad consensus among historians that the use of the atomic bomb was not an absolute prerequisite for an invasion of Japan or for an early end to the war. The president and his closest advisers were aware of alternative strategies but chose not to use them. Truman's successor President Dwight D. Eisenhower claimed that 'First, the Japanese were ready to surrender and it wasn't necessary to hit them with the awful thing. Second, I hated to see our country to be the first to use such a weapon.' (In Evans, 1998, p. 325)

A recent important work by Heinrich August Winkler offers this perspective on Truman and the bomb:

The keenest scientific criticism of the decision to drop the first atom bombs was voiced in 1965 by the historian Gar Alperovitz, the spokesman of a 'revisionist' school of thought in American historiography. His central thesis was that by the summer of 1945 Japan was on the point of military collapse and it was unnecessary to use atomic weapons to shorten the war ... In point of fact, the Japanese leadership was far from accepting the inevitability of surrender before 6 August 1945. (Winkler, 2015, p. 875)

In his *A History of the American People*, Paul Johnson states that:

On August 10 the Japanese cabled agreeing in principle to surrender without conditions. This came a few hours before the Russians, who now had 1.6 million men on the Manchurian border, declared war on Japan, following the agreement made at Yalta. It thus seems likely that the use of the two nuclear weapons was decisive in securing the Japanese surrender. That was the unanimous Allied conviction at the time ... Truman never had any qualms, at the time or later, that his decision to use both A-bombs had been right, indeed unavoidable, and he believed to his dying day that dropping the bombs had saved countless lives. (Johnson, 1997, p. 671)

Harold Evans argues:

Truman was at pains to conceal that in July 1945 the Emperor himself had been seeking peace. He never acknowledged that leading cabinet members, including Stimson, and military men repeatedly advised him from May onward that letting the Japanese know they could keep the Emperor might bring an early surrender ... He neither organised nor conducted any serious deliberations before making the most controversial decision of his Presidency ... Admiral William Leahy ... commented after the war that the United States 'had adopted an ethical standard common to the barbarians of the Dark Ages'. (Evans, 1998, p. 325)

Winkler also provides a useful analysis of Truman's personal outlook concerning the bomb:

Truman was returning home by sea from the Potsdam Conference when he heard that Hiroshima had been bombed. His reaction was one of relief and even delight. He had no moral scruples about deploying the weapon. From his point of view, it was a legitimate and even necessary means by which to end a terrible war at the earliest available opportunity with the least possible number of American casualties. Washington was happy to accept that this action would result in the deaths of an incalculable number of Japanese civilians, including women and children. (Winkler, 2015, p. 874)

Robert M. Neer, in *Napalm: An American Biography* (2013) shows the importance of napalm as opposed to the atomic bomb in bringing the Japanese to the point of surrender. As Neer says, 'The Bomb got the press, but Napalm did the work.' Neer's research demonstrates that:

By the time the war ended, around 42 per cent of Japan's urban industrial area had been burned and 330,000 civilians killed. Being burned was the leading cause of death for civilians. Japan's sixty-six largest cities save Kyoto, spared for cultural and political reasons, ceased to exist as military objectives. After the napalm attacks began, about one-quarter of Japan's urban population, an estimated 8.5 million people, fled their homes ... Tokyo shrank from over 5 million residents on January 1, 1945 to about 2.3 million on August 1. (Neer, 2013, pp. 85–86)

Finally, the occasion of the use of the atomic bomb also marks a staging-post in any discussion about the rise in the power of the presidency. Never before had so much brutal authority been exercised than when a fledgling president wrote out in his own hand a note from the Commander-in-Chief to the military to use the atom bomb for the first time.

Great American Lives: Robert Oppenheimer, 22 April 1904–18 February 1967

Robert Oppenheimer was born in New York City to wealthy parents and received the type of education reserved for the privileged class. He studied chemistry at Harvard University but had also begun to take a keen interest in experimental physics. He carried out further study in Cambridge and then the University of Göttingen where he obtained a PhD. He returned to the US and by 1936 achieved a full professorship at the University of Berkeley. His academic brilliance was now clear and he completed important work on gravitational collapse and Neutron Stars.

Oppenheimer's reputation led to his engagement by the US government to examine the process of a fast neutron chain reaction in constructing an atomic bomb. In September 1942 he was appointed director of the Manhattan Project. Authorised by President Roosevelt, the project's focus was a top-secret weapons laboratory. By November, Oppenheimer and the director of the Manhattan Project, Lieutenant General Leslie Groves, had selected a remote site in New Mexico for their work.

While some of his colleagues found Oppenheimer difficult, others found him inspirational and almost everyone recognised that he was now indispensable to the project's success. His quick grasp of the intensely complex scientific concepts was extraordinary. Meanwhile, Oppenheimer's left-leaning politics and associations led the FBI and the Army to place him under close scrutiny, and for his removal from the project to be considered.

Oppenheimer's scientific ability was demonstrated when the first nuclear device was tested near Alamagordo on 16 July 1945. The newly appointed President Truman was informed of this development as he met Stalin at the Potsdam Conference. The entire dynamic of the Cold War had changed forever. The theoretic equations scribbled on a blackboard were now translated to the physical destruction of Hiroshima and Nagasaki.

His reservations about how the atomic weapon would be used and his previous left-wing connections made Oppenheimer extremely vulnerable during the McCarthy witch hunt of the early 1950s. In December 1953 he was informed that he was now considered 'a security risk'. In 1954 he faced the humiliation of a private hearing into his conduct.

Continued

Estranged from the government but never convicted of any criminal offence, Oppenheimer spent his final years lecturing widely on science and the nature of the universe. His rehabilitation came with an award from President Kennedy in 1963 which was actually presented by President Johnson following Kennedy's assassination. He died in Princeton, New Jersey in 1967, after a long illness.

Further reading: Kai Bird & Martin J. Sherwin, *American Prometheus: The Triumph and Tragedy of J. Robert Oppenheimer* (Atlantic Books 2009)

7.9 The Iron Curtain

Winston Churchill and the Cold War

Although the Red Army had 'liberated' the people of Eastern Europe from Nazi rule, the Nazis were soon replaced by communist-dominated governments. This became a major source of superpower rivalry and was at the centre of Churchill's concerns about the future conduct of the Soviet Union. Churchill had entered the Potsdam Conference with the intention of heightening American awareness of what he saw as the Soviet threat, and with the hope that he would be returned to power in the forthcoming British general election. While he was encouraged by what he saw of Truman, he was dismayed by the verdict of the British electorate, shocked to find that the British people had rejected the Conservatives in favour of Attlee's Labour Party. Churchill submitted his resignation to King George on 26 July 1945, shattered by his election defeat. At the very height of his triumph, with Hitler vanquished, the British electorate had rejected him. Churchill retained his seat in Parliament and continued to be concerned about Stalin's actions.

Churchill's Iron Curtain Speech at Fulton Missouri, March 1946

Against a background of heightening tension between the United States and the Soviet Union, Churchill was invited to speak at Westminster College in Fulton, Missouri. Arriving in the United States in January 1946, Churchill was able to consult with President Truman, Secretary of State James F. Byrnes and Presidential Chief of Staff Admiral William Leahy. It was with their backing, and with Truman sitting on the same platform, that Churchill delivered one of the most important speeches of his career on 5 March 1946.

> A shadow had fallen upon the scenes so lately lighted by the Allied victory. Nobody knows what Soviet Russia ... intends to do in the immediate future, or what are the limits, if any to their expansive ... tendencies. From Stettin, in the Baltic, to Trieste in the Adriatic, an Iron Curtain has descended across the continent. Behind that line lie all the capitals of the ancient states of Central and Eastern Europe – Warsaw, Berlin, Prague, Vienna, Budapest, Belgrade, Bucharest and Sofia. All these famous cities ... are subject to a very high and increasing measure of control from Moscow ... The communist parties ... are seeking everywhere to obtain totalitarian control.

Some observers welcomed Churchill's speech as 'exposing ... the gravity of the peril Russia is presenting to the World' and 'putting into words what was ... in the minds of many Americans' (Yergin, 1977, p. 176).

Analysis: How important was Churchill's speech?

Churchill proposed that the way forward was to set up a permanent military alliance between the British Commonwealth and the United States. However, many Americans felt that the speech had gone too far, and urged President Truman to seek co-operation rather than conflict with Stalin. Stalin was angered by the 'Iron Curtain' speech and replied that the USSR was merely 'anxious for its future safety' while the West forgot about the colossal sacrifices made by the Soviet Union in the Second World War. Recent historians have emphasised the importance of Britain's role in the period from mid-1945 to early 1946 in heightening American awareness of the Soviet threat.

Some historians have therefore depicted the early stages of the Cold War as an Anglo-Soviet conflict, with the United States acting as a mediator. Finally, although Truman to some extent distanced himself from the speech, it is clear that Churchill's stance helped him to win approval in Congress for a huge loan from the United States to Great Britain. However, although Britain benefited from a payment of $3.75 billion, historians such as Daniel Yergin (1977) have pointed out that Britain was, in effect, acknowledging that for it to hang on to its former status it would have to become a junior partner of the United States.

7.10 The Truman Doctrine

Although Truman distanced himself to some extent from Churchill's 'Iron Curtain' speech, it gradually became apparent that his own line towards the Soviet Union was hardening. While he quickly established a reputation among his staff and advisers for selecting crisp and decisive policy options, he did not find it easy to decide upon a clear line of policy towards the Soviet Union. Privately the Soviet Union's tactics and attitudes often frustrated him. In a letter to Secretary of State James Byrnes, written on 5 January 1946, he condemned the changes Russia had made to the Polish borders as a 'high-handed outrage'. He went on to say that: 'Unless Russia is faced with an iron fist and strong language, another war is in the making. Only one language do they understand – "How many divisions have you?" I'm tired of babying the Soviets.' (Yergin, 1977, p. 161)

Meanwhile Truman's advisers were drawing his attention to what they saw as serious breaches in Soviet conduct. The promised elections in Poland had not taken place and throughout Eastern Europe communists were increasingly in control of the embryonic governments.

Iran

Further afield, Soviet and British troops had simultaneously invaded Iran in August 1941 in order to seal it off from the Axis powers and to secure Western/Soviet access to the Persian Gulf. It was agreed that these forces would withdraw within six months of the end of hostilities between the Allied and Axis forces. However, when the deadline for Soviet withdrawal from Iran arrived on 2 March 1946, Soviet troops remained in the region with some only 25 miles from Tehran. In January 1946, Truman wrote privately to Stalin that Soviet forces should withdraw immediately or face the possibility of American military action. On 16 March Secretary of State James Byrnes made a public statement reiterating this position. On 24 March 1946, the Soviet Union announced a withdrawal of its troops partly because of the threat of military force but also because of the offer of a favourable oil agreement with Iran. Meanwhile, in China the deteriorating situation meant that by the autumn of 1946 it appeared that there was a strong possibility of a communist victory against nationalist forces and the likelihood of the most populous nation on earth passing into communist hands.

Greece and Turkey

While this illustrates the broad range of American concerns, initially the focus, above all, was on Greece and Turkey. The war had taken a massive toll on Britain's physical and economic resources. As domestic economic problems came to a head in the winter of 1946–47, it became clear that some of Britain's overseas commitments would have to be scaled down. In February 1947 Britain contacted the State Department to inform it that London could no longer help the Greek and Turkish governments deal with their economic problems and the threat of communist subversion. Britain urged the United States to provide massive aid to Greece and Turkey. The critical moment in securing backing for this course of action came in what Daniel Yergin has called 'the all-out speech' given by Secretary of State Dean Acheson to a top-level meeting at the White House on 27 February 1947. Speaking in stark terms, Acheson warned that if American aid was not provided to Greece and Turkey then it was likely that:

> A highly possible Soviet breakthrough might open three continents to Soviet Union penetration. Like apples in a barrel infected by the corruption of one rotten one, the corruption of Greece would infect Iran and all to the East ... Africa ... Italy and France. (Yergin, 1977, p. 281)

The urgent tone of Acheson's speech convinced the group that aid to Greece and Turkey had to be provided, and that a presidential address was called for.

The Truman Doctrine

In a speech to Congress on 12 March, President Truman emphasised the differences between communism and democracy. Truman asserted that one way of life was 'based upon the will of the majority', with 'free elections, guarantees of individual liberty, freedom of speech and religion'. The other was 'based upon the will of a minority ... it relies upon terror and oppression'. Truman made it clear that the United States would defend 'free people who are resisting attempted subjugation by armed minorities or by outside pressures' (McCullough, 1993, pp. 547–48). It was clear that Truman was referring to communism and that he was now portraying

American–Soviet relations as a struggle between the forces of good and evil. The countries which were uppermost in Truman's mind at this time were Greece and Turkey. Truman requested that $400 million be allocated to provide these countries with humanitarian aid. Truman's fear was that mass upheaval in Greece and Turkey would lead to successful communist uprisings. These countries were now to be provided with a huge, American-funded aid programme, in order to try to prevent communism taking hold there.

Analysis of Truman's motives

Richard Crockatt (1995) observes that:

> The striking feature of the American response to the announcement of the British withdrawal is not so much the actual decision to send military and economic aid to Greece and Turkey as the manner in which Truman strove to create a consensus for a fundamental reorientation of American policy. Presenting a stark contrast between two alternative ways of life ... There seems little doubt, as historians have shown, that one of Truman's motives for pitching the rhetoric of his message so high was the need to convince a cash-conscious Congress and an American public opinion not yet fully cognizant of the extended role the United States was about to assume that the stakes in Greece and Turkey were indeed as high as he claimed. (Crockatt, 1995, pp. 73–74)

Soviet reaction to the Truman Doctrine

Stalin condemned the Truman Doctrine, accusing the Americans of using 'dollar diplomacy' to extend their capitalist empire. Meanwhile Stalin's actions showed that he was determined to safeguard the USSR from the threat of a future invasion from the West. From 1945 onwards, the Soviets installed communist regimes in Poland, Romania, Bulgaria and Hungary. In response, the White House developed a policy which became known as *containment*. This acknowledged that there was little that could be done to regain influence over Eastern Europe, which had effectively passed into the hands of the Soviet Union. The notion of containment was therefore to prevent the Soviet Union from extending its control over any new territory, either in Europe or in the wider world. The policy of containment was initially put to the test in Germany – and, in particular, Berlin.

7.11 Marshall Aid

Europe on the brink

The United States emerged from the Second World War as undoubtedly the most powerful economy on earth, controlling more than half the world's manufacturing production. No other nation came close to matching its individual capacity. However, the economic situation in Europe was a source of grave concern to President Truman and his senior advisers. On 26 April 1947, Secretary of State George C. Marshall returned from a meeting in Moscow with Stalin, overwhelmed by a sense of the Soviet leader's indifference to the suffering faced by the people of Europe. Marshall felt that Stalin was happy to see Europe descend into chaos. Famine, disease, homelessness and poverty were rife. Meanwhile a memo from Under Secretary for Economic Affairs Will Clayton warned that conditions in Europe were even more serious than had been understood. Then in a speech in London on 14 May Churchill described Europe as 'a rubble-heap, a charnel house, a breeding ground of pestilence and hate' (Schlesinger, 1965, p. 718). Truman feared that this economic situation would make the people of Europe even more vulnerable to the spread of communism.

George C. Marshall and his advisers feared that without substantial American aid, the deterioration in the economic life of Western Europe would lead to a severe slump which would have dire effects on the American economy. A major economic crisis might encourage the peoples of Western Europe to turn to communism and the Soviet Union for their salvation. After all, the communist parties of France and Italy had already attracted significant electoral support.

The Marshall Plan

In a major speech at Harvard University on 5 June 1947, Marshall called for a determined United States effort (the Marshall Plan) to promote the economic revival of Europe and thus provide for the continued prosperity of the American economy. Marshall claimed that:

> Our policy is directed not against any country or doctrine, but against hunger, poverty, desperation and chaos. Its purpose should be the revival of a working economy in the world: so as to permit the emergence of political and social conditions in which free institutions can exist. (In Reynolds, 2009, p. 381)

Between 1948 and 1952 the United States injected $13 billion into European recovery by means of the Marshall Plan: Britain received $3,000 million and West Germany $1,300 million. This included food supplies, machinery, technological expertise and cash.

The offer of help to the Soviet Union

In addition, the United States formally offered assistance to the Soviet Union and the Central and East European states. Most historians now feel that the State Department made this 'offer' in the hope that it would be refused. The prevailing Cold War atmosphere made it unlikely that Congress would give approval to a scheme involving a massive outlay on behalf of the Soviet Union. A Soviet delegation led by Molotov did attend a critical meeting of the European powers in Paris on 26 June 1947, to discuss the terms on which Marshall Aid might be available. However, they soon withdrew once they were asked by Washington DC to provide detailed economic data. Historians have pointed to Soviet attendance at this meeting as an indication that Stalin had not yet decided on a complete breach with the United States. However, there is no doubt that Stalin was deeply suspicious of America's motives and it was probably this, combined with a sense of national pride, which led to Stalin's ultimate refusal to accept any American aid. The fact was that, even if it was well intentioned, the Marshall Plan had effectively deepened the division between the two superpowers.

7.12 The Berlin blockade

Issues in Germany at the start of the Cold War

By the summer of 1946, the agreements made at the Potsdam Conference about Germany were beginning to show signs of serious breakdown. The USSR failed to meet its obligations to deliver the food and coal which it had agreed to supply from its zone. And to a large extent the Soviets stripped their section of Germany of its industrial resources and sent most of them back to the USSR. One American politician went so far as to describe the USSR as 'a vacuum into which all movable goods would be sucked' (Dobbs, 2013, p. 311). In retaliation, Britain and America ended their deliveries of industrial goods to the Soviet zone. In the late 1940s Great Britain and the United States began to take measures to consolidate their occupation zone into a German state. The Western Allies decided to make a major effort to boost the economy of their zones; by 1948 the British, French and Americans had merged their zones together to make them economically stronger. Stalin viewed these developments with apprehension. The focus of the Cold War now became Berlin, itself divided into four occupied sectors. Since 1945, Berlin had been in a unique position: the three western sectors (British, French and American) were located deep inside the Soviet zone of Germany, and more than 100 miles from West Germany. Contact between the outside world and the western zones of Berlin rested on the maintenance of the main road and rail links from West Germany.

The Berlin blockade

In April 1948, the Soviet Union halted the passage of western military supplies to West Berlin. Growing interference with road and rail traffic into Berlin culminated with the dramatic announcement on 23 June that the 'Soviet administration is compelled to halt all traffic to and from Berlin from tomorrow at 0600 hrs because of technical difficulties'. All land and water routes to the western sectors of Berlin were cut off. With food supplies to the people of West Berlin limited, the Soviets hoped that the only way in which the West could prevent the people of West Berlin from starving would be to let West Berlin become part of the Soviet Union. The West would then lose its only foothold in Eastern Europe and the division of the area would be complete.

The West refused to contemplate withdrawal from Berlin. It feared that the loss of this strategic city could lead to West Germany going the same way. It decided that its best option would be to supply West Berlin from the air, by means of three narrow air corridors. The blockade lasted from June 1948 to May 1949. The first Allied flight, on 26 June 1948, delivered 80 tonnes of milk, flour and medicine. At the height of the Berlin airlift, planes were landing in West Berlin every three minutes, 24 hours a day. To forestall the possibility of a Soviet military response, the United States moved a number of B-29 heavy bombers, capable of striking targets inside the Soviet Union, to British air bases. Stalin, faced with the danger of American retaliation, was not prepared to take any risks, and the blockade was suddenly lifted in May 1949. The episode had been a strategic and psychological victory for the West, and had ended in a humiliating climbdown for Stalin.

7.13 NATO

Although the United States made a permanent commitment to European security with the establishment of NATO (North Atlantic Treaty Organisation) in 1949, it was not always certain that this would be the direction that American policy would take. Isolationism was still an important factor in American political life. In the immediate post-war period the natural desire to 'see the boys return home' from the Far East and Europe meant that the United States was rapidly demobilising. Many Americans felt it was important that, in the wake of the Marshall Plan, Europe should be seen to contribute to its own defence rather than relying wholly on the United States. However, working against the forces of isolationism were other important trends, notably the creation of what Daniel Yergin has called the 'National Security State'. This placed the United States on a footing for 'perpetual confrontation and for war' (Yergin, 1977, p. 5). These trends meant that the United States seemed to be preparing itself for the eventuality of a war with the Soviet Union. Meanwhile in Europe anxiety about security was acute. Congress viewed the Western European Union (WEU), an embryonic Western European defence organisation, as too small to deter Soviet aggression. However, there was certainly a reluctance within the Senate to authorise the dispatch of substantial numbers of troops to Europe.

Although the United States was prepared to put its name to the NATO Treaty in April 1949, many members of Congress saw the new organisation as chiefly a morale-boosting gesture rather than a massive commitment of resources. The treaty which created NATO was signed by Britain, France, a number of other Western European nations, Canada and – most important of all – the United States. There were a number of references which reflected the primacy of the United States, particularly in Article 1, which ruled out the 'use of force in any manner inconsistent with the purposes of the United Nations'. The North Atlantic Treaty was ratified by the United States on 21 July 1949, and came into force on 24 August.

Article 5 of the NATO agreement

The central clause of the entire agreement was Article 5, which asserted that in the case of an:

> armed attack against one or more of [its members] in Europe or North America [this] shall be considered an attack against them all, and consequently ... each of them ... will assist the party or parties so attacked by taking ... such action as it deems necessary, including the use of armed force, to restore and maintain the security of the North Atlantic area.

Those who were against making a commitment to European Security were shaken by the news, in September 1949, that Soviet scientists had successfully carried out an atomic bomb test. This shattered the assumption that it would take the Soviets a long time to end the American A-bomb monopoly and also made many Americans acutely aware of the internal threat to security posed by the infiltration of the defence organisation by Soviet spies.

7.14 National Security Council Resolution 68

Now regarded by historians as of great importance in the formulation of United States foreign policy, National Security Council Resolution 68 (NSC 68) was a major review of security policy commissioned by President Truman in January 1946, submitted to the president in April and approved in September. The report advocated a rapid and major arms build-up without which containment would be 'no more than a policy of bluff'. Richard Crockatt states that 'NSC 68 epitomised the militarization of containment'. The endorsement of the report at the highest level meant that American policy makers were accepting the defence of the 'Free World', on a global scale, against the threat of communism (Crockatt, 1995, pp. 83–84).

It is vital to note the coincidence of the North Korean invasion of South Korea in June 1950, with the recommendations of military build-up advocated in NSC 68. As one aide, involved in the preparation of the report, wrote: 'We were sweating over NSC 68, and then, thank God, Korea came along.' (Crockatt, 1995, p. 83) America was decisively moving to the creation of a National Security State. A report by Special Consul Clark Clifford to President Truman concluded that in restraining the Soviet Union the United States must be prepared to wage atomic and biological warfare. Clifford advocated a highly mechanised army, which could be moved either by sea or air, capable of seizing and holding strategic areas, and supported by powerful naval and air forces. The National Security Act (1947) created a unified Department of Defense, replacing the previous separately run branches of the armed services. Consequently, two new bodies were also created: a National Security Council to co-ordinate overall security planning and the Central Intelligence Agency (CIA), charged with the co-ordination of intelligence gathering and counter-intelligence strategy.

Development of the hydrogen bomb

Meanwhile, the Soviet testing of the atomic bomb in September 1949 and the communist takeover in China a month later prompted President Truman to authorise a crash programme to rapidly develop a hydrogen (thermo-nuclear) bomb. Intensive research into the hydrogen bomb began in the 1950s. Whereas the atomic bomb involved the splitting (fission) of uranium atoms, the hydrogen bomb was based on a process of combining atoms: a small amount of matter could be converted into an incredible amount of energy. Spurred on by the Soviet Union's successful testing of the atom bomb (1949) and intelligence reports which suggested they were working on a hydrogen bomb, American scientists successfully tested a H-bomb on Elugelab Island in the Pacific, in November 1952. In March 1954, the United States exploded the first H-bomb capable of being dropped from an aeroplane.

Table 7.3 The Soviet Union and Eastern Europe, 1944–47

1944	**Poland** – a pro-Moscow provisional government was created in Lublin.
	Hungary – a communist-dominated government was formed at Debrecen.
1945	The **Yalta Conference** (February) effectively divided Europe. Roosevelt extracted only vague promises to hold democratic elections in the liberated areas.
1945–47	**Poland** gradually came under Soviet control. By 1947 a communist monopoly on power existed, with all other political groupings banned.
	Czechoslovakia briefly returned to parliamentary government after the Košice Declaration of April 1945. The communists won 38 per cent of the votes in the 1946 elections. A communist coup before the 1948 elections led to the resignation of all non-communist ministers.
	In **Hungary**, despite the Debrecen provisional government, the communists were defeated in the general election of November 1945 though they retained control of the police through the interior ministry. Gradually communist control increased until by 1947 all other parties were banned.
	Romania had fought on the side of the Germans and so was governed through an Allied Control Commission in February 1947 when a peace treaty was signed. The communists then took control of Romania.
	In **Albania**, a communist republic was created in 1945, based on the Russian system.
	In **Bulgaria**, the communists had taken control by 1947, despite the resistance of the agrarian leader Nikola Petkov who was murdered in September 1947.
	In **Yugoslavia**, under the leadership of communist ruler Marshall Tito, the country retained independence from Moscow.

7.15 Eastern Europe

As the Red Army occupied Central Europe towards the end of the Second World War there were signs that it intended to establish communist regimes wherever it could (Table 7.3). The Soviet Union took a firm grip on the countries of Eastern Europe in the period after the Yalta Conference. The following characteristics became apparent in each case:

- The adaptation of Constitutions based on the Soviet model.
- The prohibition of all political groupings except communists.
- The selection of national 'leaders' based on their willingness to comply with the Kremlin.
- The purging of dissidents or politically suspect individuals.
- A rigorous secret police and internal security mechanism and widespread use of terror.
- Economic centralisation and nationalisation, leading to the exportation of goods, food produce and raw materials by the Soviet Union at the expense of the individual states.

7.16 Relations with China, 1945–49

A Civil War between the communists, led by Mao Zedong, and the nationalists, led by Jiang Jieshi, had gripped China since the 1930s. This was temporarily put to one side during the war with Japan which lasted from 1937 to 1945. Once Japan had surrendered to the Allies in August 1945, the Civil War resumed. This posed a direct challenge to the American policy of containment of communism. Initially, America hoped that a stable post-war China would play a key role in the region and China was given one of the five permanent seats on the United Nations Security Council. These hopes were damaged by the Civil War, and Truman dispatched General Marshall to try to resolve the conflict through the creation of a coalition government. Marshall's efforts came to nothing and his departure in 1946 saw the Civil War reach a new level of intensity. America became a spectator as Jiang's armies gave way to a steady communist advance. Believing that Jiang would be able to resolve the situation himself, America did little to help. But throughout 1949 the communists captured key cities, and in the autumn Jiang was forced to leave the Chinese mainland and flee to the island of Formosa.

As Mao Zedong had prophesied:

> In a very short time, several hundred million peasants in China's central, southern, and northern provinces will rise like a fierce wind or tempest, a force so swift and violent that no power, however great, will be able to suppress it. (In Peraino, 2017, prologue)

America had enjoyed strong economic and cultural links with the Chinese and the loss of China to communism was deeply disturbing to many Americans. Critics argued that Truman had not done enough to help; they claimed that the president was 'soft' on communism, and lambasted the failure of containment. The government defended itself by saying that Jiang's inefficient, unpopular regime could have been saved only by a full-scale American intervention on the Chinese mainland, something which would not have commanded popular support. The fact remained that 1949 had contained two disastrous events for Truman; the loss of the world's most populous nation to communism and the knowledge that Stalin now possessed atomic weapons served to further heighten the anxiety and paranoia which lay at the heart of the Cold War. The loss of China also obliged American policy makers to take a fresh look at its policy regarding Japan.

7.17 Relations with Japan, 1945–52

Following the defeat of Japan in August 1945, America initially took a tough stance towards the Japanese people.

Japan was occupied by American forces under the command of General Douglas MacArthur. The Japanese army was disarmed and demobilised. The emperor was stripped of his divine status and reduced to the level of constitutional monarch. A democratic Constitution was introduced which removed the army from political influence, and war was renounced. However the communist takeover in China (1949) and the invasion of South Korea (1950) prompted a reappraisal. America now saw Japan as a vital barrier to further communist expansion. It was seen as necessary for America to bolster Japan's economic and military status to make Japan less vulnerable to communist insurgence. In 1951, a Peace Treaty was signed with Japan, despite Soviet protests. America now gained military bases in Japan, and what was a shattered nation in 1945 now began to move towards economic revival and a newfound status as an informal ally of the United States.

7.18 Historiography of the Cold War

Broadly speaking, the 'orthodox' view taken by Western historians in the late 1940s and early 1950s held that the Soviet Union bore primary responsibility for the outbreak of the Cold War. The Soviet Union was portrayed as cold-hearted and expansionist; Stalin was seen as harbouring designs on spreading communism worldwide. The wartime sacrifices of the Soviet Union tended to be forgotten in this perspective. With this perspective the actions of the United States were largely seen in a favourable light, with America depicted as acting in a fair and rational way.

A major change in the historiography of the Cold War took place during the 1960s. In this decade many experts (including from America) now argued that the United States had primary responsibility for the outbreak and continuation of the Cold War. It was now claimed that the key to the Cold War was that America had misunderstood, and overreacted to, Soviet actions. These historians felt that the Soviet Union was largely concerned with its own defence and security, prompted by the massive losses sustained in the Second World War. Significantly, this interpretation gained credibility in the 1960s as America was steadily escalating its ill-fated intervention in Vietnam. More recently, a more subtle, nuanced interpretation could be seen as the post-revisionist view. For the first time, a consensus emerged which did not seek to apportion blame for the Cold War to one side or the other. A more sophisticated stance emerged which saw the Cold War as the product of overreaction and mutual suspicion.

7.19 Overview: Crisis in Korea

Korea is a relatively small peninsula, divided by a line known as the 38th Parallel, a 200-mile boundary between North and South Korea. Today, there is a communist government in the north and a non-communist regime in the south. Traditionally, this mountainous country had been predominantly rural. However, South Korea, with its capital Seoul, has become one of the world's fastest-growing economies. The south contains the majority of the population, industry and wealth. The north remains a repressive, closed regime, with a capital at Pyongyang. Korea's proximity to China, Japan and the Soviet Union has meant that historically it has often been a source of tension, rivalry and external intervention. In the words of an old Korean proverb: 'When whales fight, the shrimp in the middle gets crushed.' Between 1910 and 1945 'the Land of the Morning Calm' (Hastings, 1988, p. 11) came under the repressive control of a Japanese military occupation. However, Japan's grip on Korea ended abruptly following America's deployment of the atomic bomb on Hiroshima and Nagasaki in August 1945; Japan's surrender meant that the future of the occupied lands was thrown into doubt.

The Soviet Union had a long-standing interest in Korea, and at the Potsdam Conference (July 1945) it was agreed that Japanese troops to the north of the 38th Parallel would surrender to the United States. Unfortunately the increasing sense of division between the superpowers evident at Potsdam was now reflected in the situation in Korea, with America dominant to the south and the Soviets to the north. Both sides pledged themselves to support an independent Korea. However, amid the atmosphere of the Cold War neither side was prepared to allow the other to dominate the Korean peninsula. The United Nations attempted to resolve the tension by calling for free general elections to establish a single, national government. However, the Soviets refused to allow the elections in the north unless certain pro-American parties were excluded. In August 1948, elections were held in the south and the independent Republic of South Korea was created with its capital at Seoul under the leadership of President Syngman Rhee. In September 1948 the Democratic People's Republic of Korea (ROK) was created in the north with its capital at Pyongyang under the communist leadership of Kim Il-Sung. This situation was in place when Russian and American troops were withdrawn in 1949.

7.20 Invasion and Truman's decision to intervene in Korea

The wet season had already begun when a massive North Korean artillery and mortar barrage began at 4 am on the morning of Sunday 25 June 1950. The first exchanges took place in the Ongjin region on Korean's west-central coast. This was followed by the opening up of North Korean artillery fire at six points along the 38th Parallel. The Korean People's Army was a highly motivated fighting unit, equipped with Russian T-34 tanks, and backed by an air force of around 200 fighter planes and bombers. In an all-out offensive thousands of communist troops armed with Soviet-made weapons crossed the border into South Korea. In the front line were troops who had recently experienced battle in the Chinese Civil War, and they met little resistance. Both South Korean and American officials were unprepared for the invasion. Within three days, the capital, Seoul, had been captured by the communists. Over the next few weeks the advance continued unchecked, until the south was almost completely overrun. The degree to which the troops from the north were able to overwhelm their counterparts in the south starkly illustrated the fact that they had been taken completely by surprise. A stronger element of resistance in the initial stages could have made the war much less protracted and costly, but it was already too late and the cost of repelling the invasion would be enormous.

Truman had planned a quiet weekend back in his home state of Missouri. In a note to a friend he mentioned plans to see family and friends and to 'order a new roof for the farm house'. As he scanned the newspapers, his routine morning activity, it must have been difficult for him to relax. The *Baltimore Sun* and the *New York Times* led with stories of mounting fears of the spread of communism in the United States. A former Army sergeant was appearing in court in New York City charged with being a member of the Klaus Fuchs spy network at the nuclear base at Los Alamos. Having enjoyed a 'pleasant family dinner' the tired president retired for the evening at 9 pm. Twenty minutes later he received an urgent telephone call from Secretary of State Dean Acheson. 'Mr. President, I have very serious news. The North Koreans have invaded South Korea. The American Ambassador in Seoul had sent reports of a very heavy attack.' (McCullough, 1993, p. 773)

In private, Truman did not attempt to conceal his dismay. His daughter wrote: 'My father made it clear, from the moment he heard the news, that he feared this was the opening of World War III.' (McCullough, 1993, p. 775) By the evening of Sunday 25 June the president was back in Washington, tersely telling reporters, 'We've got a job to do.' (McCullough, 1993, p. 776) The *New York Times* reported that 'an atmosphere of tension, unparalleled since the war days, spread over the capital' (in McCullough, 1993, p. 777). An official statement issued the next day underlined the gravity of the situation with the words: 'Our estimate is that a complete collapse is imminent.' (In McCullough, 1993, p. 779) In his diary, Truman wrote 'Must be careful not to cause a general Asiatic war.' (In McCullough, 1993, p. 783)

Many Americans were convinced that the Soviet Union was behind the communist invasion of South Korea. Following the disastrous loss of China in October 1949 Truman was under severe pressure to act decisively in Asia, and the news that the Soviets had successfully tested their own atomic device in August 1949 simply raised the stakes. Intelligence reports suggested that in addition to the invasion in Korea there were signs of communist troop activity on the Chinese border with Indochina. With crucial midterm elections looming in November, Truman knew that weakness or indecision would play into the hands of the Republican Party. Failure to act would be portrayed as weakness or, even worse, confirmation of allegations that communists had infiltrated the State Department.

The conviction that the invasion was part of a wider, Kremlin-instigated programme was enough to compel Truman to act. Within hours of the invasion the president ordered American air and naval forces in Japan to move to Korea. In a portent of what was to come, General Douglas MacArthur, the commander of United States forces in the Far East, had seized the initiative and began to ship war materials towards South Korea without prior approval from Washington. Before the end of June, Truman had committed ground troops to Korea.

Later, Secretary of State Dean Acheson wrote that the communist invasion was:

An open, undisguised challenge to our internationally accepted position as the protector of South Korea, an area of great importance to the security of American-occupied Japan. To back away from this challenge, in view of our capacity for meeting it, would be highly destructive of the power and prestige of the United States. (In Hastings, 1988, p. 53)

Many Western observers have assumed that Stalin must have encouraged Kim Il-Sung to carry out the attack. Khrushchev later wrote in his memoirs that the idea was Kim Il-Sung's but that Stalin had not objected. Recent research suggests that the initiative for the invasion came from Kim Il-Sung but that he received a clear endorsement from the Soviet Union. It seems likely that Stalin gave his approval to the invasion on the basis of Kim's assurances that the United States would not intervene. Clarity over China's role in this remains difficult for historians. Khrushchev wrote that Stalin had consulted Mao over Kim's plans and that the Chinese leader had given his approval. It has now emerged that China returned around 15,000 battle-hardened Korean troops who had fought in the Chinese Civil War. Historians have also drawn attention to a meeting that took place in April 1950 between Mao and Kim Il-Sung. The conclusion is that while Mao's ideological outlook led him to support North Korea in its plans it was probably Stalin rather than the Chinese leader who was most closely involved in the planning stages.

In retrospect, it is clear that the United States gave out ambiguous signals over Korea in the final months before the invasion. In a speech made on 12 January 1950, Secretary of State Dean Acheson gave the impression that the United States regarded Korea as outside its area of vital interest. Acheson defined the nations in the American 'defense perimeter' in the Pacific which covered a huge area, but he failed to specify Korea. He did imply that if attacked the ROK could expect support from the United Nations. On the other hand, in June 1949 Truman made a comparison between giving economic backing to the ROK and the economic assistance which was given to Western Europe. Again, conflicting signals came out of Washington when in January 1950 a bill to give economic assistance to the ROK was defeated in the House of Representatives. Given these mixed messages, Truman's quick decision to intervene took the Soviet Union by surprise. However, a rapid military conclusion was to prove elusive.

7.21 The United Nations

Crucially at the time of the invasion the Soviet Union was staging a boycott of the UN Security Council. Although Mao Zedong had taken control of China in 1949, the United Nations had refused to recognise the new communist regime. The USSR took great exception to what it saw as an anti-communist decision and refused to attend the meetings of the Security Council. In its absence the United States, with British support, was able to lead the Security Council in labelling North Korea as the aggressor and call upon its member states to come to the assistance of South Korea. The United Nations' stated objective was 'to furnish such assistance to the Republic of Korea as may be necessary to repel the armed attack and to restore peace and security in the area' (Hastings, 1988, p. 56). In a sense, the fact that the United States had chosen to operate within the framework of the United Nations offered a glimpse of hope that the conflict could be contained and brought to a peaceful conclusion. On the other hand, in the Soviet Union the United Nations was lambasted as merely a vehicle for American interests. The Moscow newspapers spoke of American 'aggression' in Korea and condemned 'arrogant US bandits'. Meanwhile, within the United Nations countries such as India and, to an extent, Great Britain, tried to shift the emphasis towards a negotiated settlement. Yet it soon became clear that the future of Korea would in the first instance be determined on the battlefield rather than in the conference room.

7.22 The initial campaigns

Altogether 15 countries sent troops to Korea, although the vast majority were American and all were under the command of General MacArthur. By the time the United Nations forces reached South Korea it had been almost entirely overrun by the communists. By September 1950 only the south east, around the port of Pusan, was outside the control of the North Korean army. It was from this base, on 15 September, that MacArthur launched Operation Chromite, a bold, amphibious landing at Inchon, in the far north of South Korea (Table 7.4).

Table 7.4   The Korean War, June–September 1950

25 June	North Korea invaded South Korea.
27 June	UN Security Council agreed to provide military aid to South Korea.
29 June	North Korean army reached Seoul.
1 July	First United States combat troops arrived in Korea.
4 July	United States troops' first contact with North Korean forces.
7 July	General Douglas MacArthur named Supreme Commander.
15 September	American X Corps made successful amphibious attack on Inchon, which allowed UN forces to break out of Pusan and push on towards the 38th Parallel.
26 September	US forces retook Seoul.
27 November	Massive Chinese forces halted progress of United States army.

MacArthur's strategy was a stroke of genius. Ostensibly no site in South Korea appeared less suitable for a landing than Inchon. Twenty-five miles west of Seoul, Inchon was on a rugged piece of coast with unpredictable currents and a tidal pattern which meant that there were only three possible dates in September and October when the harbour waters would be deep enough to prevent the large American landing craft from being trapped in mud and silt. With the typhoon season fast approaching, the North Korean leadership could not have conceived that the Americans would dare to attempt a landing at Inchon. Military historian Max Hastings is in no doubt that this marked the high point of MacArthur's career:

> Inchon remains a monument to 'can do', to improvisation and risk-taking on a magnificent scale, above all to the spirit of Douglas MacArthur ... From the early stages of the conflict, as the Eighth Army struggled to maintain fighting room in the southeast of Korea, MacArthur's thoughts had been fixed with almost mystic conviction upon a possible landing at Inchon.

At a crucial meeting on 23 August, MacArthur told his doubtful generals:

> [T]he very arguments you have made as to the impracticabilities involved will tend to ensure for me the element of surprise. For the enemy commander will reason that no one would be so brash as to make such an attempt ... I can almost hear the ticking of the second hand of destiny. We must act now or we will die ... We shall land at Inchon, and I shall crush them. (In Hastings, 1988, pp. 116–19)

On 28 August, MacArthur received formal approval for his plans from the Joint Chiefs of Staff. Operation Chromite proved a brilliant success, taking United Nations troops far behind the North Korean lines. The communists had been outmanoeuvred and MacArthur's strategic brilliance enabled the United Nations forces to push the communists back towards the 38th Parallel. By the end of September United Nations troops had retaken Seoul and cleared the south of communists. However, it was the very speed and scale of MacArthur's success which led him inexorably towards a much greater conflict.

7.23 The intervention of China

On 1 October 1950, South Korean troops moved across the 38th Parallel into North Korea. The United Nations troops had now gone beyond their original aim of restoring independence to South Korea; MacArthur saw the possibility of uniting the whole country and of freeing the north from communist control. But this took troops of MacArthur's mainly American army close to the Yalu River, which was the border between North Korea and China. This was a critical moment in the Korean War and in American foreign policy. When Truman authorised military operations north of the 38th Parallel he appeared to be going beyond the policy of containment and towards a policy of rollback. China now warned that it would intervene if the Americans continued their progress towards the Chinese border. In September–October, the Chinese press carried increasingly antagonistic coverage with slogans such as, 'Resist America, Aid Korea' and 'Preserve Our Homes, Defend the Nation'. China's acting Chief of Staff declared 'American aggression has got to be stopped. The Americans can bomb us, they can destroy our industries, but they cannot defeat us on land.' (Hastings, 1988, pp. 158–59)

These warnings were played down in Washington. On 12 October the CIA advised that 'despite statements by Zhou Enlai, troop movements to Manchuria, and propaganda charges of atrocities and border violations, there are no convincing indications of an actual Chinese Communist intention to resort to full-scale intervention in Korea' (Hastings, 1988, p. 159). Secretary of State Dean Acheson found these comments persuasive; he was convinced that China would be unwilling to run the risk of becoming involved in a war with the United States. He was wrong. The threat to Chinese security was such that China felt driven to enter the war. On 8 October, Mao ordered 'Chinese People's Volunteers' to take up arms 'against the attacks of United States' imperialism' (Hastings, 1988, p. 159). The soldiers of two great powers were about to come face to face on the battlefield (Table 7.5).

Table 7.5   China's intervention in the Korean War, October–November 1950

1 October	South Korean troops crossed the 38th Parallel.
7 October	United Stated troops crossed the 38th Parallel.
8 October	Mao Zedong ordered Chinese volunteers to resist American imperialism.
24 October	American forces in Korea reached the Yalu River.
1 November	People's Republic of China (PRC) entered the Korean War on the side of North Korea.
4 November	United Nations Forces in Korea forced to retreat.
16 November	Truman reassured China that he never intended to carry out hostilities towards the Chinese.
24 November	American offensive, launched by MacArthur, took troops close to the Chinese border.

7.24 Military deadlock and initial peace negotiations

By November 1950 the number of Chinese troops in the field was huge, and would eventually rise to 1.2 million. The United Nations troops were unable to sustain their position in the face of such forces. The impetus now seemed to be with the Chinese, and with the enemy in rapid retreat it was decided to move to an aggressive strategy which would deny the enemy breathing space. Mao hoped that a combination of Chinese and North Korean forces could take control of Seoul and go on to drive the United Nations forces out of the country completely. Foreign Minister Zhou Enlai said that as the United States had ignored the 38th Parallel in October, it could no longer be valid as a demarcation line.

On Christmas Day 1950, the Chinese troops crossed the 38th Parallel and United Nations troops were forced to retreat into South Korea. It took weeks of bloody fighting before they were able to push the Chinese back to the 38th Parallel. By January 1951, it was becoming clear that a military solution was out of reach of both sides; the war was turning into a bloody war of attrition. At this point, the differences between General MacArthur and President Truman became increasingly acute. In March 1951 MacArthur was publicly critical of Truman's concept of a limited war and stated that he wanted the resources to be able to drive the communists back before waging an unlimited offensive against the Chinese, backed up with the use of atomic weapons.

On 11 April 1951, MacArthur was removed from his command and was replaced by General Ridgway. This decision was deeply unpopular with Congress and with the American public where the returning general was greeted as an American hero. However, a subsequent investigation chaired by General Omar Bradley vindicated the president's position, concluding that taking the conflict to China would have involved America in 'the wrong war, at the wrong time, in the wrong place' (Halberstam, 2008, p. 616). By now, the front had stabilised around the 38th Parallel. Both sides had constructed extensive trench networks, leading to a military stalemate but with enormous casualties. The military deadlock was replicated in the 'on–off' saga of the peace negotiations: a great deal of ill will and mutual suspicion meant that the talks themselves were exceptionally acrimonious.

With both sides sustaining heavy casualties and with no sign of a military breakthrough, peace talks began on 10 July 1951. The Soviet Union encouraged both sides to look for peace but the talks were as difficult to bring to an end as the fighting, and dragged on for many months. A major stumbling block concerned the exchange of prisoners of war. In the summer of 1952 the United States resumed heavy bombing of the north, which had the effect of encouraging the Chinese to look for peace terms. As autumn gave way to winter, responsibility for bring the war to an end passed from Truman to Eisenhower.

Further reading

Bird K. & Sherwin M.J., *The Triumph and Tragedy of J. Robert Oppenheimer* (London: Atlantic Books 2009).

Costello J., *The Pacific War* (London: Pan Books 1985).

Crockatt R., *The Fifty Years War: The United States and the Soviet Union in World Politics, 1941–1991* (New York: Routledge 1995).

Dobbs M., *Six Months in 1945: From World War to Cold War*. (London: Arrow Books 2013).

Evans H., *The American Century: People, Power and Politics: An Illustrated History* (London: Jonathan Cape 1998).

Ferrell R.H., *Harry S. Truman: A Life* (Columbia: University of Missouri Press 1994).

Halberstam D., *The Coldest Winter: America and the Korean War* (London: Macmillan 2008).

Hastings M., *The Korean War* (London: Michael Joseph Ltd 1988).

Heale M.J., *McCarthy's Americans: Red Scare Politics in State and Nation, 1935–1965* (London: Macmillan Press 1998).

Johnson P., *A History of the American People* (London: Weidenfeld & Nicolson 1997).

McCullough D., *Truman* (New York: Touchstone – Simon & Schuster 1993).

Miller A., *The Crucible* (Penguin 1953).

Navasky V.S., *Naming Names* (The Viking Press 2003).

Neer R.M., *Napalm: An American Biography* (Cambridge Mass.: Belknap Harvard 2013).

Peraino K., *A Force So Swift: Mao, Truman and the Birth of Modern China, 1949* (New York: Crown Publishing 2017).

Pietrusza D., *1948: Harry Truman's Improbable Victory and the Year That Transformed America* (New York: Union Square Press 2011).

Reynolds D., *America, Empire of Liberty: A New History* (New York: Allen Lane 2009).

Rhodes R., *Dark Sun: The Making of the Hydrogen Bomb* (New York: Touchstone – Simon & Schuster 1996).

Schiff S., *The Witches, Salem 1692: A History* (London: Little, Brown and Company 2015).

Schlesinger A.M. Jr, *A Thousand Days: John F. Kennedy in the White House* (London: Andre Deutsch 1965).

Schrecker E., *The Age of McCarthyism: A Brief History with Documents* (Boston: Bedford Books 1994).

Stuek W., *The Korean War: An International History* (New Jersey: Princeton University Press 1995).

Winkler H.A., *The Age of Catastrophe: A History of the West, 1914–1945* (New Haven: Yale University Press 2015).

Yergin D., *Shattered Peace: The Origins of the Cold War and the National Security State* (Boston: Houghton Mifflin Company 1977).

■ ⊻ 8 The 1950s: Affluence and anxiety

8.1 Ike's background and upbringing

Dwight David Eisenhower was born in Denison, Texas, on 14 October 1890. He was raised in the small cattle town of Abilene, Kansas. Eisenhower's father was employed as an engineer in a creamery. His mother, whom Eisenhower recalled was 'by far the greatest personal influence in our lives' (Pach & Richardson, 1991, p. 2), held deeply religious and pacifist views. This did not stand in the way when Dwight left high school and commenced his college education at the United States Military Academy at West Point in New York. Eisenhower left West Point in 1915 with a reasonable academic record and with deeply held convictions about the importance of teamwork. He achieved a second lieutenant's commission in the infantry, and while stationed in San Antonio, Texas, he met and married Mamie Doud. The death, in infancy, of their first child, a son named Doud but affectionately known as Icky, cast a shadow over Eisenhower which would remain with him for the rest of his life.

Meanwhile his military career was not helped when he wrote a forthright article in 1920 advocating the development of more powerful tanks; this went against orthodox thinking, which still favoured an emphasis on infantry. However, the patronage of General Fox Conner restored the momentum behind Eisenhower's career and he was posted to the Command and General Staff School at Fort Leavenworth, Kansas, from which he graduated first in his class in 1925. Further progress came when Eisenhower was sent to Washington DC, where he worked for the staff of General Pershing. This was followed by a spell at the Army War College, a clear indication that Eisenhower was now being trained for a senior position in the army leadership. A period in France, compiling a guide to the battlefields, was followed by a return to Washington in 1929. A series of appointments culminated in Eisenhower being assigned as personal aide to the enigmatic and flamboyant General Douglas MacArthur. The two worked closely together for seven years but by 1939 Eisenhower needed a break from his general's 'regular shouting tirades'. (Pach & Richardson, 1991, p. 5)

The outbreak of the Second World War saw Eisenhower's career take off. He served in Fort Sam Houston as chief of staff of the Third Army, but shortly after Pearl Harbor he was summoned back to Washington by the Chief of Staff, General George C. Marshall. A series of challenging assignments culminated in Eisenhower being awarded his second star and being placed in command of the Operations Division. Eisenhower was flourishing under the inspiring leadership of General Marshall, and confided in one aide that he 'wouldn't trade one Marshall for fifty MacArthurs' (Pach & Richardson, 1991, p. 6). Eisenhower's growing reputation was further enhanced after a visit to England to liaise on strategy gave him the opportunity to make a tremendous personal impression on Churchill. Churchill and Marshall agreed that Eisenhower could be entrusted with the responsibility of organising the Allied assault on Nazi-occupied Europe. After the Tehran conference of November 1943, Roosevelt told Eisenhower that he would be the supreme commander of Operation Overlord, and Eisenhower's intelligence, strategic sense, clear leadership and ability to co-ordinate were reflected in the success of the D-Day landings which commenced on 6 June 1944. Although this action constituted a defining moment in the defeat of Hitler, there were those who argued that Eisenhower had been mistaken in not moving his forces on to Berlin. Nevertheless, Eisenhower's leadership meant that he was generally acknowledged as the outstanding allied military figure of the Second World War.

Although Eisenhower had achieved his military objective in Europe, the issue of whether to use the newly developed atomic bomb against Japan now came to his attention. Eisenhower attempted to persuade Truman not to use the bomb, but to no avail. While Eisenhower contemplated a quiet retirement he was nominated to become chief of staff upon the retirement of General Marshall, a post which he accepted with real reluctance and solely from a sense of duty. In this capacity, he observed the onset of the Cold War with dismay. He had established a cordial relationship with the head of Soviet forces, Marshall Zhukov, but by 1947 he had concluded that 'Russia is definitely out to communize the world' and believed that the free nations were 'under deadly, persistent and constant attack' (Pach & Richardson, 1991, p. 12). The deterioration in the political situation made Eisenhower realise that a key issue for the United States was to balance its changing security needs with its economic resources. Eisenhower stepped down as chief of staff in February 1948, and in October 1948 he accepted an academic position as president of Columbia University. Meanwhile, in early 1949, the Secretary of Defense James Forrestal persuaded Eisenhower to temporarily preside over the Joint Chiefs of Staff (JCS), an appointment designed to ease open rifts over the spending plans of the individual divisions of the armed forces.

Eisenhower's distinguished career and obvious integrity made him one of the most respected figures in America. Both political parties saw him as a potentially outstanding presidential candidate. However, Eisenhower held strong feelings about the division between military and political authority. In response to advances from both political parties, Eisenhower attempted to remove himself from the speculation in a letter written to a New Hampshire Republican in January 1948:

> I am not available for and could not accept nomination to high public office. It is my conviction that the necessary and wise subordination of the military to civil power will be best sustained ... when lifelong professional soldiers, in the absence of some obvious and overriding reasons, abstain from seeking high public office. (In Pach & Richardson, 1991, p. 15)

Eisenhower was convinced that the Republican contender Thomas E. Dewey, the Governor of New York, would defeat Truman. However, Truman's surprise victory in November 1948 led to desperation in Republican circles and a conviction that only Eisenhower could change their fortunes. Meanwhile, upon the formation of NATO in April 1949 Eisenhower accepted the position of the commander of its armed forces. It may have seemed that Eisenhower was destined to remain in military rather than political circles for the rest of his working life. However, Truman's election victory in 1948, the communist victory in China in 1949 and, most of all, the failure to secure

David Dwight Eisenhower

34th President of the United States (1953–61)
Born: 14 October 1890
Birthplace: Denison, Texas
Died: 28 March 1969, aged 78; buried at Abilene, Kansas
Education: US Military Academy, West Point, New York
Political Party: Republican
State: Texas
Occupations before presidency: Military Service: Supreme Commander of
    Allied Expeditionary Forces in Western Europe
Previous government service: None
Age at inauguration: 62
Dates of office: 20 January 1953–20 January 1961
Election: November 1952 and 1956
Vice president: Richard Milhous Nixon
Length of term: 8 years

---

victory in Korea between 1950 and 1952 created in Eisenhower a new sense of duty. Ultimately Eisenhower let it be known in Republican circles that while he would not seek high office 'there is a vast difference between responding to a duty imposed by a National Convention and the seeking of a nomination' (Pach & Richardson, 1991, p. 20). In January 1952, Eisenhower stated that while he remained duty bound to NATO he would be open to the call of an even more important service. Eisenhower's political career was about to take off.

Eisenhower received the Republican presidential nomination on 11 July 1952. Initially during the campaign Eisenhower remained aloof from the Republican criticism of Truman's record over Korea. Privately, he decided early on in the campaign that if elected he would need to visit Korea to appraise the situation. On 24 October, he publicly announced that if elected he would personally 'go there' to bring the war to an 'honourable end'. There is no doubt, given the general mood of disillusionment with the war, that this stance was a key factor in enabling him to achieve a major victory. Many voters blamed Truman for the fact that even after two years of fighting and heavy casualties, victory was still not in sight. Truman bitterly resented what he saw as Eisenhower's 'demagogic' and personal criticism of his foreign policy. While Republican strategists relished the devastating impact of Eisenhower's announcement, the candidate himself had doubts. He worried that people would imagine that he would be able to magically resolve a deeply complex issue. There is no doubt that the unpopularity of the Korean War with the American people cost the Democratic Party's presidential candidate, Adlai Stevenson, dear. Many Americans felt that Eisenhower's military experience would be invaluable in bringing the war to an end. On 4 November 1952 Eisenhower received 55.1 per cent of the total ballot. Having secured all but nine states, he had received a mandate to bring the war to an end (Table 8.1).

Candidate	Party	Electoral College votes	Popular votes
Dwight D. Eisenhower (New York)	Republican	442	33,936,442
Adlai E. Stevenson (California)	Democrat	89	27,314,992

Table 8.1 The result of the 1952 presidential election

8.2 Continuity and change between the Truman and Eisenhower administrations

Even though Truman had been unable to take much of his Fair Deal legislation through Congress, Eisenhower remained fiercely critical of his predecessor's intentions. Eisenhower believed that the Fair Deal represented a series of calculated concessions towards a range of interest groups which had traditionally enjoyed links with the Democratic Party – namely the labour unions, the elderly, African Americans and farmers. Generally, Eisenhower felt that Truman encouraged people to believe that 'only government can bring us happiness, security and opportunity'. Eisenhower contended that the Democratic brand of 'paternalistic government can gradually destroy, by suffocation in the immediate advantage of subsidy, the will of a people to maintain a high degree of individual responsibility'. The strength of Eisenhower's feelings was reflected in his pledge to 'offer myself as a political leader to unseat the New Deal–Fair Deal bureaucracy in Washington' (Pach & Richardson, 1991, p. 31). Eisenhower felt that Truman's exaggerated emphasis on the disadvantaged and the 'have-nots' exacerbated rather than soothed the potential for class conflict and unrest in a modern industrial society.

Eisenhower's vision sounded very different to that of his predecessor. 'Ike' said that he wanted to lead the United States 'down the middle of the road between the unfettered power of concentrated wealth ... and the unbridled power of ... partisan interests'. He wanted to combine 'the individual good and the common good'. He believed that the president should not seek to extend his powers but rather to exercise constraint, leading to 'progress through compromise' (Pach & Richardson, 1991, p. 32). Despite these clear ideological differences, there were some interesting similarities in the approaches of Eisenhower and Truman. Both leaders believed that governments should try to promote economic growth. Both tried to avoid creating budget deficits and the associated danger of inflation. While Eisenhower was critical of Truman's spending plans, historians have pointed out that for three of his eight years in office Truman did return a balanced budget. The historian Donald McCoy (1991) neatly points out the factor that draws these two very different presidencies together: 'The fact of the matter was that the Truman administration could not do without capitalist growth to finance its goals, any more than the Eisenhower administration could do away with earlier social reforms and still sustain stability.' (In Pach & Richardson, 1991, pp. 32–33)

8.3 The decline of McCarthyism

Ostensibly the defeat of the Democratic Party in November 1952 might have signalled the end of Joseph McCarthy's outspoken and unsupported accusations alleging the infiltration of the government by communists. However, even with Eisenhower in the White House, McCarthy continued to level accusations, particularly when he took over the Senate's Permanent Investigating Subcommittee. While Eisenhower was a committed anti-communist, he was personally appalled by McCarthy's demagogic tactics and bullying behaviour. However, Eisenhower was extremely conscious of the need to preserve the unity of the Republican Party and was reluctant to open up a split over the communist issue. In addition, although Eisenhower felt contempt for McCarthy he told his closest advisers that he refused to 'get into the gutter with that guy' (Shrecker, 1994, p. 64).

McCarthy now turned his attention away from the government and towards the army. Meanwhile a special Senate committee was set up to investigate allegations that McCarthy had pressed the army to give preferential treatment to a member of his staff. With the advent of TV, the televised Army–McCarthy hearings gripped the nation's attention when they were broadcast in April–June 1954. The television hearings showed McCarthy in a far from flattering light. As the hearings were coming to an end McCarthy's bullying instincts were revealed. He accused Joseph Welch, an associate in the law firm representing the army, of belonging to the left-wing National Lawyer's Guild while he was at college. Welch's measured and plaintive reply: 'Have you no sense of decency, Sir?' (Shrecker, 1994, p. 65) devastated McCarthy and captured the public mood perfectly. In December 1954 the Senate voted to condemn McCarthy's conduct by a vote of 67–22. The hearings destroyed McCarthy's credibility. His health, undermined by an increasingly serious drinking problem, rapidly deteriorated and he died on 2 May 1957.

Stephen Ambrose offers this verdict on Eisenhower's approach to the McCarthy problem:

> Eisenhower wanted to see Senator McCarthy eliminated from national public life, and he wanted it done without making America's record and image on civil liberties worse than it already was. But because Eisenhower would not denounce McCarthy by name, or otherwise stand up to the senator from Wisconsin, McCarthy was able to do much damage to civil liberties, the Republican Party, numerous individuals, the US Army and the executive branch before he finally destroyed himself ... Eisenhower's cautious, hesitant approach – or non-approach – to the McCarthy issue did the President's reputation no good, and much harm. (Bischof & Ambrose, 1995, p. 248)

8.4 The rise of an affluent society

In 1947, when the Cold War was increasingly influential on all aspects of the American way of life, the newsman George Putnam produced a classic statement of the difference in ideology between the capitalist United States and its communist rivals. Standing outside a typical American shopping centre, he declared it to be a 'concrete expression of the practical idealism that built America ... plenty of free parking for all those cars that we capitalists seem to acquire. Who can help but contrast them with what you'd find under communism?' (Bondi, 1995, p. 347) Three years later, in May 1950, Seattle's Northgate shopping mall, the largest in the country, opened for business. This seems an appropriate event at the start of a decade which for many Americans was one of unparalleled prosperity. Elaine Tyler May (1988) has described 'The legendary family of the 1950s, complete with appliances, station wagons, back-yard barbecues, and tricycles scattered on the sidewalks.' However, May also claims that this emphasis on consumer goods was to an extent a by-product of the fear generated by the Cold War. May contends that people saw the development of a com-fortable home as a haven from the trauma engendered by the widespread fear of a nuclear war (May, 1988, p. 11).

During the 1950s the American economy reached heights not witnessed since the consumer boom of the 1920s. By 1953, the annual income of an average American fam-ily reached $4,011. The decade was also notable for rapid developments in business technology: in 1953, the first IBM computer, the 701, was introduced. The sense of a truly booming society was further enhanced when, on 12 March, the last remaining price controls from the Korean War, on beer, coffee and domestic heating oil, were removed. In the following year the emphasis on a consumer society was maintained. In 1954 Swanson foods introduced the first frozen 'TV Dinners.' On 9 March, General Motors reported annual sales of $10.2 billion, making it the leading American com-pany in income terms.

The new suburbia was most famously demonstrated in the development of 'Levit-town.' This was based on the work of Abraham Levitt and his sons William and Alfred. They purchased a potato field in Long Island and turned it into a prefabricated suburban community named 'Levittown.' Each house cost exactly the same amount and boasted identical features. For a payment of $7,990 ($60 per month) buyers obtained a four-room house with attic, outdoor barbecue, washing machine and built-in television set. One important element in the shift to the suburbs was the view prevalent in the scientific community that the withdrawal of population from the major urban areas would leave many people less vulnerable to a nuclear strike. As Eisenhower himself stated in 1956, an improved road network would speed up evacuation in the event of a nuclear attack.

As was the case in previous decades of growth, the share in prosperity was extremely uneven. Whereas the median income for a white family in 1953 was $4,392, the figure for non-white families was $2,461. By 1960 the gap had grown between the white figure of $5,835 and the non-white figure of $3,233. Finally, Pach and Richardson provide a broad perspective of the consumer society, highlighting its strengths but also some of its limitations:

> Americans saw in 1953 an extraordinary national strength that rested on rapid popu-lation growth. The baby boom, which reached its peak during the Eisenhower years ... helped fuel a strong expansion of the economy during the 1950s. Throughout the Eisenhower Presidency, the gross national product increased at an annual rate of 2.4 per cent, from $364.6 billion to $520.1 billion. Because of the growth in the num-ber of families, many basic industries prospered, such as housing, automobiles and steel. Contemporary observers declared that Americans were a people of plenty, and indeed they were, but hardly in equal measure. The Eisenhower prosperity, in short, brought no relative improvement for blacks. (Pach & Richardson, 1991, p. 47)

Jerome David Salinger was born on New Year's Day 1919 in Manhattan where his father made a lucrative career as a cheese merchant. His success allowed the family to move into increasingly expensive areas of New York and finally into a prestigious address near Central Park. Of Lithuanian descent, his father harboured assumptions about his son's future career path – that he would uphold the family business. His mother, who was from Iowa, was much more indulgent of her son's dreams.

The family's wealth led to Sonny, as they called him, being sent to McBurney School. His academic career there was unimpressive and he was asked to leave after two years of underachievement. Fans of Salinger's most famous book, *The Catcher in the Rye* (1951), have noted that this was the school where, as captain of the fencing team, he accidentally left equipment on the New York Subway. A spell at Valley Forge Military Academy was much more successful. Despite the spartan regime there, Salinger excelled, joining a variety of extra-curricular groups, including the college's cadet programme, and above all flourished in drama and literature. He then enrolled for a Bachelor of Arts Degree at New York University in 1936. While its bohemian atmosphere and city location would appear to have suited Sonny's artistic temperament he failed to thrive. He dropped out of NYU, while a subsequent trip to see family contacts in Vienna and Poland in 1938 brought home to him the frightening reality of the menace of fascism.

By now, Salinger was determined to be a writer and a brief spell at Ursinus College in Pennsylvania provided him with further stimulus in that direction. A turning point came when he enrolled at Columbia University in January 1939 and came under the inspirational influence of a tutor called Whit Burnett, who encouraged Salinger and whose respected magazine *Story* published his story 'The Young Folks' in January 1940. Publications in popular magazines followed, but Salinger's dream was to be featured in the highly prestigious *New Yorker* magazine. He received several rejections but Salinger's creativity was indomitable and he made his *New Yorker* breakthrough in October 1941 with 'Slight Rebellion Off Madison.'

Like so many of his peers, Salinger's life was changed forever when he reported for active duty in the 1st US Signal Corps Battalion in April 1942. While he acquitted himself with great courage, the conflict was inevitably deeply traumatic, though at the time this was poorly recognised. During the war, Salinger carried about with him draft copies of *The Catcher in the Rye,* and amid the conflict he wrote whenever he could. By the time the war ended, three years of military service had taken their toll and Jerry, as his friends in the army called him, was admitted to hospital in Nuremberg in January 1945. Perhaps because of the mental health trauma he had suffered, Salinger's personal relationships were frequently complex and sometimes short-lived. A brief marriage to a German lady illustrates this point.

Salinger's unique, idiosyncratic style meant that his relationship with the somewhat staid *New Yorker* was not straightforward, but the publication of 'A Perfect Day for Banana Fish' in January 1948 perhaps showed that the

Continued

magazine's insistence on his revising his original work was helping him develop as a writer. By now Salinger's writing was widely recognised in literary circles and this recognition increased in 1950 with the very well-received 'For Esmé – with Love and Squalor'.

Salinger's intuitive insights into adolescence, quirky humour and brilliant expression appeared to perfection in his masterwork, *The Catcher in the Rye*, which was published by Little, Brown in 1951. The quality of the book was not universally understood and several publishers, including the *New Yorker*, turned it down.

However, the novel received many outstanding reviews and to Salinger's delight his work was compared to Ring Lardner. The *New York Times* called the book 'unusually brilliant' and ironically the *New Yorker* described it as 'brilliant, funny' and 'meaningful' (Slawenski, 2010, p. 197). Not least, the book contained one of the most perfect, widely celebrated opening paragraphs in American literature.

Ironically, the commercial success of the book and the intense publicity it generated brought with it an invasion of privacy and a hectic schedule which Salinger increasingly found distasteful. In February 1953 he relocated from Manhattan to the much more remote setting of Cornish, New Hampshire where he lived for the rest of his life.

Further, important work followed, including *Nine Stories* (1953), *Franny* (1954), *Raise High the Roof Beam, Carpenters* (1955) and *Zooey* (1957). At the same time, Salinger's reclusive commitment to his art saw him take to his bunker on the estate at Cornish, where he cut himself off from all family contact for days at a time.

His relationships with family, publishers, fans and an intrusive press were invariably complex. His tendency to withdraw was perhaps overstated as in this period he continued to travel and engage in correspondence. However, when his final novella, *Hapworth 16, 1924* (1965) was widely criticised, his career as a public author effectively came to an end. He continued to write for the rest of his life but had lost all interest in the publishing process. J.D. Salinger died on 27 January 2010, at the age of 91. While his career brought great joy to millions of ardent readers, Salinger's life itself was often shrouded with unhappiness. His work, though, is more revered than ever.

Further reading: Kenneth Slawenski, *J.D.Salinger: A Life Raised High* (Pomona Books 2010); David Shields and Shane Salerno, *Salinger* (Simon & Schuster 2014)

Great American Lives: Robert Lowell, 1917–77

The poetry of Robert Lowell is as difficult, and as exciting, as any that has been written in our time. It is a proud, private, hugely ambitious body of work, and it makes no obvious concessions to its readers. Lowell challenges one to be as intelligent, as imaginatively quick, and as well-read as he is himself, and the challenge is one that few readers will be able to take up with confidence. When Lowell writes about the twentieth century, he is likely to take us there via seventeenth-century poetry, mediaeval theology, ancient history and classical philosophy. To fix the present moment, he is prepared

Continued

to range up against it all that he knows of what has been thought and done and written in the past. Yet his poems are instinct with contemporaneity; they tell us more of what it means to live, painfully and difficultly, in our century than any writer has previously dared.

Jonathan Raban, *Robert Lowell's Poems: A Selection* (Faber and Faber 1982)

As these remarks by Jonathan Raban tell us, Robert Lowell is regarded as one of the foremost American poets of the twentieth century. Born in 1917 to one of the wealthiest, most influential Boston families, his life was nevertheless plagued by serious mental illness and periods of great unhappiness and self-destruction. From a young age he was often difficult to be with, and described himself at 8½ years old as 'thuggish'. In his teenage years, the powerfully built, temperamental young man was nicknamed 'Cal' (short for the crazed autocratic Roman Emperor Caligula) and people found him to be intimidating and physically aggressive.

He moved from the exclusive St Mark's preparatory school in Southborough, Massachusetts, to Harvard University, but by now he was prone to waves of great euphoria and then extremely low moods. After two increasingly unhappy years at Harvard, Lowell moved to Kenyon College in Ohio, where he studied classics. He had decided to be a great poet and his classical education equipped him with rich, complex references that would permeate his work. Lowell's relationship with his parents was difficult and his rebellious nature may be one reason why he rejected their Episcopalianism for Roman Catholicism (this itself did not last). Religious references, classicism, and evocative images of Boston's maritime history made his writing difficult, at times obscure, but at the same time startling and profound. In addition to teaching, translating poetry and his own flourishing career as a poet, Lowell also became intensely political. He was imprisoned as a conscientious objector during the Second World War and became an outspoken critic of the Vietnam War in 1960s.

Throughout his adult life Lowell suffered serious bouts of manic depression. One of many stays at the well-known McLean psychiatric hospital in Belmont, Massachusetts was immortalised in the poem 'Waking in the Blue'.

Lowell received many accolades for his work including the National Book Award for Poetry, an appointment as the Consultant in Poetry to the Library of Congress and, in 1947, the Pulitzer Prize. He wrote prolifically but some of his most important work included *Life Studies* (1959), *For the Union Dead* (1964) and *The Dolphin* (1973). He continued to publish widely into the 1970s but died suddenly after suffering a heart attack in New York City in 1977.

Further reading: Jonathan Raban, *Robert Lowell's Poems: A Selection* (Faber and Faber 1982)

8.5 The 'baby boom' of the 1950s

The 1950s was notable for the rapid increase in population which became known as the 'baby boom'. This trend began in 1945 and reached its peak during the next decade. When Eisenhower began his presidency in 1953 the population of the United States was 160 million. By 1961, when he left office, the figure had reached 181 million.

The average age of marriage came down to 20 for women and 22 for men. This helped to fuel the economic growth of the 1950s. The 'baby boom' was accompanied by the rapid development of suburban communities. A combination of post-war economic well-being and generous government subsidies enabled many middle-class families to become homeowners for the first time.

The pent-up consumer demand of the wartime period was released from August 1945 into a new wave of spending. New houses, home furnishings, consumer appliances, baby clothes and automobiles were all major sources of expenditure. On average, in each of the years between 1945 and 1949, more than a million new homes were built. Tyler May provides this summary of the post-war American economy:

> In the years following World War II the American household changed dramatically. Not only was the birth-rate exploding, but housework was transformed by technology. The new modern household now included many electronic appliances designed to make housework easier. The electric waffle maker, coffeemaker, eggbeater, egg timer, toaster, and dishwasher all came into common use. The appliances in the average household cost a total of more than two thousand dollars. (In Bondi, 1995, p. 107)

It may be tempting to assume that all of these fast-moving developments were generally beneficial to American women. Certainly some of the drudgery associated with domestic work was being removed by technology. However, the assumptions that lay behind this process were less welcome. First of all, the role of women was clearly delineated. Advertisements, films and literature frequently portrayed women embracing the prospect of motherhood as opposed to career decisions or educational opportunities. Once a house, husband and family were secured, the role of women was seen as to keep this haven clean, comforting and hospitable. Cleaning, cooking, looking after children, taking children to and from school and staying at home with them if they were ill were all regarded as fundamentally female tasks. In the workplace women found it more difficult to obtain professional positions, had to accept lower pay than men and frequently faced misogynistic attitudes in the workplace. The Eisenhower Administration, with its emphasis on successful white businessmen, did nothing to change or challenge these attitudes. Above all, the prosperous society of the 1950s carried with it an overwhelming expectation for women to comply. It would not be until the 1960s that American society's assumptions about women would be brought into question.

8.6 Eisenhower's domestic legislation

Eisenhower characterised his approach to domestic affairs as one of 'dynamic conservatism'. Key elements included reduced government intervention in the economy and a sympathetic attitude towards business, symbolised by inclusion in the Cabinet of a number of leading businessmen. For example, the Secretary of State, John Foster Dulles, was a wealthy lawyer, and Secretary of Defense, Charles E. Wilson, had served as the president of General Motors. In addition, Eisenhower was responsible for the creation of the Department of Health, Education and Welfare. This was established in 1953 and absorbed the existing Office of Education. Eisenhower also presided over the extension of unemployment and social security benefits. The administration was also responsible for the introduction of a 'soil bank' plan, designed to provide support for farmers who were being asked to reduce output so as to lessen the national problem of overproduction.

The Interstate Highway Act, 1956

In 1956 Eisenhower secured Congressional backing for a ten-year interstate highway-building programme which would ultimately cost $25 billion. America already possessed an extensive network (1940, 1.34 million miles of road; 1950, 1.68 million miles of road). But under the provisions of the Interstate Highway Act new, wider, safer four-to-eight-lane freeways were constructed, underlining the rise of private transport at the expense of public provision. The Act boosted the fortunes of the motor industry, the main beneficiaries being the 'Big Three' (Chrysler, Ford and General Motors). It could also be said that the rise of sprawling suburbs, shopping malls and domestic holidays owed a great deal to the Interstate Highway Act. However, the rise of automobile and air traffic heightened the decline of the national railroad industry. Hugh Brogan believes that the Act:

> [did more] to shape the lives of the American people than any other law passed since 1945. It reinforced the ascendancy of the private car over all other forms of passenger transport. It gave a great impetus to African American emigration from the South, and a huge boost to the automobile, engineering and building industries. (Brogan, 1985, p. 631)

Richard Layman concurs with Brogan:

> The impact of suburbia on consumer behavior can hardly be overstated ... Young people choose to marry early, to have several children in the early years of marriage, to live in nice neighborhoods, and to have cars, washing machines, refrigerators, television sets, and several other appliances at the same time. (In Bondi, 1995, p. 347)

The Tidelands Oil Act, 1953

This presidential initiative led to the state taking over the ownership of valuable offshore oil deposits in the Gulf of Mexico and off the Pacific Coast. This led to private interests being allowed to exploit these natural resources: a lucrative contract for a massive new electricity plant outside Memphis was awarded to the Dixon–Yates syndicate, as opposed to remaining under government control through the Tennessee Valley Authority (TVA).

8.7 Eisenhower's leadership style and the 'hidden hand' presidency

Eisenhower's style of presidential leadership has been the subject of widely different interpretations. It may well be that one of the reasons why Eisenhower has tended to be underrated by historians was his habit of answering difficult questions with bewilderingly complex, long-winded replies. One of the most celebrated examples, given by

Eisenhower at a press briefing when he was asked if the United States would use force in response to an attack by China on Quemoy and Matsu, is repeated below:

> I cannot answer that question in advance. The only thing I know about war are two things: the most changeable factor in war is human nature in its day-by-day manifestation; but the only unchangeable factor in war is human nature. And the next thing is that every war is going to astonish you in the way it occurred and the way it is carried out ... So for a man to predict, particularly if he has the responsibility for making the decision, to predict what he is going to use, how he is going to do it, would I think exhibit his ignorance of war; that is what I believe. So I think you just have to wait, and that is the kind of prayerful decision that may someday face a president. (In Bischof & Ambrose, 1995, p. 58)

It is now clear to historians that Eisenhower was doing this deliberately to confuse the press. At the time, many people felt that the general was just out of his depth. A more profound reappraisal of Eisenhower is summarised in an extract from an essay by Eisenhower scholar Fred Greenstein, written to commemorate the centenary of Eisenhower's birth:

> It would take little time, I reasoned, to confirm the well-established view that even to speak of Eisenhower and leadership in the same phrase was a contradiction in terms. This was the President who had been ranked twenty-first by a panel of distinguished historians in a 1961 poll of presidential greatness – a tie with Chester Arthur. The view that Eisenhower was ill suited for presidential leadership was widely shared during his years in the White House. I myself could still remember his vague, syntactically tangled answers to reporters' questions in press conferences, and his assertions that he was not familiar with matters that had been discussed in *The New York Times* ... The Eisenhower revealed to me was far from being the superannuated general who, in the phrase of the keynote speaker at the 1956 Democratic convention, whiled away his time on the 'green fairways of indifference'. Instead he was at the centre of his administration's decision making. He ran the show in the White House. (In Bischof & Ambrose, 1995, pp. 55–56)

8.8 The election of 1956

Eisenhower's decision to run for a second term of office in 1956 was not a straightforward one. Eisenhower biographers Pach and Richardson vividly describe what happened to the president as he enjoyed his vacation in September 1955:

> After a few hours of work, Eisenhower shot a round of golf, lunched on a hamburger heaped with onions ... at 1.30 the next morning, his restlessness woke his wife, and he complained of indigestion pains. Eisenhower actually suspected something far worse. 'It hurt like hell ...' he later told Vice-President Richard M. Nixon, 'but I never let Mamie know how much it hurt.' (Pach & Richardson, 1991, p. 113)

In fact, Eisenhower had suffered a 'slightly more than moderate' heart attack. Although Eisenhower had made a recovery by 1956, returning to a full work schedule as early as January, the question mark raised by his heart attack made his family and friends feel that he had done enough for the Republican Party and should now enjoy his retirement. The key factor which made him decide to ignore these concerns and run again was his fear that in his absence the Democrats would win and all of his work would be undone. Eisenhower was distinctly unimpressed by 'crackpot Democrats', including eventual Democratic nominee Adlai Stevenson, 'who did not have the competency to run the office of President' (Pach & Richardson, 1991, p. 115).

Eisenhower's closest advisers and key figures in the Republican Party came to the conclusion that he was the only man who could be trusted to virtually guarantee a Republican victory in November 1956. On 29 February 1956, Eisenhower announced his candidacy in typical style when he told a group of journalists at a briefing in Washington that:

> I would not allow my name to go before the Republican Convention unless they, all the Republicans understood, so that they would not be nominating some other individual than they thought they were nominating ... And my answer within the limits I have so sketchily observed, but which I will explain in detail tonight so as to get the story out in one continuous narrative, my answer will be positive, that is, affirmative. (In Pach & Richardson, 1991, p. 118)

Almost as tangled as his syntax was Eisenhower's agonising over his running mate. While Nixon had been a loyal, hard-working and efficient vice president he had not established a particularly close relationship with Eisenhower. Eisenhower found it hard to like Nixon and told a colleague, 'I just haven't been able to believe that he is presidential timber.' (Pach & Richardson, 1991, p. 119) Eisenhower's carefully measured ambiguity when asked by the press whether Nixon would continue as his running mate caused the vice president 'absolutely indescribable anguish' (Pach & Richardson, 1991, p. 121). It was not until August that the Republican National Convention made Eisenhower's decision for him by choosing Nixon as vice president with only one vote against. The campaign itself was more straightforward. Four years of peace and prosperity enabled the Republican campaign to claim that 'everything's booming but the guns'. As early as October, Eisenhower told his son that Stevenson was 'licked' and that he 'knew it' (Pach & Richardson, 1991, p. 126). Eisenhower did not see the need for energetic campaigning and with the foreign policy crises over Hungary and Suez becoming more demanding of his time, he cruised to an emphatic victory. Eisenhower received 35,575,420 votes, placing him 9.5 million ahead of his Democrat rival, and secured a majority in 41 states compared to 39 in the election of 1952 (Table 8.2).

Table 8.2 The result of the 1956 presidential election

Candidate	Party	Electoral College votes	Popular votes
Dwight D. Eisenhower (New York)	Republican	457	35,575,420
Adlai E. Stevenson (California)	Democrat	73	26,033,066
Walter B. Jones (Alabama)	Democratic	1	

In his second inaugural address, in January 1957, Eisenhower was able to proudly proclaim to the American people: 'We meet again, as upon a like moment four years ago, and again you have witnessed my solemn oath of service to you ... In our nation work and health abound. The air rings with the song of our industry ... the chorus of America the bountiful.' (Pach & Richardson, 1991, p. 159)

It was a landslide victory, but it would expose the ageing president to a fresh series of trials and tribulations that would often make him wonder whether he had made the right decision in running for a second term. Even so, Eisenhower believed that the victory was a personal mandate for the implementation of his beliefs and convictions. The political landscape was not quite so straightforward for Eisenhower in Congress. In the 1956 election the Democrats gained one seat in the Senate and two in the House, thus retaining their majority in both parts of Congress.

Despite Eisenhower's optimism at the time of his re-election, 1957 turned out to be a difficult year for the American economy, as summarised here by Pach and Richardson:

> The assurance and optimism of the beginning of the second term crumbled because of a series of economic, international and political shocks. The Eisenhower prosper-ity dissolved into the worst recession since the Great Depression ... The economy had turned sharply downward in summer 1957 and reached its low point in spring 1958. The hard times were severe. Industrial production declined 14 per cent, cor-porate profits fell 25 per cent, and unemployment reached a high of 7.5 per cent. Federal actions aggravated the recession. Restrictions on credit drove up interest rates and cut into consumption of durable goods, particularly automobiles. Cut-backs in defence procurement, implemented so that the federal government would not exceed the current ceiling on the national debt, also helped slow the economy ... The administration's tepid and at times, fumbling response to the recession only intensified public dissatisfaction. (Pach & Richardson, 1991, pp. 159–76)

While this period was undoubtedly challenging for Eisenhower, his economic legacy was ultimately far-reaching and positive:

> His most important contribution to the health of American society ... resulted from his management of the economy ... Eisenhower was criticised for failing to stimulate even more economic growth, since the rate of increase was lower in America than in many other industrial countries ... John F. Kennedy made economic sluggishness a major theme of his campaign ... Though the post-war period is usually thought of as one long surge of prosperity, it was during the Eisenhower years that this was most true ... A prudent manager of the economy, Eisenhower was a wise investor, too ... Much the most important program was the Interstate highway system, which Eisenhower persuaded Congress to fund in 1956. The National System of Interstate and Defense Highways was the greatest public works project in history and would ultimately blanket the country with a 42,000-mile network. (William L. O'Neill in Bischof & Ambrose, 1995, pp. 105–06)

8.9 Eisenhower's relationship with Nixon

Eisenhower made a conscious attempt to improve upon the traditionally lowly status of the role of the vice president. In a break with the recent past, Eisenhower sug-gested that Nixon should attend Cabinet meetings and make an active contribution to discussion. He also created a wide-ranging portfolio of tasks which Nixon was eager to undertake. These included liaison with Congress and with a number of groups within the Republican Party. More significantly, Nixon was also presented with the challenge of representing the United States on goodwill visits which included South and East Asia in 1953 and the Caribbean, Central America and Mexico two years later. Nixon's energetic dedication to duty and unswerving loyalty made a positive impression upon Eisenhower. However, Nixon's zealous pursuit of political enemies and his somewhat outspoken rhetoric did not endear him to the president. As a consequence, biographers of Eisenhower and Nixon alike agree that their relationship was less than intimate.

It is clear that although Nixon was given a range of responsible jobs, he was never trusted with genuine authority. The limitations of their relationship were exposed during Nixon's own campaign for the presidency. In August 1960 Charles Mohr of *Time* magazine asked Eisenhower if he could give an example of an idea of Nixon's that he had adopted. Eisenhower's reply could hardly have been more damaging to Nixon: 'If you give me a week I might think of one. I don't remember.' (Smith, 2012, p. 757) Conversely, it should be noted that during the periods when Eisenhower was seriously ill – with a heart attack in September 1955, and with a mild stroke in November 1957 – Nixon, even though he must have realised that he was close to the presidency, acted with genuine dignity and restraint.

8.10 Eisenhower's foreign policy, 1953–61 – overview

Each president faces different and at times unexpected challenges. Roosevelt had to contend with the Great Depression and then faced the enormity of the Second World War. It was Truman's fate to deploy the atom bomb, to contend with the outbreak of the Cold War and to grapple with the war in Korea. Eisenhower's successors – Kennedy, Johnson and Nixon – were to find the problem of Vietnam increasingly frustrating and challenging. The trauma of these years makes the period of peace over which Eisenhower presided even more pronounced. Tranquillity abroad combined with a thriving economy to make Eisenhower an attractive proposition to the American electorate. The verdict of historians has been less clear-cut. When Eisenhower left office in 1961 the initial judgement was not very positive. Kennedy's energy and drive made the outgoing president appear lethargic and complacent. The dazzling phrases of Kennedy's inaugural address seemed far removed from Eisenhower's baffling and long-winded speeches.

Many historians quickly concluded that Eisenhower had been fortunate to preside over a period of peace but that he had been out of his depth, unable to grasp complex issues, claiming that he was more at home on the golf course than in the Oval Office. A sense of missed opportunity led some historians to categorise the Eisenhower era as 'wasted years'. In terms of foreign policy they concluded that the passive general had been content to delegate control of his foreign policy to the able but aggressively outspoken John Foster Dulles. Pach and Richardson, two leading historians of the Eisenhower era, note that the popular view emerged that, 'While his assistants governed, Eisenhower reserved his energies for golf, bridge and fishing. The president presided over his administration, but he did not run it. As a result, the country simply drifted.' (Pach & Richardson, 1991, p. xi)

This critical interpretation has not survived intact. A number of revisionist historians with access to new archive material have argued persuasively that Eisenhower has been misjudged. A new picture has emerged of a leader who presided over the Oval Office and the Cabinet Room emphatically, but who also deployed a 'hidden hand' (Pach & Richardson, 1991, p. 42) to exercise power from behind the scenes. It is now claimed that although Dulles was allowed considerable scope in the day-to-day routine of foreign policy he was in no doubt that major decisions rested with the president. Credit for some of the major successes in foreign policy should therefore go to Eisenhower. In particular, historians have praised Eisenhower for extricating the United States from the war in Korea. They also recognise the restraint he used to avoid conflict in potential trouble spots such as Suez and Indochina. The favourable revisionist interpretation of Eisenhower gathered momentum to such an extent that by 1982 he was being rated by American historians as high as ninth in the polls of presidential performance.

8.11 Impact on the Korean War of the presidential campaign of 1952

Having committed himself to visiting Korea during what had become an increasingly bitter election campaign, Eisenhower lost no time in keeping his promise. Towards the end of November 1952, he left New York to make an undisclosed flight to South Korea. During his visit, he interviewed officers and spoke to his own son, John, who was at the front line in an infantry division. Eisenhower resolved not to allow American soldiers to 'stand forever on a static front and continue to accept casualties without any visible results' (Pach & Richardson, 1991, p. 86). However, although Eisenhower left Korea determined to end the war, he was still in search of a clear plan to break the stalemate. The president asked General Omar Bradley, the Chairman of the Joint Chiefs of Staff, about the possibility of using tactical nuclear weapons, but was told that there were few realistic targets. Nevertheless, Eisenhower concluded that if it was necessary to expand the war, atomic weapons might be deployed against targets in Manchuria and China.

Meanwhile, Dulles applied considerable pressure on China to seek terms. Dulles told Indian Prime Minister Nehru that if negotiations failed, the United States 'might well extend the area of conflict'. America's Ambassador to the Soviet Union, Charles E. Bohlen, informed the Soviet Foreign Minister that the collapse of talks would 'create a situation which the US Government is seeking most earnestly to avoid' (Pach & Richardson, 1991, p. 87).

Although Dulles later claimed that these messages had sent an 'unmistakable warning' to Communist China, historians remain divided as to whether this was the key factor in securing the peace. Historian of the Korean War William Stueck contends that 'the Chinese viewed enemy use of atomic weapons as unlikely, both because of world opinion and the Soviet Union's retaliatory capability' (Boyle, 2014, p. 39).

As late as February 1953 Mao was claiming that China could carry on in Korea for 'any amount of years'. Pach and Richardson claim that: 'More influential with the enemy than Dulles's alleged nuclear diplomacy was war weariness and pressure from the post-Stalinist leadership of the Soviet Union. The Eisenhower administration nevertheless could rightly celebrate a major achievement.' (Pach & Richardson, 1991,

p. 87) Some experts have seen the death of Stalin in March 1953 as a significant turning point. In a speech to the Supreme Soviet of 15 March, Malenkov, speaking on behalf of the new leadership, stated that 'there is not one disputed ... question that cannot be decided by peaceful means on the basis of mutual understanding of interested countries' (Stueck, 1995, p. 308).

While doubts remain about the factors which led to the breakthrough, the turning point came when North Korea and China finally agreed to compromise on the stumbling block of the exchange of prisoners of war. The atmosphere remained tense. The *New York Times* observed that 'seldom in the long story of human conflict has an armistice rested on such bad faith.' The newspaper observed that the two sides behaved as though they were 'signing a declaration of war instead of a truce.' In London, *The Times* recorded that 'there was no pretence at an exchange of courtesies, or even of civility' (Stueck, 1995, p. 342). Despite this ill-feeling the armistice was signed at Panmunjom on 27 July 1953. The terms of the armistice reflected the fact that neither side had gained a great deal. Dulles maintained that the United States' action had made the world 'infinitely safer.' In the words of William Stueck:

> The North Koreans had attacked in June 1950 only because they thought the United States would not fight. The United States had proven them wrong, and in the process North Korea had lost some 1500 square miles of territory and had seen its cities turned into 'hollow husks', its army virtually annihilated, and its population depleted and impoverished. When Eisenhower was elected President in November 1952, he made it clear that bringing the war in Korea to an end was an absolute priority, and when he made thinly veiled threats as to the possibility of nuclear weapons being deployed the Chinese and North Koreans were finally prepared to bring the conflict to a close. (Stueck, 1995, p. 345)

Bruce Cummings summarises the impact of the war as follows:

> In 1953, the Korean peninsula was a smouldering ruin. From Pusan in the South to Sinuiju in the north, Koreans buried their dead, mourned their losses, and sought to draw together the shattered remains of their lives. In the capital at Seoul, hollow buildings stood like skeletons alongside streets paved with weird mixtures of concrete and shrapnel. At American military encampments on the outskirts of the capital, masses of beggars waited to pick through the garbage that foreign soldiers tossed out. In the north, modern edifices scarcely stood anymore; Pyongyang and other cities were heaps of bricks and ashes, factories stood empty, massive dams no longer held their water. People emerged from a mole-like existence in caves and tunnels to find a nightmare in the bright of day. (Stueck, 1995, p. 361)

William Stueck observes:

> Korea's losses in the number of people killed, wounded, and missing approached three million, a tenth of the entire population ... In property, North Korea put its losses at $1.7 billion, South Korea at $2 billion, the equivalent of its gross national product for 1949 ... Each area saw 600,000 homes destroyed. The most positive light that can be put on the war from the Koreans' perspective is that, once over, it was unlikely to resume. The peninsula was now an armed camp ... but never again would the United States let down its guard there as it had in the year before

June 1950. The [US] victory extended well beyond Korea itself, as the demonstration of a willingness and an ability to combat 'aggression' combined with the military build-up at home and in western Europe to deter such action elsewhere. (Stueck, 1995, p. 361)

Finally, Max Hastings offers this analysis:

General S.L.A. Marshall, perhaps America's finest combat historian of the twentieth century, described Korea as 'the century's nastiest little war'. In those days before Vietnam, its claim to that title seemed unlikely to be eclipsed. 1,319,000 Americans served in the Korean theatre, and 33,629 did not return. A further 105,785 were wounded ... It seems reasonable to assume that China cannot have lost less than half a million men given the manner in which she fought her war. Few people of any nationality, four years earlier, would have supposed that barren peninsula would ever be worth any fraction of these lives. (Hastings, 1988, p. 407)

Dulles and Eisenhower had begun their stewardship of American foreign policy with a success, yet further challenges were ahead.

8.12 The foreign policy of John Foster Dulles

It has often been observed that John Foster Dulles seemed to have been preparing for the office of Secretary of State throughout his life. He was born into a privileged background in Washington DC, in February 1888. He was the grandson of one Secretary of State (John W. Foster) and the nephew of another. Although he graduated in law he was also attracted to the world of politics and diplomacy. He had enjoyed diplomatic experience at the Versailles Conference (1919) and the San Francisco Conference (1945). After the war, Truman's Secretary of State, James Byrnes, used Dulles as his adviser and in 1950 Dulles was appointed as a 'consultant' to the State Department. However, by this time Dulles was becoming increasingly unhappy with Truman's policy of containment, and he resigned from the State Department. He set out his views in a book *War or Peace*, published in 1950.

Dulles' dissatisfaction mounted over Truman's conduct of the Korean War. During the 1952 presidential campaign, he became increasingly outspoken, and was now entrusted with defining and drafting the Republican Party's foreign policy platform. Dulles characterised Truman's foreign policy as a 'treadmill policy which at best, might keep us in the same place until we drop exhausted'. He described containment as 'negative, futile and immoral'. Dulles proposed that the

free world ... develop the will and organize the means to retaliate instantly against open aggression by Red armies, so that, if it occurred anywhere, we could and would strike back where it hurts, by means of our choosing. (In Pach & Richardson, 1991, p. 33)

Dulles promised to embark upon a new policy which would lead to the 'rollback' of Soviet power in Eastern Europe and the 'liberation' of the people living in Soviet satellites.

Pach and Richardson (1991) offer this pen portrait of Dulles:

The secretary of state looked like an effigy on a medieval tomb. His countenance was dour and his demeanour austere. He seemed to lack elementary human warmth. He spoke with an excruciating slowness and solemnity. He had an unfortunate penchant for apocalyptic phrases, such as 'agonising reappraisal' and 'brink of war'. His personality seemed to be a deadly mixture of Presbyterian moralist and prosecuting attorney. If it was easy to like Ike, it was even easier to dislike Dulles. (Pach & Richardson, 1991, p. 85)

Even so, Eisenhower was well aware of Dulles' strengths. He felt that: 'There is probably no one in the world who has the technical competence of Foster Dulles in the diplomatic field.' (In Pach & Richardson, 1991, p. 85) The nature of the working relationship between Dulles and Eisenhower has been of considerable interest to historians. Initially, it was felt that Eisenhower had delegated enormous power to Dulles; more recent research suggests that while the president was happy to allow Dulles considerable room for manoeuvre, ultimate authority rested with Eisenhower. Finally, Bischof and Ambrose offer this analysis:

Perhaps the most notable feature of the revisionist scholarship, however, was the universal conclusion that Eisenhower was very much in command. No one could spend even one day with the documents and deny it. He did not leave domestic policy to his chief of staff, Sherman Adams, or foreign policy to his secretary of state John Foster Dulles, or defense policy to his secretary of defense, Charles Wilson. Eisenhower ran the show ... Eisenhower's deep immersion and pained grappling with nuclear weapons and deterrence theory made him the first American president to define a successful national security policy and strategy in the nuclear age. (Bischof & Ambrose, 1995, pp. 6–7)

8.13 The Cold War

The backdrop of the Cold War was very apparent when Eisenhower delivered his first State of the Union Address to Congress on 2 February 1953. The president told his audience, 'Our country has come through a painful period of trial and disillusionment since the victory of 1945.' While Americans desired a 'world of peace and co-operation' they faced 'a world of turmoil' due to the 'calculated pressures of aggressive communism'. Eisenhower stated that the 'one clear lesson' of the period 1945–52 was that the United States needed 'a new, positive foreign policy' which would make the 'free world secure' (Pach & Richardson, 1991, p. 75).

As early as February 1953, Congress passed the Captive People's Resolution, which reinforced America's support for freedom in Eastern Europe. However, three factors came into play which led to changes in the Republican approach. With the presidential victory secured, the State Department toned down its election rhetoric. In 1953, for example, Dulles commented that liberation 'must and can be a peaceful process' (Levy, 2010, p. 94). On 5 March 1953, Stalin died, indicating that a new approach to East–West relations might be about to dawn. Eisenhower rather than Dulles quickly emerged as the dominant figure in the formulation of foreign policy. It was Eisenhower's moving and conciliatory speech of April 1953, rather than the more outspoken rhetoric of Dulles, which seemed to set the tone for the new administration. Significantly, this speech, 'The Chance for Peace', was carried in full, in Russia, in the newspaper *Pravda*.

Despite this, major differences remained. At the Bermuda Conference in December 1953, Eisenhower expressed doubt as to whether the Soviet Union had genuinely changed its ways, and Dulles remained prone to making rhetorical statements. In 1953, he countered French resistance to his wish to rearm West Germany and bring her into the Western defence mechanism with the comment that an 'agonising reappraisal of American foreign policy might be necessary' (Pach & Richardson, 1991, p. 85). This was interpreted as a suggestion that the United States might reduce its commitment to Europe. A year later, Dulles spoke of 'massive retaliation' as a more cost-effective way of dealing with future communist aggression. The suggestion here was that America would redeploy its nuclear weapons rather than relying on its conventional forces. This was thrown into sharp relief by a crisis which arose off the coast of China in early 1955.

8.14 The military–industrial complex

The worst to be feared and the best to be expected [from an escalating arms race] can be simply stated. The worst is atomic war. The best would be this: a life of perpetual fear and tension; a burden of arms draining the wealth and the labor of all peoples ... Every gun that is made, every warship launched, every rocket fired, signifies, in the final sense, a theft from those who hunger and are not fed, those who are cold and are not clothed.

This world in arms is not spending money alone. It is spending the sweat of its laborers, the genius of its scientists, the hopes of its children. We pay for a single fighter plane with a half-million bushels of wheat. We pay for a single destroyer with new homes that could have housed more than eight thousand people ... This is not a way of life at all, in any true sense. Under the cloud of threatening war, it is humanity hanging from a cross of iron.

(President Eisenhower, speech to the American Society of Newspaper Editors, April, 1953) (In Bischof & Ambrose, 1995, p. 252)

Despite Eisenhower's extensive military experience and his instinctive concern about the rapid development of the arms race, he was unable to forestall its spiralling costs. By the time he left office in 1961, America's nuclear arsenal was close to 30,000 megatons. The deterioration in the relationship with the Soviet Union was matched by an intense fear of communism, which reached its peak in the period known as McCarthyism. The domestic climate became so agitated that it became impossible for any politician to ignore its clamour. The outspoken rhetoric of Secretary of State John Foster Dulles added to the prevailing atmosphere. Dulles recognised that by emphasising the 'Red Menace' he was in effect defending government defence programmes against any Congressional cutbacks. As Dulles said, 'in promoting our programs in Congress we have to make evident the international communist menace. Otherwise, such programs would be decimated' (in Powaski, 1987, p. 61).

The difficulties faced by America's conventional forces in bringing the Korean War to a conclusion added to the growing belief that America's future security rested on the development of its nuclear weapons systems. Dulles expressed this view in January 1954, when he stated that in the face of any communist aggression the Republican administration would use 'massive retaliation'. Later in that year the president told Congressional leaders that the point was to 'blow the hell out of them in a hurry if they start anything' (Powaski, 1987, pp. 62–63).

This new approach was reflected in the words of Air Force Chief of Staff General Nathan Twining, who responded to the crisis at Dien Bien Phu in 1954 with the suggestion:

> You could take all day to drop a bomb, make sure you put it in the right place ... and clean those Commies out of there and ... the French would come marching out of Dien Bien Phu in fine shape. (In Smith, 2012, p. 611)

The willingness to consider the use of atomic bombs was also in evidence in the recurring crises over the disputed islands of Quemoy and Matsu in the Taiwan Straits. These developments culminated in the emergence of what became known as the 'New Look' defence policy. This rested on a massive increase in nuclear weapons at the expense of the country's conventional forces. Between 1953 and 1957 the army was reduced in number from 1.4 million to 1 million. However, this process now boosted the air force; in the summer of 1953 the air force commissioned the first intercontinental jet bomber, the B-52. This new weapon had the capacity to deliver hydrogen bombs to targets in the Soviet Union. In 1955, it was decided to go ahead with development of the Atlas missile, which was the first intercontinental ballistic missile (ICBM). The Atlas was able to send a 1-megaton warhead over 5,000 nautical miles. At the same time, the Thor intermediate-range ballistic missile (IRBM) was also introduced. Two years later, work began on a more effective missile called the Minuteman, which was ready for use by 1962. As Ronald E. Powaski notes 'this replaced the manned bomber as the primary component of the nation's strategic forces'. Huge expenditure on these projects exerted a dynamic influence on the economy in general. Powaski points out that the Atlas, Titan and Thor missile projects involved:

> 18,000 scientists and technicians affiliated with universities and industry, and 70,000 others working in 22 industries that included 17 prime contractors, over 200 subcontractors, and innumerable small suppliers. Among the top one hundred corporations that divided three-quarters of total expenditures for military contracts, three of the largest were aircraft manufacturers: General Dynamics, Lockheed, and Boeing. (Powaski, 1987, p. 71)

Powaski argues that a range of interest groups including the defence establishment, aircraft manufacturers, trade unions, the scientific community and the educational establishment all calculated the benefits they could accrue from the development of a big-spending, military–industrial complex. America's commitment to new missile projects during the 1950s should not be taken to denote Eisenhower's enthusiasm for the arms race. Indeed, the president was disturbed by the rapid escalation in the destructive capacity of the new weapons. For example, the introduction of the hydrogen (thermo-nuclear) bomb, tested by the United States in November 1952 and by the Soviet Union in August 1953, profoundly worried him.

The American people displayed massive insecurities about the threat from the Soviet Union. A typical example came with the hysterical reporting of the Moscow

Air Show of July 1955. American reporters described in alarming terms the 'waves' of Soviet bombers which flew in the display, when in fact the same planes had circled over the spectator stands over and over again. Even more disturbing to the already frayed American psyche was the Soviets' successful launching of the Sputnik satellite on 4 October 1957. The sheer weight of the Soviet satellite (184 pounds) and the rapid development of Sputnik II (1,120 pounds) made many Americans believe that their country was falling behind the Soviet Union. Khrushchev's claim that the Soviets had developed an ICBM of their own carried real credibility for many Americans. The belief took shape in what became known as the 'missile gap'.

The Gaither Report

This was further supported by the publication of the Gaither Report, which was issued at the end of 1957. Chaired by Rowan Gaither, the chairman of the Ford Foundation, the report erroneously concluded that the Soviets had indeed opened up a missile gap which could be countered only by an immediate crash-building programme.

Ironically, whereas the press and the defence establishment simply accepted the findings of the Gaither Report, the Commander-in-Chief of the armed forces, President Eisenhower, knew full well that the report was seriously flawed. Unlike Gaither, Eisenhower had seen the top-secret findings of the U-2 reconnaissance missions. However, the secrecy which shrouded the U-2 programme was so intense that Eisenhower could not reveal to the American people the real picture. Eisenhower now faced an orchestrated campaign by the military, who eagerly took advantage of the alarm generated by the Gaither Report. Through a receptive press, leading generals made clear their desire to close the missile gap through a massive new wave of defence spending. Politicians who represented states with major defence industry projects were eager to 'bring home the bacon' by supporting 'pork-barrelling' projects which would help them get re-elected. Ronald E. Powaski cites the example of Senator Henry Jackson:

> a Democrat from Washington, a state with major aircraft industries, [who] asserted that the United States lagged far behind the Soviet Union in numbers of missiles. He called for restoration of budget reductions for missile development and increased bomber production until the United States caught up. (Powaski, 1987, p. 71)

Some historians have stated that despite the president's misgivings he was unable to counter the influence of the high-spending, unelected leaders of the military–industrial complex.

H.W. Brands has claimed that:

> Eisenhower's New Look policy was never fully implemented due to Pentagon resistance; his giving into demands both for more conventional and nuclear weapons showed that he could not control the Pentagon, that he based 'American security on possession of the latest scientific and military technology' and thereby 'surrendered to the defense bureaucrats' and 'promoted the growth of the military–industrial complex,' and that he fuelled the cold war with his 'overblown rhetoric.' (In Bischof & Ambrose, 1995, p. 8)

In a similar vein, David Alan Rosenberg (1995) has charged 'that Eisenhower was not able to contain the air force's "bootstrapping," the multiplication of targets in the Soviet

Union leading to a proliferation of nuclear weapons and thus an "overkill" nuclear capacity and a general acceleration of the arms race.' (In Bischof & Ambrose, 1995, p. 8)

By 1960, Eisenhower was increasingly frustrated by the 'astronomical' amount being spent on weapons. As he came towards the end of his presidency he prepared to deliver the speech which would become the best known of the entire Eisenhower era. Drafted by speechwriter Malcolm Moos, the speech drew attention to the:

> Conjunction of an immense military establishment and a large arms industry [that] is new in the American experience. The total influence – economic, political, even spiritual – is felt in every city, every State house, every office of the Federal government ... in the councils of government, we must guard against the acquisition of unwarranted influence, whether sought or unsought, by the military industrial complex. The potential for the disastrous rise of misplaced power exists and will persist. The free university, historically the fountainhead of free ideas and scientific discovery, has experienced a revolution in the conduct of research. Partly because of the huge costs involved, a government contract becomes virtually a substitute for intellectual curiosity. As we peer into society's future, we – you and I, and our government – must avoid the impulse to live only for today, plundering, for our own ease and convenience, the precious resources of tomorrow. (In Pach & Richardson, 1991, p. 229)

In its editorial, *The Nation* stated:

> It can be said, quite without irony that nothing became Mr Eisenhower's career in office like the leaving of it. For eight years, Mr. Eisenhower has depressed his fellow Americans by a seeming inability to grasp the major problems of his era; but now in the closing days of his Administration he spoke like the statesman and democratic leader we had so long hungered for him to become. (In Pach & Richardson, 1991, p. 230)

In their reappraisal of Eisenhower, Pach and Richardson (1991) completely reject the notion that he reached this perspective only at the end of his career. Instead, they argue that:

> Throughout his Presidency, Eisenhower worried about a militarised United States that sacrificed social improvements and democratic liberties to the goals of absolute security. The farewell address was no last-minute revelation. It was his most eloquent expression of abiding principles. (Pach & Richardson, 1991, p. 230)

Stephen E. Ambrose (1991) offers this perspective:

> His greatest successes came in foreign policy, and the related area of national defense spending. By making peace in Korea, and avoiding war thereafter for the next seven and one-half years, and by holding down, almost single-handedly, the pace of the arms race, he achieved his major accomplishments. No one knows how much money he saved the United States, as he rebuffed Congress and the Pentagon and the JCS ... and the military industrial complex ... He made peace, and he kept the peace ... Eisenhower boasted, 'the United States never lost a soldier or a foot of ground in my administration. We kept the peace. People ask how it happened – by God, it didn't just happen. I'll tell you that.' (In Bischof & Ambrose, 1995, p. 251)

8.15 SEATO

The Southeast Asia Treaty Organization (SEATO) was established by Dulles in September 1954. Its membership comprised the United States, France, Great Britain, New Zealand, Australia, the Philippines, Thailand and Pakistan.

SEATO was a defensive alliance intended to enable communist expansion in Asia to be more effectively resisted. Two weaknesses undermined this initiative. Firstly, that the key nations such as India, Indonesia, Burma and Ceylon remained outside SEATO. Secondly, that the members agreed only to consult each other in the event of attack, and their defence would rest on the military support of the United States rather than on individual members.

8.16 Formosa, Quemoy and Matsu

Republican criticism of Truman's foreign policy reached a fever pitch in the autumn of 1949, when the Democrats were accused of 'allowing' China to fall into communist hands. The Republican Party platform in 1952 had spoken of 'unleashing' the deposed Chinese nationalist leader Jiang Jieshi from Formosa on to the mainland which, since October 1949, had been in the hands of the communist regime led by Mao Zedong. In February 1953, Eisenhower changed the orders governing the conduct of the United States Seventh Fleet in the Formosa Straits: the United States fleet would no longer stand in the way of attacks from Formosa against the Chinese mainland.

However, those on the right of the Republican Party who now anticipated the 'unleashing' of Jiang Jieshi's forces were disappointed to see that this constituted no more than the occupation of the small, offshore islands of Quemoy and Matsu in the Taiwan (Formosa) Strait and the stationing of 50,000 nationalist troops there. In the autumn of 1954, the People's Republic of China (PRC) responded by shelling the two islands. Although the islands were tiny and of doubtful strategic significance it was clear to all sides that credibility and prestige were very much at stake. If America were to make the Chinese back down, then the rhetoric of Dulles would remain intact. Domestically, outspoken Republican 'Asia Firsters' such as Senator Knowland of California and Representative Judd of Minnesota would be appeased by firm American action.

However, Eisenhower was acutely aware of the dangers which escalation could entail. On 12 September 1954, at a meeting of the National Security Council (NSC), Eisenhower warned his advisers who were pressing for action that they 'must get one thing clear in their heads, and that is they are talking about war' (Pach & Richardson, 1991, p. 99). Eisenhower was always mindful of constitutional limitations and told the NSC that he risked impeachment if he sanctioned military action without Congressional consent. Equally, Eisenhower knew that the use of nuclear weapons would expose America to widespread condemnation. The strategy which Eisenhower selected was to refer the conflict to the United Nations, to draw back from committing American forces to the defence of the islands but to give a strong hint that he would not rule out the use of nuclear weapons. In the words of Dulles, the plan was to 'keep the Reds guessing'. However, this strategy was tested further in January 1955, when Chinese troops seized Ichiang Island and attacked the Tachen Islands. This prompted

Eisenhower to obtain Congressional support to commit armed forces to the defence of Taiwan. On 6 March, Dulles and Eisenhower agreed that the defence of Quemoy and Matsu 'would require the use of atomic missiles'. Within days, Vice President Nixon stated that 'tactical atomic weapons are now conventional and will be used against the targets of an aggressive force'. Indeed, a historian has commented that 'Eisenhower actually brought the country to the "nuclear brink", far closer to war . . . than most historians ever suspected' (in Pach & Richardson, 1991, pp. 101–02). However, in April 1955 China began to show signs that it was ready to defuse the crisis. The bombardment of the islands stopped, negotiations began and Taiwan's future security was guaranteed. Historians have generally praised Eisenhower's handling of this crisis. Stephen E. Ambrose (1991) has argued that 'Eisenhower himself did not know' whether he would resort to nuclear weapons and this deliberate ambiguity amounted to a 'tour de force, one of the great triumphs of his long career' (In Bischof & Ambrose, 1995, p. 103).

8.17 The 'New Look' defence policy

Eisenhower had never disguised his concern with the 'great equation' of whether defence spending could be reduced without endangering national security. He frequently spoke of the social and economic cost which resulted from money being spent on armed forces rather than on social projects. Although the Republican Party had been sharply critical of Truman's containment policy, the fact was that defence spending had soared during his last three years in office, from around $13 billion to more than $30 billion. The solution at which Eisenhower arrived was to place greater emphasis on nuclear weapons as a deterrent, while at the same time reducing the money spent on conventional forces. In addition, the Central Intelligence Agency (CIA) would play a heightened role in mounting surveillance and covert missions. Spending on the army and navy would be heavily cut back, giving 'more bang for the buck' through spending on nuclear weapons. The hydrogen bomb, which had been successfully tested in 1952, was scaled down in size, so that it could be installed in the bomb bay of the B-47. Research and development of new missiles became a priority, leading to the deployment of short-range missiles and nuclear artillery shells deployed in Europe in 1954.

Eisenhower's strategy for national security became known as the 'New Look'. Richard Crockatt (1995) highlights the role of John Foster Dulles in its development:

> In his Senate confirmation hearing as Secretary of State he spoke of the need for the 'liberation of these captive peoples' of Eastern Europe. A year later he introduced the concept of 'massive retaliation' as a means of deterring potential aggressors. 'The way to deter aggression,' he said, 'is for the free community to be willing and able to respond vigorously at places and with means of its own choosing.' Both these priorities, which constituted the main planks of the so-called 'New Look' policy of the Eisenhower administration were premised upon a dissatisfaction with the supposed negativity and passivism of Truman's containment. (Crockatt, 1995, p. 123)

Although Dulles had emphasised the concept of 'massive retaliation', this raised difficulties for the conduct of American foreign policy. For example, in Western Europe, where the United States had vital interests (such as West Berlin) the use of nuclear weapons and massive retaliation was rendered virtually impossible because it could lead to great loss of life. In 1958, when the Chinese resumed their shelling of Quemoy and Matsu, the United States again threatened the use of nuclear weapons. However, the strategy was exposed when the Soviet Union made threats that they would regard an attack on China as an attack on the Soviet Union. The 'New Look' strategy had thus created a situation where a potentially catastrophic nuclear exchange could loom up as a serious possibility over, in this case, two obscure islands. Despite these difficulties, some historians have argued that the policy instilled a compelling sense of uncertainty in the other side. The mere possibility that the United States could respond with nuclear weapons created the ultimate deterrent.

8.18 The Soviet invasion of Hungary, 1956

Events in Eastern Europe between 1953 and 1956 had created a slight thaw. The death of Stalin in March 1953 removed an enormous barrier to progress. A change in attitude among the new Soviet leadership seemed to be reflected in Soviet toleration of Tito's 'national' communism in Yugoslavia (communism, but not under direct Soviet control), illustrated by Khrushchev's visit to Yugoslavia (1955) and Tito's visit to Moscow (1956). A meeting between Khrushchev, Eisenhower and the French and British prime ministers had taken place in Geneva in July 1955, and although their arms control proposals came to nothing, the meeting did lead to a temporary improvement in East–West relations. Further signs of a thaw came with Soviet acceptance of the appointment of Wladyslaw Gomulka as General Secretary of the Polish Communist Party (he had previously been deposed under the Stalinist era). Most significant of all was Khrushchev's groundbreaking speech criticising Stalin for the first time, at the Twentieth Party Congress in Moscow in 1956.

This all created the impression that a new era was dawning. However, events in Hungary in the late autumn of 1956 dashed these hopes. In July 1956, the Hungarian people ousted Matyas Rakosi, the leader they had endured under Stalin, and replaced him with Erno Gero. Further protests and student demonstrations led to the appointment of a new government led by Imre Nagy, a reformer who had previously been expelled from the party by Rakosi. At the end of October, Nagy agreed to elections, with all parties taking part. Initially the Soviets seemed to tolerate this development, and on 30 October they issued a statement accepting the principle of complete equality and of non-interference in one another's internal affairs.

However, this was then followed by a further statement by the Hungarians announcing their withdrawal from the Warsaw Pact. This event coincided with the Suez crisis that was commanding the attention of Britain, France and the United States, as well as the countries directly involved in the Middle East. In addition, the American presidential election was taking place at the start of November. Therefore, in some respects, the timing was ideal for the Soviet Union to attack with the likelihood that the West would not intervene. On 4 November large numbers of Soviet troops moved into Hungary. Nagy was deposed and later executed. His replacement, János Kádar, clearly a puppet of the Soviet Union, issued a statement calling for the Soviet Army to come to Hungary and help to defeat the uprising.

Both Eisenhower and Dulles had expressed support for the Hungarian people. A top-secret CIA programme codenamed Red Sox/Red Cap had prepared East

European exiles to carry out covert paramilitary missions. The Hungarians broadcast desperate pleas for Western intervention over 'Radio Free Europe'. No help was forthcoming. Eisenhower hated communism, but his fear of a nuclear war between the superpowers was an even stronger emotion. Eisenhower's assessment was that direct military support carried with it colossal risks. He told his advisers that Hungary was 'as inaccessible as Tibet' (Pach & Richardson, 1991, p. 132).

The consequences of the Hungarian crisis were clear and significant. It was all too apparent that the prospect of a thaw in the Cold War was over. The Soviet hold over Eastern Europe was firmer than ever, exposing the emptiness of much of Dulles' rhetoric. Finally, the level of commitment and spending on the arms race was to reach dizzying new levels.

8.19 The Suez crisis, 1956

In 1952, Colonel Abdul Gamal Nasser, supported by a group of like-minded nationalist army officers, took control of Egypt. Nasser was deeply opposed to Western influence over the Middle East in general and Egypt in particular. Two years later he was able to secure a British agreement on the withdrawal of British troops from the Suez Canal Zone. Nevertheless, the British Prime Minister, Anthony Eden, was convinced that Nasser's anti-Western programme was supported by Moscow. In December 1955, the United States and Britain offered Nasser a substantial loan to finance the construction of the Aswan Dam on the Lower Nile. This offer was withdrawn in July 1956, after Egypt formed an anti-Israeli alliance with Syria, Saudi Arabia and the Yemen. Nasser responded by announcing the nationalisation of the French- and British-owned Suez Canal Company. Eden was convinced that Nasser had to be put firmly in his place. In the United States, Dulles looked to achieve a compromise based on the idea of a joint committee of canal users and with Egypt paying compensation to the canal owners. Meanwhile Eden had entered into secret negotiations with France and Israel to achieve a much more ambitious solution. Israel agreed to create a pretext for military intervention by invading the Suez Canal. Britain and France would then ask both sides to withdraw from the Canal Zone. Following the inevitable rejection of the ultimatum, an Anglo-French force would be sent in to occupy the area.

The bold plan began with a successful Israeli attack against Egyptian positions on 29 October 1956. Israel seized the Sinai Desert but, fatally, it took the Anglo-French forces several days to reach Alexandria. By this stage, world opinion had come out firmly against the Anglo-French action. The United States had not been fully consulted and Eisenhower now made it clear that he had no intention of supporting what he saw as a reckless piece of imperialism. Khrushchev's outspoken condemnation of Britain and France increased alarm in Washington as to the potential consequences of this ill-conceived act. The United States put forward a UN resolution calling for the withdrawal of Anglo-French forces and their replacement by an international peacekeeping force. On 22 December 1956, Anglo-French forces were withdrawn. It had been a humiliating episode for the British; it became clear that Britain had little scope for independent action without American approval. In the words of Pach and Richardson, Eisenhower 'was outraged at the brazenness and stupidity of the Suez intervention' (Pach & Richardson, 1991, p. 132). As a consequence of the Suez crisis,

Anthony Eden resigned as prime minister in January 1957, and was replaced by Harold Macmillan. It was a tribute to Macmillan's diplomatic skill that he was quickly able to rebuild the 'special relationship' between Britain and the United States.

8.20 Origins of the war in Vietnam

Abbreviations

ARVN	Army of the Republic of Vietnam
DRV	Democratic Republic of Vietnam (North Vietnam)
GVN	Government of South Vietnam
RVN	Republic of Vietnam (South Vietnam)
VC	Viet Cong

Vietnam's turbulent past

The debacle of the Vietnam War, which led to the deaths of over 3 million Vietnamese and over 58,000 US troops and brought catastrophic consequences for Vietnam, Laos and Cambodia continues to arouse heated investigation and debate. The human, psychological, economic and material cost was immense. The damage caused to America's moral standing, self-esteem and reputation remains difficult to calculate. The scale of the trauma caused to the people of South East Asia has, perhaps, not always attracted enough attention from academics who have looked in so much depth at the American experience there. As an event within the context of the end of the Second World War, the backlash against colonialism and the escalation of the Cold War it remains of pivotal importance. From the perspective of the White House surely no president can hold the office without considering its legacy. For historians so many questions remain of interest. Some of those key issues include:

- Why did America go to war in Vietnam?
- Why did the US see Vietnam as essential to American national security?
- Why did a relatively limited commitment in the 1950s escalate so sharply in the 1960s?
- Why was the United States unable to achieve its objectives in Vietnam?

It could be argued that while successive American presidents regarded Vietnam in fairly simplistic terms – a tiny, weak nation, ultimately a domino that could not be allowed to fall – the truth was that this country's history, culture and people were formidable in their complexity. Historic attachments to Confucianism, Buddhism and Catholicism were of great importance. The lives of a largely peasant population mainly occupied with rice production contrasted with urban sophistication, elegance and intellectual life. In its medieval past Vietnam had long been a Chinese protectorate creating powerful traditions of resistance in the oppressed people while at the same time instilling Confucian principles in the governance of the nation. These ideas were significant in the rise of the nineteenth-century imperial Nguyen dynasty which modelled itself on the Chinese imperial system. Since 1883, Vietnam had fallen under the control of the

French Empire which would eventually leave a legacy visible today in the elegant café society of Saigon. Over the centuries, then, a series of powerful nations had attempted to exploit, rule or subdue a proud, resourceful people.

The rise of Ho Chi Minh

Under these circumstances it would not be surprising to learn that a small, dedicated band of young Vietnamese student radicals believed that they should liberate their country from these external aggressors and place their land and people under the rule of a new ideology based on nationalism and communism but with important Confucian principles. The most important figure within this climate was Ho Chi Minh who founded the Vietnamese Revolutionary Youth League in 1925. This was a seminal moment in what would become the Vietnamese communist movement. Ho would become the dominant figure in Vietnamese nationalism with a formidable capacity to address the needs of the peasant population who formed the backbone of the nation but who had endured famine, hardship and violence as a result of military occupation.

In late 1940 forces from imperial Japan occupied Indochina so that yet again the Vietnamese people and those of Cambodia and Laos were subject to a brutal invasion. At the same time, Japan's presence in the region made her the common enemy not just of Vietnam but also of the growing force that was Chinese communism. The Chinese leaders and generals needed the support of the Vietnamese communists and nationalists and therefore lent their support to Ho, although the Sino-Vietnamese relationship was seldom straightforward or without tension.

Even at this stage, an idea of what lay in store for those who tried to suppress Vietnam could be gleaned from Ho's 'Letter from Abroad' written in 1941, in which he called for the Vietnamese people to stand together rather than accepting perpetual slavery. It was at this time that Ho's Viet Minh movement, numbering no more than 5,000 members, many of whom were languishing in colonial prisons, began creating 'national salvation associations' skilfully targeting farmers and landowners, while Ho's military associate, Vo Nguyen Giap, began the construction of an embryonic liberation army.

The First Indochina War, 1946–54

The complete military collapse of Japan in August 1945 added to the sense of rapid upheaval and helped the Viet Minh seize power in the key city of Hanoi. At the end of the month, Bao Dai, the last emperor of the Nguyen dynasty, formally gave up the throne and ceremonially handed power to the new provisional government of Vietnam, led by Ho Chi Minh. On 2 September 1945 Ho Chi Minh declared independence from France and announced the creation of the Democratic Republic of Vietnam (DRV). This was a move that France would steadfastly resist for the next nine years.

This is not to suggest that Ho had taken control of a united nation. As Mark Philip Bradley makes clear:

> The independence Vietnamese revolutionaries wrested in 1945 from French colonial rule was extremely tenuous. If Ho Chi Minh and the DRV commanded considerable prestige because of popular support for the Viet Minh's anti-French and

anti-Japanese struggle during the Second World War, its authority remained tenuous in many urban areas and in the countryside. At the same time the regime confronted an underdeveloped, war-ravaged economy. (Bradley, 2009, p. 147)

To add to the complexity of the situation, China was now only four years away from, as the US would see it, being 'lost to communism'. Mao Zedong's triumph in 1949 after years of civil war shook American policy makers to the core. Their sense of the strategic importance of the region was now heightened. To a concerned American electorate, further losses to communism in the region were inconceivable. But in 1950 when the Soviets and China both offered formal diplomatic recognition to the DRV, in the same year that the war in Korea had begun, momentum in the region seemed certain to alarm the White House. Above all, for any American leader or strategist at this time, the key element was simply the Cold War. No Cold War, no Vietnam.

American support for colonial France

Since 1945, France had been attempting to subdue nationalist forces in Vietnam. As the struggle between the French Army, who supported the Associated States government, led by the former Vietnamese emperor Bao Dai, and the Viet Minh, led by Ho Chi Minh, became more intense, the United States increased its material support to the French. As H.R. McMaster notes in *Dereliction of Duty*:

At the end of the 1940s, against the backdrop of the iron curtain's descent over Europe, the Soviet Union's successful explosion of an atomic device, and the Communist victory in China, the Truman administration concluded that Ho was part of a Soviet-sponsored, monolithic Communist movement. (McMaster, 1997, p. 33)

Early in 1950 the US formally recognised the French-backed Associated States of Vietnam and in May President Truman authorised $15 million in economic and military support to the French and the government of Bao Dai. It was a slippery slope. Before the year was over, the figure was raised to $100 million. By 1954 approximately 80 per cent of the costs of the war were being financed by the United States. We can therefore see continuity in the approach of both the Truman presidency and the Eisenhower Administration that followed.

By now, it should have been clear to any external observer that Ho was a formidable opponent. He was adept at toning down the communist nature of his movement, stressing the importance of nationalism, the 'people's war' against France and the importance of land reform and literacy programmes. Equally his benign appearance and manner should not hide the fact that the DRV was also guilty of the murder of hundreds of its domestic opponents.

Dien Bien Phu, 1954

In March 1954, the French army corps found itself surrounded at Dien Bien Phu. In the Cold War climate of this time, France was in itself a complex issue for the US. On the one hand its attempts to subdue Vietnamese independence could be seen as anachronistic. On a military level, the Americans lacked respect for French decision making and resolve. But in Europe, with the policy of containment, the loyalty and stability of France was absolutely pivotal to American foreign policy. Facing imminent catastrophe, the French asked the United States to intervene militarily. Dulles and the chairman of the United States Joint Chiefs of Staff (JCS) initially approved a plan to use air strikes against the Viet Minh forces. A leading expert on the origins of the war in Vietnam states that Eisenhower 'actively considered intervening with military force – perhaps with tactical nuclear weapons, in a heatedly debated secret plan ominously coded Operation Vulture – to try to save the French position, and came closer to doing so than is generally believed' (Logevall, 2013, p. xiv).

However, the president was more convinced by the argument of Army Chief of Staff General Ridgway that air strikes might lead to Chinese intervention. American military action was not forthcoming, and the French army at Dien Bien Phu was forced to surrender on 7 May. This resounding defeat meant that France's nine-year struggle to defend colonialism in Vietnam was over.

The division of Vietnam at the Geneva conference, 1954

Diplomatically, France now set about withdrawing from Indochina through an international conference at Geneva which began in May 1954. This resulted in the temporary partition of Vietnam along the 17th Parallel, with the DRV handed control of North Vietnam and the Bao Dai government ruling the south and appointing Ngo Dinh Diem as prime minister. Elections aimed at unifying the country were scheduled for 1956. David Anderson is critical of the policy Eisenhower followed in Vietnam, arguing that 'the Eisenhower administration simply postponed the day of reckoning in Vietnam', while his support for South Vietnam following the Geneva Accords was 'an example of flawed containment. U.S. strategy was negative. It sought to hold off defeat and wait for a better day with little regard for the internal dynamics of Vietnamese society.' (In Bischof & Ambrose, 1995, p. 12)

The Second Indochina War, 1955–75

From now on, the United States began to supply weapons and military advice to the emerging South Vietnamese government, led by the Catholic nationalist Ngo Dinh Diem. French troops finally pulled out of Vietnam in April 1956; as Ho Chi Minh's support developed in the north, the United States extended its support to the deeply flawed Diem regime in the south. By 1959, as the Eisenhower Administration drifted to its conclusion, a new war for the future of Vietnam was just beginning. The nationalist insurgency backed by Hanoi in the north began to infiltrate the south and in July 1959 the first two American servicemen of what would become more than 58,000 gave up their lives.[1] A nightmare had begun that would not formally come to an end until 1975.

8.21 The U-2 crisis

Although in personal terms Eisenhower was willing to search for an accord with the Soviet Union, the final years of his administration saw an increasingly ill-tempered relationship between the president and Premier Khrushchev. Towards the end of 1958 the Soviet leader stated that within six months he was preparing to sign a peace treaty with East Germany which would switch control of the major transport routes between West Germany and Berlin from the four powers stipulated in the Potsdam Agreement to the East Germans. Eisenhower responded in strong terms, and when further American troops were sent to Germany it appeared that Berlin could be set to become the flashpoint of the Cold War. However the six-month deadline passed without incident, and for a short time it seemed that the thaw which had preceded the invasion of Hungary was about to return.

When Nixon visited the Soviet Union in 1958, he took part in a relatively good-natured 'kitchen debate' at an American trade fair in Moscow. Khrushchev accepted Nixon's invitation to visit the United States. When Khrushchev visited the presidential retreat at Camp David in May 1959, he made a favourable impression upon Eisenhower, the media and the American public in general. It was agreed that the successful summit would be followed by a further conference to be held in Paris in May 1960 and a presidential visit to the Soviet Union later in the same year.

Against this backdrop of improved relations the United States had continued to fly high-altitude U-2 reconnaissance missions over the Soviet Union's airspace, despite earlier Russian protests. The CIA had convinced Eisenhower that the high altitude and fragile nature of the U-2 planes meant that even if one was shot down the plane would disintegrate, the sophisticated electronic instruments would be completely destroyed and the pilot would be killed. The Soviets would therefore not be able to verify the type of plane they had brought down. Just weeks before the Paris Summit came the moment Eisenhower had dreaded. Khrushchev was informed during the May Day celebrations that a U-2 had been downed. The pilot, Gary Powers, had parachuted to safety and had chosen not to take the lethal poison with which he had been equipped. Eisenhower authorised the release of a story to be planted in the inside pages of the press claiming that a NASA plane had gone missing while studying weather systems over Turkey. Khrushchev played his hand with great relish. On 5 May the Soviets announced that they had shot down an American spy plane. Eisenhower, unaware of what was coming next, stated that the NASA weather plane could have mistakenly entered into Soviet territory.

On 7 May, Khrushchev played his ace when he gleefully told his comrades on the Supreme Soviet his 'secret' that two days earlier he had failed to mention that the Russians not only had the remnants of the U-2 plane but also the pilot who was 'alive and kicking'.

Eisenhower's dismay at the humiliating turn of events (he told his secretary that he felt like resigning) grew worse when the leaders came together in Paris. Eisenhower sat turning red with anger as Khrushchev proceeded to berate the United States in front of the leaders of France and Great Britain, announcing in no uncertain terms that the invitation to visit the Soviet Union had been withdrawn. Khrushchev's demand for a personal apology from the president further inflamed the situation. The summit collapsed. Eisenhower told his advisers that Khrushchev was 'a son of a bitch', who had taken personal pleasure in insulting him. While the American public gave Eisenhower a warm welcome upon his premature return, Eisenhower was deeply depressed that the 'stupid U-2 mess' had sabotaged his hopes of bringing the costly and damaging Cold War to an end. The situation was compounded when the Democratic Senate Majority Leader Lyndon Johnson observed that Khrushchev had felt able to humiliate the president because of his lack of respect for America's future military strength. Eisenhower was drained by the U-2 crisis and his health problems were not helped by the bitter disappointment he felt as the Cold War flared around him, as his administration came to what appeared to some observers to be a rather weary conclusion.

Note

1. The first official death in Vietnam occurred in 1956 when Sergeant Richard Fitzgibbon was murdered by another member of the US military. The soldiers who died in July 1959 are the first two named on the Vietnam Veterans Memorial Wall in Washington DC. The last servicemen listed on the timeline, 18 in total, died during a rescue operation in May 1975 in Cambodia.

Further reading

Bischof G. & Ambrose S.E., *Eisenhower: A Centenary Assessment* (Baton Rouge: Louisiana State University Press 1995).

Bondi V., *American Decades 1940–1949* (Detroit: Gale Research Inc. 1995).

Boyle, P.G., *Eisenhower: Profiles in Power* (New York: Routledge 2014).

Bradley M.P., *Vietnam at War* (New York: Oxford University Press 2009).

Brogan H., *Longman History of the United States of America* (London: Longman 1985).

Crockatt R., *The Fifty Years War: The United States and the Soviet Union in World Politics, 1941–1991* (London: Routledge 1995).

Gellman I.F., *The President and the Apprentice: Eisenhower and Nixon, 1952–1961* (New Haven: Yale University Press 2015).

Halberstam D., *The Coldest Winter: America and the Korean War* (Oxford: Macmillan 2008).

Hastings M., *The Korean War* (Michael Joseph Ltd 1988).

Heale M.J., *McCarthy's Americans: Red Scare Politics in State and Nation, 1935–1965* (London: Macmillan Press 1998).

Jones M.A., *The Limits of Liberty: American History 1607–1992* (New York: Oxford University Press 1995).

Levy, M.I. (ed.) *The Korean War and the Vietnam War: People, Politics and Power* (New York: Britannica Educational Publishing 2010).

Logevall F., *Embers of War: The Fall of an Empire and the Making of America's Vietnam* (New York: Random House 2013).

Lowe P., *The Korean War* (London: Macmillan Press Ltd 2000).

McMaster H.R., *Dereliction of Duty: Lyndon Johnson, Robert McNamara, The Joint Chiefs of Staff, and the Lies that Led to Vietnam* (New York: Harper Collins 1997).

Pach C.J. Jr & Richardson E., *The Presidency of Dwight D. Eisenhower* (Lawrence, Kansas: University Press of Kansas 1991).

Powaski R.E., *March to Armageddon* (New York: Oxford University Press 1987).

Reeves T.C., *The Life and Times of Joe McCarthy: A Biography* (London: Blond & Briggs Ltd 1982).

Schrecker E., *The Age of McCarthyism, A Brief History with Documents* (Boston: Bedford Books 1994).

Slawenski, K., *J.D. Salinger: A Life Raised High* (Hebden Bridge: Pomona 2010).

Smith J.E., *Eisenhower in War and Peace* (New York: Random House 2012).

Stueck W., *The Korean War: An International History* (New Jersey: Princeton University Press 1995).

Ward G.C. & Burns K., *The Vietnam War: An Intimate History* (New York: Alfred A. Knopf 2017).

■ ⊻ 9 John F. Kennedy, 1961–63

9.1 Poetry and power – JFK in the White House

Within the space of less than three years, two events concerning the same president first of all captivated the nation and then traumatised it. When John F. Kennedy was inaugurated at the age of 43 in Washington DC on 20 January 1961, those who admired him felt that anything was possible. The dazzling phrases used in his inaugural address marked a refreshing contrast with the 'tangled syntax' of Eisenhower. Kennedy's looks, charm and sharp sense of humour also seemed to put the old general in the shade. The new sense of style and culture was emphasised when the renowned writer Robert Frost was invited to recite a poem at the inauguration.

Kennedy's beautiful wife, Jacqueline Bouvier, added to the sense of grace that enchanted so many Americans. When she tastefully redecorated the White House, the gulf between the rather drab and lethargic administration of the 1950s and the 'new generation' to whom 'the torch has been passed' seemed very substantial. Having created a tremendous impression with his first speech, the Harvard-educated president had attracted the 'best and the brightest' to work with him in the White House. During the 'Thousand Days' of the Kennedy Administration the president displayed energy, style and most of all a sense that he was developing all the time. It was this 'capacity for growth' which many historians would draw attention to when he was brutally killed. Many observers felt that had he lived, Kennedy could have gone on to be a truly great president (JFK Library, online; Jones, 1995, pp. 549–50).

Impact of JFK's assassination on historians

The trauma came less than three years later, in 1963, in Dallas, Texas. Kennedy's eagerness to bolster Democratic support and to heal rifts within the party led him to plan a couple of days visiting Houston, Fort Worth and Dallas. As was always the case on any long-haul trip, not far from the president was 'The Bagman', a Secret Service agent carrying the most potent symbol of presidential power: a locked metal suitcase with its elaborate combination code containing all that is necessary for a nuclear war to be launched. It was not just the ever-present threat of a nuclear exchange that preyed on the president's mind. Privately, Kennedy was ill at ease in the South. He sometimes called Texas 'nut country', and commented on how easy it would be for a 'lone nut' assassin to take out a president. On 22 November the president and his wife were travelling in a large motorcade procession through the streets of Dallas. They had almost reached their destination, a luncheon at the Dallas Trade Mart, when in the space of just 8 seconds several shots rang out. An initial bullet which wounded the president was followed by a devastating shot to the head. An hour later a bewildered nation watched Walter Cronkite, its most respected newsreader, struggle to retain his composure as he delivered these brief, shattering words: 'From Dallas, the flash apparently official, President Kennedy died at one o'clock Central Standard Time – two o'clock Eastern Standard Time – some thirty-eight minutes ago.' (Bugliosi, 2007, p. 153)

The dreadful manner in which the president died made it difficult for those who wrote the first histories of the Kennedy era to remain impartial. An acute sense of loss and what might have been led those who first looked at the '1,000 days' to emphasise the glamour and unfulfilled promise of the stricken president. The iconic imagery of the sombre funeral enhanced the sense of a fallen hero. Consequently, the first accounts tended to eulogise Kennedy's White House as Camelot, a 'brief shining moment' and certainly drew a veil over his less presidential activities. In the words of James N. Giglio (1991): 'In many respects how Kennedy died is as important as how he lived.' (In White, 1998, p. 1) Historians writing more recently have tended to be much more critical. Their tendency to focus on Kennedy's private life, capacity for excess and concealed health record has, on the one hand, revealed a darker side to the president and, on the other, raised more fundamental questions as to how a president should be judged.

PRESIDENTIAL PROFILE

John Fitzgerald Kennedy

35th President of the United States (1961–63)
Born: 29 May 1917
Birthplace: Brookline, Massachusetts
Died: 22 November 1963, aged 46; buried Arlington National Cemetery, Virginia
Education: Attended the Choate School; London School of Economics; Princeton University; graduated from Harvard University (1940); Stanford University
Political party: Democratic
State: Massachusetts
Occupation before presidency: Author
Previous government service: Member US House of Representatives; US Senator
Age at inauguration: 43
Dates of office: 20 January 1961–22 November 1963
Election: November 1960
Vice president: Lyndon Baines Johnson
Length of term: Less than 3 years

9.2 JFK's early political career

JFK in the House of Representatives (1946–52)

Ostensibly, JFK's early congressional career did not appear to have equipped him to seriously present himself as a presidential candidate at such a young age. Lavishly supported by the hefty finances and political clout of a pushy, ambitious father, Kennedy first served in the House of Representatives (1946–52) representing a working-class district of his home town, Boston. Blessed with good looks, charisma and an articulate manner, he clearly had potential. However, once he reached Congress Kennedy did not display the enthusiasm for case work and local issues that his Massachusetts constituents might have been hoping for. An erratic attendance record, underlying health issues and, bluntly, a lack of interest from Kennedy himself did not seem to suggest a glittering route to the highest office.

JFK in the Senate (1953–60)

This did not deter JFK himself who, after three terms in the House, successfully ran for the Senate in November 1952. The fact that the Kennedys were able to see off the challenge of an opponent as formidable as Henry Cabot Lodge Jr. suggested the scale of the operation behind him. Outspending the possibly complacent incumbent, the Kennedys not least galvanised the female vote with a string of coffee mornings at which hosts of young women were given the opportunity to gaze admiringly at the rising star of Boston politics. In November 1952 Kennedy recorded a close, but sensational, victory over his more seasoned rival.

John T. Shaw's *JFK in the Senate* presents a comprehensive analysis of Kennedy's performance in the upper house between 1953 and 1960. With its strong traditions or 'folkways', rigid sense of hierarchy, and emphasis on membership of prestigious committees, the Senate was a tough but invaluable stepping stone for the most ambitious politicians. Kennedy's record was chequered. When all Democrats in the Senate were voting to censure McCarthy in 1954, Kennedy did not vote. While it is important to note that he was in hospital at the time recovering from back surgery, even a close Kennedy aide, Ted Sorensen, believed that he was ducking the issue and 'showed no courage on that vote', with no attempt to convey his wishes to colleagues when that would have been an option open to him. While he offered support to an important piece of civil rights legislation in 1957, Shaw describes Kennedy's approach to this issue as 'tactical and even timid' (Shaw, 2013, p. 63).

Shaw offers this evaluation of JFK in the Senate:

> Kennedy's adversaries were always underwhelmed by his Senate career and took delight in criticizing it. Lyndon Johnson was famously dismissive about Kennedy as a senator. 'Kennedy was pathetic as a congressman and as a senator ...', 'He's smart enough, but he doesn't like the grunt work' ... According to biographer Robert Caro, Johnson saw Kennedy as 'little more than a joke: a rich man's son, a "playboy" ... always away from Washington because of some illness or another.' ...
>
> Most historians and political scientists who have written about Kennedy refer to his Senate years as an interlude ... Based on his own reflections on the Senate,

it's clear that John F. Kennedy was not a great U.S. senator. His Senate career is not associated with acts of historic statesmanship, novel political thought, or landmark legislation. One of the main responsibilities of a senator is to write and shape legislation, and in this area Kennedy made modest contributions ... He was not drawn to the day-to-day challenge of developing and advancing bills ... Still it was during his Senate years that Kennedy forged his political identity. He learned how to project himself as a modern, future-oriented politician who was keenly focused on the challenges of the coming decade. (Shaw, 2013, pp. 187–95)

In turn, the Senate served Kennedy well. Most importantly he used it as a vehicle to enable him to systematically enhance his knowledge of foreign affairs. In particular, a visit to Indochina in 1951 made a deep and lasting impression on the young candidate. Visits of this type meant that by 1957 he was able to gain a place on the prestigious Senate Foreign Relations Committee. His knowledge of foreign policy grew exponentially so that when he entered the cauldron of a presidential race in 1960 he would be able to successfully project himself as on the right in foreign affairs and slightly to the left in domestic issues. It would be a potent combination.

Unsuccessful campaign to be vice president (1956)

In 1956, the Democratic Party nominee, Adlai Stevenson, had thrown open the contest for vice president. Kennedy, an ambitious 39-year-old two-term senator, eventually lost out on the ballot to Senator Estes Kefauver. Far from being personally crushed by the defeat, the Kennedy camp was soon awash with positive feedback. Dallek cites a Boston journalist who felt that JFK

probably rates as the one real victor in the entire convention. He was the one new face that actually shone. His charisma, his dignity, his intellectuality, and, in the end, his gracious sportsmanship ... are undoubtedly what those delegates will remember. (In Dallek, 2003, p. 208)

9.3 The presidential election of 1960

Personal health problems – the issue of secrecy

The image Kennedy so carefully presented to the electorate, of a healthy, vigorous, sporty and happily married young man, was in some important respects very different to the reality. In fact, during his Congressional career Kennedy was plagued by constant, often severe, back pain, and was also diagnosed with a potentially life-threatening condition, Addison's disease, in September 1947. A severe episode of the disease in 1951 caused serious concern for Kennedy's family and physicians. A series of operations and procedures on his back in 1953–54 caused him massive pain and distress. A urinary tract infection in October 1954 was so serious that a priest was called to administer the last rites of the Roman Catholic Church. These health problems inevitably damaged Kennedy's attendance and voting record in the Senate. Meanwhile, the importance politically of being a married man meant that with some reluctance Kennedy married the beautiful socialite Jacqueline Bouvier at a glittering event in Rhode Island in

September 1953. Kennedy had genuinely fallen in love but Jacqueline's beauty, style, intelligence and glamour were not enough to protect her from the prodigious woman-ising of her new husband. Once again, the image of the perfect marriage did not reflect the pain that Kennedy inflicted on his wife through his predatory sexual conduct.

The launch of the Kennedy campaign

On 2 January 1960 in the Senate Caucus Room, Senator John F. Kennedy announced his candidacy for the presidency of the United States:

> The Presidency is the most powerful office in the Free World ... it is in the Executive Branch that the most crucial decisions of this century must be made in the next four years – how to end or alter the burdensome arms race, where Soviet gains already threaten our very existence – how to maintain freedom and order in the newly emerging nations – how to rebuild the stature of American science and education – how to prevent the collapse of our farm economy and the decay of our cities – how to achieve, without further inflation or unemployment, expanded economic growth benefiting all Americans – and how to give direction to our traditional moral pur-pose, awakening every American to the dangers and opportunities that confront us.
>
> For 18 years, I have been in the service of the United States, first as a naval officer in the Pacific during World War II and for the past 14 years as a member of the Con-gress. In the last 20 years, I have travelled in nearly every continent and country ... From all of this, I have developed an image of America as fulfilling a noble and historic role as the defender of freedom in a time of maximum peril – and of the American people as confident, courageous and persevering. It is with this image that I begin this campaign. (JFK Library, online)

Kennedy's rivals

Rival candidates in 1960 included Senator Stuart Symington of Missouri, Senator Lyndon B. Johnson of Texas and Senator Hubert H. Humphrey of Minnesota. Symington hoped to go forward as a compromise candidate at a deadlocked Convention; Johnson believed that his long and impressive list of powerful supporters within the Democratic Party would stand him in good stead at the Convention; Humphrey believed it would be futile to take on Kennedy in the New Hampshire primary. Kennedy had the ambition, drive and financial backing needed to get his campaign off to a flying start. Facing no serious oppo-sition in New Hampshire, Kennedy secured 85.2 per cent of the vote in the first primary. More significant was Kennedy's triumph in the Wisconsin primary where he picked up 56.5 per cent of the vote, securing 22 Convention delegates compared to Humphrey's 12.

The issue of JFK's Catholicism

Kennedy was the first Roman Catholic candidate since 1928, when Governor Alfred E. Smith of New York had won only eight states when he ran against Republican Herbert Hoover. The religious issue came to the fore in West Virginia, a state that was 95 per cent Protestant. Kennedy seized the initiative by addressing the religious issue on television. Kennedy asked why he should have been denied 'the right to be President on the day I was baptised' (Dallek, 2003, p. 284). Kennedy emphasised that he would continue to support the clear separation of Church and State. This was a turning point, and Kennedy gained 60.8 per cent of the popular vote, forcing Humphrey to withdraw. These early primary successes convinced many Democratic Party leaders that he was a candidate who could be taken seriously across the country.

The defeat of LBJ as Democratic nominee

Meanwhile, Johnson declared his candidacy less than a week before the Democratic National Convention opened on 11 July in Los Angeles. As only 16 states held primaries in 1960, Johnson believed that the Convention would determine the outcome. Johnson calculated that if he could prevent Kennedy securing a first-round victory then the Convention would go into the 'smoke-filled room' where Johnson would be able to call in payment on the number of political debts owed to him following his successful period as Senate majority leader since 1954. However, shrewd canvassing and tactical awareness, particularly of campaign manager Robert Kennedy, enabled Kennedy to secure 806 votes on the first ballot, with Johnson gaining only 406 votes. Kennedy appointed Johnson as his running mate, ensuring a more balanced ticket for the young Catholic candidate from Boston by pairing him with the older Protestant running mate from Texas. In his acceptance speech, Kennedy stated that 'the world is changing. The old era is ending'. America was 'standing on the edge of a New Frontier' (JFK Library, online).

JFK vs Nixon

Kennedy now moved on to face Republican candidate Richard M. Nixon, one of the most hard-working and gifted politicians of his generation. Having twice served as vice president in the broadly successful Eisenhower Administrations, Nixon believed that his extra experience would give him a decisive edge over his more glamorous rival. However, when the candidates entered a series of nationally televised presidential debates it became clear that Nixon would have his work cut out to contain his vigorous challenger. The most significant of the television debates took place in Chicago, where moderator Howard K. Smith told the watching audience estimated at 80 million that 'the candidates need no introduction'. While Kennedy breezed into the television studio looking youthful and vibrant his rival was much impaired by a knee injury that was causing him considerable pain. Kennedy was tanned, handsome and relaxed while his opponent looked clammy, nervous and tense.

Christopher Matthews illustrates why the first TV debate went so well for Kennedy:

To bolster his indictment of the White House, Kennedy recited a long list of national shortcomings: steel mills operating with unused capacity, West Virginia schoolkids taking their lunches home to hungry families, and the poor prospects facing the 'Negro baby' ... 'The question now is: "Can freedom be maintained under the most severe attack it has ever known?" I think it can be, and I think in the final analysis it depends upon what we do here. I think it's time America started moving again.' In eighty minutes a lean, smartly tailored young gentleman had ... shown himself as infinitely more appealing than the fellow who had been Vice President of the United States for eight years ... Kennedy was playing a hawk on foreign policy, the activist at home, the same strategy he had used in the 1952 Senate race that sent Lodge packing. By going to his rival's right on foreign policy and to his left on domestic policy, Jack Kennedy would leave Nixon scrambling for turf. After observing this tour de force, Nixon began to betray the hunted look of a man dragged from a five-dollar-a-night hotel room and thrust before the unforgiving glare of a police line-up. (Matthews, 1996, p. 151)

Elsewhere in the campaign Kennedy scored several big hits. His constant reference to the 'missile gap' and to the need to get 'America moving again' helped to undermine Nixon's desire to take credit for the Republican achievements of the 1950s. Kennedy dealt with the issue of his Catholicism by bringing it up of his own accord so that he could emphasise his belief in the separation of Church and State. To Nixon's credit, he refused to exploit the religious issue to his own advantage but he did look back at the contest with some sharp observations about the way the Kennedy campaign was run.

Other factors that led to JFK's victory

Time magazine (November 1960) observed:

Kennedy had done it all not with any specific program, or even any specific catalogue of faults. He had done it by driving home the simple message of unease, of things left undone in the world where a slip could be disastrous. But most of all, he had done it by the force of his own youthful and confident personality, which seemed to promise freshness and vigor. The US had literally taken Jack Kennedy at face value. (In Matthews, 1996, p. 187)

It should also be noted that behind the Kennedy campaign were two family members of great significance. Kennedy's father, Joseph, undoubtedly used his money and influence to great (and not necessarily legal) effect. John's brother, Robert, was the real driving force. As campaign manager, he served as his brother's attack dog, leaving nothing to chance, constantly cajoling his older brother in his distinctive, Bostonian accent, to make one more effort. In the end the outcome could hardly have been closer with a final margin of only 0.1 per cent. On 8 November 1960, Kennedy received 34,227,096 votes compared to 34,108,546 for Nixon. Although this gave Kennedy an Electoral College majority of 303 to 219, the gap in the popular vote was the smallest in American electoral history. Kennedy liked to remind himself of how narrow the margin was by keeping a piece of paper in his pocket with the figure written on it – 118,550. Nixon's day would eventually come. But for now, Kennedy held centre stage. (Table 9.1)

Table 9.1 The result of the 1960 presidential election

Candidate	Party	Electoral College votes	Popular votes
John F. Kennedy (Massachusetts)	Democrat	303	34,227,096
Richard M. Nixon (California)	Republican	219	34,108,546
Harry F. Byrd (Virginia)	Democratic	15	

9.4 The New Frontier: Kennedy's domestic legislation

Table 9.2   Legislation and domestic issues, 1961–63

1961

1 March	Peace Corps created by Executive Order.
6 March	JFK set up a Committee on Equal Employment Opportunity chaired by Vice President Johnson.
5 May	The hourly rate for work increased from $1.00 to $1.25, to be phased in over a two-year period under the terms of the Minimum-Wage Bill.

1962

11 April	President Kennedy sharply criticised proposed increases in steel prices.
13 April	Steel price increases withdrawn.
28 May	Severe slump on the Wall Street stock exchange (the worst single day since October 1929), followed by a sharp recovery the following day.
30 September – 1 October	Two people killed when demonstrators in favour of segregation orchestrate serious riot on the campus of the University of Mississippi to prevent enrolment of a black student.

1963

14 January	In his State of the Union Address Kennedy proposed tax cuts to stimulate the economy.
11 June	Governor Wallace of Alabama forced to admit two black students to the University of Alabama, after they are supported by troops from the National Guard.
12 June	JFK's Executive Order established the President's Advisory Council on the Arts.
19 June	JFK advocated sweeping civil rights legislation.
28 August	Martin Luther King Jr delivered 'I have a dream' speech to a gathering of 200,000 people in Washington DC.
22 November	President Kennedy assassinated in Dallas, Texas.

The New Frontier

When a young John Kennedy first campaigned for Congress in 1946, he had used the slogan 'The New Generation Offers a Leader'. Privately, the candidate himself admitted that he was more interested in foreign affairs than domestic matters. As a young senator he had confided to his personal adviser, Theodore Sorensen, that the only Cabinet posts that really appealed to him were those of Secretary of State or Secretary of Defense. Just 14 years later, the presidential candidate was ready to present what had by then developed into the concept of 'The New Frontier' (Table 9.2). Kennedy's acceptance speech to the 1960 Democratic Convention was delivered to an audience of 80,000 people at the Los Angeles Coliseum. The Democratic candidate told his audience:

> The problems are not all solved and the battles are not all won – and we stand today on the edge of a New Frontier – the Frontier of the 1960's – a frontier of unknown opportunities and perils – a frontier of unfulfilled hopes and threats. The New Frontier is here whether we seek it or not: unconquered pockets of ignorance and prejudice, unanswered questions of poverty and surplus. (JFK Library, online)

While it was acknowledged that the phrase 'The New Frontier' represented a catchy campaign slogan, many observers felt that the young candidate had failed to deliver a truly statesmanlike speech. His mild criticism of Eisenhower and his more outspoken attack on Nixon were by no means universally welcome. However, the sheer eloquence of Kennedy's inaugural address just a few months later signalled that he was a politician with a substantial capacity for personal growth. Kennedy told his audience: 'The torch has been passed to a new generation ... Born in this century, tempered by war, disciplined by a hard and bitter peace ... granted the role of defending freedom in its hour of maximum danger.' Although the vast majority of the speech was devoted to foreign affairs, Kennedy briefly returned to some of his domestic concerns towards the end when he asked for support in the 'struggle against the common enemies of man: tyranny, poverty, disease and war itself.' (JFK Library, online)

James N. Giglio has pointed out that Kennedy had the capacity to integrate domestic and foreign concerns which:

> enabled him to broaden the New Frontier label to include initiatives as far reaching as space, the Peace Corps, women's rights, and civil rights. No other presidential rubric, whether it be the Square Deal, the New Deal, or the Fair Deal, was as inclusive or as expansive. (In White, 1998, p. 223)

Great American Lives: Rachel Carson, 27 May 1907–14 April 1964

To a large extent the post-war United States was governed by the powerful, impersonal forces at the centre of what Eisenhower termed the Military–Industrial Complex. Many of the scientific developments of this era concerned weapons of war. Napalm, for example, a deadly, incendiary gel, was developed in a Harvard War Research Laboratory in February 1942. In similar fashion, scientists had also developed a range of pesticides, such as DDT, which was widely used from 1945 onwards in a 'war' against agricultural pests and parasites.

Huge claims were made for DDT in its early years. Its initial success against malaria and dengue fever, combined with catch-all advertisements for the 'world of tomorrow' free from troublesome insects and mosquito-borne diseases, made the new product hugely profitable to the massive companies that produced it.

But from the outset, concerns about the safety and adverse environmental impact of DDT were expressed. Turning back the huge commercial and apparent agricultural drive to eliminate pests would be a huge task. That was accomplished by a writer and scientist whose book *Silent Spring* (1962) single-handedly brought opposition to the use of DDT to the centre of the national consciousness.

Rachel Carson was raised on the family farm near Springdale, Pennsylvania. She showed a keen interest in the natural world and in her student life studied biology, zoology and genetics at Johns Hopkins University in Baltimore. In 1936 she began work as a junior aquatic biologist at the US Bureau of Fisheries. Her

Continued

first book, *Under the Sea Wind* (1941), was well received and she continued to write regularly on natural history for a range of magazines.

In 1951, her major work, *The Sea Around Us* became a best-seller and received the 1952 National Book Award for Non-Fiction. By now, the ecology and conservation movements were gathering momentum. At the same time, there were increasing concerns about the damage caused by the overuse of pesticides.

In 1962 Carson's book *Silent Spring* combined scientific data and analysis with poetic language to highlight the precarious nature of the ecological balance. While others had raised concerns about DDT, Carson's gift for expression made the arguments more accessible than ever, raising doubts about the whole notion of scientific progress in post-war America.

While the book was warmly received by liberals, intellectuals and the scientific community, powerful corporations such as Du Pont threatened legal action. Sadly, Rachel Carson's life was cut short by cancer and she passed away in April 1964. However, her impact on the use of pesticides and DDT but also in promoting wider environmental concerns still resonates today.

Further reading: *New Yorker Magazine,* 16 June 1962, 'Silent Spring: Rachel Carson'

9.5 Poverty

While the Eisenhower Administration made the 1950s a successful decade for the middle class there is no doubt that a very significant layer of poverty lay underneath the general prosperity. One estimate is that at the start of the 1960s between 40 and 60 million Americans comprised 'the hidden poor'. Bruce Schulman offers this analysis:

During the 1960s, Kennedy had become alarmed at the problem of persistent, structural poverty – the sort of tenacious deprivation that even healthy national economic growth could not alleviate. Campaigning in West Virginia, Kennedy – a man born into riches and privilege – was shocked by the appalling conditions he faced. A *New Yorker* magazine article on Michael Harrington's controversial book *The Other America* hardened JFK's determination to develop a major piece of antipoverty legislation. Harrington's book had identified an economic underworld of poor schools, substandard medical care, and dead-end jobs. (Schulman, 1995, p. 71)

In the words of the review itself:

The most obvious citizens of the Other America are those whose skins are the wrong color ... In 1939, the non-white worker's wage averaged 41.4 per cent of the white worker's; by 1958 it had climbed to 58 per cent ... The least obvious poverty affects our 'senior citizens' – those over sixty-five. Mr. Harrington estimates that half of them – 8,000,000 – live in poverty ... The problem is obvious: the persistence of mass poverty in a prosperous country. (*New Yorker Book of the 60s*, p. 564)

In December 1962, Kennedy assigned Walter Heller, chairman of the Council of Economic Advisers, to assemble the facts and figures on the poverty problem in the United States. Although Heller produced an anti-poverty package which gained the president's approval it was decided, given the legislative logjam being stored up in Congress, to leave the measures until after the 1964 election. Nevertheless, the issue remained of great importance to JFK so that as late as October 1963 he discussed with Heller how he wanted to make 'a two- or three-day trip to some of the key poverty-stricken areas to focus the spotlight and arouse the American conscience on this problem from which we are so often shielded' (Dallek, 2003, p. 640). Looking ahead to the 1964 presidential campaign Kennedy told aides that his themes would be 'peace and prosperity' and in particular he would launch 'a war against poverty in eastern Kentucky, "the most severely distressed area in the country"'. (Dallek, 2003, p. 691)

On Sunday 20 October the *New York Times* described how in eastern Kentucky:

> unemployed coal miners and subsistence farmers faced 'another winter of idleness and grinding poverty' and wrote of 'the pinched faces of hungry children,' 'listless defeated men,' a tar-paper shack school 'unfit for cattle' where 'daylight shone though gaping holes between rotting planks,' and 'pot-bellied and anaemic' children hauling water from a creek 'fouled with garbage and discarded mattresses,' so hungry they ate the dirt from chimneys. (Clarke, 2013, p. 242)

Perhaps the very fact that one of the nation's leading newspapers could describe poverty in such bleak terms shows that as Kennedy's first term was coming to an end, poverty remained a huge blight on the nation's overall health.

Following Kennedy's assassination in November 1963, the future of the anti-poverty package passed into the hands of Lyndon Johnson. Johnson told Heller, 'That's my kind of program. Go ahead. Give it the highest priority.' Within a month of taking office, Johnson used his State of the Union Address to declare 'unconditional war on poverty in America' (Dallek, 1998, pp. 60–61). Several historians have recently assessed the issue of Kennedy's attempt to reduce poverty. Sar A. Levitan (1998) concluded that Kennedy's Area Redevelopment Administration (ARA) made the mistake of trying to help in too many communities. Carl Brauer (1998) concluded that there was 'no certainty that President Kennedy would have made poverty a leading issue had he lived' (in White, 1998, p. 237).

9.6 Education in the New Frontier

When Kennedy became president in 1961, the county faced huge shortages both of qualified teachers and classrooms. Kennedy biographer Robert Dallek shows how the president may have calculated that a reticent, cautious approach to civil rights might induce southern politicians to lend support to his proposals for education and Medicare. However, as early as October 1961 his aides advised him that

> the passage of any broad-scale education legislation will be a most difficult task. A broad program of grants to States for public school construction and teacher's salaries is virtually impossible to pass. There is substantial Southern opposition to any bill for elementary and secondary schools ... Republican opposition to any general aid bill is strong, and is overwhelming against teachers' salaries. (Dallek, 2003, p. 495)

The same advisor told him that there were three fundamental barriers to educational reform:

- Southern obsession with defending segregated schools
- A general political resistance to taking away local control over education
- Steadfast opposition to giving aid to private or religion-based schools.

Despite such advice, Kennedy attempted to address the issues of school construction and teachers' salaries but Congressional opposition, fuelled by issues of religion and desegregation and centring on Republicans and Southern Democrats, led to the rejection of a number of White House initiatives such as the defeat of the omnibus School Assistance Bill in 1961. It is also interesting to note that by 1963 the president was giving greater spending emphasis to space exploration and defence than schools and education. Dallek observes: 'In October 1962, when he prepared his 1963 budget, he privately acknowledged that education reforms which would increase the annual deficit, were "not going to pass." We should "just ... start off with that realization."' (Dallek, 2003, p. 585) This somewhat downbeat assessment chimed with a comment made in his final State of the Union Address in January 1963. Kennedy lamented the fact that 'Today, an estimated 4 out of every 10 students in the 5th grade will not even finish high school.' (JFK Library, online)

Bobby Kennedy and the fight against organised crime

The new president was keen to reward his brother's outstanding service to his campaign. Once Kennedy was in the White House he appointed his brother to the post of Attorney General, the highest legal position in the government, even though he knew this would arouse charges of nepotism. In fact, Bobby turned to be just as energetic and indefatigable in this role. He considerably extended the organised crime unit which, according to Robert Kennedy biographer Larry Tye (2016), 'amassed records filling two large rooms, on twenty-three hundred triggermen, gangsters and swindlers.'

Tye demonstrates conclusively that major crime bosses in cities such as New Orleans and Chicago found the Kennedy Administration's campaign against them to be 'the largest attack on organised crime in the nation's history' (Tye, 2016, pp. 142, 144). With indictments increasing from 19 per year to 687 as he left the post and with an almost 90 per cent conviction rate, RFK took on criminal families in New York, New Jersey and Rhode Island. Just as brutal was the pursuit of the leader of the Teamsters Union, Jimmy Hoffa, who was subjected to the 'most unrelenting congressional assault ever aimed at an individual' (Tye, 2106, p. 151). It would be an understatement to say that the Kennedy family were making some very dangerous enemies.

On the other hand, the integrity of RFK's stance against organised crime has been undermined by subsequent revelations about the links between the Kennedy family and the Mob. Some historians have claimed that the administration's attempts to oust Castro from Cuba included sustained contacts with major figures from the criminal underworld and that one of Kennedy's mistresses was the girlfriend of a high-profile gangster. Meanwhile, Frank Sinatra's high-profile support for JFK placed the family uncomfortably close to a number of prominent underworld figures. Finally, historians have pointed out the incongruity between Robert Kennedy's personal hostility towards the Mob and his alleged willingness to violate civil liberties by allowing wiretapping to take place on a broad scale.

9.7 Women in the 1960s

A summary of the two preceding decades

As American women entered the decade that would be ushered in by Kennedy's New Frontier and ended with a man landing on the moon, prospects for female equality appeared bleak. In 1940 only a quarter of the female population over 14 were at work, a figure virtually unchanged since 1910. Employment opportunities for women were largely poorly paid and menial. While the Second World War had demonstrated that women had a much greater capacity for productive work than had previously been assumed, the 1950s did not see a significant improvement in the need for equality. The affluent society of the 1950s may have provided middle-class prosperity but it certainly laid few foundations for the women's liberation movement. With its emphasis on building the perfect home and its stifling conformity, the pressures on women to maintain their traditional role were profound. The fabled middle-class American household of the Eisenhower years may have given the impression of lacking for nothing, crammed with labour-saving devices and household gadgets. It seemed to many that the role of the archetypal American housewife was to keep the perfect nest clean and tidy, prepare the evening meal and await the return of the male breadwinner. In 1958 only one in three college students was female.

JFK and issues of masculinity

Even when the torch was passed to a new generation at the start of the 1960s the outlook for women did not appear encouraging. Those women who had entered the workplace by the early 1960s were generally employed in clerical or service work and were discriminated against in both employment and pay. One striking characteristic of Kennedy's 'best and brightest' administration was that it was exclusively populated by men. The only two females of note in Kennedy's immediate circle were his wife, Jackie, who attracted unending attention for her beauty and fashion sense, and the president's secretary Evelyn Lincoln. During the Cuban Missile Crisis, not a single woman was consulted. The macho culture of the Kennedy White House has recently been covered by Steven Watts in *JFK and the Masculine Mystique: Sex and Power on the New Frontier* (2016) with its coverage of the president's 'masculine mystique that informed JFK's very approach to pressing issues.' Watts argues that this masculinity 'can be seen in his decision making about Castro's Cuba, the Cold War struggle against Communism, the physical fitness program, the space program, counterinsurgency, and even the Peace Corps' (Watts, 2016, p. 8). To Norman Mailer, the fabled American writer,

> Kennedy was less a politician than a cultural icon ... a transformational leader who had appeared as an existential hero, a tough, sexually assertive masculine presence who promised to rescue the country from the swamp of timid conformity ... that it had fallen into during the Eisenhower years. (In Watts, 2016, p. 105)

The women's liberation movement

Despite the lack of role models at the highest level things were about to change. The civil rights campaign of the 1950s–60s acted as a catalyst to the women's liberation movement.

As the long-standing obstacles to black equality began to tumble, it became plain to some women that a similar process needed to take place in the liberation of women.

Great American Lives: Betty Friedan, 4 February 1921–4 February 2006

No woman did more to create an organised women's liberation movement to take on these inequalities and to challenge male assumptions than Betty Friedan. Her first, and probably most important work, *The Feminine Mystique*, published shortly before Kennedy's death in 1963, challenged notions of happy domesticity and asked whether the roles of housekeeping and raising children should be regarded as the only means to female fulfilment. The book perfectly expressed the previously stifled dissatisfaction of women with the conservative expectations of the post-war period. The book became a publishing sensation and the position of women in American society was permanently changed. The publication of the book can be seen as marking the formal start of the women's liberation movement that seemed to belong to the 1960s just as the stereotypical housewife belonged to the 1950s.

Betty Friedan (born Bettye Goldstein) was born in Peoria, Illinois to Russo-Hungarian parents. Academically gifted, she attended the prestigious Smith College in 1938. A year at Berkeley in California saw her becoming increasingly active and politically to the left. By the late 1950s her surveys of female college graduates made it increasingly clear to her that many of her respondents were deeply dissatisfied with their lives. The stifling world of the housewife was fully explored when her book was published in 1963.

Friedan went on to help in the creation of the National Organization for Women (NOW) in 1966. Initially concerned with ending sexual discrimination in employment, the movement subsequently took up causes such as childcare provision, paid maternity leave and legalised abortion. Some of these issues led to confrontation with powerful opposition to feminism and the religious pro-life movement. Even so, by the end of the decade, 17 states had passed laws to make abortion easier and the annual figure of legal abortions being performed each year reached 200,000. In addition, the increasingly widespread availability of the first oral contraceptive, the Pill, was of huge importance to women who wished to control the size of their families and to single women in terms of the sexual freedom they could now enjoy. In assessing the importance of NOW it would be fair to say that it remained a largely middle-class movement, arousing relatively little interest from working-class women. While progress for women reached a level unimaginable without Friedan's pioneering work it ran into the formidable resistance of the archly conservative President Nixon who personally vetoed Congressional programs for the extension of childcare facilities as a direct threat to American family life. Similarly, the Equal Rights Amendment was passed by Congress in 1972 but was not ratified by a sufficient number of states before it lapsed in June 1982.

Meanwhile, Friedan remained an active, influential figure into her later years and can be seen as of the highest importance in creating the feminist movement and changing relationships between men and women on a permanent basis. She passed away in the nation's capital in 2006 at the age of 85.

Spurred on by Friedan's work, women gained confidence and became more radical in their protests, staging high-profile disruptions of anachronistic events such as beauty pageants and marching into male-dominated bars and restaurants. Their actions helped to rapidly change perceptions of the role of women and stimulated a raft of federal- and state-led equal opportunity legislation. Barriers to women were falling and there was a notable increase in the early 1960s of female carpenters and electricians as well as other occupations that had hitherto been almost exclusively male. Accountancy now attracted four times as many new female entrants compared to men. Nevertheless, women were still largely excluded from management and executive roles, occupying less than 5 per cent of these posts at the start of the 1970s, and the pay gap between men and women actually widened during the 1970s.

9.8 The economy

While Kennedy was regarded by many insiders as having a keen intellect, as a presidential candidate his interest in history outweighed his understanding of economics. Although during the debates with Nixon he frequently used the phrase that he 'wanted to get America moving again' there was little of real substance to suggest how he would achieve this. However, his keen political antennae meant that the damaging political impact of a relatively mild recession in 1960 on Nixon's standing was not lost on him. In his first State of the Union Address in January 1961 Kennedy told Congress that he needed to be candid about the country's economic well-being:

> The present state of our economy is disturbing. We take office in the wake of seven months of recession, three and one-half years of slack, seven years of diminished economic growth, and nine years of falling farm income ... Our recovery from the 1958 recession, moreover, was anaemic and incomplete. (JFK Library, online)

Dallek notes that 'Kennedy's two greatest economic worries between September 1961 and June 1962 were the country's balance of payment problems, which reduced the strength of the dollar, and inflation.' (Dallek, 2003, p. 481) However, a sharp slide on the US stock market during the summer of 1962 added to the president's unease, given the imminent midterm elections due later that year. It could also be argued that the president was more suited to diagnosing problems than providing practical solutions. In April 1962 a thoughtful analysis of the shortcomings of the nation's transport system did not offer substantial answers other than the need for Congress to 'devote considerable time and effort' to the matter. (Dallek, 2003, p. 496)

However, JFK was a quick learner and by 1963 Walter Heller felt that his boss had grasped the principles of Keynesian economics to become 'a good orthodox economist' (Clarke, 2013, p. 177). With a close eye on the 1964 election Kennedy was desperate to achieve economic growth. In his State of the Union Address in 1963 the president addressed some of the central economic issues facing the nation:

> At home, the recession is behind us. Well over a million more men and women are working today than were working 2 years ago. The average factory workweek is once again more than 40 hours; our industries are turning out more goods than ever before; and more than half of the manufacturing capacity that lay silent and wasted 100 weeks ago is humming with activity. (JFK Library, online)

Proposals for tax cuts

In the same speech Kennedy proposed a fairly radical tax cut, even though general trends in employment and economic growth were healthy. The president declared that 'the mere absence of recession is not growth' and that to achieve better productivity

> one step above all is essential – the enactment this year of a substantial reduction and revision in Federal income taxes ... It is increasingly clear ... that our obsolete tax system exerts too heavy a drag on private purchasing power, profits and employment. (In Dallek, 2003, p. 585)

Kennedy's bill proposed to reduce the highest marginal rate from 91 to 70 per cent and the lowest tax rate from 20 to 14 per cent. These proposals were relatively easy to present as a 'gamble' and in the autumn of 1963 his bill was becalmed in the House Ways and Means Committee thanks to resistance from Southern Democrats. A pattern was emerging in which the president became progressively bolder in his proposals during 1963 while opposition to his ideas remained steadfast.

9.9 The space race

During his pre-presidential years Kennedy was slow to commit himself to the space programme. When the Senate debated the National Aeronautics and Space Act, he had little to say. However, during the 1960 presidential campaign, he became increasingly focused on the issue of the alleged 'missile gap' which the Democrats claimed had opened up during the Eisenhower Administration. Presidential speechwriter Theodore Sorensen noted that the constant theme that Kennedy emphasised throughout the campaign was 'the challenge of the sixties to America's security, America's prestige, America's progress' (Logsdon, 2010, p. 11).

Despite the anti-communist stance he had followed during the campaign, in his inaugural address Kennedy appealed to the Soviets: 'Let both sides seek to invoke the wonders of science instead of its terrors. Together, let us explore the stars.' (Logsdon, 2010, p. 37) The youthful, energetic image that Kennedy brought to the White House meant that he was very tempted by the attractions of the space race; he was also reluctant to see the Soviet Union steal a march on the United States in the way that it had done with its successful Sputnik mission of 1957.

Even so, financial realities meant that Kennedy was unable to support all aspects of the space programme. For example, in 1961 the president was able to support additional finance for the Saturn rocket programme but drew back from supporting the Apollo programme and manned space flight beyond Project Mercury. The climate changed dramatically when in April 1961 the Soviet spacecraft Vostok 1 took Yuri Gagarin into space. Congressman Overton Brooks commented, 'my fear is that in coming in second best on this man-in-space program, we will continue to be second best in the future.' The *New York Times* grudgingly praised the 'spectacular' Soviet achievement and noted that 'only Presidential emphasis and direction will chart an American pathway to the stars' (Logsdon, 2010, p. 73).

Kennedy was acutely aware of the political implications of falling behind the Soviets, and his burgeoning interest in the space programme was reflected in a personal

Table 9.3   The space race, 1961–63

1961	January	Kennedy received the 'Report to the President Elect of the Ad Hoc Committee on Space', which highlighted five distinct advantages for a space programme. These were identified as national prestige, national security, scientific progress, improvements in communications, navigations and meteorology, and finally opportunities for international co-operation.
	12 February	The Soviet Union sent Sputnik 8 to Venus.
	12 April	Soviet cosmonaut Major Yuri Gagarin became the first man in space when he orbited the earth in Vostok 1.
	5 May	US astronaut Commander Alan Bartlett Shepard reached an altitude in space of 116 miles.
1962	20 February	Lieutenant-Colonel John Herschel Glenn Jr became the first American astronaut in orbit; he orbited the earth three times.
1963	7 May	The communications satellite Telstar II was launched.

call to congratulate Alan Shepard following his successful mission in May 1961. At a press conference in the same month Kennedy promised a substantial increase in the national space effort (Table 9.3).

In a major speech to Congress in May 1961, Kennedy stated:

> Now it is time ... for this nation to take a clearly leading role in space achievement, which in many ways may hold the key to our future on earth ... I therefore ask the Congress, above and beyond the increases I have earlier requested for space activities, to provide the funds which are needed to meet the following national goals: First, I believe that this nation should commit itself to achieving the goal, before this decade is out, of landing a man on the moon and returning him safely to earth. No single space project in this period will be more impressive to mankind, or more important for the long-range exploration of space; and none will be so difficult to accomplish. (In Logsdon, 2010, p. 114)

At Rice University in Houston Texas on 12 September 1962, Kennedy delivered one of the most stirring speeches of his political career:

> But why, some say, the moon? Why choose this as our goal? And they may well ask, why climb the highest mountain? Why, 35 years ago, fly the Atlantic? Why does Rice play Texas? We choose to go to the moon. We choose to go to the moon in this decade and do the other things, not because they are easy, but because they are hard, because that goal will serve to organize and measure the best of our energies and skill, because that challenge is one that we are willing to accept, one we are unwilling to postpone, and one which we intend to win ...
>
> It is for these reasons that I regard the decision last year to shift our efforts in space from low to high gear as among the most important decisions that will be made during my incumbency in the office of the Presidency. (In Logsdon, 2010, p. 150)

Kennedy managed to persuade Congress to sanction a massive increase in the funding of the Apollo space programme. While space exploration may sound a relatively narrow objective, of course the programme encompassed scientific education, high-level university programmes, engineering, rocket propulsion, leading-edge design, mathematics and physics and, not least in the Cold War, matters related to defence.

The objective was now clearly defined: to land a man on the moon, and to do so before the Soviet Union. Yale University academic Gary Brewer has stated that NASA during the Apollo programme came close to being 'a perfect place' with its 'innocent clarity of purpose, the relatively easy and economically painless public consent, and the technical confidence.' Logsdon notes:

> [T]he set of judgements that led President John F. Kennedy to decide to send Americans to the Moon combined lasting characteristics of the American people, a conviction of American exceptionalism and a mission derived from that conviction, the geopolitical situation of early 1961, and the individual values and style that Kennedy brought to the White House. (Logsdon, 2010, pp. 242–43)

Although Kennedy did not live to see it, the mission achieved its objective when Neil Armstrong and Buzz Aldrin set foot on the moon's surface on 20 July 1969. While this was mankind's greatest technical achievement, the cost of this programme, approximately $24 billion, led to criticism in some quarters that this money could have been better spent on domestic concerns.

9.10 Problems with Congress

Kennedy's record as the chief executive and as a legislative leader has come under close scrutiny. In *The Dark Side of Camelot* the renowned investigative journalist Seymour Hersh states:

> The manipulation was extraordinary. The president was living a public lie as an attentive husband and hardworking chief executive ... But the Secret Service agents assigned to the White House presidential detail saw Jack Kennedy in a different light: as someone obsessed with sex, and willing to take enormous risks to gratify that obsession. They saw a president who came late many mornings to the Oval Office, and was not readily available for hours during the day to his immediate staff and his national security aides; a president, some thought, whose behaviour was demeaning to the office. (Hersh, 1998, p. 222)

At first glance, it might appear that Kennedy had a simple task in dealing with the 87th Congress which convened its two-year session at the start of 1961. In the upper chamber, the Senate, the Democrats enjoyed a majority of 64 seats over the 36 of the Republicans. In the House of Representatives, the Democrats held a majority of 263 to 174. The Democrat Speaker of the House of Representatives was John W. McCormack (1962–71), who had succeeded long-serving Democrat Sam Rayburn. However, the reality was less simple. A large bloc of conservative Southern Democrats in the 'Solid South' consistently opposed Kennedy's 'liberal' proposals and voted instead with the Republican Party.

In July 1962 the administration's proposals for medical insurance were defeated in the Senate by 52 votes to 48. This meant that even in the autumn of 1963 some of Kennedy's most important legislation was stalled in Congress. For example, in September 1963, the civil rights bill was mired in the House Judiciary Committee. A further factor making life difficult for Kennedy may have been the gloomy demeanour of someone who was much more adapt at managing the white water of the Senate – his now vice president L.B. Johnson. As one insider noted, 'LBJ's simple presence seems to bug him' (in Clarke, 2013, p. 139). This element of in-fighting did not help, given that Johnson's contacts with the Senate were legendary. In addition, Johnson's personal animosity towards the president's brother Robert – the Attorney General – was well known and LBJ was certainly willing and able to make life difficult for the Kennedys if he was so inclined.

Historiography of JFK as a legislative leader

Thomas C. Reeves is dismissive of Kennedy's handling of Congress:

> As a legislative leader, Kennedy was relatively ineffective. Weak support in Congress was part of the problem. The President's lack of conviction and personal fervor for what he was advocating was partly responsible. His reluctant approach to civil rights, until quite late in his Thousand Days, is a case in point. (Reeves, 1992, p. 416)

Mark J. White presents a valuable comparison with the domestic achievements of Eisenhower and Johnson:

> Next to the preceding Presidency of Dwight D. Eisenhower, Kennedy's domestic policies seem impressive ... More than Eisenhower, JFK sought to address the problems facing Americans, whether in education or housing or civil rights ... Compared with his successor in the White House, Lyndon Baines Johnson, Kennedy's record appears in a different light. In this case, his diplomacy appears more impressive, his domestic policies less so. Johnson's Great Society reforms, encompassing, as they did, Medicare, Medicaid, voting rights for blacks, the War on Poverty, and so much more besides, dwarf JFK's domestic accomplishments. Despite Kennedy's good intentions, he failed to get most of what he regarded as his essential pieces of legislation through Congress. (White, 1998, p. 10)

Maldwyn A. Jones is also critical:

> If Kennedy's foreign policy record was at best mixed, at home he accomplished even less. Though he had promised bold leadership 'to get America moving again', he at first acted very cautiously. To be sure he lacked effective support in Congress ... many of the key features of the New Frontier legislative program ... were either blocked or killed outright. In most cases however the margin of defeat was narrow and it may be that a President less preoccupied with foreign and defense matters and more skilled in handling Congress could have achieved more ... By the autumn of 1963 virtually all of Kennedy's domestic program was deadlocked. He hoped, however, that the 1964 elections would not only confirm him in office but also produce a more friendly Congress. (Jones, 1995, p. 548)

Kennedy biographer Robert Dallek is broadly sympathetic to the president but on JFK's legislative record he offers this appraisal:

> On roll calls involving foreign policy, he had received 96.5 per cent backing. But his overall record was much less noteworthy. Many of the bills Congress passed were relatively minor reforms, like temporarily reducing duty exemptions on Americans returning from abroad, authorizing an additional assistant secretary of labor,

extending the Sugar Act of 1948, or reorganizing the Federal Home Loan Bank Board. Most of his legislative requests – 56 per cent in 1962, to be exact – had never emerged from House and Senate committees, where conservative chairmen bottled them up. (Dallek, 2003, p. 581)

Julian E. Zelizer's analysis, *The Fierce Urgency of Now*, presents a clear contrast between the legislative achievements of JFK and LBJ:

Lyndon Johnson hated being vice president. He was at heart a legislator who had been relegated to the side-lines of legislation. For almost three years he had watched John F. Kennedy fumble most of the big domestic issues of the day, either because the president was unwilling to take on the toughest challenges of the moment, or because he was too afraid of the political fallout, or because he knew he lacked the ability to win the legislative battles he faced on Capitol Hill. At the time of Kennedy's death, most of his major domestic initiatives – including civil rights, a tax cut, federal assistance for education, and hospital insurance for the elderly – were stalled in Congress or had not yet been introduced there. Kennedy and his advisers had made a conscious decision to keep Lyndon Johnson out of their inner circle, despite his extensive experience on Capitol Hill, for fear that his well-known thirst for power would cause problems for the president. (Zelizer, 2015, p. 1)

New Frontier legislation or proposals either stalled or killed outright as of November 1963

- Federal aid to education
- Immigration policy reforms
- The introduction of a new Department of Urban Affairs
- Health insurance for the elderly (Medicare)
- Income tax reduction

These ongoing difficulties with Congress meant that the president's final year in the White House was often one in which he was frequently able to analyse particular problems but somewhat frustrated by the difficulties of providing solutions. So in January 1963 he remained concerned about 'the growing nationwide shortage of doctors, dentists and nurses', the nation's need to provide 'healthy transportation arteries' and finally, that 'the state of the economy poses a perplexing challenge to the American people. The nation is still falling substantially short of its economic potential' (JFK Library, online). A fair summary may be that Kennedy and his team had the intellectual understanding to identify the nation's failings and were not lacking in imaginative solutions, but in terms of legislation a stubborn Congress all too often curtailed the progress of a frustrated president.

9.11 Foreign policy

During the 1960 presidential election, Kennedy had portrayed himself as a hawk on all matters of foreign policy. With the White House as the glittering prize, Cold War orthodoxy was essential. In a typical campaign speech he declared:

I have strong ideas about the United States playing a great role in a historic moment when the cause of freedom is endangered all over the world. When the United States stands as the only sentry at the gate. When we can see the camp fires of the enemy burning on distant hills. (JFK Library, online)

Kennedy persistently accused the Republican administration of Eisenhower and Nixon of allowing a 'missile gap' to open up between the United States and the Soviet Union. When he made his first speech as president in January 1961, he was determined to maintain this stance. Domestically, Kennedy's inaugural address was acclaimed as a spellbinding piece of oratory. The setting lent itself to this appraisal. The pomp and circumstance of an inauguration, the atmosphere provided by the crisp January weather, Kennedy's distinctive Bostonian accent, a massive, appreciative audience and the ringing phrases all created a superb spectacle.

The president promised, 'we shall pay any price, bear any burden, meet any hardship, support any friend, oppose any foe, to assure the survival and success of liberty'. He told his audience that 'the torch is passed to a new generation ... Born in this century, tempered by war, disciplined by a hard and bitter peace ... granted the role of defending freedom in its hour of maximum danger' (JFK Library, online). However, beyond the soaring rhetoric several critical points can also be made. Kennedy's inaugural address demonstrated that his outlook remained set in the Cold War views of the late 1940s and 1950s. In setting the tone for his administration, Kennedy appeared likely to continue, rather than ease, the Cold War. James N. Giglio makes this appraisal:

President John F. Kennedy always gave his greatest attention to foreign policy matters. He was not necessarily unique in that respect. Cold War challenges and crises consumed virtually all post-World War II Presidencies. Beyond this, Kennedy had always held a deeper interest in international relations. (In White, 1998, p. 222)

Kennedy had demonstrated in unforgettable style how he could dramatise the issues of the moment with his soaring phrases. How successful was he in managing the foreign policy of the United States?

9.12 Latin America: The Alliance for Progress

Kennedy introduced the concept of the Alliance for Progress in March 1961. He had a concept of a club of the Americas. The president envisaged inviting progressive leaders from Central and South America to informal gatherings at his father's house in Palm Beach. His intention was to act against the spread of communism in Latin America by promoting economic development and much-needed social and political reform. The ousting of Castro in Cuba would be followed by the introduction of a ten-year North-to-South American sponsored aid plan, the *Alianza para el Progreso*. Kennedy launched the plan in typically grandiose terms with a speech in the East Room of the White House: 'I have called upon all people of the hemisphere to join in a new Alliance for Progress ... to satisfy the basic needs of the American people for homes, work and land, health and schools.' (JFK Library, online) However, the Alliance did not in fact lead to major changes. American aid never reached the level needed to bring economic development forward. The democratic reforms which Kennedy had hoped to promote came to very little and the elites who had ruled Latin America remained in place.

9.13 Berlin

Across the entire landscape of the Cold War no city seemed of greater psychological importance to both sides than Berlin. In *Kennedy's Wars*, Lawrence Freedman explains why Berlin presented a particular challenge to the White House:

> Berlin obliged Kennedy to address the fundamental questions of war and peace in the nuclear age. He was torn between the need to appear unyielding in the defense of America's interests and his real fear of sudden lurches into crisis and then war. The peculiar vulnerability of Berlin set an extremely demanding strategic challenge. Deep in East Germany, surrounded by Soviet and East German divisions, was not a good place to pick a fight. (Freedman, 2000, p. 93)

Many historians have drawn links between Kennedy's humiliating experience over the Bay of Pigs invasion in April 1961 and Khrushchev's decision to test his resolve even further with the construction of a wall dividing the city of Berlin in August 1961. This view remains tenable. When Khrushchev first met Kennedy he was struck by his youthful appearance; the Bay of Pigs incident encouraged Khrushchev to believe that Kennedy was weak, inexperienced and out of his depth. At the Vienna Summit in June 1961, Khrushchev told Kennedy: 'I heard you were a young and promising man.' (Zubok & Pleshakov, 1996, p. 243)

However, it also now clear that, as early as January 1961, Khrushchev was preparing to make a move over Berlin. In the same month that Kennedy was delivering his dazzling inaugural, Khrushchev told a group of party officials in Moscow that the position of the three Western powers who shared control of Berlin with the Soviet Union was 'vulnerable'. In February, the Soviet ambassador to West Germany delivered a message to the government saying that the time limits for reaching an understanding on the occupation status of West Berlin had expired. The underlying problem here was that the Soviet Union was increasingly concerned and humiliated by the fact that literally hundreds of people a week were 'voting with their feet' and moving from the drab circumstances of the Soviet-controlled section to the much more prosperous Western sectors. The Soviet embassy in Berlin reported in April 1961 that during the 1950s the population of the GDR had fallen by 1.2 million. One of Khrushchev's speechwriters made the grim joke that before long the only person left in the GDR would be the East German president himself.

In June 1961, Khrushchev announced that he was prepared to sign a separate peace treaty with East Germany concerning each of the communication routes which connected Berlin with the outside world. On 25 July, Kennedy responded by announcing American military mobilisation in the Western sector. At the same time Khrushchev decided to have a wall, barbed wire and ultimately guard posts placed along the entire border. Two Russian historians, Zubok and Pleshakov, working with newly released archive material, confirmed that Khrushchev's decision to build the wall to divide the city 'was made spontaneously coming as a surprise to friends and foes alike'. In a newly discovered speech of 3 August 1961, Khrushchev told his Warsaw Pact allies that he wanted to 'give imperialism a bloody nose'. He reaffirmed his view that the United States was 'barely governed' by Kennedy who was 'too much of a lightweight' (Zubok & Pleshakov, 1996, pp. 251–52). On 13 August, the 2.5 million people who lived in West Berlin found themselves separated by barbed wire from East Berlin. Construction of the wall itself began a few weeks later. Although Khrushchev had breached the terms of the Four-Power Agreements on Berlin, Kennedy recognised that the construction of the wall did not make military confrontation inevitable. From the Pentagon came the recommendation that the president could consider using tactical nuclear weapons to preserve Western status and access in the beleaguered city.

While the president increased spending on conventional military forces and placed American forces on alert when the US responded merely with diplomatic protests and a strengthening of their Berlin garrison, it is likely that the Soviets concluded that their strategy in the city had been a success. Although the United States displayed some belligerence over Berlin in October 1961, the crisis did not develop further. In a personal letter to Kennedy, Khrushchev expressed the hope that the two superpowers would 'plant a new orchard' on the 'ashes of the Cold War'. Yet at the same time Khrushchev convinced himself that a further, more dramatic showdown was looming over the island of Cuba.

9.14 The Bay of Pigs

The new president had only been in office for three months when he faced his first major foreign policy crisis. Until 1959, Cuba, a Caribbean island 90 miles off the coast of Florida, had been very much under the control of the United States. America had supported the country's corrupt dictator, Fulgencio Batista y Zaldivar, and at the same time exploited its resources. America controlled Cuban sugar plantations and the Mafia made huge profits from the operations which it ran there. However, in 1959 Batista was overthrown in a revolution led by a charismatic young lawyer, Fidel Castro. Castro wanted to return the island's sugar plantations to the Cuban people who worked them. He wanted to nationalise industry and spoke of 'freedom' for the Cuban people. In the United States, Castro's 'revolutionary' approach sounded alarm bells. When the new leader of Cuba visited the United States in April 1959, he was given a cold reception; he was told that Eisenhower was too busy to meet him (he was playing golf) and the vice president, Richard Nixon, made his hostility clear. Not surprisingly, Khrushchev saw this as a golden opportunity; Castro was invited to the Soviet Union, where he was given an altogether friendlier reception. The USSR embraced Castro, and provided his country with financial aid, trade deals, technical support and military supplies. During the presidential campaign of 1960 Kennedy was briefed on two occasions about the CIA's plans to overthrow Castro, although he was not provided with details.

Once he occupied the White House, Kennedy was determined to be seen as a dynamic leader. It was this factor, perhaps combined with his inexperience, which led him to quickly approve details for the anti-Castro plan which had been authorised by Eisenhower in March 1960. The plan involved the training and arming of anti-Castro Cuban exiles at secret camps in Central America and Florida. This force would then be dispatched to Cuba to carry out an invasion leading to the overthrow of Castro. On 11 March 1961, the Director of the CIA, Allen Dulles, and his chief of operations, Richard Bissell, presented Kennedy with a detailed briefing. The CIA assured Kennedy that the mission would succeed; Kennedy authorised the mission but made it clear that there would be no direct involvement of America's regular forces. Kennedy was impressed with the CIA in general and with Bissell's intellect – he had previously taught economics at Yale – in particular. Richard Reeves emphasises the importance of Kennedy's decision-making style, with his preference for informal meetings rather than rigid procedures, in what was about to unfold:

> The CIA men were making it up as they went along. They thought they had Kennedy's number already. They were calling this White House 'the floating crap game'. No regular meetings meant that all the action went with the President; if he was not looking there was no system and no guarantee that anyone was checking for him. Kennedy was at the center, but he was alone there – and Bissell was going ahead on his own. (Reeves, 1994, p. 72)

The initial invasion plan was for the Cuban exiles to land near the small city of Trinidad. Following discussions between Bissell and Kennedy, the invasion site was switched to a place known as Bahia de los Cochinos – the Bay of Pigs.

On 14–15 April 1961, approximately 1,500 men landed in Cuba on a sandy beach on the island's south coast. It soon became apparent that the CIA had grossly underestimated Castro's leadership and resources and the extent of his popularity; Castro swiftly mobilised his forces and pinned down the invading force. As the situation deteriorated for the United States, Kennedy was asked to send extra support to the exiles; Kennedy refused, and had to look on impotently as more than a hundred exiles were killed and the rest surrendered. The contrast in tone between Castro's triumphant four-hour television address and Kennedy's subdued comment at a press conference on 21 April that 'there's an old saying that victory has a hundred fathers and defeat is an orphan' could not have been more pronounced. The Bay of Pigs proved a triumph for Castro who had used the invasion to whip up patriotic feeling against the invaders. As Castro's popularity increased it was clear that Kennedy had discovered that being the president would not always be easy. In the Soviet Union, Khrushchev watched Kennedy's humiliation with keen interest, confirming his notion that American foreign policy was in the hands of a fundamentally weak and inexperienced leader.

Mark J. White offers this assessment of the impact of the Bay of Pigs on Kennedy's thinking about Cuba:

> Rather than causing JFK to re-evaluate the fundamentals of his Cuban policy, the Bay of Pigs had no discernible effect on his thinking. He continued to operate from the assumption that Castro must be overthrown, and he still believed that covert tactics were the most likely to bear fruit. (His intention had been for the Bay of Pigs to remain a secret operation.) Hence in November 1961 Kennedy launched Operation Mongoose, a well-funded clandestine CIA program designed to harass Castro and, ultimately, to trigger an anti-Castro uprising that the Kennedy administration would back militarily, if required. (White, 1998, p. 69)

In *A Question of Character*, his highly critical biography of Kennedy, Thomas C. Reeves provides this scathing verdict:

> In the Bay of Pigs fiasco, Jack rejected moral and legal obligations to an invasion; he lied, exhibited an almost adolescent macho temperament, became involved with military operations just enough to make them worse, and then blamed others for

the failure. He soon approved Operation Mongoose, the clandestine exercise in terrorism and murder. Determined to win Cuba at any cost, Jack had secret dealings with one of the top mobsters involved in the assassination attempts. This reveals an irresponsibility and lack of judgement bordering on dereliction. (Reeves, 1992, p. 416)

9.15 The Cuban Missile Crisis

Historiography

No event in the Kennedy era tested the president more fully than the Cuban Missile Crisis of October 1962 (Table 9.4), and his management of the crisis remains highly controversial. When the crisis came to an end, many observers applauded Kennedy for standing up to the Soviets, his insistence that the Soviet missiles be dismantled and taken away from Cuba earning him widespread support. More recently, some historians have admired Kennedy's restraint, praising the fact that he ruled out the options of an American air strike against the missile bases or a military invasion of Cuba. They have claimed that had Kennedy given into the strong pressure exerted by his generals and taken military action a full-scale exchange of nuclear weapons between the Soviet Union and the United States would probably have followed.

In the words of Mark J. White:

> While Kennedy's handling of Castro and Khrushchev before October 1962 was flawed, his management of the missile crisis itself proved effective. A quick but not a deep thinker, he was better at grasping immediate dangers than anticipating those down the road; and this meant he was better equipped to manage short-term crises than to implement policy of long-term benefit. There were weaknesses in Kennedy's performance in the missile crisis, especially during the first few days. But in general he handled the confrontation adroitly. (White, 1998, pp. 73–74)

On the other hand, Kennedy's handling of Cuba has also attracted severe criticism. Some historians have actually blamed him for the missile crisis developing in the first place, claiming that the president presented a weak, inexperienced image to the Soviet Union: 'Had he taken an absolutely firm stance on the matter before the spring of 1962, the missile crisis could probably have been avoided.' (Reeves, 1992, p. 366) It has also been claimed that Kennedy needlessly raised the stakes and took the world to the brink by overdramatising the crisis, with one eye on the important midterm elections which were due in November. His priority, it is alleged, was to win domestic support by taking a tough line against the Soviets, risking everything for political gain. Michael Beschloss offers some distance from the Kennedy mythology:

> Kennedy's partisans later lauded his detached ability to see things from his opponent's point of view and his care not to push them to the wall. This quality was not in consistent evidence in his relations with Khrushchev through 1961 and early 1962. The President had almost no understanding of the extent to which his allusions to American nuclear superiority and a possible first strike had made Khrushchev feel trapped and deeply insecure. (Beschloss, 1991, p. 437)

Table 9.4 Timeline: 1960–62, events leading up to the Cuban Missile Crisis

1960	**November**	Kennedy's successful election campaign included a tough stance on foreign policy. Kennedy alleged that the outgoing Republican regime had allowed a 'missile gap' to open up between the United States and its arch-rival, the Soviet Union.
1961	**January**	In a stirring inaugural address, President Kennedy announced that he would 'pay any price, bear any burden, meet any hardship, support any friend, oppose any foe, to assure the survival and success of liberty.' He told his audience that 'the torch has been passed to a new generation ... Born in this century, tempered by war, disciplined by a hard and bitter peace ... granted the role of defending freedom in its hour of maximum danger.'
	17–20 April	5,000 Cuban exiles trained in the United States landed at the Bay of Pigs in an attempt to bring about the overthrow of Cuban revolutionary leader Fidel Castro. Within hours it became clear that without further American support the mission would end in disaster. Kennedy refused to go any further and had to admit to a humiliating defeat.
	3–4 June	At the Vienna Summit the youthful president came face to face with Soviet Premier Khrushchev for the first time since his election victory. The atmosphere at the conference was tense and hostile, and Kennedy left the conference feeling that he had been mauled by a tough and skilful adversary. Khrushchev formed the impression that Kennedy was weak and inexperienced.
	12–13 August	Without warning, East German soldiers erected a wall dividing East Berlin from the West. Kennedy was unable or unwilling to do anything to physically oppose this move. However, in an emotional visit to West Berlin he pledged the inhabitants of the besieged city his support.
1962	**Spring**	Castro was convinced that the United States had decided to launch a further invasion of Cuba. Meanwhile, the CIA's anti-Castro plan, 'Operation Mongoose', was aiming to maximise disruption of the Castro regime and even examining the possibility of assassinating Castro.
	July	Castro's brother visited Moscow to urgently request military aid. Khrushchev indicated that he would be prepared to send intermediate-range nuclear missiles. Recent evidence suggests that the Soviet leader had already moved towards this decision several months before. Later, Khrushchev stated in his memoirs that they had chosen targets to inflict maximum damage and inspire terror.
	July–August	The Soviet Union began sending troops, supplies and construction workers to Cuba.
	29 August	A U-2 plane took photographs of SAM (surface-to-air missile) installations under construction. Khrushchev spent the summer at his holiday dacha on the Black Sea.
	September	Senator Kenneth Keating expressed fears that the Soviet Union were installing medium-range ballistic missiles (MRBMs) and IRBMs in Cuba.
	2 September	The Soviet Union publicly admitted for the first time that they had sent technical advisers and armaments to Cuba.

Continued

11 September	The Soviets claimed that the armaments and equipment they had sent to Cuba were for strictly defensive purposes. By early October the Soviets had installed a substantial number of fighter planes, unassembled jet bombers, tanks and anti-aircraft guns on Cuba.
10 October	Senator Keating claimed that launching sites 'to hurl rockets into the American heartland and as far as the Panama Canal Zone' (Dobbs, 2009, p. 6) were under construction in Cuba.

9.16 Why did the Cuban Missile Crisis arise?

Cuba's proximity to the United States meant that events there were watched with mounting concern in the White House. The superpower clash over Cuba can be traced to the personalities of the two key figures. The leader of the Soviet Union, Nikita Khrushchev, projected an image of himself as a tough, brash, outspoken figure. John Kennedy was eager to be seen as a man of action who would stand up to the Soviet menace. When Kennedy became president in January 1961, Khrushchev felt that an opportunity had arisen to test the resolve of the leader of the Western world.

The failure of Kennedy's invasion at the Bay of Pigs in April 1961 reinforced Khrushchev's view that the president was a weak and inexperienced leader. Even so, Khrushchev was convinced that a further, much larger American invasion of Cuba could follow. When the two leaders came face to face at the superpower summit held in Vienna in June 1961, Khrushchev pressured Kennedy to give up the West's hold on Berlin. Khrushchev threatened Kennedy with war and the president replied that they could both expect 'a very cold winter' (Zubok & Pleshakov, 1996, p. 248).

Khrushchev was aggrieved by the fact that the United States had Jupiter nuclear warheads based in Italy and Turkey and aimed at targets in the Soviet Union, and felt that this provided justification for the Soviet Union to place its nuclear missiles abroad. In the summer of 1962, Khrushchev personally issued an order for Soviet missiles to be shipped to the island of Cuba. Within months, this gamble, and Kennedy's dramatic response, would bring the world the closest it had ever been to the point of nuclear war. Kennedy was only 45 years old; responsibility for the future of the entire planet now rested in his hands. Therefore it could be said that the Cuban Missile Crisis developed because Khrushchev took a gamble and at the same time seriously underestimated the political will of President Kennedy.

9.17 American discovery of the missile bases

As early as September 1962, politicians in America were raising concerns about Russian military activity in Cuba. In October 1962, a series of reconnaissance missions were launched to establish the facts. Just before midnight on 13 October 1962 a plane, belonging to the American Strategic Air Command, took off for Cuba from Andrews Air Force Base in California. By breakfast time the following morning the aircraft was over Cuba. The focus of the mission was the area between San Cristobal and Los Palacios to the west of the capital, Havana. The crew of the U-2 reconnaissance plane completed their spying mission over Cuba without detection; at an altitude of 70,000 feet, a combination of clear skies and state-of-the art technology enabled them to take a series of photographs of stunning clarity. When the CIA developed the photographs at the National Photographic Interpretation Center, they revealed images that would bring the world to the edge of the nuclear abyss. They clearly showed a medium-range ballistic missile launch site including missile-erector launchers, canvas-covered missile trailers and a range of military vehicles. The purpose of this equipment was to deploy Russian-made R-12 missiles 74 feet long, with a 7-foot nose cone and carrying a 1-megaton warhead. Whereas the device which had devastated Hiroshima carried a force equivalent to 14,000 tonnes of TNT, these missiles could deploy 1 million tonnes of TNT. Cuba was just 90 miles off the Florida coast: with the exception of Seattle, virtually every major American city was within range of nuclear oblivion.

9.18 Thirteen days – A chronology of the Cuban Missile Crisis

Tuesday 16 October A.M.

The president was still in his White House bedroom when he was informed of the Soviet missiles on Cuba. Historian Mark White observes that while JFK was subsequently praised for his cool, considered approach to the crisis, his initial response to the news was belligerent and hawkish. His first step was to set up the emergency advisory committee which eventually became known as the Executive Committee (ExComm) which was to guide him through the most important decision-making process he had ever faced. Later that morning, President Kennedy, accompanied by a group of 14 political advisors and generals, was shown for the first time the dramatic U-2 reconnaissance photographs of Cuba. The photographic enlargements revealed the ongoing construction of medium-range ballistic missile (MRBM) sites. The 'thirteen days' of the Cuban Missile Crisis had now begun. Later, an aide recalled that at the first meeting Kennedy was 'very clipped, very tense … He seemed to me to believe that the Soviets meant business in the most real sense, and this was the biggest national crisis he'd faced.' White notes that on the first day of the crisis JFK's verbal summary of the practical alternatives was as follows: 'We're certainly going to do number one; we're going to take out these missiles … the questions will be whether, which, what I would describe as number two, which would be a general air strike. That we're not ready to say, but we should be in preparation for it. The third is the general invasion.' (White, 1996, pp. 117–19)

Given the sense of shock and crisis in the testosterone-filled room it is perhaps not surprising that by the end of the morning an air strike by the US seemed highly likely.

Continued

The president showed his ability to quickly grasp important concepts, telling the group that Soviet missiles in Cuba did not really shift the strategic balance: 'It doesn't make any difference if you get blown up by an ICBM flying from the Soviet Union or one that was ninety miles away. Geography doesn't mean that much.' (In Dobbs, 2009, p. 16) In addition, within the space of a few hours since the morning meeting, the group had begun to appreciate that an American air strike could have untold and unpredictable consequences.

Wednesday 17 October

For obvious reasons it was paramount that the administration should be seen to be going about its normal business. While the president was campaigning for the November midterm elections, the ExComm met for the third time, aware that in JFK's absence his brother Robert was of paramount importance as the de facto vessel of the president himself. Beschloss states that RFK's 'talent for criticising propositions from all angles, without the filter of ideology, helped to foreclose the perils of the Bay of Pigs deliberations' (Beschloss, 1991, p. 451).

Even so, uncertainty reigned as a wide-ranging discussion touched upon air strikes, a blockade/quarantine or a diplomatic initiative. Meanwhile, on the campaign trail in Connecticut, the president gave no hint of being a man under the most severe pressure. White is critical of the fact that Kennedy was unable to explore whether the Russian's motivation was based on aggressive instincts or alternatively a defensive manoeuvre that could therefore prompt a less risky response. (White, 1996, p. 122)

Thursday 18 October A.M.

Further U-2 photographs showed evidence of intermediate-range ballistic missile sites with a wider range and more destructive warheads. The presence of Soviet strategic bombers with the ability to deliver the nuclear payload added to the sense of alarm within the group. Some advocated a 'surgical strike', while others on the military side said the air strike should 'not be limited' (Beschloss, 1991, p. 453). Those who advocated a US bombing attack were told by the president that such a move could be seen as a 'mad act by the United States' (Stern, 2012, p. 22). Around midnight the president returned to the Oval Office to set out the gist of an unrecorded meeting that had just finished in the White House living quarters. He reported that the consensus was for a blockade.

Friday 19 October A.M.

When the president outlined his preference for a blockade, The Joint Chiefs of Staff (JCS), informed him that their favoured option was an air strike with a 'surprise attack on comprehensive targets, leading to complete blockade and invasion' (Freedman, 2000, p. 186). Under severe military pressure the

Continued

president responded that a Soviet nuclear response could inflict casualties of 80–100 million on American cities and that he wanted to avoid nuclear war by escalation. The discussion carried on into the afternoon and evening while JFK was away campaigning in the Midwest. As the tone became more belligerent RFK contacted his brother in Chicago and it was agreed that he would promptly return to the capital under the pretence of him having a cold.

Saturday 20 October P.M.

The Chairman of the Joint Chiefs of Staff argued that leaving the military sites to become operational might be a more dangerous option than a military strike. It was now that JFK placed his full weight behind the blockade option and instructed his senior speech writer Ted Sorensen to begin drafting an address to the nation in which the blockade would be announced. Meanwhile he asked his wife to return to the White House with their children in the event of an emergency. Speaking to one of his closest aides that evening JFK remarked, 'I keep thinking about the children whose lives would be wiped out.' (Beschloss, 1991, p. 469)

Sunday 21 October

Meetings in the morning and afternoon provided details of the blockade plan which would constitute a quarantine of offensive military equipment.

Monday 22 October A.M. P.M.

The morning meeting was used to finalise and approve the president's speech which would be broadcast to the nation later that evening.

At 5.00 pm the president revealed details of the military intelligence to the leaders of the House of Representatives and the Senate. Two hours later, in a national television address Kennedy informed the American people of the Soviet missile sites on Cuba:

> This government, as promised, has maintained the closest surveillance of the Soviet military build-up on the island of Cuba. Within the past week, unmistakeable evidence has established the fact that a series of offensive missile sites is now in preparation on that imprisoned island. The purpose of these bases can be none other than to provide a nuclear strike capability against the Western Hemisphere. This secret, swift and extraordinary build-up of Communist missiles is a deliberately provocative and unjustified change in the status quo which cannot be accepted by this country, if our courage and our commitments are ever to be trusted again by either friend or foe … I have directed the Armed Forces to prepare for any eventualities. I call upon Chairman Khrushchev to halt and eliminate this clandestine, reckless, and provocative threat to world peace and to stable relations between our two nations. (Dobbs, 2009, p. 49)

Continued

Kennedy announced:

> a strict quarantine on all … military equipment to Cuba. I have directed the Armed Forces to prepare for any eventualities. Any missile launched from Cuba against any nation in this hemisphere would bring a full retaliatory response upon the Soviet Union. (In Beschloss, 1991, pp. 483–85)

As he spoke, a number of Soviet ships were still steaming towards Cuba.

Tuesday 23 October A.M.

An update of photographic intelligence showed that some of the MRBM launchers were no longer visible and might have been moved. Meanwhile a letter from the Soviet leader to Kennedy accused the Americans of representing a 'serious threat to peace and security … violation of international norms of freedom of navigation on high seas' and of 'naked interference in domestic affairs of Cuban Republic, Soviet Union' (In May & Zelikow, 1997, p. 321).

Wednesday 24 October A.M. P.M.

At the same time as the American quarantine proclamation came into effect, the US Strategic Air Command moved its forces to the state of readiness known as higher Defense Condition 2, the level just below general war.

> In addition to ICBMs and submarine-based ballistic missiles, every available bomber – more than 1,400 aircraft – went on alert. Scores of bombers, each loaded with several nuclear weapons and carrying folders for preassigned targets in the Soviet Union, were kept continuously in the air around the clock. (May & Zelikow, 1997, p. 347)

By the afternoon, intelligence was indicating that the most important Soviet ships bound for Cuba appeared to have stopped dead or turned around. However, intelligence from Cuba itself suggested that the Soviets were still working quickly to make the missile sites operational.

Thursday 25 October

Given that 15 important Soviet ships had turned back, by order of the president, two ships, a Soviet oil tanker, the *Bucharest*, and an East German passenger ship, were allowed through the blockade against the wishes of the majority of ExComm. Kennedy told ExComm that he did not want to push Khrushchev into a corner.

Friday 26 October

Beyond the blockade diplomatic back channels had now been opened between the two sides and in addition the UN was urgently seeking to support a

Continued

resolution of the crisis. Several messages from the Soviet leader were sent to JFK during the crisis and offered evidence of belligerence and also attempts at conciliation. US analysts concluded that the lengthy note received on Friday evening showed a leader under severe strain. Michael Dobbs calls it, 'a rambling, almost pleading letter … raising the spectre of nuclear devastation', while at the Pentagon General Curtis LeMay was urging his colleagues not to 'swallow that syrup' (Dobbs, 2009, pp. 163, 165).

Saturday 27 October, 'Black Saturday', A.M. P.M.

When members of JFK's team looked back they universally agreed that this day was the worst part of the whole crisis. In Moscow Khrushchev outlined the terms of a deal in which 'offensive' weapons would be removed from Cuba in exchange for the US removing similar weapons from Turkey. Meanwhile, alarming intelligence showed that 'Five out of six medium-range missile sites in Cuba were "fully operational"' (Dobbs, 2009, p. 207).

Intelligence now raised suspicions about the nature of the cargo carried by the Soviet ship *Grozny*.

Meanwhile, a second letter from the Soviet leader arrived leaving the Joint Chiefs of Staff to conclude that Khrushchev had no intention of removing his missiles and that any earlier conciliatory tone was merely a ruse. Tension reached new heights when an American U-2 plane was shot down over Cuba, killing the pilot. Then news reached the Americans that a second U-2 plane on a routine mission over the North Pole had gone missing and could have strayed into Soviet airspace. As Dobbs puts it, 'The Soviets might well regard this U-2 flight as a last-minute intelligence reconnaissance in preparation for nuclear war' (Dobbs, 2009, p. 269). Fortunately by mid-afternoon Washington time the pilot had safely returned to the Arctic. Meanwhile, US reconnaissance flights over Cuba came under fire from anti-aircraft guns. Dobbs states:

> the attacks on the low-level planes appeared to represent a significant escalation by the Soviets, particularly when combined with the apparent loss of Major Anderson's U-2 over Cuba that morning … A tough new message from Khrushchev earlier in the day following more conciliatory signals on Friday. Anti-aircraft fire against low-level U.S. Navy reconnaissance planes. And now a U-2 shot down. The outlook suddenly seemed very bleak. (Dobbs, 2009 pp. 288, 293)

It was now that the pressure from the US military for a full-blown military response became acute.

Kennedy's brother, the Attorney General, now suggested that Kennedy should ignore the second, more belligerent message and reply only to the first, friendlier one. This was Robert Kennedy's most significant contribution in the crisis. Kennedy now told Khrushchev that the United States was prepared to

Continued

guarantee not to invade Cuba, but could not promise about Turkey without speaking first to its NATO allies. America demanded withdrawal of the missiles from Cuba in return. The Russians replied, saying that they were prepared to accept these terms.

Sunday 28 October A.M.

A new message from the Russian leader agreed that the Soviet Union would withdraw its missiles from Cuba. To add to the sense that the crisis was drawing to an end the Soviet vessel *Grozny* was observed to have stopped, 'dead in the water' and had clearly been instructed not to challenge the blockade. At 9.00 am Washington time a message from the Soviet leader was read out over Moscow radio:

> The Soviet government, in addition to earlier instructions on the discontinuation of further work on weapons construction sites, has given a new order to dismantle the weapons you described as offensive, and to crate and return them to the Soviet Union. (Dobbs, 2009, p. 333)

While his own generals lamented their 'defeat', President Kennedy wrote to Khrushchev praising his 'statesmanlike decision' to withdraw the missiles. (Dobbs, 2009, p. 337)

9.19 The consequences of the Cuban Missile Crisis

Kennedy was on his way to 10 o'clock mass at St Stephen's Church in Washington when he was told that Khrushchev had backed away from the brink and the missile crisis was over. Kennedy called his ExComm members together, thanked them for their contribution and warned them that in speaking to the press they must remember that 'Khrushchev has eaten enough crow. Let's not rub it in.' Kennedy instructed all of his spokesmen and advisers to avoid giving the impression that they had 'triumphed ... over the Soviets' and that the Russians had 'backed down' (Beschloss, 1991, p. 545). Several points emerged from the crisis. Both leaders realised that they had been to the brink of oblivion. This was a sobering experience and made both countries look to avoid going through a similar situation ever again. The Soviet Union now became preoccupied with a mounting division with China and was therefore less inclined to provoke the United States.

The hotline

In June 1963, both sides agreed to the creation of a 'hotline' between Moscow and Washington to avoid the sort of difficulties in communication which had contributed to the Cuban Missile Crisis. This agreement was signed in Geneva and established a wire–telegraph–teleprinter service which meant that in a future crisis coded messages could be sent between the leaders without delay. The first message sent as a practice run by American technicians to their Soviet counterparts baffled the recipients: it read, 'The quick brown fox jumps over the lazy dog.'

The nuclear test ban treaty

A month later the United States, the Soviet Union and Britain signed a Nuclear Test Ban Treaty which ruled out future testing of nuclear weapons in the atmosphere and underwater; the test ban did not extend to underground testing. It was ratified by the Senate in September, and signalled the most significant thaw in the Cold War for a decade. This extract from a speech given by Kennedy at the American University on 10 June 1963 reflects the rapid change in the international climate:

> I am talking about genuine peace – the kind of peace that makes life on earth worth living, the kind that enables men and nations to grow and to hope and to build a better life for their children ... Not merely peace in our time, but peace for all time ... let us re-examine our attitude toward the Soviet Union ... As Americans we find communism profoundly repugnant ... but we can still hail the Russian people for their many achievements – in science and space, in economic and industrial growth, in culture and acts of courage. Almost unique among the major world powers, we have never been at war with each other ... we all inhabit this small planet. We all breathe the same air. We all cherish our children's future. And we are all mortal. (JFK Library, online)

The fiasco over the Bay of Pigs seemed like a distant memory when JFK made a highly successful visit to Western Europe in June and July of 1963. Rapturously received, especially by the people of Germany, a confident president declared that 'the United States is here on this continent to stay. So long as our presence is desired and required, our forces and commitments will remain'. Then memorably, in West Berlin, in the shadow of the wall and before an audience of a million people he proclaimed:

> two thousand years ago the proudest boast was '*civis Romanus sum.*' Today, in the world of freedom, the proudest boast is 'Ich bin ein Berliner.'...There are many people in the world who really don't understand, or say they don't, what is the great issue between the free world and the Communist world. Let them come to Berlin. There are some who say that communism is the wave of the future. Let them come to Berlin. (In Dallek, 2003, p. 625)

A further consequence of the Cuban Missile Crisis can be seen with the removal of Khrushchev in August 1964. Whereas Khrushchev had been in a very powerful position during the missile crisis itself, his climbdown at the end of October was seen by the hard-line generals within the Kremlin as an unacceptable humiliation.

South East Asia

9.20 Laos

Kennedy had inherited an increasingly difficult situation in South East Asia. In both Laos and South Vietnam (two states which had been created under the Geneva Agreement of 1954) pro-American governments were looking increasingly vulnerable to mounting communist activity. As he departed office, Eisenhower told Kennedy that Laos would present the most pressing problem. Laos was a small, landlocked nation, nestled among China, Cambodia, Thailand, North Vietnam and South Vietnam with a population of less than 3 million people. Following the withdrawal of French troops in 1954, the United States had supported the Royal Lao Government led by King Savang Vatthana. The increasingly effective Pathet Lao (Patriotic Front), which received support from the growing communist movement in North Vietnam, opposed this indolent, repressive right-wing regime in a damaging and bloody civil war. The United States injected substantial money and military aid to bolster the Vatthana regime, but by 1961 it was clear that a victory for the communist guerrillas was imminent. Kennedy never forgot Eisenhower's comment that Laos was 'the cork in the bottle' in South East Asia. And as one scathing analysis later stated:

> Take the transition from the Eisenhower to the Kennedy administration ... Here are the best and the brightest, not only of the Kennedy administration but of the Eisenhower administration, and they sit there and believe – they say to each other and believe – that the fate at least of Southeast Asia and perhaps of the civilized world hinges on what happens in Laos, a landlocked country of mountain hamlets, with three million people. (Ernest R. May cited in McNamara, 1995, p. 422)

On the other hand it could be claimed that Kennedy never fully accepted the notion that Laos was absolutely critical to American security. He rejected proposals for large-scale military involvement; instead he worked with the Soviet Union to neutralise and stabilise the country. At the otherwise tense Vienna Summit of June 1961, Kennedy and Khrushchev agreed to support the creation of a neutral government in Laos. This signalled the fact that neither the United States nor the Soviet Union regarded Laos as of critical importance. By the summer of 1962 Kennedy was able to turn his attention increasingly towards a country which he felt was of much greater significance to the United States – Vietnam.

9.21 Vietnam

As a young congressman Kennedy visited Indochina on a fact-finding mission in the autumn of 1951. By now, the region was in the grip of an epic struggle between the old colonial power, France, and the burgeoning nationalism of the Viet Minh led by Ho Chi Minh, based in the north, in Hanoi, but with the powerful backing of both China and the Soviet Union. Amid the style and beauty of the capital, Saigon, the impressionable but astute young politician was informed that the Viet Minh had infiltrated the south to such an extent that they now had bases within 25 miles of the city. In a deeply informative conversation with a seasoned press bureau chief, Kennedy was told in sobering terms that the French were destined to lose their struggle. In his trip journal Kennedy noted that the hatred of the French was extending to the United States because of her support for the colonial war effort: 'We are more and more becoming colonialists in the minds of the people.' When he returned to his native Boston, JFK told the local chamber of commerce: 'In Indochina we have allied ourselves to the desperate effort of the French regime to hang on to the remnants of an empire.' Remarkably, Kennedy even acknowledged that 'a free election ... would go in favour of Ho and his Communists' (Logevall, 2013, preface, xiii–xiv).

Crucially, Kennedy's cool, detached, instinctive insights had to be balanced with electoral pragmatism. Above all, the Democrats were sensitive to the charge that they were 'soft on communism'. Both as a senator and then as president, Kennedy had been willing to publicly acknowledge the significance of Vietnam and the importance of a vigilant approach. When he was still a senator in 1956, Kennedy declared: 'Vietnam represents the cornerstone of the Free World in Southeast Asia. It is our offspring. We cannot abandon it, we cannot ignore its needs.' (In Herring, 1979, p. 47) In January 1961, when he had assumed the presidency, Kennedy warned that the threat from communism remained: 'Our problems are critical. The tide is unfavourable. The news will be worse before it is better.' (In Herring, 1979, p. 81) George C. Herring provides this analysis of the transition from Eisenhower to Kennedy concerning Vietnam:

> Inheriting from Eisenhower an increasingly dangerous if still limited commitment, he plunged deeper into the morass. Kennedy did not eagerly take up the burden in Vietnam, and his actions there contrast sharply with his rhetoric. In settling the major policy issues, he was cautious rather than bold ... He delayed making a firm commitment for nearly a year and then acted only because the shaky Diem government appeared on the verge of collapse. (Herring, 1979, p. 83)

At various stages in his short presidency, Kennedy's commitment to Vietnam was enhanced by problems he faced elsewhere. The humiliation over the Bay of Pigs, the failure to act over the Berlin Wall, the decision to avoid engagement in Laos and the difficulty of dealing with Khrushchev at the Vienna Summit all led Kennedy to want to act firmly over Vietnam. In addition, whereas he was not persuaded that Laos was of massive strategic importance he always believed that Vietnam carried greater significance.

9.22 Sending military assistance to Vietnam

In May 1961, Kennedy sent Vice President Lyndon Johnson on a visit to South Vietnam. The outcome of this was to increase the level of support to the Diem regime. Kennedy was aware of Diem's shortcomings, but felt at this stage that there was no realistic alternative but to maintain American support. A further visit in October led by Maxwell Taylor and Walt Rostow recommended that American combat troops enter South Vietnam in the guise of flood relief workers. Kennedy was quick to reject this idea and instead decided to provide further equipment and advisers to Diem. The number of American 'advisers' was increased from 3,025 in December 1961 to more than 9,000 by the end the year. Yet at precisely the same time JFK was telling his own National Security Council that he could 'make a rather strong case against intervening in an area 10,000 miles away against 16,000 guerrillas with a native army of 200,000, where millions have been spent for years with no success' (Ward & Burns, 2017, p. 91).

In February 1962, Kennedy created the American Military Assistance Command. By the summer of 1962 the number of American advisers had reached 12,000. Logevall demonstrates the scale of the commitment as well as the disturbing element of secrecy that was already enveloping the mission:

In 1962, vast quantities of the best American weapons, aircraft and armored personnel carriers arrived in South Vietnam, along with thousands of additional U.S. military advisers ... A secret American war was under way. Ostensibly, Americans were serving purely as advisers and never engaging the Viet Cong except in self-defense; in reality, their involvement extended further – in the air and on the ground. (In Ward & Burns, 2017, p. 91)

It was hoped that these measures, accompanied by a proportionate increase in equipment, would enable the South Vietnamese Army to take the initiative against the communist guerrillas so that they would be left as 'hungry, marauding bands of outlaws devoting all their energies to remaining alive' who would be forced to come out into the open and fight the Army of the Republic of Vietnam (ARVN). This ploy was accompanied by the development of the 'strategic hamlet' programme, a large-scale and costly exercise launched in the early months of 1962. Stanley Karnow provides this summary of the programme's intent: 'The plan was to corral peasants into armed stockades, thereby depriving the Vietcong of their support, which could not survive without the population.' (Karnow, 1985, p. 255)

However, he also points out that despite official claims of success, the 'reality' was that:

> The program often converted peasants into Vietcong sympathizers. Peasants in many places resented working without pay to dig moats, implant bamboo stakes, and erect fences against an enemy that did not threaten them but directed its sights against government officials ... At the working level, American soldiers and civilians in Vietnam decried the strategic hamlet scheme ... the strategic hamlets were paralyzing South Vietnamese forces that ought to be fighting the Vietcong. (Karnow, 1985, p. 257)

Further signs that despite American aid the military threat from the communists remained acute were clearly revealed in the military exchange at Ap Bac which took place in January 1963. In a grim foretaste of what was to come, 61 South Vietnamese were killed, 100 wounded and five helicopters downed. To make matters worse, as Karnow puts it, 'the Vietcong had evaporated into the darkness, leaving only three bodies behind' (Karnow, 1985, p. 262).

Despite such incidents, Kennedy was still not prepared to think in terms of sending troops into Vietnam. He told Arthur Schlesinger:

> The troops will march in; the bands will play; the crowds will cheer and in four days everyone will have forgotten. Then we will be told we have to send in more troops. It's like taking a drink. The effect wears off and you have to take another. (In Herring, 1979, p. 92)

Even so, Kennedy's commitment to the 'domino theory' remained intact and analysis of his comments in the summer indicate this was steadfast. Speaking about Vietnam at a press conference, on 17 July 1963, Kennedy told the assembled media that the US was not going to withdraw from its effort in Vietnam.

In the early autumn he was again questioned about his commitment to Vietnam in an interview with Walter Cronkite, on 9 September 1963:

> **Walter Cronkite**: Mr. President, the only hot war we've got running at the moment is of course the one in Vietnam, and we have our difficulties there, quite obviously.

President Kennedy: I don't think that unless a greater effort is made by the [South Vietnamese] Government to win popular support that the war can be won out there. In the final analysis, it is their war. They are the ones that are going to have to win it or lose it. We can help them, we can give them equipment, we can send our men out there as advisers, but they have to win it, the people of Vietnam, against the Communists ... All we can do is help, and we are making it very clear, but I don't agree with those who say we should withdraw. That would be a great mistake. (In Ward & Burns, 2017, pp. 84–85)

Furthermore, in an NBC interview of September 1963 the president was asked, 'have you any reason to doubt this so-called "domino theory" that if South Vietnam falls, the rest of Southeast Asia will go behind it?' Kennedy's reply was emphatic:

No, I believe it. The loss of Vietnam would also give the impression that the wave of the future in Southeast Asia was China and the Communists. So I believe it. (In Dallek, 2003, p. 676)

The end of the Diem Regime, November 1963

Meanwhile, the mounting unpopularity of the Diem regime was exacerbated in May 1963 when South Vietnamese troops and police opened fire on Buddhist demonstrators objecting to a ruling banning the display of flags on the anniversary of the Buddha's birth. Buddhist discontent was starkly illustrated when a monk set himself alight before an emotional crowd in downtown Saigon. This incident, dismissed by Diem's wife, Madame Nhu as a 'barbecue', unleashed an upsurge of anti-Diem opinion in the south and caused turmoil in Washington. A wave of repression orchestrated by Ngo Dinh Nhu, Diem's younger brother and political adviser, simply made the situation worse. In total, seven monks immolated themselves, and Saigon's prisons were filled with protestors. Then, in August, Nhu's special forces raided Buddhist pagodas in several major cities including Saigon and Hue. By the end of the month, Kennedy's advisers had convinced him that there was little alternative to a coup. In September Kennedy used a television interview to criticise the Diem regime. On 1 November Diem and Nhu were captured and then brutally murdered. Historians remain divided as to the extent of Kennedy's prior knowledge. Some contend that Kennedy acquiesced in the coup or did nothing to 'thwart a change of government'. Whereas some of Kennedy's advisers reacted to the murder in a matter-of-fact way, one aide recalled that Kennedy was deeply affected by the murders and reacted to the news with 'a look of shock and dismay'. Finally, American involvement in this pivotal event surely indicates that the Kennedy Administration was not, at that moment, about to abandon its commitment to Vietnam, but rather the opposite. A cable of 6 November sent by Kennedy in person 'acknowledged U.S. complicity in the coup and spoke of American "responsibility" to help the new government succeed' (Ward & Burns, 2017, p. 92).

Thomas C. Reeves is critical of Kennedy's stance over Vietnam in general, and over the Diem coup in particular:

In Vietnam the President revealed an almost reckless posture and an intense determination to win. He approved the CIA's most aggressive operations, greatly increased the American presence in the conflict, and became involved in the overthrow of the government of South Vietnam. Moral and legal objections had little or no impact on Kennedy or his advisers as they assumed, by reason of American strength and power, the right to manipulate that country's affairs. (Reeves, 1992, p. 416)

Would Kennedy have withdrawn from Vietnam?

Three weeks later, Kennedy himself was gunned down in Dallas, Texas. George C. Herring offers this assessment of Kennedy's policy in Vietnam:

> What Kennedy might have done can never be known, of course, and his brief administration must be judged on what it actually did during its brief tenure. The President and most of his advisers uncritically accepted the assumption that a non-Communist Vietnam was vital to America's global interests, and their rhetoric in fact strengthened the hold of that assumption. That the President never devoted his full attention to Vietnam ... seems clear. He reacted to crises and improvised responses on a day-to-day basis ... His cautious middle course significantly enlarged the American role and commitment in Vietnam. Like most of his advisers, he acted on the arrogant presumption that the United States knew what was best for Vietnam ... with the coup, the United States assumed direct responsibility for the South Vietnamese government. Whatever his fears or his ultimate intentions, JFK bequeathed to his successor a problem eminently more dangerous than the one he had inherited. (Herring, 1979, pp. 118–19)

Mark White examines the possibilities in Vietnam had Kennedy's life not been cut tragically short:

> The argument that if Oswald had been a lesser marksman there would have been no American war in Indochina is far from new ... From the start the thesis contained two key assertions: not merely that Americanization would have been avoided under Kennedy, but that he had already decided in favour of an unrealized alternative – to withdraw from Vietnam, even without victory – prior to his assassination. Kennedy, so this argument goes, was determined not to let Vietnam become an American war. He understood that the conflict had become a quagmire. Therefore, he planned to extricate the United States after (or perhaps before) the 1964 election, regardless of the state of the war. As evidence, these authors typically cite Kennedy's continual refusal to commit American ground troops to the war, despite the urgings of top advisers; the October 1963 declaration that 1000 US military advisers would be withdrawn by the end of 1963; his scepticism about a coup against South Vietnamese leader Diem; and his belief, stated most notably in his 2 September 1963 television interview with Walter Cronkite, that in the end this was a war that the South Vietnamese themselves would have to win. Some also refer to private comments made by Kennedy to the effect that he was determined to get out of Vietnam, come what may. (White, 1998, p 22–23)
>
> There is an additional reason to doubt that he had made any decision before Dallas to disengage from the war; namely, his administration's unbending opposition to seeking a negotiated settlement to the conflict. From its earliest days, the administration signalled its intention to pursue the war effort against the Vietcong. Neither Kennedy nor his advisers assumed office with any intention of reviewing critically the policies they inherited from the Eisenhower team ... In all likelihood,

John F. Kennedy on the day of his death had simply not decided what to do with his Vietnam problem. Like many politicians, he liked to put off difficult decisions for as long as possible. (White, 1998, pp. 30, 35)

Finally, and somewhat poignantly, we can consider this extract from President Kennedy's undelivered speech at the Dallas Trade Mart, 22 November 1963:

We in this country in this generation are the watchmen on the walls of freedom ... our assistance to ... nations can be painful, risky, and costly, as is true in Southeast Asia today. But we dare not weary of the task. (In Ward & Burns, p. 92)

One of Kennedy's closest aides, Dean Rusk, his Secretary of State, later wrote in his memoirs:

I talked with John Kennedy on hundreds of occasions about Southeast Asia and not once did he suggest or even hint at withdrawal ... Kennedy liked to bat the breeze and toss ideas around, and it is entirely possible that he left the impression with some that he planned on getting out of Vietnam after 1965 ... [had he made a decision] I think I would have known about it. (White, 1998, p. 29)

Historiography of Kennedy's foreign policy

Historians are polarised on the effectiveness of Kennedy's foreign policy. James N. Giglio observed that there were

four major international crises facing the United States at the start of the Kennedy Presidency – Laos, Berlin, Vietnam and the Congo – only one of which, Vietnam, remained a hot spot at the time of his death. And Cuba was the sole major foreign policy programme to emerge during the Kennedy years. (In White, 1998, p. 7)

However, a series of essays edited by Thomas Paterson (1991; quoted in White, 1998) has represented a highly critical view. The thesis was that a variety of factors had led Kennedy towards the pursuit of an excessively hawkish anti-communist foreign policy. Kennedy instigated a dramatic increase in military spending and at one point declared that an American first strike against the Soviet Union could not be ruled out. Therefore Kennedy's words and actions prompted the Soviet Union to increase its own defence spending and missile production to such an extent that by the early 1970s America's earlier superiority in nuclear weapons had been reduced to a state of parity. (White, 1998, p. 6)

In addition, Paterson was critical of the contention that Kennedy's personal growth and increased maturity had led to a more conciliatory approach towards the end of his presidency. Some historians as evidence of this more mature approach have cited the moderate tone of Kennedy's speech at the American University in June 1963. However, Paterson drew attention to two much more strongly worded addresses which Kennedy had been due to deliver in Texas at the time of his assassination. He argues that the tone of these undelivered speeches reveals that Kennedy had not dramatically altered his stance towards the Soviet Union at the time of his death. It is useful to consider the context within which Kennedy was operating as he attempted to construct American foreign policy. On the one hand it could be argued that in dealing with the

Soviet Union post-Stalin, Kennedy was presented with a much more favourable climate than the previous Democrat president, Harry Truman, had been. Clearly there was a stark contrast between the implacable nature of Stalin and the willingness to consider 'peaceful co-existence' offered by Khrushchev. On the other hand, Khrushchev's impetuous, risk-taking approach to foreign policy presented Kennedy with a series of difficult and unpredictable challenges.

In *A Question of Character* Thomas Reeves presents this analysis of Kennedy's foreign policy record:

> In assessing Kennedy's record as top diplomat and commander in chief, it is important to acknowledge his caution as well as his courage. Against the recommendation of top advisers, he sharply limited American's role in the Bay of Pigs invasion and refused to send American troops into Laos and Vietnam. He elected not to attack East Germany when the Berlin Wall was constructed. During the missile crisis, he did what he reasonably could to avoid an invasion of Cuba, revealing a sensitivity about nuclear war that many others in Washington and elsewhere did not share. (Reeves, 1992, p. 417)

Kennedy deserves credit for his efforts in 1963 to reduce the tension of the Cold War and achieve meaningful disarmament. The American University speech and the test ban treaty were significant achievements that signalled a measure of growth in such qualities as compassion and responsibility.

Maldwyn Jones also offers helpful insights:

> Kennedy's promise that 'a new generation of leadership' would 'cast off old slogans and delusions and suspicions' was largely unfulfilled. Especially in foreign affairs, the policies of his Administration differed little from those of its immediate predecessors. Slow to apprehend the great changes taking place in the world balance of power – the growing split between Moscow and Peking, the recovery of Europe, the upsurge of African and Asian nationalism – Kennedy continued to strike outmoded Cold War postures ... based on the glib and, as it proved, false assumption that American economic and military power was so overwhelming that the United States could police the entire world. (Jones, 1995, p. 545)

Sadly, the brutal events of November 1963 meant that Kennedy's opportunity to lead the Western world to perhaps a safer future was taken from him. Instead, the responsibilities, opportunities and dangers of the highest office passed to Lyndon Baines Johnson.

Further reading

Beschloss M.R., *Kennedy v Khrushchev: The Crisis Years 1960–1963* (London: Faber and Faber 1991).

Bugliosi V., *Four Days in November: The Assassination of President John F. Kennedy* (New York: Norton 2007).

Clarke T., *JFK's Last Hundred Days: An Intimate Portrait of a Great President* (London: Allen Lane 2013).

Dallek R., *Flawed Giant: Lyndon Johnson and his Times 1961–1973* (New York: Oxford University Press 1998).

Dallek R., *John F. Kennedy, An Unfinished Life 1917–1963* (London: Allen Lane 2003).

Dobbs M., *One Minute to Midnight* (New York: Arrow Books 2009).

Freedman L., *Kennedy's Wars: Berlin, Cuba, Laos and Vietnam* (New York: OUP 2000).

Fursenko A. & Naftali T., *One Hell of a Gamble* (London: Pimlico 1999).

Herring G.C., *America's Longest War: The United States and Vietnam 1950–1975* (New York: Wiley 1979).

Hersh S.J., *The Dark Side of Camelot* (London: Harper Collins 1998).

Jones M.A., *The Limits of Liberty: American History 1607–1992* (New York: Oxford University Press 1995).

Kaiser D., *American Tragedy: Kennedy, Johnson, and the Origins of the Vietnam War* (Cambridge Mass.: Harvard University Press 2000).

Karnow S., *Vietnam: A History The First Complete Account of Vietnam at War* (London: Century Hutchinson 1985).

Logevall F., *Choosing War: The Lost Chance for Peace and the Escalation of War in Vietnam* (Berkeley: University of California Press 1999).

Logevall F., *Embers of War: The Fall of an Empire and the Making of America's Vietnam* (New York: Random House 2013).

Logsdon J., *John F. Kennedy and the Race to the Moon* (Basingstoke: Palgrave 2010).

Matthews C., *Kennedy and Nixon: The Rivalry that Shaped Postwar America* (New York: Touchstone 1996).

May E.R. & Zelikow P.D., *The Kennedy Tapes: Inside the White House during the Cuban Missile Crisis* (Cambridge Mass.: Harvard University Press 1997).

McNamara R.S., *In Retrospect: The Tragedy and Lessons of Vietnam* (New York: Vintage Books 1995).

New Yorker Book of the 60s: Story of a Decade, ed. by Henry Finder (London: William Heinemann 2016).

Oliphant T. & Wilkie C., *The Road to Camelot: Inside JFK's Five-Year Plan* (New York: Simon & Schuster 2017).

Reeves R. *President Kennedy: Profile of Power* (London: Papermac 1994).

Reeves T.C., *A Question of Character, A Life of John F Kennedy* (Prima Publishing 1992 Rocklin California).

Reynolds D., *America, Empire of Liberty: A New History* (London: Allen Lane 2009).

Shaw J.T., *JFK in the Senate: Pathway to Presidency* (New York: Palgrave 2013).

Stern S.M., *The Cuban Missile Crisis in American Memory* (Stanford: Stanford University Press 2012).

Talbot D., *Brothers: The Hidden History of the Kennedy Years* (London: Simon & Schuster 2007).

Thomas E., *Robert Kennedy: His Life* (New York: Simon & Schuster 2000).

Tye L., *Bobby Kennedy, The Making of a Liberal Icon* (New York: Penguin Random House 2016).

Ward G.C. & Burns K., *The Vietnam War: An Intimate History* (New York: Alfred A. Knopf 2017).

Watts S., *JFK and the Masculine Mystique: Sex and Power on the New Frontier* (New York: Thomas Dunne 2016).

White M.J., *The Cuban Missile Crisis* (Basingstoke: Macmillan Press Ltd 1996).

White M.J., *Kennedy: The New Frontier Revisited* (Basingstoke: Macmillan Press Ltd 1998).

Zelizer J.E., *The Fierce Urgency of Now: Lyndon Johnson, Congress and the Battle for the Great Society* (New York: Penguin Press 2015).

Zubok V. & Pleshakov C., *Inside the Kremlin's Cold War: From Stalin to Khrushchev* (Cambridge Mass.: Harvard University Press 1996).

■ M̌ 10 LBJ: The Great Society and Vietnam

10.1 Lyndon Baines Johnson

Lyndon Baines Johnson was born in August 1908 near Stonewall, in central Texas. The Texas Hill country was a notoriously harsh, desperately poor setting and the family lived in a small shack, 'a typical Hill Country dog-run', where 'from the front porch, not another house was visible – not another human structure of any type' (Caro, 1983, p. 53). In 1911, the family, now with three children, moved to Johnson City. Lyndon's mother Rebekah Baines later remarked 'I thought I had come to the end of the earth'. The city had at most three or four cars and no paved roads. When Lyndon enrolled at the Southwest Texas State Teachers' College in San Marcos, Texas in 1927 he hitch-hiked the 30 miles from home, carrying his few belongings in a cardboard suitcase (Caro, 1983, p. 137). Short of funds and desperate for some income, Lyndon curtailed his education there to earn a living as a teacher at Welhausen Elementary School in Cotulla, in Texas from 1928 to 1929.

The 'Mexican school' in Cotulla served a poverty-stricken community. Its resources were so limited that Johnson was appointed principal on his first day. The novice teacher's drive, compassion and energy in improving the experience of the students was staggering. This was the formative period for his character, leaving him with a visceral hatred of poverty, bigotry and the way that poor Mexican Americans were treated. He returned to San Marcos in June 1929 and graduated in August 1930, when he was awarded a BS degree in education and history. By now he was ready to invest his formidable energy into politics. He made his first political speech in 1930 and a year later secured a post in Washington DC as a congressional secretary to a Texan member of the House of Representatives. Johnson worked relentlessly for his constituents but this came with fierce personal ambition.

Remarkably, in 1937 he became a congressman for central Texas in his own right, when he was still only 28 years old. His idealism and compassion were now combined with an 'utter ruthlessness' in removing anything that stood in his way, and a willingness to buy votes (the going rate was around $5 a time) which helped to make the 1937 campaign the most expensive in Texas political history. With FDR in the White House, Johnson was quick to realise the power of the executive branch and he attached himself to a circle of young, energetic New Dealers and did everything he could to ingratiate himself to 'the Boss' in the White House. His instincts for power, capacity for self-promotion, skills in lobbying for his constituents, and high-profile success in attracting investment in Texas in construction, hydro-electric power and dams, made him a formidable operator.

It was therefore ironic that corruption and fraud were instrumental in his unsuccessful run for a Senate seat in 1941. Then a brief spell of military service was impressive enough for Johnson to be awarded a Silver Star for bravery in a bombing raid over New Guinea. Johnson's political career resumed in 1942 when he returned to the House of Representatives. Six years later he took the step up the rung he so desired when he won a tightly contested seat in the US Senate. In 1951 he became majority whip of the Senate and two years later his Democratic colleagues elected him to the position of minority leader. Finally, in January 1955 he became the majority leader in the Senate.

During the Eisenhower era, Johnson earned a well-deserved reputation as a supremely skilful political operator. As Democratic floor leader in the Senate he displayed drive, tenacity, attention to detail and an ability to manage political friends and foes in an adroit manner. Johnson used this period to develop an extensive network of contacts and supporters on Capitol Hill. His personal ambition was burning as brightly as ever and he hoped that his loyal and efficient service to the Democratic Party, from 1937 as an enthusiastic New Dealer to the 1950s as Senate Majority Leader, would culminate in the Democratic Convention selecting him as their candidate to take on Nixon in the 1960 presidential race. Johnson could not conceal his dismay when the Democratic Party turned instead to someone who was in many ways his opposite.

Kennedy's wealthy Bostonian background and privileged education was in stark contrast to Johnson's tough upbringing. Whereas Johnson had undoubtedly served his time in the party, Kennedy's limited political experience had been punctuated with long absences caused by serious illness. The depth of Johnson's political conviction contrasted with Kennedy's pragmatic opportunism. Finally Kennedy's looks, sophistication and charm contrasted with what Johnson biographer Robert Caro evokes as the typical male appearance of the Johnson family from the Texas hill country: 'a tall man, always over six feet, with heavily waved coal-black hair and dramatic features: large nose, very large ears, heavy black eyebrows and eyes ... so piercing that they often seemed to be glaring.' (Caro, 1983, p. 3) Maldwyn A. Jones summarises Johnson's character in these terms:

A tough, proud, intelligent man with a compassionate understanding of the problems of poverty and deprivation, he nevertheless had some unattractive traits. His public displays of boorishness, his tendency to domineer, and his childlike love of power excited unfavourable comment. Likewise his secretiveness, his inability to be completely truthful, and his unscrupulousness in manipulating people earned him the distrust of the press. His worst faults however, were an excessive sensitivity to criticism and a stubborn refusal to admit error or change course. (Jones, 1995, p. 550)

His motivation was drawn from his acute sense of the poverty and injustice that still riddled American society. His temperament was ideally suited to the physical and mental challenges that lay ahead. Everyone who dealt with Johnson was struck by his vitality. At different stages he was described as 'a human dynamo', a 'tidal wave' and 'a tornado in pants'. Opponents were given what became known in Washington circles as 'the treatment'. Johnson was more than willing to use intimidation to get his own way. Hardened Washington journalist Ben Bradlee recalled that meeting Johnson was like going to the zoo: 'You really felt as if a St. Bernard had ... pawed you all over.' (In Dallek, 1998, pp. 4–5)

10.2 From the New Frontier to the Great Society

LBJ loathed the post of vice president and felt becalmed and isolated from his innate desire to pass important legislation. The Kennedys treated him coolly and in his absence referred to him with contempt. Johnson's relationship with Bobby Kennedy was, at best, tempestuous. So the sheer trauma of the Kennedy assassination for all concerned meant that no president could have assumed the highest office under more trying circumstances. The images remain powerful today: the motorcade through Dallas, the desperate scenes at the Parkland Memorial hospital, the blood-splattered clothing of Jacqueline Kennedy and the look of disbelief upon the face of newsreader Walter Cronkite. Then, the dramatic swearing-in of Johnson as the next president of the United States, aboard Airforce One, close to Kennedy's coffin and with Jacqueline looking on in a state of utter bewilderment. Johnson was a highly skilled politician and even in these uniquely difficult moments his trusted political instincts came into play. At times he showed real sensitivity towards the Kennedy family (although on other occasions he could be crass) and was genuinely devastated by the assassination, even though it had brought him the prize he so desired. Johnson was aware that he lacked Kennedy's charisma and was also, to an extent, inhibited by the obvious intellectual quality of Kennedy's senior staff.

It is a measure of Johnson's astute political judgement that he retained their services (with the notable exception of Bobby Kennedy, who did not want to continue to serve as Attorney General) as he tried to complete Kennedy's raft of unfinished business. This perhaps was Johnson's greatest achievement, realising that the mood of national

---

PRESIDENTIAL PROFILE

Lyndon Baines Johnson

36th President of the United States (1963–69)

Born: 27 August 1908

Birthplace: Stonewall, Texas

Died: January 22, 1973, aged 64; buried Stonewall, Texas

Education: Southwest Texas State Teachers' College, San Marcos, Texas

Political Party: Democratic

State: Texas

Occupations before presidency: Teacher; Principal, Welhausen Elementary School, Cotulla, Texas

Previous government service: Member US House of Representatives; US Senator; vice president

Age at inauguration: 55

Dates of office: November 22 1963–January 20, 1969

Election: November 1964

Vice president: Hubert Humphrey

Length of term: 5 years, 2 months

guilt and sense of what might have been which followed the assassination presented a unique 'window of opportunity' when so much legislation that had been stalled by an obdurate Congress could now be freed up and guided through the legislative process. From this exceptionally traumatic start, Johnson did remarkably well to inject considerable momentum behind what he would come to call the 'Great Society'. The scale of his ambition, from the outset, was staggering. As Zelizer puts it, he 'was determined to push through a transformative body of laws that would constitute nothing less than a second New Deal' (Zelizer, 2015, p. 2).

10.3 The election of 1964

On the Democrats' side, Johnson's legislative success in dealing with Congress and his commitment to liberal causes meant that he was nominated unanimously on the first ballot at the party convention in Atlantic City. His running mate was Hubert Humphrey from Minnesota. In contrast, the Republican Convention in San Francisco was presented with a stark contrast between the liberal wing's candidate, Nelson Rockefeller, and the extreme conservative Senator Barry M. Goldwater from Arizona. Despite Goldwater's reputation as an extremist, the Convention chose him on the first ballot. His running mate was William Miller from New York. Goldwater's campaign rested on patriotic values, vehement anti-communism, and condemnation of the Great Society's cost and its principle of 'big government'. Goldwater campaign slogans included: 'In Your Heart You Know He's Right' and 'A choice not an echo'. The Johnson campaign produced some witty retorts including: 'Yes, far right!', 'In your heart you know he might' and 'In your gut you know he's nuts.' (Reynolds, 2009, p. 437) These slogans neatly illustrated the issues at stake. Goldwater hoped to attract millions of conservatives who were alienated by the overwhelming presence of the federal government and had simply stopped voting. He believed that by presenting a radically different philosophy, the electorate would return in large numbers.

A critical moment in the campaign came with the broadcast of the 'Daisy Girl' advertisement on 7 September 1964. The brief film showed a young girl picking the petals off a daisy while she counted to ten. The girl's expression changed to a startled look against a voice-over of a man counting down from ten to one. The image of the girl's face was then replaced with the disturbing image of a nuclear explosion. Then Johnson's voice was heard saying 'These are the stakes – to make a world in which all of God's children can live, or to go into the dark. We must love each other, or we must die.' Finally, a voice urged: 'Vote for President Johnson on November 3. The stakes are too high for you to stay home.' The Democrats had successfully 'defined' their opponent as an extremist. The electorate responded with a massive endorsement of Johnson's position. Goldwater secured only six states, of which five were in the Deep South. Johnson's landslide victory extended to Congress, with a resounding 68 seats in the Senate and a majority of 155 in the House of Representatives (Table 10.1). The GOP were badly damaged and in the aftermath of the election a more moderate Republican bloc emerged, eager to distance themselves from Goldwater's extremism.

Table 10.1   The result of the 1964 presidential election

Candidate	Party	Electoral College votes	Popular votes
Lyndon B. Johnson (Texas)	Democrat	486	43,126,506
Barry M. Goldwater (Arizona)	Republican	52	27,176,799

10.4 Launching the Great Society

In an interview with CBS in March 1964, President Johnson was asked if he had decided on a phrase similar to the 'New Deal' or the 'New Frontier' which would encapsulate the 'big theme' of his presidency. Johnson replied that he had been too busy to think of a label. Yet at the same time he was pushing presidential speechwriter Richard Goodwin to devise just such a phrase. Goodwin consulted Princeton historian Eric Goldman, who suggested that 'in terms of a popular slogan, the goal of "post-affluent" America was probably best caught by the title of Walter Lippman's book of some years back, *The Good Society*' (Dallek, 1998, p. 81). Goodwin took this idea, but replaced the word 'Good' with 'Great'. Goodwin used the phrase in a speech to mark the presentation of the Eleanor Roosevelt Memorial Award to a New York judge. The phrase met with Johnson's approval and it was agreed that the president 'could fit a lot of what we were trying to do within the curve of this phrase' (Dallek, 1998, p. 81). It was decided that Johnson would formally launch the concept of a Great Society at the commencement address to be given in Ann Arbor at the University of Michigan on 22 May 1964. The speech, drafted by Richard Goodwin, was delivered in strong, stirring style to a crowd of over 80,000 in the university's sports arena.

> I have come today from the turmoil of your Capital to the tranquillity of your campus to speak about the future of your country.
>
> The purpose of protecting the life of our Nation and preserving the liberty of our citizens is to pursue the happiness of our people. Our success in that pursuit is the test of our success as a Nation … Your imagination, your initiative, and your indignation will determine whether we build a society where progress is the servant of our needs, or a society where old values and new visions are buried under unbridled growth. For in your time we have the opportunity to move not only toward the rich and the powerful society, but upward to the Great Society.
>
> The Great Society rests on abundance and liberty for all. It demands an end to poverty and racial injustice, to which we are totally committed in our time. But that is just the beginning.
>
> The Great Society is a place where every child can find knowledge to enrich his mind and to enlarge his talents.
>
> But most of all, the Great Society is not a safe harbor, a resting place, a final objective, a finished work. It is a challenge constantly renewed, beckoning us toward a destiny where the meaning of our lives matches the marvelous products of our labor. So I want to talk to you today about three places where we begin to build the Great Society – in our cities, in our countryside, and in our classrooms … Will you join in

the battle to build the Great Society, to prove that our material progress is only the foundation on which we will build a richer life of mind and spirit? (In Schulman, 1995, pp. 174–77)

A buoyant Johnson returned to Washington 'intoxicated' by the welcome that he felt his ideas had received. Despite his upbeat mood the fact remained that while his driving principle was still to 'fulfil FDR's mission', he had not yet developed his ideas of exactly what was meant by the term 'Great Society'.

The scale of the Great Society

When President Clinton proclaimed 'the era of big government is over' in his State of the Union Address of January 1996 he was signalling that even on the traditionally interventionist, Democratic end of the political spectrum, the national appetite for large-scale government planning, spending and intervention was a thing of the past. Thirty-two years earlier, LBJ's enthusiasm for legislation was boundless. As Schulman puts it:

> No president matched Johnson's skills as chief legislator. Despite the far-reaching and controversial nature of his program, LBJ won congressional approval for 58 percent of his proposals in 1964, 69 percent in 1965, and 56 percent in 1966, compared, for example, with 37 percent for Eisenhower in 1957 and just 27 percent for JFK in 1963 ... When the 'Great 89th,' the Congress which LBJ swept into office with its 1964 landslide, completed its work in the autumn of 1966, it left behind the most productive law-making record in American history. (Schulman, 1995, p. 91)

While Johnson's battle against racism and poverty continues to attract significant attention, it is sometimes forgotten that his Great Society legislation also established the National Endowments for the Arts and the Humanities, opened up access for academics and private citizens to government files, and restricted government wiretapping and surveillance as well as creating initiatives in mental health research, narcotics rehabilitation and bail reform. The Appalachian Development Act, with the construction of a major new highway, signalled an unprecedented level of investment and job creation in a historically poor region. The Water Quality Act established national standards on water to be monitored by the Water Pollution Control Administration.

The sheer scale of the Great Society is illustrated by the chart listing 'Accomplishments of the 89th Congress'.

Accomplishments of the 89th Congress

THE FIRST SESSION

1. Medicare
2. Elementary and Secondary Education
3. Higher Education
4. Farm Bill
5. Department of Housing and Urban Development

Continued

---

6. Omnibus Housing Act (including rent supplements, and low and moderate income housing)
7. Social Security Increases
8. Voting Rights
9. Immigration Bill
10. Older Americans Act
11. Heart Disease, Cancer and Stroke Research and Facilities
12. Law Enforcement Assistance Act
13. National Crime Commission
14. Drug Controls
15. Mental Health Research and Facilities
16. Health Professions Education
17. Medical Library Facilities
18. Vocational Rehabilitation
19. Inter-American Bank Fund Increases
20. Stepping Up the War Against Poverty
21. Arts and Humanities Foundation
22. Appalachia
23. Highway Beautification
24. Air Pollution (auto exhausts and research)
25. Water Pollution Control (water quality standards)
26. High-speed Ground Transportation
27. Extension and Strengthening of MTDA
28. Presidential Disability and Succession
29. Child Health Medical Assistance
30. Regional Development

THE SECOND SESSION

1. The Department of Transportation
2. Truth in Packaging
3. Demonstration Cities
4. Funds for Rent Supplements
5. Funds for Teacher Corps
6. Asian Development Bank
7. Water Pollution (Clean Rivers)
8. Food for Peace
9. March anti-inflation package
10. Narcotics Rehabilitation
11. Child Safety
12. Vietnam Supplemental
13. Foreign Aid Extension
14. Traffic Safety
15. Highway Safety
16. Public Health Service Reorganization

Continued

17. Community Relations Service Reorganization
18. Water Pollution Control Administration Reorganization
19. Mine Safety
20. Allied Health Professions Training
21. International Education
22. Child Nutrition
23. Bail Reform
24. Civil Procedure Reforms
25. Tire Safety
26. Protection for Savers (increase in Federal Insurance for savings accounts)
27. The GI Bill
28. Minimum Wage Increase
29. Urban Mass Transit
30. Elementary and Higher Education Funds

Source: Lawrence F. O'Brien and Joseph A. Califano Jr, 'Final Report to President Lyndon B. Johnson on the 89th Congress,' *Public Papers of the Presidents of the United States: Lyndon B. Johnson,* 1966, Vol. 2 (Washington: Government Printing Office 1967)

From Bruce J Schulman page 92–93

10.5 Education

Concern with American educational standards was not new. When Russia launched its Sputnik satellite in 1957 one conclusion within the Eisenhower Administration was that this reflected a gulf between the two superpowers in the standard of science education. When Kennedy became president in 1961, he drew attention to serious shortages in both qualified teachers and classrooms. The projections shown to LBJ now that he was in the Oval Office revealed that systemic, structural weaknesses would inhibit educational performance for the rest of the decade. Above all, underachievement would blight the prospects of the poor.

In this extract from *Flawed Giant*, Robert Dallek's highly acclaimed biography of Lyndon Johnson, the author highlights the importance of education to the founder of the Great Society:

Johnson's highest Great Society priority was to broaden educational opportunities and enrich the quality of school offerings. He had an almost mystical faith in the capacity of education to transform people's lives and improve their standard of living. He shared with earlier generations of Americans an evangelical faith in educational opportunity as a public good. 'He was a nut on education,' Hubert Humphrey said. 'He felt that education was the greatest thing he could give to the people; he just believed in it, just like some people believe in miracle cures.' (Dallek, 1998, pp. 195–96)

For these reasons, education was at the very centre of Johnson's 'Great Society' speech.

Today, 8 million adult Americans, more than the entire population of Michigan, have not finished five years of school. Nearly 20 million have not finished eight years of school. Nearly 54 million – more than one quarter of all America – have not even finished high school. In many places, classrooms are overcrowded and curricula are outdated. Most of our qualified teachers are underpaid, and many of our paid teachers are unqualified. So we must give every child a place to sit and a teacher to learn from. Poverty must not be a bar to learning, and learning must offer an escape from poverty ... The Great Society is a place where every child can find knowledge to enrich his mind and to enlarge his talents. A place to build the Great Society is in the classrooms of America. There your children's lives will be shaped. Our society will not be great until every young mind is set free to scan the farthest reaches of thought and imagination. We are still far from that goal. (In Schulman, 1995, p. 176)

Public education had been Lyndon's ticket out of poverty in rural Texas, and he wanted all children in the country to have the same chance to advance themselves. He was confident that federal funds could make a significant difference in expanding and improving education at every level. Indeed, with the post-war 'baby boom' causing overcrowded classes in run-down schools short of competent teachers, Johnson believed that there was no choice but for Washington to take the initiative in meeting the problem. In his message to Congress of January 1964 the president called education 'the number one business on this Nation's agenda' (Dallek, 1998, pp. 196–97). He set out a vision for a national goal of Full Educational Opportunity and asked Congress to double educational spending to $8 billion.

However, there were three major factors that had routinely blocked presidential initiatives in this area.

1. To many in the South, federal aid to schools was seen as a 'Trojan horse', a device designed simply to enforce desegregation.
2. Any support to parochial schools was seen as unconstitutional.
3. Federal involvement in education was seen as promoting excessive government control at the expense of local school boards.

Of course, Johnson was not deterred and at the centre of his new proposals came the Elementary and Secondary Education Act, which proposed, in Title 1, to provide $1 billion in compensatory education funding for the poorest students. Johnson's skill in piloting such a controversial and costly bill through Congress was masterly. As Dallek relates it: 'in only eighty-seven days the Congress had passed a billion-dollar law, deeply affecting a fundamental institution of the nation ... The House had approved it with no amendments that mattered; the Senate had voted it though literally without a comma changed.' (Dallek, 1998, p. 200)

In order to secure support from local school districts, they were given direct responsibility for planning and implementing the compensation programme. Bruce Schulman provides an insightful analysis of the hidden problems this created:

The government allocated money to a district based on the number of poor students enrolled in it, but the districts selected which schools, students, and programs received the funds. Most districts pocketed the money and continued business-as-usual. In fact ... few Title 1 dollars actually benefitted poor students; most of the funds supported programs for the middle class and well-to-do ... President Johnson always believed that Title 1 was an anti-poverty program. The local school districts made sure that it was not. (Schulman, 1995, p. 95)

Two critical weaknesses in the strategy of the Great Society were emerging. Firstly, that in the frenzied haste of getting legislation though, Johnson made major compromises so that he diluted the programmes and hampered their implementation. Secondly, and of profound importance, LBJ himself showed little interest in following through on the progress of the various agencies his team created. Nevertheless, his interest in education remained and in 1965 a Higher Education Act created community service programmes at college and university level aimed at lending support to urban and suburban areas. Most of all, this provided significant investment in previously underfunded black colleges. In particular, scholarships, student loans and work–study programmes were all given significant support (Table 10.2).

Table 10.2 The Great Society, 1963–68

1963	**22 November**	After the assassination of President Kennedy in Dallas, Lyndon B. Johnson was sworn in as the 36th President of the United States.
1964	**January**	President Johnson used his State of the Union Address to declare 'unconditional war on poverty'.
	May	At a graduation day address at the University of Michigan at Ann Arbor, President Johnson introduced the concept of the Great Society.
	July	Johnson signed the Civil Rights Act of 1964.
	20 August	Johnson signed the Economic Opportunity Act to launch the War on Poverty programme.
1965	**15 March**	President Johnson calls for action to improve voting rights for African American southerners at a joint session of Congress.
	11 April	Johnson signed the Elementary and Secondary Education Act at Johnson City, Texas.
	June	At Howard University, Johnson delivered the commencement address, demanding 'equality as a fact and result' for African Americans.
	6 August	Johnson signed the Voting Rights Act.
	12 August	Serious riots at Watts, Los Angeles.
1966	**January**	In his State of the Union Address Johnson stated that he intended to maintain a commitment to the Great Society at the same time as waging the war in Vietnam.
	November	The midterm elections showed the electoral tide to be turning against the president, as the backlash from Vietnam, domestic inflation and concerns about racial tension in the cities all took their toll on LBJ's standing.
1967	**July**	Further race riots in Detroit and Newark, New Jersey.
	August	Johnson proposes an Income Tax Bill to Congress to finance the Vietnam War.
1968	**31 March**	Johnson announced his decision to withdraw from the 1968 presidential campaign and to de-escalate the war in Vietnam.
	11 April	Johnson signed the Civil Rights Act of 1968.

10.6 Poverty

Johnson was convinced that federal action against poverty represented a sound investment. He saw the money spent on helping the young unemployed as a 'hand up' rather than a 'hand out'. The individual who did most to assist Johnson in preparing legislation was President Kennedy's brother-in-law, Sargent Shriver. By March 1964, they had put together the Economic Opportunity Act (EOA). This called for the establishment of a Job Corps, work training and study programmes to provide young people with education and vocational skills. It also proposed a Community Action Program, designed to allow each American community the chance to develop its own local plan to fight poverty. The Act also proposed the creation of Volunteers in Service to America (VISTA) for people who wanted to support the War on Poverty and the setting up of the Office of Economic Opportunity to co-ordinate the War on Poverty.

The EOA was passed in August 1964 backed by almost $1 billion worth of funding. Commentators such as Joseph A. Califano Jr (1995) and Allen J. Matusow (1995) remain divided about the effectiveness of Johnson's War on Poverty. Califano retorts:

> Ask the 8 million children who have been through Head Start whether the poverty program failed ... And what of the overall impact of the Great Society on poverty in America? In 1960, 22 per cent of the American people lived below the official poverty level. When Lyndon Johnson left office in 1969, that had dropped to 13 per cent ... Lyndon Johnson's Great Society provided: liberalization of welfare, food stamps and unemployment compensation; Medicaid and Medicare; community health centers; work training; housing; and a host of other programs. (In Schulman, 1995, pp. 178–85)

However, Matusow offers a very different perspective:

> I think that the root problem of the War on Poverty was a political problem. President Johnson was a politician of consensus in a middle-class country, and that meant whatever he did for the poor, he had to do with the permission of the affluent classes. And that, I think, was the root of the difficulties that followed. The truth of it is, if you want to fight a real war on poverty, you are going to have to recognize that the interests of the poor will at some crucial point be in conflict with the interests of the middle classes ... In 1964, when the President declared war on poverty, the 20 per cent of the population he said were poor received 5 per cent of the money income. And today, the bottom 20 per cent receives 5 per cent of the national income. By that measurement ... there has been no reduction in the incidence of poverty. (In Schulman, 1995, pp. 185–89)

10.7 Medicare and Medicaid

The Medicare Act, 1965

The relative prosperity of the Eisenhower years had not necessarily created a healthy nation and, like in all advanced countries, in the US a longer lifespan meant diseases of the elderly were hugely problematic and expensive. Johnson's personal awareness of this was heightened by the shock of his own heart attack, which he suffered at the age of 46. Beyond this, as a young legislator he had backed federal support for health care and research as early as the 1940s. In 1956, he personally proposed an amendment to a social security bill to include federal health insurance for the elderly.

Full of energy and resolve at the start of his first term, he asked Congress to make 'the wonders of modern medicine' available to all Americans. Robert Dallek describes how the president 'urged hospital insurance for the aged, more modern hospitals, increased and better medical manpower, and greater spending on mental health'. Johnson demanded the creation of a Commission on Heart Disease, Cancer and Strokes (HDCS) given that 'two-thirds of all Americans now living will ultimately suffer or die from one of them' (Dallek, 1998, p. 204).

Although federal proposals for the provision of health care for the elderly and a national medical programme had been made under Roosevelt and Truman, respectively, they had not been able to overcome Congressional opposition. The combination of the general improvement in the standard of living and the steady advance in medical knowledge meant that by the time Johnson occupied the White House there was a rapid rise in the number of Americans reaching old age. The cost of providing medical care to this group was immense. Johnson wanted to provide medical insurance benefits for the elderly through the social security system. The scheme approved by the president offered '60 days of hospital coverage, 180 days of skilled nursing home care, and 240 days of home health visits for Social Security recipients sixty-five and older'.

His proposals were opposed by the American Medical Association (AMA), the powerful doctors' lobbying group, and by private insurance companies. It was felt that federal intervention might reduce the earnings of private health care groups. Johnson's Medicare Act was effectively a compromise with these groups, and although the president claimed that his Bill would offer 'care for the sick and serenity for the fearful' it did not provide the kind of comprehensive medical insurance that he would have liked. Importantly, Dallek notes 'staggering increases in medical costs to the entire society. Where total Medicare expenditures were $3.5 billion in the first year of the program, they had risen to $144 billion by 1993' (Dallek, 1998, p. 211).

The Medicaid Act

The Medicaid Act aimed to provide for the poor in the same way that the Medicare Act sought to provide for the elderly. Some historians have claimed that this Act was less significant than advocates of the Great Society have claimed, because poor people were already catered for by an extensive system of charity medicine. Allen J. Matusow provides this critique of Medicaid:

It's quite often implied by people who talk about Medicaid that in the old days if you didn't have money, you didn't have access to medical services. That is not true. There was an extensive system of charity medicine before Medicaid was passed ... Poor people saw doctors on an average of 4.3 times a year compared to 5.1 times for more affluent classes. This doesn't mean that access was not a problem. There were pockets of poor people in America that did not have access to medical treatment. But if you were the average poor person, you had access to a fairly well-developed charity medical system ... most of the medical services received by poor people after

Medicaid would have been received anyway under the charity medical system ... the primary beneficiaries were the doctors and hospitals who received payment for services they once rendered free of charge or at reduced payment. (In Schulman, 1995, pp. 187–88)

Matusow (in Schulman, 1995, pp. 185–89) identifies four key criticisms that have been made about the Medicaid scheme:

1. Those who gained the most from the new system were the doctors and hospitals who were paid for delivering services that had previously been free.
2. The programme was exceptionally expensive, quickly accounting for more than half of all money spent on public assistance.
3. The two-tier element of the medical system remained so that both before and during Medicaid people were allocated to the charity side of the medical system.
4. Debate remains as to whether the extra medical services provided by Medicaid actually led to improved health.

Finally, Dallek provides this analysis of the two schemes:

The benefits to the elderly and the indigent from Medicare and Medicaid are indisputable. But they did not solve the problem of care at reasonable cost for all Americans. Johnson's reforms were only a partial and imperfect solution to a dilemma that other industrialized societies had addressed more successfully. (Dallek, 1998, p. 211)

The Immigration Act, 1965

A long-standing legacy of the Red Scare of the 1920s was the sharp change in attitudes to immigration. The American tradition of welcoming people from overseas regardless of their nationality had been replaced with a quota-based, national origins system, specifically designed to restrict immigrants from Asia and also eastern and southern Europe. Johnson denounced the 1920s legislation as incompatible with American tradition and the ethnic quotas were abandoned. This was of long-standing cultural, social and economic importance as it led to the large-scale arrival of immigrants from countries including Korea, Vietnam and Japan so that the impact of Johnson's change of outlook was profound, particularly in the western United States.

Conservation and the environment

The booming post-war economy, conspicuous consumption of the affluent society, love of gas-guzzling cars and Eisenhower's commitment to highway construction meant that the 1940s–50s were not environmentally friendly decades. Despite Johnson's formidable commitments in Vietnam and a crowded domestic agenda, he was nevertheless determined to reverse the impact of economic growth on the natural world. His willingness to commit time, leadership and resources to green issues places him in the front rank of 'conservation' presidents. Indeed, by the time he prepared to leave office, the chairman of the National Geographic Society called Johnson 'our greatest conservation president' (Schulman, 1995, p. 92). His administration aimed to reduce air and water pollution, beautify highways, extend national wildlife refuges, protect wilderness areas and allocate more land to the great national parks. While the 1960s saw some improvement in public awareness of environmental issues, at the same time opposition to federal action came from powerful lobbying from the automobile and petroleum industries. Johnson's willingness to take on the industrialists contradicted the stereotypical view of him as a Texan who would be in the pocket of the big oil interests so powerful in his home state.

10.8 The Supreme Court

Whereas Johnson's efforts to build a Great Society provoked fierce opposition in some quarters, he received emphatic support from the Supreme Court. Between 1953, when he was appointed by President Eisenhower, to 1969, Chief Justice Earl Warren made a number of rulings which helped to promote a fairer society. Warren's landmark ruling came in Brown vs Board of Education of Topeka (1954). Warren's liberal tendencies also resulted in the relaxation of censorship in the arts. In a sign of how far the nation had travelled since the decline of McCarthyism, Yates vs United States (1957):

> ruled that mere membership of the Communist Party was not enough to convict on the charge of conspiracy to overthrow the government by force. In Gideon v. Wainwright (1963); Miranda v. Arizona (1966) a series of rulings that established the right of suspects to remain silent and to be able to see a lawyer before facing interrogation. Then in Baker v. Carr (1962) and Reynolds v. Sims (1964) the Court ruled in favour of equalised electoral districts, thereby removing the traditional rural control over state legislatures. (Jones, 1995, p. 552)

10.9 The decline of the Great Society

Given the sheer energy and commitment expended by Johnson on all aspects of the Great Society, the endless telephone calls and meetings cajoling Congress and the billions of dollars spent on government programmes, the president expected to feel a sense of gratitude from his people in return. However, the president's personal approval ratings were gradually falling as he paid the price for the urban riots that frightened so many of his erstwhile supporters. Yet to fully understand why Johnson's fortunes were on the wane, we need to look beyond domestic disturbances to consider the impact of foreign policy on Johnson's civil rights programme. If scenes of rioting at home were disturbing to television viewers, then the images that began to appear night after night from Vietnam were even more damaging.

Despite his strong personal feelings of foreboding, Johnson's instinctive combativeness and desperation not to fail in the struggle against communism was to lead him into an abyss. In the spring of 1965, Operation Rolling Thunder launched an intense bombing campaign against the North Vietnamese, which was accompanied by a surge of American ground troops. The more Johnson prosecuted the war in Vietnam, the greater was the damage to his domestic standing. The consequences of this for the president, the civil rights campaign and the Great Society were profound. The administration became increasingly mired in controversy and recrimination. Johnson was unusually thin-skinned and found the criticism that came his way hurtful and difficult to understand. Doris Kearns Goodwin, a Johnson biographer, shows how upset the president was with the student protests that became a daily ritual outside the White House:

> Then take the students. I wanted to help them, too. I fought on their behalf for scholarships and loans and grants. I fought for better teachers and better schools. And look what I got back. Young people by the thousands leaving their universities, marching in the streets, chanting that horrible song about how many kids I had killed that day. (In Kearns Goodwin, 1991, p. 340)

Despite the tide of criticism that was beginning to flow his way Johnson was initially resolute that he would continue to wage war in Vietnam while at the same time maintaining the impetus of the Great Society. In his message to Congress on the State of the Union, 12 January 1966, Johnson declared:

> Our Nation tonight is engaged in a brutal and bitter conflict in Vietnam ... But we will not permit those who fire upon us in Vietnam to win a victory over the desires and the intentions of all the American people. This Nation is mighty enough, its society is healthy enough, its people are strong enough, to pursue our goals in the rest of the world while still bringing a Great Society here at home. Because of Vietnam we cannot do all that we should, or all that we would like to do ... We will continue to meet the needs of our people by continuing to develop the Great Society ... Carry forward with full vigor, the great health and education programs that you enacted into law last year ... Prosecute with vigor and determination our war on poverty. Rebuild completely, on a scale never before attempted, entire central and slum areas of several of our cities. (In Schulman, 1995, p. 234)

Despite these defiant words it is now clear that the momentum of the Great Society was ebbing away. The escalation of the Vietnam War in 1967–68 would ensure that. However, it should also be noted that while some of the Great Society programmes came under severe pressure, initiatives in Medicare and education not only survived but were an important element of future presidential administrations.

Johnson's foreign policy

10.10 The Dominican Republic

Johnson's unquestioning acceptance of the fundamental principle that the United States was dealing with a communist conspiracy masterminded by Moscow led him to intervene directly in the Dominican Republic in April 1965. Having served on the Executive Committee (ExComm) during the Cuban Missile Crisis, Johnson believed it was essential to prevent further communist insurgence in the Caribbean. When the ruling right-wing military junta came under pressure from rebel forces containing communist elements, Johnson felt obliged to act. A Pentagon official later recalled that

Johnson 'was immediately drawn into that and took a very active and vigorous stand' (in Dallek, 1998, p. 263). With the situation rapidly becoming more volatile, Johnson went on national television and told the American people: 'At stake are the lives of thousands, the liberty of a nation, and the principles and values of all the American Republics.' Johnson went on to say that without American forces, 'men and women – Americans and those of other lands – will die in the streets' (in Dallek, 1998, p. 265).

Johnson dispatched 30,000 American troops to dissuade the rebels but the incident had the potential to develop into a long-running problem. However, it was resolved when the Organization of American States (OAS, created at a conference in Bogota in 1948) sent in a peacekeeping force. When the situation on the island became more stable, Johnson was able to withdraw his troops and bring the matter to a close. An election held in June 1966 produced a victory for the left but was acclaimed by the Johnson Administration as a triumph for democracy. Despite the short-term nature of the problem in the Dominican Republic, the press was by no means universally favourable. *Newsweek* commented that the complexities of foreign affairs soon rendered the president 'touchy, bitter and exasperated.' As the Dominican crisis faded into the past, the problem of Vietnam loomed ever larger for Johnson. The incident had convinced Johnson of the wisdom of firm action and an unwavering course. He would eventually realise that these principles could be extremely problematic.

10.11 Johnson's foreign policy team

From the moment Johnson assumed the presidency, doubts were cast about his ability to deal with the sheer complexity of foreign relations. In January 1964, the *New York Herald Tribune* described the 'mounting evidence' that Johnson had not developed 'an effective technique for the day-by-day conduct of foreign affairs' (Dallek, 1998, pp. 84, 87). While Johnson bitterly resented this criticism, he personally accepted that he was more comfortable with domestic issues. The trauma of the Cuban Missile Crisis, in which Johnson had initially supported 'an unannounced air strike' while President Kennedy had opted for the option of a blockade, had graphically illustrated to Johnson the pitfalls of foreign policy. Therefore the new president came to rely heavily on the experience of Kennedy's foreign policy advisers: Defense Secretary Robert McNamara, National Security Adviser McGeorge Bundy and Secretary of State Dean Rusk. This factor led to a considerable degree of continuity in the foreign policy of Kennedy and Johnson.

Robert McNamara – Defense Secretary

A brilliant graduate of Berkeley and Harvard Business School, following successful service as an officer in the air force McNamara secured a job at the Ford Motor Company. His flair for management meant that by 1961 he had become the chief executive officer. When Robert McNamara entered the Kennedy White House as the secretary of defense he enjoyed a reputation as one of the most brilliant young minds in American society. Summoned from Ford – whose fortunes he is credited with single-handedly turning round – by President Kennedy, McNamara's talent for modern decision making enhanced the reputation of the 'Camelot' White House as attracting the 'best and the brightest'. His reputation for updating the management of Ford had attracted national attention and prompted Kennedy to offer him the post of defense secretary. He was described as the 'can-do man in the can-do society in the can-do era' (Dallek, 1998, p. 88). Johnson had observed McNamara at close quarters and was impressed by him to the point of being 'worshipful'. Johnson summed McNamara up as

> enormously energetic ... he is the first one at work and the last to leave. When I wake up, the first one I call is McNamara. He is there at seven every morning, including Saturday. The only difference is that Saturday he wears a sports coat. (In Dallek, 1998, p. 89)

Between November 1963 and May 1968, McNamara served as Johnson's secretary of defense. Together, these two powerful figures led the United States deeper and deeper into a conflict of the most traumatic scale imaginable.

McGeorge Bundy – National Security Adviser

A highly gifted individual, Bundy enjoyed a glittering academic career at Groton and then Yale. He then became a junior fellow at Harvard, served in the army during the Second World War, taught in the Harvard Government Department and finally, at the age of 34, was appointed as the youngest Dean of Faculty in Harvard's distinguished history. He was appointed by Kennedy as special assistant for national security affairs. In turn, Johnson soon came to rely heavily on Bundy's crisp memos on every aspect of American foreign policy.

Dean Rusk – Secretary of State

From a modest background in Georgia, Rusk's academic ability had enabled him to obtain a Rhodes scholarship to Oxford University. Rusk became Professor of Government at Mills College on the West Coast. Rusk also served as president of the Rockefeller Foundation. He was appointed by Kennedy as Secretary of State as a compromise candidate and did not develop a close relationship with the president – Rusk's reserved temperament was reflected in the fact that he was the only member of the Cabinet who Kennedy did not address by his first name. However, Rusk's deferential attitude towards Johnson meant that LBJ looked favourably upon him when he became president.

10.12 Johnson's initial response to the problem of Vietnam

George C. Herring presents this summary of the role of LBJ in the escalation of the Vietnam War:

> Between November 1963 and July 1965, Lyndon Baines Johnson transformed a limited commitment to assist the South Vietnamese government into an open-ended

commitment to preserve an independent, non-Communist South Vietnam. Johnson inherited from Kennedy a rapidly deteriorating situation in South Vietnam. Fearing that large-scale involvement might jeopardize his chances of election in 1964 and threaten his beloved Great Society domestic programs, he temporized for over a year, expanding American assistance and increasing the number of advisers in hopes that a beefed-up version of his predecessor's policy might somehow stave off disaster. South Vietnam's survival appeared more in doubt than ever in early 1965, however, and over the next six months Johnson made his fateful decisions, authorizing a sustained air offensive against North Vietnam and dispatching ground forces to stem the tide in the south. By July 1965, the United States was engaged in a major war on the Asian mainland. (Herring, 1979, p. 108)

In essence, Johnson's perception of Vietnam was very similar to Kennedy's. Less than a week after Kennedy's assassination Johnson approved National Security Action Memorandum No. 273, which reaffirmed an American pledge to support the South Vietnamese 'to win their contest against the externally directed and supported communist conspiracy'. Johnson portrayed North Vietnam as a 'ragged ass little fourth rate country' (Dallek, 1998, p. 99) which would not be able to resist a truly determined United States. Despite this bravado, Robert McNamara later reflected that Johnson 'inherited a mess' from Kennedy in terms of Vietnam (Lowe, 1998, p. 101). Although Johnson committed himself to maintaining Kennedy's policy of supporting South Vietnam against the Viet Cong and the North Vietnamese, the possibility of complete continuity had been prevented by the murder of Diem in November 1963.

At an early meeting to discuss the future Johnson told an aide, 'I am not going to lose Vietnam. I am not going to be the President who saw Southeast Asia go the way China went ... I don't think Congress wants us to let the Communists take over South Vietnam.' (In Dallek, 1998, p. 99) In December 1963, McNamara returned from a visit to Vietnam and told the president, 'the situation is very disturbing. Current trends, unless reversed in the next 2–3 months will lead to neutralization at best and more likely to a Communist controlled state ... We should watch the situation very carefully.' Two months later, Johnson remarked to a journalist that to withdraw would be to 'run and let the dominoes start fallin'' over, and God Almighty what they said about us leaving China would be just warmin' up compared to what they'd say now' (in Dallek, 1998, pp. 101–02).

Nevertheless, some senators did urge him to withdraw. Senate Majority Leader Mike Mansfield told Johnson that 'we are close to the point of no return in Viet Nam' and that further commitments would lead to 'massive costs'. Senator Richard Russell told Johnson to 'spend whatever it takes to bring to power a government that would ask us to go home' (in Dallek, 1998, p. 102). Meanwhile, following the assassination of Diem, control of South Vietnam passed into the hands of General Nguyen Khanh. Although Johnson's instincts regarding Vietnam were clear, he was also acutely aware of the difficulties that lay in store. In a private remark to McGeorge Bundy in May 1964, Johnson made it clear that there would be no easy solution:

Looks like to me that we're getting into another Korea ... I don't think it's worth fightin' for and I don't think we can get out. And it's just the biggest damn mess that I ever saw. (In Dallek, 1998, p. 145)

10.13 The Gulf of Tonkin and military escalation

While Johnson seems to have been aware of the pitfalls represented by further military involvement in Vietnam, he was unable to accept the option of complete withdrawal. Given that fact, the only alternative seemed to be to increase the level of support given the rapidly deteriorating situation in South Vietnam since the murder of Diem in November 1963. As early as December 1963, Defense Secretary Robert McNamara was warning Johnson that unless action was taken in the near future South Vietnam could be lost. Johnson's commitment to his domestic programme – the Great Society – was immense. He feared that a weak posture in Vietnam would increase southern conservative disapproval of his leadership. This, combined with his explicit commitment to the Kennedy agenda, made him resolve to address the Vietnam problem and reject the option of withdrawal. A key moment came in August 1964, with an alleged attack on the American destroyer *USS Maddox* by a group of North Vietnamese torpedo boats. This was followed by a further exchange with the *Maddox* and the destroyer *C. Turner Joy*.

Controversy still surrounds these exchanges. The point was that the United States presented them as acts of North Vietnamese aggression. In private, Johnson told an aide 'what happened was we've been playing around up there and they came out, gave us a warning, and we knocked hell out of 'em.' Furthermore, new evidence now shows that McNamara met with the Joint Chiefs of Staff to support the claim that an attack on the destroyers had occurred. The Pentagon then issued a statement saying that the two destroyers were attacked by the patrol boats. In the face of what was presented as Vietnamese aggression, Congress responded with almost unanimous support for a resolution which allowed the president to 'take all necessary steps, including the use of force' to prevent further aggression in Southeast Asia. (Beschloss, 1997, pp. 494, 506). It is important to recognise that while Johnson had handled the situation with his customary skill, he was not seeking to obtain a 'blank cheque' with the objective of waging an unlimited war. He still believed he could achieve his objectives without having to wage such a war.

Even so, formidable force was deployed at the start of 1965. A huge bombing campaign over North Vietnam coincided with a rapid escalation in the deployment of ground troops. By the end of the year 180,000 troops had been sent to South Vietnam; 12 months later, the figure had risen to 350,000. Increasingly the Johnson Administration, supported by the advice of Defense Secretary McNamara and urged on by urgent requests from General Westmoreland for more men and materials, responded to setbacks by sending more and more troops to Vietnam. As Johnson put it: 'We have kept our guns over the mantel and our shells in the cupboard for a long time now ... I can't ask our American soldiers out there to continue to fight with one hand behind their backs.' (In Herring, 1979, p. 129)

As 1967 came to a close, and with casualties steadily mounting, half a million troops were in Vietnam. By the time Johnson stepped down in January 1969, American expenditure in Vietnam had reached $30 billion a year and 30,000 American troops had been killed. Despite this massive application of military might, the resistance of North Vietnam remained implacable. Huge casualties and massive damage to Vietnamese towns and villages seemed only to alienate the Americans and increase the determination of the Vietnamese to carry on the fight. General Vo Nguyen Giap, the communist commander in the field, said that even with the loss of 'a hundred, a thousand, tens of thousands' the struggle would carry on until 'final victory' had been achieved. When the war was over, the American leader, General Westmoreland, ruefully observed that 'any American commander who took the same vast losses as General Giap would have been sacked overnight' (Karnow, 1985, p. 18). In the face of these disturbing signs, the United States, once it had committed itself to a full-scale war, seemed unable to change course. As Herring puts it:

> The President staked everything on the casual assumption that the enemy could be quickly brought to bay by the application of American military might ... The United States never developed a strategy appropriate for the war it was fighting, in part because it was assumed that the mere application of its vast military power would be sufficient. The failure of one level of force led quickly to the next and then the next, until the war attained a degree of destructiveness no-one would have thought possible in 1965. (Herring, 1979, p. 145)

Maldwyn A. Jones offers further reasons for the American failure to achieve its objectives:

> While American strategic bombing caused terrible damage and casualties, it failed to cripple the enemy's predominantly agricultural economy. Likewise concentrated artillery fire and search-and-destroy missions proved ineffective in what was essentially a guerrilla war. Nor could American attempts to create an effective Vietnamese army overcome the apathy of the mass of the peasants. (Jones, 1995, p. 555)

10.14 Internal criticism: Opposition in Congress

When President Johnson first obtained Congressional sanction for his actions in 1964 the Senate voted 88 to 2 in his favour; in the House of Representatives, the vote was unanimous. The questioning of the basic assumptions which led the United States down the path to war was confined to a few individuals. Early opposition came from George Ball, an Undersecretary of State who wrote a long memorandum in October 1964 questioning the assumptions that led to war. Paul Kattenburg, a senior State Department official, argued that the United States should withdraw from Vietnam, and found himself posted to Guyana as a result. Democratic Senator Mike Mansfield (Montana) cautioned against increased involvement from the fall of 1962 onwards. However, by 1967 a combination of spiralling costs, enormous casualty figures and the realisation that a conclusion was nowhere in sight meant that the tide began to turn.

A group of highly influential senators adopted a critical approach to the war. Prominent critics of the administration's stance included Robert F. Kennedy, Eugene McCarthy and J. William Fulbright. As the influential chairman of the Senate Foreign Relations Committee, Senator Fulbright had lent powerful support to the Gulf of Tonkin Resolution. However, he aired strongly critical views in the televised committee hearings of spring 1966. Fulbright's book *The Arrogance of Power* (1966) argued that America had become overconfident and brash in its outlook. McCarthy sought

Table 10.3		The anti-Vietnam protest movement, 1963–68
1963		Limited, low-key protests against the war in Vietnam. With the notable exception of Senator Morse, there was little opposition in Congress.
1965	**Spring**	At various college campuses a number of 'teach-ins' were staged, allowing debates between academic staff and students and representatives of the government.
		At the same time, the first national demonstration against the war organised by the Students for a Democratic Society (SDS).
	Autumn	SANE organised an anti-war rally in Washington.
		At the Pentagon building near Washington, a Quaker called Norman Morrison set himself alight near the office of the Defense Secretary Robert McNamara.
1966		Three army privates sent to prison for two years following their refusal to serve in Vietnam.
1967		Martin Luther King Jr criticised the war.
	April	More than 300,000 protestors took part in a demonstration in New York.
		Senator Eugene McCarthy announced his candidacy as a Democratic candidate with an anti-war platform.
1968		Following McCarthy's performance in the New Hampshire primary, Johnson announced his decision not to run for re-election in November 1968.

the Democratic nomination as an anti-war candidate, and came close to defeating President Johnson in the New Hampshire Democratic primary. The result of this poll brought home to Johnson how unpopular the war had become. Others maintained that the principle of the 'domino theory' was fundamentally unsound.

The unprecedented television coverage of the war brought graphic images onto the screens of both politicians and the electorate. By 1968, a growing sense of unease permeated American society. The events of 1968, such as the assassinations of Martin Luther King Jr and Robert Kennedy and the violent scenes at the Democratic Convention in Chicago, created a deep sense of malaise. These factors were made more significant by the shocking turn of events at the start of 1968 in Vietnam. The sheer unexpected nature of the Tet Offensive lent credence to those who opposed the war and made many other Americans who had supported the war question America's role for the first time. By the time 1968 came to a close, there were even fewer Americans who were prepared to support the war (Table 10.3).

10.15 Vietnam and the media

The American news media accurately reflected the public mood during the Vietnam War. As in the country at large, initial approval was forthcoming for Johnson's early show of resolve. News coverage tended to be positive and the reasons for American involvement seemed to be broadly accepted. By 1967–68, the situation had drastically changed. The key to the problem was the increasing discrepancy between the official picture presented by the White House and the Pentagon and the reality observed by an increasingly sophisticated and questioning news media. This divergence was reflected in damaging circumstances when the previously supportive newsreader Walter Cronkite, the most respected news reporter in the United States, made this powerful statement, related here by Stanley Karnow:

> Cronkite was apple-pie American, a Missouri boy who expressed the mood of the heartland as much as he presumably influenced its pulse beat. His views on the war had mostly been balanced, nearly bland. Now, on the evening of February 27, he delivered a fresh verdict. Just back from Saigon, he rejected the official forecasts of victory, predicting instead that it seemed 'more certain than ever that the bloody experience of Vietnam is to end in a stalemate.' The broadcaster shocked and depressed Johnson, who assumed that Cronkite's despondent comment would steer public opinion even farther away from support for the war. But Cronkite, like all other journalists, was lagging behind the American public – reflecting rather than shaping its attitudes. (Karnow, 1985, pp. 547–48)

Cronkite's change of heart reflected the mood of the public at large. Damaging images abounded. Children mutilated by American air strikes, apparently wanton destruction of villages, the deaths of innocent civilians and the depressing sight of American troops being brought back home in body bags. The Tet Offensive of 31 January 1968 (Table 10.4) was yet another moment when coverage of the war seemed to add new weight to the conviction that it could not be won. In September 1968, CBS launched its first news magazine show '60 Minutes', presented by Harry Reasoner and Mike Wallace. Although it took a long time for the format to be more widely accepted, it contained some notable Vietnam programmes including a powerful interview with Captain Ernest Medina, a participant in the My Lai Massacre. Coverage like this merely underlined what had already been said. The war had turned into a nightmare that was being observed on a daily basis in the living rooms of the American people.

Table 10.4		Vietnam: A summary of military events, 1964–68
1964	**3 August**	North Vietnamese patrol boats allegedly attacked American ships in the Gulf of Tonkin. The United States responded by passing the Gulf of Tonkin Resolution, giving the president Congressional approval for his future conduct of the war.
1965	**7 February**	The Vietcong launched an attack on the American barracks at Pleiku. The United States retaliated by launching 'Flaming Dart', a series of air raids on North Vietnam.
	24 February	American aircraft began bombing Vietcong targets in South Vietnam.
	March	Operation Rolling Thunder, aimed at forcing North Vietnam into abandoning their support for South Vietnam. This operation, a series of bombing raids, lasted with interruptions until the autumn of 1968.

Continued

	March	The first United States combat troops sent to Vietnam; earlier forces had been deployed as military advisers.
	October	In the first large-scale conventional battle of the war, American troops defeated North Vietnamese units in the la Drang Valley.
	December	The number of American troops stationed in Vietnam reached 180,000. Johnson suspended bombing of North Vietnam over Christmas in a bid to bring the communists to negotiate.
1966	31 January	Johnson ordered resumption of the bombing campaign.
	June	United States bombed oil depots in Hanoi.
	December	American troop strength reached nearly 400,000 by the end of the year.
1967	May	United States bombed Hanoi's major power plant.
	December	American troop strength reached 475,000.
1968	31 January	Tet offensive began. North Vietnamese and Vietcong attacked a wide range of towns and cities in South Vietnam. General Westmoreland's call for 206,000 further troops rejected by McNamara's replacement as secretary of defense, Clark Clifford.
	March	• General Westmoreland appointed Army Chief of Staff and replaced in the Vietnam Command by General Creighton Abrams. • President Johnson announced he would not stand for re-election and called a partial bombing halt. • My Lai Massacre. • Johnson announced that he was halting the bombing of North Vietnam. • American troops in Vietnam exceed half a million.

10.16 What was it like to serve in Vietnam?

No picture could duplicate the complexity of the beauty: over there, the sun lighted a bomb scar in the forest, and next to it smoke filled the bowl in a valley; a column of rain from one fugitive cloud slanted on another slope and the blue gave way to black green, to rice green on the flat fields of shoots, which became, after a strip of sand, an immensity of blue ocean ... Who has mentioned the simple fact that the heights of Vietnam are places of unimaginable grandeur? (Paul Theroux – American travel writer)

In seeking to answer this question the most obvious response would be to examine letters from soldiers to their loved ones. These represent the main source shown here but initially there are also extracts from government publications which were intended to support the soldiers in their bid to come to terms with an exceptionally demanding situation. The vocabulary itself is chilling.

Extracts from a guide for soldiers to some basic Vietnamese language

English	Vietnamese
Halt	Dung Lai
Lay down your gun	Buong sung xuong
Put up your hands	Dua tay len
Keep your hands on your head	Dua tay len dau
I will search you	Toi kham ong
Do not talk	Dung noi chuyen
Walk there	Lai dang kia

Nine rules issued to American soldiers on arrival in Vietnam

1. Remember we are guests here. We make no demands and seek no special treatment.
2. Join with the people! Understand their life, use phrases from their language and honor their customs and laws.
3. Treat women with politeness and respect.
4. Make personal friends among the soldiers and common people.
5. Always give the Vietnamese the right of way.
6. Be alert to security and ready to react with your military skill.
7. Don't attract attention by loud, rude or unusual behaviour.
8. Avoid separating yourself from the people by a display of wealth or privilege.
9. Above all else you are members of the US Military Forces on a difficult mission, responsible for all your official and personal actions. Reflect honor upon yourself and the United States of America.

> Source: Peter Lowe (ed.), *The Vietnam War* (Macmillan Press Ltd 1998), p. 203.

The extracts which follow are taken from the collection, *Dear America: Letters Home From Vietnam* (Edelman, 1985) and reproduced with kind permission of The New York Vietnam Veterans Memorial Commission; they explain, in a deeply moving way, what it was like to fight in Vietnam.

July 3rd [1966]

Dear Mom and Dad,

I don't know how I can say this without alarming you, but I know I'll have to tell you about it because NBC News was there and I'm afraid you might have seen me on film or read about the dreadful fighting.

When I think about the hell I've been through the last few days. I can't help but cry and wonder how I am still alive. My company suffered the worst casualties – I believe something close to 50 dead and wounded ...

I was carrying the bodies of wounded and dead onto helicopters that were in a clearing when I saw, I believe, Ron Nessen of NBC, and they were taking pictures ... The area is less than two miles from Cambodia, where VCs have regiments, and they ambushed us ... Try to hold up ...

Love, Kenny (Edelman, 1985, p. 73)

May 8, 1968

My Dearest Bev,

For the last week we have been waiting for an attack, and last night it came in full force. Honey, I was never so scared in my whole life. We got hit by 12 mortars and rockets and some even hit our ammo dumps, which really hurt the battery. A mortar landed about 30 feet from me and I was lucky enough to have my head down, but the sergeant next to me didn't and we think lost an eye ... this was my first look at war, and it sure was an ugly sight ... It was an experience you can never explain in a million words.

The noise from shooting is enough to drive a person crazy. Even after the attack last night, we had to stay up and wait for a ground attack ... We expect to catch a lot of hell through May because it seems that the VC are really putting a big push on ... I hope I don't have to go through what we did last night in a long time (like never!)

All my love, Al (Edelman, 1985, p. 51)

September 17, 1969

Red

Anyone over here who walks more than 50 feet through elephant grass should automatically get a Purple Heart. Try to imagine grass 8 to 15 feet high so thick as to cut visibility to one yard, possessing razor-sharp edges. Then try to imagine walking through it while all around you are men possessing the latest automatic weapons who desperately want to kill you. You'd be amazed at how much a man can age on one patrol ...

George (Edelman, 1985, p. 50)

September 2, 1966

Dear Mom, Dad, Shrub, the Egg and Peach,

Sorry to be so long in writing, but I have just come back from an abortion called Operation Jackson. I spent a three-day 'walk in the sun' and paddies and fields and mountains and impenetrable jungle and saw grass and ants, and screwed-up radios and no word and deaf radio operators, and no chow, and too many C-rations, and blisters and torn trousers and jungle rot, and wet socks and sprained ankles and no heels ... finished off by a 14,000-meter forced march on a hard road ...

Love Sandy (Edelman, 1985, p. 61)

April 1967

Dear Ma,

Vietnam has my feelings on a seesaw. This country is so beautiful, when the sun is shining on the mountains, farmers in their rice paddies, with their water buffalo, palm trees, monkeys, birds and even the strange insects. For a fleeting moment I wasn't in a war zone at all, just on vacation, but still missing you and the family.

There are a few kids who hang around, some with no parents. I feel so sorry for them. I do things to make them laugh. And they call me 'dinky dow' (crazy). But it makes me feel good. I hope that's one reason why we're here, to secure a future for them. It seems to be the only justification I can think of for the things I have done!

Love to all.

Your son, George (Edelman, 1985, p. 105)

June 1966

Dear Madeline,

Hello my dear sister.

It's good to have someone to tell your troubles to. I can't tell them to my parents or Darlene because they worry too much, but I tell you truthfully I doubt if I'll come out of this alive.

In my original squad I'm the only one left unharmed. In my platoon there's only 13 of us. It seems every day another young guy 18 and 19 years old like myself is killed in action. Please help me, Mad. I don't know if I should stop writing my parents and Darlene or what.

I'm going on an operation next month where there is nothing but VC and VC sympathizers. The area is also very heavily mined. All of us are scared cause we know a lot of us won't make it ...

Oh, and one more favor. I'd like the truth now. Has Darlene been faithful to me? I know she's been dating guys, but does she still love me best? ... See ya if it's God's will. I have to make it out of Vietnam though, cause I'm lucky. I hope. Ha ha.

Miss ya,

Love Ray (Edelman, 1985, pp. 127–28)

March 1968

Dear Mom and Dad,

Well, I've had my baptism by fire, and it's changed me I think. Two days ago my platoon was on a mission to clear three suspected minefields ... We spent the whole day clearing the three fields and came up with a big zero.

The tracks were then returning to us where we would stay overnight. When we reached our spot we jumped off the tracks, and one of my men jumped right onto a mine. Both his feet were blown off, both legs were torn to shreds – his entire groin area was completely blown away. It was the most horrible sight I've ever seen ... I've developed hate for the Vietnamese because they come around selling Cokes and beer to us and then run back and tell the VC how many we are, where our positions are, and where the leaders position themselves.

All Love, Mike (Edelman, 1985, p. 180)

October 20, 1966

Dear Aunt Fannie,

This morning, my platoon and I were finishing up a three-day patrol. Struggling over steep hills covered with hedgerows, trees, and generally impenetrable jungle, one of my men turned to me and pointed a hand, filled with cuts and scratches, at a rather distinguished-looking plant with red flowers waving gaily in the downpour and said, 'That is the first plant which I have seen today which didn't have thorns on it.' I immediately thought of you.

The plant, and the hill upon which it grew, was also representative of Vietnam. It is a country of thorns and cuts, of guns and marauding, of little hope and of great failure. Yet in the midst of it all a beautiful thought, gesture, and even person can arise among it waving bravely at the death that pours down upon it. Someday this hill will be burned by napalm, and the red flower will crackle up and die among the thorns... The flower will always live in the memory of a tired, wet Marine, and has thus achieved a sort of immortality.

Love Sandy (Edelman, 1985, pp. 137–38)

10.17 The role of Robert McNamara (Defense Secretary, 1961–68)

Lyndon Johnson valued intellectual strength, work rate and leadership in his closest advisers and for this reason he became an enthusiastic devotee of McNamara during the height of Kennedy's 'Camelot'. From the moment that LBJ occupied the Oval Office the two men worked intimately on the process that led to the full-scale conflict in Vietnam in 1965. With the considerable benefits of hindsight, some experts have not held back in their criticism of the defense secretary who was so instrumental in the White House decision-making process. As the title of this particular book suggests, H.R. McMaster, in *Dereliction of Duty: Lyndon Johnson, Robert McNamara, The Joint Chiefs of Staff, and the Lies That Led to Vietnam* is one such critic:

> As American involvement in Vietnam deepened, the gap between the true nature of that commitment and the President's depiction of it to the American people, the Congress, and members of his own administration widened. Lyndon Johnson, with the assistance of Robert S. McNamara and the Joint Chiefs of Staff, had set the stage for America's disaster in Vietnam ... What Johnson feared most in 1964 was losing his chance to win the Presidency in his own right. He saw Vietnam

principally as a danger to that goal ... The war in Vietnam was not lost in the field, nor was it lost on the front pages of *The New York Times* or on the college campuses. It was lost in Washington, DC, even before Americans assumed sole responsibility for the fighting in 1965 and even before they realized the country was at war; ... The disaster in Vietnam was not the result of impersonal forces but a uniquely human failure, the responsibility for which was shared by President Johnson and his principal military and civilian advisers. (McMaster, 1997, pp. 322, 326, 333–34)

At some point in 1966, McNamara began to develop grave doubts about the ability of the United States to bring the war in Vietnam to a successful conclusion; in February 1968, just a month after the launching of the Tet offensive, he stepped down. Privately, he had reached the conclusion that the war in Vietnam could not be won. Clark Clifford replaced him as secretary of defense, and one of his first actions was to consult a small group of high-level former government officials, known as the 'Wise Men'. In a major turning point, this group offered Clifford the recommendation that the United States should begin the process of disengagement. Westmoreland's post-Tet request for a further 206,000 additional troops was met with approval for only 13,500 more men.

To this day McNamara's role remains highly controversial. How much was he to blame for what went wrong? Should he have expressed his doubts more emphatically, and at an earlier date? Does he deserve credit for eventually reaching the conclusion he did, and also for subsequently having the courage to admit that he was wrong? Thirty years after the United States entered the war in Vietnam, Robert S. McNamara described in his work *In Retrospect: The Tragedy and Lessons of Vietnam* some of the fundamental mistakes he had personally made:

I had never visited Indochina, nor did I understand or appreciate its history, language, culture or values ... We also totally underestimated the nationalist aspect of Ho Chi Minh's movement. We saw him first as a Communist and only second as a Vietnamese nationalist ... We failed to analyze our assumptions critically, then or later. The foundations of our decision making were gravely flawed. (McNamara, 1995, p. 33)

McNamara's willingness to honestly admit his own mistakes gained him the respect of some but not all reviewers of his work. In the words of Richard Rusk, writing in the *Washington Post* in April 1995:

Of that small circle who made Vietnam policy in the 60's, only one was able to stare into the abyss, challenge his own assumptions and confront that horrible question: 'What if I am wrong?'
    That man was Robert McNamara. He may have been weak in conversion, irresolute in pressing his doubts. But a shattered Bob McNamara did try to change policy. He lost that argument within the administration, out of public view, and resigned. (In McNamara, 1995, p. 451)

Richard Harwood, also writing in the *Washington Post* in April 1995, offered these remarks:

The punishment of Robert McNamara for his role in the Vietnam War has begun anew with the publication of his apologetic memoirs. 'We were wrong, terribly wrong,' he tells us now. On the talk shows the 'war criminal' charge is heard. In other quarters 'moral condemnation' is proposed. *The New York Times*, in a scathing editorial, 'Mr. McNamara's War,' writes of 'how fate dispensed rewards and punishment for [his] thousand days of error. Three million Vietnamese died. Fifty-eight thousand Americans got to come home in body bags. Mr. McNamara ... got a sinecure at the World Bank and summers at the Vineyard.' Mickey Kaus in the New Republic asks: 'Has any single American of this century done more harm than Robert McNamara?'

But to lay all of this heavy burden on McNamara's frail shoulders too easily lets a lot of us, both living and dead, off the hook. He did not single-handedly make the war. It was the American Establishment – political, military, journalistic and academic – that wrote the script ... A virtually unanimous consensus supported the judgment that the war had to be fought. That judgment was strongly supported by the American people as well. (In McNamara, 1995, p. 387)

10.18 The Tet offensive, 1968

If McNamara's doubts about whether the war in Vietnam could ever be won had reached the surface by 1967, then many of his colleagues were to come to similar conclusions in 1968. The reason for this can be expressed in one word – Tet. No one military event had a more direct bearing on perception of the Vietnam War than the Tet (New Year) offensive of 31 January 1968. For months, the American people had been given the impression by their government that there was light at the end of the tunnel. Then, in a stunning development, the North Vietnamese launched a sudden and totally unexpected assault on every major town and city in South Vietnam, including the capital, Saigon. The scale of the offensive showed that despite America's best efforts the Vietnamese were still able to carry out operations on a massive scale.

Historians are in agreement that the Tet offensive was a highly significant episode in the Vietnam War; however, the precise nature of its impact remains highly controversial. The traditional view has been that although it was a military victory for the United States, this was totally overshadowed by the psychological triumph achieved by the North Vietnamese. The original aims of the offensive are set out in the following extract drawn up by the North Vietnamese in Hanoi at the end of 1967.

The aims of the Tet offensive

After several deceptive moves militarily and diplomatically, on New Year's Eve of the lunar calendar, 31 January 1968, the general offensive and general uprisings, or the Tet offensive began. The VWP (Vietnam Workers' Party) Central Committee Resolution of

December 1967 had set the objectives for a decisive victory through the general offensive and general uprisings:

- 'To break down the bulk of the puppet troops, topple the puppet administration at all levels, and take power into the hands of the people.'
- 'To destroy the major part of the US forces and their war material and render them unable to fulfil their political and military duties in Vietnam.'
- 'On this basis, to break the US will of aggression, force it to accept defeat in the south, and put an end to all acts of war against the north. With this, we will achieve the immediate objectives of our revolution – independence, democracy, peace and neutrality for the south – and we can proceed to national reunification.'

Source: Nguyen Vu Tung, 'Hanoi's Search for an Effective Strategy,' from Peter Lowe (ed.), *The Vietnam War* (Macmillan Press Ltd 1998), p. 48.

The senior American soldier in Vietnam, General Westmoreland was eager to deny that the Tet offensive represented anything other than a major defeat for the North Vietnamese, claiming in 1968 that their well-laid plans had failed and that the enemy's poor strategy had led to heavy casualties. With the passage of so much time a clearer perspective may now be possible. David L. Anderson sees things very differently to General Westmoreland:

Many writers have advanced a 'stab in the back argument', which alleges that the pessimistic reporting and analysis of the Tet fighting turned a military success into psychological defeat. Actually, Tet was a military as well as psychological defeat from which the US effort to impose its power on Vietnam never fully recovered. Despite Westmoreland's public confidence, military leaders privately acknowledged that the enemy offensive exposed serious weaknesses in the American war effort. The massive American air and ground war had not deterred infiltration into the South. The Tet combat had weakened the ranks of the Viet Cong, but the PAVN [People's Army of North Vietnam] could and would continue to pour a virtually limitless supply of men into the [Republic of Vietnam] RVN. US and ARVN losses had been high, and the fighting generated thousands of refugees, further destabilising the South. In an 'eyes only' message to Westmoreland on 1 March, Army Chief of Staff General Harold K. Johnson concluded: 'We suffered a loss, there can be no doubt about it.' (In Lowe, 1998, p. 108)

Ngo Vinh Long measures the impact of Tet by the diplomatic consequences that followed:

Although the Tet Offensive did not overthrow the Saigon government it was successful in accomplishing its main objective of forcing the United States to de-escalate the war in the North and to begin negotiations. On 1 November 1968, President Johnson ordered the unconditional cessation of the bombing of North Vietnam and announced a four-party conference with the participation of NLF (National Liberation Front) and Saigon representatives. This negotiation process would eventually lead to a peace agreement based on NLF terms in January 1973. (In Lowe, 1998, p. 80)

10.19 President Johnson's decision not to stand for re-election, 1968

Perhaps most telling of all in appreciating the impact of the Tet offensive is the response of the president himself. The anguish of the war took a huge personal toll on Johnson. Photographs taken at his desk in the Oval Office in 1968 just three years after the war had begun show how much he had aged. To his advisers the president looked tired. The super-human energy he had displayed since taking up office had waned. However, the news he broke to the American people in a televised address to the nation on 31 March 1968 still came as a complete surprise:

> Tonight I want to speak to you of peace in Vietnam and Southeast Asia ... I am taking the first step to de-escalate the conflict. Tonight I have ordered our aircraft and our naval vessels to make no attacks on North Vietnam, except in the area of the Demilitarized Zone ... I call upon President Ho Chi Minh to respond positively and favorably to this new step of peace ... This country's ultimate strength lies in the unity of our people. There is division in the American house now. There is divisiveness among us all tonight. And holding the trust that is mine, as President of all the people, I cannot disregard the peril to the progress of the American people and the hope and prospect of peace for all people. With America's sons in the fields far away, with America's future under challenge right here at home ... I do not believe that I should devote an hour or a day of my time to any personal partisan causes ... Accordingly, I shall not seek, and will not accept, the nomination of my party for another term as your President. (LBJ Presidential Library, online)

It was a momentous speech by any standards. The self-confident, even brash leader who had tried to build a Great Society and fight a victorious war in Vietnam had now reached the personal decision that he could no longer shoulder the burden of these two conflicting enterprises. For the Democratic Party it would be hard to say that Johnson's term of office was coming to a successful conclusion. As the president himself had admitted, his country was now bitterly divided. To the North Vietnamese perhaps, the speech sent a signal that American commitment to the war was visibly waning. To the American soldiers in Vietnam it must have raised questions about how long they would be asked to remain in the field and whether their mission was to be curtailed. The election of November 1968 resulted in a landmark victory for the Republican candidate, Richard Nixon. If the people of Vietnam believed that the bombing raids they had endured for so long were about to come to an end, they were sadly mistaken. Nixon had entered the Oval Office.

Further reading

Beschloss M.R., *Taking Charge: The Johnson White House Tapes, 1963–1964* (New York: Simon & Schuster 1997).

Caro R.A., *The Years of Lyndon Johnson: Volume 1: The Path to Power* (New York: Vintage 1983).

Caro R.A., *The Years of Lyndon Johnson: Volume 4: The Passage of Power* (London: The Bodley Head 2014).

Dallek R., *Flawed Giant: Lyndon Johnson and his Times 1961–1973* (New York: Oxford University Press 1998).

Edelman B. (ed.), *Dear America: Letters Home from Vietnam* (New York: Simon & Schuster 1985).

Herring G.C., *America's Longest War: The United States and Vietnam 1950–1975* (New York: John Wiley and Sons 1979).

Jones M.A., *The Limits of Liberty: American History 1607–1992* (New York: Oxford University Press 1995).

Karnow S., *Vietnam: A History The First Complete Account of Vietnam at War* (London: Century Hutchinson 1985).

Kearns Goodwin D., *Lyndon Johnson and the American Dream* (New York: St Martin's Griffin Press 1991).

Lowe P. (ed.), *The Vietnam War* (Basingstoke: Macmillan Press Ltd 1998).

McMaster H.R., *Dereliction of Duty: Lyndon Johnson, Robert McNamara, The Joint Chiefs of Staff, and the Lies that Led to Vietnam* (New York: Harper Collins 1997).

McNamara R.S., *In Retrospect: The Tragedy and Lessons of Vietnam* (New York: Vintage Books 1995).

Purdum T.S., *An Idea Whose Time Has Come: Two Presidents, Two Parties, and the Battle for the Civil Rights Act of 1964* (New York: Picador 2014).

Reynolds D., *America, Empire of Liberty: A New History* (London: Allen Lane 2009).

Schulman B.J., *Lyndon B. Johnson and American Liberalism, A Brief Biography with Documents* (Boston: Bedford Books 1995).

Updegrove M.K., *Indomitable Will: LBJ in the Presidency* (New York: Crown Publishers 2012).

Ward G. C. & Burns K., The Vietnam War: An Intimate History (New York: Alfred A. Knopf 2007).

Zelizer J.E., *The Fierce Urgency of Now: Lyndon Johnson, Congress and the Battle for the Great Society* (New York: Penguin Press 2015).

Online resources

LBJ Presidential Library: www.lbjlibrary.org, last accessed in 2018.

▮ ▾ ▮▮ The shift to the right

11.1 Introduction

There was probably no man who desired the power of the presidency more avidly than Richard Nixon and yet who experienced so much trauma when he finally reached the White House. During his 2,026 days in office, the 37th President was prepared to abuse power, sanction acts of sheer criminality and then lie and ask others to do the same in the obstruction of justice. While he had always emphasised his support for law and order, when he reached the highest office he worked to undermine it. Perhaps the defining trait of his administration was the emergence of an 'imperial presidency' with immense power concentrated in the hands of the chief executive and his closest aides. Nixon's complex character continues to command attention. His ability, intelligence, work ethic and political skill are not in doubt.

Early in his career Nixon established himself as a formidable opponent, perfectly capturing the anxiety felt by many Americans as their country emerged from World War II and entered the Cold War. By his early forties he had been elected to the House, the Senate and twice to the vice presidency of the United States. Yet at the same time Nixon's obsession with secrecy and power brought a darker side to the presidency than any of his predecessors. His simmering sense of rage against his enemies led him to sanction illegal wiretapping, break-ins and cover-ups. The Internal Revenue Service (IRS), FBI and CIA were all misused for political purposes. Unprecedented power was amassed in Nixon's Oval Office.

Stanley I. Kutler presents this appraisal of Nixon:

> Richard Nixon was a very complicated man. Essentially a loner, he was at the same time the most public of public men. Few leaders have ... [e]xposed themselves to such scrutiny as did Richard Nixon. His countless appearances through almost five decades on the public stage, and numerous writings, gave him extraordinary visibility, with all the inherent advantages – and risks. Whether it was the perspiration on his upper lip that betrayed his innate uneasiness with us, the maudlin sentimentality he invoked in his 'Checkers' speech, the pride he displayed at his daughter's wedding, the unbounded joy of his triumphs and the unspeakable burden of his dramatic defeats – this man exposed his multifaceted humanity in extraordinary, vivid ways. (Kutler, 1997, p. xix)

Nixon's background

A brief glance at Richard's childhood indicates that some of these character traits were clearly visible in his early years. He was born in the small, homespun town of Yorba

Linda, California, in 1913. His mother, Hannah, a very private person, was of Quaker stock; his father, Frank, a farmhand, was temperamental and moody. A small farm, with lemon trees, and land that was dusty and arid, made it difficult to prosper. Nixon biographer John A. Farrell says that as Richard grew up 'the two sides clashed and swirled: the good Quaker son, trying to win Hannah's love, against Frank's battling, angry boy' (Farrell, 2017, p. 50). At school, he worked hard, read prodigiously, absorbed knowledge and sought praise. But family life had tragedy in store when Richard's little brother, Arthur, whom he doted upon, died in 1925 after a short illness. Richard was only 12 years old but tried to deal with the family bereavement as stoically as possible. Just two years later, Harold, the oldest of the brothers, became ill with symptoms of tuberculosis. He would suffer for six years before he too, passed away.

So Richard had to deal with terrible loss and, at the same time, economic hardship. The soil of Yorba Linda could not sustain citrus fruit and the lemon ranch project had to be abandoned in 1922. Frank opened a gas station with a small store instead. Success in the new business did not improve Frank's mood and he was frequently angry or involved in petty, never-forgotten, disputes. Tellingly, Farrell notes:

> his legacy to Richard was a distinct brand of Republicanism, built upon resentment of the big forces – crooked Business or profligate Government – that exploited hard-pressed common folk. Among his fancied banes were big chain stores, owned by Jews, out to crush small operators like the Nixons. (Farrell, 2017, p. 55)

Shrouded in raw grief, driven by the need for success and praise, endowed with an intense work ethic and with an increasing interest in history and politics, Richard excelled academically at Fullerton High School but was strikingly awkward and socially isolated. He was clearly talented and the opportunity of a scholarship to outstanding universities such as Harvard and Yale was offered to him. Sadly, by now, America was facing the worst depression in its history and the family decided that they could not afford the expense of sending Richard to the East. Instead, in the fall of 1930 he enrolled at the homely, somewhat less distinguished, Whittier College, ten miles from his birthplace. Further ingredients of Nixon's outlook were being put in place: relentless energy and drive coupled with resentment, a bitter sense of the haves and the have-nots, an acute belief that life was not fair and a capacity for feeling sorry for himself. On the sports field, Nixon lacked the size or athleticism to excel but his determination to make the college football team meant that he spent a disproportionate amount of time being pummelled and getting up off the floor: further Nixon characteristics.

Things picked up for Nixon when he was admitted to Duke University where, with his usual application, he flung himself into the study of law. He worked hard but was often unsettled, having to do mundane jobs in his spare time to pay his way. Law graduates from America's Ivy League found the transition to high-flying firms in Manhattan to be straightforward, but at that time those graduating from Duke found the going less clear-cut. It fitted with Nixon's sense of resentment that he was unable to secure a glamorous position and instead headed back to Whittier where he joined a local firm, in Farrell's words, 'helping farmers draft their wills' (Farrell, 2017, p. 70). In 1938 he met and fell in love with Pat, his future wife. Finally, in 1940, Nixon secured a post he felt happier with when he joined the newly formed Office of Price Administration in Washington DC. War was now imminent and while his Quaker background and government position could have been used to steer away from the conflict, Nixon was more than willing to serve his country. Patriotism was a further Nixon character trait.

Military service and political career

Nixon undertook naval officer training in 1942 and was sent to the South Pacific in 1943. He served with genuine bravery and, like all service men there, witnessed terrible suffering and came close to serious harm. Nixon was an officer and endeared himself to his men with his personal valour. He escaped the war with nothing more serious than a nasty fungal infection. Charged with responsibilities in the nation's complex transition from war to peace, there were plenty of career paths and opportunities available. One he had not anticipated was a suggestion from a well-placed banker from his home town of Whittier that he consider running for Congress against Jerry Voorhis, a long-standing Democratic incumbent. Nixon's looks, college-developed skills in debate, academic record and military service had begun to make an impression. The phrase that stands out, from the ensuing correspondence over whether Nixon would take up the challenge, was when he promised his sponsor that he would 'tear [his opponent] to pieces' (Farrell, 2017, p. 12). Even more worrying was his note to himself, scribbled on the yellow legal pads that he would one day use in the Oval Office, to 'set up spies' in his opponents' 'camp' (Farrell, 2017, p. 17). Finally, even at this first electoral hurdle, Nixon quickly decided in the emerging Cold War climate that falsely defining his opponent as being further left than was actually the case was a trick that, in this instance, he was happy to employ.

1946–50 (Two consecutive terms in the House of Representatives)

A resounding victory followed in November 1946 and Nixon entered the House of Representatives at the same time as his future rival, John F. Kennedy. In his first speech in Congress in February 1947 Nixon criticised the 'foreign-directed conspiracy' whose 'aim and purpose was to undermine and destroy the government of the United States' (Farrell, 2017, p. 95). The press in the nation's capital recognised political talent when they saw it, describing Nixon as: 'Serious and energetic, he is indicative of the change in political trends, the increasing emphasis on youth and a genuine desire to serve the country. If he bears out his promise he will go far.' (Farrell, 2017, p. 42) It was no surprise to anyone when he easily secured re-election two years later.

Three factors were instrumental in Nixon's rapid rise. The first was the war. Military service was everything to Nixon's fledgling career. The second was the Cold War. Nixon was skilled in using the mood of McCarthyism to define his opponents and to further himself. His personal impact on the House Un-American Activities Committee was substantial. Farrell demonstrates that in Nixon's initial work with the HUAC 'he steered clear of the committee's most abusive practices', leading the respected *New York Times* to conclude that he 'is at pains to try and keep the committee on a legally sound path and has a considerable reputation for fairness to witnesses' (Farrell, 2017, p. 101). At the same time, he was not above leaking confidential HUAC files to conservative supporters and at times the actions swirling around him on the committee were less than honourable.

The Hiss trial, 1949–50

Above all, though, it was the sensational trial of Alger Hiss, a former high-ranking State Department official, which brought Nixon to national attention. Hiss, a highly qualified, Ivy League-educated diplomat, was so well regarded that he had been part of Roosevelt's personal delegation at the crucial Yalta Conference of February 1945. When Hiss was accused in 1948 of passing sensitive material to the Russians, the nation, in the grip of McCarthyism, was transfixed. The Hiss case, the first House hearing to be televised, brought Nixon's brooding intensity to the fore. Hiss denied the allegations but was prosecuted for perjury. The first trial in July 1949 was eventually declared a mistrial but at a second hearing in early 1950 he was convicted and imprisoned. Nixon's desperation to secure a guilty verdict and overwhelming desire to win positive headlines divided opinion. To some he was strong-jawed, tenacious, deeply patriotic and simply defending his nation against the 'Red Menace'. Alternatively, he could be seen as a stop-at-nothing, unscrupulous demagogue who would pursue the accused like a hellhound as long as it served his ambitions.

The Senate, 1950

Nixon's notable work on the Taft–Hartley bill and his bipartisan support for the Marshall Plan, both accomplished when he was still new to the workings of the Capitol, signalled that he was now close to the front rank of the Republican Party. Drive, intellect, and an instinctive understanding of the impact of the Cold War on the public mood had combined to form a consummately gifted politician. Following Voorhis and Hiss, the next person to stand in Nixon's way was Helen Douglas, a Democratic congresswoman from the rapidly growing and crucially important state of California. As the 1950 campaign for the Senate seat became more intense the Nixon team increasingly characterised their opponent as the 'pink lady'. In the autumn the Nixon campaign said that 'the contest centers on ... Communism.' Nixon accused Douglas of a failed policy of appeasement that had led to the outbreak of war in Korea and stated: 'If there is a smear involved, let it be remembered that the record itself is doing the smearing. Mrs. Douglas made that record. I didn't.' (Farrell, 2017, pp. 153–54) The win, when it came, was divisive. For now, Nixon's burgeoning ambition was sated and Republicans celebrated his tough, no-holds barred approach, which seemed to deliver results. To the liberal left, Nixon was an unprincipled, even malicious demagogue, 'Tricky Dick'.

The vice-presidential campaign of 1952

Christopher Matthews provides this summary of Nixon's meteoric rise:

> During the early years, Nixon was the man to beat. He was the best politician of his time, articulating more ably than anyone else the nervous mood of post-World War

II America. By the age of forty-three, he had been elected to the House, the Senate, and twice to the vice presidency of the United States. Even the respected liberal columnist Murray Kempton called the 1950s the 'Nixon decade'. (Matthews, 1996, p. 15)

When, in 1952, Herbert Brownell Jr told Dwight D. Eisenhower that his advisers had selected Richard M. Nixon as his running mate, the General readily concurred. Ike saw in Nixon a young, talented politician who, like himself, was a strong foe of communism and had distinguished himself as a congressman in 1948 by his pursuit of Alger Hiss, later shown to have spied for the Soviet Union. Eisenhower would come to value Nixon's political insight and his ability to connect with his Republican constituency. Not yet 40 years old at the time he was nominated, Nixon saw his place on the 1952 ticket as a priceless opportunity, and he never lost his determination to make the most of it.

Against the backdrop of the unpopular war in Korea and McCarthyism at home, the Eisenhower–Nixon ticket looked ready to cruise to victory. But in his short career Nixon had already alienated many observers and made plenty of enemies. From Nixon's perspective, those enemies coalesced around the East Coast establishment, the Ivy League universities, the State Department and the liberal press. Within days of securing his place on the Eisenhower ticket, rumours of financial impropriety began to circulate. An expenses fund, created by his backers, lay at the heart of the potential scandal and stories of lavish spending, including a mink coat for his wife Patricia, began to appear in the press. This was damaging because Nixon had nailed his flag to the issue of public integrity.

The 'Checkers' speech, 1952

Amid calls for Nixon to be dropped from the ticket and with Eisenhower privately considering a replacement, it was decided that the candidate should give a televised speech to the nation in order to clear his name. On 23 September 1952, with his career hanging in the balance, Nixon made the speech of his life, 'as a candidate for the Vice Presidency, and as a man whose honesty and integrity has been questioned'. Nixon gave details of his financial affairs and stated that 'not one cent of the $18,000' raised as a fund by his supporters 'ever went to me for my personal use'. He spelt out his humble background, the 'modest circumstances ... the grocery store ... my mother and dad had five boys and we all worked in the store'. Every item of Nixon's personal finances was placed before the American public and then the words that captured attention:

> It isn't very much. But Pat and I have the satisfaction that every dime that we've got is honestly ours. I should say this, that Pat doesn't have a mink coat. But she does have a respectable Republican cloth coat, and I always tell her she'd look good in anything.
>
> One other thing, I probably should tell you, because if I don't they'll probably be saying this about me, too. We did get something, a gift after the election. A man down in Texas heard Pat on the radio mention the fact that our two youngsters would like to have a dog. And believe it or not, the day before we left on this campaign trip we got a message from Union Station in Baltimore, saying they had a package for us. We went down to get it. You know what it was? It was a little cocker spaniel dog, in a

crate that he had sent all the way from Texas, black and white, spotted, and our little girl Tricia, the six year old, named it Checkers. And you know, the kids, like all kids, love the dog, and I just want to say this, right now, that regardless of what they say about it, we're gonna keep it. (In Farrell, 2017, pp. 192–94)

Corny, maudlin in the extreme, the speech was spectacularly well-received by enough of the American public to convince Eisenhower that Nixon was the ideal election partner. Farrell remarks that 'in one half hour of television, Richard Nixon had done more than save his career, he had reset the calculus of American politics ... Nixon's speech added impetus to the Roosevelt coalition's unravelling. A man and a moment had arrived, together ...' The sophisticates ... sneer,' wrote columnist Robert Ruark, but Nixon's speech

> came closer to humanizing the Republican Party than anything that has happened in my memory ... Tuesday night the nation saw a little man, squirming his way out of a dilemma, and laying bare his most private hopes, fears and liabilities. This time the common man was a Republican. (Farrell, 2017, pp. 198–99)

The pair swept to an emphatic victory, winning all bar nine states, with some new success in the South and the fracturing of the Democratic bloc in the North. It was a personal triumph for Eisenhower, and for Nixon it would mean two terms as vice president, gaining vital experience for what was to come. Fate had decreed that his presidential race would be against a man of similar youth, proud military service and who had entered the House of Representatives at exactly the same time. Kennedy vs Nixon would be one of the most compelling presidential races of all time.

Note: Nixon's vice presidency is covered in Chapter 8. His election defeat of 1960 is covered in Chapter 9.

11.2 The election of 1968

Nixon looked back at his narrow defeat of 1960 almost in awe of the 'dirty tricks' the other side had used against him. As a master of the political black arts it still seems remarkable to hear Nixon complain.

> I had been through some pretty tough campaigns in the past, but compared to the others, going into the 1960 campaign was like moving from the minor to the major leagues. I had an efficient, well-financed and highly motivated organization. But we faced an organization that had equal dedication and unlimited money that was led by the most ruthless group of political operatives ever mobilized for a presidential campaign. Kennedy's organization approached dirty tricks with a roguish relish and carried them off with an insouciance that captivated many politicians and overcame the critical faculties of many reporters. The way the Kennedys played politics and the way the media let them get away with it left me angry and frustrated. (In Matthews, 1996, pp. 182–83)

Nixon's capacity to pick himself up from the floor had been there since his college football hidings and so it was not long before he had his sights on another campaign. As a native of California, the state's gubernatorial election of 1962 held obvious appeal.

California was a hugely important prize and would act as a presidential springboard for Ronald Reagan in the future. For now, Nixon's attention focused on the relatively popular but apparently beatable Democratic incumbent Pat Brown. Nixon had carried California in the 1960 presidential race, so it seemed an eminently winnable seat. He was therefore devastated when an increasingly bitter campaign ended in his second defeat in two years.

The beaten candidate could not conceal his anger. In a remarkable, impromptu set of remarks at a press conference Nixon said:

> Now that all the members of the press are so delighted that I have lost, I'd like to make a statement of my own … you don't have Nixon to kick around anymore, because, gentlemen, this is my last press conference. (In Farrell, 2017, p. 310)

It appeared that Nixon would be true to his word when he melted into the background as his party lurched to the right. In 1964 the Republican candidate Barry Goldwater was heavily beaten in LBJ's landslide victory. Goldwater was an extreme candidate and his positions, particularly on foreign policy and the atomic bomb, were badly exposed during a poor campaign. This meant that the stage was set for a relatively more moderate candidate to lead the Republicans back from the political wilderness. That man, remarkably, was Richard Nixon.

The presidential election campaign of 1968, the most highly charged in decades, was dominated by the issue of Vietnam. When the Republican Party Convention took place at Miami Beach, Florida, the party nominated Richard M. Nixon on the first ballot, with Nelson Rockefeller in second place and future president Ronald Reagan a distant third. Nixon selected Spiro Theodore Agnew, the conservative Governor of Maryland, as his running mate with the intention of bolstering the Republican campaign in the South, where George Wallace, the Democratic Governor of Alabama, was running as an independent candidate on a pro-segregation ticket in the name of the American Independent Party. Wallace announced his intention to stand in February 1968. His fervent opposition to desegregation made him a potentially potent electoral force in the South. Wallace also adopted an aggressive campaign style; with outspoken attacks on the Great Society with its welfare mothers, he derided liberals, intellectuals, hippies, feminists and left-wingers. These targets struck a chord in working-class areas in the North and among blue-collar workers. Wallace's emphasis on returning 'law and order' to the streets further broadened his appeal.

However, the selection of General Curtis LeMay as his running mate was a serious tactical error. LeMay did not try to conceal his enthusiasm for air power, and even nuclear weapons; when he had served as air force chief of staff, he had threatened to 'bomb North Vietnam back into the Stone Age' (Hersh, 1983, p. 575). Wallace's lack of judgement in selecting such an extreme running mate underlined the fact that, despite his personal charisma, he remained a third-party candidate.

The death of Robert Kennedy

Whereas the Republicans had been able to reach a clear-cut decision, the search for the Democratic Party candidate opened deep internal divisions. The faction of the party which supported peace produced two candidates – Eugene McCarthy, who initially exposed the president's vulnerability, and Robert Kennedy, who entered the race when it was clear that Johnson could be beaten. The first sign that the election campaign was to carry enormous stakes came when McCarthy, campaigning on an anti-war ticket, came desperately close to defeating President Johnson in the New Hampshire primary. This demonstration of public opinion contributed to Johnson's decision of March 1968 that the time had come to step down. Only after the president had been pushed so close in New Hampshire did Kennedy decide he could beat Johnson. Kennedy was an able and charismatic figure, carrying a deep personal animosity towards Johnson that dated back to his brother's assassination in 1963. By 1968, he was profoundly uneasy about the way in which Johnson had conducted the war. Kennedy and McCarthy fought out a tight contest which reached its conclusion when Kennedy achieved a narrow victory over his rival in the California primary of 5th June 1968.

Yet on the same day, an Arab nationalist, Sirhan Sirhan, gunned down Kennedy. Following hard on the heels of the murder of Martin Luther King Jr, the latest atrocity added to the sense of 1968 as a succession of traumatic events. In the words of James T. Patterson: 'The death of Robert Kennedy further smashed the already beleaguered forces of American liberalism and devastated people who had looked to him as the only remaining hope to heal a fragmented nation.' (Patterson, 1996, p. 693)

Hubert Humphrey and the Democratic Convention of 1968

McCarthy failed to build further support in the wake of Kennedy's death and the initiative passed to Johnson's vice president and the approved candidate of the party hierarchy, Hubert Humphrey.

Humphrey defended Johnson's handling of the war but the division within the party erupted at the Democratic Convention in Chicago in August. Although Humphrey was nominated on the first ballot, it was the scenes on the streets outside the convention hall that received the most attention. The Mayor of Chicago, Richard Daley, despised anti-war protestors and by the time the convention began he had deployed 12,000 police who were aware of his hostility towards the students and young anti-war protestors coming to his city. The violent scenes, with the police using tear gas and clubs without restraint, shocked a nation that was already reeling from the terrible events that had already marked 1968 as the most traumatic year since 1963.

The damaging comments of LeMay and the riots at the Democratic Convention seemed to hand the election to the untroubled campaign run by Nixon. His team produced a series of highly effective 60-second commercials, with Nixon's voice promising to bring an end to the war, set against film clips of war footage. However, events took a further dramatic turn when Humphrey's campaign received a last-minute boost on the eve of the election. Johnson's announcement in October of a total halt to the bombing of North Vietnam seemed to undermine Republican campaign pledges and encouraged Humphrey to campaign energetically to the finish. Some historians now claim that Nixon did his best to undermine the peace talks by encouraging the Thieu regime in South Vietnam not to attend the peace talks in Paris because they would get a better deal under Nixon than Johnson. The crucial point was that the peace talks served to make the election much closer than it might have been (Table 11.1).

Table 11.1   The result of the 1968 presidential election

Candidate	Party	Electoral College votes	Popular votes
Richard M. Nixon (California)	Republican	301	31,710,470
Hubert H. Humphrey (Minnesota)	Democratic	191	30,898,055
George C. Wallace (Alabama)	American Independence Party	46	9,446,167

Note: Nixon received 55.9% of the Electoral College votes (301 votes, 32 states); Humphrey received 33.5% (191 votes, 13 states and DC); Wallace received 8.5% (46 votes, 5 states)

PRESIDENTIAL PROFILE

Richard Milhous Nixon

37th President of the United States (1969–74)
Born: 9 January 1913
Birthplace: Yorba Linda, California
Died: 22 April 1994, aged 81; buried at Yorba Linda, California
Education: Whittier College
Political Party: Republican
State: California
Occupation before presidency: Lawyer
Previous government service: Member US House of Representatives (1946);
    US Senator (1950); 91st–93rd Congresses
Age at inauguration: 53
Dates of office: 20 January 1969–9 August 1974
Election: November 1968 and 1972
Vice president: Spiro Theodore Agnew
Length of term: 5 years, 201 days

11.3 The Nixon Administration and the end of the Great Society

Nixon's political outlook when he became president was undoubtedly less dogmatic than it had been when he had served as Eisenhower's vice president. While he empha-sised his opposition to drug abuse and sexual permissiveness, and placed an onus on law and order, the wishes of the 'silent majority' and American values, the more stri-dent element of his character seemed less evident. Nevertheless, he was convinced that the 'big government' solution represented by the Great Society was not the way forward. As Nixon entered the White House, several factors, many of them beyond his control, came together to ensure that the Great Society did not just come to an end but was systematically unravelled. Bruce Schulman indicates some of the social and economic problems which acted as a powerful backdrop in the transition from Johnson to Nixon:

> The economic turmoil of the late 1960s did not merely discredit the New Economics and its liberal adherents in the White House. It brought real uncertainty and hardship to many Americans; wages could not keep up with gains in prices, inflation ate away the value of savings and fixed incomes. At the same time, long-term economic trends, most of them out of control of the White House, signalled an end to the long period of unprecedented prosperity that had blessed the United States for a generation ... by 1969, the rest of the world was beginning to catch up. The United States, to be sure, remained the world's largest, most productive, richest economy, but its lead had dwindled, its unchallenged dominance eroded. Japan passed the United States as the world's fastest-growing national economy, the European Economic Community became the world's largest economic entity, and America's share of world trade declined. (Schulman, 1995, p. 159)

Americans had become accustomed to a steady increase in their standard of living. As the 1960s came to an end, with the depressing shadow of Vietnam still hanging over them, the uncertainties raised by high inflation, strong competition from overseas, rising unemployment, higher income taxes and a general sense of economic difficulty meant that American society now faced some fairly profound adjustments. In this climate many middle-class Americans came not just to question but to actually resent the 'big spending, big government' programmes that had now become so strongly tied to the Democratic Party. The public knew that the Democrats had spent vast sums of money on programmes such as the War on Poverty. Having invested this money they looked at the inner-city areas where they believed most of the money had been spent and witnessed a combination of simmering racial tension, violent crime, drug abuse and urban decay. A crucial factor in making America turn its back on the Great Society was the alarming rise in crime. The deteriorating situation in the urban ghettos led to an explosion in violent crime, which terrified many middle-class Americans. What was the point of Johnson's huge spending programme if this was its legacy?

Nixon was sympathetic to this outlook. Urging Americans to return to the principles of 'self-help' and 'local control', the president took apart Johnson's social welfare programmes and used the power of the veto to derail incomplete liberal initiatives in areas such as health and education. If the climate of 1964 was right for building a Great Society, then the climate of 1968, with the violent deaths of Martin Luther King Jr and Robert Kennedy, and the uproar at the Democratic Convention, was right for its destruction.

11.4 The Supreme Court

The rapidly changing political landscape was reflected in the new president and also in the new Chief Justice in the Supreme Court. Since 1953, Judge Warren had established a reputation for liberalism in civil rights and the legal system and in relaxed attitudes towards censorship in the arts. Nixon's appointment of Warren's successor suggested that a further blow to liberalism was about to be struck. The new Chief Justice, Warren E. Burger, had established a reputation for taking a tough stance on crime. Surprisingly, the Burger court did not quite fulfil expectations. In particular, the ruling in *Furman* vs *Georgia* (1972) stated that, in the majority of cases, the death penalty was unconstitutional. To Nixon's dismay the Court also moved to legalise abortion in the landmark case of *Roe* vs *Wade* (1973).

The incoming president inherited a challenging economic situation. The war in Vietnam, rising inflation, the cost of the Great Society and increasingly dynamic competition from overseas meant that Nixon found it difficult to restore prosperity. Nixon entered the election year of 1972 with what Jones describes as a 'dismal economic record which included the doubling of unemployment' (Jones, 1995, p. 561).

11.5 The presidential election of 1972

Despite the obvious economic difficulties Nixon was grappling with, the incumbent was nominated on the first ballot in the Republican Party Convention at Miami Beach, Florida. He received 1,347 votes with just one vote against, registered by Paul McCloskey of California. Nixon was almost without parallel in his sense of paranoia yet when the campaign began he was so confident of victory that he was able to leave most of the campaigning to his vice president, Spiro Agnew. The reason for this self-assurance in a politician who generally left nothing to chance was that Nixon knew that the public were by no means ready to return to the Democrats whom they had thrown out just four years earlier. This conviction was reinforced when George Wallace, the right-winger who was probably the Democratic Party's most effective campaigner, was shot and paralysed during the campaign. This opened the door to George S. McGovern, who was very much on the liberal wing of the party. At the Democratic Party Convention, also held at Miami Beach, McGovern was nominated on the first ballot. However, his running mate, Thomas Eagleton, dropped out of the race just 19 days later when it was revealed that he had previously been treated for psychiatric illness. McGovern initially backed Eagleton and then dropped him when he sensed that public support was draining away. Robert Shriver replaced him, but it was already too late for the Democratic Party.

McGovern's proposals on tax and welfare failed to strike a chord with the public mood. His ill-judged comment that he would 'crawl to Hanoi' to secure peace in Vietnam cost him further support. Finally, his liberal view on issues such as abortion and drugs did not endear him to Middle America. The result was a forgone conclusion, and Nixon knew it. The contrast between this victory and the narrow defeat by Kennedy in 1960 could hardly have been more pronounced. The Nixon–Agnew ticket was returned with 47,169,911 votes, more than 60 per cent of the popular vote. The McGovern–Shriver partnership received only 29,170,383 votes. Nixon captured 520 votes in the Electoral College and 49 states. McGovern obtained just 17 Electoral College votes and was successful only in Massachusetts and Washington DC. Despite this massive rejection of McGovern, the Democrats retained their control of the House and gained two more seats in the Senate (Table 11.2).

Table 11.2 The result of the 1972 presidential election

Candidate	Party	Electoral College votes	Popular votes
Richard M. Nixon (California)	Republican	520	47,169,911
George S. McGovern (South Dakota)	Democrat	17	29,170,383
John Hospers (Iowa)	Libertarian	1	

11.6 Watergate

The triumph of the second election victory would turn out to be short lived. Although Nixon found peace in Vietnam, it was not achieved without further suffering in the period between his re-election and the signing of the ceasefire in January 1973. In fact, the Christmas campaign of 1972 saw the Vietnamese exposed to a level of bombing which was unprecedented in its severity. Even this was overshadowed, however, by the scandal which became known as Watergate.

Having lost by the narrowest of margins to Kennedy in 1960 and having defeated Humphrey by a hair's breadth in 1968, Nixon became increasingly obsessed with holding on to presidential power. While he was all too aware of the enormous antipathy towards the Democrat model of big government, and scathing in his assessment of his likely opponents, he was determined that nothing should be left to chance in the run-up to the election in 1972. With this objective in mind, Nixon's former Attorney General John Mitchell organised the Committee to Re-Elect the President (CREEP).

In a sense, much that became so disturbing in the Nixon presidency was not new. The long-term trend of steadily increasing presidential power that was identified under Nixon could be dated back to FDR. The bugging of opponents was not without precedent; both Kennedy and Johnson had resorted to that tactic. They were also prepared to misuse the lawful functions of the FBI and the CIA for political purposes. However, under Nixon bugging, entrapment, smear stories, sabotage and the driving need to 'get' his opponents became central to the very fabric of the presidency. Effectively this moved the administration from questionable methods to sheer criminality.

The Pentagon Papers

Meanwhile in 1971 the leak of the 'Pentagon Papers' to the press – a large amount of explosive material relating to the conduct of the Vietnam War – prompted the White House to create the Special Investigative Unit that became known as the 'Plumbers'. This unit was briefed to 'stop security leaks and to investigate other security matters' (Kutler, 1997, p. 7). Within days of the publication of the 'Pentagon Papers', Nixon advised his closest aides (Haldeman, Ehrlichman and Kissinger) to order a search for classified documents at the Brookings Institution. The release of hitherto secret taped conversations from the Oval Office show Nixon saying, 'Do you remember [the] plan for White House-sponsored break-ins as part of domestic counter-intelligence operations? Implement it ... Godamnit, get in and get those files. Blow the safe and get it.' (Farrell, 2017, p. 425)

The road to Watergate, 1971

Table 11.3   The road to Watergate

1971 February	Nixon and his chief of staff, H.R. Haldeman, installed an improved recording system in the White House. The system was subsequently extended to include the President's Office in the Executive Office building, the presidential retreat at Camp David and the telephone system at the White House and Camp David.
13 June	The *New York Times* featured the first instalment of the 'Pentagon Papers', classified documents leaked by Daniel Ellsberg, a former security official. Within a week the president responded to the leak by creating a secret White House unit to stop future leaks. This group became known as the 'Plumbers'.
1 July	On the tapes, the president condemned the *New York Times* for publishing the 'Pentagon Papers': 'Those sons of bitches are killing me ... We're up against an enemy, a conspiracy. They're using any means. We are going to use any means. Is that clear?' (Kutler, 1997, p. 8)
3 September	Break-in at the California office of Dr Lewis Fielding, the psychiatrist of Daniel Ellsberg, the man who leaked the 'Pentagon Papers' to the *New York Times*.

These activities brought into the orbit of the president bizarre characters such as E. Howard Hunt and G. Gordon Liddy. Endorsed by Charles 'Chuck' Colson, the Special Counsel to the President, as 'good healthy right-wing exuberants', they would become central to the break-in at the Watergate building and the subsequent cover-up. Liddy sought to impress people who would work for him by briefing them at the same time as holding his left hand and forearm over a candle, enduring the burns that followed without expression. Liddy's plans included 'burglary, bugging, and blackmail ... with prostitutes, spy planes, thuggery and kidnapping' (Farrell, 2017, p. 433). Even more damaging was the fact that when Liddy made an elaborate flip-chart presentation of illegal intelligence operations (Operation Gemstone) to senior White House staff, including the Attorney General, he was rebuked merely because of the $1 million which he said his plans would cost (Table 11.3).

Watergate – the break-in, 1972

During May and June 1972, repeated attempts were made by a small group of men working for CREEP to break into the Democratic National Committee (DNC) head-quarters in the Watergate complex in Washington DC. The episode, which would ultimately undo the president's power and see his closest advisers sent to jail, began on an almost comic note with a number of botched attempts to get into the building. On the night of 17 June the police apprehended the burglars; they were indicted for burglary and illegal bugging. The White House Press Secretary Ron Zeigler tried to minimise the event as a 'third-rate burglary'. This line was followed by the president himself in a statement given by Nixon at a press conference on 22 June 1972, in which he emphatically denied any White House involvement in the Watergate incident.

However, the extracts that follow, taken from Nixon's own tapes, which were of course, top secret at this time, show beyond doubt that knowledge of what had taken place extended to the very highest level. In the words of Watergate expert Stanley Kutler:

> What did the President know and when did he know it? ... The answer is conclusive: The President knew virtually everything about Watergate and the imposition of a cover-up, from the beginning. The new tapes painstakingly revealed his repeated manoeuvres to deny that knowledge for more than a year and, in turn, tell us much about the man. (Kutler, 1997, p. xiv)

Tape transcript

June 21, 1972: The President, Haldeman, and Colson, 9.30–10.38 a.m., Oval Office

President Nixon: What's the dope on the Watergate incident? Anything break on that?

Haldeman: No. We talked about that. We don't talk about it at the staff meeting; there's nothing new. The whole question now is, Mitchell's concern is the FBI, the question of how far they're going in the process. He's concerned that, they be turned off, and then they're working on John.

President Nixon: My God, Ehrlichman, are you talking – it's got to be done by Ehrlichman.

Haldeman: Well, we were told yesterday in the discussion on this that we should not go direct to the FBI.

President Nixon: Think of anything.

Haldeman: Start maybe now. John [Mitchell] laid out a scenario ... which would involve this guy Liddy at the committee confessing and talking, moving the thing up to that level, saying 'Yeah, I did it, I did it; I hired these guys, sent them over there, because I thought it would be a good move and build me up in the operation; I'm a little guy.'

President Nixon: Isn't there some way you can get a little better protection, get a little better protection for the White House on that?

Haldeman: The problem is that there are all kinds of other involvements and if they started a fishing thing on this they're going to start picking up tracks.

President Nixon: You mean you'd have Liddy confess and say he did it unauthorized.

Haldeman: Unauthorized.

(Kutler, 1997, p. 50)

The next extract, just 24 hours later, underlines the extent to which within days of the burglary, Nixon was discussing with his most senior aides how to limit the damage and avoid a proper investigation. It also shows the White House directly attempting to impede the FBI.

Tape transcript

June 23, 1972: The President and Haldeman, 10.04–11.39 a.m., Oval Office

Haldeman: Now on the investigation, you know, the Democratic break-in thing, we're back to the ... problem area because the FBI is not under control ... and their investigation is now leading into some productive areas, because they've been able to trace the money, not through the money itself, but through the bank ... And it goes in some directions we don't want it to go ... Mitchell came up with yesterday, and John Dean analysed very carefully last night and concludes – concurs – now with Mitchell's recommendation that the only way to solve this ... is for us to have [Deputy CIA Director Vernon] Walters call Pat Gray [Acting Director of the FBI] and just say, 'Stay the hell out of this ... this is ah, business here we don't want you to go any further on it.'

17 June	Break-in at the Democratic National Committee (DNC) Headquarters in the Watergate building in Washington DC.
29 June	Nixon told Haldeman that their attempts to cover up the break-in are 'a time bomb.'

(Kutler, 1997, p. 67)

Watergate – the cover-up, 1973

Despite the official denials from the White House, a combination of intrepid investigative reporting by the *Washington Post*, the determination of trial judge John J. Sirica to get to the truth, and the decision of one of the burglars to come clean ultimately exposed a much more serious crime. The probings of a Senate investigative committee revealed that senior White House staff, including the President's Chief of Staff H.R. Haldeman and his domestic adviser John Ehrlichman, knew about the break-in and took part in the cover-up. Given the proximity of these figures to the Oval Office, many observers came to doubt Nixon's denials of presidential involvement. The various lines of enquiry in the press and in Congress also revealed for the first time the existence of hours of taped conversations from the Oval Office. Public support, already draining from the president, dwindled further in October 1973 when Nixon dismissed Archibald Cox, the Special Prosecutor who had been appointed by the Attorney General to unravel the whole affair, after he had attempted to subpoena the tapes: Nixon claimed that executive privilege entitled him to hang on to them. He also claimed that issues of national security were at stake (Table 11.4).

Table 11.4   The cover-up, 1973

16 March	Nixon to John Dean: 'You've always got to think in terms of the Presidency and the President should not appear to be hiding and not be forthcoming ... The problem is the cover-up, not the facts ... But you cannot have the President take the rap on a cover-up.' (In Kutler, 1997, p. 232)
17 April	The president set up an investigation into the Watergate break-in and cover-up. He appointed Archibald Cox of the Harvard Law School to head the enquiry; he was replaced by Leon Jaworski on 20 October.
30 April	A distraught Nixon fired his two closest aides Haldeman and Ehrlichman against a background of criminal charges. Nixon now totally exposed in the White House.
16 July	The Senate Select Committee informed that 'there is tape in the Oval Office.'
10 October	Vice President Spiro Agnew resigned in face of charges of tax evasion.

Table 11.5	Resignation of Nixon, 1974
April	Almost 40 hours of Nixon tapes released.
5 August	Nixon accepted the Supreme Court's order in *United States* vs *Nixon* to release transcripts of the 'smoking gun' conversations of 23 June 1972 in which Nixon and Haldeman had discussed the possibility of using the CIA to disrupt the FBI's investigation of the Watergate break-in.
8 August	At 9.00 pm Nixon announced in a nationally televised speech that he would resign the next day. He became the first president to resign the office.
9 August	Nixon's resignation came into effect at noon. The president said goodbye to his staff in the morning and left with his family for San Clemente, California. Nixon did not attend the noon swearing-in of Gerald Ford as the 38th President of the United States.

Watergate – resignation, 1974

In April 1974 a reluctant president finally handed over edited transcripts; the tapes exposed the unattractive side of the president's character to public view: a crude, foul-mouthed, petty and deceitful man. As John Farrell puts it, the President of the United States was 'hip deep in sabotage and surveillance' (Farrell, 2017, p. 433).

In the words of Stanley I. Kutler:

> When the first tapes of less than forty hours were released in April 1974, they provided a rough outline of Nixon's 'abuse of power' and 'obstruction of justice', the principal charges for his proposed impeachment. The charges made his position untenable and forced his resignation in August 1974, less than two years after his magnificent re-election. They mortally wounded Nixon's Presidency and sent many of his associates to jail. (Kutler, 1997, p. xiv)

In July, the Supreme Court ordered the president to hand over all relevant tapes to Leon Jaworski, who had replaced Cox as Special Prosecutor. At the end of the month the House Judiciary Committee recommended three charges of impeachment, based on obstruction of justice, abuse of power and refusal to comply with the committee's subpoenas. On 5 August the president complied with the Supreme Court's order in *United States* vs *Nixon*, and released transcripts of the 'smoking gun' conversations of 23 June 1972. This showed the President, just six days after the break-in, discussing with Haldeman the possibility of using the CIA to thwart the FBI's investigation. Any last vestige of support for the president had now disintegrated. On 9 August 1974, with impeachment charges looming, Nixon became the first man to resign the presidency (Table 11.5).

11.7 The resignation of Nixon

Broadcast by President Nixon, 8 August 1974, 9.00 pm

> Throughout the long and difficult period of Watergate, I felt it was my duty to persevere, to make every possible effort to complete the term of my office to which you elected me. In the past few days, however, it has become evident to me that I no longer have a strong enough political base in the Congress to justify continuing the effort ...

I would have preferred to carry through to the finish whatever the personal agony it would have involved ...

I have never been a quitter. To leave office before my term is completed is opposed to every instinct in my body. But as President I must put the interests of America first. America needs a full-time President and a full-time Congress ...

To continue to fight through the months ahead for my personal vindication would almost totally absorb the time and attention of both the President and Congress in a period when our entire focus should be on the great issues of peace abroad and prosperity without inflation at home.

Therefore, I shall resign the Presidency effective at noon tomorrow.

(Richard Nixon Foundation, online)

Farewell to his staff, 9 August 1974

On Friday 9 August, the shattered president performed his final official duties. He signed a letter addressed to the senior member of the Cabinet, Secretary of State Henry Kissinger. In just 11 words it etched a stunning moment in American history. It said: 'I hereby resign the office of President of the United States.' Then, before a transfixed audience of millions of Americans, he gave his resignation address. An emotional Nixon thanked his staff and told then how proud he was of them. He claimed that 'no one in his administration ever profited at the public expense or the public till ... Mistakes yes, but for personal gain never' (Werth, 2006, pp. 4–9).

Nixon then lurched into rambling recollections of his family:

I remember my old man. I think that they would have called him sort of a little man, a common man. He didn't consider himself that way. You know what he was? He was a streetcar motorman first, and then he was a farmer, and then he had a lemon ranch. It was the poorest lemon ranch in California, I can assure you ... my mother was a saint. And I think of her, two boys dying of tuberculosis, nursing four others in order that she could take care of my older brother.

Nixon moved on to say:

[T]he greatness comes and you are really tested, when you take some knocks, some disappointments, when sadness comes, because only if you have been in the deepest valley can you ever know how magnificent it is to be on the highest mountain. (In Werth, 2006, p. 9)

He was then ushered to the presidential helicopter, Marine One, waiting on the White House lawn. Moments later, he was whisked away to Andrews Air Force Base for the flight home to California. It had been a long and painful road.

All the president's men

Charles Colson
Presidential aide, 1970–73.

John W. Dean III

Counsel to the President, 1970–73

Served 4 years in jail.

John Ehrlichman

Advance man, Nixon for President, 1960

Campaign aide, Nixon presidential campaign, 1968

Assistant to President Nixon for domestic affairs, 1969–73

Served 18 months in jail.

H.R. 'Bob' Haldeman

Advance man, Nixon presidential campaign, 1960

Campaign manager, Nixon for Governor, 1962

Head of advance, Nixon for President, 1968

White House Chief of Staff to President Nixon, 1969–73

Served 18 months in jail.

E. Howard Hunt

Central Intelligence Agency (CIA)

Presidential aide, 1971–72.

G. Gordon Liddy

White House 'plumber'

Led the Watergate break-in

Served 52 months in jail.

11.8 President Ford

PRESIDENTIAL PROFILE

Gerald Rudolph Ford

38th President of the United States (1974–77)

Born: 14 July 1913

Birthplace: Omaha, Nebraska

Died: 26 December 2006, aged 93; Rancho, Mirage, California

Buried: Grand Rapids, Michigan

Education: University of Michigan, Ann Arbor

Political party: Republican

State: Michigan

Occupation before presidency: Lawyer

Previous government service: Member US House of Representatives (1948); member of the Warren Commission enquiry into the assassination of President Kennedy (1963–64); House Minority Leader (1965); vice president to President Nixon after resignation of vice President Agnew (December 1973); sworn in as president after resignation of Nixon

Age at inauguration: 61 years

Dates of office: 9 August 1974–20 January 1977

Vice president: Nelson Rockefeller (New York)

Length of term: 2 years, 5 months

As the former president left, the new one was sworn in, in the most trying of circumstances. Gerald Ford, a long-standing, staunchly conservative, Republican congressman from Grand Rapids, Michigan, became the first man to serve as vice president and then president without facing the electorate. An unassuming man, Ford had worked closely with Nixon since the 1940s and placed loyalty to Nixon at a premium. A former Republican leader in the House of Representatives, he had served as vice president since the resignation of Vice President Agnew, who had stepped down in October 1973 in the light of charges of income tax evasion and extortion from his time as the Governor of Maryland. Responsible and good-natured, it now fell to Ford to restore belief in the highest office. Beyond this, he simply wanted to balance the books and reduce government intervention in the economy and in the wider society. The 61-year-old, caretaker president tried to strike the right chord in his first address to the American people:

> The oath I have taken is the same oath that was taken by George Washington and by every President under the Constitution. But I assume the Presidency under extraordinary circumstances, never before experienced by Americans. This is an hour of history that troubles our minds and hurts our hearts. Therefore, I feel it is my first duty to make an unprecedented compact with my countrymen. Not an inaugural speech, not a fireside chat, not a campaign speech, just a little straight talk among friends. And I intend it to be the first of many. I am acutely aware that you have not elected me as your President by your ballots. So I ask you to confirm me as your President with your prayers ... I have not sought this enormous responsibility, but I will not shirk it ... My fellow Americans, our long national nightmare is over ... Our Constitution works; our great republic is a government of laws and not of men. (In Werth, 2006, pp. 11–12)

In a limited sense the initial challenge facing Ford was relatively straightforward. As a man of obvious integrity he was able to provide a clear contrast with his predecessor. However, the country he now led was badly damaged by the trauma of Watergate. As Americans prepared for the 200th anniversary celebrations of the Constitution, a president left the White House who had lied to his people and besmirched the highest office. A nation that had made glib assumptions about boundless energy supplies now faced an energy crisis. A country that prided itself as a superpower had been humbled in Vietnam. To make matters worse, it would soon become apparent that the new president's personal limitations were painfully clear. Within a month of his appointment, Ford faced his first major controversy and one from which he never really recovered. On Sunday 8 September 1974, he announced that he had decided to grant Nixon a 'full, free and absolute pardon ... for all offenses against the United States which he (Richard Nixon) has committed or may have committed or taken part in during the period of his five and a half years as president' (Werth, 2006, p. 321). While Ford justified his decision as an act of healing, the public reaction was largely unfavourable. The president's press secretary, Jerald terHorst, resigned in protest (Table 11.6).

Gerald Ford

Evidence that the electorate were deeply disenchanted with their elected representatives came in the midterm elections of November 1974. Republican seats in the House

Table 11.6   Key events in the administration of Gerald Ford

11 October 1973	President Nixon offers Gerald Ford the nomination of the vice president, following the resignation of the previous post-holder, Spiro T. Agnew, over charges of income tax evasion.
9 August 1974	Richard Nixon becomes the first man to ever resign the presidency. Gerald Ford is sworn in as the 38th President of the United States.
8 September 1974	Ford grants a 'full, free and absolute pardon' to Nixon. Ford claimed that it was in the country's best interests to bring the Watergate controversy to an end. He said his decision to pardon Nixon was based on the need for 'domestic tranquility'. While the decision was hugely unpopular and Ford's personal approval rating fell dramatically, his use of the presidential pardon under Article II, section 2 of the US Constitution represented an enhancement of presidential power that was beyond Congress or the judicial branch to challenge.
16 September 1974	Ford's administration launches a clemency so that draft evaders could return to US society by performing alternative duties.
15 October 1974	The Federal Elections Campaign Act, the most important attempt to reform campaign finance for 50 years.
11 November 1974	A major swing to the Democrats gives them a majority in both Houses of Congress.
17 November 1974	Ford becomes the first US president to visit Japan.
21 November 1974	Despite Ford's veto, the Freedom of Information Act provides unprecedented access to government records.
4 January 1975	A presidential commission, the 'Rockefeller Commission', is set up to examine abuses by the CIA.
13 January 1975	Ford uses his State of the Union Address to put forward a proposed tax cut of $16 billion.
27 March 1975	The South Vietnamese city of Saigon falls to the North Vietnamese.

of Representatives fell to their lowest level in almost 40 years. The Democrats gained four seats in the Senate. Behind these figures the more worrying trend was that the turnout was only 38 per cent.

Beyond the presidential pardon, Ford was able to find precious little room for manoeuvre in managing the economy. Tension in the Middle East erupted into full-blown war in October 1973. Consequently the oil-exporting Arab states sharply increased their prices and placed an embargo on Israel's allies, most notably the United States. Through the winter of 1973–74 prices at the petrol pumps rose by 50 per cent. A gasoline panic gripped the nation and added to the sense of malaise that had swirled around the country since the Watergate scandal had first unravelled. Facing rising unemployment and economic stagnation in the spring of 1975, Ford had little choice but to jettison his principles as he tried to stimulate growth with a major tax cut that produced only limited results. For the rest of his time in office, Ford merely established a reputation as the most prolific user of the veto since the days of Grover Cleveland in the late nineteenth century. Legislation aimed at job creation, increasing farm prices and promoting social welfare were all obstructed by the White House.

Further disenchantment with the government came with the findings of the Rockefeller Commission, established by President Ford in January 1975, and through the hearings of Congressional Committees on Intelligence. These inquiries revealed that the CIA had supported plots to assassinate foreign political leaders and had infiltrated anti-war groups. The FBI had conducted a campaign to discredit the civil rights leader Martin Luther King Jr and had violated the civil rights of citizens involved in dissident groups. In November 1976, the American people were given their opportunity to express their opinion as to whether the time had come to forgive the Republican Party for the scandal of Watergate.

11.9 The election of 1976

As the primary campaign season began, Gerald Ford surprised many observers by announcing that he would go beyond the caretaker role which many people had assumed was his limit. His desire to secure the nomination was challenged by the growing ascendancy of Ronald Reagan as the foremost right-wing candidate of the party. Reagan had served two terms as Governor of California. His homely style, laconic sense of humour, and above all his yearning for America to regain 'military superiority' and to 'restore America' itself made him an extremely effective communicator. Ford secured a narrow victory over Reagan on the first ballot at the Republican Convention in Kansas City in August 1976. His running mate was Robert (Bob) Dole from Kansas. Four years later, Reagan's time would come.

Meanwhile, on the Democratic side, James Earl Carter (Jimmy Carter) the former Governor of the southern state of Georgia, emerged from a competitive field as the chosen candidate. Carter was nominated on the first ballot at the convention held in New York in July 1976. Carter went against the trend of Southern Democrats with his reputation for a liberal approach towards the race issue, and had the distinct advantage of being patently honest. When he promised 'never to tell a lie to the American people' he seemed sincere. He was far removed from the Washington establishment and this seemed enough to guarantee success. However, under the glare of the national news media, he seemed uncertain and doubts were raised about his ability to fulfil the role of president. Neither candidate was able to stir the public imagination, and after a low-key campaign Carter emerged with a narrow victory in November 1976. A critical factor in tipping the balance was Carter's almost unanimous support among African American voters. This was enough to secure important states, including New York and Mississippi (Table 11.7).

Table 11.7 The result of the 1976 presidential election

Candidate	Party	Electoral College votes	Popular votes
James E. Carter (Georgia)	Democratic	297	40,830,763
Gerald R. Ford (Michigan)	Republican	240	39,147,793

Note: Carter received 55 per cent of the Electoral College votes (297 votes, 23 states); Ford received 44 per cent (240 votes, 27 states).

James Earl (Jimmy) Carter

39th President of the United States (1977–81)
Born: 1 October 1924
Birthplace: Plains, Georgia
Education: Georgia Southwestern College; US Naval Academy Graduate 1946
Political party: Democrat
State: Georgia
Occupations before presidency: Farmer; warehouseman; businessman
Previous government service: Georgia State Senator (1962–66); Governor of
 Georgia (1971–75)
Age at inauguration: 52
Dates of office: January 1977–January 1981
Election: November 1976
Vice president: Walter F. Mondale
Length of term: 4 years

11.10 The Carter presidency

Domestic

James Earl Carter was raised in the small town of Plains in Georgia, where his father made a living as a peanut farmer. He came through local politics to become governor of Georgia from 1971 to 1975. Carter's sincerity, faith and homespun simplicity seemed to some to offer the chance for redemption after the trauma of Watergate. The newly sworn-in president's decision, immediately after his inaugural address, to get out of his bulletproof car and walk, hand in hand with his wife, down Pennsylvania Avenue to the White House seemed to symbolise a new beginning. Less concerned with the trappings of the highest office, Carter's humility seemed to signal a move away from the 'imperial presidency' and offered the first couple the chance to reconnect with the American people.

In the White House however, Carter came up short. In Jones' words:

> Seemingly ill at ease with the power of the Presidency, he proved incapable of wielding it effectively. He gave the impression of reacting to crises rather than anticipating them and of being unable to foresee the implications of his own actions ... He rarely looked or sounded like a President, appearing rather to be naïve, capricious and prone to error. (Jones, 1995, p. 568)

Carter's determination not to become an insider meant that he failed to build up the necessary strategic alliances to work effectively with Congress. Thus, despite significant Democratic majorities in both sides of Congress his domestic policy agenda was either rejected or eviscerated by the House and the Senate. His proposals on reorganisation of the government, wider health care provision and tax reform came to nothing.

Carter and the Equal Rights Amendment (ERA)

In his unexpected election victory of 1976, Jimmy Carter gained support not just from southern blacks but, having expressed support for the Equal Rights Amendment (ERA), from women too. Less sure-footed was his attempt to straddle the middle ground on the divisive issue of abortion. While his strong faith made him 'personally opposed to abortion' he stressed that he would be guided by the law and would not overturn the landmark Supreme Court judgement of *Roe* vs *Wade*. This attempt not to alienate feminists was limited by his opposition to federal funding to pay for abortions for women with low incomes. On the other hand, the powerful and vociferous pro-life movement were furious that President Carter was not prepared to overturn *Roe* vs *Wade*. Carter's failure to truly commit to either side on the challenging issue of abortion came to illustrate a man who seemed increasingly out of his depth in the Oval Office. Jones offers a damning appraisal: 'Far from providing the "new leadership" he had promised, Carter turned out to be a political tyro and, what was worse, one with only a limited capacity to grow into the job.' (Jones, 1995, pp. 567–68)

Worst of all, the fledgling president now faced an almost perfect storm of economic adversity. The crisis in the Middle East and its accompanying uncertainty, the resultant fuel crisis, rising unemployment and inflation all combined to make Carter look increasingly ineffective and hard-pressed. Once again, a clear, consistent policy seemed difficult to find. Carter initially believed that generous spending was the best way to set the country back on the road to prosperity. As prices rose, he was forced to abandon this approach and take a much more cautious one aimed at tackling the scourge of inflation. As the 1980 election loomed, the country faced a budget deficit of $50 billion and rapidly rising unemployment and inflation. The combination of domestic malaise and impotence abroad paved the way for a candidate who could promise Americans a brighter future. That future would pass into the hands of Ronald Reagan (see Chapter 13).

American foreign policy, 1968–80

11.11 Overview of Nixon's foreign policy, 1968–74

Much of the difficulty Nixon faced stemmed from the conduct of American foreign policy. He had an acute sense of presidential history and was obsessive about the fact that one day his actions would come under the review of historians. He was particularly determined that they would not conclude that he was the first president to lose a war. As the difficult legacy of Vietnam crumbled in his hands, his determination to salvage honour became a mental and physical craving. Publicly, Nixon's commitment to peace seemed laudable. In his oath of office he made a 'sacred commitment to consecrate my office and wisdom to the cause of peace among nations'.

The more Hanoi resisted his attempts to bring the war to an honourable conclusion, the more infuriated he became. Nixon's basic political instincts prompted him to lash out at the 'enemies' that he so readily saw all around him. The communists in Vietnam, the 'student bums' protesting on campus and the 'biased' journalists who scrutinised his every move all aroused Nixon's anger. In his bid to retain America's prestige, the Nixon White House developed many of the characteristics of an imperial court, with Nixon, remote, difficult and all-powerful, protected by able but sycophantic aides who flattered him and encouraged his neuroses.

Yet at the same time it should be emphasised that Nixon was a highly intelligent and able man. Stimulated by the often shrewd analysis of Henry Kissinger, a political scientist lured from Harvard University to the White House, Nixon came to realise that America's position on the world stage had fundamentally shifted, appreciating, in a way that some of his less talented successors might not have done, that a new configuration had emerged. Nixon saw that the Sino-Soviet split, the growing division between Communist China and the Soviet Union, was of immense importance and called for a new response from the United States.

11.12 Nixon's aims in Vietnam

Nixon came to the White House in January 1969 with an unambiguous electoral commitment to withdraw from the war in Vietnam by achieving 'Peace with honor'. However, George C. Herring (1979) contends that Nixon did not enter the White House with the tactic of Vietnamisation clearly in mind. He paints a picture of a president infuriated by the implacable resistance of the North Vietnamese government in Hanoi. Herring says that as peace efforts floundered in the summer of 1969, Nixon was sorely tempted to launch massive air strikes and a blockade against North Vietnam. He shows that Kissinger asked a National Security Council study group to devise plans to deliver 'savage, punishing' blows against North Vietnam, to include huge bombing raids, a blockade of key ports and the consideration of tactical nuclear weapons in 'controlled' situations. Herring argues that close advisers such as Secretary of State William Rogers and Secretary of Defense Melvin Laird begged Nixon to refrain from taking the drastic military action that would further inflame the already volatile situation at home. It could be argued that one of the most significant features of the domestic anti-war movement was that it served to dissuade Nixon from further, massive escalation. Herring's theory is that it was only when Nixon had been through this process that the White House finally took up a plan initially looked at by Johnson and which the Nixon Administration called 'Vietnamisation' (Herring, 1979, Chapter VII).

11.13 Vietnamisation of the war

'Vietnamisation' had two strands. The first was to gradually withdraw American troops from Vietnam. Whereas at the height of the war 550,000 troops had been in Vietnam, by December 1971 the number of American troops was down to 140,000 men. By September 1972, the total had dwindled to just 40,000. The last troops to return home left Vietnam on 29 March 1973. The second strand of this endgame was to place a steadily increasing onus on the South Vietnamese Army. In a major speech delivered in November 1969, Nixon outlined to the American people what he had in mind. He claimed that a simple American withdrawal would result in a 'bloodbath'. He contended that America's entire status as a world leader could be undermined if the United States were to meekly withdraw. Finally, he contrasted the peace protestors who had done so much to undermine the war effort with the 'great silent majority' who had stood behind American troops in the field. He concluded, 'North Vietnam cannot humiliate the United States. Only Americans can do that.' (In Herring, 1979, p. 225) Herring points out the sheer extent of the Vietnamisation programme:

> While US combat forces kept the North Vietnamese and NLF off balance by relentlessly attacking their supply lines and base areas, American advisers worked frantically to build up and modernize the South Vietnamese armed forces. The force level, about 850,000 when Nixon took office, was increased to over one million, and the United States turned over to South Vietnam huge quantities of the newest weapons: more than a million M-16 rifles, 12,000 M-60 machine guns, 40,000 M-79 grenade launchers, and 2000 heavy mortars and howitzers. The Vietnamese were also given ships, planes, helicopters, and so many vehicles that one congressman wondered whether the objective of Vietnamization was to 'put every South Vietnamese soldier behind the wheel' ... Literally overnight the South Vietnamese Army had become one of the largest and best-equipped in the world. (Herring, 1979, p. 226)

Despite these monumental efforts it could be argued that the entire programme was doomed to failure.

Fundamentally the Thieu government in South Vietnam was unable to build the type of support which the regime in the North had commanded. The battle for the hearts and minds of the people of South Vietnam could not be won merely by the provision of further military hardware. A critical point which came to haunt Kissinger was put forward with great effect by North Vietnamese negotiator Le Duc Tho. During a

---

Table 11.8 The final stages of the Vietnam War

1969	**June**	Nixon announced withdrawal of 25,000 troops.
	September	Ho Chi Minh died in Hanoi.
	December	American troop strength reduced by 60,000 by the end of the year.
1970	**April**	Nixon announced that American and South Vietnamese forces had attacked communist havens in Cambodia.
	October	The last week of the month saw the lowest number of American combat deaths (24) since October 1965.
	December	American troop strength in Vietnam reduced to 334,600 by the end of the year.
1972	**Christmas**	Nixon ordered a massive bombing campaign over North Vietnam.
1973	**23 January**	Kissinger and Le Duc Tho initialled the peace agreement in Paris.
	27 January	Ceasefire agreement formally signed.
	14 August	United States ceased to bomb Cambodia in line with Congressional approval.
1974		Thieu declared the war had resumed.
		Communist build-up of troops and supplies.
1975	**29 March**	Last American troops left Vietnam.

tense moment in the peace talks he wondered out loud that if the United States could not win with half a million of its own troops, 'how can you succeed when you let your puppet troops do the fighting?' So despite Nixon's efforts, it could be seen in retrospect that the inexorable force was with the North rather than the South (Table 11.8).

11.14 Cambodia

In terms of American casualties, the opening months of 1969 were intensely damaging. For some time it had been apparent that North Vietnamese forces were using the adjoining, neutral state of Cambodia as a base, storing military personnel and supplies there and using Cambodia as a safe haven when they needed to take refuge from American attacks. Cambodia was also being used by the North Vietnam Army (NVA) as an infiltration point for their attacks into South Vietnam. Nixon believed that as the NVA had already violated Cambodia's neutrality, his initiative could be justified both morally and militarily. In March 1969, Nixon secretly ordered the American air force to bomb Cambodia, even though it was technically a neutral country; the targets were communist bases and arms stores and the scale of the bombing was immense. The extent of the subterfuge involved has been best documented by Seymour Hersh who explains that even the pilots involved were not fully aware of what was taking place:

> Sixty B-52 aircraft would be sent on the mission. Twelve of them would drop their bombs on legitimate targets inside South Vietnam; the others would be bombing Cambodia ... The B-52 pilots would be briefed en masse before their missions on targets that were in South Vietnam – that is, the cover targets. After the normal briefing, some crews would be taken aside and told that shortly before their bombing run they would receive special instructions from a ground radar station inside South Vietnam. The radar sites, using sophisticated computers, would in effect take over the flying of the B-52s for the final moments, guiding them to their real targets over Cambodia and computing the precise moment to drop the bombs. (Hersh, 1983, p. 61)

The damage caused not just to the innocent people caught in the bombing raids but by the wider turmoil to the country at large was almost incalculable. Initially the raids targeted border areas but the intensity of these attacks prompted the communist forces to move deeper and deeper into Cambodia, effectively taking the conflict to the heart of a neutral country. The trauma this caused can be said to have directly led to the collapse of the Cambodian government and ultimately the rise of the genocidal Khmer Rouge regime. The raids, conducted by high-altitude B-52s, were concealed from public knowledge for two months, until the *New York Times* exposed details in May 1969.

In March 1970 the neutral leader of Cambodia, Prince Sihanouk, was overthrown in a military coup. A further, more tragic consequence was that the North Vietnamese stepped up their opposition to the United States-sponsored government, led by Lon Nol, by supporting the Cambodian forces of the Khmer Rouge, led by Pol Pot. Administration officials took the decision to launch an incursion into Cambodia led by the South Vietnamese Army but supported by American artillery, aircraft and even

US troops on the ground. Domestically, Nixon now faced the accusation that he was extending the scale of the conflict rather than extricating the United States. At the end of April Nixon tried to justify his actions claiming: 'If when the chips are down, the world's most powerful nation, the United States of America, acts like a pitiful, helpless, giant, the forces of totalitarianism and anarchy will threaten free nations and free institutions throughout the world.' (Farrell, 2017, p. 403)

Although NVA operations were temporarily affected, and the border became much less porous, the domestic protest in the United States, not least now the secret bombing of Cambodia, brought the anti-war movement to an unprecedented pitch. When four students were shot dead by National Guardsmen in a peace protest at Kent State University in May 1970 Nixon was placed in a profoundly embarrassing position and his standing was undermined still further. Just days before, Nixon had expressed his displeasure with the privileged students at the centre of the peace protests, referring to them as 'bums'. In the wake of the Kent State shootings, campus protests reached an intensity that shook the entire nation. Therefore although American action in Cambodia was short lived, it had overwhelmingly negative consequences for the war effort in Vietnam.

11.15 Losing the battle of hearts and minds

The My Lai Massacre

Events in the summer of 1971 served to further alienate the public from the war in Vietnam. President Nixon seemed increasingly sensitive to what many observers regarded as legitimate questions about the conduct of the war. It could be argued that the growing divergence between public opinion and Nixon's outlook became instrumental in the path that ultimately led to the Watergate scandal, his resignation and ignominy in South East Asia.

The massacre of South Vietnamese villagers, including women and children, in a small hamlet called My Lai in March 1968 had taken place before Nixon entered the Oval Office. However, Nixon had become president by the time the hitherto covered-up incident was revealed by investigative journalist Seymour Hersh in November 1969. Olson and Roberts note that 'the revelations triggered a storm of controversy throughout the United States. For anti-war activists, the massacre and cover-up stood as stark totems to the evil of the Vietnam War' (Olson & Roberts, 1998, p. 24). Farrell clearly shows that the president's response was to mislead the American people:

> [R]ather than seeking justice – as he promised the American people in a December 8 press conference – his response was to direct his aides to use the necessary 'dirty tricks' and discredit the army witnesses who had intrepidly refused to participate in a cover-up. (Farrell, 2017, p. 370)

In March 1971 William Calley was found guilty of 'at least twenty-two murders' in the My Lai Massacre of 1968. He was sentenced to life imprisonment with hard labour. In August 1971, following Nixon's intervention, the life sentence was reduced to 20 years, and in November 1974 the Secretary of the Army, Howard Calloway, paroled him.

The Pentagon Papers

Nixon's controversial support for William Calley coincided with the furore that surrounded the publication in the *New York Times* of the 'Pentagon Papers' in June 1971. These exposed to public view previously secret documents based on a 7,000-page report commissioned by former Defense Secretary Robert S. McNamara. The papers concerned top-secret, high-level discussions in the Pentagon; the conclusion most people drew from them was that both Kennedy and Johnson had actually misled the public about the situation in Vietnam. While the documents did not directly relate to Nixon's administration, he instinctively reacted against this open exposure of the decision-making process. Nixon was also outraged by the fact that a former Pentagon official (Daniel Ellsberg) had leaked the documents to the press. Central to Nixon's defensive outlook was his personal conviction that the press in general, and the *New York Times* and the *Washington Post* in particular, was biased against his Republican administration. Nixon was ill at ease with the Ivy League-educated intellectuals whom he believed controlled the country's top newspapers.

11.16 The peace process and the bombing of Vietnam

The peace process in Vietnam was a protracted affair characterised by mutual distrust. The decision to search for a peaceful solution can be dated back to the trauma of the Tet offensive in January 1968. In the aftermath of the North Vietnamese offensive Johnson, aided by new Defense Secretary Clark Clifford, came to the conclusion that a military victory could not be achieved. On 31 March Johnson signalled the end of his personal commitment to winning the war when he wearily announced that he would not be standing for re-election in November. Within a few days of his announcement, Hanoi indicated its willingness to accept his suggestion of peace talks. Initial negotiations began in Paris in May 1968, and the war cast an ugly shadow over the 1968 presidential election. However, with Election Day looming, Johnson announced a halt to the American bombing of North Vietnam. It appeared that peace was approaching, and this prospect gave the Democratic candidate, Hubert Humphrey, a massive and timely boost.

However, recent research indicates that on the eve of the election Richard Nixon moved to disrupt the peace talks, which he felt threatened the Republican Party's prospects. It seems that Nixon advised South Vietnam that if they did not attend the peace talks and waited instead for a Nixon victory, he would secure them a better deal at the conference table. Nixon secured victory in the November 1968 election and set about achieving 'Peace with honor.' The president brought to this process a curious combination of a desire for peace, an obsession with avoiding humiliation and a willingness to exact terrible destruction on the people of North Vietnam. In his memoirs, *RN*, Nixon claimed that the Christmas bombing raids of 1972 were designed solely to compel the Vietnamese to come to terms. He vividly remembered how Eisenhower had succeeded in giving the Chinese the impression that he was prepared to consider the use of nuclear weapons if they did not agree to peace terms over Korea. Some historians have

Table 11.9		Protests and peace in Vietnam, 1968–72
1968	November	Nixon elected president with a clear commitment to bring an honourable end to the war in Vietnam.
1969	April	100,000 people in an anti-war demonstration in New York City.
	August	Secret talks in Paris between Henry Kissinger and North Vietnamese representative Xuan Thuy.
	October	A left-wing group, the Weatherman, organised its controversial 'Days of Rage' protest, leading to violent clashes with police on the streets of Chicago. Across the country over 2 million people took part in the largest protest so far.
1970	February	Kissinger returned to Paris for secret talks with North Vietnamese negotiator Le Duc Tho.
	May	Kent State, Ohio: four students shot dead by the National Guard during a campus protest against an escalation of the war to Cambodia.
1972	January	Nixon revealed the existence of secret negotiations between Kissinger and the North Vietnamese.
	March	North Vietnam launched an offensive across the demilitarised zone.
	May	Nixon stepped up bombing raids over North Vietnam in a bid to force the communists to come to terms.

claimed that in 1969 he told his adviser H.R. Haldeman of his 'madman theory', which could help to end the struggle in Vietnam:

> I want the North Vietnamese to believe I've reached the point where I might do anything to stop the war. We'll just slip the word to them about that, 'for God's sakes, you know Nixon is obsessed about communists. We can't restrain him when he's angry – and he has his hand on the nuclear button' – and Ho Chi Minh himself will be in Paris within two days begging for peace. (In Farrell, 2017, p. 362)

It does seem that the ferocity of the bombing raids made the communist government in Hanoi accept the fact that the time had come to conclude peace. The long-awaited peace terms were signed in Paris in January 1973; all American troops were withdrawn from Vietnam. However, North Vietnamese troops did not pull back across the 17th Parallel, and in April 1975 Saigon and the remainder of South Vietnam finally fell into the hands of the communists (Table 11.9).

Why did the United States fail to achieve its objectives in Vietnam?

While the casualties suffered by the North Vietnamese Army and its general population were horrendous, their capacity to keep going aroused incredulity in their enemies. As George C. Herring states in *America's Longest War: The United States and Vietnam 1950–1975* (1979):

> North Vietnam demonstrated great ingenuity and dogged perseverance in coping with the bombing. Civilians were evacuated from the cities and dispersed across

the countryside; industries and storage facilities were scattered and in many cases concealed in caves and under the ground. The government claimed to have dug over 30,000 miles of tunnels, and in heavily bombed areas the people spent much of their lives underground. An estimated 90,000 North Vietnamese, many of them women and children, worked full time keeping transportation routes open, and piles of gravel were kept along the major roadways, enabling 'Youth Shock Brigades' to fill craters within hours after the bombs fell ... B-52s devastated the narrow roads ... leading to the Ho Chi Minh Trail, but, to the amazement of the Americans, trucks moved back through the pass within several days. (Herring, 1979, pp. 148–49)

It would be easy to conclude from Herring's analysis that the corollary of Vietnamese doggedness and perseverance might be that American troops were lacking in their commitment. However, Herring completely rejects this view: 'American troops fought well, despite the miserable conditions under which the war was waged – dense jungles and deep swamps, fire ants and leeches, booby traps and ambushes, an elusive but deadly enemy.' (Herring, 1979, p. 153) This would suggest that in military terms the two sides were closely matched, one fundamentally suited to the conditions and terrain, the other backed by monumental resources and military hardware. This might point to the conclusion that the reason for America's defeat lay away from the jungles of Vietnam but was rather due to the political consequences of the war back home in the United States (Table 11.10).

Stanley Karnow's very substantial work on Vietnam includes this somewhat damning verdict:

The US army in Vietnam was a shambles as the war drew to a close in the early 1970s. With President Nixon then repatriating the Americans, nobody wanted to be the last to perish for a cause that had clearly lost its meaning, and the name of the game for those awaiting withdrawal was survival. Anti-war protests at home had by now spread to the men in the field, many of whom wore peace symbols, and refused to go into combat ... Soldiers not only disobeyed their superiors but, in an alarming number of incidents, actually murdered them with fragmentation grenades. (Karnow, 1985, p. 22)

Table 11.10   Vietnam War in numbers

58,220	US troops killed
Unknown	number of Vietnamese who fled the country or disappeared at sea
3 million	North and South Vietnamese killed
1.5 million	South Vietnamese who underwent indoctrination
30,357	tonnes of US napalm bombs dropped
36,000	tonnes of bombs dropped in Christmas bombing raid (Linebacker II)
320,000	Chinese soldiers who served in North Vietnam
500,000	US troops in South Vietnam
80%	proportion of US soldiers drafted that could be defined as working class
5 million	acres of upland forest destroyed by Agent Orange
500,000	acres of crops destroyed by Agent Orange
2%	proportion of US officer corps who were black

11.17 Henry Kissinger

Dr Henry Kissinger served as Nixon's National Security Adviser between 1969 and 1973 and as Secretary of State under Nixon and Ford from 1973 to 1977. A Jew born in Germany in 1923, his family fled to the United States in the 1930s. Kissinger served in the American forces during the Second World War and then embarked upon a dazzling academic career as a student and eventually as Professor of Government at Harvard University between 1958 and 1971. His published work on nineteenth-century statesmen commended the virtues of realpolitik, a pragmatic foreign policy which recognised and worked within the limitations created by the internal systems of other nations. Nixon was impressed by Kissinger's intelligence and recruited him as an adviser in his presidential campaign in 1968. He was rewarded with the post of White House National Security Adviser between 1969 and 1973. It soon became clear that Kissinger's contribution to the formulation of American foreign policy was overshadowing that of the Secretary of State, and in 1973 he became Secretary of State on the resignation of William Rogers.

Nixon valued Kissinger's grasp of international relations, and together they came to understand that the relatively simple dynamics of the Cold War had given way to a more complex configuration. The resulting Nixon Doctrine was based on the belief that the United States must put its own interests first; other nations had to take prime responsibility for their own defence. The United States had in the recent past overreached itself by trying to take on too many responsibilities on a global scale. Kissinger and Nixon were quick to appreciate the deteriorating relationship between the Soviet Union and China. They also understood that Western Europe and Japan were increasingly significant, particularly in economic terms.

11.18 Relations with the Soviet Union: The arms race, detente and the SALT talks

Richard Nixon was inaugurated as president in January 1969. The new president was intelligent and well-read and appointed a very capable National Security Adviser in Henry Kissinger. However, this able partnership assumed responsibility at a time when the United States faced severe difficulties in foreign policy. Critically, Nixon had inherited the problem of the war in Vietnam. In addition to the massive cost of the war in Southeast Asia, Nixon and Kissinger recognised that the sheer cost of the Cold War and the arms race which accompanied it had become a crippling burden. Faced with rising inflation and pressing domestic issues, Nixon concluded that unless something was done, the world's richest nation could veer towards bankruptcy.

By 1969, it was also clear that the Soviet Union had achieved parity with the United States in terms of nuclear missiles. Neither side could hope to win a nuclear war; yet both sides continued to spend billions of dollars on military research and development. Meanwhile, Nixon and Kissinger watched with interest as tension grew between the Soviet Union and China. In September 1969, fighting on the border between the two nations escalated; Kissinger felt that this was a good point to establish closer relations with both sides than they did with each other. At the same time, their Soviet counterparts had drawn the same conclusion. These factors came together during the late 1960s, to create a process known as detente (a word meaning 'relaxation of tension') which began, lasting, despite some considerable setbacks, until 1979. As well as an improvement in relations between the United States and the Soviet Union, this period also saw a dramatic improvement in relations between the United States and China.

In 1969, the Soviet Union and the United States began talks called SALT (Strategic Arms Limitation Talks). Following the success of his visit to China of February 1972 Nixon took part in a second high-profile summit when he became the first president to visit Moscow. Kissinger's prodigious hard work and political skill were instrumental in making the meeting possible. The thought of an American president going into the heart of the communist empire had been unthinkable for generations. Now, when Air Force One took off for Moscow in May 1972 Kissinger could not conceal his excitement. He bounded into Nixon's cabin saying: 'This has to be one of the great diplomatic coups of all time!' (Thomas, 2015, p. 379) Privately, Nixon was wary of the reception the tough men in the Kremlin would give him. Unable to sleep, he instilled panic in his security detail when he slipped out of his ornate base in the Grand Palace in the Kremlin to stretch his legs on the streets of Moscow at 4.30 am.

Once the talks began, some initial wariness on both sides began to develop into an increasingly warm personal rapport between Nixon and his host. Substantive issues were on the agenda. In a summit meeting with Soviet leader Leonid Brezhnev, the two men agreed the final details of the Strategic Arms Limitation Talks (SALT I). Thomas describes how the two leaders, from the opposite ends of the political spectrum, '[e]xuberantly drank cognac toasts to each other and to peace' (Thomas, 2015, p. 382). This was a personal high point in Nixon's career, a landmark in the process of detente and a substantial event rather than a PR exercise.

The background talks had begun in November 1969, and were brought to a conclusion with the signing of the treaty in May 1972. The aim of this process was to limit the stockpiles of long-range nuclear weapons. After complex talks, some limitations, over a five-year period, were agreed on certain types of missile. President Nixon stated that: 'A declaration of this magnitude could only have been taken by two countries which had chosen to place their relations on a new foundation of restraint, co-operation, and confidence.' (American Presidency Project, online) The agreement was technically extremely complex but the key points are summarised in the list that follows.

SALT I, May 1972

- The treaty placed a ceiling on the future build-up of intercontinental ballistic missiles for a period of five years.
- In a further treaty, both sides agreed to restrict the deployment of anti-ballistic missile (ABM) systems.
- The treaty did not cover the construction of ICBMs already in production.
- Both agreements were ratified by the Senate in 1972.
- The second round of talks (SALT II) began in November 1974 and led to a treaty in June 1979, but when the Soviet Union invaded Afghanistan in December 1979 the Senate refused to ratify the agreement.
- Despite these curbs on the arms race, further development of long-range bombers and MIRVs (multiple independently targeted re-entry vehicles) occurred.

Just over a year after SALT I, in June 1973, Nixon welcomed Brezhnev to Washington for a second superpower summit between the two men. The rapport remained; this time Nixon presented the Soviet leader with a specially made Lincoln Continental which the delighted Russian even got to take on a test drive with the President of the United States in the passenger seat! While an Agreement on the Prevention of Nuclear War was signed by the two men it was of limited importance and discussions on a peace deal in the Middle East did not acquire any real momentum. (Indeed when Israel was suddenly attacked by Egypt and Syria in October 1973, the Nixon Administration was caught completely off guard.) When the two men met for the last time in Nixon's presidency, in Moscow in the summer of 1974, the chemistry between them from their first meeting was difficult to re-kindle. Kissinger later described Nixon as 'preoccupied and withdrawn' on that particular trip (Thomas, 2015, p. 488). Meanwhile, Brezhnev was himself under pressure from hardliners in the military and the Kremlin who felt that the rapport with the United States had gone too far.

11.19 Communist China

The traumatic 'fall' of China to communism in 1949 had shaken American society to the core. Ever since, relations between 'Red China' and the United States had been exceptionally cold, fuelled by America's consistent defence of Taiwan and the powerful China Lobby in the US and made worse by periodic reports of purges and atrocities committed by the Chinese communists. The war in Korea in the early 1950s had led China and the United States to become the first of the superpowers to confront each other directly on the battlefield. China's support for North Vietnam meant that relations in the mid-1960s remained extremely tense. At first glance, it seemed completely unimaginable that Nixon, a politician who had based his early political career on his staunch opposition to communism, would be the president who would achieve better relations with Communist China. Indeed, President Kennedy had aborted a plan to normalise relations with China because he knew that Nixon and other conservatives would criticise him. China's development of the atomic bomb in 1964 further fuelled American suspicion.

However, by the time Nixon entered the Oval Office his outlook had become more sophisticated and the political climate was rapidly changing. The fundamental assumptions that had formed the framework of American diplomacy since 1945 – The Cold War, containment, a bipolar world – were giving way to new power configurations. Nixon knew that China's future standing in world affairs would be of immense importance. The key factor in the changing constellation was the Sino-Soviet rift, the split between the Soviet Union and China. Nixon recognised that China would not want to move away from the Soviets *and* remain on bad terms with the United States. When Beijing made it clear that they were ready to move towards better relations, Nixon was ready to respond.

Nixon and Kissinger correctly calculated that a shift in the posture towards China would make the Soviet Union distinctly uneasy and more willing to compromise in the future. Speaking in Kansas City in July 1971 Nixon envisaged a future with five great '"superpowers": the United States, the Soviet Union, Japan, Western Europe – and China'. The old firebrand told his audience of news editors:

> The doors must be opened and the goal of U.S. policy must be ... ending the isolation of Mainland China and a normalization of our relations. Looking down the road

– and let's just look ahead 15 to 20 years – the United States could have a perfectly effective agreement with the Soviet Union for limitation of arms; the danger of any confrontation there might have been almost totally removed. But Mainland China, outside the world community, completely isolated, with its leaders not in communication ... would be a danger to the whole world. (In Farrell, 2017, p. 435)

Nixon had realised, before anyone else, that the time to think the unthinkable – an American president visiting Communist China – had arrived. In the spring of 1971 Kissinger was sent on a top-secret mission to meet with Chinese premier Zhou Enlai. On 10 June 1971, Nixon announced that he would drop the 21-year-old embargo on American trade with China, and in October the United States dropped its opposition to Chinese admission to the United Nations.

The symbolic high point of the improved relationship came in February 1972, when Nixon became the first American president to visit China. Air Force One touched down in Beijing on 21 February 1972. With prime-time television coverage in mind, the visit was carefully choreographed but Nixon's emphatic, outstretched handshake with Zhou was spontaneous and demonstrated the importance of the trip to the Americans. It was only after Nixon had arrived at his villa that he was informed that a meeting with Mao Zedong had been arranged. At Mao's home, the two leaders spoke warmly for an hour setting the tone for what was to come. It is hard now to find the words to explain how extraordinary these moments really where. The press provided saturation coverage at home and Nixon's standing, as a world statesman, could hardly have been higher. In the grand setting of a state dinner, Nixon paid the tribute of using the words of Mao himself in his speech: 'Seize the day, seize the hour', before continuing:

What legacy shall we leave our children? Are they destined to die for the hatreds which have plagued the old world, or are they destined to live because we had the vision to build a new world? This is the hour, this is the day. (In Farrell, 2017, p. 462)

With its television-friendly images of the Great Wall and giant pandas, and with Nixon himself on excellent form, the trip was a resounding success. As Kissinger put it, 'He had indeed wrought a genuine historic achievement. He had thought up the China initiative ... he had fostered it, had run the domestic political risks of going it alone and had conducted himself admirably during the journey.' (In Farrell, 2017, p. 463) Following the high-profile visit, however, little changed. It took until 1979 for the United States to formally recognise the People's Republic of China (PRC). In addition, the United States continued to lend support to the Chinese nationalists on the island of Formosa. In a wider sense it certainly made the Soviet Union much more willing to improve its relationship with the United States and for a little while it depicted American foreign policy in a better light than the constant nightmare of Vietnam. Finally, it could be claimed that Nixon's visit to China took place when it did because no politician was ever more mindful of an election year than Richard Nixon.

11.20 The Middle East

Despite Nixon's visit to Moscow, the emergence of detente did not go so far as to undo the spiralling tension in the Middle East which so firmly divided the superpowers. The United States had traditionally led emphatic support to the state of Israel. On the other hand, the Soviet Union was clearly committed to the cause of the Arab nations. Both sides had heightened the potential for disaster in the Middle East by supplying arms on a large scale to the two sides. The outbreak of war in October 1973 when Egypt, Syria and Jordan attacked Israel during the religious festival of Yom Kippur caused worldwide alarm. Henry Kissinger's status as a major diplomatic figure was enhanced even further when a series of frenetic visits to the capitals of the Middle East – 'shuttle diplomacy' – led to a ceasefire and a limited peace settlement.

11.21 President Ford's foreign policy, 1974–76

Just as Watergate hemmed in the president domestically, the Vietnam War meant that any appetite for initiatives abroad was strictly limited. Nixon's closest foreign policy adviser, Henry Kissinger, had survived the Watergate cull and remained as influential as ever. However, the charismatic Secretary of State had been accused by opponents of being too willing to concede ground to the Soviets during the period of detente. In September 1975, Ford sacked his defense secretary, James R. Schlesinger, in a move that was widely interpreted as offering backing to Kissinger. In a continuation of the previous administration's policy of relaxing tension between the superpowers, President Ford met with the Soviet leader, Leonid Brezhnev, at Vladivostok in November 1974. Brezhnev was entrenched in his outlook but the two leaders nevertheless agreed to a second round of SALT talks.

At Helsinki in August 1975 Ford added his signature to that of Brezhnev and 33 other heads of state supporting principles to respect territorial boundaries, allow freedom of information and travel, and respect human rights. The complexity and protracted nature of the SALT discussions meant that when Ford lost the election in 1976 the negotiations were still taking place. The responsibility for their conclusion passed to Jimmy Carter and in particular his Secretary of State, Cyrus Vance, in the talks that would take place in Moscow early in 1977.

The War Powers Act and the fall of Saigon

While Ford's positive steps with the Russians did not attract any serious criticism at home the nation was not forthcoming with support for interventions elsewhere. In the wake of the US withdrawal from Vietnam in 1973 the regime in the South faced complete collapse. When Ford asked for support from Congress to provide emergency military aid to the South Vietnamese it was not forthcoming. As a reaction to Vietnam, Congress had introduced the War Powers Act in November 1973, while Nixon was still in office. This stipulated that the president could not deploy US troops in combat for more than 60 days without congressional approval. The Act was passed despite Nixon's veto. With depleted powers and massive budget cuts, and a psychological aversion to further overseas commitments, presidential opportunities for military action were now significantly reduced. Within two years of American withdrawal, the North Vietnamese were poised to take Saigon and complete the process of national unification. When the last American helicopter took off from the roof of the US Embassy in Saigon in April 1975 the symbolism of American decline was striking. Ten years after Johnson had begun a full-scale war, the American commitment to Vietnam was over.

Before the year was out, Laos and Cambodia had also become communist states. As 1975 drew to a close, attention briefly shifted to Angola, an oil-rich nation in southern Africa, where the anachronistic Portuguese colonial empire was entering its death throes. Despite the process of detente it was clear that the Angolan uprising was receiving massive military support from Russia and Cuba. From Kissinger's geopolitical perspective the support of the Soviet–Cuban Marxist axis to the Angolan rebels was deeply troubling. Kissinger proposed to provide arms and equipment to anti-communist forces in the government's struggle against Soviet-backed guerrillas and 15,000 troops provided by Cuba's Castro regime. By spring 1976 the Marxist forces had taken control of Angola, but once again Congress flatly refused Kissinger's proposals. This offered confirmation that the painful lessons of Vietnam were sinking in but at the same time opened Ford to criticism from the American right over his alleged weakness. The word 'detente' was becoming discredited and Ronald Reagan, the emerging Republican candidate for the 1976 election, was happy to take advantage. While he was unable to secure the nomination on this occasion, his time would come just four years later. By this time President Carter's foreign policy would be in ruins.

11.22 President Carter's foreign policy 1976–80

Carter's foreign policy had some high points but equally was plagued with the inconsistency which marked his domestic leadership. The policies he initially outlined seemed, in the context of Watergate, Vietnam, Kissinger and Nixon, to be reasonable. Moving away from 'balance of power politics' and 'excessive military spending' Carter promised to be guided by his overriding concern for universal human rights. While Carter was hoping to take a new direction from Nixon in masterminding foreign policy, he was happy to continue with those trends Nixon had set in motion which seemed to augur well for peace. Most noteworthy was the successful conclusion of the journey of reconciliation with Communist China. On New Year's Day, 1979 the US established full diplomatic relations with Beijing. The inevitable corollary of this was to terminate relations with the Chinese Nationalists in Taiwan ending a defensive treaty that dated back to Eisenhower and 1954. While the American people appreciated the sense of additional peace and security that this agreement heralded, Carter's actions over the issue of the Panama Canal were much more difficult for the public to understand. The recurring narrative pursued by the Republican Party, and by Ronald Reagan in particular, would be that Carter was fundamentally weak.

The Panama Canal

The Isthmus of Panama, also referred to historically as the Isthmus of Darien, is the narrow strip of land that lies between the Pacific Ocean and the Caribbean Sea. The president's commitment to human rights as opposed to American imperialism was exemplified in his approach to the controversial issue of the Panama Canal. As long ago as 1903, the US had signed a treaty with the government of Panama which gave America the right to construct and operate a canal through the Isthmus of Panama for all time. While the value of the canal to the US both in war and during peacetime was unquestionable it had come about in a different, imperialist era and been negotiated for in some hard bargaining to recognise Panama's breakaway from Columbia. From a post-Vietnam perspective the deal seemed anachronistic and difficult to justify. Nixon and Kissinger recognised this and it was their formative work that culminated in the Panama Canal Treaty being placed before the Senate in the spring of 1978. The treaty passed through the Senate and set the scene for complete withdrawal by America from the Canal Zone by the end of the twentieth century.

While President Carter was eventually able to persuade the Senate to ratify the treaty after months of intense debate, it was less easy for all Americans to understand what once again appeared to be a move that diminished the US abroad. Nevertheless, Carter looked back at the issue of Panama as one of his greatest achievements. To liberal observers an enlightened president was finally coming to terms with a post-colonial world and making clear to those who had claimed that America had ridden roughshod over smaller nations in the colonial past that those days were over. To the Republican right, however, the surrender of 'our canal' to Marxist pressure was simply another example of a weak president signing away America's strategic interests.

The Middle East and the Camp David agreement

Few could argue that Carter's brokering of the March 1979 peace treaty between Israel and Egypt marked the high point of his foreign policy and of his own political career. Throughout the 1960s and into the following decade the issue of the rights of the Palestinian people had been pushed down the agenda of successive American presidents by events in Indochina and by the Cold War. However, the worldwide fallout from the Yom Kippur War of 1973 underlined how damaging instability in the Middle East was for the fuel hungry nations in the west. Israel's military success in the wars of 1967 and 1973 had extended her control over the Palestinian territory and heightened her reliance on the immensely powerful Jewish lobby in Washington DC. By the time Carter entered the Oval Office no other nation on earth received more military support and US foreign aid than Israel.

Carter's critics often portrayed him as a 'wimp' but his courageous pursuit of peace in the Middle East suggests a level of personal tenacity at odds with this perspective. The sheer complexity and propensity for armed conflict in this region made this an unlikely destination for any president timidly seeking a quiet life. Few American statesmen had invested so much personal energy and political capital in the Middle East peace process as Carter. In particular, he hosted an intense 13-day summit at Camp David, his presidential retreat in Maryland, and personally shuttled between Cairo and Jerusalem to maintain the diplomatic initiative. The symbolic handshake when the treaty was signed between the hitherto bitter rivals, Menachem Begin and Anwar Sadat, was an iconic moment that seemed to finally herald a genuine breakthrough. While the treaty did not address the status of the Palestinians, Carter earned great praise for his calm and dignified manner and determination to seek peace. Sadly, this moment of triumph was short lived and was overwhelmed by events in Iran that were to fatally damage his presidency.

Lawrence Wright's verdict, in his in-depth study of Camp David, *Thirteen Days in September*, shows that Carter had, more than most presidents perhaps, a capacity for bad luck, even when his personal effort was above and beyond normal expectations.

So many neglected issues had piled up while Carter had devoted himself to making peace in the Middle East. The shah of Iran was overthrown and replaced by a radical Shiite theocracy. Inflation was running out of control, and unemployment remained persistently high. Even Carter's accomplishments – normalizing relations with China, advancing human rights, creating an energy policy, cutting the federal deficit, signing the Panama Canal treaties – were overshadowed by the extended turmoil of the Camp David process. (Wright, 2014, p. 267)

Iran

Iran's size and strategic position combined with its immense reserves of fossil fuel made it an attractive proposition to the United States, while at the height of the Cold War its long border with Russia gave cause for concern. To understand the events of 1979 that virtually overwhelmed President Carter, we need to briefly return to the Eisenhower Administration and a fateful decision made in 1953. It was in August of that year when the British and American intelligence networks combined to engineer a coup against the prime minister of Iran, Mohammad Mossadegh. Mossadegh was a nationalist who had briefly nationalised the lucrative Iranian oil industry.

Alarmed by what they saw as an alarming upsurge in Iranian nationalism, the US and Britain supported the second and last monarch of the royal House of Pahlavi, Mohammad Reza Shah, who immediately restored the oil industry to foreign control. Over time, this regime became increasingly corrupt and autocratic. However, the Shah retained American support primarily perhaps because Iran's oil assets were of critical and long-standing importance to the United States. With Russia on Iran's doorstep it was essential to Western oil supplies to keep this friendship intact. The Shah's increasing unpopularity led to a series of large-scale violent demonstrations and strikes culminating in the overthrow of the Shah and the monarchy in February 1979; these were replaced by an Islamic republic run by Muslim clerics who denounced the US as 'the Great Satan'. The Shah left for exile in Egypt never to return.

The virulence of the sheer hatred of the Americans that came from the new Islamic Republic sent shockwaves through the region. Violent, and to the eyes of foreign observers, almost hysterical anti-Western demonstrations became routine in the capital city, Tehran. While this wave of fundamentalism was frequently shown in international news coverage, the Americans seemed surprisingly ill-prepared for the dramatic events which consumed their embassy in Tehran in November 1979. A huge, orchestrated, revolutionary crowd stormed the American compound, overwhelming limited security and taking 73 US diplomats as hostages. Having faced increasing charges of weakness and impotence from his right-wing opponents and the press, the President of the United States now found himself in the most trying situation of all: a hostage crisis, a fanatical, wildly popular new opponent riding on the crest of a revolutionary wave and a demand that the strongest nation on earth should secure the return of the Shah to Iran with all of his financial assets.

SALT II

If the mood of detente provided a general improvement in superpower relations then the SALT talks provided a detailed technical framework for the reduction in weapons that could realistically accompany a general relaxation in tension. Following the signing of the SALT I Treaty in May 1972, a second series of talks resumed with SALT II under President Nixon, followed by Ford and then Carter. President Carter called SALT II 'The most detailed, far-reaching, comprehensive treaty in the history of arms control.' (American Presidency Project, online) However, the talks did not proceed in the straightforward way that this description might imply. Secretary of State Vance was dispatched to Moscow with proposals for further dramatic reductions in nuclear weapons on both sides but his plans were spectacularly derailed when the Russians made clear that Carter's accompanying agenda of human rights discussions would not be on the agenda.

Carter was forced to make concessions and it was only when the human rights guarantees were dropped that the substantial talks resumed. This meant that the talks did not reach a conclusion until June 1979 when Carter and Brezhnev signed the SALT II talks in Vienna. In essence, little had changed since the Ford agreement. Both Moscow and Washington would reduce their totals of long-range bombers and nuclear missile systems. But the international climate was changing, detente was becoming discredited and the SALT Treaty was heavily criticised in the Senate. Yet again, Carter seemed to be providing his opponents with a simple narrative to sell to the electorate: a weak president who was always prepared to concede ground and whose opponents now understood this.

The Soviet invasion of Afghanistan

While Carter was regularly mocked and vilified in the American press it was not at home but in Afghanistan that the SALT II Treaty met its demise. In December 1979 the world was shocked by Russia's decision to launch a full-scale military invasion of Afghanistan. The SALT II accord was fatally damaged. Intrinsically a man of peace, Carter was forced into a dramatic rethink of his entire foreign policy. Limited sanctions were applied to the Soviet Union, including an embargo on grain sales and a proposed boycott of the Olympic Games, scheduled to be held in Moscow in the summer of 1980. Carter's proposed budget cuts for the military were now replaced with proposals to increase it. The SALT II Treaty was withdrawn from Senate consideration. These damaging foreign policy episodes suggested that the incumbent might be placed in the unedifying position of failing to secure the party's support for a second term. However, the rallying effect upon the nation of the hostage situation and the Soviets' actions in Afghanistan secured some further vestige of support for the beleaguered president. Even some sympathetic observers felt that the events of 1979 had taken their toll on a visibly tired and shaken Carter. From this perspective the proposed candidature of Senator Edward Kennedy from Massachusetts seemed to offer the Democratic Party new hope. However, Carter was determined to continue and inflicted some damaging defeats upon Kennedy in the primary season.

Put simply, the longer the hostage crisis continued the weaker Carter looked. In the words of the *Washington Post*:

The United States, far from earning respect for its restraint and forbearance, is increasingly seen as a country that shrinks from asserting what even its enemies recognize as a legitimate interest in protecting its diplomats from a mob ... The United States has made concessions of the sort one might expect from a nation that had lost a war. Each concession has been met with a demand for another. (In Bowden, 2006, p. 1294)

For the self-confident Republican candidate, Ronald Reagan, the public longing for a more aggressive posture presented the perfect electoral opportunity to define his opponent as weak. Always fond of a soundbite, Reagan made clear: 'There comes a time in negotiations with people of this kind that you have to say, 'No, this is our last offer.' (In Bowden, 2006, p. 1294)

Any sense that Carter may have had that his personal fortunes had turned a corner were horribly dashed by the tragic events of April 1980. A dramatic attempt to rescue the hostages, whose fate was in the balance, by an airborne mission to Iran ended in technical disaster when of the eight helicopters deployed, only five came through the opening stages unscathed. When it was decided to abort the mission, one of the helicopters crashed into a transport aircraft causing a fire in which a total of eight servicemen were killed. The consequences for Carter were disastrous.

Further reading

Bernstein C. & Woodward B., *All the President's Men* (London: Quartet Books 1974).
Bowden M., *Guests of the Ayatollah* (New York: Grove Press 2006).
Brinkley D. & Nichter L.A., *The Nixon Tapes 1971–1972* (Boston: Mariner Books 2015).
Dallek R., *Nixon and Kissinger: Partners in Power* (London: Penguin Books 2007).
Emery F., *Watergate: The Corruption and Fall of Richard Nixon* (London: Pimlico 1995).
Farrell J.A., *Richard Nixon: The Life* (New York: Doubleday – Random House 2017).
Ferguson N., *Kissinger 1923–1968: The Idealist* (London: Allen Lane 2015).
Herring G.C., *America's Longest War: The United States and Vietnam 1950–1975* (New York: Wiley 1979).
Hersh S.J., *The Price of Power: Kissinger in the Nixon White House* (New York: Summit Books 1983).
Jones M.A., *The Limits of Liberty: American History 1607–1992* (New York: Oxford University Press 1995).
Karnow S., *Vietnam: A History* (London: Century Hutchinson Ltd 1985).
Kutler S.I., *Abuse of Power: The New Nixon Tapes* (New York: Touchstone – Simon & Schuster 1997).
Matthews C., *Kennedy and Nixon: The Rivalry that Shaped Postwar America* (New York: Touchstone 1996).
Olson J.S. & Roberts R., *My Lai: A Brief History with Documents* (Boston: Bedford Books 1998).
Patterson J.T., *Grand Expectations: The United States, 1945–1974* (New York: Oxford University Press 1996).
Perlstein R., *Nixonland: The Rise of a President and the Fracturing of America* (New York: Scribner – Simon & Schuster 2008).
Reeves R., *President Nixon: Alone in the White House* (New York: Simon & Schuster 2001).

Schulman B.J., *Lyndon B. Johnson and American Liberalism, A Brief Biography with Documents* (Boston: Bedford Books 1995).

Shawcross W., *Sideshow: Kissinger, Nixon and the Destruction of Cambodia* (New York: Cooper Square Press 2002).

Thomas E., *Being Nixon: A Man Divided* (New York: Random House 2015).

Werth B., *31 Days: Gerald Ford, The Nixon Pardon and a Government in Crisis* (New York: Anchor Books 2006).

Wright L., *Thirteen Days in September: Carter, Begin and Sadat at Camp David* (London: Oneworld 2014).

Online resources

American Presidency Project: presidency.ucsb.edu, last accessed in 2018.

Richard Nixon Foundation: www.nixonfoundation.org, last accessed in 2018.

▣ Ṿ 12 African Americans 1945–2000

12.1 President Truman, civil rights and the transition from war to peace

Raised expectations at the end of the Cold War

If we take 1945 as a starting point for our examination of the position of African Americans, particularly in the Deep South, then the situation was horrendous. As David Reynolds puts it: 'Segregation had become almost an American way of life. The American Red Cross even segregated the plasma of white and black blood donors.' (Reynolds, 2009, p. 367) Victory in the war against fascism, and its associated ideas of racism and intolerance, unleashed powerful forces against segregation and raised expectations among black people, especially among those who had risked their lives in military service to their country.

The contrast between the America that had fought for freedom and the America that racially divided its own people was more striking than ever. While it is always tempting to think of individual presidents, in this case Truman, and their personality in terms of an approach to civil rights, on the other side of the 'role of the individual' in history was the factor of war as an immense catalyst for social change. In addition, with the Cold War in its infancy, American racism could be seen as profoundly embarrassing to the United States in the battle of propaganda with Communist Russia, although it should also be noted that, conversely, in the witch-hunt era of McCarthyism all forms of dissent would be stifled. Finally, in the post-1945 context, the horror of the Holocaust, the end of some overseas empires and the demise of colonialism all seemed at odds with the perpetuation of segregation in 'the land of the free and the home of the brave.'

Truman and civil rights

At first glance, Truman may appear an unlikely supporter of civil rights, and his background in Missouri offered no particular preparation for the role. Analysis of his personal papers and documents has shown that as late as 1945 he was using damaging and unacceptable racial remarks. Sone historians have spoken of the president's conversion to the black cause while some would say that he needed to look for black support because of his unpopularity elsewhere. (Problems with labour strikes, food shortages and inflation led to a poor performance in the 1946 midterms and to real concerns about the 1948 presidential election.)

At the same time, in the difficult post-war period of transition, Truman's relationship with Congress was tempestuous. The passage by Congress of the Taft–Hartley Act despite a presidential veto underlined this tension and angered labour unions and urban voters in the North. With the November 1948 presidential election looming, Truman and his advisers were well aware of the pivotal importance of the African American vote. While the president had not previously displayed a particular knowledge of, or passion for, the civil rights movement, his personal commitment to the cause of African Americans now became evident. In February 1948 Truman dispatched a special message to Congress recommending legislation to:

- end segregation in interstate travel
- make lynching a federal crime
- take measures to end the poll tax
- create a permanent Fair Employment Practices Commission.

Resistance to Truman and the emergence of the Dixiecrats

These proposals were pressing and of critical importance but Truman was unable to secure any progress in these areas. Southern filibustering sealed the fate of his civil rights bill and his actions prompted a violent white backlash in the South. In addition, Truman's initiatives prompted a splintering of the Democratic Party with the emergence of a new group called the Dixiecrats that rallied around a militant anti-civil rights platform under the leadership of the Governor of South Carolina, Strom Thurmond. Despite these difficulties, an important landmark came in July 1948 with an executive order which ended segregation in the armed forces. When American troops were sent to fight in Korea in 1950 they were no longer subject to racial division.

Great American Lives: Jackie Robinson, 1919–72

Like Muhammad Ali in the 1960s, Jackie Robinson was not just a sporting icon but also a courageous opponent of racial oppression. While Ali was revered for his style and skill in the boxing ring and for his steadfast opposition to the Vietnam War, Robinson's glorious exploits took place within 'America's sport', from the baseball diamond. It was a sport which, in the 1940s, was rigidly based on segregation and without a single African American in the Major League.

Jackie Robinson was born in rural Georgia in 1919 but raised in Southern California where he would later win an athletics scholarship to Pasadena City College. A prodigiously talented athlete, he attended the University of California, Los Angeles (UCLA). During World War II he served as an army lieutenant based at Fort Hood in Texas. His refusal to comply with the racist demands of a bus driver led to him being 'honourably relieved from active duty'.

At age 26 he joined a black-only baseball league, playing for the Kansas City Monarchs in 1945. Despite his obvious prowess, he was overlooked following a trial with the Boston Red Sox, the Major League side, in 1945. While Boston had denied itself the most talented player of his generation, the Brooklyn Dodgers realised that 'this guy can take us to the World Series'. In April 1947 he

Continued

---

was formally signed and handed the team's uniform with the number 42. His subsequent performances, in the face of bigotry, abuse and intimidation, are so revered that today the number 42 has been permanently retired by every club in Major League Baseball.

Further reading: Scott Simon, *Jackie Robinson and the Integration of Baseball* (Wiley 2002)

12.2 President Eisenhower and the civil rights campaign

The durability of the Jim Crow system

Despite Truman's efforts, the problems faced by African Americans in the United States at large, and in the Deep South in particular, were crying out for attention as America entered the 1950s. In the words of Hugh Brogan:

> In spite of all the aspirations to a 'New South' the region still stood supreme in disease, poverty, ignorance, sloth, hunger and cruelty ... Eisenhower completed the desegregation of the armed services and followed Truman's policy of making numerous black appointments. But if the Afro-Americans allowed their progress to wait on the actions of the federal government it would be very slow. (Brogan, 1985, p. 634)

In the Deep South the 'Jim Crow' system of racial segregation remained the norm as Eisenhower entered the Oval Office. Public amenities were separated for African Americans and whites. Children attended separate schools. African Americans could not get service in many restaurants or even use the rest rooms available for white people. White supremacist organisations such as the Ku Klux Klan remained active. The black electorate were deterred by a battery of poll taxes, exclusion clauses, literacy tests and, if all this failed, violent intimidation. In every indicator of socio-economic well-being, African Americans were consistently losing out to their white counterparts. Inferior housing, jobs, schools and status supported by endemic racism made black lives exceptionally difficult. Higher infant mortality, lower life expectancy, greater risk of imprisonment, greater risk of conviction for the same crime as white people and a general exclusion from the professions, the police force and the legal system made the position of African Americans in the Deep South completely unacceptable.

12.3 Brown vs Topeka Board of Education (May 1954)

With so much focus in the American century on executive power, it is interesting to note that the step change in civil rights in the 1950s came from the Judicial rather than the executive branch. It was not the president but the Supreme Court, under the dynamic liberal leadership of Eisenhower's appointee, Chief Justice Earl Warren of California, that led the way. When Eisenhower appointed Warren to the position of Chief Justice he had assumed that he would take the path of careful conservatism. But within six months of his appointment, on a Monday in May 1954, he made one of the most important legal decisions of the century. The Supreme Court unanimously accepted the argument put forward by the National Association for the Advancement of Colored People (NAACP) that the notion of 'separate but equal' as it was applied to education was a contradiction in terms. The NAACP was America's oldest civil rights organisation and through its Legal Defense and Education Fund had contested this issue for literally decades.

The decision was actually based on five separate cases involving racial discrimination which through the appeals system eventually came to the highest court in the land. The impact of the NAACP, incidentally a largely middle-class organisation, and its dogged determination to continue with their case was due in no small part to the outstanding work of Thurgood Marshall, a celebrated black lawyer from Baltimore. 'Separate but equal' was a concept dating back to the Supreme Court's judgement in *Plessy* vs *Ferguson* (1896). For decades this ruling was used to support racial segregation in the education system on the grounds that black and white children could be educated separately as long as they received equal quality. Now this was totally overturned by a new ruling that segregation in public schools was unconstitutional because 'separate educational facilities are inherently inferior'. As Timothy Tyson puts it, 'nine white men in black judicial robes dropped the bomb on public school segregation' (Tyson, 2017, p. 90).

In the nation as a whole the decision was broadly welcomed, and seen as responsive to the changing interpretation of the Constitution. The *New York Times* observed:

> In such decisions as the one rendered yesterday, we move toward a more perfect democracy ... The highest court in the land, the guardian of our national conscience, has reaffirmed its faith – and the undying American faith – in the equality of all men, and all children before the law. (In Martin, 1998, p. 201)

In similar vein the *Chicago Defender* stated:

> Neither the atom bomb nor the hydrogen bomb will ever be as meaningful to our democracy as the unanimous declaration of the Supreme Court that racial segregation violates the spirit and the letter of our Constitution. This means the beginning of the end of the dual society in American life and the ... segregation which supported it. (Martin, 1998, p. 203)

Reaction to Brown vs Topeka in the South

While not all newspapers in the South expressed hostility to the ruling, some certainly did. The *Daily News* in Jackson, Mississippi, spoke of 'Bloodstains on the White Marble Steps' of the Supreme Court; the *Cavalier Daily* in Virginia bitterly complained about the 'violation' of the southern way of life (Martin, 1998, pp. 204, 207). Robert Cook provides an excellent analysis of the power and significance of the judgement which now made clear that:

> the fiction of 'separate but equal' education had no place in a meritocratic, capitalist democracy ... Segregation represented a negation of modern American democracy ... Although *Brown* neither resulted in the immediate demise of the caste system in the Deep South nor prompted a major grass-roots revolt against Jim Crow, it did crystallise the hitherto inchoate white opposition to the profound changes under way in southern society. Public opinion in parts of the region was polarised dramatically, forcing moderate whites to abandon thoughts of gradual reform and causing blacks to reassess their tactics and strategy. (Cook, 1998, pp. 87–88)

Finally, a decision that had sounded like a step change when it was announced in 1954 sounded more ambiguous a year later when the Court ruled in May 1955 that the process of desegregating schools should begin 'with all deliberate speed'. The ambiguity of the word 'deliberate' was not wasted on those who wanted to do everything in their power to retain segregation in the South.

12.4 White resistance and violence

White Citizens' Councils

It was one thing for a group of learned judges in the hallowed chambers of the Supreme Court to make a ruling with profound national implications but the response to the ruling in the Deep South showed that years of struggle lay ahead. Robert Cook states that: 'The most adverse reaction came from the core states of the old Confederacy – Georgia, South Carolina, Alabama, Mississippi and Louisiana – states where regional distinctions were most highly prized and white supremacy was most firmly entrenched.' (Cook, 1998, p. 89)

The re-emergence of the Ku Klux Klan brought terror and violence to the lives of many black people in the Deep South. Yet the less ritualised but possibly more effective campaigns of predominantly middle-class White Citizens' Councils showed that the South would not resist integration by violence alone. Within days of *Brown* vs *Board of Education*, Judge Tom Brady, a Yale University-educated judge based in Mississippi, issued a pamphlet denouncing 'Black Monday', the 'totalitarian' judgement, the NAACP and the international communist conspiracy. The document effectively became the handbook of middle-class resistance to desegregation that manifested itself as the White Citizens' Council movement. The first White Citizens' Council was formed at Indianola, Mississippi, but the movement spread rapidly and by conservative estimates may soon have numbered 300,000 members across seven states.

Who joined the White Citizens' Councils?

Crucially the membership consisted of 'people of influence' who could skilfully operate within the social hierarchy to resist the process of desegregation and to impose heavy economic sanctions on their opponents. Historian Charles Payne states: 'The Councils were eminently respectable and in Mississippi were hard to distinguish from the state government.' (In Tyson, 2017, p. 98)

In the words of Lillian Smith:

Some of these men are bankers, doctors, lawyers, engineers, newspaper editors, and publishers; a few are preachers; some are powerful industrialists. It is a quiet, well-bred mob. Its members speak in cultivated voices, have courteous manners, some have university degrees, and a few wear Brooks Brothers suits. They are a mob, nevertheless. For they not only protect the rabble, and tolerate its violence, they think in the same primitive mode, they share the same irrational anxieties, they are just as lawless in their own quiet way, and they are dominated by the same 'holy ideal' of white supremacy. (In Tyson, 2017, p. 97)

Just as depressing was the spectacle of white elected officials almost falling over themselves to proclaim their racist credentials in the sure knowledge that in the Deep South at this time it was the best way to be re-elected. With the honourable exception of Senator Estes Kefauver of Tennessee, most southern governors, senators and congressmen fell into this pattern.

The murder of Emmett Till, 1955

The horrific murder of Emmett Till, a boy of just 14 years of age, in Mississippi showed that daily life in the Deep South would not be altered by a judicial ruling. It may be that the brutal, swaggering thugs who carried out the murder of a young boy were not thinking of the wider legal implications as they perpetrated their crime. But perhaps the culture they lived in encouraged a response to the Supreme Court that showed indifference to its distant authority. Till, a much-loved young man raised in Chicago, was in Mississippi visiting family and friends in the sweltering summer of August 1955. The exact content of a verbal exchange between a self-confident, friendly but naive youth from Chicago and a white shop assistant remains uncertain. Unfortunately, Till was not accustomed to the racial etiquette of the Deep South. The wrong words, direct eye contact, or even placing money directly into the hand of the female assistant would all have been enough to place him in extreme danger.

What is clear is that around 2.00 am the next day a small group of armed men arrived at a home in East Money in the Mississippi Delta and abducted 'the boy from Chicago' who had done 'the smart talking' at the store in Money. Till's mutilated, brutalised body was found in the Tallahatchie River a few days later. Remarkably, when Till's body was returned to Chicago, Emmet's mother found the strength to insist that his body lie in state in an open casket. Timothy Tyson explains how:

> The sociologist Adam Green observes that the spectacle surrounding Emmett Till's death 'convened' black Chicago and black Mississippi into one congregation that trumpeted the tragedy to the world ... Green writes, 'northern city and southern delta seemed the same place, and the need for collective action among African Americans across the nation seemed as urgent as never before.' (Tyson, 2017, p. 75)

12.5 The civil rights movement

The bus boycott, 1955–56

In December 1955, Rosa Parks refused to give up her seat on a crowded bus. A simple but courageous act of defiance in a society used to submission and deference became iconic in the whole history of the civil rights movement. The subsequent high-profile involvement of the emerging Martin Luther King Jr in the protracted and ultimately successful boycott means that the spectacular activity of one man has sometimes dominated our picture of a movement that was in fact complex, wide-reaching and with church-based, grass-roots support spread widely across the Deep South. The setting for Parks' protest was Montgomery, a large, rapidly growing city in Alabama, in which almost 40 per cent of the total population of 120,000 were black.

Rosa Parks

Born in Tuskegee in 1913, Rosa Parks had been raised by a strong-minded mother, with a powerful commitment to civic affairs and with family members who had stood up to racial oppression. At what would become the landmark moment in her life she was 42 years old and worked as a seamstress. While she has sometimes been depicted as a lady who was 'too tired' to give up her seat, in her autobiography Parks pointed out that she was in fact tired of giving in to segregation. Although a similar protest had taken place in Baton Rouge, Louisiana in 1953, it was the arrest in Montgomery that proved pivotal, sparking a boycott of the City Lines bus company that would last for more than a year and inflict unsustainable damage on the revenue of the company itself and the local economy. Moreover, by charging Parks with violating a statute on segregated transport the authorities now faced an appeal to a federal court and then the US Supreme Court, bringing the issue to national scrutiny and judgement.

The emergence of Martin Luther King Jr

The response to Parks' arrest illustrates the issues concerning the centrality of Martin Luther King's 'leadership' of the civil rights movement. Did the momentum of the movement stem from an outstanding, charismatic 'messiah' such as King or the less well-known work of the church, civil rights organisations, local leaders, community institutions and a range of committed activists both male and female? While King's charisma and oratory have made him famous, scholars have also now drawn attention to the role played in the bus boycott by local black activists such as Jo Ann Robinson and Edgar D. Nixon, and to direct action emanating from important centres of resistance such as Nashville, Tennessee and Birmingham, Alabama.

The 'Jim Crow' system gradually began to crumble not just because of the much publicised work of King but also because, as the 1950s wore on, an increasing number of African Americans from a broad range of backgrounds, ages and occupations began to act together, encouraged by each further step along the way to desegregation. Transport, schools, lunch counters and stores each became focal points for the burgeoning movement. This is not to say that King himself was not becoming of national importance. Within days of Parks being arrested, King declared:

> There comes a time when people get tired. We are here this evening to say to those who have mistreated us for so long that we are tired – tired of being segregated and humiliated, tired of being kicked about by the brutal feet of oppression. We have no alternative but to protest. For many years, we have shown amazing patience. We have sometimes given our white brothers the feeling that we liked the way we were being treated. But we come here tonight to be saved from that patience that makes us patient with anything less than freedom and justice.
> (In Oates, 1998, p. 279)

While there is no doubt King brought bravery, conviction and exceptional oratory skills to the campaign, the civil rights movement was so effective because it became such a broad-based and widely supported protest of the people and assumed a momentum beyond the capacity of any one individual.

Education and Little Rock High School, 1957

In 1957, the nation's attention was drawn to a previously white-only Central High School in Little Rock, Arkansas. When the local school board attempted to begin desegregation it aroused the wrath of the White Citizens' Councils and the Governor of Arkansas, Orville Faubus. While Faubus had a reputation as a relatively moderate figure, he knew that in the highly charged summer of 1957 his appeal to 'state's rights' would guarantee his political future. At the start of term in September 1957, Faubus responded to the fact that a handful of children would be attempting to enrol at Little Rock High School by personally sending in the state's National Guard to prevent them joining. When the National Guard had to be withdrawn under federal law they were replaced by a baying mob which by Monday 23 September numbered up to a thousand.

The intervention of President Eisenhower

Eisenhower was dismayed by what he called the 'disgraceful behaviour' of 'a mob of extremists'. Reluctantly, the president dispatched 1,000 troops from the 101st Airborne Division to Little Rock. The press now carried pictures of American troops, bayonets fixed, patrolling a high school. Eisenhower lamented the use which 'our enemies' would make of such scenes, and pleaded with the people of Arkansas to return to 'their normal habits of peace'. Eisenhower's decision to send in the troops has earned praise from historians who recognise that his commitment to defend the Constitution and to combat mob action was the right thing to do at a critical point in time. In the words of Stephen E. Ambrose: 'He could not have done otherwise and still been President.' (In Pach & Richardson, 1991, p. 154) The black children were admitted to the school, but within a year the school itself was closed down by opponents of desegregation. As late as 1963, significantly less than 10 per cent of schools in the Deep South were desegregated. As a depressing postscript, it is worth noting that Faubus went on to be elected governor on a further four occasions.

12.6 Martin Luther King Jr

King's emergence in the 1950s

While Faubus used the fears and anger of the white community to further his career, a man of formidable talent and boundless energy was emerging as the leader of the campaign to bring down the system of segregation. That man was Martin Luther King Jr. Hugh Brogan summarises King's contribution in these words:

> Born in Atlanta, with a doctor of theology's degree from Boston University, he combined the traditional fervour of Southern black Christianity with trained philosophical insight. Profoundly influenced by the example of Mohandas Gandhi, who by displaying moral authority through non-violence had overthrown the British Empire in India, King's peculiar contributions were his perception that the same philosophy and similar tactics could overthrow white supremacy in America and his ability to dramatize this doctrine for millions. (Brogan, 1985, p. 649)

King's achievements in the face of terror, death threats, physical attacks and repeated incarceration were immense. At his peak he captured the conscience of the nation.

In particular, his ideas impacted upon many of the white middle class and on influential members of the East Coast establishment. King would have a very direct, personal impact on two successive presidents, Kennedy and Johnson, and this helped to bring about landmark legislation in the Civil Rights Act and the Voting Rights Act. In some respects, his strategy of non-violence was the perfect technique in the face of the brutality used by those who fought to preserve segregation. Moreover, King displayed a level of empathy that was truly profound for those who suffered from racism.

Key campaigns against segregation in transport and for voter registration, and iconic moments such as the March on Washington speech and the Selma campaign perhaps marked the highlights of his career. The lasting impact of his oratory and his skill as a preacher is still striking today. King's skill in combating the vile racism of men like 'Bull' Connor helped to undermine those who tried to defend segregation with violence. In addition, King of course, mobilised a large section of the black community, not least through the foundation of the Southern Christian Leadership Conference (SCLC).

King's early life

Martin Luther King Jr. was born in the segregated city of Atlanta, Georgia in January 1929. His upbringing was steeped in the values of the African American Southern Baptist Church. While his family, church and religious beliefs were African American, some of King's academic career took place in largely white institutions. When he graduated from high school in 1944 at the age of 15, he enrolled in Morehouse, the same college attended by his father and by his maternal grandfather. In 1948, King attended the predominantly white Crozer Theological Seminary in Chester, Pennsylvania, where he graduated in Divinity. Boston College, Massachusetts, where King studied for his PhD, was also a largely white organisation.

By now, King had fallen in love with Coretta Scott, a gifted musician from Alabama. Music was intrinsic to African American worship so this was a perfect match for the young divinity scholar. They were married in June 1953, by which time King was looking for a pastoral role. In April 1954 he was appointed Pastor at the Dexter Avenue Baptist Church in Montgomery, Alabama. King's career was blossoming and he was awarded his doctorate in the summer of 1955 (Table 12.1).

Table 12.1 Key civil rights events in the Eisenhower era and the emergence of Martin Luther King Jr

---

1953	A bus boycott predating the more well-known protest of Mrs Rosa Parks and adapting the tactic of car pools took place in Baton Rouge, Louisiana.
	Martin Luther King Jr, married Coretta Scott in Marion, Alabama.
	In *Terry* vs *Adams*, the Supreme Court ruled that segregated primary elections were in breach of the Fourteenth Amendment.
1954	Following two years of hearings and deliberation the Supreme Court ruled in *Brown* vs *Board of Education* (*Brown I*) that separate black and white schools were no longer allowed; this overturned the ruling of *Plessy* vs *Ferguson* which stated that facilities could be 'separate but equal'.

Continued

Organisation of White Citizens' Councils in Mississippi and beyond to combat deseg-regation.

Martin Luther King Jr became the pastor at Dexter Avenue Baptist Church in Montgomery.

1955 In *Brown II*, the Supreme Court made the somewhat ambiguous ruling that schools should be desegregated 'with all deliberate speed'.

Emmett Till, a 14-year-old boy, was murdered and thrown in a river in Mississippi.

In Montgomery, Alabama, in December, Mrs Rosa Parks arrested after she refused to give up her seat on a crowded bus to a white person; a bus boycott was organised in Montgomery and after more than a year segregation ended.

Martin Luther King Jr began to emerge as the most significant leader in the struggle for civil rights; he was elected president of the Montgomery Improvement Association (MIA).

Having graduated with a BA in Sociology from Morehouse College in 1948, King obtained his PhD in Systematic Theology from Boston University.

1956 King's house in Montgomery bombed.

King arrested on a minor speeding charge.

Montgomery Improvement Association (MIA) issued suits against the city's system of bus segregation; King subsequently convicted of inciting an illegal boycott.

In response to the Supreme Court's *Brown* ruling a group of 19 senators and 77 con-gressmen, led by Strom Thurmond, issued the Southern Manifesto: 'With the gravest concern for the explosive and dangerous condition created by this decision and inflamed by outside meddlers.' (Martin, 1998, p. 221)

The Supreme Court upheld a Federal District Court ruling that Alabama's bus segrega-tion laws were unconstitutional.

Montgomery bus boycott reached a successful conclusion.

1957 Foundation of the Southern Christian Leadership Conference (SCLC), with King as president.

Passage of the Civil Rights Act under President Eisenhower – the first such legislation since Reconstruction; in the face of Southern Democratic opposition the bill was wa-tered down to such an extent that some considered it a sham, yet it could also be seen as a small step forward in terms of Congressional action after decades of inactivity.

Major disturbances outside Central High School in Little Rock, Arkansas, as nine black students attempted to enrol; President Eisenhower sent in troops to escort the students into school.

1958 King arrested in Montgomery.

King stabbed in a bookstore in New York City; the wound was life-threatening but he survived.

12.7 Appraisal of Eisenhower's record on civil rights

The Eisenhower White House did not instigate the gradual wearing down of this powerful system. Indeed, most historians would agree that Eisenhower's record on civil rights was probably the weakest element of his entire administration. Eisenhower's upbringing in states like Kansas and Texas, and his long career in the military, had equipped him with many qualities, but had not instilled a clear vision for leadership in the area of civil rights.

While he was prepared to complete the process of desegregation of the armed forces begun by Truman, and made some encouraging appointments of African American officials, Eisenhower had an abiding distrust of African American militancy. His conservative, gradualist approach meant that it fell instead to the Supreme Court to set in motion the tide of events which would reach their peak in the Kennedy, and particularly the Johnson, Administrations. In the area of civil rights Eisenhower was a reactive rather than proactive leader. As late as 1958, Eisenhower was still advising leaders of the African American community that while they had his support, 'you must be patient.' Stephen E. Ambrose presents this perspective on the Eisenhower Administration in general, but on the civil rights campaign in particular:

> William Ewald, in *Eisenhower the President*, concludes that 'In the fifties, many terrible things that could have happened, didn't. Dwight Eisenhower's Presidency gave America eight good years – I believe the best in memory.' There were no wars, no riots, no inflation – just peace and prosperity. Most white middle-class and middle-aged Republicans would heartily agree with Ewald. But a black American could point out that among the things that did not happen were progress in civil rights or school desegregation ... But although Eisenhower's record on civil rights ... is more negative than positive, he did leave us with some valuable legacies. He hated having to send American troops into Little Rock in 1957 to enforce court-ordered desegregation, but he did it ... He did not agree with the Court's ruling in *Brown* v. *Topeka* but he acted on the basis of a deeply held belief ... 'I hold to the basic purpose. There must be respect for the Constitution – which means the Supreme Court's interpretation of the Constitution – or we shall have chaos.' (In Bischof & Ambrose, 1995, p. 248)

William L. O'Neill is arguably even more critical:

> It must be admitted, Eisenhower did not understand the civil rights revolution and failed to meet its challenge. That he was unprejudiced personally and, by appointing Chief Justice Earl Warren to the Supreme Court, had an indirect responsibility for some of the positive changes make his record here all the more disappointing. The reasons for his failure are plain enough. Eisenhower was a child of the nineteenth century, and as such he did not believe that desegregation could, or should, be brought about by coercion ... As Stephen Ambrose puts it, 'He missed a historic opportunity to provide moral leadership.' In fact, until Little Rock in 1957 he provided almost no leadership at all 'on the most fundamental social problem of his time.' That is a grave indictment, and also the worst thing to be said about Eisenhower's social policy. (In Bischof & Ambrose, 1995, p. 104)

While the civil rights movement began during the Eisenhower Administration, the issues they had raised were passed to Kennedy and then Johnson under the heading of 'unfinished business.'

12.8 Grass-roots resistance

Sit-in protests

Far from the majesty of the White House or the oratory of Dr King, attention now switched to a setting just as prosaic as a seat on a bus. This time, the protest came with a 'sit-in' at a lunch counter in a Woolworth store. In a similar way to the bus boycott, the first use of the sit-in technique is much less well known than the iconic protest that followed. In August 1958, predating the better known Woolworth protest of 1960, young activists in Wichita, Kansas, staged a sit-in which eventually led to the end of segregation practices there. Then on 1 February 1960, acting on their own initiative, four young men at the Woolworths counter in Greensboro, North Carolina refused to move when they were refused service. The protest was simple but devastatingly effective. Encouraged by the stand taken by the Greensboro Four, the sit-in movement rapidly spread through the South. By April 1960, 78 similar sit-ins had taken place, not just in North Carolina but also in Nashville, Tennessee and Atlanta, Georgia. 2,000 people had been arrested but the momentum given to grass-roots activism was immense.

The Freedom Rides

Having witnessed the success of the bus boycott and the sit-in movement, a further bastion of segregation in transport now came under attack. As early as 1947 a relatively little-known but important campaign predating the activity of the 1960s took place in the upper South, aimed at raising the issue of desegregating transport. This incident illustrates the fact that a decade before King became famous, the civil rights movement was already underway. Once again, ordinary people at the grass roots were taking part in protests and we can see the shortcomings of a messianic explanation of the civil rights campaign.

The early protest may have put down a marker but as late as 1961 segregation in transport and in its associated facilities remained firmly in place. In April 1961 13 volunteers, black and white, received training in non-violence strategies ahead of their proposed 'Freedom Ride' travelling from Washington DC to New Orleans through the Southern states. The key events are summarised in Table 12.2.

Table 12.2   Key events of the Freedom Rides

- The Ride through Georgia passed without major incident but in Anniston, Alabama, the riders came under sustained attack. The bus was set alight and a baying mob were only just kept at bay.
- A second group were badly beaten at the Anniston bus depot.
- In Birmingham, Alabama, the riders suffered a further brutal attack. Congress of Racial Equality (CORE) activists had to be flown to New Orleans, leaving Student Nonviolent Coordinating Committee (SNCC) members to complete the Freedom Ride.
- Further violence in Montgomery prompted the Attorney General, Robert Kennedy (RFK), to demand that the Governor of Alabama provide better protection.
- June 1961 – A further wave of Freedom Riders arrived in large numbers in Jackson, Mississippi.
- November 1961 – RFK forced the Interstate Commerce Commission (ICC) to bring an end to all segregation on interstate buses.
- By 1964 the Civil Rights Act brought to a complete end the dwindling practice of segregation in transport or transport facilities.

12.9 President Kennedy and the civil rights issue

The first rehearsal had been in the bathtub where Kennedy could relieve his aching back. The second run-through was over bacon rolls and coffee: 'Ask not what your country can do for you – ask what you can do for your country.' The president's advisers and speechwriters liked what they were hearing. Yet during the dry run for what would be acclaimed as one of the most stirring inaugural addresses ever delivered, one of the president's aides was less impressed than most. He was Harris Wofford, a professor of law at Notre Dame University and now the president's adviser on civil rights. He had listened in vain to the first draft to find a single reference to civil rights. On the same day that Wofford raised his objections to the omission, 23 African American students had demanded to be served at segregated lunch counters in two department stores in Richmond, Virginia. Kennedy's response was simply to insert the words 'at home' in the sentence: '... unwilling to witness or permit the slow undoing of those human rights to which this nation has always been committed and to which we are committed today *at home* and around the world' (Reeves, 1994, p. 39).

During the campaign itself, Kennedy had simply asked Wofford to tell him the ten things he needed to know about civil rights. Kennedy was certainly without personal prejudice towards African Americans. He personally removed his campaign team from a hotel in Paducah, Kentucky, when he discovered that a black reporter had been denied a room there. A more public gesture came on 20 October 1960, when Kennedy phoned Mrs Coretta King to offer support following the sentencing of her husband Martin Luther King Jr to four months of hard labour in a Georgia prison following a traffic violation. This public show of support is seen by many historians as a turning point in the 1960 election, and Kennedy consequently secured around 70 per cent of the African American vote.

Analysis of President Kennedy as a civil rights leader

How much attention did Kennedy pay to the civil rights issue once he was in office? Maldwyn A. Jones observes that:

> After his death Kennedy was remembered as a fearless champion of racial equality. But he was slow to take a strong stand on the issue. When he became President he was unwilling to propose a civil-rights bill, or even to support one drafted by Congressional liberals, for fear of jeopardising other New Frontier measures. Executive action, he believed, could do more for blacks than legislation. (Jones, 1995, p. 548)

Kennedy certainly made some outstanding appointments of black officials to high office. Thurgood Marshall, the NAACP's foremost lawyer, became a US Circuit Court Judge. Robert Warren was made head of the Housing and Home Finance Agency. More dramatically, Kennedy sent troops to Mississippi in 1962 to enforce the admission of a black student to the state university. The Attorney General, Robert Kennedy, used the power of the law to extend African American voting rights and to reduce segregation in schools and public amenities.

However, even those historians most favourably inclined towards Kennedy have conceded that the president displayed an ambivalent attitude towards the civil rights issue when he first entered the White House. In his prize-winning book *A Thousand Days: John F. Kennedy in the White House*, historian Arthur M. Schlesinger contended that Kennedy believed that an all-out drive to support civil rights would have simply alienated southern support for other New Frontier measures such as a minimum wage increase and further support for educational projects. Schlesinger argued that black leaders 'never doubted that Kennedy was on their side' (Schlesinger, 1965, p. 793). Many subsequent interpretations have been much more critical. Several historians have drawn attention to Kennedy's appointment of segregationist judges in the South and to his approval of the FBI's wiretapping of Martin Luther King Jr.

Kennedy's capacity for growth as a supporter of civil rights

An area of interest for all students of the Kennedy era is the notion that the young president had an exceptional capacity for personal growth. This concept can be applied to Kennedy's increasing commitment to civil rights as his presidency developed. Some experts have discerned a turning point when Kennedy witnessed on national television the dramatic events unfolding in Birmingham, Alabama, in April and May 1963. Kennedy watched with a mounting sense of revulsion as local police commissioner Eugene 'Bull' Connor unleashed dogs, high-pressure fire hoses and baton-wielding policemen on civil rights marchers including large numbers of children. On Friday 4 May an Associated Press photographer captured the image of a large German shepherd dog mauling a 15-year-old bystander. When the picture appeared on the front of the *New York Times*, Kennedy privately remarked that he 'felt sick'. Within a month Kennedy gave a national television address from the Oval Office on the issue of civil rights:

> We are confronted primarily with a moral issue. It is as old as the Scriptures and is as clear as the American Constitution. If an American, because his skin is dark, cannot eat lunch in a restaurant open to the public, if he cannot send his children to the best public schools available, if he cannot vote for the public officials who represent him ... then who among us would be content with the counsels of patience and delay ... It is time to act in the Congress ... I am therefore asking the Congress to enact legislation giving all Americans the right to be served in facilities which are open to the public – hotels, restaurants, theatres, retail stores and similar establishments ... I am also asking Congress to authorize the Federal government to participate more fully in lawsuits designed to end segregation in public education ... Other features will also be requested, including greater protection for the right to vote. (JFK Library, online)

The verdict of historians on JFK and civil rights

Although at the time of the groundbreaking speech Kennedy had not yet devised detailed legislation, he had, at last, made a public commitment to the civil rights campaign. Bruce Miroff criticises Kennedy for not committing himself to civil rights as a moral issue until the summer of 1963, and points out that even in the last few months of his life he continued to see civil rights as 'an intrusion rather than a priority' (White, 1998, p. 226). Thomas C. Reeves (1992) claims that Kennedy's domestic programmes floundered because of 'his lack of conviction and personal fervor' (p. 228). More sympathetic historians have balanced their approach by stressing the narrowness of

Kennedy's electoral mandate, the ideological opposition of the Southern Democrats and the partisan approach of the Republicans. They contend that these factors were significant in reducing the president's room for manoeuvre. Indeed, it is worth noting that following Kennedy's commitment to civil rights in the summer of 1963 his support in Congress visibly diminished. Alonzo Hamby (1985) has presented Kennedy in a more favourable light, arguing that he made an impressive commitment to civil rights for moral rather than political reasons (in White, 1998, pp. 228–29). Although as late as the spring of 1963 Martin Luther King Jr felt that the president had accepted 'token' measures, the massive demonstrations in the summer of 1963 prompted Kennedy to lend full executive support to a broad-ranging civil rights bill. (White, 1998, pp. 226–29)

12.10 The transition from Kennedy to Johnson (1963)

'Come let us reason together' (Johnson's favourite biblical quote – from Isaiah)

The brutal, untimely nature of Kennedy's death undoubtedly created a climate which was more conducive to social reform. A combination of the public mood of guilt, grief and a sense of unfulfilled potential meant that it was now possible to present radical reform with a sense of optimism. Bruce Schulman provides this analysis of the transition from the Kennedy Administration to the Johnson era with regard to civil rights:

> Of all the holdover measures from the Kennedy administration, LBJ devoted the greatest effort to civil rights. In the wake of Kennedy's death, a number of civil rights leaders feared that LBJ, the master of Senate compromise, would dilute the bill as he had the Civil Rights Act of 1957. But LBJ quickly assured the nation that he would accept no compromises this time around. (Schulman, 1995, p. 73)

When he addressed a Congress still reeling from the murder of his predecessor, Johnson proclaimed: 'No memorial oration or eulogy could more eloquently honor President Kennedy's memory than the earliest possible passage of the civil rights bill for which he fought so long' (in Dallek, 1998, p. 60):

> During the first two weeks of his Presidency, he met with the principal leaders of the civil rights movement – Whitney Young, James Farmer, A. Philip Randolph and Martin Luther King, Jr. – and warned them to lace up their sneakers because he was going to move so fast on civil rights that they would have trouble keeping up with him. (Schulman, 1995, p. 73)

12.11 The Civil Rights Act, 1964

Amid a raft of important Great Society legislation, the Civil Rights Act of July 1964 stands out as a landmark moment in the history of the struggle against racism. In its own words the act enforced 'the constitutional right to vote ... to provide injunctive relief against discrimination in public accommodations ... to protect constitutional rights in public facilities and public education' and 'to prevent discrimination in federally assisted programs'. Henceforth, the law, in theory at least, would outlaw discrimination on the grounds of race, colour, religion, gender, or national origin.

In his memoirs, LBJ explained: 'There comes a time in every leader's career when he has to put in all his stack. I decided to shove in all my stack on the Civil Rights Act of 1964.' (In Schulman, 1995, p. 73) Johnson enjoyed several advantages as he prepared to take his civil rights legislation through Congress. The post-Kennedy assassination mood, creating the idea that the time had come for the nation to act, combined with Johnson's legislative experience and his undoubted commitment, seemed to bode well for groundbreaking legislation. However, formidable barriers remained. To better understand those barriers we need to briefly look at particular features of the US Congress.

The Southern Democrats

Within Congress the hostility of Southern Democrats towards civil rights legislation was well known. Zelizer explains how

> the primary base of power for the Right was Congress, dominated by a coalition of powerful southern Democratic and Midwestern Republican representatives and senators. The southern Democrats represented primarily rural constituencies of farmers, agribusiness, poor whites, poor African Americans and individuals involved in military contracting. Most of the Republicans in the coalition represented rural interests, fiscally conservative small-town voters, and small- and midsize business leaders. (Zelizer, 2015, p. 13)

Zelizer also points out that what united these diverse forces was a determination to resist any legislation designed to benefit African Americans. The political skill and power of individuals within this system should not be underestimated. LBJ's campaign against the Jim Crow system was opposed by highly effective political operators such as Richard Russell, a senior Democratic senator from Georgia who warned Johnson that his bill would mean that 'it's going to cost you the South and cost you the [1964] election ' (Dallek, 1998, p. 112). Russell was shrewd enough to understand that public opinion was shifting and the civil rights movement had acquired a momentum that was unprecedented. More nuanced still was his sense that some of his younger southern colleagues now felt that the future economic well-being of the South was more important than the cause of segregation. While Russell was actually willing to give Johnson some room for manoeuvre with a bill, this was only on the premise that its content would be so diluted as to be acceptable to the South.

The committee system

It is frequently said that it is in the committees that the real work of Congress is done. This is where proposals for legislation are debated and the detailed content of bills is drafted before being passed to the House or Senate for general floor debate. So these committees can be seen as gatekeepers to the whole legislative process. Membership of committees, especially the most prestigious ones, is highly prized. Not least, the legislators use the committees to deliver benefits to their home state – 'bringing home the bacon'. The chairmanship of these committees confers real power and status and, in particular, reflects the seniority of the post-holder. In the JFK/LBJ era conservative Southern Democrats held the chair in almost half of the major committees in the House and Senate. This included committees of the highest importance including the House Ways and Means Committee with its myriad fiscal responsibilities and, crucially, the House Rules Committee, which controlled the schedule and rules for debate on the floor.

Kennedy's civil rights bill had emerged from the House Judiciary Committee in October 1963 but in December of that year it was marooned in the Rules Committee, whose chairman, Howard Smith of Virginia, was a dyed-in-the-wool opponent of civil rights legislation. Indeed, at the start of 1964 Smith was still insisting on a hostile scrutiny of the bill, line-by-line, word-by-word. Even when the bill came out of the Rules Committee it remained vulnerable to 'poison-pill' amendments in which those opposed to the bill could add clauses actually designed to make the bill even less palatable to those who might support a more modest act.

The filibuster

Early in 1964, the threat from Johnson's people of a humiliating 'discharge petition' helped to persuade the House of Representatives to forward the bill to a final vote. In February, the House passed the civil rights bill by 290 to 130, with 91 Democrats voting against the bill, of whom 88 were from the Old Confederacy. But it was in the Senate that the battle lines were drawn, and it seemed likely that the technique of 'filibustering' would be used to mire the bill in unlimited debate. This tactic, first employed in 1837, was based on an interpretation of the Senate's rules concerning extended debate. Effectively, any member of the Senate could prevent a bill from being voted on providing that they continuously occupied the floor and kept talking. Notoriously, for example, the white supremacist Allen Ellender from Louisiana took down an anti-lynching bill by staging a filibuster that lasted for six weeks in 1938. Four times in the 1940s, anti-poll tax legislation had been blocked by filibustering Southern Democrats. While these practices might almost sound quaint, the stark fact was that between the end of the Reconstruction era and 1956 not a single civil rights bill had been able to overcome the committee system or the filibuster tactic.

'Cloture'

The way to overcome the filibuster was to 'invoke cloture', which required 67 of the 100 senators to agree to terminate the debate. This device for bringing the interminable talking to an end was introduced by senators for the first time in 1917. However, 67 votes represented a huge barrier to anyone presenting any type of 'liberal' bill and, most of all, to civil rights legislation. In the past, the Senate had never voted for cloture where civil rights legislation was concerned. Johnson's ability to reach across the political divide was remarkable and, in particular, he secured the co-operation of the Senate Minority Leader, Everett Dirksen of Illinois. As Todd S. Purdum states:

Dirksen was the single most flamboyant senator of his day … the consummate Senate show horse, he was also a master of rules and procedures and a meticulous legislative draftsman, an expert on the fine print of pending bills, with crackerjack legal staff. (Purdum, 2014, p. 211)

With Johnson steadfastly refusing to present a watered-down bill Southern Democrat conservatives initially tried to delay the legislation in its committee stages.

The Senate debate, March 1964–June 1964

When the bill finally came to the floor of the Senate, the segregationists reverted to the filibuster. In his epic opening speech, Johnson's ally Hubert Humphrey pointed out that there were hotels in South Carolina that allowed guests to bring in dogs, but did not accommodate African Americans. But a determined band of southerners had organised themselves into platoons, with each member speaking for around four hours a day. While the opponents of the bill spoke of the dire threat to the Constitution, in constituencies across the country senators who remained on the fence faced mounting pressure to support the vote for cloture. In particular, grass-roots civil rights organisations belonging to the Jewish, Catholic and Protestant faiths added to the clamour for the bill to be passed. Meanwhile, in the Oval Office, LBJ was happy to support lucrative, 'pork' projects – for example the Central Arizona Project to provide water to that state – in return for support from, in this particular case, Senator Hayden. Perhaps most important of all in turning the tide was Johnson's relationship with Republican Minority Leader Dirksen. All of these factors combined so that the longest filibuster in the history of the Senate finally came to an end in June 1964. In the end, the vote for cloture was 71 to 29.

Johnson had decided to risk the consequences of alienating a powerful section of his own party, and it fell to a combination of Northern Democrats and moderate Republicans to push through the vote for cloture. The Civil Rights Act became law in 1964: segregation of public amenities in the South became illegal. This was Johnson's finest hour.

12.12 'The freedom summer', 1964

The gradual stirring of long overdue legislation in Congress was not enough to satisfy the burgeoning momentum of the civil rights movement. Perhaps the most notable event of the summer of 1964 took place in the state of Mississippi. As with other civil rights initiatives, this was instigated not by M. L. King Jr but, in this case, largely by individuals within the Student Nonviolent Coordinating Committee (SNCC). The broad target of this protest was the denial of African American voting rights and, more specifically, corruption among the all-white Mississippi Democratic Party. Ultimately, as the protest unfolded, the combined efforts of the SNCC, local people and King exerted pressure on the city of Selma over black voter registration. The pinch-point of the protest came to be the Edmund Pettus Bridge, where a peaceful march came under attack from law enforcement officers armed with billy-clubs and tear gas. The images of brutality were, in a sense, 'perfect' for the civil rights movement, promoting widespread sympathy, presidential outrage and the mobilisation of thousands of white supporters who headed to the city to take part in the Selma–Montgomery march.

12.13 The Great Society and the Voting Rights Act, 1965

A combination of physical and verbal intimidation, literacy and residency tests and the economic sanction represented by the poll tax combined to make African American electoral turnout in the South exceptionally low. At the start of the 1940s only 3 per cent of the 5 million African Americans eligible to vote in the south were actually registered to vote. Nevertheless, despite the success of the Civil Rights Act and Goldwater's calamitous defeat in the presidential election, Johnson had to be pushed by Martin Luther King Jr to prioritise voter registration over education and health care legislation. Meanwhile, King's focus had switched to Selma, Alabama, a city notorious for its commitment to segregation and with a police sheriff, James Clark, with a reputation for violence. Predictably, Selma's police responded to unarmed protestors with unrestrained brutality. Television coverage of 'Bloody Sunday' shocked the nation and, not least, members of Congress. The murder of a white civil rights campaigner and Unitarian minister, James Reeb, created a sense of national outrage and forced the president to act without further delay. President Johnson signalled his determination to take back the initiative with his dramatic appearance before a joint session of Congress on 15 March 1965:

> Rarely in any time does an issue lay bare the secret heart of America itself. Rarely are we met with a challenge, not to our growth or abundance ... but rather to the values and the purposes and the meaning of our beloved Nation. The issue of equal rights for American Negroes is such an issue. And should we defeat every enemy, should we double our wealth and conquer the stars, and still be unequal to this issue, then we will have failed as a people and as a nation. There is no Negro problem. There is no Southern problem ... There is only an American problem. [On] Wednesday I will send to Congress a law designed to eliminate illegal barriers to the right to vote. This bill will strike down restrictions to voting in all elections – Federal, State and local – which have been used to deny Negroes the right to vote ... Their cause must be our cause too. Because it is not just Negroes, but really it is all of us, who must overcome the crippling legacy of bigotry and injustice. And we shall overcome. As a man whose roots go deeply into Southern soil I know how agonizing racial feelings are. I know how difficult it is to reshape the attitudes and the structure of our society. But a century has passed, more than a hundred years, since the Negro was freed. And he is not fully free tonight ... The time of justice has now come ... And when it does, I think that day will brighten the lives of every American. (In Dallek, 1998, pp. 218–19)

Opponents of civil rights legislation who had seemed so powerful in 1964 now seemed relatively impotent. The filibuster in the Senate against the Voting Rights Act went on for less than half the time of the 1964 protest and the bill was eventually passed with only 19 votes in dissent. In the House of Representatives the forces of liberalism swept all before them. The passage of the Voting Rights Act in August 1965 amid a whirlwind of Great Society legislation marked a major step forward in civil rights legislation. In the face of white southern resistance to black voting, the Act provided federal registration of African American voters in any county where less than 50 per cent of the eligible voters took part in presidential elections. A further sign of progress came with the Twenty-Fourth Amendment to the Constitution (1964) which outlawed poll taxes: the African American voter was no longer deterred from going into the voting booth by the thought of having to pay for the privilege. A substantial increase in African American voting and in African American representatives now followed in the South. Within months, almost a quarter of a million new African American voters were added to the register.

12.14 The Watts riots, 1965

Even at the height of his executive power, LBJ had always known that the time he would get to achieve his goals was strictly limited. While the election landslide of 1964 seemed so empowering, there were signs within less than a year that any consensus he had achieved could quickly unravel. Ironically, it was the very act of wielding presidential power, particularly in foreign policy, that in some senses curtailed Johnson's authority.

In August 1965, just five days after Johnson signed the Voting Rights Act, a serious riot erupted in the Watts district of Los Angeles. The city's mayor, Sam Yorty, had failed to deal with repeated allegations of police brutality when a further police arrest in the ghetto sparked six days of rioting. This resulted in 34 deaths, at least 1,000 injuries and more than $200 million damage to property. The importance of Watts was profound. Many broadly sympathetic white people were shocked and frightened by the violence shown on TV and were mystified as to why black people would cause so much damage to their own neighbourhood. Zelizer's analysis is that 'there would be more riots that would nurture the view of the Great Society as a cause of rather than a solution to urban violence' (Zelizer, 2015, p. 222).

12.15 The Black Power movement

The successful civil rights legislation of 1964 and 1965 had raised expectations among the African community, but as the focus shifted from the ballot box to the inner city it became plain to many that in one sense nothing had really changed. Poverty, drug abuse, unemployment, crime, poor housing and residential discrimination remained to blight the lives of many ordinary people. While the focus of many black activists turned to matters such as housing, the white community demanded a sharper focus on the enforcement of law and order in the American city.

By the middle of the 1960s it was becoming evident, not least to King himself, that not all Black Americans agreed with the direction and style of his leadership. In particular, many young black people who were growing up in an urban setting in the North East or on the West Coast were attracted to a new, more militant brand of leaders who were committed to the notion of Black Nationalism. In this context, King's leadership appeared conservative and conciliatory. The Black Muslims rejected Christianity in favour of Islam and claimed that all white people were devils. In the summer of 1966, under the radical leadership of Stokely Carmichael, the SNCC dropped the word 'nonviolent' from its name, signalling a more aggressive approach than its predecessor. His phrase 'We want black power!' unsettled many Americans who had previously been sympathetic to the civil rights movement. This middle-class anxiety was exacerbated in 1967, when racial tension flared in over 100 cities in a disturbing summer of discontent.

The degree to which race was again becoming a divisive issue can be seen in the language used by future president Gerald Ford, speaking in Illinois in September 1966. Labelling the Democrats as the party 'with the big riots in the streets', he asked voters:

> How long are we going to abdicate law and order – the backbone of any civilization – in favor of a soft social theory that the man who heaves a brick through your window or tosses a firebomb into your car is simply the misunderstood and underprivileged product of a broken home? (In Zelitzer, 2015, p. 247)

The Republican Party that had been in despair in November 1964 seemed resurgent, with candidates such as Richard Nixon and Ronald Reagan happy to exploit Johnson's growing vulnerability over Vietnam, inflation, the budget deficit (projected to rise from $3.7 billion to $8.64 billion for 1967), urban disorder and its connections with the civil rights movement. These factors coalesced in the midterm elections of 1966 to signify a dramatic shift away from liberalism and public spending and towards conservatism and austerity.

Great American Lives: Muhammad Ali, 1942–2016

While lists of the greatest sportsmen and women can be contentious, surely many people would place Muhammad Ali as the greatest athlete of the twentieth century. His skill, flamboyance and courage in his boxing career came to be matched by his willingness to stand up for his beliefs outside of the ring. His conversion to Islam, rejection of his 'slave name' Cassius Clay, support for the civil rights movement and dignified opposition to the Vietnam War meant that he distinguished himself just as much in civic life as in his sporting career.

Raised in a warm, loving family in Louisville, Kentucky, Cassius Clay grew up amid the harsh system of racial segregation. Entering the boxing gym at the age of 12, his precocious talent was quickly recognised. A succession of amateur titles culminated in a spectacular success when he won the Light Heavyweight Gold Medal at the Rome Olympics in 1960. What would be a glittering professional career began in October 1960 and a string of sensational wins followed, with the majority by a knockout. The young boxer did not lack self-confidence and his outrageous comments, predictions for when he would knock people out and flamboyant entry into the ring attracted vocal criticism as well as a huge fan base. Clay's taunting of opponents sometimes crossed over a line between amusing and cruel and unacceptable.

Following his surprise victory over the much-feared Sonny Liston in 1964 the new Heavyweight Champion of the World proclaimed himself 'the greatest! I shook the world ... I'm the prettiest thing that ever lived'. Clay subsequently changed his name to Cassius X and then, after converting to Islam, to Muhammad Ali.

While success in the ring continued unabated, Ali's refusal to be drafted into military service led to a five-year prison sentence, the loss of his boxing

Continued

licence and the removal of his passport. The enforced period of inactivity in the ring lasted from March 1967 to October 1970, but Ali's opposition to the war in Vietnam remained steadfast. His conviction was overturned in 1971, by which time Ali was ready to embark on the defining fights of his career.

1. Ali vs Joe Frazier. Madison Square Garden. March 1971. 'The Fight of the Century'. After 15 brutal rounds Ali was knocked down in the final round. He quickly got back to his feet but suffered his first professional defeat by a unanimous decision.
2. Ali vs Frazier. January 1974. The re-match with 'Smokin' Joe' took place in New York City again. This time, Ali prevailed by a unanimous decision.
3. Ali vs George Foreman. October 1974. 'The Rumble in the Jungle' against one of the hardest-hitting fighters of all time was staged in Zaire. Foreman was a clear favourite with the bookmakers but his ferocious style floundered when he was confronted by Ali's 'rope-a-dope' tactic. Showing incredible bravery, Ali spent most of the fight on the ropes, soaking up punishment from an increasingly tired and bewildered Foreman. In the spectacular eighth round, Ali suddenly cut loose and knocked out his exhausted opponent. Ali had regained the title in perhaps the most iconic moment of his career.
4. Ali vs Frazier. 3 October 1975. The final, definitive fight with his old adversary Frazier was known as the 'Thrilla in Manilla'. In a brutal, astonishing fight both fighters reached the point of exhaustion. Frazier was withdrawn by his corner before the start of the 15th round. Ali later remarked that he had come close to death.

Too many more fights followed as time caught up with the 'Greatest'. He absorbed too much punishment against lesser opponents, as concerns mounted about the long-term damage to his health. His last fight, a defeat, took place in 1981, and a diagnosis of Parkinson's disease was confirmed in 1984. Ali's dignity in the face of serious illness in later life, his concern for the underprivileged both in the US and abroad and his warmth whenever he met fans ensured that his later years were filled with love and appreciation. The image of him lighting the Olympic Flame at the Atlanta Games of 1996 despite his trembling hands touched millions around the world. When he died in June 2016, athletes, boxers, film stars and politicians mourned his loss and paid tribute to his outstanding achievements. The Mayor of Louisville, Greg Fischer, proudly commented that: 'Muhammad Ali belongs to the world. But he has only one hometown.'

Ali's professional boxing record		
61 fights	56 wins	5 losses
By knockout	37	1
By decision	19	4

Further reading: Jonathan Eig, *Ali* (Simon & Schuster 2017)

12.16 1967 – Further rebellion and a presidential Commission of Enquiry

In 1967, racial tension flared in over 100 cities in a summer of discontent. In July 1967 in Newark, New Jersey, 26 people were killed and 2,000 were injured during five days of disturbances, and in the same month 43 people were killed in Detroit. Johnson responded to the 1967 upheaval by setting up a Commission of Enquiry. In the spring of 1968, its report concluded that the root cause of the racial tension was 'pervasive discrimination and segregation in employment, education and housing' (Haas Institute, online).

However, the tide of events in the country at large was no longer flowing in the direction of further legislative measures for African Americans. The war in Vietnam had drained Johnson's energy and the nation's finances. White sympathy for the civil rights cause ebbed away in the face of nationally televised images of looting and violence. This was particularly evident in great cities like Chicago, where concerns about fair housing legislation were expressed by people worried about the impact of African Americans moving into hitherto largely white communities.

Meanwhile, also in 1966, in Oakland, California, the Black Panther movement, with its paramilitary style, came to national attention, under its charismatic 'minister of information', Eldridge Cleaver. The Black Panthers were confrontational towards the police and to white authority, famously using the medals ceremony in the 1968 Mexico Olympic Games to raise a black-gloved salute during the playing of the Star Spangled Banner. More than any of these gifted and formidable leaders, it was Malcolm X who was most able to articulate the anger of so many black people at this time.

12.17 Malcolm X

Upbringing

Malcolm Little's upbringing could hardly have been more traumatic. Born in 1925 in Omaha, Nebraska, his parents were violent and the family dysfunctional. One of Malcolm's earliest childhood memories was of his paternal uncle being lynched. Malcolm's father, a full-blooded, hot-headed preacher was a 'dedicated organizer' (Dierenfield & White, 2012, p. 171) for Marcus Garvey and his 'back to Africa' movement. His outspoken views may have provoked an attack by Klansmen, resulting in the Little family being driven out of town, but the details of this incident remain unclear. At any rate, the family moved to Lansing, Michigan where a mysterious arson incident once again left the family homeless. When Malcolm was just 6 years old his father was killed, either at the hands of a white supremacist group, as the family maintained, or in an accident as ruled by the police and the coroner. Malcolm's mother was later sectioned on the grounds of insanity and in 1941 Malcolm left school and moved to live with his older half-sister in Roxbury, a black ghetto in Massachusetts.

From Malcolm Little to Malcolm X

By now, the young man's sense of hostility and anger at the cards he had been dealt was complete. A series of increasingly more serious crimes meant that at the age of just 20 he was given a seven-year prison sentence. Despite the brutality of these circumstances he became a prolific reader and, through family members on the outside, a convert to the Nation of Islam. Upon release in 1952 he met with Elijah Muhammad who enlisted him as a member of the Nation and replaced the name Little with the surname X. Moving to Harlem, he proved to be a powerful, instinctive and charismatic speaker. He preached the orthodox Black Muslim doctrine to an increasingly sizeable congregation. Malcolm's message was particularly receptive to young black people from the poor ghettos.

Malcolm's message regarding King was scathing: 'The goal of Dr. Martin Luther King is to give Negroes a chance to sit in a segregated restaurant besides the same white man who has brutalized them for 400 years.' (In Dierenfield & White, 2012, p. 175) In turn, Malcolm was becoming increasingly frustrated with what he was coming to see as the conservatism of his mentor Elijah Muhammad. At times, Malcolm's angry rhetoric was distorted by the press, and a comment that President Kennedy's murder was a matter of 'chickens coming home to roost' (Marable, 2011, p. 273) because of the violence America itself had perpetrated was widely condemned.

The split with the Nation of Islam

It was no surprise when Malcolm X broke from the Nation of Islam but the bitterness of the spilt caused Malcolm to predict that it would only be a matter of time before he was killed as a result. Meanwhile, in New York City, Malcolm founded a new religious, black nationalist, direct-action group called the Muslim Mosque Inc. The new organisation advocated black participation in political, economic and social programmes while condemning King's tactics of non-violence: 'It is criminal to teach a man not to defend himself when he is the constant victim of brutal attacks ... When our people are being bitten by dogs, they are within their rights to kill those dogs.' (In Dierenfield & White, 2012, p. 178)

Malcolm was strongly influenced by a visit to the Muslim holy city of Mecca in 1964. Upon his return he formed the Organization of Afro-American Unity (OAAU). The political platform of his new group has been seen by some scholars as predating the beliefs of the Black Power movement which began in 1966. The tone of some of its literature was less confrontational and even offered support to more mainstream civil rights leaders. Even so, Malcolm remained afraid of no one and a message offering physical support to King proclaimed:

> If the federal government will not send troops to your aid, just say the word and we will immediately dispatch some of our brothers there to organize self-defence units among our people and the Ku Klux Klan will then receive a taste of its own medicine. The day of turning the other cheek to these brute beasts is over. (In Dierenfield & White, 2012, p. 180)

Analysis of the importance of Malcolm X

Malcolm's unique brand of agitation, black nationalism and commitment to the spiritual and economic elevation of African Americans was a fire which remained undimmed, even though he was roundly condemned by the white press as the 'angriest Negro in America' for stirring up a long, hot, summer of violence and confrontation in 1964. Malcolm's retort to this was emphatic: 'It takes no one to stir up the sociological dynamite that stems from the unemployment, bad housing and inferior education already in the ghettoes.' (In Dierenfield & White, 2012, p. 181) Malcolm had predicted that he would be murdered and in February 1965, while speaking in Harlem, he was brutally gunned down by three members of the Nation of Islam.

12.18 A change in direction for the civil rights movement

The emergence of the Black Power movement was one factor among several in forcing King to shift position, between the passage of the Voting Rights Act in 1965 and his tragic death in April 1968. King's relationship with President Johnson gradually deteriorated from 1965 onwards. Johnson's commitment to escalating the increasingly unpopular war in Vietnam made it difficult for the two leaders to remain on good terms. The fact that young black men were making up a disproportionate share of the US military effort meant that in the words of King himself America was sending blacks to 'guarantee liberties in South East Asia which they had not found themselves in Southwest Georgia and East Harlem' (in Jones, 1995, p. 554).

In the months before his brutal murder in April 1968, King and others in the civil rights movement were broadening their attention to issues of wider economic justice and the damaging war in Vietnam. Firstly, in the words of Piven and Cloward, 'blacks became more indignant over their condition – not only as an oppressed racial minority in a white society but as poor people in an affluent one' (in Alexander, 2012, p. 38). The civil rights campaign was shifting towards a movement that represented a broad swathe of poor people. In the spring of 1968 King looked at bringing together disadvantaged people, from the rural poor to those who lived in the ghetto, from poor white families in the Appalachians to Native Americans, Mexicans and Puerto Ricans. King's focus was shifting from the battle against segregation in the South to the national issue of economic equality.

12.19 King in perspective

The scrutiny and extensive academic research to which King has been subject means that inevitably some criticisms and reservations have emerged (Table 12.3). As a reader, you may wish to consider how much importance you would attach to each of these individual points.

Table 12.3   King's leadership in perspective

- Acclaimed for his charismatic leadership, King actually suffered from periods of intense self-doubt.
- King has been accused of plagiarism both in his work for his doctorate and also subsequently in his preaching.

Continued

- It is now very clear that King was a prolific womaniser. Some analysts have said that this undermined King's moral authority.
- King's leadership style could be extremely autocratic and this alienated some members of the civil rights movement.
- It has been claimed that King was unable or unwilling to develop a genuinely grass-roots movement.
- The civil rights movement was dominated by men and perhaps slow to recognise the inherent problem of this fact.

12.20 From LBJ to President Nixon

John A. Farrell's outstanding biography of Nixon presents some disturbing material in relation to the president's attitudes towards African Americans. In a private conversation with close aides Ehrlichman and Haldeman, for example, Nixon said that black people 'live like a bunch of dogs'. Further recent research on Nixon reveals more damaging evidence that Johnson's successor was capable of expressing horrendous views on black people. It is, perhaps, a measure of how bizarre Nixon could be that he was also capable of writing to his aides that 'my feelings on race, as you know, are if anything ultra-liberal' (in Farrell, 2017, pp. 385–86).

As Farrell puts it:

> The civil rights movement, in the late 1960s, had grown more militant and off-putting to many white Americans. The photographs of nonviolent martyrs in Birmingham and Selma – being beaten by state troopers, bitten by police dogs, or tossed by fire hoses as they fought for their rights as citizens – had given way to images of 'black power' advocates like Stokely Carmichael, defiant sports figures like Muhammad Ali, and the gun-toting revolutionaries of the Black Panther Party.
>
> The movement had shifted its agenda as well. With the fundamental rights of citizenship now legally secured, civil rights leaders like King had pressed for economic benefits and tax-supported social programs, irritating the white working and middle class, who were starting to chafe at rising income and property taxes. In the year before his death, King joined the opposition to the Vietnam War, yet another polarizing issue. (Farrell, 2017, p. 387)

Political scientists have long been clear that the black vote for John F. Kennedy cost Nixon dearly and was instrumental in his narrow defeat in the 1960 presidential election. Nixon was unforgiving of any individual or group whom he felt had cost him votes. The 1968 presidential campaign pitted Nixon not just against the Democrats but also against the American Independent candidate George Wallace, the outspoken, brooding, segregationist Governor of Alabama.

The busing programme

A major issue at this time was 'busing,' a key part of the programme to achieve racial desegregation in the North. Under busing schemes, pupils were moved away from traditional neighbourhood schools and taken a distance to schools in other areas to achieve a racial balance. Even before Nixon entered the White House, busing was controversial. In the city of Boston, for example, implementation of busing was accompanied by widespread violence, protests and school closures. Nixon's opposition to busing was accompanied by his high-profile condemnation of the permissive society and drug culture, all of which was designed to out-flank potential right-wing support for Wallace who, nevertheless, secured almost 10 million votes.

When Nixon entered the Oval Office the vast majority of black children in the Deep South were still attending segregated schools. Any momentum to change this came not from the president but from the Supreme Court. The struggle between the executive branch and judicial authority was reflected in the Court's ruling in *Alexander* vs *Holmes* (1969) which went against Nixon's attempts to slow down the process of school desegregation in Mississippi. Despite the president's hostility to the busing programme, in 1971 the Supreme Court ruled in its favour. The decision handed cities and counties the authority to use the busing strategy to end the segregation of their school districts. In a note to senior figures in his administration Nixon commented that 'segregated white education is probably superior to education in which there is too great a degree of integration of inferior black students with the white students'. Nixon's conclusion was that students and teachers from ethnic minorities 'dragged the others down with them' (in Farrell, 2017, p. 385).

Farrell makes the following observations:

- The task of integrating schools was deliberately shifted from the more progressive Health, Education and Welfare Department (HEW) to the Attorney General, Mitchell, and the Department of Justice, so that the pace would be slowed down.
- Spiro Agnew was given nominal responsibility for school desegregation and promptly proposed watering down changes in the Voting Rights Act.
- Nixon asked the courts for 'more time' for enforcing the rulings regarding school desegregation.

As a consequence of these actions, well-respected columnists Evans and Novak concluded at the time that Nixon would push only for 'token integration', thus taking 'the first serious backward step from racial integration by any national administration in a generation' (in Farrell, 2017, p. 385).

Given Nixon's damaging personal comments sampled here, the overall conclusion of his policy on civil rights is perhaps unexpected. In a white paper on civil rights issued in March 1970 Nixon stated that: 'Deliberate racial segregation of pupils by official action is unlawful wherever it exists, in the words of the Supreme Court it must be eliminated, "root and branch" – and it must be eliminated at once.' (In Farrell, 2017, p. 391) Nixon could be the arch pragmatist. Seeing the historic inevitability of school desegregation and at the same time desperate to avoid a 'Little Rock'-style stand-off, Nixon dramatically changed course. In the words of Dean Kotlowski: 'A confluence of presidential leadership, federal persuasion, Supreme Court rulings, Justice Department lawsuits and the threat of HEW denying holdout districts federal aid, broke white southern resistance.' (In Farrell, 2017, p. 393)

Out of a total school population of 3 million, only 186,000 African American children attended desegregated school in the South prior to 1969. During autumn 1969, after the Nixon administration began to desegregate schools via litigation, 600,000 southern blacks entered desegregated schools ... [and by the end of 1970] two million more African Americans were attending desegregated schools ... In this sense, Nixon was the greatest school desegregator in American history. (Kotlowski in Farrell, 2017, p. 393)

12.21 From Ford to Carter, 1974–80

Ford's short spell in the White House as effectively a caretaker president made it unlikely that he would devote any significant attention to the civil rights issue. To be sure, dealing with the immensely toxic fallout from the Watergate scandal would have preoccupied any politician, particularly one judged by historians as being of relatively limited ability. Ford will always be best remembered for his controversial pardon offered to his disgraced predecessor, Richard Nixon. He also attracted some controversy for offering a partial pardon to those who had been found guilty of dodging the draft during the Vietnam War. Some historians have commented wryly that the leniency offered by the Oval Office at this time was not extended to the judicial system as it applied to ordinary people and, in particular, African Americans.

Therefore we can move on briskly from President Ford, and consider the work of his successor, James Earl ('Jimmy') Carter, a politician from the South. Whereas previous prominent politicians from the Deep South had fanned the flames of racial bigotry, Carter, a Southern Baptist, spoke during the presidential campaign of reconciliation with the South, 'to be accepted as equals, to re-join the mainstream of American political life' (Reynolds, 2009, p. 498). Unwilling to attach himself to the old guard of southern conservatives and with a distance between himself and the more strident voices of the moral majority, Carter made clear he was a political outsider. This path enabled him to win huge support from African American voters.

However, Kendi states:

Black hopes were high until the austere Carter administration, to boost the economy, started unprecedented cuts in social welfare, health care, and educational programs while increasing military spending. From the lowest Black poverty rate in US history in 1973, the decade ended with record unemployment rates, inflation, falling wages, rising Black poverty rates, and increasing inequality. (Kendi, 2016, p. 425)

With the 1970s drawing to an end it seemed that the plight of the black poor was effectively becoming worse. Although a sizeable black middle class was also now evident the success of this minority in achieving the education, career and 'breaks' needed to achieve this status could not detract from the fact that the poor seemed worse off than ever. It would fall to Ronald Reagan, the two-term president of the 1980s, to decide whether addressing this gulf in equality would be a priority for his new administration.

12.22 President Reagan

Iwan Morgan's biography of Ronald Reagan makes it plain that African Americans were a group for whom the president's claim to have restored 'Morning Again in America' 'was largely a mirage'. He states:

> the racial gap in wages and employment had started to widen again in the stagflation-hit 1970s, a trend that continued in the supposedly prosperous decade that followed. Inner-city poverty, family breakdown, and gang violence further blighted many black lives. Making matters worse, the police offensive against the crack-cocaine epidemic in the second half of the 1980s and beyond was clearly targeted at young black males. By 1989, one analysis calculated, 23 per cent of African American men aged 18 to 29 were caught up within the criminal justice system – whether in prison, on parole, or on probation ... It was later estimated that a black male born in 1991 had a 29 per cent chance of spending life in prison at some stage of his life, compared to 1 per cent for a white male. (Morgan, 2016, p. 241)

Accordingly, many African Americans thought Reagan's celebration of America's renewal manifested wilful disregard of their plight. Morgan claims that Reagan stood alone in this approach, breaking from the policy of the past that ran from Franklin D. Roosevelt to Jimmy Carter. He argues:

> Despite lacking personal bigotry, he had already proved himself the most successful racial-backlash politician in US history before entering the White House. All of his campaigns, at both state and national level, featured rhetorical assaults on able-bodied welfare cheats that carried strong racial imagery ... As president, Reagan espoused a colour-blind conservatism that denied any racial intent in his anti-statist agenda, which hit African Americans harder than white people because they relied on government to mitigate the structural inequalities of American society. Lack of interest rather than prejudice blinded him to this reality. (Morgan, 2016, pp. 241–42)

A further important attack on Reagan's War on Drugs came with the publication in 2010 of *The New Jim Crow* by Michelle Alexander. Alexander states:

> Most people assumed the War on Drugs was launched in response to the crisis caused by crack cocaine in inner-city neighbourhoods. This view holds that the racial disparities in drug convictions and sentences, as well as the rapid explosion of the prison population, reflect nothing more than the government's zealous – but benign – efforts to address rampant drug crime in poor, minority neighbourhoods. This view, while understandable, given the sensational media coverage of crack in the 1980s and 1990s is simply wrong ... there is no truth to the notion that the War on Drugs was launched in response to crack cocaine. President Ronald Reagan officially announced the current drug war in 1982, before crack became an issue in the media or a crisis in poor black neighbourhoods. A few years after the drug war was declared, crack began to spread rapidly in the poor black neighbourhoods of Los Angeles and later emerged in other cities across the country. The Reagan administration hired staff to publicise the emergence of crack cocaine in 1985 as part of a

strategic effort to build public and legislative support for the war. The media campaign was an extraordinary success. (Alexander, 2012, p. 5)

12.23 George H.W. Bush

In terms of race, the Bush Campaign of 1988 was disturbing. Labouring to create a 'vision' and trailing the Democratic candidate, Michael Dukakis, Bush deliberately resorted to 'negative' campaigning. The most notorious example of this was a television advertisement about a black man, Willie Horton, who had been convicted of murder and rape in Dukakis's home state of Massachusetts. Under a state furlough scheme supported by Dukakis, Horton had received ten weekend passes from prison. On one of these weekends Horton fled and kidnapped a young couple, stabbing the man and repeatedly raping his girlfriend. Some observers claimed that the advert cynically blended an anti-crime message with racism. Beyond the advert itself, Bush's 'tough' stance on crime saw him enthusiastically endorse the use of capital punishment, even though statistics showed extraordinary disparities between the treatment of black and white people.

If the campaign was, to say the least, concerning, then it also signified that there would be little coming from the White House to advance the lives of black people. Bush's promise of a 'kinder, gentler America' was not evident for African Americans in the late 1980s. In the same decade that Wall Street gorged itself in greed, in the great American cities homicide rates were often terrifying. During the mid- to late 1980s a crack cocaine epidemic generated a growing culture of gangs, guns and violence. Poor educational standards for the disadvantaged, a lack of sympathetic law enforcement in the most difficult areas, the failure of a largely white police force to build positive relations with black communities in the inner city, a culture dominated by young men aged 15–30, the easy availability of alcohol and a proliferation of black-on-black violence all combined to create a terrible reputation for crime in great cities such as Detroit, New York City, Chicago and Washington DC.

Acute deprivation, racially motivated law and order systems and a demography towards younger males were all contributory factors in making some urban areas particularly dangerous. Statistics showed 1980 to be the worst for crime in New York City's history, in terms of recorded murders, robberies and burglaries since records had started to be kept some 50 years earlier. In Far South Side Chicago '[a] mortician from nearby Cedar Park Cemetery had drawn press attention by publicizing his offer of free funerals and burials to victims of ... gun violence.' (Garrow, 2017, p. 200) With young black men statistically much more likely to be in prison, a further generation faced being brought up by lone parents and without the presence of a father figure in the home. In summary, 'a kinder, gentler' America was also a nation that in almost every sense seemed predicated against giving black people the same opportunities as whites. The institutionalised racism of the police was particularly striking.

Rodney King, 1991–92

The savage beating, following a high-speed car chase, of black motorist Rodney Glen King in March 1991 by four out-of-control white policemen from the Los Angeles

Police Department (LAPD) received worldwide attention. Their subsequent acquittal, a year later, brought a degree of racial tension to the country that was as intense as the Watts riots of 1965 or the fallout from the assassination of Martin Luther King in 1968. The 1992 Los Angeles riots lasted for six days and resulted in 55 deaths and more than 2,000 injuries. These events placed President Bush in a situation he seemed ill-equipped to deal with or even comprehend. The man who had managed the Gulf War in a calm, statesmanlike manner now seemed far removed from the daily plight of those who lived in the inner cities.

President Bush's nomination of Clarence Thomas to the Supreme Court

Kendi states that President Bush 'fanned the fury on July 1, 1991, when he nominated a Black jurist, Clarence Thomas to replace civil rights icon Thurgood Marshall on the Supreme Court' (Kendi, 2016, p. 447). Kendi claims that Thomas:

> had been the backseat driver of antiracist and racist forces throughout his career. And now, Bush had called Thomas to the Supreme Court, claiming he was the 'best qualified at this time,' a judgement that sounded as ridiculous as those officers trying to justify the beating of Rodney King. (Kendi, 2016, p. 447)

Maldwyn Jones is no less critical of the nomination. He points out that Thomas 'had questioned the constitutionality of the right to abortion, criticized affirmative action programs, and spoken dismissively of civil-rights leaders' (Jones, 1995, p. 620).

The formal confirmation hearings in the Senate in the autumn of 1991 were equally contentious. Anita Hill, who had worked closely with Thomas, now accused the nominee of sexual harassment and gender discrimination. While Thomas dismissed the allegations as a 'high-tech lynching for uppity blacks' (Kendi, 2016, p. 448), Hill maintained that 'the defamation of Black womanhood and the lack of awareness of sexual harassment was preventing Americans from believing her testimony' (Kendi, 2016, p. 448). The Senate eventually voted to confirm Thomas by the narrow margin of 52–48. The months of bitter argument merely showed the extent of division not just on matters of race, but also on the treatment of women and sexual harassment in the workplace.

Cultural response to racial injustice

In his important book *Stamped from the Beginning*, Ibram X. Kendi provides this analysis of the response to this injustice from the black community:

> Like their ancestors, young urban blacks resisted the law enforcement officials who condemned them to twentieth-century slavery. And they resisted sometimes to the beat. Hip Hop and rap blossomed in 1988 after a decade of growth from the concrete of the South Bronx. BET and MTV started airing their popular Hip Hop shows. *The Source* hit newsstands that year, beginning its reign as the world's longest-running rap periodical. It covered the head-slamming rhymes of Public Enemy – and 'Fuck tha Police,' the smashing hit of N.W.A. or Niggaz Wit Attitudes, from straight out of Compton. (Kendi, 2016, p. 442)

12.24 President Clinton

Empathy vs votes?

In handing authority to another southern president, Bill Clinton from Arkansas, and his vice president, Al Gore from Tennessee, there seemed a striking opportunity for the neglect of the Reagan/Bush years to be addressed. During his skilful election campaign of 1992 Clinton perhaps trod a fine line between his genuine empathy for people and his unwillingness to be portrayed as a typical 'tax and spend' Democrat. In January 1992 the candidate briefly returned to his home state where he was governor. In sanctioning the execution of a mentally limited black man, Ricky Ray Rector, he demonstrated his capacity to seek votes over principle. Clinton was well aware that previous Democratic candidates had been badly damaged by appearing to be 'weak' on crime.

The first Clinton Cabinet – 'A Cabinet that looks like America'

Once in power, Clinton's record in appointments and the selection of his Cabinet was more promising. During the campaign Clinton promised that he wanted his first Cabinet to 'look like America', in terms of both gender and race. Clinton's initial pick of six Cabinet nominations included two African Americans but only one woman. While the new president was initially criticised for not reflecting the support he had so substantially received from women, the new Cabinet as it emerged was ultimately more diverse in terms of gender and race than its predecessors. Three women, four African Americans and two Hispanic Americans ensured that there was a marked break with tradition.

In general, historians have been reasonably positive in terms of Clinton's attitude towards African Americans. His empathetic temperament, 'liberal' outlook, insistence on racial tolerance and his ability to attract a large number of votes from the African American community have all been recognised. A speech he made to black ministers in Memphis in the autumn of 1993 was interesting because the president felt sufficiently close to black people to be able to express some contentious points to effectively ask his audience to face some difficult truths. Furthermore, his express support for affirmative action programmes in the build-up to the 1996 campaign reflected the fact that times had changed to the extent that 'all-white' teams, either presenting in the media or in corporate offices, were no longer acceptable.

On the other hand, Ibram X. Kendi is scathing in his assessment of some of Clinton's key policies. Kendi is critical of Clinton's first State of the Union Address in which he called for a 'strong, smart, tough crime bill'. This came into existence as the Violent Crime Control and Law Enforcement Act, in the summer of 1994. It injected billions of dollars into the urgent expansion of police forces, prisons and consequently into a massive increase in the incarceration of black people. As Kendi puts it:

> The net effect would be the largest increase of the prison population in US history, mostly on nonviolent drug offenses. Clinton fulfilled his campaign vow that no Republican would be tougher on crime than him – and crime in America was

colored Black. As Tupac Shakur rhymed in 'Changes', 'Instead of war on poverty they got a war on drugs so the police can bother me.' (Kendi, 2016, p. 454)

So while President Clinton promised that his administration would 'Build a bridge to the Twenty-First Century' (Klein, 2002, p. 13) it is clear that not all analysts would agree that he was really able to do so in regard to the general life opportunities presented to the black population of the United States.

12.25 The fundamentals of racism in American society in the twenty-first century

Earlier in this book, the coverage of the lives of African Americans at the turn of the twentieth century painted a depressing picture of the structural and institutional barriers to racial equality that were so firmly in place. Now at the end of our coverage of this matter it may be helpful to consider some of the fundamental barriers to an equal society that remain in place and for readers to consider how much progress has been made. The huge racial disparity of punishment in America is not the mere result of neutral state action. Effectively, a mass incarceration of black people has taken place based on intense police surveillance and hostile police action. In addition, the massive use of state power has been deployed to imprison hundreds of thousands of poor, black male (and increasingly female) young people in the 'War on Drugs'. Beyond this, the systemic breakdown of black and poor communities has been brought about through mass unemployment, social neglect and economic abandonment.

This somewhat depressing picture is not intended in any way to disparage those who have worked so hard to combat racism in the United States. Huge progress has undoubtedly taken place, including the landmark election of a Black American to the highest office. The emergence of an extremely successful black middle class has shown that people of colour can reach the highest levels of success in all aspects of professional, cultural, artistic and sporting life. Nevertheless, at the time of writing, even after the two-term presidency of Barack Obama the areas raised in the list above surely need to be urgently addressed.

Further reading

Alexander M., *The New Jim Crow: Mass Incarceration in the Age of Colorblindness* (New York: The New Press 2012).

Bischof G. & Ambrose S.E. (eds.), *Eisenhower: A Centenary Assessment* (Baton Rouge: Louisiana State University Press 1995).

Branch T., *Parting the Waters: America in the King Years 1954-63* (New York: Simon & Schuster 1989).

Brogan H., *Longman History of the United States of America* (London: Longman 1985).

Coates T., *We Were Eight Years in Power: An American Tragedy* (London: Hamish Hamilton 2017).

Cook R., *Sweet Land of Liberty?* (London: Longman 1998).

Dallek R., *Flawed Giant: Lyndon Johnson and his Times 1961–1973* (New York: Oxford University Press 1998).

Dierenfield B.J. & White J.W., *A History of African-American Leadership* (Harlow: Pearson 2012).

Farrell J.A., *Richard Nixon: The Life* (New York: Doubleday Random House 2017).

Garrow D.J., *Rising Star: The Making of Barack Obama* (London: William Collins 2017).

Jones M.A., *The Limits of Liberty: American History 1607–1992* (New York: Oxford University Press 1995).

Kendi I.X., *Stamped from the Beginning: The Definitive History of Racist Ideas in America* (London: Penguin Random House 2016).

Kirk J.A. (ed.), *Martin Luther King, Jr and the Civil Rights Movement* (New York: Palgrave Macmillan 2007).

Klein J., *The Natural: The Misunderstood Presidency of Bill Clinton* (New York: Doubleday 2002).

Marable M., *Malcolm X: A Life of Reinvention* (London: Penguin 2011).

Martin W.E. Jr (ed.), *Brown v Board of Education: A Brief History with Documents* (Boston: Bedford/St Martin's 1998).

Morgan I., *Reagan: American Icon* (London: I. B. Tauris 2016).

Oates S., *Let the Trumpet Sound: A Life of Martin Luther King Jnr* (Edinburgh: Canongate 1998).

Pach C.J. Jr & Richardson E., *The Presidency of Dwight D. Eisenhower* (Lawrence: University Press of Kansas 1991).

Purdum T.S., *An Idea Whose Time Has Come: Two Presidents, Two Parties, and the Battle for the Civil Rights Act of 1964* (New York: Picador 2014).

Reeves R., *President Kennedy: Profile of Power* (London: Papermac 1994).

Reeves T.C., *A Question of Character: A Life of John F. Kennedy* (Rocklin, California: Prima Publishing 1992).

Reynolds D., *America, Empire of Liberty: A New History* (London: Allen Lane 2009).

Schlesinger A.M. Jr, *A Thousand Days: John F. Kennedy in the White House* (London: Andre Deutsch 1965).

Schulman B.J., *Lyndon B. Johnson and American Liberalism: A Brief Biography with Documents* (Boston: Bedford Books 1995).

Thomas E., *Being Nixon: A Man Divided* (New York: Random House 2015).

Tyson T.B., *The Blood of Emmett Till* (New York: Simon & Schuster 2017).

White M.J., *Kennedy: The New Frontier Revisited* (London: Macmillan Press Ltd 1998).

Zelizer J.E., *The Fierce Urgency of Now: Lyndon Johnson, Congress and the Battle for the Great Society* (New York: Penguin Press 2015).

Online resource

JFK Presidential Library: www.jfklibrary.org, last accessed in 2018.

13 The end of the American century: 1980–2000

13.1 The 1980s and the shift to the right

While incumbent candidates often go into presidential elections with significant inherent advantages, that can scarcely be said of President Carter in 1980. Domestic indicators could hardly have been worse. Carter had presided over a doubling of unemployment and inflation while the budget deficit had reached an eye-watering $50 billion. If this was not enough, the calamitous fate of the American mission to rescue its hostages in Iran dragged Carter's approval ratings down even further. Although Carter was able to secure enough delegates at the New York convention to see off the challenge of Edward Kennedy, he received, at best, a lukewarm endorsement. This was in marked contrast to the Republican Party's enthusiasm for Ronald Reagan.

In retrospect, the shift to the right that this signalled had a fairly long gestation period. In spite of hugely expensive liberal programmes such as the Great Society in the 1960s there seemed little to show for it by 1980. America's inner cities were crumbling, African Americans continued to live in poverty, educational standards were modest, crime rates soaring, prison populations burgeoning and to some observers this came together as a picture of American decline and moral decay.

In his outstanding book *The Unwinding*, George Packer paints a picture of a relentless downward spiral. In this extract he describes the fate of once-thriving areas in Youngstown, Ohio from the perspective of a lady called Tammy Thomas.

> As Tammy drove over the crumbling asphalt of the streets, she was still amazed by the gaps and silence where there had once been so much life. It was as if she had still expected to see the old families, and the east side had just disappeared. Where had it all gone? The things that made it a community – stores, schools, churches, playgrounds, fruit trees – were gone, along with half the houses and two-thirds of the people, and if you didn't know the history, you wouldn't know what was missing. The east side had never been the best part of Youngstown, but it had the most black homeowners, and to Tammy it had always been the greenest, the least dense, the most beautiful – you could pick peaches around Lincoln Park – and now parts of it were almost returning to nature with deer wandering across overgrown lots where people came to dump their garbage. (Packer, 2013, p. 28)

Packer makes clear that this sad decline was not confined to one area. 'It was happening in Cleveland, Toledo, Akron, Buffalo, Syracuse, Pittsburgh, Bethlehem, Detroit, Flint, Milwaukee, Chicago, Gary, St. Louis and other cities across a region that in 1983 was given a new name: the Rust Belt.' (Packer, 2013, p. 53)

The damaging process of de-industrialisation that scarred these great, sometimes iconic, cities was part of a deeper malaise. As the cities fell apart and jobs disappeared, America's standing in the world seemed also to be in terminal decline. Not just the trauma of the failure in Vietnam but more recent episodes such as the drawn-out hostage crisis in Iran, and the rise of the highly competitive Far East economy, had badly damaged American morale and certainty.

As the Democratic experiment in big government appeared to be discredited, neo-conservatives set out an alternative picture of a minimalist state, while economists like Milton Friedman espoused the free market and intellectuals of the New Right used prestigious think-tanks to argue that the counter-culture of the 1960s, lax treatment of criminals and tolerance of a permissive society needed to be replaced by a new political order. If these ideas were complex, then Ronald Reagan's gift was to be able to 'translate' them into simple slogans that would find considerable traction as the American people came to decide who would lead them at the start of the new decade.

13.2 Ronald Reagan

Ronald Reagan was born in February 1911. The son of an itinerant shoe salesman travelling across Northern Illinois, he lived an archetypal but remarkable American life. Nicknamed 'Dutch' he left Dixon High School for Eureka College and by the time he became a summer lifeguard, at Lowell Park Beach, he had developed an impressive physique and stature that remained with him throughout his long life. He derived enormous satisfaction from this job and even in his final years, his mind ravaged by Alzheimer's disease, he would fondly recall how he had 'saved seventy-seven lives'. He loved swimming and horse-riding and in later life was never happier than when he was riding out on his ranch near Santa Barbara. With his film star looks he exuded a kind of Western hero charm, wrapped in all-American patriotism that would serve him well. Twice married, he was devoted to his second wife Nancy, but was remarkably detached from his four children, to the extent that it was said he did not even recognise his own son at his high school graduation ceremony.

A sportscaster in Des Moines, blessed with a melodious, reassuring voice, he became an enthusiastic supporter of the New Deal. Renowned most of all for his career as a Hollywood film star he also enlisted in the forces as a cavalry officer and as a member of the air corps, though his actual service was curtailed due to poor eyesight. Politically he travelled on a journey from left to right, working in the film industry as the president of the Screen Actors Guild, but then becoming an outspoken anti-communist. He became a television host, acquiring the comic timing which would serve him so well in later life. He then worked for the General Electric Company as the host of 'General Electric Theatre' and finally in the political arenas served as Governor of California from 1967 to 1975. By then he was wealthy, well-connected and a committed Republican in the mould of Eisenhower. He believed he was ready to secure the Republican nomination for the highest office.

13.3 The presidential election of 1980

Thwarted in 1976, even though he completely overshadowed the chosen candidate, the lacklustre Ford, Reagan arrived at the Republican Convention in Detroit in 1980 certain of victory. The primary campaign saw him record emphatic victories against future president George H.W. Bush and John Anderson. Bush was wealthy, well-connected and an important figure in the East Coast Republican establishment so Reagan's decision to choose him as his running mate made them the perfect team to deliver a strongly right-wing agenda. Carter's foreign policy agenda left him wide open to allegations of weakness in the face of the Soviet threat. The discredited policy of detente, the weakness of the SALT II treaty, the humiliation in Iran and fears over Soviet adventurism in Afghanistan all created a climate in which Reagan's cheerful personality, easy one liners and, most important of all, promises to end the painful spectacle of American decline achieved much more traction than Carter's weary disposition.

The sharp difference in their demeanour was underlined in the one and only televised debate of the campaign when Reagan spoke directly to the electorate and provided a devastating critique of Carter's presidency.

> It might well be if you would ask yourself, are you better off than you were four years ago? Is it easier for you to go and buy things in the stores than it was four years ago? Is there more or less unemployment in the country than there was four years ago? Is America respected throughout the world as it was? Do you feel that our security is as safe, that we're as strong as we were four years ago? (In Morgan, 2016, p. 141)

Carter's earnest attempts to deal with serious issues such as human rights and post-imperialism were lost in the simplicity of Reagan's appeal to reverse the country's moral and international decline. Carter suffered the worst defeat of an incumbent since Herbert Hoover in 1932. Reagan, at the age of 69, became the oldest man ever to win the presidency. His winning margin in the Electoral College of 489 to 49 had been bettered only twice, by Roosevelt in 1936 and Nixon in 1972. In the popular vote Reagan achieved 50.7 per cent compared to Carter's 41 per cent and the independent candidate John Anderson's score of 6 per cent. On Reagan's coat tails, the Republicans won control of the Senate and gained 33 seats in the House (Table 13.1).

If the presidency had been brought to its knees by the Iranian hostage crisis, then Ronald Reagan was the man who would reinvigorate the highest office. In the words of his biographer Edmund Morris,

> We became so positive a society under Ronald Reagan that we forget how low our national morale had sunk before he raised his right hand on January 20, 1981, and by plain force of character, reinvested the Presidency with authority and dignity ... Reagan will be remembered, with Truman and Jackson, as one of the great populist Presidents, an instinctual leader who, in body and mind, represented the better temper of his times. (Morris, *The New Yorker*, 28 June 2004)

Table 13.1   The result of the 1980 presidential election

Candidate	Party	Electoral College votes	Popular votes
Ronald W. Reagan (California)	Republican	489	43,899,248
Jimmy Carter (Georgia)	Democrat	49	35,481,435
John B. Anderson (Illinois)	Independent	–	5,719,437

Ronald Wilson Reagan

40th President of the United States (1981–89)
Born: 6 February 1911
Birthplace: Tampico, Illinois
Died: 5 June 2004, aged 93; buried in California
Education: Eureka College, Illinois
Political party: Republican
State: California
Occupations before presidency: Sports broadcaster and actor
Previous government service: Governor of California 1967–75
Age at inauguration: 69
Dates of office: 20 January 1981–20 January 1989
Election: November 1980 and 1984
Vice president: George H.W. Bush
Length of term: 8 years

13.4 Ronald Reagan's first term: 1981–85

The end of big government

In the honeymoon period after his first presidential triumph, Reagan stated that his election 'was not so much a victory of politics as it was a victory of ideas'. Then in his inaugural address in 1981, Ronald Reagan, perhaps the most effective spokesman for the right wing, told the American people: 'Government is not the solution to our problem. Government is the problem.' As Iwan Morgan puts it:

> Reaganism as a governing ideology promoted unfettered capitalism as a social good, rewarded individualism, and limited the state's role in mitigating inequality in American society ... From the outset, Reagan's holy trinity consisted of cutting taxes, reducing government, and restoring America's defences. (Morgan, 2016, pp. 174–75)

Reagan's obvious limitations and self-deprecating sense of humour meant that his political opponents often fell into the trap of underestimating his capacity for getting things done. In fact, his personal charm, ability to connect with grass-roots America and highly skilled public speaking meant that the 'Great Communicator' was a highly capable political operator. His bravery and good humour when an assassination attempt in March 1981 left him with life-threatening injuries further enhanced his standing. Aided in his first term by a Republican majority in the Senate (for the first time since 1952) and a reduced Democratic margin in the House of Representatives, the new president was able to cut a swathe through what he saw as the dense undergrowth of big government. In what Morgan describes as 'the most significant domestic spending retrenchment since World War II' a projected income tax cut of 30 per cent in three years was put forward as the means to 'stimulate growth, productivity and employment' (Morgan, 2016, p. 176).

A range of government programmes were to be put to the sword. Welfare measures including employment training, food stamps, child nutrition, disability benefits and public assistance schemes were all sharply reduced. Other areas suffering savage cuts included education, law enforcement, the arts and transport. The president's handling of an air traffic controllers' dispute in the summer of 1981 showed that Reagan's authority was difficult to counter. A brief strike was declared illegal and when the deadline set by the president for a return to work was ignored, the controllers were abruptly dismissed and replaced. This outcome illustrated the fact that the power and size of the labour unions was in progressive decline. While millions of new jobs were created, many of these were in newer, non-unionised service industries and small businesses. Furthermore, appointments to the National Labor Relations Board were carefully chosen to reflect sympathy to business rather than the workforce. Meanwhile deregulation in major industries such as mining, banking, oil drilling and transport illustrated the president's belief that government interference in the economy was both costly and inefficient.

The Supreme Court

In a similar vein, Reagan also wished to change the outlook of the judicial branch of the government to bring it into line with the more conservative climate of the early 1980s. This was quickly achieved with circuit and district judges but changing the complexion of the Supreme Court was more challenging and extended into the second term. Reagan appointed Sandra Day O'Connor to become the first woman to serve as a Supreme Court justice. Her conservative outlook was matched by the appointment of another conservative, Antonin Scalia, and the promotion of William H. Rehnquist to the Chief Justiceship upon the retirement of Warren E. Burger (1986). However, it was only with the nomination of Robert Bork in 1987 that the president would have achieved the composition of the court as he desired. Bork's professional competence was not in doubt but his questioning of the Civil Rights Act of 1964 meant that black groups were steadfastly opposed to his promotion. There was opposition to Bork also from women's groups, and after a long and bitter confirmation process which the president at times likened to a 'lynch mob', the Senate eventually rejected him by 58–42. It was not until Reagan reached a third nominee, Judge Kennedy, that the Senate finally relented. While the Court went on to pass routinely conservative judgements in matters of criminal law and civil rights, the judges were also prepared to assert their independence when they unexpectedly refused to withdraw their earlier prohibition of school prayer or more controversially still, to overthrow the landmark decision of 1973 which established a constitutional right to abortion.

Reaganomics

Despite his personal authority, Reagan was pragmatic enough to appreciate that some areas of spending were off limits and so was unwilling to reduce spending on critical elements such as Medicare, social security or farm subsidies. However, in order to forestall major spending by various Congressional standing committees the administration proposed to replace all committee allocations with a single omnibus reconciliation measure. This enabled the president to anticipate 'the greatest reduction in government spending that has ever been attempted' (Morgan, 2016, p. 179). When complete the Omnibus Budget and Reconciliation Act (OBRA) of 1981 curtailed 200 domestic spending programmes with projected savings of $140 billion over three years.

Meanwhile, within three years Congress reduced income tax rates by 25 per cent with a particularly striking reduction in the top rate from 70 to 50 per cent. As the 'Reagan Revolution' took hold, public spending flowed into the defence budget with a 10 per cent increase year on year for the next five years. Fiscal responsibility was not part of the defence equation as new money poured into nuclear weapons, cruise missiles, B-1 and B-2 bombers, an extended navy and new levels of spending on military research and development.

The president's economic strategy was supported by theorists who claimed that lower tax rates would promote free enterprise and the growth of business opportunities for both large and small companies and therefore more job creation across the economy. Not least in the president's formidable armoury was his ability to express what some people might make complicated into simple, folksy home truths.

> If you reduce tax rates and allow people to spend or save more of what they earn, they'll be more industrious ... The result: more prosperity for all – and more revenue for the government. A few economists call this principle supply-side economics. I just call it common sense. (In Reynolds, 2009, p. 510)

On prime-time television in July 1981, the president once again simplified the issue to great effect: 'If the tax cut goes to you, the American people ... that money won't be available to the Congress to spend, and that, in my view, is what this whole controversy comes down to.' (Ronald Reagan Presidential Foundation & Institute, online)

13.5 The presidential election of 1984

Given the clear links between an incumbent's economic performance and their prospects for re-election, Reagan and his supporters were entitled to view the 1984 campaign with some optimism. Economic recovery had been strong – albeit with a huge budget deficit – the dollar was riding high on the international exchanges, inflation was relatively low and employment was high. Grateful for the confidence he had restored in both the Republican Party and the country at large, the GOP re-nominated by acclamation their president at an uneventful convention in August. For the Democrats a bitter, drawn-out struggle for the party's presidential nomination eventually saw them discard the relative youth and 'new ideas' of Senator Gary Hart of Colorado and the powerful oratory of the Reverend Jesse Jackson, the first African American to launch a credible presidential campaign, and instead place their faith in Walter Mondale of Minnesota, an old-style New Deal liberal, who had served as Carter's vice president. Mondale sought to extend his appeal by choosing a woman as his running

Table 13.2 The result of the 1984 presidential election

Candidate	Party	Electoral College votes	Popular votes
Ronald W. Reagan (California)	Republican	525	54,281,858
Walter F. Mondale (Minnesota)	Democratic	13	37,457,215

mate: Geraldine Ferraro, a congresswoman from New York. Reagan's campaign was typified by a hugely uplifting and optimistic political commercial that was referred to as 'It's Morning Again in America' and which celebrated America's economic and military strength. Despite a lacklustre performance in the first presidential debate in Louisville, Kentucky, which prompted questions about the president's age and health, the outcome was seldom in doubt. The country's mood was solidly conservative and Reagan's reassuring tone swept all before him.

Mondale's campaign focused on the less fortunate and advocated budget deficit reduction through higher taxes but this failed to garner support from any group other than the African American community, the lowest-income voters and Latinos. Reagan was returned by 525 to 13 votes, the greatest Electoral College margin since F.D. Roosevelt's landslide win of 1936. Protestants, Catholics, the middle class, the old and the young and, in spite of the Ferraro vice-presidential candidate, women, all went with Reagan by a significant margin. In the popular vote the totals were devastating for the Democrats, with 54 million votes for Reagan compared to 37 million for Mondale. The victory was a personal triumph for the old campaigner but in the Senate the Republicans had a slightly reduced majority while they gained only a small number of seats in the House (Table 13.2).

13.6 Ronald Reagan's second term

Despite his resounding personal triumph in 1984 and the fact that when Ronald Reagan left the White House in 1989 he was more popular than ever, the second term was in many ways a period of frustration, disappointment, scandal and at times tragedy. The much-vaunted 'Reagan Revolution' did not really transpire in the way the president had hoped. The 1980s were undoubtedly a period of economic growth but a series of tax cuts and huge expenditure on the military, with year-on-year defence spending increases of 10 per cent over five years, came at a heavy price. Reagan presided over a more than doubling of the national debt, which reached an eye-watering $2.2 trillion by 1989. The trade deficit, measured at $42 billion during the Carter presidency, reached $150 billion by 1988.

As in the 1920s, economic well-being was extremely uneven. While huge profits were made by big business, the stock market provided extraordinary returns and the technology sector boomed, those at the lowest end of the income scale continued to suffer, with only a very marginal fall in measurements of poverty during the Reagan years. Even the tax reforms which were emblematic of the Reagan presidency were difficult to secure. Following division within his own party in December 1985, his original plans were derailed. It was not until after months of presidential lobbying that Congress finally passed the Tax Reform Act in September 1986. This simplified the number of tax brackets down to just two and almost halved the maximum personal tax rate from 50 to 27 per cent. Economists in favour of Reagan's changes referred to the concept of 'supply-side economics' with the notion that lower tax rates would encourage harder work, personal endeavour and career progress, free enterprise and the generation of wealth that would trickle down throughout the economy. However, the tax changes did not seem to translate into success at the polls as the midterm elections of November 1986 saw the Democrats gain eight seats in the Senate and an increased majority in the House of Representatives.

Tragedy came in January 1986 when a huge television audience watched NASA's space shuttle, *Challenger*, with seven astronauts on board, lift off from Cape Canaveral. For the first minute everything appeared normal. Then the words from NASA being broadcast with the TV pictures said: 'One minute 15 seconds, velocity 2,900 feet per second, altitude 9 nautical miles, down range distance 7 nautical miles ... [Long Pause] ... Flight controllers here looking very carefully at the situation ... Obviously a major malfunction.' (NASA 1986) Since the days of JFK, the space programme had epitomised America's technological prowess and sense of derring-do. President Reagan spoke movingly in the aftermath of the tragedy, reading a poem including the words: 'They slipped the surly bonds of earth to touch the face of God.' The aftermath of the disaster was hugely damaging. The official investigation identified a fault with a rubber seal on one of the solid-rocket boosters. It then emerged that NASA had known about the problems with the design of the seal but had allowed the mission to go ahead anyway. The whole space programme was suspended and it would be more than two years before the next flight took place. While of course the president could not be held responsible for the *Challenger* tragedy, the scandal that engulfed his administration in late 1986 was certainly directly at his door.

13.7 The Iran-Contra affair

Origins of a scandal

At his best, Reagan seemed serenely comfortable in the White House; his calm good humour seemed to remove tension from almost any situation. But even the Great Communicator was placed in harm's way by the damage that unfolded from the Iran-Contra affair. This episode could have been as damaging to Reagan as Watergate was to Nixon. In both cases, an 'imperial' president had flagrantly ignored the constitutional limits upon their authority and on both occasions the unravelling of the scandal followed landslide election victories. Reagan did not seek to conceal his motives for the actions he sanctioned which he maintained were in the interests of national security. His desire to roll back communism was underlined in his State of the Union Address in 1985. Reagan told Congress: 'We must not break faith with those who are risking their lives – on every continent, from Afghanistan to Nicaragua – to defy Soviet-supported aggression and secure rights which have been ours from birth.' (In Morgan, 2016, p. 260) While the actions taken on Reagan's behalf in this case were often incompetent they were also shrouded in secrecy, covered up dishonestly and at times were completely illegal.

As with Nixon, these covert operations only came to light because of an outstanding tradition of high-quality investigative journalism. In late autumn 1986 news emerged suggesting that the US, aided by Israel, had been secretly selling arms to Iran to try to secure the release of the American hostages captive in Lebanon in the hands of Islamic-inspired Iranian terrorists. This was in spite of the fact that the Reagan White House had publicly insisted there could be no negotiations with terrorists and had insisted to its allies that they should play no part in arming Iran.

As the investigative thread ran deeper it became clear that a group of US officials from inside the White House had covertly passed the proceeds of the arms sales to Iran to the Nicaraguan Contras. This went directly against the express instructions of Congress. While the authority for these actions came from National Security Adviser Vice-Admiral Poindexter and the director of the CIA, William Casey, most of the wheeling and dealing was actually conducted by Lieutenant-Colonel Oliver P. North.

Strategy of rollback in Afghanistan

The rollback strategy outlined in the State of the Union Address could be said to have achieved its objectives in Afghanistan. Since 1979 the Soviet Army had been at war against the Mujahideen resistance forces and by 1985 many analysts believed a final Russian victory was in sight. Determined to avoid this at all costs, the Americans secretly provided a massive range of military hardware to the Afghan rebels, including shoulder-fired Stinger anti-aircraft missiles which inflicted devastating losses against the Russian's helicopter gunships. This amounted to the largest covert operation in the whole history of the American military and tipped the balance against the Russian mission to the extent that Gorbachev announced in 1988 that a full withdrawal was planned.

Central America

While Congress supported the operation in Afghanistan, there was no such agreement to endorse a similar policy in Central America, where Reagan sought to depose the Marxist Sandinista regime from Nicaragua. To the Democrats on Capitol Hill, Reagan's intentions in Central America were the type of 'Yankee Imperialism' long discredited to those with a liberal outlook. Unbeknown to Congress, though, Oliver North was busily encouraging the airlifting of military supplies paid for by Saudi Arabia to the Nicaraguan counter-revolutionaries known as the Contras. By 1986 the president himself was hosting expensive photo opportunities in the Roosevelt Room of the White House to add further funds to provide military supplies to the Contras.

While some limited activity against the Sandinistas was in the public domain, it was only through the oversight of the Democrat-controlled House Intelligence Committee (HIC) and the diligent investigative journalism of American correspondents, that the degree of Contra activity became clear. As opposition to Reagan's plans mounted in the House, the president felt obliged to issue a clarion call for support to Congress in April 1983.

The national security of all the Americas is at stake in central America. If we cannot defend ourselves there, we cannot expect to prevail elsewhere. Our credibility would collapse, our alliances would crumble, and the safety of our homeland would be put in jeopardy. (In Morgan, 2016, p. 264)

While the 'Great Communicator' was normally unerring in aligning himself with popular sentiment, on this occasion he was unable to generate the support he needed. In the public mind, Nicaragua and El Salvador were difficult to locate geographically, let alone the places to open new military adventures that seemed to readily evoke memories of Vietnam.

Investigations into the Contra scandal

The frustration Reagan felt at failing to garner support was as nothing compared to the damage he sustained as investigations into the Contra scandal gathered pace. In the initial round of questioning Reagan insisted that arms had been shipped to Iran solely to promote links with moderate groups in Tehran, rather than to secure the release of US hostages, but this assertion was quickly withdrawn. While initially eyebrows were raised as to the president's detached leadership style, a joint Congressional investigating committee of 1987 was less forgiving. It established that the climate of dishonesty and lack of regard for Congress emanated from President Reagan himself. It emerged that documents had been interfered with or destroyed, and in 1990 Poindexter was given a six-month jail sentence while North was also found guilty but was not imprisoned on a technicality.

Analysis of the Iran-Contra scandal

The whole affair was a damaging one for the president and helped to drain energy and support from his second term. While some were willing to believe that Reagan himself would not have sanctioned acts of sheer criminality others felt that he had significantly harmed relations between the executive branch and Congress, damaged critical alliances and fatally undermined the public image of the affable president. In Iwan Morgan's outstanding biography of Ronald Reagan, the author amply demonstrates that the president's claim that 'The United States gives terrorists no rewards and no guarantees. We make no concessions, we make no deals' had no 'basis in reality' (Morgan, 2016, p. 270). When the Tower Commission looked into the Iran-Contra case the president's final words in his written submission were: 'The simple truth is that I don't remember.' However, it is worth noting that in early 1984 the president gave a verbal instruction to his National Security Advisor Robert McFarlane to 'do everything you can' to bypass congressional restraint in supporting aid to the Contras. When McFarlane passed the president a note to say that the Saudi royal family had offered $1 million a month for the Contras, Reagan returned the note with the phrase 'Mum's the word' written on it. (Morgan, 2016, p. 267) It was, in many senses, a sad ending to the Reagan presidency and its legacy. Towards the end, the Iran-Contra affair became linked with concerns about the president's personal health and state of mind. Trusted biographer Edmund Morris believed he discerned signs of depression in the president by 1987 and Reagan's deeply loyal wife Nancy later observed that her husband 'always had a reputation for integrity, and it went right to his soul to see his character being questioned every day … It was a dark and hurtful time' (in Morgan, 2016, p. 279).

Morgan offers this fascinating conclusion:

What angered Reagan above all was the decrepit, detached, and disoriented image that had been his salvation during the Iran-Contra investigations. As a consequence, his tongue occasionally strayed from denial of personal wrongdoing. In one exchange with reporters, he objected to being depicted as uninformed and ignorant about everything. 'I was very definitely involved in the decisions about support to the freedom fighters,' he remarked. 'It was my idea to begin with.' Fortunately for Reagan, his success in negotiating arms control with the Soviet Union would soon overshadow his Iran-Contra ignominy and have far greater significance in defining his presidential legacy. (Morgan, 2016, p. 285)

13.8 George H.W. Bush, 1989–92

Bush as vice president

Despite George Bush's privileged background, Ivy League education, standing in the Republican Party, and substantial experience, he came very close to missing out on the vice presidential ticket with Ronald Reagan in 1980. The two men had endured a gruelling, at times bitter and personal campaign for the Republican nomination in 1980. While Reagan was generally slow to anger, he resented Bush's description of his ideas for the American economy as 'voodoo economics' and, even worse, that the younger candidate had implied that his rival may be too old to face the physical demands of the highest office. With this in mind, Bush was extremely relieved when Reagan called him in July 1980 to ask if he would join the ticket. By then, the presumption in the press and in the GOP was that Reagan would take the unique step of teaming up with Gerald Ford, who of course had already served as president. It seems likely that Ford's lingering desire to assume very significant responsibilities once installed in the White House may have led Reagan to believe that Bush would be a more straightforward second-in-command. It was a wise decision, and from the outset Bush showed himself to be intensely loyal, discreet and determined never to attempt to outshine his boss.

Bush's relationship with Reagan

During the two terms, the men came to share an extremely close working relationship and Reagan knew that he could always count on Bush to do the right thing. This was illustrated most graphically when an assassination attempt against Reagan in 1981 inflicted life-threatening injuries. Whereas Al Haig alarmed some insiders with his apparent eagerness to assume responsibilities beyond the constitutional guidelines, the vice president conducted himself with faultless dignity and decorum.

13.9 The presidential election of 1988

Those eight years of loyal service guaranteed the support of the moderate elements of the party when Bush decided to run in his own right for the 1988 presidential election. But first Bush had to deal with the challenge of Robert Dole, the abrasive Senate minority leader from Kansas, and the more flamboyant candidacy of the right-wing television evangelist Pat Robertson. Reagan's support, and Bush's experience and solid character meant that he had a relatively untroubled primary campaign. While some derided Bush's lack of passion and 'the vision thing', he rose to the challenge and delivered a consummate acceptance speech at the party convention in August 1988. However, the momentum he had established was badly shaken by his quirky choice of running mate in Dan Quayle, a young senator from Indiana who was palpably ill-qualified for such a significant step-up. Despite significant misgivings about Quayle, Bush himself ran a solid, if at times very negative, campaign against the Democratic choice, Michael Dukakis of Massachusetts. Following his victory over Gary Hart (ruled out by a sex scandal and a boat called 'Monkey Business') and over the gifted orator and civil rights activist Jesse Jackson, Dukakis had classically attempted to broaden his appeal by choosing a conservative running mate, Senator Lloyd Bentsen from Texas. While Bentsen savaged Quayle in the vice presidential debate after the hapless senator tried to compare himself to a young JFK, the presidential debates went much more smoothly for Bush.

Dukakis was easy to characterise as a 'liberal' and took repeated criticism for his 'weak' record on crime and for an alleged lack of patriotism. Finally, Dukakis's cold personality and vague, rambling style put paid to his chances, enabling Bush to become the first sitting vice president since Martin Van Buren in 1836 to be elected directly to the presidency. Despite his lethargic campaign, Dukakis was able to claim 46 per cent of the popular vote (41.8 million votes) but only ten states, including some states in the North East, the Midwest and the Pacific North West. Bush prevailed in 38 states, with 426 Electoral College votes and 48.8 million votes, and emphatic victories in the South, the South West, the crucial state of California, most of the Midwest farm belt and all of New England (Table 13.3). It was a deserved victory and one that he would cherish. He loved the White House, respected the Constitution and devoted himself to the presidency. He did not have the easy manner of the Gipper (a name associated with Reagan following his portrayal of Notre Dame football star George Gipp) or a philosophical framework for his ideas but he was desperate to succeed though hard work, a sense of decency, a desire to govern and a capacity to build consensus.

Table 13.3   The result of the 1988 presidential election

Candidate	Party	Electoral College votes	Popular votes
George H.W. Bush (Texas)	Republican	426	48,881,221
Michael S. Dukakis (Mass)	Democratic	112	41,805,422

George Herbert Walker Bush

41st President of the United States (1989–93)
Born: 12 June 1924
Birthplace: Milton, Massachusetts
Education: Phillips Academy, Andover, Massachusetts and Yale University
Political party: Republican
State: Texas
Occupations before presidency: Oil industry executive
Previous government service: Member US House of Representatives (1967–71);
    US Ambassador to UN (1971–73); Director of CIA (1976–77)
Age at inauguration: 64
Dates of office: 20 January 1989–20 January 1993
Election: November 1988
Vice president: J. Danforth Quayle
Length of term: 4 years

13.10 President Bush and the Reagan legacy

Reagan departed the centre stage more popular than ever. The rich had grown richer and the middle class had enjoyed a mainly prosperous decade. But in certain respects the Reagan legacy was more problematic than it might first appear. To be clear, some of the difficult trends we will consider now cannot be solely accredited to the Reagan years but rather point to the fact that Bush inherited a country with some challenging and divisive issues that would not be easy to face. In his acceptance speech at the Republican Convention in August 1988 Bush expressed his heartfelt desire to lead his country so that it became 'a kinder, gentler nation'. He went on to say 'I want a drug-free America and this will not be easy to achieve'. Finally, he promised: 'I will keep America moving forward, always forward – for a better America, for an endless enduring dream and a thousand points of light.' (In Meacham, 2015, p. 340)

13.11 Newt Gingrich and the rise of political partisanship

While the sentiment was not unwelcome it was more difficult to deliver. Firstly, the reality was that during the election campaign Bush had shown that he was prepared to indulge in exceptionally negative campaigning against Dukakis. One particularly controversial advertisement encompassing ideas of crime and race led the *Washington Post* to ask whether the Republican candidate was guilty of running 'A Racist Campaign?' Secondly, once elected the new president quickly appreciated that

Congress was moving in the direction of a much more hostile polarisation between Republicans and Democrats. During his own congressional career and as vice president Bush skilfully cultivated warm working relationships with both Republicans and Democrats. The traditional manners and protocols encompassed in the Senate's long-standing 'folk ways' came easily to President Bush.

While Bush was committed to orderly governance he watched in horror as the dividing line in Congress became increasingly bitter, partisan and ideological. This was exemplified by the confrontational approach of the rising star of the Republican Right, Newt Gingrich from Georgia, who became the Republican Minority Leader in 1989 at the age of only 45. Gingrich emerged from a tough upbringing and some family dysfunction as a driven, well-read, somewhat socially isolated young man. He entered Congress in 1978, when 'with vandalism in the cities, stagflation across the country, and a humourless moralizer in the White House preaching sacrifice, the public's mood was sour, frustrated, suspicious of bureaucracies and special interests, anti-government, anti-tax – populist and conservative'. It was the perfect time for the Georgia firebrand to make his presence felt on the Hill. From the outset he railed against the 'corrupt elite'. As Packer puts it: 'The Moral Majority was about to take Washington by storm' (Packer, 2013, p. 21). Gingrich made his name by launching relentless verbal attacks upon the Democrats. He described his opponents as 'sick' and used emotional language to drum up a war of civilisations between 'true' conservatives like himself and 'liberals' whom he despised.

13.12 The environment

Far away from Capitol Hill, toxicity was not confined to the political climate. Of course, environmental pollution had been a long time in the making and can certainly not be placed at the door of any particular politician. For example, a notorious incident in Donora, Pennsylvania in October 1948 saw a malodorous fog seep across this small but heavily industrialised town of steel and zinc smelters to the extent that 20 people died and 7,000 were hospitalised. In the same year, ozone was identified for the first time as a component of Los Angeles' increasingly evident smog. In 1962, the scientist Rachel Carson wrote the influential book *Silent Spring*, a searing indictment of the damage being caused by the use of harsh chemical pesticides, most notably DDT. But during the Reagan years it could be claimed that conspicuous consumption and the pursuit of wealth became obsessions, at the expense of environmental concerns. During the 1980s the environmental cost of America's prolific use of fossil fuels, gas-guzzling motor vehicles and ever-spiralling consumer demand became more apparent. Sprawling metropolitan areas such as Los Angeles, the San Joaquin Valley in California and the city of Chicago were facing urgent issues of smog and acid rain. The need for closer regulation, environment guidelines and targets, technological innovation and greater public awareness and responsibility were all evident by the time Bush became president.

13.13 Corruption

On the East Coast the 1980s had also been a period of excess, in the financial markets and on Wall Street. Illicit manipulation of stock prices, insider dealing and reckless investments were all endemic. As Maldwyn Jones states: 'a number of investment bankers ... made vast profits, especially in the market for the high-risk, high-yield "junk bonds" which fuelled the decade's corporate takeover boom' (Jones, 1995, p. 606). In his scrupulously fair biography of Ronald Reagan, Iwan Morgan observes:

> In the get-rich-quick atmosphere of the 1980s ... Reagan had remarked, 'What I want to see above all is that this country remains a country where someone can always get rich' ... Corruption was everywhere but nested most comfortably in New York City, the seat of financial power, and in Washington, the seat of government power ... By Reagan's final year in office, more than 100 of his appointees were being or had been investigated for corruption ... Although much of the wrongdoing was exposed after Reagan left office, it marked his administration as the most corrupt of modern times. (Morgan, 2016, pp. 256–57)

Grants had been rigged, wealthy contributors to the Republican Party had been rewarded with generous contracts and corruption exposed in the multi-billion dollar business of military procurement.

13.14 Bush and domestic policy

With a Democratic Congress it became necessary for Bush to legislate from the centre while shoring up his defence against those in his own party who had moved sharply to the right and who would be ready to obstruct either financial commitments or legislative overreach. Given these constraints, Bush made a positive start. Meacham offers this summary of the early legislative record of the Bush Administration:

> Bush's understanding of Washington especially in his first two years, brought him domestic achievements. He sought and passed increased funding and tax credits for families with children, including enhancements for Head Start. He signed the Financial Institutions Reform, Recovery, and Enforcement Act of 1989 to bail out troubled savings and loans and create the Resolution Trust Corporation. Bush banned the importation of most semi-automatic rifles. After a veto, he signed the Fair Labor Standards Amendments of 1989 raising the minimum wage ... On education ... Bush called for national performance goals in K-12, establishing a key policy principle. (Meacham, 2015, p. 393)

As vice president, Bush had seen at close quarters the Reagan Administration oppose legislation for clean-air-and-water bills. With a growing groundswell of concern for the environment and visible signs of the damage caused by pollution from Los Angeles to Chicago, the new incumbent put his weight behind the complex Clean Air Act Amendments which were implemented with bipartisan support in 1990. A further piece of landmark legislation came with the Americans with Disabilities Act which tried to give people with disabilities access to their workplace and other buildings. In such cases, Bush was more than happy to use all of the presidential powers of persuasion open to him to generate sufficient Congressional support for his legislation.

13.15 The economic recession

During the soaring euphoria of his Gulf War victory, few would have foreseen how quickly George Bush's fortunes would be reversed but the events of 1992 could hardly have been more calamitous. The stunning acquittal in April 1992 of four white policemen charged with the beating of Rodney King took President Bush into a situation where he seemed detached from the lives of Black Americans. At the Republican Convention in New Orleans in August 1988 Bush, renowned for his caution, took a leap into the dark, with an elaborate, personal promise on taxation: 'My opponent won't rule out raising taxes, but I will, and the Congress will push me to raise taxes, and I'll say no, and they'll push again and I'll say to them, "Read my lips: no new taxes". (In Meacham, 2015, p. 339)

Doubtless this clear water between Bush and Dukakis played its part in the Republican victory. But by late spring 1990 the promise was seldom out of the president's thoughts. Sleepless nights, tension and a stiff neck bothered the president as it began to emerge that any serious attempt to address Reagan's record budget deficit would depend on raising additional new revenue. The deficit had assumed menacing proportions and was seen by many experts as a serious threat to the well-being of the American economy.

Then, at the Federal Reserve, the renowned economist Alan Greenspan announced that the American economy had entered a 'meaningful downturn'. The emerging recession can be traced back to 1990 and would persist until the middle of the following year. The sharp downturn in the nation's economy dragged the president's personal approval rating to just above 30 per cent in the election year. The extravagant economic success enjoyed by so many in the 1980s came to an abrupt halt with a recession in the summer of 1990 followed by economic stagnation that lasted for the remainder of Bush's time in office. This downturn took a severe toll upon the middle classes and professionals in the service sector, finance, technology and on Wall Street. Unemployment went through the 10 million barrier, to reach the highest level for ten years, rising from 5.9 per cent in 1989 to 7.8 per cent halfway through 1991. Property values collapsed, personal debt and bankruptcy grew exponentially.

As Meacham states in his major biography of Bush:

> Trapped between his own campaign rhetoric of 'Read my lips' and economic and political reality, he was coming to understand that movement towards a balanced budget might well require more revenue – more taxes. The business cycle was also working against him. After the deep recession of 1981–1982 the country had had several good years under the Reagan presidency.

However, as Meacham explains:

> Beginning in 1989 the economy grew at below typical rates. Bush was thus caught in a depressing spiral. The higher deficits from the Reagan years meant slower economic growth and slower economic growth exacerbated the deficit since tax receipts were lower in leaner times.

In May 1990 as the president moved in on the agonising decision to reverse his campaign pledge, Bush took to his diary to get things off his chest. 'The big subject this morning is taxes. The shit has hit the fan ... We're getting pounded, and the right wing is the worst.' Faced with the choice of a government shut down and reversing the most important domestic pledge of the 1988 campaign, Bush opted for the latter. (Meacham, 2015, p. 412)

13.16 The impact of the recession upon President Bush

Bush felt his own energy and emotional well-being sapped by the damaging nature of the recession. In his diary he lamented: 'We're going to be facing these humungous deficits and the economy is still down, down, down.' In May 1991 the president was suffering with an irregular heartbeat and was diagnosed with the thyroid disorder Graves' disease, which drained his energy. While the 66-year-old leader was in excellent personal shape it is possible that the strain of leadership and his exacting work regime was beginning to take its toll. Some of those close to him felt that with the election looming in 1992 President Bush had lost some of his old vigour. Sadly, Lee Atwater, central to the Bush victory of 1988, passed away in the spring of 1991 and was never effectively replaced. Despite this, Bush remained committed to his re-election and in the summer of 1991 he confided to his diary: 'I firmly believe that elections are won or lost by the state of the economy and ours appears to be improving.' (Meacham, 2015, p. 469)

The force of the recession meant that Bush was no longer guaranteed the support of his party. His most striking opponent was Patrick Buchanan, a newspaper and television commentator renowned for his outspoken views on issues such as family values, abortion, homosexuality, immigration and prayers in school. While Buchanan was evidently not presidential material, his 'protest' campaign pushed Bush and Quayle to the right. By the time Bush received the nomination for a second time he had begun to sound increasingly strident in his eagerness to accommodate the religious right. His fate was now inextricably linked to the fortunes of an outsider: a little-known governor, William Jefferson Clinton, from one of the poorest states in the union, Arkansas.

13.17 Bill Clinton and the presidential election of 1992

With election victories in 1992 and 1996, William Jefferson Clinton would become the first Democrat to be elected to a second term since Franklin D. Roosevelt in the 1936 campaign. For the second time in the recent past, the American people would choose a southern governor to run their country. In 1976, Jimmy Carter from Georgia and now Bill Clinton, from Arkansas, a small state with low budgets and considerable poverty, would take up the highest office. The two men were both from the South but in no other way were they alike.

Clinton was also the first president to lead in the post-Cold War period, 'the end of history' as it was termed by the political analyst Francis Fukuyama. As the fresh-faced, relatively unknown Governor of Arkansas, he announced his candidacy for the presidency at the Old State House in Little Rock on 3 October 1991, telling the crowd, 'I refuse to be part of a generation that celebrates the death of communism abroad with the loss of the American dream at home.' (Clinton Library, online)

13.18 Clinton's background

Clinton was bright and ambitious, a graduate of Yale Law School and a Rhodes Scholar at Oxford. He had formed a formidable political partnership with his wife, Hillary Rodham, who was exceptionally gifted, driven and well organised. Representing the new, dynamic face of the American South, and ditching the tax and spend baggage of traditional Democrats, the charismatic 45 year old had paid his dues, starting with an energetic but unsuccessful campaign for Congress in 1974 at the age of just 28. Two years later he had secured the state's post of Attorney General and then, in 1978, became the youngest-ever governor in the nation's history. A defeat in the gubernatorial election two years later taught the incumbent more valuable lessons than his early victories. Shrewd shifts in policy positions away from the overtly liberal, activist, tax and spend, progressive character of his first term and an ability to show a more humble public demeanour enabled him to make the first of what would become his celebrated 'comebacks', when he was restored to the governorship in 1982.

In the 1982 campaign Clinton visibly moved his platform to one of financial responsibility, a more pragmatic, centrist stance and a greater emphasis on law, order, crime and punishment that reflected the conservative political mood in Arkansas at that time. His willingness to indulge in some ferocious negative campaigning, combined with a contrite TV advertisement in which he apologised for raising motor vehicle licence fees during his first term, helped to secure Clinton a substantial 55 to 45 per cent victory. Not least, it was striking that one of Clinton's key strengths was his ability to secure support from large numbers of African American voters without alienating the white vote. Furthermore, Clinton was able to attract external investment to previously 'unfashionable' Arkansas and to demonstrate very positive progress in educational standards within his state.

By the 1990s, presidential campaigns had become so expensive, and the fear of reputational damage so intense, that some of the most high-profile candidates in the Democratic Party wanted victory to be more than likely before they committed themselves and put everything on the line. Bush's surgical victory in the 1991 Gulf War made him so popular that many of the Democratic Party's big hitters decided not to run at all in 1992. Their unwillingness to lose a fruitless campaign left the way open for younger, less-seasoned candidates to take their chance. Most notably, Bill Clinton, awash with natural empathy, savvy to new forms of media and quick on his feet in political debate, decided to throw his hat into the ring when others had chosen to wait until 1996.

13.19 The Clinton campaign

Campaigning under national scrutiny raised issues for Clinton, including questions of morality and character, alleged affairs, draft-dodging in the Vietnam War and drug use. But as the recession took hold, the sharp-witted, energetic Clinton campaign team zeroed in on the issues they believed could propel their young candidate into the White House. In Bill Clinton's campaign 'War Room', his strategists, George Stephanopoulos and James Carville, posted messages that became famous in themselves: 'Change v. more of the same', 'The Economy, stupid' and 'Don't forget health care.' (Reynolds, 2009, p. 439) Meanwhile, a book entitled *America: What Went Wrong?* by Donald L. Barlett and James B. Steele attracted national attention with its indictment of the country's economic malaise and the argument that the US had lost its historic edge in productivity and technology to the emerging Asian economies. (Harris, 2006, p. xiii)

Beyond the slogans, Clinton proved to be a skilled and resilient campaigner, able to distance himself from the traditional burden of being defined as a 'tax and spend' candidate but rather a 'New Democrat' with innovative ideas for the future. Clinton's 'new thinking' was seen when he took the bold step of selecting another young southerner, Al Gore from Tennessee, as his running mate. Conventional wisdom held that the ticket should always be balanced, so the traditional choice would have been a Northern liberal with much greater experience than the candidate himself. Instead, this new pairing seemed bright, energetic and forward-thinking.

13.20 Shortcomings in the Bush campaign

While Clinton made headway targeting 'the forgotten middle class', Bush's prospects suffered a further blow when Ross Perot, a billionaire from Texas who had made his fortune in IT, threw his hat into the ring. Perot's quirky, populist campaign, with the slogan 'Make Ross the Boss!' captured the imagination of those who were becoming increasingly alienated from the two major parties. As an avowed outsider Perot derided the 'political nobility' in Washington who had 'forgotten that they worked for the people'. Perot's character was questioned when he withdrew from the race but then dramatically re-entered the contest in October 1992, with little more than a month to go; it would soon become clear that he could still command sizeable support.

Meanwhile, Clinton was able to portray America under Bush as 'in a ditch' and by October, trailing badly in the polls, the Bush campaign was imploding. Frustrated and lacking direction, Bush lashed out in a way that made him appear shrill and undignified. He claimed that his dog Millie knew 'more about foreign policy' than the Democratic 'bozos' challenging him and referred to Clinton's running mate, Al Gore, as 'Ozone Man' (Meacham, 2015, p. 519) because of his preoccupation with environmental issues. Finally, with horrendous timing for the incumbent, the former defence secretary Caspar Weinberger was indicted for his involvement in the Iran-Contra scandal. When handwritten minutes clearly showed that Bush had strongly supported the arms-for-hostage deal, Bush's five-year-old claim that he had been 'out of the loop' was exposed to devastating effect.

13.21 Analysis of the 1992 election

One of the healthiest aspects of the November 1992 election was that voter turnout, for so long in decline, reached its highest level for 24 years. 55.9 per cent of the electorate cast their vote, with Clinton carrying 32 states plus the District of Columbia, while Bush secured just 18 states. In the Electoral College, Clinton secured 370 votes compared to Bush's figure of 168. Clinton captured 43 per cent of the popular vote with Bush managing just 37.5 per cent, which was the worst performance by a Republican since Howard Taft in 1912. In a sign of things to come, perhaps, Perot, as an Independent, took 18.9 per cent of the popular vote, or almost 20 million votes (Table 13.4). This was the best performance by an Independent since Theodore Roosevelt's Bull Moose

Table 13.4 The result of the 1992 presidential election

Candidate	Party	Electoral College votes	Popular votes
Bill J. Clinton (Arkansas)	Democrat	370	43,682,624
George H.W. Bush (Texas)	Republican	168	38,117,331
H. Ross Perot (Texas)	Independent	–	19,217,213

campaign, also in 1912. It was a sign that the politicians in Washington DC could not take public support for granted. Although these figures gave Clinton victory he had failed to capture a majority and so was the first minority president since 1968. Moving from almost national anonymity to centre stage, Clinton attracted support from women, black people, young people, Catholics, Jews and in the suburbs. He carried New England, the key industrial states in the Middle Atlantic region and most of the Midwest. Surprisingly, perhaps, the Clinton–Gore, southern ticket failed to prise most of the former Confederate states from the Republicans. It was clear that the flow of support for Perot had fatally damaged Bush. To make matters even worse for the Republicans, the Democrats took control of both Houses of Congress. The long period of conservative, Republican ascendancy was over. It was time for change in the White House.

PRESIDENTIAL PROFILE

William Jefferson (Bill) Clinton

42nd President of the United States (1993–2001)

Born: 19 August 1946

Birthplace: Hope, Arkansas

Education: Georgetown University, Washington DC; Oxford University, England; Yale Law School, Connecticut.

Political party: Democrat

State: Arkansas

Occupations before presidency: Lecturer in Law at University of Arkansas (1973–75)

Previous government service: Arkansas Attorney General (1977–78); Arkansas Governor (1979–81, 1983–92)

Age at inauguration: 46

Dates of office: 20 January 1993–20 January 2001

Election: November 1992 and 1996

Vice president: Albert Gore

Length of term: 8 years

13.22 President Clinton in the White House

Health care reform

The United States stands alone among the wealthy, developed nations in its failure to provide a universal system of health care through compulsory insurance schemes or taxation. While the Medicare programme introduced by Johnson in the 1960s provided a safety net to some degree, for the majority of US citizens health care was linked to their employment package. Consequently, those without a job who were injured or fell ill could find themselves in a perilous position. According to President Clinton, as he began what would become a traumatic campaign to introduce reform, 'Over 37 million Americans, most of them working people and their little children, have no health insurance at all.' (Address to a Joint Session of Congress on Health Care Reform, 22 September 1993, in The American Presidency Project, online). This constituted 15 percent of the total population. It was clear that any politician trying to reform the complex, bureaucratic system would face massive resistance from huge pharmaceutical companies, wealthy private hospitals, the powerful medical establishment and the health insurance industry, all of whom were invested heavily in maintaining the status quo.

Because of the searching demands of this task, Clinton gave the job to the most able, trusted person he knew. His wife, Hillary Rodham Clinton, seemed spectacularly well-equipped to take on this challenge. A brilliant student, she had graduated from Wellesley College and met her future husband at Yale Law School. He was beguiled by her intellect, drive and ambition. Her guidance and support for him in his early political career in Arkansas was central to his rise to power. Now, in the White House, she prepared to deliver the mother of all reforms. Typically, Hillary applied herself with energy and diligence but in a sense this was also her downfall. Her report, more than 1,000 pages long, was easily shredded by her opponents, who could highlight the cost and complexity of the Clintons' Health Care Plan.

13.23 Opposition to the Health Care Plan

By now, Clinton's enemies were circling. The Speaker of the House of Representatives, Newt Gingrich, treated most things to do with the Clintons with revulsion, but his bile was mostly reserved for the Health Care Plan and for Clinton's adultery, which was, by now, an open secret. Gingrich had long believed that his own personal political future was best placed on the far right of the Republican Party. Gingrich argued that the Health Care Plan was part of a larger malaise. In the build-up to the 1994 midterm elections he put forward his 'Contract with America' which advocated 'the end of government that is too big, too intrusive, and too easy with the public's money' (Johnson & Broder, 1997, p. 546). He proposed swingeing cuts to welfare and social programmes and to tax rates. Welfare and Medicaid schemes would be moved to the orbit of the individual states rather than that of the federal government. Crucially, Gingrich tied this message to a broader moral crusade for the restoration of American family values.

The rivalry with Clinton was becoming increasingly bitter and personal. This reached a stand-off of tumultuous proportions in the winter of 1995. Constitutionally, the House, with Gingrich as its leader, controlled the purse strings but the budget it proposed had to be approved by the president. When Clinton vetoed the 1996 budget proposals the federal government and all of its associated programmes and agencies came to a juddering halt. During a three-week stand-off around Christmas time almost a million federal employees went without their December pay packet. Finally, the Republicans gave way and Clinton's revised budget was passed. While Clinton may have secured a victory on this occasion, the fact was that political life was becoming increasingly bitter and polarised.

13.24 The Oklahoma City bombing

The common purpose that the nation had shown in earlier times of difficulty seemed to have been lost. Faith in the federal government was once again under attack, sometimes in the most extreme ways possible. By the mid-1990s several groups and individuals with a paranoid hatred of the federal government, a sense of alienation from the political mainstream, and at times a genuine belief in myriad conspiracy theories, formed armed militia groups that proposed taking matters into their own hands. One such individual was Timothy McVeigh, a veteran, whose anger against the government prompted him to explode a truck packed with explosives outside the largest federal building in the centre of Oklahoma City.

On 19 April 1995, President Clinton was taking part in a photo opportunity with the Turkish prime minister when the White House press secretary Michael McCurry leant forward and whispered into his ear, with the news that CNN were reporting that a bomb had destroyed part of a federal building in Oklahoma City. More details were provided by Leon Panetta, White House Chief of Staff, who passed a note that said, 'Half of federal building in O.K. City blown up – expect heavy casualties.' It was perhaps a measure of Clinton's personal growth that he was able to combine firing off a score of practical questions and commands about the security response to the incident, express genuine concern for the casualties and display an inner determination not to be accused of being detached from a public disaster, as he had been depicted in the aftermath of the Waco disaster two years earlier. In the White House briefing room the president denounced the 'evil cowards' who had perpetrated the latest atrocity and pledged that 'we will find the people who did this' and that 'when we do, justice will be swift, certain and severe. These people are killers and they must be treated like killers' (in Harris, 2006, p. 179). It soon became clear that the casualty figures were terribly high. 168 people had been killed, including 19 children. Clinton correctly claimed that the Oklahoma City bombing went beyond the twisted actions of one angry individual. Paranoia, hatred, armed militia groups, extreme right-wing radio talk-show hosts and extremist websites were all ingredients in a toxic wave of anti-government sentiment at its most extreme.

13.25 The presidential election of 1996: Clinton vs Dole

Clinton's draining battles with Gingrich, the federal shutdown, an increasingly ideological struggle with the Republican Party, the damaging midterm campaign of 1994 and lingering accusations of financial impropriety and sexual scandal meant that the president could not face the prospect of re-election in 1996 with any certainty.

Table 13.5 The result of the 1996 presidential election

Candidate	Party	Electoral College votes	Popular votes
Bill J. Clinton (Arkansas)	Democrat	379	47,402,357
Robert J. Dole (Kansas)	Republican	159	39,198,755
H. Ross Perot (Texas)	Reform Party	–	8,085,402

However, Clinton was stubborn, personally resilient and convinced that he still had important work to do in the White House. To the dismay of his opponents, the self-styled 'Comeback Kid' began to show signs of a resurgence in 1996. Clinton's sensitive political antennae, not to mention astute use of focus groups, told him that many people were uncomfortable with the more extreme members of the Republican Party.

Clinton skilfully shifted his position towards the centre ground and, as in the old days in Arkansas, was able to glide away from issues that could damage his campaign. With a focus on reducing welfare and combating youth crime, Clinton was further boosted by the Republican's selection of the veteran senator from Kansas, Bob Dole. Dole's age, terse manner and commitment to anti-abortion all played into Clinton's hands. Crucially, the campaign was well-timed for the incumbent in that it coincided with an economic uplift. With prosperity in the air, Dole seemed to have little to offer those voters who wanted to support a political moderate. Many Americans did not doubt that the president's personal conduct may have been lax, but in a broader sense they felt that the country itself was moving in the right direction. However, Clinton's emphatic victory in 1996 (Table 13.5) did not mean that the rumours would go away. Two years later, the denials that the president had frequently made came back to haunt him.

13.26 The Lewinsky scandal, 1998

In the days of Nixon and Watergate, the journalists of the *Washington Post* brought to the nation's attention the skulduggery at the Democratic Party headquarters that, thanks to the diligence of Woodward and Bernstein, was eventually traced directly back to the Oval Office itself. Now, on 21 January 1998 the same, formidable newspaper was once again bringing the nation's leader to account. The *Post* now told its readers that Bill Clinton had indulged in a sexual relationship with White House intern Monica Lewinsky. To make matters worse, the president had lied under oath – in a sexual harassment claim brought by Paula Jones – in denying an affair with Lewinsky. With speculation swirling around him an agitated president angrily claimed: 'I did not have sexual relations with that woman – Miss Lewinsky.' Clinton was lying and this led to a protracted, unedifying process as his opponents reacted to new, damaging details with glee.

No matter how significant the achievement of turning a trillion dollar deficit into a projected surplus, Clinton's ideological enemies were in no mood to call off the hounds. The man charged with investigating the charges against the president was Kenneth Starr, an 'independent counsel' initially tasked with examining questions relating to the Clintons' financial affairs. Starr's investigation, supported by Congress, was now asked to encompass the matter of Monica Lewinsky. For months, political partisanship, lurid details, highly personal questions and an element of religious morality engulfed the president. In August 1998, Clinton was at bay and forced to admit how he had lied the previous January. On national TV he admitted:

> Indeed, I did have a relationship with Ms. Lewinsky that was not appropriate. In fact, it was wrong. It constituted a critical lapse in judgement and a personal failure on my part for which I am solely and completely responsible ... I misled people, including even my wife. (In Reynolds, 2009, p. 547)

Clinton had not been a fan of formal government meetings and so it emerged that of only two cabinet meetings to take place between January and August 1998, the first one had been used by the president to assure his colleagues that there was no truth in the Lewinsky rumours. The second meeting was for the president to apologise to the cabinet for lying to them in January.

13.27 Impeachment

Amid the zealous clamour from the far right, Starr presented a lurid, explicit report to Congress in September and stated that the president's lies and misconduct 'may constitute grounds for an impeachment.' The Republican leadership in the House smelt blood and Clinton became the first president since Andrew Jackson in 1846 and only the second in US history to face impeachment. In fact, the House leaders had placed themselves beyond the public mood. Some observers felt Congress itself was being demeaned by the lurid nature of the content being placed before it and the momentum against the president began to ease. The Republicans were disappointed by the results of the 1998 midterm elections and Gingrich, having badly overplayed his hand, resigned. Nevertheless, it took until February 1999 for the charges of perjury and obstructing justice that had been made against the president to be rejected and for it to become certain that the two-thirds majority needed in the Senate to impeach a president would not materialise.

13.28 Clinton's economic record

Despite the economic well-being of the Reagan years, it could be argued that the huge federal debt built up during the Republican period was unsustainable. The debt issue under Reagan and the recession under Bush were followed by a significant upturn in the nation's economic well-being and stability. Iwan Morgan sees Clinton's economic record as the 'defining achievement' of his presidency, and cites one Harvard analyst as describing 'macroeconomic performance in the 1990s' as 'exceptional.' Clinton possessed a genuine interest and some expertise in economics, advocating a 'third way' between Reagan's conservatism and the big spending of a liberal, interventionist government. (Morgan, 2012, pp. 65–66) The rise of the Chinese economy meant that America found it increasingly difficult to compete with manufacturers in the Far East. In response, Clinton and his economic strategists understood that the US needed to direct its renewal through high wages, high productivity and the latest technology while making a serious, systematic attempt to tackle the deficit. Within a year of entering the White House Clinton pushed through a new budget aimed at drastically lowering the national debt. In addition, the Bush recession began to steadily recede, boosting confidence that happier times were ahead. In particular, investment in new communications technology grew spectacularly, as did share values on the Dow Jones index.

The president used the 1996 State of the Union Address to proclaim that the era of big government was over. His subsequent victory in the presidential election of 1996 gave Clinton the opportunity to further advance his economic agenda. In legislative terms, this led to the Balanced Budget Act and the Tax Relief Act of 1997. These bills offered a combination of preserving some domestic programmes and favourable tax cuts for middle and lower income families.

Just after 9 pm on 27 January 1998, President Clinton strode into the House of Representatives to make his annual State of the Union Address. With the Lewinsky scandal swirling around him, some observers believed that the strain upon the president would be manifest. But as he opened his speech, it became clear that Clinton was in an upbeat mood:

> We have fourteen million new jobs; the lowest unemployment in twenty-four years; the lowest core inflation in thirty years; incomes are rising and we have the highest home ownership in history. Crime has dropped for a record five years in a row. And the welfare rolls are at their lowest levels in twenty-seven years. Our leadership in the world is unrivalled. Ladies and gentlemen, the state of the union is strong.

But then came the zinger!

> For three decades, six presidents have come before you to warn of the damage deficits pose to our nation. Tonight, I come before you to announce that the federal deficit – once so incomprehensibly large that it had eleven zeros – will be simply zero.

Given the scale of this achievement it might have been tempting for the president to stop there and bask in the moment. But now he went further.

> If we balance the budget for next year, it is projected that we will have a sizeable surplus in the years that immediately follow. What should we do with this projected surplus? I have a simple four word answer: Save ... Social ... Security ... First! (In Klein, 2002, p. 18)

Finally, Morgan offers this perspective on Clinton's overall economic record (also see Table 13.6):

> Overall, Clinton's record was marginally superior to those of fellow Democrats Harry Truman, John Kennedy and Lyndon Johnson, who were also in the running for the title of 'economic champ' ... a persuasive case can be made that Clinton was a particularly effective economic president. Firstly, he developed a coherent agenda for promoting economic growth and followed this plan throughout his presidency. Secondly, he took political risks – such as the 1993 deficit reduction plan, the drive for NAFTA [North American Free Trade Agreement] ratification, the 1995 bailout of Mexico, and denying the steel industry the tariffs it wanted – in the long-term interests of the economy. Thirdly, he introduced a significant institutional reform to improve the coordination of economic policy by creating the National Economic Council. (Morgan, 2012, p. 81)

Table 13.6   President Clinton's economic organisations

NAFTA: The North American Free Trade Agreement	This agreement was signed by the United States, Canada and Mexico and came into operation on 1 January 1994. It was effectively a three-way trade bloc for North America. Although this was signed by President Clinton, talk of a North American free trade zone can be dated back to the 1980 presidential campaign and Ronald Reagan.
NEC: National Economic Council	This came into being in January 1993 and its first Director was Robert Rubin. It was tasked with the brief of providing economic policy advice to the president. It remains in place today.

American foreign policy, 1980–2000

13.29 President Reagan's foreign policy

El Salvador

Given Reagan's ideological leanings and political instincts he was bound to be sensitive to any communist threat close to home. So events in the small Central American republic of El Salvador where a military junta had seized power in 1979, before Reagan entered the White House, quickly attracted his attention. The junta represented the economic interests of the republic's landowning elite at the expense of the peasants who were largely landless and poverty-stricken. A left-wing insurgency sprung up, representing the oppressed majority and receiving arms from sympathetic neighbours Nicaragua and Cuba. This prompted the Reagan Administration to commit significant financial and military aid to the military junta. The junta's brutal response to the insurgency was to offer some degree of support to right-wing death squads who took a heavy toll in killing rebels or those even suspected of resistance. It is estimated that 75,000 people were killed by execution and massacres, or in landmine explosions and bombing raids.

While the president was made aware of these atrocities, he was not prepared to countenance a communist regime in El Salvador. Despite American journalists reporting details of atrocities the president told Congress, 'The Salvadorian battalions that have received US training have been conducting themselves well on the battlefield and with the civilian population.' Iwan Morgan offers this scathing verdict on American policy in El Salvador: 'The outcome of this policy was that El Salvador did not fall to Marxism but the cost in innocent blood besmirched any American claim to stand for freedom in that country.' (Morgan, 2016, p. 204) Circumstances there were moderated to some extent, when the alleged leader of the death squads was defeated in elections in 1984 by the more moderate figure of Jose Napoleon Duarte. However, this did not bring the civil war to an end and it was not until 1992 that the government and the rebels signed a peace treaty.

Nicaragua

Nicaragua is the largest country in the Central American isthmus and borders Honduras to the north and Costa Rica to the south. Its capital, Managua, is the third largest city in Central America. Since 1927 this ethnically diverse country had been ruled by a hereditary dictatorship under the control of the Somoza family. Throughout the 1970s, the family presided over a series of scandals and injustices, including the syphoning of overseas aid, following the devastating earthquake of 1972, into the family coffers, at the expense of the poverty-stricken majority. In 1978, the country's leading journalist, Pedro Chamorro, who had exposed the excesses of the Somoza regime, was assassinated. It was widely believed that this murder had been sanctioned at the highest levels of the government.

These scandals, combined with the long-standing neglect of ordinary people, led to a mounting degree of unrest which culminated in the overthrow of the government by the Communist Sandinistas in 1979. The Sandinistas' National Liberation Front (FSLN) had been founded in 1961. While the new regime was given provisional official recognition by President Carter, when Ronald Reagan entered the White House in January 1981 he was much more hostile. The Sandinistas' Marxist ideology, close ties to the Soviet Union, support for El Salvador and campaigns for ambitious social reforms at the expense of the landed class all gave Reagan cause for concern. He believed that if the communist movement in Nicaragua was not supressed then the insurgency could spread to South America and Mexico.

The president's sense of urgency was reflected in the fact that as early as December 1981 he had directed the CIA to train and equip a small band of Nicaraguan counter-revolutionaries (Contras) to launch attacks upon the Sandinistas from nearby Honduras. As Reagan noted in his diary on 1 December 1981, 'We're proceeding with covert activity in Nicaragua to shut off supplies to the Guerrillas in El Salvador.' (In Morgan, 2016, p. 263) While Reagan did not go as far as to send American troops to Nicaragua, it gradually became clear that the CIA had carried out several missions, for example the mining of Nicaragua's harbours, that were completely illegal. Details of the Iran-Contra affair would prove to be extremely damaging to the Reagan Administration and to the president's legacy, but it was not until his second term that details of the whole programme began to emerge.

Grenada

If Nicaragua was damaging to Reagan because of the covert activity he sanctioned and because he was unable to secure the Congressional support he needed, the intervention in Grenada was carried out with popular approval and in the glare of publicity. Reagan's ever-watchful concern for the spread of communism was aroused in October 1983, when the left-wing Prime Minister Maurice Bishop, ruler of the tiny island of Grenada in the Caribbean, was deposed and executed by a far-left military junta. Grenada's near neighbours were alarmed by these developments and looked for support from the United States. Reagan's prompt response saw US marines and paratroops quickly remove the new junta. The mission was accomplished quickly and with minimal casualties and was broadly welcomed by the Grenadian people and by the American public. This view was not shared by the UN General Assembly which condemned Reagan's intervention and many in Latin America felt it heralded a return to the 'big stick' diplomacy of the turn of the twentieth century.

The Middle East

Reagan was not the first president or the last to find out how difficult an arena the Middle East could be. Support for Israel was the cornerstone of his policy and this was linked to the broader objective of constraining the influence of the Soviet Union and its ally Syria. Robert Dallek's analysis is that 'the administration's failure to shift its focus decidedly "from primary concern over the Soviet strategic threat to the underlying indigenous problems of the region" contributed to the deterioration of conditions for peace' (Dallek, 1999, p. 186). In the complex, volatile landscape of the Middle East the focus of attention for the US at this time was the Lebanon, where the Palestine Liberation Organization (PLO) was using its bases to launch attacks on Israeli settlements in the north.

In June 1982 Israel launched a full-scale invasion of the Lebanon, using American-provided planes and weaponry to attack Syrian missile sites in the Bekka Valley. Weaknesses in the American position here were manifold. Reagan was unable to establish a positive working relationship with Israel's President, Menachem Begin. Tacit American support for the Israeli invasion of the Lebanon was given but did not foresee the damaging international consequences of the brutality that was about to be unleashed. Israel's relationship with the US was made more difficult by what they saw as the unacceptable policy of massive American arms sales to Saudi Arabia.

The complex sectarian tensions there erupted into conflict not just between troops from Israel and Syria but also between Christians and Muslims. Israel's relentless pursuit of the PLO in the Muslim sections of Beirut led to massive civilian casualties and heartbreaking images of the dead and wounded, including children. With international opinion increasingly against Israel, Reagan had to ask more than once for Israel to stop. Following an emotionally charged personal phone call to Begin, it was agreed that the Israeli army would withdraw and a multinational force (MNF) would supervise a PLO evacuation. However, as soon as this task was complete and the MNF had withdrawn, the Israeli troops promptly returned. These troops then turned a blind eye when a terrible massacre took place in August 1982, in the refugee camps of west Beirut, in which Christian Phalangist militia killed up to 2,000 Palestinians including women and children.

Reagan was deeply shocked by these events and genuinely believed he could broker an even-handed solution in the Lebanon with the MNF under the aegis of the United Nations keeping apart the warring factions. A well-intentioned, even-handed Reagan was becoming more personally involved in a desperate, complex problem. Naively, he believed that the new leader of the Lebanon, Amine Gemayel, could be the focal point for US support, with Israeli withdrawal, while urging the moderate Arab states to put pressure on Syria to also pull its forces out of the Lebanon. Reagan failed to grasp the depth of Gemayel's commitment to the Maronite Christians at the expense of the Lebanese Muslim factions who would seek support from Syria. The MNF became increasingly beleaguered and at times helpless and besieged. In particular, the US contingent was regarded with increasing hostility by Gemayel's opponents who were legion.

When US warships fired in support of Lebanese operations against anti-government forces, the sense that America had moved from being a referee to taking sides was becoming more pronounced. At a Pentagon briefing the president was urged to withdraw but his sense that the US was obliged to stay and his concerns about the loss of American prestige led him to resist this advice. While Reagan knew he was entering 'a nest of adders' the geopolitical complexity of the region was difficult to grasp. Crucially, the formation in 1982 of Hezbollah, 'the party of God', with its militant concept of a holy war against Israel and its American backer, placed the United States within a conflict which would bring suffering directly to the people of the United States.

On 23 October 1983, the president was woken at 2.30 am eastern time to be told that a Hezbollah suicide bomber had driven a lorry packed with 12,000 pounds of TNT into a US marine barracks at Beirut airport. 241 American servicemen were killed on a day that Reagan himself recorded as 'the lowest of the low points' of his presidency. By early 1984 the pressure from the military intelligence community to withdraw and the unpopularity of the whole enterprise with the American public left Reagan with no choice but to remove the peacekeeping force. For the violent militants the message was that the US could be forced out of its commitments by acts of terrible violence. This would have consequences long after Reagan had left the White House.

13.30 The Strategic Defence Initiative (SDI), 'Star Wars'

Reagan was an emotional politician who trusted his own instincts and his gift was that these so often chimed with the American people themselves. His profound distrust of the Soviet Union was matched by his deep aversion to the prospect of a nuclear exchange between the two superpowers. In the summer of 1979 his powerful emotions came to the fore when he visited the remote, mountain headquarters of NORAD, America's nuclear command centre in Colorado. Impressed by the huge steel doors that protected the installation, Reagan is said to have asked what would happen if the centre was hit by a nuclear strike. When the almost casual response from a commander came, that the whole system would be decimated, Reagan was aghast. Despite all of its might and technology, one missile could render the United States helpless.

Four years later, Reagan's Cold War rhetoric reached its most confrontational point. In a now notorious speech to the National Association of Evangelicals in Florida in March 1983 the president spoke of the 'aggressive impulses of an evil empire'. Reagan claimed that the Cold War was a struggle 'between right and wrong and good and evil' (in Morgan, 2016, pp. 214–15). These remarks, perhaps fortunately, came when the Kremlin was still in the grip of a trio of somewhat ossified leaders, Brezhnev, Andropov and Chernenko, all of whom fitted the template of a 'typical' Soviet leader and who characterised the Americans as 'imperialists' and 'warmongers'. It was Andropov who was in place when the president made a televised address to the nation in March 1983 in which he unveiled his proposal for a Strategic Defence Initiative (which some of his opponents mockingly termed 'Star Wars'). This envisaged a hugely ambitious and expensive programme which would provide some type of defensive shield using lasers or particle beams from space to neutralise enemy missiles in flight.

Reagan had already alarmed the Russians with his approval of the neutron bomb in 1981 but the SDI proposal came as a bombshell to the Soviet Union, who feared that their strike capability against the US could be rendered obsolete. The initiative, almost uniquely for a development of this financial scale, came from within the president's own mind, although there were scientists around him who claimed to be able to deliver the system Reagan desired. The Cold War context of these developments was heightened when the Russians deployed SS-20 intermediate-range nuclear missiles in Eastern Europe, while American cruise missiles were positioned in the United Kingdom and West Germany.

The sense that the nuclear clock was getting unnervingly close to midnight was made worse when a Korean airliner flying out of New York strayed into Soviet airspace and was taken down, killing all of the passengers and crew, including 61 American citizens. Beyond his public condemnation of this incident, Reagan privately worried how close the world was to the nuclear precipice. The broadcast in the autumn of a harrowing television movie *The Day After*, which imagined the complete destruction of Kansas City, Missouri and the resulting fallout, further convinced the president that urgent action was needed to move the world back from the brink. In Moscow, however, his tough talk, high spending and futuristic plans all made the Russians more paranoid than ever, believing the US was preparing for a first strike.

13.31 The rise of Mikhail Gorbachev

It was fortunate for all concerned, then, that the death of Chernenko in March 1985 brought to power a leader who seemed to many influential figures in the West to be cut from a very different cloth to his ageing, conservative predecessors. In an important meeting at the Chequers country house in December 1984, British Prime Minister Thatcher met and was immediately impressed by the new, dynamic force in the Kremlin, Mikhail Gorbachev. Famously, Mrs Thatcher, whom the White House knew could be exceptionally abrasive and difficult, said that the new Soviet leader was someone the West 'could do business with'. Gorbachev's dynamic new programmes of openness – glasnost – and restructuring – perestroika – became watchwords for a style of leadership in the Kremlin that had seemed out of the question only months earlier. Critically for the West, Gorbachev realised that the ongoing nuclear arms race was one that the Soviets could never win and one which would preclude the type of large-scale domestic reform that he believed could no longer be delayed.

Lake Geneva

The two most powerful men in the world came face to face for the first time at a summit meeting in Lake Geneva, Switzerland, in November 1985. The American delegation were nervous, worried that their leader, never the most comfortable with detail, could be outwitted by the younger, highly intelligent Russian. However, both men later recalled that from the moment they met there seemed to be a natural warmth and chemistry between them. By the end of the first day, the two men revealed to their staffers that they had already arranged further meetings in Washington and Moscow.

Reykjavik

The second meeting, in October 1986, in Reykjavik, Iceland was even more dramatic. While at the first summit Gorbachev had raised an eyebrow at Reagan's reliance on cue cards, this time the personal relationship and growing trust soon took the two men to the brink of a deal to dismantle most of their nuclear weapons over the next decade. But it was the SDI programme that proved a fatal barrier to what could have been a spectacular arms deal. Gorbachev's steadfast refusal to proceed until the SDI was dropped and Reagan's unwillingness to drop his pet policy meant that the Iceland summit ended up in bitter disappointment.

Gorbachev changes his stance on SDI

Meanwhile, American spending on SDI reached staggering proportions. By the time Reagan left the White House $22 billion had been spent and by the end of the century the figure had reached almost three times that amount. Despite the fact that this expenditure failed to produce a workable defence system, it seems likely that its psychological impact on the Russians was of immense value. While the Russians doubted that an SDI scheme was practically possible, they could not be certain and that made their desire for an arms deal even more urgent. Consequently, when Gorbachev dropped his insistence that the Star Wars programme should form part of the arms deal and while the scheme itself remained a monumentally expensive exercise with no tangible end product, the stage was set for a genuine arms deal between the two superpowers.

Washington DC

With the earlier difficulties removed, a summit in Washington in 1987 finally allowed the two men the chance to sign a treaty reducing their intermediate-range nuclear weapons. In May 1988 when Reagan made a reciprocal visit to Moscow the president withdrew his comment that the Soviet Union was an 'evil empire' with the historic words, 'I was talking about another time, another era.' (In Morgan, 2016, p. 311)

13.32 President Bush and foreign policy

The certainties of the Cold War were in a sense straightforward to manage. The American public were used to seeing the Soviet Union as their traditional enemy and were prepared to support the United States in outspending it, to ensure that their country would retain its clear military supremacy. In addition, the firm grip of the Russians had brought a stability of sorts to the world since 1945. But under the leadership of Mikhail Gorbachev rapid change replaced years of stagnation. In 1989 the Soviet Union demonstrated its new thinking by withdrawing from its interminable war in Afghanistan. This was followed by a major speech in Strasburg in which Gorbachev made the striking comment that Russian interference in the domestic affairs of any other country was unacceptable. There followed a spectacular unravelling of the old Soviet bloc in Eastern Europe. Countries which had been subject to Soviet domination for so long, such as Poland, Hungary, Czechoslovakia and Bulgaria left the crumbling empire without bloodshed. These were followed by East Germany and then Romania.

This meant that the focus of the end of the Cold War was now drawn to Berlin. In November 1989, in a manner that would have been unthinkable only months earlier, the Berlin Wall, the symbol of Cold War division, was taken down. Bush had entered the White House as ill-disposed towards the Soviet Union as any of his counterparts but as Reagan's vice president he could see that Gorbachev was changing everything. Gorbachev's wide-ranging reforms and intelligent, charismatic personality had swept all before him in the West, with favourable feedback from political leaders, the press and the general public. In the *New York Times* one analyst observed: 'In the image wars, Mikhail S Gorbachev, even in translation, effortlessly demolishes George Bush' (in Plokhy, 2014, p. 18). In contrast, Bush appeared somewhat heavy-footed and cautious but his incremental approach may well have provided a valuable counter-balance given the pace at which events were about to move.

Domestically, the situation was reversed. Poor living standards, terrible food shortages and a sense that Russia was rapidly losing its sense of power and status all made Gorbachev hugely unpopular at home. Gorbachev was now vulnerable to attack from the disgruntled hardliners in the military elite who saw him as completely out of step with the old-style Russian military-industrial complex, and the party apparatchiks who desired a return to traditional Soviet leadership. The leader understood that Russia could not win the Cold War and was doomed to trail a distant second in the nuclear arms race. Therefore, drastic arms reduction was essential if Russia was to remain economically viable. By April 1989 the CIA had reported to the president that the pace and scale of Gorbachev's changes were 'threatening the stability of the [Soviet] regime' and 'could lead to a conservative reaction' (Meacham, 2015, p. 380).

However, to the Americans this smacked of surrender and desperation, giving the US the opportunity to dictate the terms in virtually all details of any nuclear arms treaty. In *Time* magazine, American analyst Strobe Talbott wrote: 'On almost every major question in START [Strategic Arms Reduction Treaty], the U.S. demanded and got its own way ... In the START treaty Gorbachev is tacitly accepting a position of overall inferiority.' (In Plokhy, 2014, p. 15) When the treaty was signed at the end of July 1991, long-range nuclear weapons were now reduced rather than being limited. Sweeping reductions initiated under Gorbachev would be continued under his successor Boris Yeltsin, so that by June 1992 the two superpowers had agreed to reduce their total numbers of strategic nuclear weapons to 3,500 for the US and 3,000 for Russia.

In the face of these truly tumultuous events, Bush adopted his now trademark policy of caution. He was skilful in avoiding any sense of triumphalism as the Russians dealt with their internal and external crises. He was able to influence Gorbachev's thinking in the acceptance of German reunification and in not using significant force against any of Russia's opponents in the Baltic or from within the Soviet Empire. So it was with real sympathy, concern and a sense of impotence that he watched the dramatic events of August 1991, as Gorbachev appeared to have been removed by communist hardliners.

China

It could be argued that a totalitarian dictatorship such as the communist regime in China was relatively easy for an American president to manage. Perhaps it is when change comes that the more difficult decisions arise. For decades all aspects of reform had been supressed by the Chinese Communist Party and a population of more than one billion people had been held in check. But in the period after the death of Mao Zedong a gradual loosening of the command and control economy had taken place. In addition, it is possible that the rapid decline of communism in Eastern Europe in 1989 had further raised expectations for change, especially among young people. In the spring of 1989 it seemed that student demonstrators for democracy were emboldened and clashes between the reformers and the military became increasingly intense. For several days the world watched as a tense stand-off between the two sides took place, focused on a huge demonstration in Tiananmen Square in Beijing.

As President Bush looked on from his holiday home in Kennebunkport, the hardliners in the Chinese regime had their way and in June 1989 the demonstrators were subjected to a devastating assault. Several hundred people were killed and perhaps three thousand more injured. Deng Xiaoping's regime had demonstrated the lengths it would go to in order to retain power and suppress reform. Bush's decision making in the days that followed seemed uncertain and, at times, weak. While the president made a measured speech deploring the use of force and imposing sanctions on military contacts and high-level exchanges between the two countries, he appeared to believe that personal diplomacy based on his earlier experience as the US ambassador to China could win the day. Bush's highly trusted national security adviser Brent Scowcroft was sent to China on a top-secret diplomatic mission. However, when news of the visit was leaked the response at home was uniformly hostile. To make matters worse, Scowcroft's Chinese hosts made it clear they were in no mood for softening their approach.

Panama

During the Reagan years, the American government gave close support to a regime that was, to say the least, unsavoury and corrupt. The dictatorship of General Manuel Noriega which was established in 1981 was notorious for drug trafficking and money laundering. Despite these well-known excesses, such was the president's all-consuming hostility towards the Sandinistas in Nicaragua that the CIA was prepared to deal with Noriega in exchange for information and intelligence in Central America. Noriega's position was undermined when details of the Iran-Contra scandal emerged in 1987. The relationship was toxic and needed, from the American standpoint, to be brought to an end.

In February 1988 a federal grand jury in Florida indicted Noriega on the charge of conspiracy with a Colombian drugs cartel to smuggle drugs into the United States. The Panama Canal remained critical to American interests in the region and tolerance for the Noriega regime was at an end. Somewhat bizarrely, Noriega declared war on the United States in December 1989. As ever, Bush was cautious, but two violent incidents against Americans in Panama, including the murder of a US marine, now prompted him to act. Under the codename Operation Just Cause, 26,000 American troops were sent to Panama. While the casualties among the Panamanian people were heavy, only 23 American servicemen perished, so the operation was seen as a decisive success. Noriega was eventually brought to trial in March 1992 and sentenced to 40 years in prison.

13.33 The invasion of Kuwait

It was late in the day on 1 August 1990 and in Washington DC the president was taking the opportunity to unwind from the manifold stresses of his job. A session hitting golf balls was followed with a massage in the medical wing of the White House. It is possible that not least in Bush's mind as he attempted to order his thoughts was how to react to the dramatic events taking place in Eastern Europe. The collapse of communism, at breathtaking speed, highlighted by the dismantling of the Berlin Wall, was demanding a coherent strategic response. The rare opportunity to spend time with his own reflections was soon cut short when an adviser came in to say that intelligence revealed that the president's gaze needed to shift from Europe to the Middle East. Armed forces from Saddam Hussein's Iraq were massed on the border with Kuwait.

Since 1982 Iraq had been involved in a bitter, attritional conflict with Iran. The hostage crisis under Carter had cast a long shadow on relations between the US and Iran and for this reason the Americans had supplied very substantial military resources to Iraq. But for Saddam, eight years of war had drained his country of the resources needed to secure victory. Kuwait, a small emirate on Iraq's border, was militarily insignificant but phenomenally wealthy and important because of its extensive oil reserves. Indeed it was these rich oil supplies that explained Saddam's willingness to take the risk of venturing into Kuwait without provocation. Closer analysis suggests that the dictator had calculated that the West's fixation on the unravelling of communism in Eastern Europe would mean that it would not be motivated to become involved in a potentially bloody and protracted conflict with Iraq.

Bush's security briefing proved entirely accurate. Within hours, Iraqi forces had occupied Kuwait City and the emirate's inland oil fields and were also perilously close to the border of Saudi Arabia. The potential for Saddam to control up to 20 per cent of the world's oil reserves, combined with the military implications of boosting Iraq's capacity for further aggression, was alarming to the West. While Bush had looked to the lofty prospect of a 'post-Cold War world order', Iraq's initiative jolted these assumptions to their core. While some of the president's advisors wondered out loud if this was a 'fait accompli', presenting only dangers to American intervention, Bush himself was quick to reach a different, more emphatic conclusion. Speaking to the press on the White House's South Lawn on the Sunday after the invasion began, the president made two comments that remain important. 'This will not stand. This will not stand, this aggression against Kuwait.' And then, his final parting comment to the press and perhaps for Iraqi consumption as well: 'I've got to go. I have to go to work. I've got to go to work.' (In Meacham, 2015, p. 433)

Not for the first time, the Iraqi dictator had made a profound miscalculation. As events unfolded during a humid summer in the US capital it became clear that George H.W. Bush was a wise and skilled opponent who would be more than capable of dealing with the first great crisis of the post-Cold War era that had been thrust upon him. Firstly, Bush reacted cautiously and gave himself time to think and avoided an immediate display of American belligerence that could have cost him dearly. In the UN in New York, an emergency meeting of the Security Council condemned the Iraqi invasion, demanded a withdrawal and imposed a damaging trade and financial embargo. Bush's skilled, determined but restrained approach allowed him to build a coalition against

Saddam that would have seemed unlikely on other occasions. Bush not only secured the support of his natural allies, but more remarkably the moderate Arab states as well as the Soviet Union.

However, Saddam had shown in the past that he was a resourceful and calculating opponent who would not easily respond to mere words. So by November 1990 the US had taken steps to assemble a force of 400,000 troops in the Gulf. Bush certainly did not dispatch these troops with any sense of recklessness. In his diary he noted: 'The troops are under way.' He called it 'the biggest step of my presidency' (in Meacham, 2015, p. 436). The first American troops to enter Saudi Arabia did so under an operation to provide military protection that was known as 'Desert Shield.'

Meanwhile, with UN backing an ultimatum for Iraqi withdrawal was set for 15 January 1991. The passage of time made it inevitable that in Congress, the press and the wider community a movement to avoid armed conflict in the Gulf gathered considerable momentum. Concerns about American casualties or the use of foreign citizens as 'human shields' and the nightmare scenario of hostage-taking, so soon after the Tehran crisis, were all put forward as reasons to change course. The peace movement campaigned under the banner of 'no blood for oil', while in private, an anxious, soul-searching president repeatedly reassured himself that he was doing the right thing; at the same time allies such as the UK stressed the damaging precedent that would be set if Saddam's aggression went unchecked. As the deadline for Iraqi withdrawal approached, the House, by a considerable margin, and the Senate by a much closer one, voted to authorise the use of force.

More than half a million US troops had now amassed in the Gulf, backed by a further quarter of a million from the rest of the coalition. Led by the charismatic and telegenic American general, H. Norman Schwarzkopf, Operation Desert Storm was launched on 17 January 1991. President Bush had steeled himself against American losses and was worried about Iraq's capabilities, the strength of Saddam's elite Republican Guard and above all the terrible possibility of chemical weapons being used against coalition forces. In the event, the display of American prowess and military technology was overwhelming. The gap between America's capacity for destruction and Iraq's ability to defend itself quickly became apparent.

The Iraqi capital Baghdad, military installations and air fields were targeted to devastating effect. With the Iraqi air force quickly neutralised and rudimentary defence systems rendered obsolete by America's laser-guided missiles, it became relatively straightforward to extend the attack to take out key roads, bridges, communication systems and power stations. Iraq's 'command and control' was quickly paralysed, leaving the Americans with unchallenged air supremacy over Kuwait and the rest of the Persian Gulf.

Under relentless US assault, an increasingly desperate Saddam used Scud missiles to target Saudi Arabia and Israel. Not least in the coalition's achievements was to persuade the Israelis not to retaliate which would have played into Saddam's hands in provoking a wider conflict between the Arabs and Israelis. America's hastily installed Patriot anti-missile batteries were able to repel the Scud attacks. A final, desperate ploy of setting fire to around 600 Kuwaiti oil wells caused lasting damage to the environment but did not seriously deflect the allies from their course. The preparation for a ground war was complete. A final ultimatum to Saddam to withdraw completely or face a ground offensive came and went, so that on the night of 23 February President Bush entered the briefing room to state: 'The liberation of Kuwait has now entered a final phase.' (In Meacham, 2015, p. 463) News from the battlefield itself exceeded Bush's wildest expectations. Within 100 hours, the complete evisceration of Iraq's army was complete and the Iraqis were in full retreat out of Kuwait. The difference between the casualty rates was stark. The Defense Department calculated that approximately 100,000 Iraqi soldiers had been killed, with 300,000 wounded. 4,000 tanks, 90 per cent of the total tanks and 3,000 artillery weapons had been destroyed. Fewer than 200 allied troops lost their lives, including 137 Americans.

13.34 The aftermath of the Gulf War

Almost 90 per cent of Americans expressed support for Bush's leadership of the war against Iraq. But the rapid success, marked by a conditional ceasefire on 27 February 1991, raised further issues: chiefly, what to do next. The Iraqis were clearly in disarray but with the residual elements of the Republican Guard still loyal, Saddam remained in power. Jon Meacham, author of an outstanding recent biography, offers this balanced appraisal:

> There was no swagger, no self-satisfaction, in the wake of the victory in the Persian Gulf ... Bush made mistakes at the end of the Gulf War. By failing to force Saddam to the surrender table at Safwan, where Schwarzkopf received the Iraqi capitulation on Sunday, March 3, 1991, the president enabled Saddam to save some personal face. (Bush had not insisted for fear that Saddam might refuse to come.) He regretted the decision. 'It hasn't been clean, there is no Battleship Missouri surrender,' he told his diary. 'This is what's missing to make this akin to World War II, to separate it from Korea, and Vietnam.'
>
> More substantively, Bush had encouraged Iraqis to rise up against the regime. When Shiites and Kurds did, in fact, rebel against Saddam after Safwan, though, everything went wrong. The United States did nothing to support the insurgents, and the uprising was put down in part by Iraqi helicopters that the coalition had allowed Saddam's army to keep. (Meacham, 2015, p. 467)

While the US-led victory was greeted euphorically at home, the longer-term consequences for American policy and the wider stability in the Gulf were difficult and costly. Maldwyn Jones observes:

> [T]he war had done little or nothing to advance America's less explicit goals in the Middle East. Saddam Hussein, now widely hailed as an Islamic hero, was as firmly in control of Iraq as ever, able both to obstruct the work of UN inspectors charged with finding and destroying his weapons of mass destruction and to renew his persecution of minority Kurds and Shiites ... Far from improving the prospects for democracy and human rights in the Gulf States, the war propped up corrupt and despotic regimes, of which the restored Al Sabah family in Kuwait was one of the shabbiest examples. Further, the war did not bring peace and stability to the Gulf, nor pave the way for Arab-Israeli understanding. (Jones, 1995, p. 618)

Finally, James Carroll in this extract from *House of War* argues that the very nature of American military prowess was in itself problematic in the Middle East.

> In the past, American interests in the region had been advanced by surrogates – the shah, the Saud family, Israel – but now those hundreds of thousands of U.S. soldiers were

bivouacked on the sands of Saudi Arabia, where many regarded the American presence as blasphemy pure and simple. And the more significant the performance of this fighting force turned out to be – thirty-eight days of unimpeded precision bombing, followed by a four-day rout on the ground – the more deeply humiliated the whole house of Arab Islam had to feel ... As the hundreds of thousands of GIs littered the Arabian desert with empty Evian bottles, their very presence profaned a sacred territory. One of those motivated to a new militancy by this combined experience of sacrilege and shame was a self-anointed messianic mujahedeen member named Osama bin Laden. What George H.W. Bush really inaugurated ... was a new world disorder that would show itself with staggering brutality exactly eleven years later. (Carroll, 2006, p. 437)

13.35 President Clinton's foreign policy

Bill Clinton entered the White House relatively inexperienced in foreign affairs and as John F. Harris explains in *The Survivor*:

It was commonly accepted wisdom in these early years of the Clinton administration that this was a president with little spontaneous interest in foreign policy. The popular image was wrong. Clinton had a fluid mind that was curious and knowledgeable about all manner of topics. (Harris, 2006, p. 120)

Clinton knew that the success of his presidency required a cohesive foreign policy. This included the management of the delicate relationship between the US and the volatile new leader of post-Cold War Russia, Boris Yeltsin, but also led to American intervention in some of the most challenging scenarios possible.

Somalia, 1993

Clinton's involvement in Somalia was limited in time and scale but disastrous and painful nevertheless. Somalia is a considerable expanse of territory on the Horn of Africa, reaching from the Awash Valley in the north to beyond the Tana River in northern Kenya in the south. The area has great cultural significance and the capital, Mogadishu, houses some of the most ancient mosques on the East African coast. Torn apart by warring clans, the brutal activities of unaccountable warlords created famine and suffering on a monstrous scale. One of the most notorious warlords was General Aidid who had effectively taken control of the capital by the end of January 1991. Heavy fighting, revenge killings, famine and an exodus of refugees to Ethiopia and Kenya meant that the issue of Somalia gained worldwide attention. The territorial nature of clan domains meant that aid workers and foreigners were in serious danger in this region, even when they were endeavouring to bring relief to a famine-stricken people.

In the White House, the outgoing President Bush was somewhat demoralised and world weary after his election defeat in November 1992, but he nevertheless recognised that a humanitarian mission safeguarded by the US military would demonstrate that America did care about suffering in Africa and among Muslims. At the end of November 1992 it was announced that almost 30,000 American troops would join a multinational force in Somalia. The strictly humanitarian mission was intended to open up vital food supplies and ameliorate the threat of famine and was given the title 'Operation Restore Hope'.

While relief supplies were initially getting through, conditions on the ground remained extremely volatile. On 5 June 1993 a group of Pakistani UN blue berets were ambushed and killed, leading to international condemnation. By now the United Nations intervention was shifting from providing humanitarian assistance and opening up food supplies to attempting to restore order in a lawless city in a failed state. The sense of 'mission creep' was illustrated when, from Washington, it was decided that the renegade warlord Mohammed Aidid should be captured and deposed. Remarkably, President Clinton authorised a mission with only a limited understanding of how it would be executed. He assumed that his military advisers would only authorise actions that while inherently dangerous were also designed to minimise risk. In Clinton's mind it was feasible that a night-time mission would snatch the warlord from his lair. In practice, the mission began in broad daylight and quickly lurched into a disaster.

The operation unravelled in brutal fashion at the start of October 1993. Flying low through the dangerous streets of Mogadishu, two Black Hawk helicopters were brought down, killing Special Forces soldiers and leaving US troops in a desperate firefight against insurgents in the Somali capital. Eighteen US Army Rangers were killed and horrific images of the body of a soldier being dragged through the streets were shown by the American news channels.

In the face of intense Congressional opposition and a lack of public support, Clinton had little choice but to announce that all American forces would withdraw from Somalia, no later than the end of March 1994. The episode was humiliating for the US and led to the resignation of Defense Secretary, Les Aspin. It was a personal disaster for Clinton, impotent in his rage when things went wrong, and a brutal demonstration of the limits of executive power. Subsequently, the abandoned UN base was looted and a new group of clan leaders and warlords replaced the earlier ones. As Francis Fukuyama puts it:

> The failed state problem that was seen previously as largely a humanitarian or human rights issue, suddenly took on a major security dimension. In the words of Michael Ignatieff (2003), 'It was also, in the 1990s, a general failure of the historical imagination, an inability of the post-cold-war-West to grasp that the emerging crisis of state order in so many overlapping zones of the world – from Egypt to Afghanistan – would eventually become a security threat at home.' (Fukuyama, 2005, p. 126)

Rwanda

The bloody nature of events in Rwanda that came to world prominence in April 1994 almost defied belief. In this central African state approximately 800,000 members of the Tutsi people and those who tried to defend them were killed in a government-sponsored genocide. Still haunted by the painful mistakes in Somalia, it became clear that both President Clinton and the United Nations were capable of sitting on their hands rather than risk a disastrous intervention. Four years later, during an extensive speaking tour across six African nations, the president briefly visited Rwanda, where he met with survivors and apologised for not taking action to reduce the slaughter. In Somalia, Clinton's intervention was disastrous. In Rwanda, his failure to intervene in the face of the most horrific slaughter was condemned at home and in the wider international community.

Haiti

Haiti, an island in the Caribbean, was geographically close to the United States but a world apart in terms of its poverty and political instability. In 1991 the democratically elected president, Jean-Bertrand Aristide, was removed in a coup led by the brutal military dictator Raoul Cedras. In October 1993 the USS *Harlan County* was dispatched to Port-au-Prince, carrying US engineers and civil affairs officials, who it had been agreed would enter the country as part of a United Nations plan to restore Aristide to his rightful position. Cedras, it was planned, would voluntarily step aside. All hope of a smooth transition was dashed when an angry crowd threw missiles and shouted threats and abuse at the Americans. With no contingency plan for a forced entry, the ship was eventually turned around rather than risking a repeat of the Mogadishu disaster. For Clinton's reputation as Commander-in-Chief, the sight of the world's only superpower being chased out of a harbour by one of the poorest nations on earth added further layers of humiliation to those accrued in Somalia.

The Balkans

The disintegration of the former Yugoslavia began in 1991. By the time the torch was passed from George H.W. Bush to Bill Clinton, a major conflagration was developing in an area of Europe that was little known to the American people. Intervention in the horrific conflict which engulfed the component nations in the early 1990s did not come easily to the Clinton White House. The president was a voracious reader of history and politics and was all too aware of the heavy price paid by some of his predecessors for intervening in tangled foreign conflicts. But at the same time, Clinton's compassion, empathy and open-minded nature meant that he was willing to be persuaded on any particular issue and was not given to compartmentalising his thinking. At times, horrific television images were enough to make him believe that the US must intervene.

To any outsider, it was painfully clear the Bosnian Civil War involving Serbs, Croats and Muslims was complex, bloody and not likely to be resolved in an easy settlement. As the former Yugoslavia disintegrated, bitter civil, religious and ethnic differences made the wars there amount to the most serious crisis on European soil since the Second World War. For two years, Clinton and his advisors watched from the sidelines, so that American involvement was minimal. This meant that those most responsible for atrocities and war crimes in the region may have reached the conclusion that they would be free to carry out the most brutal 'ethnic cleansing' without the risk of American intervention.

It was only when Serbian atrocities against Bosnian civilians reached the most appalling level that the president finally decided to act. The Americans did so by urging NATO forces to commence the bombing of Serb positions. At the same time, the well-respected American diplomat, Richard Holbrooke, Clinton's Assistant Secretary of State for European Affairs, managed to persuade the three major players – Croats, Serbs and Bosnian Muslims – to come to the conference table. The Dayton Peace

Accords, hammered out in the confines of an American air force base in Ohio in November 1995, brought an end to the conflict. It was a complex settlement but Holbrooke's role in the tense negotiations was immense. The settlement has been hailed as a particularly impressive example of conflict resolution, while others have claimed that the agreement left in place ethnic discontent and unresolved human rights abuses.

The ceasefire agreed at Dayton was protected by a huge NATO peacekeeping force which included 20,000 American troops. With unfettered elections taking place in September 1996, the troops played a huge part in restoring an uneasy stability to Bosnia and Herzegovina. America did not suffer any casualties and the whole episode reflected well on the Clinton Administration after a hesitant start.

Kosovo

The brutality and disregard for international law that was synonymous with the name Slobodan Milosevic returned to the world's attention with the Serbian programme of ethnic cleansing against the Albanian people of the Kosovo region. Highly trained Special Forces and paramilitaries who had bloody experience from the early Bosnian wars now forced hundreds of thousands of Albanians to leave their homes. This was barbaric in itself and caused terrible suffering but in addition Serb forces also murdered thousands of ethnic Albanians. With the country still wary of setting troops on the ground but, like the rest of the world, appalled by haunting television images reminiscent of the Holocaust, inaction seemed morally reprehensible.

Consequently, in 1999 President Clinton worked with NATO to commence an intensive bombing campaign against the Serbian government. This time, surgical military precision, alongside diplomatic pressure from the Russians, combined to bring an end to the slaughter. The Serbs were obliged to withdraw from the region, and US troops and a multinational NATO force helped to keep the peace. Under the peace terms, Kosovo remained a nominal part of Yugoslavia but the Kosovan people were given autonomy. Without incurring any casualties, the United States had demonstrated not just its military might but also its capacity to do the right thing and to rescue an oppressed people from brutal aggression. Milosevic was brought to justice in The Hague and President Clinton was rightfully given credit for his leadership in this process (Table 13.7).

Table 13.7   Further positive achievements in Clinton's foreign policy

---

- A positive relationship with Boris Yeltsin allowed Clinton to persuade Russia to withdraw troops from the Baltic Republics of Estonia and Latvia (1994).

- Two major trade agreements were ratified by Congress: NAFTA (North American Free Trade Agreement) (1993) and GATT (General Agreement on Tariffs and Trade) (1994).

- Timely and practical intervention to prevent likely collapse of the Mexican economy (1995).

- With Clinton's backing, his emissary, George Mitchell, brokered the peace talks between the United Kingdom, Sinn Fein and the Irish Republic, which culminated in the much-heralded Good Friday Agreement (1998).

George Walker Bush

43rd President of the United States (2001–09)
Born: 6 July 1946
Birthplace: New Haven, Connecticut
Education: Yale University; Harvard Business School
Political party: Republican
State: Texas
Occupations before presidency: Oil industry
Previous government service: Governor of Texas (1995–2000)
Age at inauguration: 54
Dates of office: January 2001–January 2009
Election: November 2000 and 2004
Vice president: Dick Cheney
Length of term: 8 years

13.36 The presidential election of 2000

Al Gore

Given the familiarity of the two candidates it seemed possible that the first American presidential election of the twenty-first century might be somewhat predictable or mundane. Instead, the clash between Al Gore, twice Clinton's vice president, and George W. Bush, son of the former president, turned out to be the most controversial election in US history, not for the campaign itself but for the way in which the votes were counted and the outcome decided. The 1990s had been marked by a bitter partisanship between the two main parties and the two candidates on this occasion had little in common. Al Gore was a committed environmentalist and conservationist, noted for his film, *An Inconvenient Truth,* which highlighted the perilous nature of the earth's eco-systems and the damaging consequences of global warming. Alongside President Clinton he had alienated the powerful gun lobby, the tobacco industry and the pro-life movement. In the more conservative areas of the country his support for gay issues caused further discontent. However, in the second term the Clinton/Gore team had delivered good numbers economically and generally avoided damaging foreign entanglements.

George W. Bush

George W. Bush was the Governor of Texas where he had courted controversy with his support for the death penalty. Educated at Yale University, Bush was teetotal (after a period of heavy drinking in his earlier life), a born-again Christian and a passionate opponent of abortion under almost any circumstances. However, he was an experienced campaigner and presented himself as a compassionate conservative rather than

Table 13.8	The result of the 2000 presidential election		
Candidate	Party	Electoral College votes	Popular votes
George W. Bush (Texas)	Republican	271	50,455,156
Albert A. Gore (Tennessee)	Democrat	266	50,992,335
Ralph Nader (Connecticut)	Green	–	2,882,738

an ideologue. With the experience of Karl Rove as his chief strategist and Dick Cheney, who had served as defense secretary during the administration of President George H.W. Bush, the Republican team was not lacking in substance. No one, though, on either side, could have foreseen what happened next.

As the polls closed on 7 November 2000, the Bush dynasty gathered for a private family dinner at the Shoreline Grill restaurant in Austin. But the exit polls and early calls from the major networks caused dismay in the Bush entourage. It appeared that Gore had carried Pennsylvania, Michigan and the key state of Florida, where George W.'s brother, Jeb, was governor. Then through the night the news changed and it appeared that Florida had gone to Bush. Gore called Bush to concede, but then the networks reported that the numbers were too close to call and Gore retracted his concession. The definitive numbers began to emerge. In the popular vote, it appeared that Gore had prevailed but by as small a margin as 500,000 votes (Table 13.8). However, what counted was the Electoral College, in which 538 votes were allocated on a state-by-state basis. After all of the votes had been counted, and in some cases, re-counted, all of the attention focused on the key state of Florida. With an electorate of about 5.8 million people, a recount placed Bush just 500 votes ahead of Gore. This was so close that Gore insisted on re-counts in several of the individual counties where the votes had been cast. As the Constitution set out, the issue now passed to the Supreme Court. It took until 12 December 2000, more than a month after the election, for the definitive verdict to be reached. By five votes to four the Supreme Court rejected demands for a state-wide recount and this effectively passed the presidency to George W. Bush. The next day, in a moment of statesmanship that was simply outstanding, Gore delivered the most gracious of concession speeches. In a moment when the Electoral College, the Supreme Court and the bitter nature of adversarial politics caused anger and turmoil Gore's speech pointed to the chance for the United States to come together. But the circumstances in which that would happen, on a crisply perfect, blue-skied beautiful day in September 2001, were unimaginable.

Further reading

Baker P., *Days of Fire: Bush and Cheney in the White House* (New York: Anchor Books 2013).
Branch T., *The Clinton Tapes: Wrestling History in the White House* (London: Simon & Schuster 2009).
Carroll J., *House of War: The Pentagon and the Disastrous Rise of American Power* (New York: Houghton Mifflin 2006).
Clarke R.A., *Against All Enemies: Inside America's War on Terror* (New York: Free Press 2004).
Clift E. & Brazaitis T., *War Without Bloodshed: The Art of Politics* (New York: Simon & Schuster 1997).

Dallek R., *Ronald Reagan: The Politics of Symbolism* (Cambridge Mass.: Harvard University Press 1999).

Duncan R. & Goddard J., *Contemporary America* (New York: Palgrave Macmillan 2005).

Fukuyama F., *State Building: Governance and World Order in the Twenty-First Century* (London: Profile Books 2005).

Harris J.F., *The Survivor: Bill Clinton in the White House* (New York: Random House 2006).

Johnson H. & Broder D.S., *The System: The American Way of Politics at the Breaking Point* (Boston: Little Brown 1997).

Jones M.A., *The Limits of Liberty: American History 1607–1992* (New York: Oxford University Press 1995).

Klein J., *The Natural: The Misunderstood Presidency of Bill Clinton* (New York: Broadway Books 2002).

Levine P. & Papasotiriou H., *America since 1945: The American Moment* (London: Palgrave Macmillan 2005).

Mann J., *George W. Bush* (New York: Times Books 2015).

Meacham J., *Destiny and Power: The American Odyssey of George Herbert Walker Bush* (New York: Random House 2015).

Morgan I., A New Democrat's New Economics in *The Presidency of Bill Clinton: The Legacy of a New Domestic and Foreign Policy,* ed. by Mark White (London: I.B. Tauris 2012).

Morgan I., *Reagan: American Icon* (London: I.B. Tauris 2016).

Morris E., *Dutch: A Memoir of Ronald Reagan* (London: Harper Collins 1999).

Packer G., *The Unwinding: Thirty Years of American Decline* (London: Faber & Faber 2013).

Peele G., Bailey C.J., Cain B. & Peters B.G. (eds.), *Developments in American Politics 5* (London: Palgrave Macmillan 2006).

Plokhy S., *The Last Empire: The Final Days of the Soviet Union* (London: Oneworld 2014).

Renshon S.A., *High Hopes: The Clinton Presidency and the Politics of Ambition* (New York: Routledge 1998).

Renshon S.A., *In His Father's Shadow: The Transformations of George W. Bush* (New York: Palgrave Macmillan 2005).

Reynolds D., *America, Empire of Liberty: A New History* (New York: Allen Lane 2009).

Smith J.E., *Bush* (New York: Simon & Schuster 2016).

Online resource

Clinton Library: www.clintonlibrary.gov, last accessed in 2018.

■ ▽ Questions and Exercises

Chapter 1: The beginning of the American twentieth century: 1900–20

Essay questions

The United States at the turn of the century

1. What factors led to the development of American imperialism in the period 1890–1914?
2. Why was the Republican Party so dominant in US politics in the period from 1896 to 1912?
3. 'The rapid expansion of the US economy was due primarily to the expansion of the railway system.' How far would you agree with this verdict?
4. 'By 1917 ... the American nation had already passed through a remarkable period of economic change.' (Hawley) Provide your analysis of the consequences of this for the people of the United States in the period 1900–17.

Source analysis: Urban living conditions

Study Sources A–C and then answer the questions which follow.

Source A

Description of the New York Triangle Fire of 1911

The sight was more than New York could bear: Young women jumping to their deaths from the ninth-floor windows of the blazing Triangle Shirtwaist Company. Sometimes they join hands for their leap. A girl jumps with hair ablaze streaming around her head. Another sails her broad-brimmed hat over the crowds below, flings a few bills and coins of her pay after it and hits the pavement just after the coins. A man is seen gently handing girls onto a windowsill, 'as if he were helping them onto a streetcar instead of into eternity.'

One of the girls turns to embrace him and she kisses him before she leaps. Then he climbs out and follows her in her fall to the pavement.

At least 46 died that way on the afternoon of March 25, 1911. Another 100 charred bodies were recovered from the building, mainly young Jewish and Italian women who sewed tailored blouses on a piecework basis. The tallest

Continued

---

fire ladders reached only to the sixth floor, and the factory was on floors eight through ten. Altogether in New York, more than 300,000 people worked in lofts higher than ladders could reach.

Source: Harold Evans, *The American Century: People, Power and Politics: An Illustrated History* (Jonathan Cape 1998).

Source B

Description of immigrant life in the New York City tenements

The staircase is too often a dark well in the centre of the house, and no direct through ventilation is possible, each family being separated from the other by partitions ... When once I asked the agent of a notorious Fourth Ward alley how many people might be living in it I was told: One hundred and forty families, one hundred Irish, thirty-eight Italian, and two that spoke the German tongue. Barring the agent herself, there was not a native-born individual in the court. The answer was characteristic of the cosmopolitan character of lower New York, very nearly so of the whole of it, wherever it runs to alleys and courts ...

Life in the tenements in July and August spells death to an army of little ones whom the doctor's skill is powerless to save ... sleepless mothers walk the streets in the gray of the early dawn, trying to stir a cooling breeze to fan the brow of the sick baby. There is no sadder sight than this patient devotion striving against fearfully helpless odds ... Turn and twist it as we may, over against every bulwark for decency and morality which society erects, the saloon projects its colossal shadow, omen of evil wherever it falls into the lives of the poor ...

The sea of a mighty population, held in galling fetters, heaves uneasily in the tenements.

Source: Jacob Riis, *How the Other Half Lives: Studies Among the Tenements of New York* (Hill & Wang 1957).

Source C

Statistics relating to the tenement population

Population of tenements in New York (1888) (Census)	1,093,701
Population of Eleventh Ward (1880)	68,778
Density of population to the square mile (1880)	224,576
Number of persons to a dwelling in New York (1880) (Census)	16.37
Number of persons to a dwelling in London (1881) (Census)	7.9
Number of persons to a dwelling in Philadelphia (1880) (Census)	5.79
Number of persons to a dwelling in Boston (1880) (Census)	8.26
Death rate of New York (1889)	25.19
Death rate of London (1889)	17.4
Death rate of Philadelphia (1889)	19.7
Death rate of Boston (1889)	24.42

Source: Jacob Riis, *How the Other Half Lives: Studies Among the Tenements of New York* (Hill & Wang 1957).

1. Source A was written in the 1990s and describes a traumatic event which took place in 1911. As an historian, would you be happy to accept all of its details as accurate? (3 marks)
2. What can you infer from Source A about the type of problems faced by the urban workforce in New York City at the turn of the century? (3 marks)
3. What problems are described in Source B? (3 marks)
4. To what extent does the material in Source B support the impression of New York life given in Source A? (3 marks)
5. Define the 'tenements' type of housing, as described in Sources B and C. (3 marks)
6. Use Sources A–C and your own knowledge to answer the following essay question:

   'To what extent was the ideal of a new life in the United States realised by immigrants who arrived there at the end of the nineteenth century?' (10 marks)

Source analysis: Theodore Roosevelt and Progressivism

Source

Our relations with the other powers of the world are important; but still more important are our relations among ourselves. Such growth in wealth, in population, and in power as this nation has seen during the century and a quarter of its national life is inevitably accompanied by a like growth in the problems which are ever before every nation that rises to greatness. Power invariably means both responsibility and danger ... Modern life is both complex and intense, and the tremendous changes wrought by the extraordinary industrial development of the last half-century are felt in every fiber of our social and political being. Never before have men tried so vast and formidable an experiment as that of administering the affairs of a continent under the forms of a Democratic Republic. The conditions which have told for our marvelous material well-being, which have developed to a very high degree our energy, self-reliance, and individual initiative, have also brought the care and anxiety inseparable from the accumulation of great wealth in industrial centers. Upon the success of our experiment much depends, not only as regards our own welfare, but as regards the welfare of mankind. If we fail, the cause of free self-government throughout the world will rock to its foundations, and therefore our responsibility is heavy, to ourselves, to the world as it is today and to the generations yet unborn.

Source: (Inaugural address 4 March 1905, millercenter.org)

1. Read the extract containing Roosevelt's exposition of Progressivism.
2. Explain in your own words the meaning of Roosevelt's speech.
3. Assess the relative importance of the factors which led to the birth of the Progressive movement.
4. How far was Roosevelt's administration able to meet the challenges outlined by the president in his inaugural address?
5. When and why did the Progressive era come to an end?

Source analysis: The administration of Woodrow Wilson

Study Sources A and B and then answer the questions which follow.

Source A

Woodrow Wilson: 1

He left the academic world to become one of the most important presidents
in the nation's history and a leader of movements for progressivism and
international peace. Working with a progressive-minded Congress, he signed
more reform legislation into law than Roosevelt and Taft combined. He also
pursued an active foreign policy. His response to the events of World War
1 made him one of the world's leading statesmen. A forceful leader, Wilson
nevertheless differed sharply from Roosevelt in personality and style. Slim and
unbending, with a long, angular face and cold, steely eyes peering through
pince-nez glasses, Wilson looked and acted like a schoolmaster to the nation ...
He lectured the public and won its loyalty through eloquent appeals to moral
principles and ideals.

 A long-time admirer of the parliamentary system, Wilson helped to
transform the Presidency into an instrument of party leadership and a vehicle
for directing legislation. Acting like a prime minister, he boldly led Congress
into enacting his proposals ... In his substantive policies he understood that
the country wanted reform and that the Democratic Congress was prepared to
act. 'We are greatly favoured,' he remarked early in his administration, 'by the
circumstances of our time.'

 Although he was an effective and courageous leader with great skill
and inspiring strength and purpose, Wilson was in many ways his own
nemesis. His character was that of the protagonist in a Greek tragedy, a
heroic figure containing the seeds of his own destruction ... **the flaws in his
own temperament** – pride, ambition, overconfidence, stubbornness and
intolerance – often changed differences over issues into bitter personal quarrels
... A combination of recurring physical disability, aggressive overconfidence,
and impatience could lead this man ... to become petty, vindictive, intractable,
and ultimately self-destructive.

Source: John Whiteclay Chambers II, *The Tyranny of Change: America in the Progressive
Era 1890–1920* (St Martin's Press 1992).

Source B

Woodrow Wilson: 2

He relied more on intuition, when it came to decision-making, than on
logic, and was absolutely stubborn in defending his intuitive conclusions
... He developed new techniques of leadership, or perhaps it should
rather be said that he revived old ones. Realizing, as befitted the author
of Congressional Government, that it was essential to collaborate with

Continued

Congress, he spent long hours on the Hill, cajoling and reasoning with Congressmen and Senators ... Even when the economy slid into a recession in 1914, leading to the loss of many Democratic seats in Congress ... He was able, by appropriating several leading ideas of Roosevelt's New Nationalism – by accepting, above all, that the powers and activities of the federal government must be increased and therefore feeling free to propose further legislation, for instance, a law forbidding child labour in factories and sweatshops – to find new work for the legislature and enhanced authority for himself. By the elections of 1916 he had compiled the most impressive record of legislation proposed and passed of any President since George Washington ... Wilson, with the great liberal lawyer Louis D. Brandeis at his elbow, might orate of the **New Freedom** ... in fact ... Wilson's actions strengthened the capitalist order by reforming it; they increased the functions and size of the federal bureaucracy; and they gave added power and authority to the Presidency.

Source: Hugh Brogan, *The Penguin History of the United States of America* (Penguin 1990).

1. Using Sources A and B and your own knowledge, explain the significance of the following terms:
   (i) '**The flaws in his own temperament**' (Source A). (3 marks)
   (ii) '**New Freedom**' (Source B). (3 marks)
2. To what extent do the two historians agree about the qualities and weaknesses of Wilson's administration? (4 marks)
3. Use Sources A and B and your own knowledge to answer the following essay question:

   To what extent can Woodrow Wilson be regarded as a great reformer in the light of his administration's achievements between 1913 and 1917? (10 marks)

Chapter 2: Foreign Policy 1900–20

Essay questions

American entry into the First World War

1. To what extent was Woodrow Wilson's policy of neutrality doomed from the start?
2. How far was unlimited German submarine warfare chiefly responsible for American entry into the First World War?
3. How powerful was the United States when it entered the First World War in April 1917?
4. Would you agree that economic self-interest was the key element in America's support for the Allied powers in the period 1914–18?
5. To what extent did Wilson go to war to 'make the world safe for democracy'?

Source analysis: The role of Wilson in America's entry into the First World War

Study Sources A–C and then answer the questions which follow.

Source A

American neutrality

Historians of American neutrality from August 1914 until April 1917 have often found it tempting to show how events changed policy: Germany's invasion of Belgium in 1914 ... the destruction of Louvain ... and a **submarine policy** that, unlike the equally illegal British blockade, killed people in torpedoings at sea; and all the while, the gradual infiltration of what a later generation described as British propaganda but in fact was the bond of a common language and heritage binding America to Britain.

But for the nation to go to war a catalyst was necessary, and it proved none other than President Wilson, whom everyone had presumed to be as neutral as it was possible to be. Wilson, it now is clear, was un-neutral from the beginning. He waited for sentiment to change so that forces ... positioned themselves in such a way that a careful Chief Executive could reasonably make a move ... As early as August 1914, Wilson told his brother-in-law ... that a German victory would be a disaster to the world, for it would mean universal militarism ... In December 1915 the President heard his minister to Belgium, Brand Whitlock, say that he, the minister, was heart and soul for the Allies. "'So am I" was the response. No decent man, knowing the situation and Germany, could be anything else. But that is only my own personal opinion and there are many others in this country who do not hold that opinion. In the West and Middle West frequently there is no opinion at all. I am not justified in forcing my opinion upon the people of the United States and bringing them into a war which they do not understand.'

Source: Robert H. Ferrell, *Woodrow Wilson & World War I, 1917–1921* (Harper & Row 1985).

Source B

U-boat warfare: 1

It was the Atlantic which eventually made the United States an unwilling belligerent in Europe's suicidal conflict ... German U-boat warfare had a catastrophic effect on America's view of Germany, at any rate at a popular level. On May 7, 1915 a German U-boat sank the British North Atlantic **passenger liner Lusitania**, without warning. It was an international crime without precedent or mitigating circumstance. Nearly 1200 passengers drowned, 128 of them American.

In retrospect this was a clear and adequate pretext for America entering the war, and thus shortening it – or even bringing it to a negotiated conclusion. But Wilson contented himself with securing German assurances that such atrocities would never be repeated.

Source: Paul Johnson, *A History of the American People* (Weidenfeld & Nicolson 1997).

U-boat warfare: 2

There is no evidence that bankers or businessmen attempted to persuade
Wilson to declare war. They did not believe American intervention was
necessary to avert an Allied defeat. Indeed virtually no one in the United States
was aware of the gravity of the Allied position in April 1917. Everyone believed
that the Allies were winning.

It was undoubtedly the U-boat that brought the United States into the
First World War. Without it there would have been no quarrel with Germany
capable of producing armed conflict. If Germany had been prepared to restrict
submarine warfare in the way Wilson wanted, the United States may have
remained neutral ... he spoke not merely for Americans but for the world in
condemning unrestricted submarine warfare. That was why he felt that its
resumption left him no alternative but war.

Source: Maldwyn A. Jones, *The Limits of Liberty: American History 1607–1992* (Oxford
University Press 1995).

1. Consult Sources A and B. With reference to these extracts and using your own
   knowledge, explain what was meant by the following phrases as they applied to
   American foreign policy and the First World War:
   (i) '**submarine policy**' (Source A). (3 marks)
   (ii) '**passenger liner Lusitania**' (Source B). (3 marks)
2. Consult Sources A–C. To what extent are historians in agreement concerning President Wilson's approach to the issue of neutrality? (4 marks)
3. 'Neutral in thought as well as in deed.' To what extent was President Wilson able to
   abide by this premise between 1914 and 1917? (10 marks)

Source analysis: Woodrow Wilson and the Versailles Peace Settlement

On 22 January 1917, almost two years before the war in Europe came to an end,
President Woodrow Wilson addressed the Senate with his vision of the peace
he would like to see:

It must be a peace without victory ... Victory would mean peace forced upon
the loser, a victor's terms imposed upon the vanquished. It would be accepted
in humiliation, under duress, as an intolerable sacrifice, and would leave a
sting, a resentment, a bitter memory upon which terms of peace would rest,
not permanently, but only as upon quicksand. [Such a peace was the] only ...
sort of peace that the peoples of America could join in guaranteeing.

1. What impact did the First World War have on the 'home front' in the United States in the period 1917–18?
2. Use Sources A–D and your own knowledge to assess the validity of the following view: 'The impact of the United States' entry into the First World War was predominantly economic.'

Chapter 3: The 1920s

Essay questions

1. Outline the most important elements of the Red Scare and explain why they occurred when they did.
2. With reference to the period 1917 to the early 1920s, was the US dominated by nativism or the defence of democracy?
3. How damaging were the domestic repercussions of American entry into the First World War?
4. Why was Prohibition introduced?
5. Was 'the noble experiment' a success or a failure?
6. 'The 1920s were a time of phenomenal economic progress in the United States.' How far would you agree with this statement?
7. To what extent is it possible to commend the Republican presidents for their management of the American economy in the 1920s?
8. Why did the general prosperity of the 1920s culminate in the Crash of 1929?

Source Analysis: The 'Red Scare'

Study Sources A–C and then answer the questions which follow.

--- **Source A** ---

Mitchell Palmer's reaction: 1

The country was in a **wild mood of fear and reaction**: after some bomb outrages, culminating in an attack on the House of Morgan on Wall Street – attacks which were presumably the work of the sort of crazed, conceited fanatics who have done so much harm since – the fear of Bolsheviks swept the country as the fear of German spies had done two years previously. It was urged on by the Attorney-General, Mitchell Palmer, himself the victim of an attempted assassination: but he was moved less by vengefulness than by his hope that the Red Scare would launch a successful Palmer-for-President boom. He arrested a thousand anarchists and socialists, and deported many of them to Russia. Five members were expelled from the New York state legislature because they were socialists. Strikes were ruthlessly broken by industrialists determined to regain control of the economic process which the war had compelled them partly to yield.

Source: Hugh Brogan, *Longman History of the United States of America* (Longman 1985).

Mitchell Palmer's reaction: 2

The first law officer of the United States, the Attorney General himself, had his house in Washington blown up. He was A. Mitchell Palmer ... the archetype of the paranoid witch hunter with which the Republic is regularly afflicted whenever an unpleasant turn of history – a spy scare, a wave of violence, a dramatic plunge of the stock market – cannot be logically explained or seems to be beyond the control of the government of the United States. He ordered or condoned raids on magazine offices, public halls, private houses, union headquarters, meetings big and small of anyone – socialists, liberals, atheists, freethinkers, social workers – who could be identified or accused as Bolsheviks.

Source: Alistair Cooke, *Alistair Cooke's America* (BBC Books 1973).

Source C

Impact on immigrants

1919 brought an **upsurge of radicalism**, bomb outrages and labour unrest. That the radical threat to social stability and industrial peace should have been blamed on the immigrant is not difficult to understand. Immigrant workmen were prominent both in violent textile strikes of the spring of 1919 and in the great steel strike of the succeeding summer. The newly formed American Communist parties, too, as well as numerous other radical organisations, claimed a large foreign-born membership, the Red Scare, therefore, erupted with special force upon the foreign-born group.

Source: Maldwyn A. Jones, *American Immigration* (University of Chicago 1960).

---

1. With reference to Sources A and C and to your own knowledge, explain the importance of the following phrases as they applied to the United States in the aftermath of the First World War.
   (i) '**wild mood of fear and reaction**' (Source A). (3 marks)
   (ii) '**upsurge of radicalism**' (Source C). (3 marks)
2. Consult Sources A and B:
   To what extent do these sources contain material which is critical of the role in the Red Scare of the Attorney General, A. Mitchell Palmer? (4 marks)

3. Consult all three extracts and use your own knowledge to answer the following essay question:
   'The Red Scare: a cynical manipulation of prejudice and racial hatred by the authorities or a genuine fear of revolution caused by the trauma of the First World War and the disorder of 1919.' Which view of the events of 1919 do you feel is closest to the truth? Give detailed support to your answer. (10 marks)

Source analysis: The presidency of Warren G. Harding

Study Sources A–C and then answer the questions which follow.

Source A

Harding as President: 1

Harding's platitudinous oratory, intellectual shallowness, and **inveterate parochialism** contrasted painfully with Wilson's high-minded rhetoric, disciplined mind, and breadth of vision. An amiable, gregarious man who had been a local newspaper editor before entering politics, Harding had made little effort to outgrow his origins. As President he enjoyed the trappings of office but found complex issues beyond him.

Source: Maldwyn A. Jones, *The Limits of Liberty: American History 1607–1992* (Oxford University Press 1995).

Source B

Harding as President: 2

Harding was not intelligent or firm or hard-working enough to be a successful President. His other personal weaknesses hardly mattered. True, he committed adultery in a coat-cupboard at the White House because he was too afraid of his wife to take his mistress to more comfortable quarters ... True he was rather too fond of giving government posts to **poker-playing cronies** whose honesty turned out to be inadequate.

Source: Hugh Brogan, *Longman History of the United States of America* (Longman 1985).

Source C

Harding as President: 3

Historians have long looked upon the Presidency of Warren G. Harding as a major debacle ... Often missing from their accounts is the fact that the Harding era also came close to combining full employment and rising living standards with stable prices and international peace. For all the scandals the new administration presided over a series of developments that made the American economy the envy of much of the world.

Source: Ellis W. Hawley, *The Great War and the Search for a Modern Order: A History of the American People and Their Institutions, 1917–1933* (St Martin's Press 1979).

---

1. With reference to Sources A and B and your own knowledge, explain what is meant by the following phrases as they applied to the presidency of Warren Harding:
   (i) '**Inveterate parochialism**' (Source A).
   (ii) '**Poker-playing cronies**' (Source B). (6 marks)

2. Consider the criticisms of Harding contained in Sources A and B.
   'These statements demonstrate that Harding was not fit to be president.' How far do you agree with this judgement? (4 marks)

3. Consider Source C in relation to Sources A and B. To what extent do these sources demonstrate that the time has come for historians to reconsider their interpretations of the Harding presidency? Use Sources A–C and your own knowledge to illustrate your answer. (10 marks)

Source analysis: Immigration and the asylum tradition

Study Sources A–D and then answer the questions which follow.

Source A

From the inscription on the Statue of Liberty

Give me your tired, your poor, Your **huddled masses** yearning to breathe free, The wretched refuse of your teeming shore ...

Source B

Bartolomeo Vanzetti: Statement made before his execution, April 1927

I not only am not guilty of these crimes, but I never commit crime in my life – I have never steal and I have never kill and I have never spilt blood ... My conviction is that I have suffered for things that I am guilty of. I am suffering because I am a radical and indeed I am a radical; I have suffered because I was an Italian, and indeed I am an Italian.

Source: Hugh Brogan, *Longman History of the United States of America* (Longman 1985).

Source C

Mobs in the Italian district, Illinois, 1920

During the night of August 5, 1920, and all through the following day, hundreds of people laden with clothing and household goods filled the roads leading out of West Frankfort, a mining town in southern Illinois. Back in town their homes were burning. Mobs bent on driving every foreigner from the area surged through the streets. Foreigners of all descriptions were beaten on sight, although the Italian population was the chief objective. Time and again crowds burst into the Italian district, dragged cowering residents from their homes, clubbed and stoned them, and set fire to their dwellings. The havoc went on for three days although five hundred state troops were rushed to the scene.

Source: John Higham, *Strangers in the Land* (Rutgers University Press 1978).

Senator Albert Johnson, speaking in 1924

It is no wonder, therefore, that the myth of the **melting pot** has been discredited. It is no wonder that Americans everywhere are insisting that their land no longer shall offer free and unrestricted asylum to the rest of the world … The United States is our land … we intend to maintain it so.

Source: Hugh Brogan, *Longman History of the United States of America* (Longman 1985).

1. Read Sources A–D, and use your own knowledge. Explain the following terms in the context of American society in the 1920s:
   (i) **'huddled masses'** (Source A). (3 marks)
   (ii) **'melting pot'** (Source D). (3 marks)
2. Read the words from the inscription on the Statue of Liberty in Source A, and then with reference to Sources A–D and your own knowledge produce a **balanced** response to the question which follows. Remember to include in your answer evidence which contradicts the assertion in this question as well as material which supports it.

'To what extent was the ideal of the United States as a melting pot repudiated in the 1920s?' (14 marks)

Themes: Across Chapters 1–3: The power of the presidency

To what extent does an overview of the presidencies of Roosevelt, Taft, Wilson and Harding suggest that the power of the presidency depended largely upon the ability and personality of the president himself?

Source analysis: The Great Depression and the election of 1932

This extract from a Hoover campaign speech in New York in October 1932 shows the incumbent bitterly opposing FDR's ideas:

This campaign is more than a contest between two men … They are proposing changes and so-called new deals which would destroy the very foundations of our American system. Our system is founded on the conception that only through freedom to the individual, will his initiative and enterprise be summoned to spur the march of progress.

With reference to this extract, explain why Hoover suffered such a resounding defeat to FDR in the presidential election of 1932.

Chapter 4: FDR: The Great Depression and the New Deal

Essay questions

1. How new was the New Deal?
2. How central was Franklin Delano Roosevelt to the New Deal?
3. Was the purpose of the New Deal to reform American society or to save capitalism?
4. How successful was the New Deal?
5. How far did the New Deal reshape the lives of many Americans?

Source analysis: Interpretations of the New Deal

Study Sources A–E and then answer the questions which follow.

Source A

FDR and America

At bottom, Franklin Roosevelt was a man of power and vision. He was a **master politician**, who took command with absolute authority; he knew ... that he could save the country and that no one else could ... Thanks to Franklin Roosevelt, in short, six years (1933 to 1938) transformed America from a country which had been laid low by troubles which its own incompetence had brought on it, and which it was quite unable to cope with, to a country, as it proved, superbly equipped to meet the worst shocks the modern world could hurl at it. It was enough.

Source: Hugh Brogan, *Longman History of the United States of America* (Longman 1985).

Source B

The New Deal: 1

The success of the New Deal's efforts to secure industrial recovery was strictly limited. Between 1933 and 1937 the American economy grew at an annual rate of 10 per cent, but output had fallen so low after 1929 that even this growth left 14 per cent of the work force unemployed. A recession in 1937 quickly shot the unemployment rate back up to 19 per cent. Well into 1941 unemployment remained at over 10 per cent ... It was World War II, not the New Deal, that was to shape the political economy of industrial and financial America ... [Roosevelt] undoubtedly lifted the paralysing fear that had settled on the country ... He was ... the first American President who could carry his message directly to the people ...

The deficiencies of the New Deal were glaring. As the 9,000,000 unemployed in 1939 testified, the policies for industrial recovery did not work ... Roosevelt never pretended that his aim was anything other than to save and preserve capitalism.

Source: Anthony Badger, *The New Deal: The Depression Years, 1933–1940* (Macmillan 1989).

The New Deal: 2

[The New Deal] never demonstrated that it could achieve prosperity in peacetime. As late as 1941, the unemployed still numbered 6 million and not until the war year of 1943 did the army of jobless finally disappear.

Source: William Leuchtenburg, *Franklin D. Roosevelt and the New Deal* (Harper & Row 1963).

Source D

The New Deal: 3

Recent historical interpretations of the New Deal have tended to emphasize its limitations as a reforming, radical force. Many of its achievements helped to institutionalize and consolidate the existing status quo in both economic and political spheres. Certainly, it also reinforced the prevailing gender stereotypes, incorporated organized labor into a regulated contractual relationship with capital and failed to address critical issues such as the racial discrimination endemic in American society. Many of its longest-lasting effects were virtually coincidental, most notably the changes in the role of the federal government, the strengthening of the executive branch and the beginning of an 'imperial presidency'.

Source: Fiona Venn, *The New Deal* (Edinburgh University Press 1998).

Source E

The New Deal: 4

Yet for all its failures and limitations the New Deal can claim achievements which have stood the test of time and have become part of the national consensus. It laid the foundations of the welfare state and created a new legal framework for industrial relations. It introduced much-needed controls on banks and stock exchanges. It established the principle that government had the primary responsibility for regulating the economy ...

Roosevelt ... restored national morale ... The New Deal permanently enlarged the role of the Federal government. It gave American capitalism a more humane aspect. While it did nothing to redistribute wealth or income, it redistributed power between capital and labor ... Finally, Roosevelt raised the presidential office to a new peak of prestige and power. He revitalized and dramatized the Presidency.

Source: Maldwyn A. Jones, *The Limits of Liberty: American History 1607–1992* (Oxford University Press 1995).

Use Sources A–E and your own knowledge to answer the following questions.

1. Look at Sources A and B. Explain what you understand by the following phrases as they applied to FDR and the New Deal:
   (i) '**master politician**' (Source A). (3 marks)
   (ii) '**The success of the New Deal's efforts to secure industrial recovery was strictly limited**' (Source B). (3 marks)
2. Consider those sources which are critical of the New Deal. To what extent are historians in agreement as to the weaknesses of the New Deal? (4 marks)
3. Consider Sources A–E and use your own knowledge to answer the following essay question:
   'How successful was the New Deal in restoring economic prosperity to the United States?' (10 marks)

Chapter 5: Roosevelt's foreign policy, 1933–45

Essay questions

1. Why did the United States enter the Second World War when it did?
2. Would you describe the Yalta Conference as a success or failure for the United States?
3. Who was to blame for the outbreak of the Cold War?
4. Account for the contrast between the mood at Yalta and Potsdam.
5. To what extent can the decision to use the atomic bomb against Japan in August 1945 be justified?

Source analysis: FDR and the Second World War

I have seen blood running from the wounded. I have seen men coughing out their gassed lungs. I have seen the dead in the mud. I have seen cities destroyed. I have seen two hundred limping, exhausted men come out of line – the survivors of a regiment of one thousand that went forward forty-eight hours before. I have seen children starving. I have seen the agony of mothers and wives. I hate war. (FDR, 1936)

Explain why the United States entered the Second World War in 1941 despite the sentiments put forward by the president in 1936.

Source analysis: The impact of the Second World War upon American society

Study Sources A–D and then answer the essay question which follows.

--- Source A ---

The United States at war: 1

In countless other domains of wartime American life things changed, often dramatically. The winds of war lifted up a people dazed and inert after a decade of paralyzingly hard times. As a thunder squall ionizes the sultry summer air,

World War II left the American people energized, freshened, and invigorated. Depression America had been a place of resignation, fear and torpor. America at war was quickened by confidence, hope, and above all by movement.

Fifteen million men and several hundred thousand women – one in nine Americans – left home for military training camps. Three-quarters of them eventually ended up overseas, six times the number that had gone to France with the American Expeditionary Force in 1917–18.

Source: David M. Kennedy, *Freedom from Fear: The American People in Depression and War, 1929–1945* (Oxford University Press 1999)

— **Source B** ————————————————————

The United States at war: 2

'We must raise our sights all along the production line,' Roosevelt told the Congress in his State of the Union message on January 6, 1942. 'Let no man say it cannot be done.' He then proceeded to outline a staggering set of production goals for 1942: sixty thousand planes, forty-five thousand tanks, twenty thousand aircraft guns, six million tons of merchant shipping. 'The figures,' US news reported, 'reached such astronomical proportions that human minds could not reach around them. Only by symbols could they be understood; a plane every four minutes in 1943; a tank every seven minutes; two seagoing ships a day.'

Source: Doris Kearns Goodwin, *No Ordinary Time: Franklin and Eleanor Roosevelt: The Home Front in World War II* (Simon & Schuster 1994).

— **Source C** ————————————————————

Federal expenditures

The economic recovery of World War II was the result of massive federal expenditures for defense. The government spent approximately $360 billion on the war, at times as much as $250 million a day. A little under half of these expenditures were raised by taxes; bond sales and deficit spending accounted for the rest. Throughout the war the government operated in the red; by 1945 the national debt was a staggering $260 billion ... buying war bonds became an act of patriotism, a way for people on the home front to help the men and women fighting the war.

Source: Victor Bondi, *American Decades 1940–1949* (Gale Research Inc 1995).

— **Source D** ————————————————————

Women at war

Women welded, riveted, cut steel, assembled bombs and tanks. Half of them were married, and one in five had a husband away in the armed services. Every second worker in ordnance and electrical manufacturing plants and every third worker in aircraft factories was a woman. Women were thought to be better than men for welding in tight corners and fiddling with fuses because of their smaller fingers. They made the fuses for most of their bombs ... Yet on average Rosie earned only 60 per cent of the male wage. Women pilots got 20 per cent less than men of the same grade ...

Nor did the influx of women transform social attitudes. Women were hissed in some workplaces where men feared they would be taking their work ... The working women helped to win the war, but they had no effective champion for their social concerns. The middle-class women's organizations were preoccupied with more general civic issues than Rosie the Riveter's problems in being worker, wife, mother and housekeeper.

Source: Harold Evans, *The American Century: People, Power and Politics: An Illustrated History* (Jonathan Cape 1998).

1. With reference to Sources A–D and using your own knowledge, explain whether you would agree with the notion that, in domestic terms, the Second World War was, in many respects, a positive experience for the people of the United States.

Chapter 6: African Americans 1900–45

Essay questions

1. Outline the key difficulties faced by African Americans at the start of the twentieth century.
2. Explain whether presidential attitudes helped or hindered the progress of African Americans in the period 1900–45.
3. How successful was African American leadership in improving the situation faced by black people from 1900 to 1945?
4. Did the New Deal help or hinder the progress of African Americans?

Source analysis: The Ku Klux Klan

Study Sources A–C and then answer the questions which follow.

___ **Source A** _____

The Klan and American values: 1

The Klan, therefore, has now come to speak for the great mass of Americans of the **old pioneer stock**. We believe that it does fairly and faithfully represent them, and our proof lies in their support. To understand the Klan, then, it is necessary to understand the character and present mind of the mass of old-stock Americans ... They decided that the melting pot was a ghastly failure ... they saw, too, that the alien was tearing down the American standard of living.

Source: Extract from Hiram W. Evans, 'Imperial Wizard, The Klan's Fight for Americanism' in *North American Review* 223 (March 1926).

The Klan and American values: 2

[The Klan's] greatest selling point was the protection of traditional American values. These were to be found in the bosoms and communities of white, native-born, Anglo-Saxon, Protestants ... The changing world of the 1920s, which saw post war restlessness and new waves of immigration combined with ... the erosion of both the small town and **fundamentalist morality**, brought the Klan millions of recruits.

Source: David M. Chalmers, *Hooded Americanism: The History of the Ku Klux Klan* (Duke University Press 1981).

Source C

The Klan and American values: 3

An organiser of the Ku Klux Klan was in Emporia the other day, and the men whom he invited to join his band at ten dollars per join turned him down .... The proposition seems to be:

- Anti-foreigners
- Anti-Catholics
- Anti-Negroes

The whole trouble with the Ku Klux Klan is that it is based upon such deep foolishness that it is bound to be a menace to good government in any community.

Any man fool enough to be Imperial Wizard would have power without responsibility and both without any sense. That is social dynamite. To make a case against a birthplace, a religion, or a race is wickedly un-American and cowardly.

Source: Extract from William Allen White, *A Letter on the Ku Klux Klan* (1921) (Emporia State University, online)

1. With reference to Sources A–C and to your own knowledge, explain what was meant by the following phrases as they applied to American society in the period after the First World War:
   (i) **'old pioneer stock'** (Source A). (3 marks)
   (ii) **'fundamentalist morality'** (Source B). (3 marks)
2. Source A shows a speech by the Imperial Wizard. Refer to Sources A and B. To what extent is the accuracy of the historian's analysis of the appeal of the Klan in Source B supported by the tone and content of the Imperial Wizard's speech given in Source A? (4 marks)
3. Using Sources A–C and your own knowledge, account for the rapid rise and fall of the Ku Klux Klan between 1915 and 1927. (10 marks)

Chapter 7: Post-war America

Essay questions

1. Did Truman consolidate or undermine the New Deal?
2. To what extent was Truman able to successfully manage the transition from war to peace?
3. Why did the United States decide to intervene in the war in Korea and to what extent can that intervention be judged a success?
4. To what extent was the rise of McCarthyism due to the personal influence of Joseph McCarthy?
5. How damaging was the period of McCarthyism for American society?

Source analysis: McCarthyism

Study Sources A–D and then answer the questions which follow.

Source A

Senator Joseph McCarthy, Speech at Wheeling, West Virginia, 9 February 1950

Six years ago ... there was within the Soviet orbit 180,000,000 people ... Today ... there are 800,000,000 people under the absolute domination of Soviet Russia – an increase of over 400 per cent ... As one of our outstanding historical figures once said, 'When a great democracy is destroyed, it will not be because of enemies from without, but rather because of enemies from within.'

The truth of this statement is becoming terrifyingly clear as we see this country each day losing on every front ...

The reason why we find ourselves in a position of impotency is not because our only powerful potential enemy has sent men to invade our shores, but rather because of the traitorous actions of those who have been treated so well by this Nation. It has not been the less fortunate or members of minority groups who have been selling this Nation out, but rather those who have had all the benefits that the wealthiest nation on earth has had to offer – the finest homes, the finest college education, and the finest jobs in Government we can give.

This is glaringly true in the **State Department**. There the bright young men who are born with silver spoons in their mouths are the ones who have been worst ...

In my opinion the State Department, which is one of the most important government departments, is thoroughly infested with Communists.

I have in my hand fifty-seven cases of individuals who would appear to be either card carrying members or certainly loyal to the Communist Party, but who nevertheless are still helping to shape our foreign policy.

Source: Ellen Schrecker, *The Age of McCarthyism* (Bedford Books 1994).

'McCarthyisms'

McCarthy was a gifted demagogue whose wildly irresponsible charges of communism brought him the publicity he craved. But his antics distracted the attention of contemporaries and historians and caused them to overlook the more profound and enduring aspects of the anti-Communist crusade of the 1940s and 1950s ... The word McCarthyism creates problems. Identifying the anti-Communist crusade with Senator McCarthy narrows the focus and slights the more important roles played by people like FBI Director J. Edgar Hoover and President Harry Truman ...When we look beyond ... the rantings of Joe McCarthy to the thousands of unpublicized firings, FBI investigations, speakers' bans, passport denials and other sanctions against political dissenters during this period, it becomes clear that that there was not one, but many McCarthyisms. They were all linked by a common concern with domestic communism and with a desire to eliminate its alleged threat to the American way of life.

Source: Ellen Schrecker, *The Age of McCarthyism* (Bedford Books 1994).

Source C

McCarthyism

Some years ago a conference held at Harvard University on the topic 'Anticommunism and the US' was advertised by a poster presenting the brooding, baleful face of Senator Joe McCarthy. The image was a powerful one but it was also misleading, because, as most of the conference participants knew perfectly well, the late Senator had done little or nothing to create the phenomenon he had come to personify ... One limitation of the term McCarthyism is that it slights the long history of red scare politics in the United States before Joe McCarthy's high-pitched whine was first heard in the United States Senate ...

Even the red scare associated with Senator McCarthy was not triggered by his celebrated speech at Wheeling, West Virginia, in February 1950. Several scholars have pointed to the significance of episodes and policies associated with President Harry Truman's first beleaguered term, and some have emphasized the rightward thrusts of American politics during the later part of the New Deal, as illustrated by the foundation of the **House Committee on Un-American Activities (HUAC)** in 1938 ... Scholars have rightly pointed to the demoralizing impact of the course of foreign affairs on both public opinion and policy-makers, most evidenced by the extension of Soviet control over eastern Europe after the Second World War and by the unnerving '"loss" of China and the revelation of Soviet possession of the A-bomb in 1949' ... In some states red scares arrived early and in others late ... But if there was a foreign crisis which had a clear impact on state politics it was the outbreak of the Korean War ... the evidence suggests that Korea was more important than McCarthy in precipitating anticommunist programmes ... For many Americans, McCarthyism was a cry of pain for the sundry worlds they had lost.

Source: M.J. Heale, *McCarthy's Americans: Red Scare Politics in State and Nation, 1935–1965* (Macmillan Press 1998).

Judge Irving Kaufman, remarks in the sentencing of Julius and Ethel Rosenberg, 5 April 1951

I consider your crime worse than murder. Plain deliberate contemplated murder is dwarfed in magnitude by comparison with the crime you have committed ... In your case, I believe your conduct in putting into the hands of the Russians the A-bomb years before our best scientists predicted Russia would perfect the bomb has already caused, in my opinion, the Communist aggression in Korea, with the resultant casualties exceeding 50,000 and who knows but that millions more of innocent people may pay the price for your treason. Indeed by your betrayal you undoubtedly have altered the course of history to the disadvantage of our country. No one can say that we do not live in a constant state of tension. We have evidence of your treachery all around us every day – for the civilian defense activities throughout the nation are aimed at preparing us for an atom bomb attack ...

It is not in my power, Julius and Ethel Rosenberg, to forgive you. Only the Lord can find mercy for what you have done.

The sentence of the Court upon Julius and Ethel Rosenberg is, for the crime for which you have been convicted, you are hereby sentenced to the punishment of death, and it is ordered upon some day within the week beginning with Monday, May 21st, you shall be executed according to law.

Source: Ellen Schrecker, *The Age of McCarthyism* (Bedford Books 1994).

1. Explain what was meant by the following phrases as they applied to the period of McCarthyism:
   (i) **'State Department'** (Source A). (3 marks)
   (ii) **'House Committee on Un-American Activities (HUAC)'** (Source C). (3 marks)
2. Was McCarthyism a product of internal or external problems facing the United States in the period 1945–54? (10 marks)

Chapter 8: The 1950s: Affluence and anxiety

Essay questions

1. Was the 1950s predominantly characterised by affluence or anxiety?
2. Historian Elaine Tyler May (1988) has described '[t]he legendary family of the 1950s, complete with appliances, station wagons, backyard barbecues, and tricycles scattered on the sidewalks.' To what extent does this present an accurate image of the American family in the 1950s?
3. 'We must guard against the acquisition of unwarranted influence, whether sought or unsought, by the **military industrial complex**.' What did Eisenhower mean by this term and to what extent was he able to resist its influence?
4. William Ewald, in *Eisenhower the President*, concludes: 'In the fifties, many terrible things that could have happened, didn't. Dwight Eisenhower's Presidency gave America eight good years – I believe the best in memory.' How far would you agree with this view of the Eisenhower presidency?

Source analysis: The Affluent Society

Study Sources A–F and then answer the questions which follow.

Source A

The consumer society: 1

In the years following World War II **the American household changed dramatically**. Not only was the birthrate exploding, but housework was transformed by technology. The new modern household now included many electronic appliances designed to make housework easier. The electric waffle maker, coffeemaker, eggbeater, egg timer, toaster, and dishwasher all came into common use. The appliances in the average household cost a total of more than two thousand dollars.

Source: Elaine Tyler May, *Homeward Bound: American Families in the Cold War Era* (Basic Books 1988).

Source B

Extract from a 1960 study into the psychology of spending

The impact of suburbia on consumer behavior can hardly be overstated ... Young people choose to marry early, to have several children in the early years of marriage, to live in nice neighborhoods, and to have cars, washing machines, refrigerators, television sets, and several other appliances at the same time.

Source: Victor Bondi, *American Decades 1940–1949* (Gale Research Inc 1995).

Source C

The consumer society: 2

While McCarthyites worried about the corrupting influences of modern society, other Americans saw in 1953 an extraordinary national strength that rested on rapid population growth. The baby boom, which reached its peak during the Eisenhower years ... helped fuel a strong expansion of the economy during the 1950s. Throughout the Eisenhower Presidency, the gross national product increased at an annual rate of 2.4 per cent, from $364.6 billion to $520.1 billion. Because of the growth in the number of families, many basic industries prospered, such as housing, automobiles and steel. Contemporary observers declared that Americans were a people of plenty, and indeed they were, but hardly in equal measure ... **The Eisenhower prosperity**, in short, brought no relative improvement for blacks.

Source: Chester J. Pach and Elmo Richardson, *The Presidency of Dwight D. Eisenhower* (University Press of Kansas 1991).

Extract from Eisenhower's second inaugural address, January 1957

We meet again, as upon a like moment four years ago, and again you have witnessed my solemn oath of service to you ... In our nation work and health abound. The air rings with the song of our industry ... the chorus of America the bountiful.

Source: Chester J. Pach and Elmo Richardson, *The Presidency of Dwight D. Eisenhower* (University Press of Kansas 1991).

__ Source E __

The downturn in Eisenhower's second term

The assurance and optimism of the beginning of the second term crumbled because of a series of economic, international and political shocks. The Eisenhower prosperity dissolved into the worst recession since the Great Depression ... The economy had turned sharply downward in summer 1957 and reached its low point in spring 1958. The hard times were severe. Industrial production declined 14 per cent, corporate profits fell 25 per cent, and unemployment reached a high of 7.5 per cent. Federal actions aggravated the recession. Restrictions on credit drove up interest rates and cut into consumption of durable goods, particularly automobiles. Cutbacks in defence procurement, implemented so that the federal government would not exceed the current ceiling on the national debt, also helped slow the economy ... The administration's tepid and at times, fumbling response to the recession only intensified public dissatisfaction. The President did not appreciate the seriousness of the downturn until mid autumn 1957. Even then, he was convinced that the economy would recover quickly, as it had in 1954, and so issued a series of optimistic public statements the principal effect of which was to create the impression that he did not care about workers who had lost their jobs.

Source: Chester J. Pach and Elmo Richardson, *The Presidency of Dwight D. Eisenhower* (University Press of Kansas 1991).

__ Source F __

Infrastructure and public works

His most important contribution to the health of American society ... resulted from his management of the economy ... Eisenhower was criticized for failing to stimulate even more economic growth, since the rate of increase was lower in America than in many other industrial countries ... John F. Kennedy made economic sluggishness a major theme of his campaign ... Though the post-war period is usually thought of as one long surge of prosperity, it was during the Eisenhower years that this was most true ... A prudent manager of the economy, Eisenhower was a wise investor, too ... Much the most important program was the Interstate highway system, which Eisenhower persuaded Congress to fund in 1956. The National System of Interstate and Defense Highways was the greatest public works project in history and would ultimately blanket the country with a 42,000-mile network ... Thus it was the expanded infrastructure and booming economy Eisenhower bequeathed to Kennedy and Johnson that made the Great Society possible.

Source: William L. O'Neill, 'Eisenhower and American society' in G. Bischof and S.E. Ambrose (eds), *Eisenhower: A Centenary Assessment* (Louisiana State University Press 1995).

1. With reference to Sources A–F, and using your own knowledge, explain what is meant by the following phrases as they applied to American society in the 1950s:
   (i) **'The American household changed dramatically'** (Source A). (3 marks)
   (ii) **'The Eisenhower prosperity'** (Source C). (3 marks)
2. Consult extracts D and E. How would you explain their contradictory viewpoints? (4 marks)
3. Consult Sources A–F and use your own knowledge to answer the following essay question:

   'How appropriate is the term "affluent society" in describing America in the 1950s?' (10 marks)

Chapter 9: John F. Kennedy, 1961–63

Essay questions

1. Account for Kennedy's narrow victory over Nixon in the 1960 presidential election.
2. Was the New Frontier a success or a failure?
3. 'Ineffective domestically, increasingly effective on the world stage.' How far would you agree with this assessment of the Kennedy Administration?
4. How successful was Kennedy's foreign policy in relation to Cuba?
5. How close to nuclear war did Kennedy come in the Cuban Missile Crisis?

Source analysis: JFK's foreign policy

Historian George C. Herring (1979) provides this analysis of the transition from Eisenhower to Kennedy concerning Vietnam:

   Inheriting from Eisenhower an increasingly dangerous if still limited commitment, he plunged deeper into the morass. Kennedy did not eagerly take up the burden in Vietnam, and his actions there contrast sharply with his rhetoric.

1. How much continuity was there in Kennedy's policy in Vietnam, compared with Eisenhower?
2. Why did JFK plunge the United States deeper into the morass of Vietnam?

3. Assess the conflicting views of historians concerning Kennedy's intentions in Vietnam. Do you believe he would have escalated or reduced America's commitment in Vietnam had he served a second term?

Chapter 10: LBJ: The Great Society and Vietnam

Essay questions

1. To what extent did the Great Society represent a major departure from previous American reform movements?
2. Account for Johnson's landslide victory in the presidential election of 1964.
3. How successful was the Great Society?
4. Who was more successful in dealing with the issue of poverty, LBJ or JFK?
5. Account for the factors which led to the increasing involvement of the United States in Vietnam, from Eisenhower, through Kennedy, to Johnson.
6. How far would you agree that the trauma of Vietnam overwhelmed LBJ's domestic achievements?
7. How deep and widespread were the divisions in American society by the time LBJ left the Oval Office?

Chapter 11: The shift to the right

Essay questions

1. To what extent did the Watergate affair undermine the power and credibility of the presidency in the 1970s and 1980s?
2. To what extent was domestic opposition responsible for the failure of the United States to achieve its objectives in Vietnam?
3. How powerful was President Nixon?
4. To what extent did Nixon create an Imperial Presidency?
5. How successful was Nixon's foreign policy?
6. 'In the end, Vietnam was lost on the political front in the United States, not on the battlefront in Southeast Asia.' How far would you agree with Maldwyn Jones' assessment of the Vietnam War?

Source analysis: Watergate

What did the President know and when did he know it? The answer is conclusive: The President knew virtually everything about Watergate and the imposition of a cover-up, from the beginning. The new tapes painstakingly revealed his repeated manoeuvres to deny that knowledge for more than a year and, in turn, tell us much about the man.

Source: Stanley I. Kutler, *Abuse of Power: The New Nixon Tapes* (Touchstone – Simon & Schuster 1997).

1. Explain the significance of the term 'Watergate'. (3 marks)
2. Explain what was involved in the subsequent 'cover-up'. (3 marks)
3. Why were these two things so damaging to the Nixon presidency? (4 marks)
4. What was the longer-term impact of the Watergate scandal on the American people? (10 marks)

Chapter 12: African Americans 1945–2000

Essay questions

1. How far did the position of African Americans improve in the period 1945–60?
2. Was the leadership of Martin Luther King Jr or Malcolm X more effective in advancing the cause of African Americans?
3. 'The amazing thing about our movement is that it is a protest of the people. It is not a one-man show. It's the people. The masses of this town, who are tired of being trampled on, are responsible. The leaders couldn't stop it if they wanted to.' Was the civil rights movement led from the top or from the grass roots?
4. 'It must be admitted, Eisenhower did not understand the civil rights revolution and failed to meet its challenge.' How valid is William L. O'Neill's analysis (in Bischof & Ambrose, 1995) of Eisenhower as a civil rights leader?
5. Who was the more effective civil rights president, Truman, Eisenhower or Kennedy?

Chapter 13: The end of the American century: 1980–2000

Essay questions

1. Analyse the key issues facing the United States in the last 20 years of the twentieth century.
2. Account for President Carter's emphatic defeat in the presidential election of 1980.
3. How successful was the presidency of Ronald Reagan?
4. Account for Reagan's landslide victory in 1984.
5. Which of Reagan's two terms was more successful in regard to a) domestic b) foreign policy?
6. Why was the Iran-Contra affair so significant to the Reagan Administration?
7. How successful was the American economy from 1980 to 2000?
8. Account for Clinton's defeat of Bush in the 1992 presidential election.
9. Was Clinton's presidential leadership more successful at home or abroad?

◼ ﹀ References

Ahamed L., *Lords of Finance: The Bankers Who Broke the World* (London: Windmill Books 2010).

Alexander M., *The New Jim Crow: Mass Incarceration in the Age of Colorblindness* (New York: The New Press 2012).

Alter J., *The Defining Moment: FDRs Hundred Days and the Triumph of Hope* (New York: Simon & Schuster 2007).

Badger A.J., *The New Deal: The Depression Years, 1933–1940* (London: Macmillan 1989).

Bair D., *Al Capone: His Life, Legacy and Legend* (New York: Doubleday 2016).

Berg A.S., *Lindbergh* (New York: Macmillan 1998).

Berg A.S., *Wilson* (London: Simon & Schuster 2013).

Bernstein C. & Woodward B., *All the President's Men* (London: Quartet Books 1974).

Beschloss M.R., *Kennedy v Khrushchev: The Crisis Years 1960–1963* (London: Faber and Faber 1991).

Beschloss M.R., *Taking Charge: The Johnson White House Tapes, 1963–1964* (New York: Simon & Schuster 1997).

Beschloss M.R., *The Conquerors: Roosevelt, Truman and the Destruction of Hitler's Germany 1941–1945* (New York: Simon & Schuster 2002).

Bischof G. & Ambrose S.E. (eds.), *Eisenhower: A Centenary Assessment* (Baton Rouge: Louisiana State University Press 1995).

Bird K. & Sherwin M.J., *American Prometheus: The Triumph and Tragedy of J. Robert Oppenheimer* (London: Atlantic Books 2009).

Bondi V., *American Decades 1940–1949* (Detroit: Gale Research Inc. 1995).

Bowden M., *Guests of the Ayatollah* (New York: Grove Press 2006).

Boyle P.G., *Eisenhower: Profiles in Power* (New York: Routledge 2014).

Bradley M.P., *Vietnam at War* (New York: Oxford University Press 2009).

Brogan H., *Longman History of the United States of America* (London: Longman 1985).

Brogan H., *The Penguin History of the United States of America* (London: Penguin 1990).

Brown, D.S. *Paradise Lost: A Life of F. Scott Fitzgerald* (Cambridge, Mass.: Belknap Press 2017).

Bugliosi V., *Four Days in November: The Assassination of President John F. Kennedy* (New York: Norton 2007).

Caro R.A., *The Years of Lyndon Johnson, Volume 1: The Path to Power* (New York: Vintage 1983).

Carroll J., *House of War: The Pentagon and the Disastrous Rise of American Power* (New York: Houghton Mifflin 2006).

Chalmers D.M., *Hooded Americanism: The History of the Ku Klux Klan* (Durham: Duke University Press 1981).

Clarke T., *JFK's Last Hundred Days: An Intimate Portrait of a Great President* (London: Allen Lane 2013).

Clements K.A., *The Life of Herbert Hoover: Imperfect Visionary 1918–1928* (New York: Palgrave Macmillan 2010).

Coates T., *We Were Eight Years in Power: An American Tragedy* (London: Hamish Hamilton 2017).

Coffey P., *American Arsenal: A Century of Waging War* (New York: Oxford University Press 2014).

Cooke A., *Alistair Cooke's America* (London: BBC Books 1973).

Cook R., *Sweet Land of Liberty?* (London: Longman 1998).

Cooper J.M., *Woodrow Wilson: A Biography* (New York: Vintage Books 2011).

Costello J., *The Pacific War* (London: Pan Books 1985).

Crockatt R., *The Fifty Years War: The United States and the Soviet Union in World Politics, 1941–1991* (London: Routledge 1995).

Dallek R., *Flawed Giant: Lyndon Johnson and His Times 1961–1973* (New York: Oxford University Press 1998).

Dallek R., *Ronald Reagan: The Politics of Symbolism* (Cambridge, Mass.: Harvard University Press 1999).

Dallek R., *John F. Kennedy, An Unfinished Life 1917–1963* (London: Allen Lane 2003).

Dallek R., *Franklin D. Roosevelt: A Political Life* (London: Allen Lane 2017).

Dierenfield B.J., & White J.W., *A History of African-American Leadership* (Harlow, UK: Pearson 2012).

Dobbs M., *One Minute to Midnight* (New York: Arrow Books 2009).

Dobbs M., *Six Months in 1945: From World War to Cold War* (London: Arrow Books 2013).

Edelman B. (ed.), *Dear America: Letters Home from Vietnam* (New York: Simon & Schuster 1985).

Egan T., *The Worst Hard Time* (Boston: First Mariner Books 2006).

Eig J., *Ali* (New York: Simon & Schuster 2017).

Evans H., *The American Century: People, Power and Politics: An Illustrated History* (London: Jonathan Cape 1998).

Farrell J.A., *Clarence Darrow: Attorney for the Damned* (London: Scribe 2011).

Farrell J.A., *Richard Nixon: The Life* (New York: Doubleday – Random House 2017).

Felzenberg A.S., author of 'Calvin Coolidge and Race: His Record in Dealing with the Racial Tensions of the 1920s' (1988) speaking in a forum held at the President Kennedy Museum in Boston, in 1988.

Fernandez-Armesto F., *Our America: A Hispanic History of the United States* (New York: W.W. Norton 2015).

Ferrell R.H., *Woodrow Wilson & World War I 1917–1921* (New York: Harper & Row 1985).

Ferrell R.H., *The Presidency of Calvin Coolidge* (Kansas: University Press of Kansas 1998)

Fitzgerald F.S., *The Great Gatsby* (Sussex: Vigo Books 2011).

Freedman L., *Kennedy's Wars: Berlin, Cuba, Laos and Vietnam* (New York: OUP 2000).

Fukuyama F., *State Building: Governance and World Order in the Twenty-First Century* (London: Profile Books 2005).

Galbraith J.K., *The Great Crash 1929* (London: Hamish Hamilton 1955).

Garrow D.J., *Rising Star: The Making of Barack Obama* (London: William Collins 2017).

Gerstle G., *Liberty and Coercion: The Paradox of American Government from the Founding to the Present* (New Jersey: Princeton University Press 2015).

Gordon L., *The Second Coming of the KKK: The Ku Klux Klan of the 1920s and the American Political Tradition* (New York: Liveright Publishing 2017).

Gordon R.J., *The Rise and Fall of American Growth* (New Jersey: Princeton University Press 2016).

Halberstam D., *The Coldest Winter: America and the Korean War* (London: Macmillan 2008).

Harris J.F., *The Survivor: Bill Clinton in the White House* (New York: Random House 2006).

Hastings M., *The Korean War* (London: Michael Joseph Ltd 1988).

Hawley E.W., *The Great War and the Search for a Modern Order: A History of the American People and Their Institutions, 1917–1933* (New York: St Martin's Press 1979).

Heale M.J., *McCarthy's Americans: Red Scare Politics in State and Nation, 1935–1965* (London: Macmillan Press 1998).

Herring G.C., *America's Longest War: The United States and Vietnam 1950–1975* (New York: Wiley 1979).

Hersh S.J., *The Dark Side of Camelot* (London: Harper Collins 1998).

Hersh S.J., *The Price of Power: Kissinger in the Nixon White House* (New York: Summit Books 1983).

Higham, J., *Strangers in the Land: Patterns of American Nativism, 1860–1925* (New Brunswick: Rutgers University Press 1978).

Hoover, H., *The Memoirs of Herbert Hoover, Volume 3: The Great Depression 1929–1941* (New York: Macmillan 1952).

Jackson K.T., *The Ku Klux Klan in the City, 1915–1930* (Chicago: Elephant Paperback 1992).

Jeansonne G., *The Life of Herbert Hoover: Fighting Quaker 1928–1933* (New York: Palgrave 2012).

Johnson H. and Broder D.S., *The System: The American Way of Politics at the Breaking Point* (Boston: Little Brown 1997).

Johnson, P., *A History of the American People* (London: Weidenfeld & Nicolson 1997).

Jones M.A., *American Immigration* (Chicago: University of Chicago 1960).

Jones M.A., *The Limits of Liberty: American History 1607–1992* (New York: Oxford University Press 1995).

Karnow S., *Vietnam: A History* (London: Century Hutchinson 1985).

Katznelson I., *Fear Itself: The New Deal and the Origins of Our Time* (New York: Liveright 2013).

Kearns Goodwin D., *Lyndon Johnson and the American Dream* (New York: St Martin's Griffin Press 1991).

Kearns Goodwin D., *No Ordinary Time: Franklin & Eleanor Roosevelt: The Home Front in World War II* (New York: Simon & Schuster 1994).

Kendi I.X., *Stamped from the Beginning: A Definitive History of Racist Ideas in America* (London: Penguin Random House 2016).

Kennedy D.M., *Freedom From Fear: The American People in Depression and War 1929–1945* (New York: Oxford University Press 1999).

Klein J., *The Natural: The Misunderstood Presidency of Bill Clinton* (New York: Doubleday 2002).

Kutler S.I., *Abuse of Power: The New Nixon Tapes* (New York: Touchstone – Simon & Schuster 1997).

Lang D., *Fallout (On Radioactive Debris) in The New Yorker Book of the 1950s: Story of a Decade* (London: William Heinemann 2015).

Lelyveld J., *His Final Battle: The Last Months of Franklin Roosevelt* (New York: Alfred A. Knopf 2016).

Lentin A., *Guilt at Versailles* (London: Methuen & Co Ltd 1985).

Leuchtenburg W.E., *Franklin D. Roosevelt and The New Deal* (New York: Harper & Row 1963).

Levy M.I. (ed.), *The Korean War and the Vietnam War: People, Politics and Power* (New York: Britannica Educational Publishing 2010).

Logevall F., *Embers of War: The Fall of an Empire and the Making of America's Vietnam* (New York: Random House 2013).

Logsdon J., *John F. Kennedy and the Race to the Moon* (Basingstoke: Palgrave 2010).

Lowe P. (ed.), *The Vietnam War* (Basingstoke: Macmillan Press Ltd 1998).

Marable M., *Malcolm X: A Life of Reinvention* (London: Penguin 2011).

Martin W.E. Jr (ed.), *Brown v Board of Education, A Brief History with Documents* (Boston: Bedford/St Martin's 1998).

Matthews C., *Kennedy and Nixon: The Rivalry that Shaped Postwar America* (New York: Touchstone 1996).

May E.R. & Zelikow P.D., *The Kennedy Tapes: Inside the White House During the Cuban Missile Crisis* (Cambridge, Mass.: Harvard University Press 1997).

May, E.T., *Homeward Bound: American Families in the Cold War Era* (New York: Basic Books 1988).

McCullough D., *Truman* (New York: Touchstone – Simon & Schuster 1993).

McCullough D., *The Wright Brothers: The Dramatic Story behind the Legend* (London: Simon & Schuster 2015).

McElvaine R., *Down and Out in the Great Depression: Letters from the Forgotten Man* (North Carolina: Chapel Hill 1983).

McGirr L., *The War on Alcohol: Prohibition and the Rise of the American State* (New York: Norton 2016).

McMaster H.R., *Dereliction of Duty: Lyndon Johnson, Robert McNamara, The Joint Chiefs of Staff, and the Lies that Led to Vietnam* (New York: Harper Collins 1997).

McNamara R.S., *In Retrospect: The Tragedy and Lessons of Vietnam* (New York: Vintage Books 1995).

Meacham J., *Destiny and Power: The American Odyssey of George Herbert Walker Bush* (New York: Random House 2015).

Meigs M., *Optimism at Armageddon: Voices of American Participants in the First World War* (London: Macmillan 1997).

Miller A., *The Crucible* (Penguin 1953).

Morgan I., A New Democrat's New Economics in *The Presidency of Bill Clinton: The Legacy of a New Domestic and Foreign Policy*, ed. by Mark White (London: I.B. Tauris 2012).

Morgan I., *Reagan: American Icon* (London: I.B. Tauris 2016).

Morgan T., *FDR: A Biography* (New York: Simon & Schuster 1985).

Morris C.R., *The Tycoons* (New York: Holt 2005).

Morris C.R., *A Rabble of Dead Money, The Great Crash and the Global Depression: 1929–1939* (New York: PublicAffairs 2017).

Morris E., *The Rise of Theodore Roosevelt* (New York: Random House 1979).

Morris E., *Theodore Rex* (New York: Random House 2001).

Murdock C.G., *Domesticating Drink: Women, Men, and Alcohol in America, 1870–1940* (Baltimore: Johns Hopkins 1998).

Neer R.M., *Napalm: An American Biography* (Cambridge, Mass.: Belknap Harvard 2013).

Neiberg M.S., *The Path to War: How the First World War Created Modern America* (New York: Oxford University Press 2016).

Nelson, C., *Pearl Harbor: From Infamy to Greatness* (London: Weidenfeld & Nicolson).

New Yorker Book of the 60s: Story of a Decade, ed. by Henry Finder (London: William Heinemann 2016).

Oates S., *Let the Trumpet Sound: A Life of Martin Luther King Jnr* (Edinburgh: Canongate 1998).

O'Brien, L.F. & Califano, J.A. Jr, 'Final Report to President Lyndon B. Johnson on the 89th Congress', *Public Papers of the Presidents of the United States: Lyndon B. Johnson*, 1966, Vol. 2 (Washington: Government Printing Office 1967).

Oliphant T. & Wilkie C., *The Road to Camelot: Inside JFK's Five-Year Plan* (New York: Simon & Schuster 2017).

Olson J.S. & Roberts R., *My Lai: A Brief History with Documents* (Boston: Bedford Books 1998).

Pach C.J. Jr & Richardson E., *The Presidency of Dwight D. Eisenhower* (Lawrence, Kansas: University Press of Kansas 1991).

Packer G., *The Unwinding: Thirty Years of American Decline* (London: Faber & Faber 2013).

Page J., *In the Hands of the Great Spirit* (New York: Free Press 2003).

Patterson J.T., *America's Struggle Against Poverty 1900–1994* (Cambridge, Mass.: Harvard University Press 1994).

Patterson J.T., *Grand Expectations: The United States, 1945–1974* (New York: Oxford University Press 1996).

Peraino K., *A Force So Swift: Mao, Truman and the Birth of Modern China, 1949* (New York: Crown Publishing 2017).

Plokhy S.M., *Yalta: The Price of Peace* (New York: Penguin 2011).

Plokhy S., *The Last Empire: The Final Days of the Soviet Union* (London: Oneworld 2014).

Powaski R.E., *March to Armageddon* (New York: Oxford University Press 1987).

Purdum T.S., *An Idea Whose Time Has Come: Two Presidents, Two Parties, and the Battle for the Civil Rights Act of 1964* (New York: Picador 2014).

Raban J., *Robert Lowell's Poems: A Selection* (Faber and Faber 1982).

Rappleye C., *Herbert Hoover in the White House: The Ordeal of the Presidency* (New York: Simon & Schuster 2016).

Reeves R., *President Kennedy: Profile of Power* (London: Papermac 1994).

Reeves T.C., *A Question of Character: A Life of John F. Kennedy* (Rocklin, California: Prima Publishing 1992).

Reynolds D., *America, Empire of Liberty: A New History* (London: Allen Lane 2009).

Riis J., *How the Other Half Lives: Studies among the Tenements of New York* (New York: Hill & Wang 1957).

Schiff S., *The Witches, Salem 1692: A History* (London: Little, Brown and Company 2015).

Schlesinger A.M. Jr, *A Thousand Days: John F. Kennedy in the White House* (London: Andre Deutsch 1965).

Schrecker E., *The Age of McCarthyism: A Brief History with Documents* (Boston: Bedford Books 1994).

Schulman B.J., *Lyndon B. Johnson and American Liberalism: A Brief Biography with Documents* (Boston: Bedford Books 1995).

Shaw J.T., *JFK in the Senate: Pathway to Presidency* (New York: Palgrave 2013).

Shields D. & Salerno S., *Salinger* (Simon & Schuster 2014).

Shlaes A., *Coolidge* (New York: Harper Perennial 2014).

Simon L., *Lost Girls: The Invention of the Flapper* (London: Reaktion Books 2017).

Simon S., *Jackie Robinson and the Integration of Baseball* (Hoboken, New Jersey: John Wiley & Sons 2002).

Slawenski K., *J.D. Salinger: A Life Raised High* (Hebden Bridge: Pomona Books 2010).

Smith J.E., *Eisenhower in War and Peace* (New York: Random House 2012).

Smith J.E., *FDR* (New York: Random House 2007).

Smith J.E., *Bush* (New York: Simon & Schuster 2016).

Stern S.M., *The Cuban Missile Crisis in American Memory* (Stanford: Stanford University Press 2012).

Stueck W., *The Korean War: An International History* (New Jersey: Princeton University Press 1995).

Temkin M., *The Sacco-Vanzetti Affair: America on Trial* (New Haven: Yale University Press 2009).

Terkel S., *Hard Times, An Oral History of the Great Depression* (New York: Pantheon Books 1986).

Thomas E., *Being Nixon: A Man Divided* (New York: Random House 2015).

Thompson J.A., *Journal of American Studies* (Cambridge: Cambridge University Press 1988).

Traynor J., *Roosevelt's America 1932-1941* (London: Macmillan Education 1987).

Traynor J., *Challenging History 1890-1990* (London: Macmillan 1991).

Traynor J., *Mastering Modern United States History* (London: Palgrave 2001).

Traynor J., *USA 1918-1941* (London: Nelson 1997).

Twain M., *Autobiography of Mark Twain: Volume 1* (Berkeley: University of California Press 2010).

Tye L., *Bobby Kennedy: The Making of a Liberal Icon* (New York: Penguin Random House 2016).

Tyson T.B., *The Blood of Emmett Till* (New York: Simon & Schuster 2017).

Venn F., *The New Deal* (Edinburgh: Edinburgh University Press 1998).

Wallace M., *Greater Gotham: A History of New York City from 1898 to 1919* (Oxford University Press 2017).

Ward G.C. & Burns K., *The Vietnam War: An Intimate History* (New York: Alfred A. Knopf 2017).

Watts S., *JFK and the Masculine Mystique: Sex and Power on the New Frontier* (New York: Thomas Dunne 2016).

Werth B., *31 Days: Gerald Ford, The Nixon Pardon and a Government in Crisis* (New York: Anchor Books 2006).

White M.J., *The Cuban Missile Crisis* (Basingstoke: Macmillan Press Ltd 1996).

White M.J., *Kennedy: The New Frontier Revisited* (Basingstoke: Macmillan Press Ltd 1998).

White R.D. Jr, *Kingfish: The Reign of Huey Long* (New York: Random House 2006).

Whiteclay Chambers J. II., *The Tyranny of Change, America in the Progressive Era 1890-1920* (New York: St Martin's Press 1992).

Whitman J.Q., *Hitler's American Model: The United States and the Making of Nazi Race Law* (Princeton: Princeton University Press 2017).

Williams T.H., *Huey Long: A Biography* (New York: Alfred A. Knopf 1969).

Winkler H.A., *The Age of Catastrophe: A History of the West, 1914-1945* (New Haven: Yale University Press 2015).

Wood A.L., *Lynching and Spectacle: Witnessing Racial Violence in America, 1890-1940* (Chapel Hill: University of North Carolina 2009).

Wright L., *Thirteen Days in September: Carter, Begin and Sadat at Camp David* (London: Oneworld 2014).

Yergin D., *Shattered Peace: The Origins of the Cold War and the National Security State* (Boston: Houghton Mifflin Company 1977).

Zelizer J.E., *The Fierce Urgency of Now: Lyndon Johnson, Congress and the Battle for the Great Society* (New York: Penguin Press 2015).

Zubok V. & Pleshakov C., *Inside the Kremlin's Cold War: From Stalin to Khrushchev* (Cambridge, Mass.: Harvard University Press 1996).

Online resources

A short list of sites I found most useful in preparing this book. All were accessed in 2018.

American Presidency Project: presidency.ucsb.edu

Emporia State University: emporia.edu

Haas Institute: haasinstitute.berkeley.edu

University of Virginia, Miller Center: virginia.edu

Presidential Libraries – each US president has their own online library and collection of documents

Wilson Presidential Library: woodrowwilson.org

FDR Library: www.fdrlibrary.org

JFK Library: www.jfklibrary.org

LBJ Presidential Library: www.lbjlibrary.org

Richard Nixon Foundation: www.nixonfoundation.org

Ronald Reagan Presidential Foundation & Institute: www.reaganfoundation.org

Clinton Library: clintonlibrary.gov

◼ ✓ Index

Note: Entries in **bold** type indicate items in the questions and exercises section featured at the back of this book.

Printed and bound by PG in the USA

USA2018PGIL